ISAIAH, AHAZ,
AND THE
SYRO-EPHRAIMITIC CRISIS

SOCIETY OF BIBLICAL LITERATURE

DISSERTATION SERIES
David L. Petersen, Old Testament Editor
Charles Talbert, New Testament Editor

Number 123

ISAIAH, AHAZ, AND THE SYRO-EPHRAIMITIC CRISIS

by
Stuart A. Irvine

Stuart A. Irvine

ISAIAH, AHAZ, AND THE SYRO-EPHRAIMITIC CRISIS

Scholars Press
Atlanta, Georgia

ISAIAH, AHAZ, AND THE SYRO-EPHRAIMITIC CRISIS

Stuart A. Irvine

Ph.D., 1989
Emory University

Advisor:
John H. Hayes

© 1990
The Society of Biblical Literature

Library of Congress Cataloging in Publication Data

Irvine, Stuart A.
    Isaiah, Ahaz, and the Syro-Ephraimitic crisis / Stuart A. Irvine.
    p. cm. -- (Dissertation series / Society of Biblical
Literature ; no. 123)
    Originally presented as the author's thesis (Ph.D.--Emory
University, 1989)
    Includes bibliographical references and index.
    ISBN 1-55540-447-2 (alk. paper). -- ISBN 1-55540-448-0 (pbk. :
alk. paper)
    1. Bible. O.T. Isaiah--Criticism, interpretation, etc.
2. Isaiah (Biblical prophet) 3. Ahaz, King of Judah. 4. Syro
-Ephraimitic War, ca. 734 B.C. I. Title. II. Series: Dissertation
series (Society of Biblical Literature) : no. 123.
BS1515.2.I73 1990
224'.1067--dc20   90-46977
                                                                      CIP

Printed in the United States of America
on acid-free paper

To Sam and Lou

TABLE OF CONTENTS

Abbreviations ix

Preface xv

Chapter One. Introduction 1

    A. Ahaz and Isaiah as Antagonists 3
    B. Traditio-historical Studies 7
    C. The Immanuel Prophecy 10
    D. The Organization and Purpose of the *Denkschrift* 13
    E. Critique 15
    F. Overview of the Dissertation 18

Part I: THE SYRO-EPHRAIMITIC CRISIS

Chapter Two. The Assyrian Texts Relating to the
                Syro-Ephraimitic Crisis 23

    A. The Eponym List 24
    B. The Royal Inscriptions 26
        1. Layard 72b+73a 28
        2. Layard 29b 32
        3. Layard 66 37
        4. II R 67 40
        5. ND400 44
        6. ND4301+4305 56
        7. III R 10,2 62
    C. Conclusions 69
        1. Participants in the Revolt 69
        2. The Assyrian Campaign "against Philistia"
           in 734/733 70

3. The Assyrian Campaigns in 733/732 and 732/731 71
Appendix. The Royal Chronology of Israel and Judah 73

Chapter Three. Biblical Accounts of the Syro-Ephraimitic Crisis 75

    A. Second Kings 16 75
        1. The Deuteronomistic Introduction 76
        2. The Cultic Reform of Ahaz 79
        3. The Syro-Ephraimitic Crisis 83
    B. Second Chronicles 28 90
    C. Reconstructing the Syro-Ephraimitic Crisis 95
        1. Joachim Begrich 96
        2. Herbert Donner 97
        3. Bustanay Oded 99
        4. Critique 101
            a. The Cause and the Purpose of the War 101
            b. The Date of the War 104
            c. The Payment of Ahaz 107
    D. Summary 109

Part II: ISAIAH AND THE SYRO-EPHRAIMITIC CRISIS

Chapter Four. The Source Material 113

    A. The Selection of Texts 113
    B. The *Denkschrift* Hypothesis 120
        1. Isaiah 6:1–9:6 as an Interpolation 121
        2. Stylistic Cohesion 125
        3. Thematic and Structural Unity 126
    C. Summary 131

Chapter Five. Isaiah 7 133

Chapter Six. Isaiah 8:1–20 179

Chapter Seven. Isaiah 8:21–9:6 215

Chapter Eight. Isaiah 9:7–10:4 235

Chapter Nine. Isaiah 10:5–27c 251

Chapter Ten. Isaiah 10:27d–12:6 273

Part III: CONCLUSION

Chapter Eleven. Conclusion.. 297

Bibliography.. 303

Indexes 337

ABBREVIATIONS

AASOR	Annual of the American Schools of Oriental Research
AB	Anchor Bible
ABC	*Assyrian and Babylonian Chronicles*, by A. K. Grayson (Locust Valley, NY: J. J. Augustin, 1975)
AcOr	*Acta orientalia*
AEL	*Ancient Egyptian Literature: A Book of Readings*, by M. Lichtheim (3 vols.; Berkeley/London: University of California Press, 1973–1980)
AfO	*Archiv für Orientforschung*
AJSL	*American Journal of Semitic Languages and Literature*
ALBO	Analecta lovaniensia biblica et orientalia
ALUOS	Annual of Leeds University Oriental Society
AnBib	Analecta biblica
ANET	*Ancient Near Eastern Texts Relating to the Old Testament* (ed. J. B. Pritchard; 3d ed.; Princeton: Princeton University Press, 1969)
AnOr	Analecta orientalia
Ant	*Jewish Antiquites*, by Josephus
AOAT	Alter Orient und Altes Testament
ARAB	*Ancient Records of Assyria and Babylonia*, by D. D. Luckenbill (2 vols.; Chicago: University of Chicago Press, 1926–1927)
ARI	*Assyrian Royal Inscriptions*, by A. K. Grayson (2 vols.; Wiesbaden: Otto Harrassowitz, 1972–1976)
ArOr	*Archiv orientální*
ARW	*Archiv für Religionswissenschaft*
ASTI	*Annual of the Swedish Theological Institute*
ATANT	Abhandlungen zur Theologie des Alten und Neuen Testaments

ATD	Das Alte Testament Deutsch
ATR	Anglican Theological Review
AUSS	Andrews University Seminary Studies
BA	Biblical Archaeologist
BASOR	Bulletin of the American Schools of Oriental Research
BAT	Die Botschaft des Alten Testaments
BBB	Bonner biblische Beiträge
BEvT	Beiträge zur evangelischen Theologie
BFCT	Beiträge zur Förderung christlicher Theologie
BH	Biblia hebraica, edited by R. Kittel
BHS	Biblia hebraica stuttgartensia
Bib	Biblica
BibLeb	Bibel und Leben
BibOr	Biblica et orientalia
BibS(N)	Biblische Studien (Neukirchen, 1951–)
BK	Bibel und Kirche
BKAT	Biblischer Kommentar. Altes Testament
BN	Biblische Notizen
BR	Biblical Research
BRev	Bible Review
BT	The Bible Translator
BTB	Biblical Theology Bulletin
BWANT	Beiträge zur Wissenschaft vom Alten und Neuen Testament
BZ	Biblische Zeitschrift
BZAW	Beihefte zur ZAW
CAH	Cambridge Ancient History
CBQ	Catholic Biblical Quarterly
CBQMS	Catholic Biblical Quarterly—Monograph Series
CJ	Conservative Judaism
CT	Cuneiform Texts from Babylonian Tablets, &c., in the British Museum
CTM	Concordia Theological Monthly
DTT	Dansk teologisk tidsskrift
ErFor	Erträge zur Forschung
ErIsr	Eretz Israel
EncJud	Encyclopedia judaica (1971)

ETL	*Ephemerides theologicae lovanienses*
EvT	*Evangelische Theologie*
ExpTim	*Expository Times*
FB	Forschung zur Bibel
FOTL	The Forms of the Old Testament Literature
FRLANT	Forschungen zur Religion und Literatur des Alten und Neuen Testaments
GKC	*Gesenius' Hebrew Grammar*, edited by E. Kautzsch, translated by A. E. Cowley (2d ed.; Oxford: Clarendon, 1910)
GS	*Gesammelte Studien*
HAT	Handbuch zum Alten Testament
HBD	*A Dictionary of the Bible* (5 vols.; ed. J. Hastings; Edinburgh/New York: T. & T. Clark/Charles Scribner's Sons, 1900–1904)
HTR	*Harvard Theological Review*
HUCA	*Hebrew Union College Annual*
IA	*Die Inschriften Asarhaddons, Königs von Assyrien*, by R. Borger (Graz: Im Selbstverlags des Herausgebers, 1956)
IB	*Interpreter's Bible*
ICC	International Critical Commentary
IDB	*Interpreter's Dictionary of the Bible*
IDBSup	Supplementary volume to *IDB*
IEJ	*Israel Exploration Journal*
Int	*Interpretation*
JAOS	*Journal of the American Oriental Society*
JB	Jerusalem Bible
JBC	*Jerome Biblical Commentary*
JBL	*Journal of Biblical Literature*
JCS	*Journal of Cuneiform Studies*
JNES	*Journal of Near Eastern Studies*
JNSL	*Journal of Northwest Semitic Languages*
JQR	*Jewish Quarterly Review*
JSOT	*Journal for the Study of the Old Testament*
JSOTSup	Journal for the Study of the Old Testament—Supplement Series
JSS	*Journal of Semitic Studies*
JTS	*Journal of Theological Studies*

KAI	*Kanaanäische und aramäische Inschriften*, by H. Donner and W. Rollig (3 vols. Wiesbaden: Otto Harrassowitz, 1962–1964)
KAT	Kommentar zum Alten Testament
KD	*Kerygma und Dogma*
KJV	King James Version
KS	*Kleine Schriften*
LQ	*Lutheran Quarterly*
LR	*Lutherischer Rundblick*
LTQ	*Lexington Theological Review*
MDB	*Le Monde de la Bible*
MIO	*Mitteilungen des Instituts für Orientforschung*
NASB	New American Standard Bible
NEASB	*Near East Archaeological Society Bulletin*
NEB	New English Bible
NIV	New International Version
NJPSV	New Jewish Publication Society Version
NKZ	*Neue kirchliche Zeitschrift*
NTT	*Norsk Teologisk Tidsskrift*
Numen	*Numen: International Review for the History of Religions*
OLZ	*Orientalische Literaturzeitung*
Or	*Orientalia* (Rome)
OTS	*Oudtestamentische Studiën*
PAPS	*Proceedings of the American Philosophical Society*
PJB	*Palästina Jahrbuch*
RB	*Revue biblique*
RGG	*Religion in Geschichte und Gegenwart*
RSR	*Recherches de science religieuse*
RSV	Revised Standard Version
RTP	*Revue de théologie et de philosophie*
SANT	Studien zum Alten und Neuen Testament
SBLDS	SBL Dissertation Series
SBLMS	SBL Monograph Series
SBS	Stuttgarter Bibelstudien
SBT	Studies in Biblical Theology
SEÅ	*Svensk exegetisk årsbok*
ScrHier	*Scripta Hierosalymitana*

SJT	Scottish Journal of Theology
ST	Studia theologica
SThU	Schweizerische theologische Umshau
TA	Tel Aviv
TEV	Today's English Version
TGl	Theologie und Glaube
TLZ	Theologische Literaturzeitung
TS	Theological Studies
TSBA	Transactions of the Society of Biblical Archaeology
TSK	Theologische Studien und Kritiken
TUAT	Texte aus dem Umwelt des Alten Testaments (ed. O. Kaiser; Gütersloh: Gerd Mohn, 1982–)
TWAT	Theologisches Wörterbuch zum Alten Testament (eds. G. J. Botterweck and H. Ringgren; Stuttgart: Kohlhammer, 1970–)
TZ	Theologische Zeitschrift
UF	Ugarit-Forschungen
VD	Verbum domini
VT	Vetus Testamentum
VTSup	Vetus Testamentum, Supplements
WBC	Word Biblical Commentary
WD	Wort und Dienst
WHJP	World History of the Jewish People
WMANT	Wissenschaftliche Monographien zum Alten und Neuen Testament
WO	Die Welt des Orients
ZAW	Zeitschrift für die alttestamentliche Wissenschaft
ZDMG	Zeitschrift der deutschen morgenländischen Gesellschaft
ZDMGSup	Zeitschrift der deutschen morgenländischen Gesellschaft, Supplements
ZDPV	Zeitschrift des deutschen Palästina-Vereins
ZRGG	Zeitschrift für Religions- und Geistesgeschichte
ZTK	Zeitschrift für Theologie und Kirche

Preface

The Syro-Ephraimitic crisis and the speeches of Isaiah relating to it have long been subjects of scholarly interest. Countless articles and books over the years, and especially in recent times, have treated the war and the prophet's message during it. It is important then to identify the contributions and distinguishing features of the present volume on Isaiah, the Judean king Ahaz, and the Syro-Ephraimitic crisis.

(1) The dissertation examines all of the biblical and non-biblical evidence relating to the crisis in far greater detail, and perhaps with a more critical eye, than previous works on the war. This is particularly true with regard to the Assyrian inscriptions, but also, to some degree, with regard to the biblical accounts as well.

(2) The analysis of the Assyrian and biblical texts allows for a new understanding of the Syro-Ephraimitic crisis, particularly as it concerns the foreign policy and actions of Ahaz, and the complex political dynamics within Judah at the time. It is argued, specifically, that the king adhered to a neutralist course throughout the episode, despite the inclination of many Judeans to join Syria and Israel in revolt against Assyria.

(3) Scholars generally view 2 Kgs 16:5-9 as the interpretive key to the speeches of Isaiah relating to the war. The present work challenges this correlation, at least as it is usually made, by calling into question the reliability of the Kings text. The notice on Ahaz's alliance with Assyria comes particularly under attack.

(4) Another distinguishing feature of the dissertation is its selection of prophetic material for examination. The analysis argues that nearly all of Isaiah 7-12 makes sense against the background of the Syro-Ephraimitic crisis. Few earlier studies of the prophet and the war have as broad a textual basis as this.

(5) Previous works on Isaiah and the Syro-Ephraimitic crisis have generally emphasized the antagonism between Isaiah and Ahaz. This dissertation presents a very different picture of the relations between the king and prophet. It argues, specifically, that Isaiah supported

Ahaz throughout the war, applauding and encouraging the king in his isolationist stand.

The relation of the present volume to three specific publications requires special comment. The research of the dissertation began while J. M. Miller and J. H. Hayes were writing *A History of Ancient Israel and Judah* (1986). Conversations with them and the mutual sharing of ideas account for the similarities between our views of the Syro-Ephraimitic crisis. Some of my preliminary insights, particularly with regard to Second Kings 16 and the relationship between Isaiah and Ahaz, were incorporated into the volume of Miller and Hayes.

Work on the dissertation also coincided with the writing of *Isaiah, the Eighth-Century Prophet: His Times and His Preaching* (1987), which J. H. Hayes and I co-authored. Again, some of the dissertation's preliminary research and ideas were included in Part I of that volume ("The Historical Background—750–700 B.C.E."), as well as in Part IV ("Isaiah's Preaching and the Isaianic Narratives"). I was responsible specifically for the analyses of Isaiah 7–12.

Finally, the dissertation utilizes the chronology worked out by J. H. Hayes and P. K. Hooker in *A New Chronology for the Kings of Israel and Judah and Its Implications for Biblical History and Literature* (1988). Hayes and Hooker worked out the chronology after the publication of *Isaiah, the Eighth-Century Prophet*, and in light of their work, the Isaiah volume needs minor revision. This dissertation makes some of the required changes in its treatment of the Syro-Ephraimitic crisis and the analysis of Isaiah 7–12.

Several people supported the completion of this work, and I wish to acknowledge them. The Deutsches Akademisches Austausch Dienst funded a year of research in Munich, and made my stay in Germany a pleasureful experience overall. In Munich, Professor Jörg Jeremias read an early draft of Chapter Three and made several helpful suggestions. At Emory University, Professors Gene Tucker and Max Miller read parts of the dissertation very closely. I am grateful for their detailed comments. I also thank Professors Martin Buss and Walter Brueggemann for participating in the dissertation defense.

A special word of gratitude goes to Professor John Hayes, my director and friend. His strong interest in the dissertation sustained my own, and his many suggestions always stimulated my thinking. His good humor and sage counsel carried me through dark periods of the project, and taught me a little courage along the way.

At Scholars Press, Jeff Kuan gave generously of his time to proofread the text and point the Hebrew. I am grateful to Scholars Press for publishing the book in a remarkably short time.

Finally, I wish to thank Elizabeth Irvine, my wife, for her confidence in me, and for all the sacrifices she had to make during my graduate years. The book is dedicated to my parents.

CHAPTER ONE

INTRODUCTION

Twenty-five years ago H. Donner stated that "our knowledge of the ancient Near East in general and of the Syro-Palestinian region in particular has gained considerably in recent decades; the results must be made fruitful for the interpretation of the prophets' speeches."[1] With this claim Donner called for renewed study of the long-discussed relationship of the prophets to historical events and politics. It is safe to say that the issue merits reinvestigation with each new understanding of the historical circumstances in which the prophets were active. This is particularly true in the case of the eighth-century prophet Isaiah. The present work reexamines the relationship of the prophet to the Judean king Ahaz during the so-called Syro-Ephraimitic crisis. Such a study involves two main tasks. First of all, the nature and course of the Syro-Ephraimitic crisis will be interpreted on the basis of a close critical examination of all relevant evidence, both biblical and non-biblical. Secondly, the speeches of Isaiah which can be reasonably related to this crisis will be determined and analyzed in light of an appraisal of Ahaz's actions and policies during the crisis.

The relations between Isaiah and Ahaz is an issue which cuts across several related lines of research. Properly the topic belongs under the general rubric of prophetic politics. Early studies of the prophets', and particularly Isaiah's, relationship to politics fall roughly within the first half of the twentieth century and exhibit a preoccupation with general issues, for example, the perspective from which the prophets addressed politics and the practical astuteness of their advice.[2] With H. Donner's *Israel unter den Völkern* (1964), a sec-

---

[1] H. Donner, *Israel unter den Völkern. Die Stellung der klassischen Propheten des 8. Jahrhunderts v. Chr. zur Aussenpolitik der Könige von Israel und Juda* (VTSup 11; Leiden: E. J. Brill, 1964) xi.
[2] See H. Winckler and H. Zimmern, eds., *Die Keilinschriften und das Alte Testament* (3d ed.; Berlin: Reuther and Reichard, 1902-3) 170-75; F. Küchler, *Die Stel-*

ond phase of study began. This work emphasizes the need for a detailed analysis of the individual prophetic speeches within their respective historical settings. Donner does not ignore the broader issues of prophetic politics, but simply postpones their treatment until he obtains the preliminary exegetical base. The result of this procedure is an appreciation of the variety of attitudes which the different prophets had toward the political issues of their time.[3] Works which follow in the wake of Donner's study take note of this variety and consequently focus narrowly either on the politics of a single prophet or on the different postures of several prophets toward a single political event.[4]

Isaiah's relationship with Ahaz arises as an issue also in treatments of the so-called Isaianic *Denkschrift* (Isa 6:1–9:6).[5] This is understandable, for here one finds a large deposit of the prophet's thought about the Syro-Ephraimitic crisis and its principal figures.

---

lung des Propheten Jesajas zur Politik seiner Zeit (Tübingen: J. C. B. Mohr [Paul Siebeck], 1906); F. Wilke, *Jesaja und Assur. Eine exegetisch-historische Untersuchung zur Politik des Propheten Jesaja* (Leipzig: Dieterich'sche Verlagsbuchhandlung, 1905); idem., *Die politische Wirksamkeit der Propheten Israels* (Leipzig: Dieterich'sche Verlagsbuchhandlung, 1913); W. Staerk, *Das assyrische Weltreich im Urteil der Propheten* (Göttingen: Vandenhoeck & Ruprecht, 1908); E. Troeltsch, "Das Ethos der hebräischen Propheten," *Logos* 6 (1916) 1–28; F. Weinrich, *Der religiös-utopische Charakter der "prophetischen Politik"* (Giessen: A. Töpelmann, 1932); O. Procksch, *Der Staatsgedanke in der Prophetie* (Gütersloh: Bertelsmann, 1933); K. Elliger, "Prophetie und Politik," *ZAW* 53 (1935) 3–22; M. Buber, *Der Glaube der Propheten* (Zurich: Manesse, 1950); and H.-J. Kraus, *Prophetie und Politik* (Munich: Chr. Kaiser, 1952). For reviews of this literature, see the volume by Kraus (pp. 5–15) and N. K. Gottwald, *All the Kingdoms of the Earth: Israelite Prophecy and International Relations in the Ancient Near East* (New York/Evanston/London: Harper and Row, 1964) 350–62.

[3]The work of Donner accordingly concludes with individual summaries of the distinctive views of Isaiah, Hosea, and Micah.

[4]See for example B. Childs, *Isaiah and the Assyrian Crisis* (SBT II/3; London: SCM, 1967); G. Rice, *The Syro-Ephraimite Crisis and the Witness of Isaiah, Chapters Seven and Eight, to the Prophet's Involvement* (dissertation, Columbia University, 1969); F. Huber, *Yahwe, Juda und die anderen Völker beim Propheten Jesaja* (BZAW 137; Berlin/New York: Walter de Gruyter, 1976); W. Dietrich, *Jesaja und die Politik* (BEvT 74; Munich: Chr. Kaiser, 1976); J. M. Asurmendi, *La Guerra Siro-Efraimita: Historia y Profetas* (Valencia/Jerusalem: Institución San Jerónimo, 1982); and M. E. W. Thompson, *Situation and Theology: Old Testament Interpretations of the Syro-Ephraimite War* (Sheffield: Almond, 1982).

[5]The widespread interpretation of Isa 6:1–9:6, or a part thereof, as the prophet's personal memoir from the period of the Syro-Ephraimitic crisis derives largely from K. Budde. See K. Budde, *Geschichte der althebräischen Litteratur* (Leipzig: C. F. Amelangs Verlag, 1906) 76–77; idem., "Über die Schranken, die Jesajas prophetischer Botschaft zu setzen sind," *ZAW* 41 (1923) 154–203; idem., *Jesaja's Erleben. Eine gemeinverständliche Auslegung der Denkschrift des Propheten (Kap. 6,1–9,6)* (Gotha: L. Klotz, 1928).

The individual interpretive problems which the material poses are as difficult as any in the Hebrew Scriptures and consequently have developed into separate, though related, subjects of study. These include the genre and meaning of the temple vision (6:1–13), the significance of She'ar-yashub as a symbolic name (7:3), the structure and purpose of Isaiah's warning to the royal house (7:3–9), the meaning of the Immanuel saying (7:10–17), the prophet's use of traditions throughout 6:1–9:6, and the organization and purpose of the *Denkschrift*. Many of these issues are related inextricably to the historical question: how precisely did Isaiah react toward the Judean king and his policies during the Syro-Ephraimitic crisis?

These remarks demonstrate the relevance of the present work to numerous areas of Isaianic research. They show as well how so many variable factors enter into the study of Isaiah's posture during the war. The result has been an almost endless and not easily schematized number of interpretations. The survey of research in this chapter is primarily introductory in character; it cannot and need not treat the variety of interpretations exhaustively. The aim is rather to highlight and assess the persistence of a particular but widespread conception of the relations between the king and prophet.

A. Ahaz and Isaiah as Antagonists

Scholars traditionally have viewed Isaiah and his younger contemporary, Micah, as antagonists of the Davidic monarchs, Ahaz and Hezekiah. The conclusion of G. von Rad is typical: "All the evidence suggests, however, that these prophets increasingly wrote off the reigning members of the house of David of their own day, and even that they regarded the whole history of the Monarchy from the time of David as a false development."[6] As for Isaiah's attitude toward Ahaz specifically, the prophet's change from support to opposition is thought to have occurred during the course of the Syro-Ephraimitic crisis. A detailed explanation of this shift and a delineation of the issues were given classical formulation in K. Budde's *Jesaja's Erleben* (1928).

In this highly influential work, Budde first investigates the integrity of Isa 6:1–9:6 as an originally independent unit.[7] Several reasons, he contends, justify viewing this block as the prophet's memoir from the period of the Syro-Ephraimitic war. The chronological notice which begins chapter 6 and its parallel in 7:1 link the two chapters and set them apart from Isaiah 1–5. At the same time the autobio-

---

[6] G. von Rad, *Old Testament Theology* (2 vols.; New York: Harper and Row, 1965) 2. 171.
[7] *Jesaja's Erleben*, 1–5.

graphical style throughout chapters 6–8 binds all three chapters together and demonstrates their character as a prophetic memoir.[8] Isaiah 9:1–6 first refers to the dark fate of the people described in 8:20–22, but then concludes the memoir with a view toward future salvation. The child figure around which that salvation centers (v 5) parallels the child figures of chapters 7 and 8: She'ar-yashub (7:3), Immanuel (7:14), and Maher-shalal-hash-baz (8:3). With Isa 9:7, a new unit clearly distinct from the memoir begins.

The rest of Budde's work examines closely the individual parts of Isa 6:1–9:6, tracing in the course of the analysis the progressive experience of the prophet throughout the Syro-Ephraimitic crisis. As early as the temple vision, Isaiah realized that Yahweh was bringing judgment against his people in the guise of the Assyrian western campaigns (6:9–13).[9] The harshness and inevitability of this punishment, Budde explains, was already clear to the prophet at the time of his call. His preaching would meet resistance until destruction had swept over the land (vv 10–12). At the same time, however, Isaiah also anticipated salvation in the distant future. Out of the devastated people would emerge a pious remnant, a "holy seed" (v 13bb).

The imminence of the divine judgment, Budde argues, became apparent to Isaiah years later when he met with Ahaz shortly before the Syro-Ephraimitic siege of Jerusalem (7:1–25).[10] At first, the prophet's word was both encouraging and admonitory: the efforts of Rezin and Pekah to conquer Judah and replace the Davidic king with a certain ben Tabeel would fail (vv 6–7).[11] Yahweh would protect Zion and safeguard the king's throne on the condition that he "take heed," remain "quiet," "not fear," nor let his "heart fail" (v 4a). If the royal court would not "believe" in Yahweh's promise, it would not "remain" (v 9b). The threat implicit in the name of Isaiah's son, She'ar-yashub (v 3), would be fulfilled: only a small remnant would survive the destruction, turn to Yahweh, and receive divine mercy.

What "belief" entailed concretely in the eyes of the prophet is not explicit in the text. The interpretive key, Budde contends, lies in 2 Kgs

---

[8]Budde emends $\rangle el$-$y\check{e}\check{s}a^c y\bar{a}h\hat{u}$ in 7:3 and $wayy\bar{o}\rangle mer$ in 7:13 to first person forms, $\rangle\bar{e}lay$ and $w\bar{a}\rangle\bar{o}mar$ respectively.

[9]*Jesaja's Erleben*, 5–31. Budde views the temple vision as the inaugural call of Isaiah and dates the event to 740.

[10]*Jesaja's Erleben*, 31–68.

[11]Budde (41–42) rejects the thesis classically formulated by J. Begrich ("Der syrisch-ephraimitische Krieg und seine weltpolitischen Zusammenhänge," ZDMG 83 [1927] 213–37), that the Syro-Ephraimitic attack aimed at securing Judah as a member of a broad anti-Assyrian coalition. He views the episode as strictly an internal Syro-Palestinian conflict. In a later article ("Jesaja und Ahaz," ZDMG 84 [1931] 125–38), Budde argues at length against Begrich's interpretation of the war.

16:5, 7–9.[12] This passage reports that Ahaz, when faced with the Syro-Ephraimitic invasion, appealed to Tiglathpileser III, the Assyrian king, for military aid against the attacking troops, submitting at the same time to Assyrian vassalage. Isaiah's warnings in 7:4 and 9 supposedly were aimed against this appeal. "Belief" involved Ahaz's full trust in the promise of Yahweh (vv 7–9a) and his refusal to resort to foreign alliances.

The exchange between the king and prophet in 7:10–13 is, according to Budde, the turning point in their relationship.[13] In order to assure Ahaz of Yahweh's protection, Isaiah instructed the king to request a divine sign (vv 10–11). The latter, however, refused: "I will not put Yahweh to test" (v 12). The fraudulence of this excuse, Budde argues, is clear from the prophet's angry retort (v 13). Ahaz was bent upon appealing to Assyria and realized that the bestowal of a sign might force him to abandon the plan. The response of the prophet exposed the king's lack of faith and marked the decisive break between the two. Yahweh was no longer the God of Ahaz, but rather stood alone with Isaiah against the king.[14] The stubborn resistance which the prophet's mission was to meet (6:9–10) became fully manifest in this moment.

Budde's interpretation of the Immanuel saying (7:14–16) is determined in large part by his analysis of the preceding verses. After Ahaz rejected the first sign and with it Yahweh's promise of protection, the new sign offered by Yahweh himself could only mean disaster for the king and people.[15] The young woman and the child whom she would bear were representatives of the future generation. With them alone would Yahweh mercifully reside. As for the present generation, judgment in the form of Assyrian domination—a fate which they ironically brought upon themselves by appealing to the foreign king—was imminent: "Before the child will have learned to reject evil and to choose what is good, the land [Judah!] will be desolated."[16] Only the young mother and Immanuel would survive this punishment and learn through the subsequent hardship, symbolized by the child's meager diet, to choose the good which the generation of Ahaz spurned.[17] They would form the small but holy remnant to whom Yahweh's salvation would be given.

---

[12]*Jesaja's Erleben*, 36, 42, and 49.

[13]*Jesaja's Erleben*, 48–50.

[14]According to Budde, the shift from $'ĕlōhêkā$ (v 11) to $'ĕlōhāy$ (v 13) is highly significant.

[15]*Jesaja's Erleben*, 49–57.

[16]Budde excises the relative clause, $'ăšer 'attâ qāṣ mippĕnê šĕnê mĕlākêhā$, from v 16b as a gloss.

[17]Budde construes $lĕda'tô$ in v 15b as an expression of purpose.

The rest of the prophet's memoir, Budde explains, develops in detail the messages of judgment and salvation set forth in the Immanuel saying. Isaiah 7:17 announces in general terms the disaster which is soon to befall the Judean king and people. The threat is elaborated in vv 18–20: Assyria, the "hired razor" (an allusion to Ahaz's appeal to Tiglathpileser), will afflict not only Israel and Syria but Judah as well (v 20). The result will be the devastation of the land's culture, a disaster out of which, however, a new and righteous generation will emerge (vv 23–25, 21–22).[18] Chapter 8 reiterates the theme of doom: Tiglathpileser will not only crush the Syro-Ephraimitic alliance (8:1–4) but, as the result of Ahaz's voluntary submission to Assyrian vassalage, will sweep over Judah as well (8:5–8), bringing upon its inhabitants days of gloom and sorrow (8:18–22). Isaiah 8:23–9:6 concludes the memoir with a note of hope: the remnant that survives the Assyrian oppression will develop into a new Judean kingdom with a new and righteous ruler.[19]

What emerges so strikingly in this review of Budde's study is the central role which 2 Kgs 16:5–9 plays in the exegesis. Isaiah's initial warning to Ahaz (7:4–9), the king's refusal to request a sign (vv 10–13), the Immanuel saying (vv 14–16), and the subsequent announcements of judgment against the king and people (vv 17–25; 8:5–22) are all referred to the Assyrian alliance which the Kings text reports. Budde is certainly aware that nowhere in Isa 6:1–9:6 is Ahaz's appeal explicitly mentioned, but he is no less convinced that it forms the essential historical background of the prophetic speeches. The text does not refer explicitly to the appeal because it assumes the readers' knowledge of it. Isaiah had no need to specify the policy which he attacked because his readers were contemporary with it. They would have understood the Assyrian alliance as the prophet's concern.[20]

Analyses of Isa 6:1–9:6 which follow in the wake of Budde's work continue to assign 2 Kgs 16:5–9 a key role in the exegesis. The opinion becomes almost universal that, without a knowledge of the Assyrian alliance reported there, the prophet's speeches would remain "a sealed book."[21] Consequently, the general picture of Isaiah and Ahaz at odds with one another also persists. New interpretations of Isaiah's posture during the Syro-Ephraimitic crisis adjust the details of Budde's analysis along various interrelated lines. Particularly sig-

---

[18]Budde (63) argues that vv 23–24a, 25 originally preceded vv 21–22. He eliminates v 24b as a gloss.
[19]Budde (120–21) suggests Hezekiah as the royal "child."
[20]According to Budde in a later article ("Das Immanuelzeichen und die Ahaz-Begegnung Jesaja 7," *JBL* 52 [1933] 22–54), the fact that the text assumes so much as already known to the readers actually testifies to the genuine Isaianic authorship of the text, distinguishing it from legend. See n. 56 below.
[21]E. G. Kraeling, "The Immanuel Prophecy," *JBL* 50 (1931) 280.

nificant here are: (1) the study of the traditions which Isaiah used in his preaching during the crisis; (2) the reconsideration of the precise moment when the prophet broke with Ahaz, whether before or after the Immanuel saying; and (3) the organization and purpose of the *Denkschrift* as a whole.

B. Traditio-historical Studies

In *Der Heilige Krieg im Alten Testament*, G. von Rad examines Isa 7:4–9 and sees in the prophet's warnings to Ahaz the ideology of holy war.[22] Holy war, he explains, originally envisioned the cooperation of the Israelites and Yahweh in battle: the former are to fight fearlessly because the latter stands within their midst. In a later form of the tradition,[23] Yahweh's combat in Israel's wars excludes all human military participation. Faith in the absolute miracle of Yahweh's deliverance is emphasized. It is this later form of the holy war tradition, von Rad argues, which Isaiah takes up and actualizes during the Syro-Ephraimitic crisis. The prophet's purpose in 7:4–9 is to persuade the Judean king to abandon all defense measures.[24]

E. Würthwein subsequently modifies von Rad's thesis in two significant ways.[25] First, he contends that Isaiah's warnings in 7:4 take up the tradition of holy war in its original form. Just as the priestly address to troops in Deut 20:2–4 does not recommend military passiveness, but rather urges Israel to fight fearlessly, trusting upon Yahweh, so Isaiah exhorts Ahaz to forswear only those defense measures which exhibit faithlessness. Concretely in mind is the appeal to Assyria for military aid.[26] Würthwein admits that the political advisability of such counsel is difficult to evaluate.[27] The thrust of his

---

[22]G. von Rad, *Der Heilige Krieg im Alten Testament* (ATANT 20; Zurich: Zwingli, 1951) 56–58.
[23]Von Rad (33–49, 58) speaks of Solomonic and post-Solomonic *Novellisten*, for example, Exodus 14, Joshua 6, First Samuel 14, and Second Samuel 24.
[24]Von Rad's interpretation tends to agree with earlier estimations of prophetic politics as "utopian" (F. Weinrich, *Charakter der "prophetischen Politik"*) or "unclever and impractible for actual situations" (H. Gressmann, *Der Messias* [Göttingen: Vandenhoeck & Ruprecht, 1929] 238, n. 1).
[25]E. Würthwein, "Jesaja 7,1–9. Ein Beitrag zu dem Thema: Prophetie und Politik," in *Theologie als Glaubenswagnis. Festschrift für Karl Heim zum 80. Geburtstag* (Hamburg: Furche-Verlag, 1954) 47–63 = his *Wort und Existenz. Studien zum Alten Testament* (Göttingen: Vandenhoeck & Ruprecht, 1970) 127–43.
[26]"Jesaja 7,1–9," 54–55.
[27]The author (58) states: "It is vain to ask whether Isaiah or Ahaz had made the correct decision. Even if much could be said for submission to Assyrian vassalage, from the religious perspective of Judah it appeared as a mistrust in its God, out of which, according to the prophet's opinion, nothing good could grow."

argument is simply that the prophet's advice does not amount to what H. Gressmann describes as "sticking the hands in the pockets and waiting for divine help."[28]

Second, Würthwein also detects in Isa 7:1-9 the tradition of Yahweh's promise to David.[29] The divine saying in vv 7-9a is elliptical, he argues, and would logically be continued: "The head of Judah is Jerusalem and the head of Jerusalem is the Davidic house." The allusion is particularly apt in the context of the Syro-Ephraimitic crisis, for the plan of Rezin and Pekah (vv 5-6) threatened principally the royal house.

The prophetic warning in v 9b also alludes to the Davidic promise. The verbs, $ta\!\!\,^{\!\!,}ămînû$ and $tē\!\!\,^{\!\!,}āmēnû$, are forms of the root, $\!\!\,^{\!\!,}mn$, which also appears in 2 Sam 7:16: "And your (David's) house and kingship will be established ($wĕne\!\!\,^{\!\!,}man$) forever." The similar vocabulary, Würthwein argues, indicates that the whole of Isa 7:1-9 should be understood against the background of the Nathan prophecy. The aim of Isaiah's warning is that Ahaz realize for himself in the present moment of political crisis the Davidic promise: Yahweh will maintain his throne if he reciprocally keeps faith with Yahweh's covenant. Such faith dictates against all foreign alliances, particularly the one with Assyria which Ahaz was presumably considering.

Scholars have generally accepted Würthwein's interpretation, either wholly intact or with slight adjustments.[30] At the same time, they have extended the traditio-historical analysis to other parts of 6:1-9:6. W. Vischer detects the vocabulary and concepts of the Davidic tradition in 7:10-17.[31] Ahaz's refusal to request a sign from Yahweh allegedly reflects his disbelief in Yahweh's pledge to the Davidic house. Despite the prophet's assurance that Yahweh will protect the king's throne if only he "believes," Ahaz is bent on appealing to Assyria. Isaiah subsequently breaks with the king and announces his

---

[28]H. Gressmann, *Der Messias*, 237, quoted by Würthwein, "Jesaja 7,1-9," 50.

[29]"Jesaja 7,1-9," 139-43.

[30]W. Vischer (*Die Immanuel-Botschaft im Rahmen des königlichen Zionsfestes* [Zurich: Evangelischer Verlag, 1955]) seems to have detected the Davidic tradition in 7:1-9, and elsewhere within 6:1-9:6, independently of Würthwein. He proposes a royal Zion festival as the original setting of the tradition (following H.-J. Kraus, *Die Königsherrschaft Gottes im Alten Testament* [Tübingen: J. C. B. Mohr (Paul Siebeck), 1951]). R. Kilian (*Die Verheissung Immanuels. Jes 7,14* [SBS 35; Stuttgart: Katholisches Bibelwerk, 1968] 26-30) questions whether 7:7-9a is elliptical, but otherwise follows Würthwein's interpretation. K. Seybold (*Das davidische Königtum im Zeugnis der Propheten* [FRLANT 107; Göttingen: Vandenhoeck & Ruprecht, 1972] 68-69) buttresses the interpretation by comparing Isaiah 7 and Psalm 2. J. M. Asurmendi (*La Guerra Siro-Efraimita*, 84) argues that the holy war and Davidic traditions had already combined in the royal ideology that Isaiah inherited.

[31]W. Vischer, *Die Immanuel-Botschaft*, 20-25.

replacement by Immanuel, the son of David par excellence. For him and through him Yahweh will realize his promise to David as it is recounted annually in the royal Zion festival.

Other tradition streams have been detected in the Immanuel saying. E. Hammershaimb sees in v 14 a quotation from the Jerusalem royal cult, promising the queen's pregnancy and the subsequent birth of a royal heir.[32] Ugaritic parallels to the motif, he contends, point to Canaanite mythology as the ultimate tradition source.

Alternatively, H. W. Wolff sees in 7:10–17 the language and thought of holy war.[33] In refusing to ask a sign from Yahweh (vv 10–12), Ahaz rejects his call as the deliverer of Yahweh's people in holy war, choosing instead to rely on Assyrian aid. The king, Wolff suggests, appears here as an antitype to Gideon, the savior of Israel par excellence, who requested and received a divine sign confirming his deliverer role (Judg 6:14–24, 36–40). Similarly, the promise of a child in Isaiah 7 echoes Judg 13:3–5, the birth-announcement of Samson, another deliverer of Israel. Also significant, Wolff contends, is the very name Immanuel ("God-with-us"): it echoes the promise of Yahweh's presence with Israel in holy war (see Deut 20:4; Judg 6:12, 16). The circle which the name describes is the prophet and his few followers, the holy remnant which puts its faith in Yahweh. For Ahaz and the royal court, the sign functions ironically. By appealing to Assyria, they forfeit Yahweh's saving presence and ultimately bring judgment upon themselves.

Scholars have discerned the Davidic tradition in the remainder of 6:1–9:6, though the nature of the evidence varies from text to text. In 8:6, for example, the "waters of Shiloah" are understood by Vischer, and more recently by J. M. Asurmendi, as a symbolic reference to the royal house.[34] The rejection of these waters by "this people," Vischer argues, amounts to disbelief in the Davidic promise: "melting in fear before Rezin and the son of Remaliah" (emending v 6b), they appealed to Tiglathpileser.[35] Or again in 8:11–15, the charge of

---

[32]E. Hammershaimb, "The Immanuel Sign," *ST* 3 (1949) 124–42 = his *Some Aspects of Old Testament Prophecy from Isaiah to Malachi* (Copenhagen: Rosenkilde og Bagger, 1966) 9–28.

[33]H. W. Wolff, *Frieden ohne Ende. Jesaja 7,1–17 und 9,1–6 ausgelegt* (BibS[N] 35; Neukirchen-Vluyn: Neukirchener Verlag, 1962) 26–52.

[34]W. Vischer, *Die Immanuel-Botschaft*, 25–26; J. M. Asurmendi, *La Guerra Siro-Efraimita*, 66–68.

[35]Asurmendi retains the reading of the Masoretic Text ("rejoice in Rezin and the son of Remaliah") and consequently arrives at a very different understanding. The verse, he explains, testifies to Judean support for the coalition, widespread opposition to Ahaz, and the people's rejection of the Davidic promise. As we will see, this interpretation, if combined with other considerations, could lead one to reassess the overall relationship between the king and

"conspiracy" (*qešer*), whether levelled against Isaiah who opposed the Assyrian alliance (Vischer) or against the Syro-Ephraimitic coalition which was attacking Jerusalem (Asurmendi), designates action against the royal house.[36] Yahweh's pledge to David is thus at stake in the present crisis. Finally, in 8:23–9:6, the language and concepts of the royal ideology have been widely recognized and are most recently reviewed by Asurmendi.[37] The evidence includes the motif of the enemies' destruction (vv 1–4; compare Pss 2:5, 8; 21:9–12; 2 Sam 7:9), the mention of a royal "child" (v 5; compare 2 Sam 7:14; Pss 2:7 and 89:27–28), the titles of the child,[38] and the description of his reign as just and righteous (v 6; compare Pss 89:15, 97:2, Isa 11:3–5, 32:1). These features of the text characterize the royal figure as an ideal Davidic ruler and present him as an antitype to the contemporary Davidide.[39]

C. *The Immanuel Prophecy*

In addition to and in part overlapping with the traditio-historical questions, scholars debate the precise moment when Isaiah rejected Ahaz. The issue centers upon the meaning of the Immanuel saying: is it encouragement to the king or an announcement of his demise? The latter interpretation is presented by Budde and subsequently defended by most scholars.[40] The following arguments are frequently

---

prophet. Asurmendi, however, continues to view Isaiah at odds with Ahaz over the king's appeal to Assyria.

[36] W. Vischer, *Die Immanuel-Botschaft*, 29–30; J. M. Asurmendi, *La Guerra Siro-Efraimita*, 69–73.

[37] J. M. Asurmendi, *La Guerra Siro-Efraimita*, 75–79.

[38] "Wonderful Counsellor," Asurmendi explains (78), calls to mind Isa 7:5–7, 8:9–10, 11:2, 28:29, 29:14, Ps 20:5 and Judg 13:18–19. "Heroic God" echoes Pss 20:7–8, 24:8, 45:7, 89:20, and Isa 10:21. "Everlasting Father" supposedly reflects the thought of II Sam 7:14. "Prince of Peace" is reminiscent of Ps 72:7, Isa 11:6–9, Mic 5:4, Judg 6:24, and the names of David's two sons, Absalom and Solomon.

[39] See for example G. von Rad, *Old Testament Theology*, 2. 171; K. Seybold, *Das davidische Königtum*, 88–89; H. W. Wolff, *Frieden ohne Ende*, 69–70; H. Gressmann, *Der Messias*, 242–46; S. Mowinckel, *He That Cometh* (Oxford/Nashville: B. H. Blackwell/Abingdon, 1956) 165–86; M. E. W. Thompson, *Situation and Theology*, 14, 45–48; idem., "Isaiah's Ideal King," *JSOT* 24 (1982) 79–88. A minority opinion identifies the child with Hezekiah; see for example M. Buber, *Der Glaube der Propheten*, 200–208; J. Lindblom, *A Study on the Immanuel Section in Isaiah. Isa. vii,1–ix,6* (Lund: CWK Gleerup, 1958) 25; and J. M. Asurmendi, *La Guerra Siro-Efraimita*, 79.

[40] Here we associate interpretations of the passage as entirely judgment and readings which see in the saying a measure of hope as well. All agree that the verses announce doom for the king. See the review of literature on the Immanuel saying in J. J. Stamm, "Neuere Arbeiten zum Immanuel-Problem, *ZAW* 68 (1956) 46–53; idem., "Die Immanuel-Perikope im Lichte neuerer Veröffentlichungen,"

given. (1) The prophet accuses Ahaz of exhausting Yahweh's patience and implies that Yahweh is no longer the king's God (v 13). (2) The *lākēn* ("therefore") which introduces the Immanuel sign connotes a threat (v 14). (3) The diet of the child, "curds and honey," symbolizes an end to all culture in the land (v 15). (4) Verse 17 appears to announce judgment against the royal house and Judah.

Two elements within 7:14–17 do not easily fit the interpretation of the saying as judgment. First, v 16 in its present form threatens Rezin and Pekah and thus appears to function indirectly as encouragement to Ahaz. The incongruity is recognized by many and resolved in one of three ways: (a) by discarding the whole of v 16 as a late editorial addition[41]; (b) by eliminating v 16b, or at least the final relative clause, as secondary, thereby transforming the verse into an announcement of disaster against Judah[42]; or (c) by transposing the whole of v 16 to a place where its hopeful meaning is appropriate.[43] Others, however, question whether the threat against the enemies implies salvation for Ahaz and so allow v 16 to stand as it is.[44] Divine judgment in the guise of the Assyrian westward campaigns will sweep not only over Syria and Israel (already implied in vv 7–9), but also over Judah. Ahaz's short-term relief from the Syro-Ephraimitic coalition is insignificant in comparison to the long-term punishment which he and his people will suffer at the hand of Assyria.

Second, the name of the child, Immanuel, means "God with us" and, in accordance with the expression's hopeful meaning elsewhere in the Hebrew Bible, would seem to signify salvation for Ahaz. Schol-

---

ZDMGSup 1 (1969) 281–90. More recent interpretations of the passage as judgment against Ahaz include R. Bartelmus, "Jes 7,1–17 und das Stilprinzip des Kontrastes. Syntaktisch-stilistische und traditionsgeschichtliche Anmerkungen zur 'Immanuel-Perikope,'" *ZAW* 96 (1984) 50–66; R. E. Clements, *Isaiah 1–39* (Grand Rapids/London: Eerdmans/Marshall, Morgan & Scott, 1980) 89; W. Dietrich, *Jesaja und die Politik*, 75–81, 95–96; J. Jensen, "The Age of Immanuel," *CBQ* 41 (1979) 220–39; R. Kilian, *Jesaja 1–39* (ErFor 200; Darmstadt: Wissenschaftliche Buchgesellschaft, 1983) 12–26; G. Rice, "The Interpretation of Isa 7:15–17," *JBL* 96 (1977) 363–69; idem., "A Neglected Interpretation of the Immanuel Prophecy," *ZAW* 90 (1978) 220–27; M. E. W. Thompson, *Situation and Theology*, 29–30.

[41]See for example A. H. J. Gunneweg, "Heils- und Unheilsverkündigung in Jes. VII," *VT* 15 (1965) 27–34; G. Rice, "The Interpretation of Isa 7:15–17," 363–69.

[42]See K. Budde, *Jesaja's Erleben*, 49–57; O. Procksch, *Jesaja I* (KAT 9; Leipzig: A. Deichert, 1930) 124; R. Kilian, *Die Verheissung Immanuels*, 41–44; G. Fohrer, *Das Buch Jesaja* (2 vols.; 2d ed.; Zurich/Stuttgart: Zwingli, 1966) 1. 110–17; O. Kaiser, *Isaiah 1–12* (2d ed.; London/Philadelphia: SCM/Westminster, 1983) 151–72.

[43]See, for example, W. Dietrich, *Jesaja und die Politik*, 79–82.

[44]See for example W. Vischer, *Die Immanuel-Botschaft*, 20–25; H. W. Wolff, *Frieden ohne Ende*, 41–47; K. Seybold, *Das davidische Königtum*, 72–78; O. H. Steck, "Beiträge zum Verständnis von Jesaja 7,10–17 und 8,1–4," *TZ* 29 (1973) 161–78; H. Wildberger, *Jesaja 1–12* (BKAT 10/1; 2d ed.; Neukirchen-Vluyn: Neukirchener Verlag, 1980) 294–97; and M. E. W. Thompson, *Situation and Theology*, 29–30.

ars who construe 7:14–17 as judgment against Ahaz handle the apparent discrepancy in one of two ways. (a) The hopeful meaning of "God with us" is admitted, but referred to someone other than Ahaz and the royal court. The likely candidate is Isaiah himself and the small group of followers who "believe." They alone form the holy remnant with whom God will be present.[45] (b) The name is interpeted as a threat. "God-with-us" signifies God's presence with Ahaz and Judah for judgment and punishment.[46] Alternatively, the name is construed as a cry of distress ("God be with us!") by someone in dire circumstances. As applied to the king and royal house, the expression emphasizes the disaster that will soon befall them.[47]

A small but nonetheless significant number of scholars construe the Immanuel saying as encouragement to Ahaz. Most notable are the analyses of E. G. Kraeling, E. Hammershaimb, J. Lindblom, J. Coppens, J. J. Scullion, H. Donner, and J. J. M. Roberts.[48] Their collective arguments include the following. First, the prophet's rebuke of Ahaz in v 13, together with the shift here from "your God" (v 11) to "my God," reflect Isaiah's anger with the king, but not necessarily a decisive break between the two. Second, the *lākēn* ("therefore") which introduces the Immanuel sign does not invariably signal announcements of disaster. Third, the child's name "God-with-us" is a quotation from the Jerusalem royal cult and, as a sign given to the king, likely bears a hopeful meaning. Fourth, Ugaritic parallels to the promise of a young woman's pregnancy and the birth of a son suggest that the woman is the Judean queen. The birth of a royal child can only function as encouragement to Ahaz: he and his house will survive the present crisis.[49] Fifth, the diet of the child (v 15) symbolizes the future well-being and fruitfulness of Ahaz's realm. Sixth, while v 16 proclaims disaster against Rezin and Pekah, v 17 functions as a promise to Ahaz: under Davidic rule the Judean and Israelite kingdoms will be reunited.

One might expect this interpretation of the Immanuel saying to lead to a radical reappraisal of the relations between the king and

---

[45]See for example H. W. Wolff, *Frieden ohne Ende*, 43.
[46]See for example N. K. Gottwald, *All the Kingdoms of the Earth*, 157.
[47]See especially T. Lescow, "Das Geburtsmotiv in den messianischen Weissagungen bei Jesaja und Micha," *ZAW* 79 (1967) 176–80.
[48]E. G. Kraeling, "The Immanuel Prophecy," 277–97; E. Hammershaimb, "The Immanuel Sign," 124–42; J. Lindblom, *The Immanuel Section*, 15–28; J. Coppens, *La Prophétie de la ʿAlmah* (ALBO II/35; Louvain: Publications universitaires de Louvain, 1952); J. J. Scullion, "An Approach to the Understanding of Isaiah 7:10–17," *JBL* 87 (1968) 288–300; H. Donner, *Israel unter den Völkern*, 16–18; J. J. M. Roberts, "Isaiah and His Children," in *Biblical and Related Studies Presented to Samuel Iwry* (eds. A. Kort and S. Morschauser; Winona Lake: Eisenbrauns, 1985) 193–203.
[49]See especially E. Hammershaimb, "The Immanuel Sign," 126–35.

prophet. This reappraisal, however, does not occur, largely because Second Kings 16 continues to play a central role in the exegesis. The Assyrian alliance remains the assumed point of contention between Isaiah and Ahaz and the cause of their alleged falling out. Construing the Immanuel sign as encouragement to the king, scholars redate the saying to a time preceding the appeal and reinterpret its function as an attempt to dissuade Ahaz from that course of action. The prophet's failure in this regard and his subsequent break with the king are supposedly evident in other passages like 8:5–8.

D. *The Organization and Purpose of the Denkschrift*

The organization and purpose of the *Denkschrift* are also matters of ongoing debate. Relevant here are those studies which ascribe the document, either in its present or an earlier form, to Isaiah.[50] Budde, as seen above, believes that the speeches proceed in rough chronological order and, with respect to content, exhibit the following progression. (1) Isaiah foresees the failure of his mission, divine judgment, and the survival of a holy remnant (6:1–13). (2) The prophet recounts how Ahaz rejected his advice and appealed to Assyria for help (7:1–13). (3) He announces imminent disaster against both the Syrian-Israelite alliance and Judah (7:14–8:22). (4) Isaiah anticipates the future salvation of a remnant (9:1–6). The purpose of the *Denkschrift* as a whole is to justify retrospectively Isaiah's posture during the Syro-Ephraimitic war. K. Marti adjusts this interpretation only slightly.[51] (1) He detects a gap between chapters 6 and 7 and so hypothesizes a lost piece which related the birth of She'ar-yashub and explained the name's symbolic meaning. (2) Marti ascribes the texts that speak of salvation (for example, 6:12–13, 8:8b–10, and 9:1–6) to a late redactor. The *Denkschrift* in its original form portrayed Isaiah's rejection, first predicted in the call vision (6:1–11), and concluded with repeated announcements of disaster against Ahaz and Judah. Only with the addition of editorial passages did the prophet's message gain a hopeful eschatological element.

Renewed attention to the *Denkschrift* in recent years has detected increasingly detailed schemes. T. Lescow limits the original document to 7:1–9, 10–19, 8:1–8, 11–15, and 16–18.[52] The first three units, he argues, are formed on the same structural pattern: (1) a description

---

[50]Besides the works of Budde, K. Marti, T. H. Lescow, and H.-P. Müller which we discuss below, see O. H. Steck, "Rettung und Verstockung. Exegetische Bemerkungen zu Jesaja 7,3–7," *EvT* 33 (1973) 73–90. We comment on Steck's interpretation of the *Denkschrift* in Section E below.
[51]K. Marti, "Der jesajanische Kern in Jes 6,1–9,6," *BZAW* 34 (1920) 113-21.
[52]T. Lescow, "Jesajas Denkschrift aus der Zeit des syrisch-ephraimitischen Krieges," *ZAW* 85 (1973) 315–31.

of the situation (7:1–3, 10–14a, 8:1–3a); (2) an oracle (7:4, 14b–16, 8:3b–4); and (3) an announcement of disaster (7:5–9, 17–19, 8:6–8). Isaiah 8:11–15 and 16–18 also begin with prose descriptions of the situation (vv 11–13, 16–18a), and then continue with metrical sayings—either an announcement of disaster (vv 14–15) or a liturgical conclusion (v 18b). The progression of the units, Lescow contends, is not, as traditionally argued, a conditional promise to Ahaz giving way to an unconditional threat against Syria, Israel, and Judah alike. Rather, what was at first a prediction of disaster for the Syro-Ephraimitic coalition and a warning to Ahaz against hasty defense measures evolves into an announcement of judgment against all three nations. The shift in Isaiah's preaching allegedly occurs because Ahaz did not "remain still," as the prophet had urged. Because the king appealed to Tiglathpileser for help, the Assyrians would overrun not only Syria and Israel, but also Judah. The *Denkschrift* concludes with an expression of hope in Yahweh's future mercy.

According to H.-P. Müller, the internal cohesion of the *Denkschrift* consists in the programmatic development of the prophet's concept of faith.[53] The central part of the original document (7:2–17, 8:1–15) consists of a series of paired expressions of salvation and disaster, the dialectically related aspects of the faith-concept. In the first pair, an unconditional promise to Ahaz (Rezin and Pekah would be defeated; 7:4–9a) is followed by a conditional threat (the Davidic House would fall; v 9b). In each of the subsequent pairs (7:14–16 and v 17; 8:1–4 and vv 6–8a; 8:9–10 and vv 12–15), the unconditional promise that the Syrian-Israelite coalition would fail is followed by the unconditional announcement of disaster for Ahaz and Judah. Because of Ahaz's lack of faith, evidenced in his appeal to Assyria, the "either-or" relation of promise and threat in 7:4–9 gives way to a "both-and" relation between the two. The plans of Rezin and Pekah will fail, but Ahaz and Judah will suffer too at the hands of Assyria.

To this central corpus, Müller explains, Isaiah added the account of his call (6:1–13) and the concluding instructions for the written preservation of the *Denkschrift* (8:16–18). The purpose of the document is to emphasize how, in the fulfillment of the collected oracles, Isaiah's status as a genuine prophet of Yahweh is vindicated. The prefixing of the call account explains the meaning of the prophet's failed mission: Yahweh had intended his prophecy to effect the impenitence of "this people."[54]

---

[53]H.-P. Müller, "Glauben und Bleiben. Zur Denkschrift Jesajas Kapitel vi 1–viii 18," *VTSup* 26 (1974) 25–54.
[54]C. Hardmeier ("Verkündigung und Schrift bei Jesaja. Zur Entstehung der Schriftprophetie als Oppositionsliteratur im alten Israel," *TGl* 73 [1983] 119–34) emphasizes the function of Isaiah's *Denkschrift* as instruction to the prophet's few

E. Critique

The above survey has highlighted two facts. First, amidst the various interpretations of Isaiah's relationship with Ahaz, a basic two-part concensus persists. (a) The prophet rejected the king midway through the Syro-Ephraimitic crisis. (b) Ahaz's appeal to Assyria precipitated the break. Second, this concensus rests on the correlation of Isaiah's speeches with the historical notice in 2 Kgs 16:5–9. Several considerations undermine this correlation, at least as it has traditionally been made, and raise doubts about the resulting picture of Isaiah and Ahaz at odds with one another.

The speeches of Isaiah provide strikingly little clear evidence that he rejected Ahaz. If in fact the break occurred, one might expect to read at least one unambiguous statement about it. Nowhere, however, is the king's rejection explicit. The threats in 8:5–8 and 11–15 denounce the behavior of "this people," but say nothing against Ahaz and his policies specifically. Isaiah 7:17, as it now stands, does announce disaster upon the royal house. Once, however, the concluding reference to the Assyrian king is removed as a secondary addition,[55] the verse can be understood as encouragement to Ahaz, promising the reunion of the Israelite and Judean kingdoms under Davidic rule. Isaiah 7:18–25 announce Yahweh's punishment of the "land," but again the verses neither reproach nor threaten the Davidic House specifically. In 7:10–13, the cryptic exchange between the king and prophet certainly reflects tension between the two, but not necessarily a decisive falling out.

If one reads the speeches of Isaiah in isolation, one would never guess that the point of contention between him and Ahaz was the latter's thought of appealing to Assyria. It may be reasonable to suppose in light of Isa 30:1–17 and 31:1–5 that the prophet would have opposed such an appeal, but that this was in fact Isaiah's concern during the Syro-Ephraimitic crisis is not indicated by the prophetic texts themselves. One must infer it from the notice in 2 Kgs 16:5–9.

The failure of the prophetic texts to refer explicitly to the Assyrian alliance has frequently been explained by suggesting that the prophet, writing for his contemporaries, could assume his readers' knowledge of the alliance. According to Budde, the fact that the material, particularly in Isaiah 7, can assume this information is precisely

---

followers in the wake of the Syro-Ephraimitic crisis. The progression which he sees in the content of the document is similar to that laid out by Müller.

[55]The vast majority of commentators view the reference as a late addition. M. E. W. Thompson ("Isaiah's Sign of Immanuel," *ExpTim* 95 [1983/84] 69) is one of the few to retain "the king of Assyria" as an original part of the text, but he does not argue the point.

what marks it apart from legend and vouchsafes its historicity.[56] This interpretation is certainly possible. The silence of the prophetic texts, however, admits another explanation as well. What remains unsaid may not be assumed, but simply unknown. Again, it is striking how, in all of the Isaianic material, the supposed assumption of the speeches—Ahaz's appeal to Assyria—does not once come to clear expression. What one finds rather is a series of ambiguous, if not obscure, warnings, promises, and exchanges which may or may not indicate a break between the king and prophet. The strategy of Budde and the majority of subsequent scholars is to construe these as evidence of Isaiah's rejection of Ahaz and to cite the Assyrian alliance reported in Second Kings 16 as the obvious issue of dispute.

In recent years a few dissident voices have questioned the quick correlation of Isaiah's speeches and the Kings text. P. R. Ackroyd examines the presentations of the Syro-Ephraimitic crisis in Second Kings 16, Isaiah 7 and 8, and Second Chronicles 28, highlighting the differences of detail and interest among the three accounts.[57] He concludes with a warning against conflating the traditions, lest in search of the history behind them one obscures the distinctive theological contours of each. Ackroyd makes the same point in a more recent study where he remarks on Isaiah 7 and 8:

> It is often stated, as if it were self-evident, that Isaiah warned Ahaz against appealing to Assyria for help, but this is not in the text. If it is proper to regard it as a logical position for the prophet to hold . . . we must still ask why the text does not make the point explicit.[58]

Ackroyd answers that the appeal, assuming that it did occur, is irrelevant to the theological interest of the tradition. The Isaiah material emphasizes only that "because of divine protection Ahaz and his court had no need to fear Aram and Israel" and that "a king who lacks faith in Yahweh must expect doom at the hands of Assyria."[59]

---

[56]"Das Immanuelzeichen," 36–54. Budde dialogues here with H. Gressmann (*Der Messias*, 235–42) and E. Kraeling ("The Immanuel Prophecy," 277–97), both of whom describe Isa 7:1–17 as a prophetic legend. Legend, Budde argues, guards carefully against misunderstanding at every step of the narrative. In contrast, Isaiah 7 assumes a great deal as known to the reader, particularly the historical background given in Second Kings 16. "Everything [in Isaiah 7] reflects the immediate present, the discussion between individuals whose personal interests are involved, between persons who are totally informed about matters. Only the prophet himself can be made responsible for such a depiction of events" (39).

[57]P. R. Ackroyd, "Historians and Prophets," *SEÅ* 33 (1968) 22–37.

[58]P. R. Ackroyd, "The Biblical Interpretation of the Reigns of Ahaz and Hezekiah," in *In the Shelter of Elyon: Essays on Ancient Palestinian Life and Literature in Honor of G. W. Ahlström* (eds. W. B. Barrick and J. R. Spencer; Sheffield: JSOT Press, 1984) 250.

[59]"The Reigns of Ahaz and Hezekiah," 250.

The exegetical remarks on Isa 7:3–9 by O. H. Steck move in the same direction.[60] Whether Isaiah advised Ahaz to abandon all defense measures or simply the plan to appeal to Assyria is difficult to decide, Steck explains, because both choices make the text more precise than it really is by introducing data which stands behind the present text. Within the context of the *Denkschrift*, the pericope is oriented neither toward the king's difficult political situation nor toward the right or wrong policy decision. It focuses rather on the encounter between Yahweh and Ahaz, on the response of the king to the divine word, whether faithful or not. The unit and those which follow were brought together with the intention of demonstrating the resistance to Yahweh's word (the *Verstockung*) proleptically announced in 6:9ff. Steck concedes that one may move behind the present text to address the historical question—what concrete policies of the king did Isaiah oppose? He emphasizes, however, that in so doing, one cannot expect a decisive answer from the prophetic material alone, because it itself is interested in other matters.[61]

Neither Ackroyd nor Steck doubt that the Assyrian appeal occurred, nor do they question its importance in the actual preaching of Isaiah. Their point is exegetical, not historical. The silence of the prophetic text is a reflex of its distinctive theological *Tendenz*, in light of which the appeal and other untold details of the war are simply irrelevant.

Chapter Four of this study will examine closely and evaluate the *Denkschrift* hypothesis and the various understandings of the material's editorial arrangement. The critique will argue that the overall *Tendenz* of Isaiah 7 and 8 is not as evident as Ackroyd, Steck, and others suggest. The material sets forth a variety of messages, but these do not follow one another schematically in a way that expresses a clear overarching theological point. It is difficult, then, to explain the silences of the material by appealing to its distinctive *Tendenz*.

Interpreting Isaiah's preaching during the Syro-Ephraimitic crisis requires the use of outside sources and/or a working reconstruction of the crisis. His speeches are not general theological statements understandable on their own. Rather, they are concrete sayings for a definite circle pursuing specific policies at a particular time.[62] As such, they are fraught with assumptions which the exegete and historian must seek to recover with all the evidence available. If previous treatments of Isaiah's preaching during the Syro-Ephraimitic crisis

---

[60] O. H. Steck, "Rettung und Verstockung," 77–90.
[61] "Rettung und Verstockung," 87–88.
[62] E. Würthwein ("Jesaja 7,1–9," 140) also stresses the particularity of Isaiah's message: "With Isaiah, like all prophets, it is a matter of an entirely concrete saying to a well-defined audience in a unique situation. The more we keep that in mind, the sharper we will see what he intended."

can be faulted, it is not because they import outside data into the exegesis of his speeches. Rather, the fault lies in their not having scrutinized the reliability of that data sufficiently. This criticism pertains specifically to the widespread use of Second Kings 16.

One aim of the present work is to argue that Ahaz paid Assyrian tribute only after the Assyrians had invaded Palestine in 734/733. The special appeal reported in Second Kings 16 is not likely historical. While the arguments for this conclusion are not conclusive individually, their cumulative force weighs against the appeal as the factual background of Isaiah's speeches.

Once the idea of the appeal is set aside as the interpretive key to the prophetic material, new possibilities for understanding Isaiah's posture toward Ahaz arise. Our interpretation of Isaiah's speeches during the Syro-Ephraimitic crisis construes the prophet as a fervent legitimist for the Davidic dynasty and a loyal supporter of Ahaz specifically. Far from rejecting the Judean king, he denounced the majority of Judeans for opposing Ahaz and his isolationist foreign policy.

F. Overview of the Dissertation

The work falls largely into two sections. Part I focuses on the nature and course of the Syro-Ephraimitic crisis. Any proposed reconstruction of the crisis and of Ahaz's policy in that crisis must rely heavily on the Assyrian texts relating to Tiglathpileser's activity in the west (Chapter Two). Of particular concern here are the number of states which opposed Assyria in 734–731, the role of Syria and Rezin in the revolt, the specific goals and strategies of the individual coalition members and of Assyria, and the general outline of events. Chapter Three analyzes and assesses the biblical accounts of the Syro-Ephraimitic crisis, Second Kings 16 and Second Chronicles 28, and concludes with a comprehensive sketch of the war.

Part II studies the speeches of Isaiah delivered during the crisis against the historical background recovered in Part I. Scholars dispute which texts derive from the prophet and relate to the Syro-Ephraimitic crisis. Chapter Four accordingly discusses the selection of prophetic texts for study and addresses the question of their editorial arrangement. We then analyze the prophetic material en route toward sketching Isaiah's posture during the war, particularly his attitude toward and relation to Ahaz and the royal house (Chapters Five through Ten).

Part II clearly depends on the results of Part I, but the reverse is also true. The speeches of the prophet and their historical background relate in fact as poles of a dialectic: one's view of the Syro-Ephraimitic crisis informs the interpretation of the speeches; conversely, the speeches themselves provide crucial information about the political dynamics of the war. Historical reconstruction thus goes on throughout the study. Part I arrives at a general outline of the Syro-Ephraimitic crisis; Part II fills out that outline with important historical details. These details in turn aid in understanding the meaning of Isaiah's speeches. An hermeneutical circle is thus unavoidable.

Parts I and II are mutually dependent in another way. In sketching the background of Isaiah's speeches, Part I marshals arguments against the claim in Second Kings 16 that Ahaz appealed to Tiglath-pileser for military help. These arguments include the utter silence about the appeal in the Assyrian texts and the tendentious character of Second Kings 16. The case gains strength, however, from the analysis of Isaiah's speeches in Part II. There we see that the prophet nowhere mentions the appeal, but alludes rather to another issue of concern, namely, the pressure on Ahaz from many Judeans to join the anti-Assyrian coalition. The skepticism towards Second Kings 16 is partly vindicated by the fact that the prophetic material makes good sense apart from the idea of an appeal to Assyria.

Part III (Chapter Eleven) concludes the entire study. Here we combine the results of Parts I and II in a brief, general summary.

PART I

THE SYRO-EPHRAIMITIC CRISIS

CHAPTER TWO

THE ASSYRIAN TEXTS RELATING TO THE
SYRO-EPHRAIMITIC CRISIS

The biblical accounts portray the Syro-Ephraimitic crisis as a regional conflict largely between Rezin of Syria, Pekah of Israel, and Ahaz of Judah. It is widely thought, however, that the episode in fact related to a broad anti-Assyrian movement in Syria and Palestine during the late 730s.[1] This conclusion depends primarily on the interpretation of Assyrian inscriptions from the reign of Tiglathpileser III, but also, to a limited degree, on biblical materials that presumably fill in the Assyrian evidence. No previous study of the Syro-Ephraimitic crisis has examined and interpreted all of the relevant Assyrian texts closely. This chapter thus provides a detailed and comprehensive treatment of the inscriptions.

Because the Assyrian and biblical accounts refer alike to the kings of Israel and Judah, questions about how and when the kings rose to power are important to any historical treatment of the texts. We recognize that the royal chronology of Israel and Judah during the second half of the eighth century is a very difficult problem, and that any set of dates proposed for the kings depends on many assumptions and hypotheses.[2] Nevertheless, if we are going to use the

---

[1] J. Begrich ("Der syrisch-ephraimitische Krieg," 213–37) was the first to emphasize the "world-political connections" of the Syro-Ephraimitic crisis and most scholars subsequently have shared this view of the war. B. Oded ("The Historical Background of the Syro-Ephraimite War Reconsidered," *CBQ* 34 [1972] 153–65) is a notable exception. He views the crisis as primarily a regional conflict. Compare also R. Bickert, "König Ahas und der Prophet Jesaja. Ein Beitrag zum Problem des syrisch-ephraimitischen Krieges," *ZAW* 99 (1987) 361–84.

[2] For extensive bibliography on the subject and a brief delineation of the issues, see J. H. Hayes and J. M. Miller, eds., *Israelite and Judean History* (Philadelphia: Westminster, 1977) 678–83. More recent studies of the biblical chronology include the following: W. H. Barnes, *Studies in the Chronology of the Divided Monarchy of Israel* (dissertation, Harvard University, 1986); J. R. A. Hughes, *The Secrets of the*

Assyrian and biblical texts to reconstruct the Syro-Ephraimitic crisis, at least a tentative chronology is necessary at the outset. We adopt the chronology recently proposed by J. H. Hayes and P. K. Hooker.[3] An appendix at the end of this chapter presents it briefly.

A. The Eponym List

The Assyrians named each year after a different government official and compiled lists of the eponym years.[4] Two major lists have survived. One (so-called Canon A) records only the eponyms; the other (Canon B) lists both the eponyms and their titles and records as well the most important event of each year. The second list is obviously more valuable to the historian and fortunately is well preserved for the reign of Tiglathpileser III (745–727). It documents the following campaigns of the king.[5]

Nisan 745 – Nisan 744	On the 13th day of Airu Tiglathpileser sat on the throne. In the month of Tashritu he marched to the territory between the rivers.
Nisan 744 – Nisan 743	against Namri
Nisan 743 – Nisan 742	in the city of Arpad. A massacre took place in the land of Urartu.
Nisan 742 – Nisan 741	against Arpad
Nisan 741 – Nisan 740	against Arpad. After three years it was conquered.
Nisan 740 – Nisan 739	against Arpad
Nisan 739 – Nisan 738	against Ulluba. The fortress was taken.
Nisan 738 – Nisan 737	Kullani was captured.
Nisan 737 – Nisan 736	against Madai
Nisan 736 – Nisan 735	to the foot of Mount Nal

Times: Recovering Biblical Chronologies (Sheffield: JSOT Press, 1989); N. Na'aman, "Historical and Chronological Notes on the Kingdoms of Israel and Judah in the Eighth Century B.C.," *VT* 36 (1986) 71–92; J. Reade, "Mesopotamian Guidelines for Biblical Chronology," *Syro-Mesopotamian Studies* 4/1 (1981) 1–9; and H. Tadmor, "The Chronology of the First Temple Period: A Presentation and Evaluation of the Sources," *WHJP* 4/1 (1979) 44–60, 318–20 = J. A. Soggin, *A History of Ancient Israel* (London/Philadelphia: SCM/Westminster, 1984) 368–83, 408–11.

[3]J. H. Hayes and P. K. Hooker, *A New Chronology for the Kings of Israel and Judah and Its Implications for Biblical History and Literature* (Atlanta: John Knox, 1988).

[4]For detailed descriptions of the Assyrian eponym lists, see A. Ungnad, "Eponym," in *Reallexikon der Assyriologie* (6 vols.; eds. E. Ebling and B. Meissner; Berlin: Walter de Gruyter, 1932) 2. 412–57; also A. K. Grayson, *Assyrian and Babylonian Chronicles* (Locust Valley, NY: J. J. Augustin, 1975).

[5]Since the Assyrians used a spring calendar, each year began in Nisan (March/April). Unfortunately the Eponym List does not date the campaigns more precisely.

Nisan 735 – Nisan 734	against Urartu
Nisan 734 – Nisan 733	against Philistia
Nisan 733 – Nisan 732	against the land of Damascus
Nisan 732 – Nisan 731	against the land of Damascus
Nisan 731 – Nisan 730	against Sapia
Nisan 730 – Nisan 729	in the land
Nisan 729 – Nisan 728	The king took the hand of Bel.
Nisan 728 – Nisan 727	The king took the hand of Bel. The city of Da[mascus . . .][6]
Nisan 727 – Nisan 726	against the city of [Damascus] [Shalma]neser [sat] on the throne.

Although the notices are brief, they nevertheless establish important dates for events relating to the Syro-Ephraimitic crisis. In 734/733 Tiglathpileser campaigned in the southwestern part of Palestine "against Philistia." In 733/732 and 732/731 the Assyrian army was busy subjugating the "land of Damascus." The Eponym List does not record the outcome of these campaigns. If, however, Tiglathpileser marched against Sapia in southern Babylonia in 731/730,[7] it is reasonable to assume the fall of Damascus in 732/731 (compare 2 Kgs 16:9).

The campaigns of 734–731 were not the first time that Tiglathpileser intervened in the west. The Eponym List records his presence in north Syria from 743/742 to 740/739 and again in 738/737. The list provides few details about these early campaigns, but the corresponding inscriptions of the king report action against several north Syrian states (see *ARAB* 1. 271–76). These states were in league, at least initially, with the Urartians, Assyria's chief rival for control of the region, and Mati'ilu of Arpad was the local leader of the resistance until the capture of Arpad in 740. With Tiglathpileser's absence from the region in 739/738, north Syrian states again rebelled against Assyria, this time under the leadership of Tutammu, the king of Unqi, whose capital was Kullani (Calneh/Calno; see Amos 6:2 and Isa 10:9). The Assyrian army returned to the region the following year, suppressed the coalition, and received tribute from rulers as far south as Rezin of Damascus, Hiram of Tyre, Menahem of Israel, and Zabibe the "queen of Arabia." For the next three years, Tiglathpileser campaigned in the east, fighting among others the Urartians. In 734–731, however, the Assyrian king was again in the west, this time fighting the small kingdoms of southern Syria and Palestine.

---

[6]Only the first sign of toponym remains. G. Smith ("On a New Fragment of the Assyrian Canon Belonging to the Reigns of Tiglath-pileser and Shalmaneser," *TSBA* 2 [1873] 331) is probably correct in guessing that the line originally recorded the revolt of Damascus.

[7]For the location of Sapia, see A. K. Grayson, *Assyrian and Babylonian Chronicles*, 262; also J. A. Brinkman, *A Political History of Post-Kassite Babylonia, 1158–722 B.C.* (AnOr 43; Rome: Pontificium Institutum Biblicum, 1968).

Two salient points emerge from the above scenario. First, the campaigns of 734–731 were part of Assyria's ongoing effort to control the entire Eastern Mediterranean Seaboard. Second, the states of the region were determined to retain their independence. Usually by forming coalitions, they were able to offer significant, though ultimately unsuccessful, resistance.

B. The Royal Inscriptions

British excavations at Nimrud (ancient Calah) have recovered reliefs and texts of Tiglathpileser.[8] Most of these were carved or written on stone slabs and were brought to light by A. H. Layard in the late 1840s. H. Rassam, W. K. Loftus, and G. Smith led expeditions in 1853, 1854, and 1873 respectively, but they found few new inscriptions. In the 1950s, however, the British resumed digging at Nimrud under the directorship of M. Mallowan and recovered several additional, though fragmentary, inscriptions of Tiglathpileser on clay tablets.

The inscriptions recount in detail the king's campaigns noted only briefly in the Eponym List. Several factors, however, complicate the interpretation of the texts and their use for historical reconstruction.

(1) The inscriptions are of two types: annals and summary texts.[9] The former narrate the military accomplishments of the king in rough chronological order. Summary texts, in contrast, usually list events in geographical sequence. Horizontal lines often divide these texts into sections focusing on different areas. The distinction between annalistic and summary inscriptions is obviously important for understanding the course of Tiglathpileser's campaigns. A false reconstruction results if one mistakes the geographical association of events in a summary text for a chronological sequence.

(2) The inscriptions are fragmentary and in terrible disarray. This is particularly true of the annals. Tiglathpileser apparently had them

---

[8]For a good review of the discovery of Tiglathpileser's inscriptions and their subsequent treatment, see H. Tadmor, "Introductory Remarks to a New Edition of the Annals of Tiglath-pileser III," *Proceedings of the Israel Academy of Sciences and Humanities* II/9 (1967) 168–87. The discussion below is largely dependent on Tadmor's study.

[9]H. Tadmor ("The Historical Inscriptions of Adad-nirari III," *Iraq* 35 [1973] 141) proposes the label, "summary inscription," in place of the older and more widespread name, "display inscription" (in German, *Prunkinschrift*). "Display inscription" is inaccurate because many texts belonging to this category were not intended for display, but rather were buried in the foundation of a building. For a recent description of these two types of inscriptions and their differences, see A. K. Grayson, "Histories and Historians of the Ancient Near East: Assyria and Babylonia," *Or* 49 (1980) 150–55 and 177.

installed on the walls of the Central Palace at Nimrud, but Esarhaddon (680–669) later decided to re-use them as decoration for the walls of his own building, the Southwest Palace. Transferring the annals, however, had only begun when fire destroyed the Southwest Palace. When Layard excavated the two palaces in 1845, he found many of the slabs out of order on the floors, awaiting either their transfer to the Southwest Palace or re-installment on the walls there. Several of the reliefs and inscriptions, he reports, were badly damaged.The treatment of the inscriptions after their discovery worsened the textual problems. Layard removed some slabs to the British Museum in London, but others he only copied and left at the ruins of Nimrud. Furthermore, in order to lighten the slabs for the trip to London, Layard had some of the inscriptions sawed off in favor of the accompanying reliefs. He discarded the inscribed parts, but first made squeeze copies. When G. Smith excavated the site in 1873, the inscriptions left by Layard were badly damaged. Smith made new copies and squeezes, but these unfortunately were never published.

The squeezes made by Layard also suffered a sad fate. When Smith examined them in 1866, they were already very fragmentary. Twenty some years later, P. Rost studied the squeezes in preparation of his edition of Tiglathpileser's inscriptions.[10] Seven of the original twenty-two squeezes were missing at that time. All have been lost since Rost's study.

(3) The extant annals of Tiglathpileser are not only badly damaged but incomplete as well. H. Tadmor estimates that the existing slabs cover less than half of the original annals.[11] Layard's copies of texts left at Nimrud fill in some of the gaps, but many still remain.

(4) The original sequence of the annals is uncertain. Layard did not find them "in situ" but largely out of order on the floors of the Central and Southwest Palaces. Compounding the problem is the matter of different recensions. H. Tadmor reconstructs six parallel series of the annals (A, B, C1, C2, D, and E), each presumably intended for a different hall in the Central Palace.[12]

(5) When the Assyrian scribes compiled the royal inscriptions, they often used sources. They might, for example, copy directly from an earlier inscription or reproduce part of it in abridged form. Sometimes the scribes inherited different inscriptional accounts of the same episode and simply conflated them. Other sources include booty and tribute lists and possibly campaign diaries. Detecting the use of such

---

[10]P. Rost, *Die Keilschrifttexte Tiglat-Pilesers III* (Leipzig: E. Pfeiffer, 1893).

[11]H. Tadmor, "Introductory Remarks," 173.

[12]Tadmor (*Introductory Remarks*, 177–84) uses three criteria to distinguish the different series: (a) whether the inscriptions are written over the reliefs or between upper and lower registers of reliefs; (b) the number of lines of text in each column; and (c) paleographic features.

sources is important to any judgment on the historical reliability of an inscriptional text.[13]

(6) The royal inscriptions are propagandistic accounts of the king's campaigns, narrating events to his glorification.[14] Consequently, the Assyrian scribes never admit military difficulty, let alone defeat. When a campaign did not fully succeed, the scribes either ignored the episode, lied about it flatly, or confused the narrative in a way that hid the truth and gave the impression of an easy and complete victory. Sensitivity to this scribal bias prevents us from naively taking the inscriptional accounts at face value.

A modern critical edition of the inscriptions of Tiglathpileser III is not presently available. H. Tadmor has been working several years on a new edition of the king's annals, but it has not yet appeared in print. The older work by P. Rost is problematic for a variety of reasons, but particularly unsatisfactory is the way Rost conflates the different annalistic fragments and numbers the lines consecutively.[15] Nevertheless, Rost's volume remains the one widely available edition of the Assyrian texts. For this reason, the presentation of three inscriptions below—Layard 72b+73a, Layard 29b, and Layard 66—follows his numbering of the lines.

1. Layard 72b+73a

Layard 72b+73a is a composite slab belonging to Tadmor's Series C2 of the annals.[16] The opening and concluding lines of the original inscription are lost; otherwise, however, the text is relatively well preserved.

195) . . . his war[riors] I cap[tured] . . . I overthrew with my weapons.
196) . . . his face
197) The chariot-commanders . . . their weapons I broke
198) and their wagons, their horses I [seized] . . . his fighters who carried bows

---

[13]For more detailed discussions of the compilation of the royal inscriptions, see L. D. Levine, "The Second Campaign of Sennacherib," *JNES* 32 (1973) 312–17; M. Cogan and H. Tadmor, "Gyges and Ashurbanipal: A Study in Literary Transmission," *Or* 46 (1977) 65–85; A. K. Grayson, "Histories and Historians," 164–70; and J. Van Seters, *In Search of History: Historiography in the Ancient World and the Origins of Biblical History* (New Haven/London: Yale University Press, 1983) 60–68.

[14]See the remarks of A. K. Grayson ("Histories and Historians," 171) on the *Tendenz* of the royal inscriptions.

[15]Tadmor ("Introductory Remarks," 173–75) gives a full critique of the various editions of the inscriptions of Tiglathpileser, including the volume by Rost.

[16]H. Tadmor, "Introductory Remarks," 180.

199) ... [who carried] great shields and spears, I over[threw] with my own hands and their battle formation ...
200) I [broke up]. He fled alone in order to save his life and
201) ... [like] a mouse he entered the gate of his city. His officers alive
202) [I seized], had them impaled, and showed (them) to his land ... soldiers[17]
203) I assembled in the vicinity of his city and like a bird in a cage I shut him in. His gardens
204) ... trees without number I cut down and left not one (standing).
205) ... [the city], Ḫadara, the ancestral seat of Rezin, (the ruler) of the land of Damascus,
206) where he was born, I besieged, I captured. 800 people, together with their possessions
207) ... their cattle, their sheep I took as spoil. 750 captives from the city of Kuruṣṣa
208) ... [captives] from the city of Irma, 550 captives from the city of Metuna, I took as spoil. 591 cities ...
209) ... of the 16 districts of the land of Damascus I destroyed, (leaving them) like ruins after a flood.
210) ... Samsi, the queen of Arabia, who broke the oath by Shamash and ...

Most of the fragment recounts the Assyrian campaign against Syria in 733/732.[18] Lines 195–204 narrate the defeat of the Syrian army, Rezin's escape to Damascus, and the subsequent siege of the capital city.[19] Lines 205–208 review the conquest of towns lying to the south of Damascus.[20] Lines 208–209 summarize the entire campaign by giving the total number of destroyed Syrian cities throughout the whole of Rezin's kingdom. A new section on Samsi, the queen of Arabia, begins in l. 210, but the inscription abruptly breaks off.

The text gives the impression that the Assyrian victory was easy and decisive. Tiglathpileser reportedly decimated the Syrian army,

---

[17]Rost's version records "XLM" (40,000) before the noun, ṣabi ("soldiers"), but indicates with a question mark that the number is uncertain. D. D. Luckenbill (*ARAB* 1. 279) suggests reading a lower figure, 45. The translation in *TUAT* (1. 372) also reads the number as 45, but construes the reference temporally: "45 days I assembled my soldiers...."

[18]H. Tadmor, "Introductory Remarks," 180; and I. Eph'al, *The Ancient Arabs: Nomads on the Borders of the Fertile Crescent: 9th–5th Centuries B.C.* (Jerusalem/Leiden: Magnes/E. J. Brill, 1982) 26.

[19]Without the opening lines of the original inscription, the antecedent of the third-person pronouns throughout ll. 195–204 must be guessed. Rezin of Syria-Damascus is the probable referent.

[20]E. Forrer (*Die Provinzeinteilung des assyrischen Reiches* [Leipzig: J. C. Hinrichs, 1920] 62–65) identifies Ḫadara with j. el-Ḥadhr, 52 kilometers southwest of Damascus; Kuruṣṣa with el-Breqa, at the foot of the mountains called the Hami-Qurṣuh; and Metuna with Imtan, 11 kilometers southeast of Salhad. These lie, then, in what became after 732/731 the Assyrian provinces of Qarnini and Haurini.

forcing Rezin to retreat to Damascus. The capital city was besieged by myriad Assyrian forces; the surrounding region was devastated; other cities were taken and sacked as well. The concluding summary intends to dispel any doubt about the military success of the Assyrian king: he subjugated Syria, destroying cities throughout Rezin's kingdom.

Certain features of the account indicate that Syrian resistance may have been more substantial than the Assyrian scribes were willing to admit. First, the text does not actually report the fall of Damascus, but only hints at its inevitability. Rezin reportedly was "shut in like a bird in a cage."[21] His captured officers were executed, apparently within view of the city walls. Assyrian troops stood ready to take Damascus. Yet now, precisely when we expect to read of battle and the city's capture, the account narrates only the Assyrian actions against the outlying fields and forests (ll. 203–204). Admittedly, the subsequent listing of conquered towns (ll. 205–208) and the concluding summary might lead the reader to infer the fall of the capital city as well. The impression, however, is likely one artificially created by the Assyrian scribes intent upon concealing the fact that Rezin's forces within Damascus had been and were still able to hold out against the Assyrian attack. Such resistance was not conducive to the praise of the Assyrian king, before whom, ideally, all enemies were to fall easily.

Second, the report of the Syrian defeat in ll. 195–199 is quite general. Although the capture of warriors and the seizure of booty are impressively recounted, nowhere are actual figures given. This vagueness contrasts strikingly with the specificity of ll. 205–209. There, concrete data abounds. The suspicion arises that ll. 195–199 do not rest on detailed information such as that which the scribes could have derived from booty lists. While the report is unlikely a fabrication altogether, it may very well exaggerate the ease and completeness of the Assyrian victory.[22] Enough of Rezin's forces apparently survived to defend the capital city. The strength of their resistance is reflected by the fact that the siege of Damascus dragged on into the following year, 732/731.

The precise course of the Assyrian campaign is uncertain. The literary order of the inscription suggests that the siege of Damascus be-

---

[21] The Assyrian scribes are drawing here on stereotypical military imagery. Sennacherib's annals use the identical phrase in reference to Hezekiah (*ANET* 288).

[22] The scribes of Shalmaneser's III annals similarly resorted to vagueness and generality as a means of glossing over the ambiguous results of the battle of Qarqar (*ANET* 279). The same technique can be seen in Sennacherib's account of his campaign to Palestine in 701 (*ANET* 287–88). See J. M. Miller and J. H. Hayes, *A History of Ancient Israel and Judah* (Philadelphia: Westminster, 1986) 362.

gan before the conquest of towns to the south. However, stylistic and other tensions between ll. 195–204 and ll. 205–209 indicate that a single source does not underlie both sections.[23] The Assyrian scribes likely inherited the list of conquered southern towns and appended it to their own account in ll. 195–204, thereby concealing the inconclusive results of the siege of Damascus. Accordingly, the true chronological order of the events may not coincide with their literary order. The Assyrians may have first quelled the rebellion in the peripheral districts of Rezin's kingdom and then have turned against the capital city, where Syrian resistance would make its final stand.

Line 210 begins an account of the Assyrian actions against Samsi, the queen of Arabia. While only a small part of the original report has survived,[24] two details of the episode can still be noted here. First, the text describes Samsi as one who "broke the oath by Shamash." It thus assumes that the queen had submitted earlier to Assyrian vassalage. When precisely she first paid tribute to Tiglathpileser is uncertain, whether during the Assyrian campaign to Palestine in 734/733 or earlier.[25] In any case, Samsi subsequently reversed her policy and rebelled.

Second, the literary sequence of events in Layard 72b+73a suggests that the Assyrian action against Samsi followed the subjugation of Syria. While there is no reason to doubt a temporal connection between the two campaigns, we should again be careful not to press the chronological order of the inscription too far. It is safe to assume that the queen would have ventured an encounter with the Assyrians at a time when rebellion against the Assyrians still seemed to have a reasonable chance of success. Such would not have been the case after the final defeat of the Syrians in Damascus. If Samsi's realm was east of Palestine, bordering on the Hauran region,[26] the Assyrians might have engaged her army while they were still campaigning in the southern part of Rezin's kingdom (ll. 205–208). Fighting in this area, we suggested above, may have taken place in 733/732, before the Syrian king withdrew to Damascus.

---

[23]Specifically, three features reflect the scribes' use of a distinct source in ll. 205–209: (1) the seemingly unnecessary specification of Rezin's country in l. 205; (2) the sudden shift from an expansive narrative style in ll. 195–204 to a summarizing style in ll. 205–209; and 3) the wealth of concrete figures in ll. 205–209, as compared to the vagueness of the preceding lines.

[24]The campaign against Samsi is reported more fully in Layard 66:213–218, ND4301+4305 rev. 17–22, and III R 10,2:19–26. See sections B3, B6 and B7 below.

[25]A tributary list from 734/733 (II R 67 rev. 7–13) does not mention Samsi, but her absence there may be due to the fragmentary character of the preserved text (see section B5 below). Another tributary list from 738 names her predecessor, Zabibe (see *ARAB* 1. 276).

[26]See I. Eph'al, *The Ancient Arabs*, 85, and section B5 below.

2. Layard 29b

Layard 29b belongs to Tadmor's Series C1.[27] The original slab may have had as many as twenty lines of text, but portions of only twelve have survived.

229) [like] a hurricane
230) ... [captives from] ... districts of the land of Beth-... [I] took away ...
231) ... [captives from the city] -bara, 625 captives from the city -a- ...
232) ... [captives from] the city Hinatuna, 650 captives from the city Qana ...
233) [400 captives from the city Ia]tbiti, 650 captives from the city Ir[una] ... .[28]
234) ... people together with their possessions [I took as spoil] ... the city Aruma, the city Marum ...
235) ... [Mitinti of the land of] Ashkelon against [my] oath [transgressed and against me
236) rebelled. The defeat of Re]zin he saw and into [misfortune (?) fell][29]
237) [Rukiptu, the son of Mitinti], sat[30] on his throne ...
238) ... and implored me. 500 ...
239) ... and into his city I entered.[31] 15 cities ...
240) ... the Idibi'ilu of the land of Arabia ...

Despite the poor condition of the text, scholars generally agree on three points. First, the towns listed in ll. 231–234 fall within the Galilean region.[32] Second, ll. 235–239 report the demise of Mitinti, the

---

[27]H. Tadmor, "Introductory Remarks," 180.

[28]The restoration of the two toponyms, Iatbiti and Iruna, follows Y. Aharoni's translation of the text (*The Land of the Bible: A Historical Geography* [2d ed.; Philadelphia: Westminster, 1979] 372).

[29]The text is obscure here. P. Rost (*Keilschrifttexte*, 38) suggests completing the phrase, *ina miqit*, with *ṭimi imqut* and translating the whole, "and he fell into insanity." D. D. Luckenbill (*ARAB* 1. 280) construes *miqit* (construct of *miqtu*) in the well-attested sense of "fire" and translates the line, "he died in a conflagration." The more general meaning, "downfall or misfortune," is also possible for *miqtu*. Compare the variant, *miqittu*, which carries this sense.

[30]The Akkadian verb *ušib*, normally translated "he (Rukiptu) sat" (see G. Smith, *Assyrian Discoveries* [London: S. Low, Marston, Searle, and Rivington, 1876] 284; P. Rost, *Keilschrifttexte*, 38; and *TUAT* 1. 373). Compare the translation, "I (Tiglathpileser) set/installed," by Luckenbill (*ARAB* 1. 280) and J. M. Asurmendi (*La Guerra Siro-Efraimita*, 25).

[31]"He (Rukiptu) entered" is also a possible translation of the Akkadian *TU-ub*. See G. Smith, *Assyrian Discoveries*, 284.

[32]Y. Aharoni (*Land of the Bible*, 372-374) gives the following identifications: Marum (biblical Merom) = Tell el-Khirbeh; Iruna (biblical Yiron) = modern Yarun; Hinatuna (biblical Hannathon) = Tell el-Bedeiwijeh; Qana (biblical Kanah

king of Ashkelon, the rise of his son, Rukiptu, to the throne, and Rukiptu's submission to Assyrian vassalage. Third, both the Galilean campaign and the events in Ashkelon likely occurred in 733 or 732.[33] Apart from this minimal consensus, however, several details are debatable.

The inscription does not clearly state from whom the Assyrians seized the Galilean region. The uncertainty stems in part from the fragmentary toponym in l. 230: both "Beth-Omri" (Israel) and "Beth-Hazael" (Syria) are possible restorations. The latter reading would assume that the line is parallel to the passage in Layard 72b+73a, which speaks of the "16 districts of the land of Damascus" (l. 209). Yet even if Beth-Hazael is correctly restored in l. 230, it is still unclear whether what follows concerns Syria or Israel. The issue has to do with the division of literary units. Do ll. 229–230 and ll. 231–234 belong to one and the same section of the annals and so together report actions against the extended realm of Rezin, king of Damascus? Or do they form two distinct sections, the first regarding the land of "Beth-Hazael," the second concerning the realm of Pekah, the king of Israel?

Interpreters commonly hold that ll. 231–234 recount the Assyrian advance against Israel. The position rests partly on the observation that Israel had traditionally claimed the Galilean region and on the assumption that Israel had in fact controlled it during much of the preceding two and a half centuries. It would seem reasonable to assume that the area was Israelite on the eve of the Assyrian invasion, barring evidence to the contrary. Second Kings 15:29, it is usually thought, confirms this view. There it is reported:

> In the days of Pekah the king of Israel, Tiglathpileser the king of Assyria came and took Ijon and Abel-beth-maacah and Janoah and Kedesh and Hazor and Gilead and Galilee, all the land of Naphtali, and took them captive to Assyria.

The Kings text and ll. 231–234 of Layard 29b are correlated as parallel accounts of Tiglathpileser's campaign against the realm of Pekah.[34]

---

of Galilee) = Khirbet Qana; and Iatbiti (biblical Jothbah) = Khirbet Jefat. E. Forrer (*Provinzeinteilung*, 60–61) identifies Aruma with J. Ḥirbet Rume.

[33]See A. Alt, "Das System der assyrischen Provinzen auf dem Boden des Reiches Israel," *ZDPV* 52 (1929) 228–30 = his *KS* (Munich: C. H. Beck, 1953) II. 195–96; J. M. Asurmendi, *La Guerra Siro-Efraimita*, 24–25; J. Bright, *A History of Israel* (3d ed.; Philadelphia: Westminster, 1981) 274–75; H. Donner, *Israel unter den Völkern*, 6; I. Eph'al, *The Ancient Arabs*, 26; M. Noth, *The History of Israel* (2d ed.; New York/Evanston: Harper & Row, 1960) 260; H. Tadmor, "Philistia under Assyrian Rule," *BA* 29 (1966) 89; idem., "Introductory Remarks," 180.

[34]See, for example, H. Donner, *Israel unter den Völkern*, 6, especially n. 5; Y. Aharoni, *Land of the Bible*, 371–74.

This interpretation is certainly possible, but its correctness is far less certain than scholars often suppose. Four observations and/or arguments indicate that another reconstruction of the history is at least as tenable.

(1) A closer look at 2 Kgs 15:29 reveals that this passage is actually just as ambiguous as its Assyrian parallel. The conquered cities and regions are listed, but their political status, whether Israelite or Syrian, is not explicit. This vagueness contrasts strikingly with a similar account in 1 Kgs 15:20. The latter text carefully states that the Galilean cities attacked by Benhadad I of Syria during the early ninth century had been Israelite. One might expect the same specification in 2 Kgs 15:29, if the writer or editor of this account believed that the Assyrians had confiscated the region from Pekah's realm. Instead, the Galilean campaign is presented simply as the prelude to Hoshea's revolt (v 30). It is true that the revolt would have gained popular support, if the Galilean cities had previously belonged to Israel but were lost during Pekah's tenure. Yet a different scenario is just as plausible. Having moved against Syria's holdings in Galilee and elsewhere, Assyrian forces were now approaching the very border of Israel and were threatening to push onward to Samaria. The severity of the threat was enough to catalyze a pro-Assyrian, anti-Pekah movement within Israel, led by Hoshea.

(2) Although Israel traditionally claimed the Galilean region, Syria-Damascus periodically competed for the area.[35] During the ninth and eighth centuries, the two states alternately controlled the region. Benhadad I, we noted above, invaded Galilee during the reign of Baasha (903–882). It is unclear whether the Syrian king actually confiscated the area, and if so, how long the Syrians controlled it. In any case, Galilee probably belonged to Israel during the reigns of the powerful Omride kings.[36] Under the leadership of Hazael, Syria embarked again on an aggressive expansionist policy. Israel's holdings in Transjordan and along the Philistine coast were seized from Jehoahaz (2 Kgs 10:32–33, 12:17), the Israelite army was practically destroyed (2 Kgs 13:7), and the country was reduced virtually, if not

---

[35]Both states were interested in the region for its economic value. Important trade routes passed through Galilee to the coastal cities of Sidon, Tyre, Achzib and Akko. Whoever controlled these routes could enjoy significant commercial benefits. See A. Šanda, *Die Bücher der Könige* (2 vols.; Münster: Aschendorff, 1911–12) 1. 389; M. F. Unger, *Israel and the Arameans of Damascus* (Grand Rapids: Zondervan, 1957) 58; and J. Gray, *I and II Kings* (Philadelphia: Westminster, 1963) 321.

[36]Archaeological evidence at Dan and Hazor is consistent with this conclusion. The architectural style of public buildings at both sites is reportedly similar to that of Ahab's construction at Samaria and Medido. See Y. Yadin, *Hazor: The Recovery of a Great Citadel of the Bible* (New York: Random House, 1975) 162–70; A. Biran, "Tell Dan—Five Years Later," *BA* 43 (1980), 175.

actually, to a Syrian vassal. It would be most surprising if Hazael at this time did not also take the coveted Galilean region.[37]

The western campaigns of Adadnirari III greatly reduced the power of Damascus, paving the way for a resurgence of Israel during the reigns of Joash and Jeroboam II. Second Kings 14:20 and 25 seem to indicate that Jeroboam retook the north Transjordan area (compare Amos 6:13–14). At the same time he probably also extended Israel's border due north to include the Galilean region.[38] From this moment to the Assyrian invasion in 733, Second Kings passes over the history of the area in silence. It is conceivable, however, that Galilee reverted back to Syrian control during the last years of Jeroboam and the first part of Menahem's reign.

(3) In Layard 29b, the section on events in Ashkelon assumes that Rezin has already been introduced and his "defeat" previously recounted (l. 236). A straightforward reading of the inscription would see that account at least partly in ll. 229–234.

(4) If ll. 231–234 form a distinct section on Israel, one would expect l. 231 to have originally provided a brief introduction, mentioning Beth-Omri and perhaps Pekah as well. The lacuna at the beginning of the line, however, is doubtfully large enough for this. What is preserved launches immediately into a list of Galilean captives, as though continuing the report on Syria in ll. 229–230. This line of reasoning assumes, of course, that "Beth-Hazael" is the correct restoration in l. 230.

The above remarks have suggested the possibility of reading ll. 229–234 as a report on Assyria's actions against the territorial holdings of Rezin in Galilee. Further treatment of the issue must await the analysis of Tiglathpileser's other inscriptions (see sections B3 and B7 below).

Lines 235–239 report on events in Ashkelon. If Mitinti's name is correctly restored in l. 235, it appears that Mitinti first paid tribute to the Assyrians in 734/733, but quickly reversed his decision and rebelled the following year.[39] The anti-Assyrian policy did not escape the attention of the Assyrian king.

---

[37]See E. Meyer, *Geschichte des Altertums* (2nd ed.; 5 vols.; Stuttgart/Berlin: J. G. Cotta'sche, 1931) 2. 341–42; M. F. Unger, *Israel and the Arameans*, 78, 84; and W. T. Pitard, *Ancient Damascus: A Historical Study of the Syrian City-State from Earliest Times until its Fall to the Assyrians in 732 B.C.E.* (Winona Lake: Eisenbrauns, 1987) 151–58.

[38]The prophet Amos in Amos 8:14 assumes that Israel's territory extended northward as far as Dan. Regarding Jeroboam's retaking of Galilee, see M. F. Unger, *Israel and the Arameans*, 90.

[39]The tributary list, II R 67 rev., 11, records Mitinti's payment (see section B4 below).

Less clear is how Mitinti subsequently fell from power. The text reports cryptically that he suffered some misfortune and that his son, Rukiptu, afterwards ascended the throne. Apparently the Assyrian king did not himself depose Mitinti, but simply approved the succession of Rukiptu after the fact. Possibly Mitinti had fled before the approaching Assyrian army, but more likely he had fallen in a coup d'etat.

Why the citizens of Ashkelon would have overthrown their rebel king is easy to understand. In late 733 or 732, the anti-Assyrian revolt led by Rezin of Syria must have seemed doomed to fail. Tiglathpileser had defeated the Syrian army in the field and had begun the siege of Damascus (Layard 72b+73a). Assyrian troops had overrun Galilee and moved down the coast toward Ashkelon. Gezer perhaps was placed under siege at this time[40] and action against towns under Mitinti's control had been taken.[41] In such circumstances, Mitinti's own subjects must have anticipated the siege of Ashkelon and its fall. In an effort to avert the disaster, they likely executed Mitinti, set his son on the throne, and had him implore Tiglathpileser for lenient treatment. The plan seems to have worked. The Assyrian king recognized Rukiptu as the new king of Ashkelon, although perhaps only after receiving a substantial monetary gift and entering the city himself (l. 239).[42]

Layard 29b concludes with a reference to the Idibi'ilu, an Arab tribe located in the north Sinai (l. 240). From other inscriptions of Tiglathpileser (Layard 66:226; II R 67 rev., 6; and III R 10,2:34), it is evident that the Assyrians assigned them a measure of authority in the region south of Philistia. The strategy behind this appointment will be examined later. Here it is necessary only to comment on the possible connection of the Idibi'ilu with the Assyrian treatment of Ashkelon. The issue again hinges on the division of literary units. Reading l. 240 as the continuation of the section on Ashkelon, A. Alt suggests that Tiglathpileser reduced the realm of Rukiptu, setting fifteen cities formerly controlled by Mitinti (l. 239) under the author-

---

[40]One of Tiglathpileser's reliefs depicts the conquest of *Gazru* (Gezer). See B. Meissner, "Palästinensische Städtebilder aus der Zeit Tiglatpilesers IV.," *ZDPV* 39 (1916) 261–63; H. Tadmor, "Philistia under Assyrian Rule," 89, n. 15; and H. D. Lance, "Gezer in the Land and in History," *BA* 30 (1967) 34–47. For Layard's drawing of the Gezer relief, see R. D. Barnett and M. Faulkner, *The Sculptures of Tiglatpileser III (745–727 B.C.) from the Central and Southwest Palaces at Nimrud* (London: Trustees of the British Museum, 1962) 112.

[41]This is the likely meaning of the reference to fifteen cities in l. 239.

[42]See, however, n. 31 above. The text might claim only that Rukiptu returned to Ashkelon after personally doing homage before the Assyrian king.

ity of the Arab tribe.[43] The proposal falters, however, on the fact that the territories of Ashkelon and of the Idibi'ilu did not share a common border, separated as they were by the realm of Hanno, the king of Gaza.[44] Accordingly, it is best to take l. 240 as the beginning of a new section of the annals which treats of the Idibi'ilu.[45]

3. Layard 66

Classifying Layard 66 is difficult. Tadmor views the text as the sole surviving remnant of Series E of Tiglathpileser's annals.[46] He does so, however, with some reservation, noting that the order of the reported events may not be entirely chronological. Eph'al similarly stresses the chronological disorder of the text.[47] He notes also, however, the difficulty in taking Layard 66 as a summary inscription, for the geographical sequence, Arab groups—Israel, is unusual. Other summary texts of the Assyrian king (see ND4301+4305 rev. 9–22 and III R 10,2:15–33) treat Israel before the Arabs. As long as the organization of Layard 66 remains unclear, we do well not to draw chronological conclusions from the sequence of the reported events.

The inscription is extremely fragmentary. However, with the help of parallel passages from other inscriptions of Tiglathpileser (see II R 67 rev. 2–6; ND400:24–27; ND4301+4305 rev. 17–22; and III R 10,2:19–34), lost parts of Layard 66 can be restored.

> 211) ... the city of ...
> 212) ... [a]gainst the city I'za[si] ...
> 213) [Samsi, queen of] the Arabs[48] in the land of Sa- ...[49]
> 214) [her people] in her camp ... [of my powerful
> 215) weapons] she was afraid and [camels, she-camels] ...
> 216) ... in[to my presence she brought. A *qepu*-officer

---

[43]A. Alt, "Neue assyrische Nachrichten über Palästina," *ZDPV* 67 (1945) 128–46 = his *KS* II. 237, n. 5; idem., "Historische Geographie und Topographie des Negeb" in his *KS* (Munich: C. H. Beck, 1959) III. 420, n. 1.
[44]According to ND 400:17–18, ND 4301+4305 rev. 13–14, and III R 10,2:9–15, Tiglathpileser's actions against Gaza in 734/733 had left the city-state politically intact. See sections B5, B6, and B7 below.
[45]See I. Eph'al, *The Ancient Arabs*, 24–25.
[46]H. Tadmor, "Introductory Remarks," 180.
[47]I. Eph'al, *The Ancient Arabs*, 32–33.
[48]Read [ŠAL Samsi šarrat mat] Aribi. This reconstruction seems to underlie G. Smith's translation (*Assyrian Discoveries*, 285) and finds support in Layard 29b:210 and III R 10,2:19.
[49]Rost restores the toponym as Saba', but Saqurri is the more likely reading (compare ND400:24). I. Eph'al (*The Ancient Arabs*, 33–35) indicates that G. Smith's unpublished copies of III R 10,2:19 also mention Mt. Saqurri in connection with Samsi.

217) over her I] set and war[riors⁵⁰
218) at] my feet I made bow [down. The people of Massa', Tema,
219) Saba', Hayappa, Badanu
220) Hat]te, the [Idiba'ilu] . . .
221) [on the bor]der of the lands where sets the sun, [whose region is far away,
222) the re]pute of my majesty . . .
223) [majesty.] Gold, silver, ca[mels, she-camels]
224) all kinds of spices—their tribute as [one they brought before me and
225) kis]sed [my feet] . . .⁵¹
226) . . . the Idibi'ilu as *qe[pu*-officers] over the land of Egypt I appointed.
227) On my former campaigns, all the cities . . . I counted.
228) . . . his . . . I carried off and Samaria⁵² alone I [le]ft . . . their king . . .

The content of the inscription divides into four sections. (1) Lines 211–212 conclude an account of Assyrian action against an unnamed country. (2) Lines 213–218 report Samsi's capitulation and payment of tribute. Apparently, Tiglathpileser decided not to depose the rebellious queen, but only to place her under the watch of an Assyrian

---

⁵⁰The Akkadian text reads, *LU.ERIN* . . . *-ia ušak-* . . . . Rost (*Keilschrifttexte*, 37) construes *LU.ERIN* as a reference to an Arab tribe and so proposes reading "the Bireans." I. Eph'al (*The Ancient Arabs*, 28, n. 73), however, astutely notes that the parallel passage in ND4301+4305 rev. 22 reads: 10 *LIM.LU.ERIN.MEŠ* . . . (that is, "10,000 warriors"). In Layard 66 the number was omitted, thus opening the way for misunderstanding *LU.ERIN* as a reference to a separate Arab group. The line in fact concludes the preceding section on Samsi.

⁵¹The Akkadian continues but is extremely fragmentary. Eph'al (*The Ancient Arabs*, 35) indicates that the copy of the text in Layard's notebooks reads only: . . . *-ši-qú* . . . *di-x-*[*ni*]*-šú-nu* . . . *a* . . . *GAL* (or *ma ina*) . . . *ad* . . . . Compare Rost's restored version and translation of l. 225 (*Keilschrifttexte*, 38–39) and the translation by Luckenbill (*ARAB* 1. 279). In *TUAT* (1. 372), all but the beginning of the line is wisely left untranslated.

⁵²The determinative, *URU*, which generally designates a city, precedes "Samaria" (*Samirina*). How literally the determinative should be taken, however, is questionable. In Layard 50a (see P. Rost, *Keilschrifttexte*, 24–26, ll. 141–52), one sees listed among the various Syro-Palestinian tributaries of 738 *Miniḫimmi URU Samirinai* ("Menahem of Samaria"). This text likely has more in mind than the city of Samaria. Significantly, *Miniḫimmi KUR Sam*[*e*]*rina* ("Menahem of the land of Samaria") is listed in another tributary list from about the same time (see L. D. Levine, *Two Neo-Assyrian Stelae from Iran* [Toronto: Royal Ontario Museum, 1972] 18; idem., "Menahem and Tiglat-Pileser: A New Synchronism," *BASOR* 206 [1972] 40–42). It thus appears that the Assyrian scribes were not always precise in the designation of place-names through determinatives. (Note that in the above mentioned tributary lists *URU* and *KUR* are both used as determinatives for Byblos also.) In Layard 66:228, *URU Samirina* likely designates more than the capital city.

qepu-officer.⁵³ Her army was forced to declare its allegiance to the Assyrian king (ll. 217–218).

(3) Lines 218–225 report the submission of several Arab groups located along the trade routes in northern Arabia and the north Sinai.⁵⁴ The text here gives no hint of armed conflict. The presentation of tribute seems, rather, to have been voluntary. Having seized the northern termini of the trade routes during the campaigns against Philistia and Syria-Damascus, Tiglathpileser was in a position to affect adversely commerce all along the routes. Presumably it was this capacity that persuaded the distant Arab tribes to accept vassalage status. The section closes with a reference to the appointment of the Idibi'ilu as *qepu*-officers "over the land of Egypt."⁵⁵

(4) Lines 227–228 recount the results of earlier campaigns. Against whom precisely these actions were aimed is not, however, clear. Minimally, one gathers from the text only that cities were incorporated into the Assyrian provincial system, booty was carried off, and "Samaria" alone was "left."⁵⁶ Presumably the account went on originally to narrate something about Pekah, "their king," perhaps his rejection by a faction of his own people (compare 2 Kgs 15:30 and III R 10,2:17–18).

Scholars generally have seen in this last section a picture of Israel's territorial reduction.⁵⁷ The lines are correlated with Layard 29b:(230) 231–234 and 2 Kgs 15:29; all three passages are then construed as evidence of Assyrian action against Pekah's realm. The "Israel" which survived the war was only the "rump state" of Ephraim with the capital city of Samaria at its center.

Two considerations undercut the force of this interpretation. First, we have already seen that Layard 29b and 2 Kgs 15:29 might describe the confiscation of Syrian, not Israelite, territory. Second, l. 227 does not explicitly characterize as Israelite the cities seized by Assyria. This must be inferred from the mention of Samaria which follows. The text, of course, is fragmentary and so might have originally contained

---

⁵³For a description of this official, see especially A. Godbey, "The Kepu," *AJSL* 22 (1905) 81–88; also A. Spalinger, "Esarhaddon and Egypt: An Analysis of the First Invasion of Egypt," *Or* 43 (1974) 314.

⁵⁴See I. Eph'al, *The Ancient Arabs*, 87–92.

⁵⁵The Idibi'ilu had authority over the region south of Gaza in the vicintiy of the Wadi Besor. See N. Na'aman, "The Brook of Egypt and Assyrian Policy on the Border of Egypt," *TA* 6 (1979) 68–90. The Idibi'ilu were probably appointed in 734, when the Assyrians were actually campaigning in the area.

⁵⁶"Samaria" in l. 228 probably refers not just to the capital city, but rather to the broader Israelite state. See n. 52.

⁵⁷See, for example, E. Forrer, *Die Provinzeinteilung*, 59; J. Begrich, "Der syrisch-ephraimitische Krieg," 27; M. Noth, *The History of Israel*, 260; H. Donner, *Israel unter den Völkern*, 6, especially n. 5; Y. Aharoni, *Land of the Bible*, 371–74; H. Cazelles, "Problemes de la Guerre Syro-Ephraimite," *ErIsr* 14 (1978) 73–74, 78.

"Beth-Omri" in l. 227. Just as plausibly, however, one could restore the name of Rezin or "Beth-Hazael" to the line. The account in this case would read tolerably well, narrating military action against the extended realm of Rezin (l. 227), which in turn isolated the Israelite state[58] and perhaps set the stage for an internal revolt against Pekah (l. 228).

The opening clause, "on my former campaigns," can be understood as a broad reference to Tiglathpileser's treatment of Syria-Damascus in 733–731. If the account originally continued with a report on the rise of Israelite opposition to Pekah, it may have presented such opposition as the indirect consequence of Assyria's victories over Pekah's ally, Syria.

4. II R 67

II R 67 is the surviving portion of a long summary inscription dating to 728.[59] It culminates in a lengthy report on the construction of Tiglathpileser's palace at ancient Nimrud, but the greater part of the inscription reviews the military and political achievements of the king during the first seventeen years of his reign.[60] Our focus is on the tributary list which concludes the review (rev. 7–13).[61]

> 7) [The tribute] of Kushtashpi of Qummuh, Urik of Que, Sibittibi'il of [Byblos] . . .

---

[58]This isolation would be the meaning of Tiglathpileser's claim, "Samaria alone I left."

[59]Reference to the inscription is frequently made by its tablet number, K3751. For a copy of the cuneiform text, see H. C. Rawlinson, *Cuneiform Inscriptions of Western Asia* (5 vols.; London: British Museum, 1861–1909) 2. plate 67. P. Rost (*Keilschrifttexte*, 55–77) provides a transliteration of the text with a German translation. English translations are given by D. D. Luckenbill (*ARAB* 1. 282–89) and G. Smith (*Assyrian Discoveries*, 254–66).

[60]The sequence of subjugated states and peoples moves from the southeastern to northeastern to northwestern to southwestern part of the Assyrian empire. Horizontal lines divide the text into paragraphs, each of which treats a specific region. For reviews of the inscription's contents and overall structure, see A. T. E. Olmstead, *Assyrian Historiography: A Source Study* (The University of Missouri Studies, Social Science Series III/1; Columbia, MO: University of Missouri Press, 1916) 32–35; and W. Schramm, *Einleitung in die assyrischen Königsinschriften* (Handbuch der Orientalistik I/5, part 2; Leiden/Cologne: E. J. Brill, 1973) 133–35.

[61]The list is part of a larger section, ll. 3–13, marked off by horizontal lines. Lines 3–6 report the surrender of various Arab tribes and the appointment of the Idibi'ilu as *qepu*-officers "over the land of Egypt." Originally the historical review came to a close in l. 13. Notes on the deposal of Uassurme of Tabal (ll. 14–15) and the receipt of tribute from Metenna of Tyre (l. 16) are secondary additions. See A. T. E. Olmstead, *Assyrian Historiography*, 34; and I. Eph'al, *The Ancient Arabs*, 28–29.

8) [I'n]il of Hamath, Panammu of Sam'al, Tarhulara of Gurgum, Sul[umal of Melid] . . .
9) [U]assurmi of Tabal, Ushitti of Tuna, Urballa of Tuhan, Tuhammi [of Ishtunda] . . .
10) [M]atanbi'il of Arvad, Sanipu of Beth-Ammon, Salamanu of Moab . . .
11) [M]itinti of Ashkelon, Jehoahaz of Judah, Kaushmalaka of Edom, Muṣ- . . .[62]
12) [Ha]nno of Gaza—gold, silver, lead, iron, tin, colored garments, linen, the purple garments of their land(s) . . .
13) [all kinds of] costly things, products of the sea and land, the commodities of their lands, horses, mules broken to the yoke . . . [I received].

The names here fall into two groups. (1) Lines 7–9 list the rulers of small states in northern Syria and Anatolia. Each of these is mentioned in two earlier tributary lists: one dating to 740, or earlier, and incorporated in an Iranian stela recently published by L. D. Levine;[63] the other dating to 738 and incorporated in the annals of Tiglathpileser (*ARAB* 1. 273, 276; *ANET* 283).[64] (2) Lines 10–12 list vassals who, with the exception of Matanbi'il of Arvad, were located to the far south in Palestine. These include the Transjordanian rulers, Ahaz of Judah, and the Philistine kings of Ashkelon and Gaza. Rezin of Damascus, Pekah of Israel, Hiram of Tyre, and Samsi, queen of the Arabs, are conspicuously absent from the list, at least as it has survived.

The textual uncertainty of the list, the possibility of its redactional growth, and its use for historical reconstruction are closely related issues. J. M. Asurmendi treats the list as an original unit and dates it to 728, the year when the inscription as a whole was composed. The list would thus reflect the political situation in Syria and Palestine during the late aftermath of the Syro-Ephraimitic crisis.[65] The interpretation fails, however, to account for the mention of Mitinti of Ashkelon in l. 10. Layard 29b, we saw above, indicates that this king, having rebelled against Assyria, fell from power shortly after an Assyrian de-

---

[62]*Muṣ[ri]* (Egypt) is the traditional reading (see, for example, P. Rost, *Keilschrifttexte*, 72–73; *ARAB* 1. 287; *ANET* 282). H. Tadmor ("Philistia under Assyrian Rule," 89, especially n. 13) proposes, however, *Mušehu-* or *Mušepak-*, possibly the king of Ekron or Ashdod.

[63]See L. D. Levine, *Two Neo-Assyrian Stelae*, 11–24. Levine dates the list and the inscription as a whole to 737, but M. Cogan ("Tyre and Tiglathpileser III: Chronological Notes," *JCS* 25 [1973] 96–99) convincingly argues that the list must pre-date 738 and suggests the year 740.

[64]For the Akkadian text, see P. Rost, *Keilschrifttexte*, 14–16 (ll. 82–89) and 26 (ll. 150–155). The original slabs which record the tributaries of 738 are Layard 50a+50b+67a, Layard 69b2+69a1 and Layard 45b. See H. Tadmor, "Introductory Remarks," 180, 185; and M. Cogan, "Tyre and Tiglath-Pileser III," 96–97.

[65]J. M. Asurmendi, *La Guerra Siro-Efraimita*, 34–35.

feat of Rezin. If Mitinti's demise occurred in 733 or 732, he could not appear among tributaries of 728. His mention in II R 67 rev. 10 indicates, rather, that the list, or at least its second half, dates to 734/733. This is the year when Tiglathpileser first intervened in Palestine and likely received the voluntary tribute of states such as Ashkelon and Judah.

The matter of dating is complicated by attempts to discern in ll. 7–13 the conflation of originally separate lists. I. Eph'al, for example, dates only ll. 10–12 to 734. Lines 7–9, he believes, were copied from the tributary list of 738.[66] M. Weippert expresses a similar view of the text's redaction and draws the inevitable historiographical conclusion: the list "cannot be used as evidence to show that the kings named in it all paid tribute to Tiglathpileser III at one specific historical moment."[67]

Eph'al does not actually demonstrate that ll. 7–9 derive from the 738 list of tributaries; he merely asserts it as "obvious." What in fact is obvious is only that those mentioned in ll. 7–9 paid Assyrian tribute as early as 738. It is quite possible that the same rulers continued as subservient vassals in subsequent years and so appear among tributaries of 734/733.

Weippert's reasons for dating ll. 7–9 to 738 are clearer. By restoring the kings of Syria, Israel, and Tyre at the end of l. 7, the kings of Carchemish and the Kashkeans at the end of l. 8, and the ruler of Hubisna and the queen of the Arabs at the end of l. 9, he brings these lines into closer agreement with the two earlier lists of tributaries. Weippert furthermore comments on the specific arrangement of the three lists. In the 738 and 740 lists, Qummuh, Syria, Israel, Tyre, Byblos, and Que are mentioned in sequence. Weippert explains the peculiarity of this grouping by suggesting that the states in question were members of the anti-Assyrian coalition which arose in 738, but quickly collapsed. If the same grouping of states were originally evidenced in II R 67 rev. 7–9, these lines too would seem to derive from 738.[68]

The argument here is unconvincing. The grouping of Syria, Israel, and Tyre with the northern states of Qummuh, Que and Byblos does not actually appear in II R 67 rev. 7. Weippert restores the three southern states to the line, thereby creating himself the distinctive sequence which he thinks bears on the date of ll. 7–9. Furthermore, while the grouping of Qummuh, Syria, Israel, Tyre, Byblos and Que is peculiar, there is no evidence to suggest the collaboration of these

---

[66]I. Eph'al, *The Ancient Arabs*, 29, n. 76.

[67]M. Weippert, "Menahem von Israel und seine Zeitgenossen in einer Steleninschrift des assyrischen Königs Tiglathpilser III. aus dem Iran," *ZDPV* 89 (1973) 53.

[68]M. Weippert, "Menahem und seine Zeitgenossen," 39–40, 46, and 53.

states in the anti-Assyrian revolt of 738. The hypothesis in fact contradicts indications elsewhere of hostilities between Syria and Israel and of Israel's pro-Assyrian posture during the reign of Menahem (see Isa 9:10–11 and 2 Kgs 15:19–20). Accordingly, the enigmatic grouping of tributaries, even if it were attested in II R 67 rev. 7–9, would not demand the dating of these lines to 738.

II R 67 rev. 7–13 should be taken as an original whole and dated to 734/733. The list reflects the conditions in Anatolia, Syria and Palestine immediately after Tiglathpileser's campaign "against Philistia." These included: the continued submission of most of the states which had paid Assyrian tribute in 738; the forcible subjugation of Gaza and possibly also Arvad (see section B5 below); and the voluntary submission to vassalage status by Ashkelon, Judah, and the Transjordan kingdoms.

Still unclear is the political posture of Rezin of Damascus, Pekah of Israel, Hiram of Tyre, and Samsi, queen of the Arabs, in 734/733. Does their absence from II R 67 rev. 7–13 indicate their refusal to submit to Tiglathpileser? Were it not for the fragmentary condition of the list, an affirmative answer would be certain. Possibly, however, the missing names once appeared in the lacunae of the text.

At the end of its report on the events of 733/732, Layard 72b+73a refers to Samsi as one "who broke the oath by Shamash" (l. 210). The inscription thereby indicates that Samsi previously had been an Assyrian vassal. When exactly she first submitted to the Assyrians is uncertain, but Tiglathpileser's Palestinian campaign in 734/733 is a reasonable guess; the Assyrian records relating to earlier years mention only Zabibe, Samsi's predecessor.[69] If this scenario is correct, Samsi's name should be restored to the list in II R 67, either at the end of l. 9 or among the Palestinian rulers which follow.

Whether the tributary list originally mentioned Rezin, Pekah, and Hiram is harder to decide. Weippert believes that the names of the three kings and their countries once stood at the end of l. 7, thereby completing the same group of states as that evidenced in the earlier lists of 738 and 740. In the earlier lists, however, what is distinctive of the group is not simply its members, but also the sequence in which they are named: Qummuh-Syria/Damascus-Israel-Tyre-Byblos-Que. If II R 67 rev. 7 once attested to the same pattern, one would expect to find the lacuna in the middle of the line and the kings of Que and Byblos in reverse order. It is unlikely that Rezin, Pekah, and Hiram were once named in this part of the list.

---

[69]It is perhaps noteworthy that the Assyrian annals single out Samsi and Mitinti of Ashkelon as rulers who broke their oaths of vassalage. Others like Rezin and Hiram were equally guilty of the same charge. The Assyrian scribes may have applied the charge especially to Samsi and Mitinti, because their treachery was most recent, following their payment of tribute in 734/733.

Alternatively, the three rulers might have appeared among the Palestinian rulers in ll. 10–12. J. M. Asurmendi, however, contends that the lacuna at the end of l. 10 allows for only fifteen to twenty-four additional signs and thus probably contained the name of only one ruler and his country.[70] The lacuna at the end of l. 11 allows even fewer additional signs. Furthermore, if Tadmor is correct in taking the last preserved sign of l. 11 as the beginning of a fourth ruler's name, *Mu-še-hu/pak-* of Ekron or Ashdod,[71] space for more than one additional ruler would doubtfully be left. At most then, only two of the three kings—Rezin, Pekah, and Hiram—could with any likelihood have been named in this part of the list, and only then if Samsi were restored to l. 9.

A conclusive answer to the textual question is impossible. We strongly suspect, however, that none of the three rulers originally belonged to II R 67 rev. 7–13. Our reasons are two. (1) It seems highly coincidental that Syria, Israel, and Tyre—precisely those states which formed the core of the revolt against Assyria during the late 730s—should all be missing from the list. (2) The anti-Assyrian alliance, we will see, probably did not arise suddenly in the wake of Tiglath-pileser's campaign "against Philistia," but had begun to take shape earlier, before the Assyrian king intervened in the area (see section B5 below). The absence of Rezin, Pekah, and Hiram from the tributary list of 734/733 likely reflects their determination to carry on the resistance.

5. ND400

ND400 is the surviving part of a summary inscription found at Nimrud in 1950.[72] It consists of two sections, ll. 1–19 and 20–27, marked apart by a horizontal line. The inscription is fragmentary: only the middle part of each line remains. Consequently, the narrative throughout is very disjointed.

1) ....
2) ... on the mainland ...
3) ... [their lives] I poured out. That city I ...
4) ... in the midst of the sea I trod them down and up to ...

---

[70]J. M. Asurmendi, *La Guerra Siro-Efraimita*, 35.
[71]H. Tadmor, "The Philistines under Assyrian Rule," 89.
[72]D. J. Wiseman ("Two Historical Inscriptions from Nimrud," *Iraq* 13 [1951] 21–28) first published and translated the text, providing as well a brief commentary. A recent translation of the entire inscription appears in *TUAT* (1. 375–76).

5) [Fear of my weapons upon him fe]ll[73] and his courage failed. In sackcloth he dressed himself...
6) ... of willow set with precious stones and gold together with ...
7) ... ivory, fine oil, spices of all kinds, hordes from the land of ...
8) ... from Kashpuna which is on the coast ...[74]
9) ... into the charge of my official, the governor of Ṣi[mirra] ...
10) ... [like gra]ss with the corpses of their warriors I filled [the open field] ...
11) ... their [pos]sessions, their cattle, their flocks, their asses ...
12) ... in the midst of his palace ...
13) ... their [tribute] I received from them and their land I ...
14) ... [Han]no of Gaza before my powerful weapons was terrified and ...
15) ... gold, 800 talents of silver, people together with their possessions, his wife, [his] sons ...
16) ... an image of the great gods my lords, a golden image of my royal person ...
17) ... I set up and that one from Egypt like a bird ...
18) ... of Ashur I counted. An image of my royal person at the Brook of Egypt ...[75]
19) ... silver I seized[76] and to Assyria ...

---

20) ... [to the kings][77] my predecessors he did not humble himself nor send his embassy, the conquest of ...
21) ... he became afraid.[78] His leaders[79] for the purpose of showing servitude ...
22) ... -ruatti of the land of the Meunites who are below [Egypt] ...[80]

---

[73]E. Vogt ("Die Texte Tiglat-Pilesers III. über die Eroberung Palästinas," *Bib* 45 [1964] 349) proposes this restoration.

[74]The text probably read originally: "Kashpuna which is on the coast of the Upper Sea" (*URU Ka-aš-pu-na ša aḫ tam-tim e-li-ti*).

[75]The determinative *URU* precedes *Nahal Muṣur*, but probably does not refer to a specific city at the Brook of Egypt. See N. Na'aman, "The Brook of Egypt," 69.

[76]The verb *nasaḫu* probably refers to the forcible confiscation of booty. (The verb *maḫaru* is usually used for the simple receipt of tribute.) Wiseman translates the line, "I tore out the silver and [carried it back] to Assyria." See I. Eph'al, *The Ancient Arabs*, 31, n. 86.

[77]The parallel passage in ND4301+4305 rev. 23 reads clearly: "to the kings, my predecessors, he did not humble himself" (*ana šarrani alikut paniya la išpiluma*).

[78]This translation assumes the reading, *ir-ša-a na-kut-tú*, and treats what follows as an independent sentence. See R. Borger and H. Tadmor, "Zwei Beiträge zur alttestamentliche Wissenschaft aufgrund der Inschriften Tiglathpilesers III," *ZAW* 94 (1982) 250.

[79]Wiseman ("Two Historical Inscriptions," 23-24) translates *LÚ.MAḪ.MEŠ* as "prophets." In numerous Assyrian letters and other documents, however, the Akkadian term refers to political officials and ambassadors. See H. W. F. Saggs, "Nimrud Letters, 1952—Part II," *Iraq* 17 (1955) 135.

[80]The Akkadian in l. 22 reads: ... *ru-at-ti KUR Mu-'u-na-a-a šá šapal* (*KI.TA*) .... Before *ru-at-ti*, however, there is a fragment of a sign, which can be restored either as *URU* or *si*. Compare the different readings and translations of Wiseman

23) ... superior, the great conquest of my hands ...[81]
24) ... at the Saqurri mountains 9400 of [her] warriors ...
25) ... her [gods], the weapons (and) scepter of her goddess ...
26) ... [like] a wild [she-ass, she set] her face. The rest ...
27) ... camels, she-camels to[gether with] ...[82]

Lines 1–19 describe the Assyrian campaign "against Philistia" in 734/733.[83] The account narrates the advance of Tiglathpileser southward along the east Mediterranean coast in that year. It divides into three parts, each treating a phase of the campaign. (1) Lines 1–9 recount action along the Phoenician coast: a city described as lying "in the midst of the sea" is subjugated and Kashpuna[84] is set under the authority of the Assyrian governor at Ṣimirra.[85] (2) Lines 10–13 report the conquest of a state whose name unfortunately is not preserved. (3) Lines 14–19 narrate the subjugation of Gaza and of territory in the vicinity of the "Brook of Egypt."[86]

Scholars debate the precise focus of ll. 1–9. The issue centers on the identity of "that city ... in the midst of the sea" (ll. 3–4). A. Alt proposes Arvad because of its proximity to Ṣimirra mentioned in l.

("Two Historical Inscriptions," 23–24), R. Borger and H. Tadmor, ("Zwei Beiträge," 250–51), and I. Eph'al, *The Ancient Arabs*, 91.

[81]Wiseman's copy of the cuneiform text ("Two Historical Inscriptions," 27) shows *iš* as the last readable sign of l. 23. It is apparently the beginning of a new word which R. Borger and H. Tadmor ("Zwei Beiträge," 250) restore and translate "he perceived."

[82]For the translation of ll. 24–27, we depend on I. Eph'al's reading of the Akkadian text (*The Ancient Arabs*, 33–36). See also *TUAT* 1. 376.

[83]See A. Alt, "Tiglathpilesers III. erster Feldzug nach Palästina," in his *KS* II. 150–62; H. Donner, *Israel unter den Völkern*, 5; idem., *Geschichte des Volkes Israel und seiner Nachbarn in Grundzügen* (Göttingen: Vandenhoeck & Ruprecht, 1987) 305; H. Tadmor, "Philistia under Assyrian Rule," 88; E. Vogt, "Die Texte Tiglat-Pilesers," 348–54; and J. M. Asurmendi, *La Guerra Siro-Efraimita*, 28. The account may have been part of a larger annalistic source before the Assyrian scribes incorporated it into ND400 as a distinct paragraph. Compare, however, the view of N. Na'aman ("The Brook of Egypt," 69), who questions whether ll. 1–19 all relate to the Philistine campaign.

[84]Only in ND400 and ND2715 (Nimrud Letter XII) is the name, Kashpuna, fully preserved. The toponym survived partially in Tiglathpileser's annals (see Rost, *Keilschrifttexte*, 21, l. 126) and K2649 (Rost, *Keilschrifttexte*, 86, l. 1), but it was often restored erroneously as Rashpuna and identified with Rishpon ('Arsuf), north of Tel Aviv.

[85]Ancient Ṣimirra (modern Ṣumra, a coastal town north of Tripoli) was the capital of a province which Tiglathpileser established in 738 and which included several towns formerly under the control of En'il of Hamath (Arqa, Zimarra, Usnu, Siannu, etc.). Kashpuna also had belonged to this province (see Rost, *Keilschrifttexte*, 21, l. 126), but apparently the town asserted its independence sometime after 738.

[86]Parallel accounts appear in ND4301+4305 rev. 13–16 and III R 10,2:8–15.

9.⁸⁷ Wiseman also suggests Arvad, observing that the annals of Ashurbanipal describe Arvad as lying "in the midst of the sea" (see *ANET* 296).⁸⁸ E. Vogt notes, however, that Tyre and Sidon are similarly designated in the annals of Esarhaddon (see *ANET* 290–91).⁸⁹ The subjugation of the former, Vogt asserts, occurred in the course of Tiglathpileser's 734 campaign. Tyre would thus seem the likely focus of ND400:1–9.⁹⁰ In support of this interpretation, one might also solicit the testimony of ND2715 (Nimrud Letter XII) which, according to H. W. F. Saggs, locates Kashpuna in the vicinity of Tyre.⁹¹

While the argument for Tyre cannot be easily dismissed, three considerations undercut its force. (1) The tributary list of 734/733, we saw above, does not mention Tyre. Its conspicuous absence, along with that of Syria and Israel, is plausibly explained by the assumption that the Assyrians conquered these three states only later. Arvad, on the other hand, apparently was first subjugated in 734/733 and so was listed in the tributary list of that year.

(2) Another summary inscription, ND 4301+4305, indicates that the Assyrian move against Tyre involved extensive and doubtlessly time-consuming military action (rev. 5–8). Not only Maḥalab, the "stronghold" of Hiram, but several "great cities" under his control were forcibly taken. If the episode were part of the 734/733 campaign, it would seem that Tiglathpileser was willing to put off his intervention in Philistia until the northern cities were firmly under his control. This assumption, however, conflicts with the overall appearance of the Philistine campaign as a kind of *Blitzkrieg*, the essential goals of which were three: the suppression of anti-Assyrian activity among the Philistine city-states; the control of commerce in the area of Gaza; and the prevention of Egyptian intervention in Palestine.⁹² Time would have been a crucial factor in the easy attainment of these objectives. The lack of Philistine opposition to the advancing Assyrian army seems to reflect the suddenness with which the army appeared in the area.⁹³ The delay involved in conquering Tyre would

---

⁸⁷A. Alt, "Erster Feldzug," 152–53.
⁸⁸D. J. Wiseman, "Two Historical Inscriptions," 24. Note that Tiglathpileser I speaks of crossing over "in ships to Arvad from Arvad which is on the seashore . . . ." (*ANET* 275). Apparently Arvad included both mainland and island settlements.
⁸⁹E. Vogt, "Die Texte Tiglat-Pilesers," 349–50.
⁹⁰Vogt ("Die Texte Tiglat-Pilesers," 351) implies that the report of the subjugation of Hiram of Tyre in ND4301+4305 rev. 5–8 is parallel to ND400:1–9.
⁹¹H. W. F. Saggs, "Nimrud Letters," 149–50. The author dates the letter approximately to 738–734.
⁹²See the discussion of ND 400:14–19 below and of ND 4301+4305 rev. 16 in section B6.
⁹³A. Alt, "Erster Feldzug," 157–58.

have cost Tiglathpileser the important element of surprise which he in fact seems to have enjoyed.

(3) The mention of Kashpuna in ND400:8 cannot count much in the identification of the city "in the midst of the sea," for the data relating to Kashpuna's location is far from clear. In Nimrud Letter XII, an Assyrian official reports on events in Tyre, Sidon and Kashpuna. The close geographical proximity of the three cities would thus seem a reasonable, though not altogether necessary, conclusion. The annals of Tiglathpileser, however, list Kashpuna with Usnu, Siannu, Ṣimirra and other cities "as far as Mt. Saue," which the Assyrian king reduced to provincial status in 738.[94] The city would thus appear to lie in north Phoenicia. A third Assyrian text, III R 10,2:1–6, describes Kashpuna, Byblos, Ṣimirra, Arka, Zimarra, Usnu, Siannu, Ri'raba, and Ri'sisu as cities lying "on the Upper Sea." The literary structure of the text, however, separates Kashpuna from the other northern coastal towns and treats it in connection with southern inland cities "on the border of Beth-Omri."[95] Another inscription, K2649, confuses the picture still more. This text describes Kashpuna as lying "on the Lower Sea"[96] and treats it as part of a geographical and administrative region separate from Gilead and other towns adjoining Beth-Omri.[97] Finally, possible references to Kashpuna in 1 Macc 5:26 (Kaspho) and 2 Macc 12:13 (Kaspin) have in mind a town in Gilead.[98]

The above evidence can be explained by the assumption that there were several Kashpunas in antiquity, more than one of which were located along the Mediterranean coast. While the Kashpuna mentioned in Nimrud Letter XII may have been a southern Phoenician town near Tyre, the Kashpuna in ND400:8 likely lay in the vicinity of Ṣimirra, under the control of whose governor it was again set.[99]

Arvad's proximity to Ṣimirra and its mention in the tributary list of 734/733, the absence of Tyre from the same list, and the unlikelihood that Tiglathpileser delayed his campaign against Philistia to conquer Tyre—all speak in favor of Arvad, not Tyre, as the focus of ND400:1–9. When the Assyrian king swept down the coast in

---

[94]See Rost, *Keilschrifttexte*, 20, l. 126.

[95]Notices on the appointment of Assyrian officials in ll. 4–5 and 8 mark divisions within the account.

[96]See Rost, *Keilschrifttexte*, 86. H. Tadmor ("The Southern Border of Aram," *IEJ* 12 [1962] 117, n. 18) tries to harmonize the reference with the one in III R 10,2:5 by suggesting that *aḥ tamtim šapliti* (Lower Sea) was a scribal error for *aḥ tamtim eliti* (Upper Sea). A. Alt ("Erster Feldzug," 153, n. 4) draws the same conclusion.

[97]A horizontal line separates ll. 1–2 and ll. 3–4. See H. Tadmor, "Southern Border," 116–17.

[98]See J. Goldstein, *I Maccabees* (AB 41; Garden City: Doubleday, 1976) 301; idem., *II Maccabees* (AB 41A; Garden City: Doubleday, 1983) 439. Note also the location of modern-day Haspin and Khisfin in the southern Golan.

[99]A. Alt, "Erster Feldzug," 153.

734/733, the city's king, Matanbi'il, apparently offered some initial resistance. The extent of the fighting, however, is uncertain. Tiglathpileser claims that he "poured out" enemy lives and "trod them down in the midst of the sea." The language here is somewhat stereotypical, however, and may be little more than high-flung rhetoric. An actual siege of the island-city seems unlikely, given the delay in the Assyrian march that would have resulted. At some point during the episode, Matanbi'il abjectly surrendered. Booty and/or tribute were collected, but the state was otherwise left intact.[100] Tiglathpileser permitted Matanbi'il to continue as king of Arvad.

The connection between the subjugation of Arvad and the annexation of Kashpuna is difficult to determine. We noted above that in 738 Kashpuna became part of an Assyrian province centered around Ṣimirra.[101] If ND400:8–9 speaks of Kashpuna's return to provincial status, the town likely asserted its independence between 738 and 734.[102] While the details of its emancipation remain obscure, we suspect that Arvad may have been stirring up revolt in the province of Ṣimirra and that Kaspuna had become involved.[103] In any case, placing the town again under the control of the Assyrian governor at Ṣimirra re-established the previous status quo. Matanbi'il of Arvad undoubtedly pledged his loyalty to the Assyrian regime and promised to refrain from subversive activity among his southern neighbors.[104]

ND400:10–13 narrate the subjugation of a country whose name unfortunately is lost. Tiglathpileser claims to have decimated the enemy forces in the open field, seized booty, and received tribute. He

---

[100]Contrary to Alt's opinion ("Erster Feldzug," 153), nothing in ll. 1–9 hints clearly at the territorial reduction of Arvad.

[101]B. Oded ("The Phoenician Cities and the Assyrian Empire in the Time of Tiglathpileser III," *ZDPV* 90 [1974] 44–45) argues that the Assyrians first annexed Kashpuna to the province of Ṣimirra in 734. He does not convincingly explain why the annals of Tiglathpileser list the town among other cities included in the province of Ṣimirra in 738.

[102]Another possible explanation is that the Assyrians reduced Kashpuna to provincial status in 738, but subsequently granted the city more independence. Sargon II treated the Philistine city of Ashdod in a similar way.

[103]Arvad depended upon maritime trade for the bulk of its revenue and likely competed with other Phoenician cities for goods exported from Egypt. If the Assyrians, after 738, implemented in Ṣimirra commercial policies detrimental to Arvad's trade, Arvad would have had reason to stir up trouble in the Assyrian province. See Nimrud Letter XII (H. W. F. Saggs, "Nimrud Letters," 149–50), which documents Assyrian efforts during the 730s to monopolize the maritime trade.

[104]Alt ("Erster Feldzug," 154) correctly characterizes the subjugation of Arvad as a "subordinate task which Tiglathpileser undertook personally only because he was underway toward more distant and greater goals in the same direction."

also refers to actions both within the palace of the opposing king and relating to his territory, but the meaning is obscure.

A. Alt argues that the report narrates Assyrian action against Israel.[105] If ll. 1–19 recount the sequential stages of the Philistine campaign and if the first and third sections of the account deal with Arvad and Gaza respectively, the country treated in the middle section, ll. 10–13, should lie somewhere between north Phoenicia and southernmost Philistia. Israel, Alt contends, appears as the likely candidate, especially in view of another inscription, III R 10,2. There, in ll. 5–15, the progression Kashpuna-Israel-Gaza is supposedly clear.[106] The Assyrians, Alt concludes, defeated Pekah's army in the plain of Sharon or Acco, annexed the coastal area,[107] and then proceeded southward to Gaza. Tiglathpileser's final settlement with Israel followed in 733–732.

Alt's interpretation is unconvincing for two reasons. First, ND400:1–19 and III R 10,2:5–15 are not strictly parallel. Lines 5–8 of the latter text, which Alt believes treat Israel, concern in fact Syria-Damascus (see section B7 below). Second, l. 12 of ND400 refers to the palace of the opposing king. The allusion is cryptic, but probably in mind are measures which Tiglathpileser took in the capital city.[108] If ll. 10–13 concern Israel, as Alt contends, it would seem that the Assyrian king moved inland from the coast to take action against Samaria. Such a detour is unlikely, as Alt himself argues, given the primary aims of the larger campaign—the subjugation of Philistia and the control of its maritime trade.

The focus of the text, if not Israel, is difficult to know without new inscriptional evidence. Whichever state it may be, Tiglathpileser easily defeated its army in 734/733.

A report on the conquest of Gaza and its environs to the south follows immediately in ll. 14–19. The text thus passes over in silence other Philistine cities by which the Assyrian army must have

---

[105] A. Alt, "Erster Feldzug," 155–57.

[106] Alt ("Erster Feldzug," 156) explains the significance of this series: ". . . Thereby the most important events of the same campaign [734] are enumerated as in the new fragment [ND 400], and from this parallelism it undoubtedly follows that the middle sub-section of the latter [ND400:10–13] describes a military clash of Tiglathpileser with the kingdom of Israel." (Brackets are ours.)

[107] According to Alt ("Erster Feldzug," 157), this is the origin of the Assyrian province, Du'ru. See also A. Alt, "Das System der assyrischen Provinzen," 233–38.

[108] Alt believes that the text originally reported actions by Pekah in his residence at Samaria. Alternatively, N. Na'aman ("Historical and Chronological Notes," 72) suggests that l. 12 refers to the coup of Hoshea in 731. Most likely, the text originally reported that Tiglathpileser set up a temporary throne for himself in the palace of the opposing king (compare Rost, *Keilschrifttexte*, 16, l. 97) or perhaps a stela (compare III R 10,2:9–11).

marched. This silence is best explained as an indication that these cities submitted voluntarily to Tiglathpileser. If he had moved swiftly down the coastal plain, he would have caught the Philistines by surprise, leaving them little time to organize a defense. The tributary list of 734/733 (II R 67 rev. 11) attests to the capitulation of one of their numbers, Mitinti of Ashkelon.

With the help of parallel accounts (see ND4301+4305 rev. 13–16 and III R 10,2:8–15 in sections B6 and B7 below), the gist of the report on Gaza can be understood. As the Assyrian army approached the city, its ruler Hanno fled to Egypt (l. 14). Tiglathpileser was thus able to occupy Gaza without a fight. His initial treatment of the town seems to have been harsh: booty was seized; a portion of the population, including members of the royal family, was taken into exile; images of the Assyrian king and his god were set up within the palace (ll. 15–16).[109] At some point during the proceedings, Hanno returned to Gaza and with Assyrian permission resumed the throne (l. 17).[110] Subsequently, Tiglathpileser marched about ten kilometers to the south and, in the vicinity of the "Brook of Egypt" (Wadi Besor),[111] set up a royal stela and took booty (ll. 18–19). Permanent defense troops may have been stationed in the area.

If the bare facts of the Assyrian action against Gaza are clear, their broader historical significance is debatable. What objectives lay behind the move against Gaza? What was the purpose of the subsequent action at the "Brook of Egypt"? Why did Hanno flee to Egypt rather than submit voluntarily to Tiglathpileser in the manner of other Philistine rulers? What induced the Assyrian king to pardon Hanno and restore him to the throne? How did the entire episode relate, if at all, to the anti-Assyrian movement in the west? A full treatment of the Gaza episode must await our study of the parallel accounts. We limit ourselves here to three points.

First, Alt contends that Tiglathpileser initially intended to reduce Gaza to provincial status, but with the return of Hanno from Egypt, the Assyrian king altered his plan and agreed to leave the city as a vassal state.[112] ND400, however, is utterly silent about the appointment of an Assyrian governor over the city. Also lacking is the kind of language typically used to describe the incorporation of a

---

[109]III R 10,2:10 also reports the spoliation of the local gods. For the significance of these measures, see M. Cogan, *Imperialism and Religion: Assyria, Judah, and Israel in the 8th and 7th Centuries B.C.E.* (SBLMS 19; Missoula: Scholars Press, 1974) 22–41.

[110]III R 10,2:13 describes Hanno's pardon clearly: "and like a bird . . . he fled and . . . to his place I returned him. . . ."

[111]For this identification of the "Brook of Egypt," see N. Na'aman, "The Brook of Egypt," 68–90.

[112]A. Alt, "Erster Feldzug," 160–61.

state into the provincial system.¹¹³ Furthermore, the Assyrians rarely annexed a state which did not border directly on previously formed provinces.¹¹⁴ As a province in 734/733, Gaza would have been isolated by vassal states like Ashkelon and Judah. For these reasons, it is likelier that, from the outset of the Philistine campaign, Tiglathpileser intended to make Gaza a vassal state. The plan was in keeping with Assyrian policy toward other Philistine and Phoenician seaports.¹¹⁵

Second, H. Donner contends that nothing in ND400 suggests a connection between the Philistine campaign and a broader anti-Assyrian revolt.¹¹⁶ The claim, however, is only partially correct. Nowhere in the text is clear reference made to Hanno's participation in an alliance of states opposing Assyria. However, the singular flight of the Philistine ruler and the initially harsh treatment of Gaza by Tiglathpileser seem to reflect Hanno's deep involvement in some sort of anti-Assyrian activity. One may reasonably guess that Hanno, like Pekah of Israel, had fallen in league with Rezin of Syria, and that, as a member of the coalition, he was the principal opponent to the Assyrians in southern Palestine. Concern to safeguard Gaza's maritime trade would have induced Hanno to join the rebel cause.¹¹⁷

Third, Alt argues that the Assyrian measures in Gaza and at the "Brook of Egypt" were not aimed at warding off an expected attack by Egypt.¹¹⁸ Egypt at this time was supposedly too weak to be of much concern to Tiglathpileser. The establishment of a defense outpost in southern Philistia, Alt explains, simply accorded with Assyrian policy elsewhere along the periphery of the empire. H. Donner concurs in this opinion and emphasizes that ND400 says nothing

---

¹¹³The technical terminology for the establishment of a province is *ana eššuti ṣabatu* ("to re-organize"). Alternative expressions include "restoring to the land of Assyria," "reckoning them with the Assyrians," and "setting the yoke of Ashur my lord upon them just as upon the Assyrians."

¹¹⁴See H. Tadmor, "Philistia under Assyrian Rule," 88.

¹¹⁵The Assyrians feared that converting these coastal cities into provinces could jeopardize the lucrative maritime trade. See H. Tadmor, "Philistia under Assyrian Rule," 88; B. Oded, "Phoenician Cities," 47; N. Na'aman, "The Brook of Egypt," 87–90; G. L. Mattingly, "The Role of Philistine Autonomy in Neo-Assyrian Foreign Policy," *NEASB* 14 [1979], 49–57.

¹¹⁶H. Donner, "The Separate States of Israel and Judah," in *Israelite and Judean History*, 428.

¹¹⁷Isaiah 9:11 hints at the cooperative relations between Syria and Philistia during the 740s and/or 730s. The Chronicler's account of the Syro-Ephraimitic crisis (2 Chr 28:1–21) records attacks on Judah by both Syria and the Philistines, but does not link the aggressive actions of the two states directly. Regarding the sea trade of the Philistine cities and the Assyrian efforts to control it, see G. L. Mattingly, "The Role of Philistine Autonomy," 49–57.

¹¹⁸A. Alt, "Erster Feldzug," 160–61.

about the participation of Egypt in any anti-Assyrian coalition.[119] He adds as well that the pardoning of Hanno would have been very odd, if he had recently fled to Egypt to request military aid.

Several considerations undercut the force of these arguments. The Assyrian royal inscriptions are principally interested in glorifying Tiglathpileser and so portray him as omnipotent as possible. Accordingly, we would not necessarily expect ND400 to acknowledge a potential threat from Egypt.

The Assyrians did not invariably replace vassals who had revolted or had acted in some way against the interests of the empire. Their policy was particularly flexible in the case of the Phoenician and Philistine cities, which they preferred to leave semi-independent.[120] If a rebellious monarch did acceptable obeisance before the Assyrian king, he might retain his throne.[121] Thus in the case of Hanno, Tiglathpileser might have pardoned him, even if he had recently sought Egyptian aid.

Competition over the east Mediterranean sea trade was increasingly a source of tension between Egypt and Assyria during the 730s. Nimrud Letter XII attests to Assyria's efforts to monopolize the control of this trade by prohibiting Tyre and Sidon from selling timber to the Egyptians.[122] Egyptian economic interests were similarly threatened when Tiglathpileser moved into Palestine. The Assyrian king probably understood this and so perhaps anticipated Egyptian intervention.

Although Egypt in fact could not have seriously challenged Assyrian hegemony in Palestine during the 730s, its past reputation as a military power probably persisted and so perhaps gave the Assyrians cause for concern.[123] Furthermore, Egypt had a history of

---

[119]H. Donner, "The Separate States," 428.

[120]J. L. Mattingly, "The Role of Philistine Autonomy," 49–57; and B. Oded, "Phoenician Cities," 47.

[121]For example, Samsi of the Arabs and Hiram of Tyre were allowed to continue their reigns after they capitulated to Tiglathpileser (see sections B6 and B7 below). Similarly, the Assyrian king Esarhaddon pardoned Ba'lu of Tyre, who "had put his trust upon his friend Tirhakah, king of Nubia, and had thrown off the yoke of Ashur," but who subsequently "bowed down and implored me [Esarhaddon] as his lord" (see *ANET* 290–91, 533–34).

[122]See H. W. F. Saggs, "Nimrud Letters," 128.

[123]Pharaohs of the Eighteenth and Nineteenth Dynasties had campaigned continually in Syria and Palestine, thereby establishing not only Egypt's control of the region during the Late Bronze and Early Iron ages, but also its international image as a military power. After a period of political decline during the twelfth and eleventh centuries, Egyptian power resurged briefly toward the end of the tenth century when Sheshonk I invaded Palestine (see *ANET* 242–43, 263–64; 1 Kgs 14:25–28). Although Egypt did not control the region again until the seventh century, 2 Kgs 7:6 indicates that its reputation as a military force, able to intervene in Palestine, continued during the interim period.

supporting anti-Assyrian movements in Syria and Palestine.[124] Although military help from its quarter was not forthcoming in 734–731, it persisted as an expectation among the states of the region during the following decade[125] and finally materialized in 720 and 701 (see *ANET* 285, 287; compare 2 Kgs 18:19–25).[126]

In the twentieth year of his reign, the powerful Ethiopian king, Piye, re-established Ethiopian hegemony in Lower Egypt by invading the Delta region (see *AEL* 2. 66–84).[127] If Piye had begun to rule in 753, as some scholars now believe,[128] his invasion would have occurred in 734, precisely the same year as Tiglathpileser's campaign against Philistia. If this scenario is correct, it is reasonable to surmise that Piye's aggression was a factor in the Assyrian strategy. As events unfolded, the Ethiopians did not directly challenge Assyria's control of Palestine in 734–731, but only later in 701 (see *ANET* 287 and 2 Kgs 19:8–9).[129] Nevertheless, we might reasonably guess that Tiglathpileser intended his actions against Gaza and at the "Brook of Egypt" partly as precautions against a possible Ethiopian attack.

A decision on the role of Egypt/Ethiopia in the anti-Assyrian revolt of the late 730s depends ultimately on whether one is inclined toward a minimal or maximal interpretation of the evidence. Strictly interpreted, ND400 records only that Hanno fled to Egypt. Refuge there may have been his only goal. The episode, however, may have been more involved, as we suggested above. That Hanno sought assistance from Egypt in 734/733 is a very plausible assumption, espe-

---

[124]Osorkon II of the Twenty-second Dynasty contributed a division of soldiers to the coalition of Syro-Palestinian states which fought Shalmaneser III at Qarqar in 853.

[125]See 2 Kgs 17:4; Isa 30:1–7, 31:1–3, and Hos 7:11. During the revolt of Ashdod in 715–711, Egyptian aid was requested but not received (see Isa 20:1–6; *ANET* 287).

[126]N. Na'aman ("Brook of Egypt," 83) rightly concludes: "From the Assyrian point of view, the seizure of the Philistine coast meant pushing the Egyptians back to their homeland, with the intervening expanses of Sinai preventing any immediate threat to their holdings in Philistia. From the outset of the Assyrian campaigns to Philistia, Egypt was the main threat to Assyria from the south."

[127]Earlier, during the reign of Piye's father, Kashta, Ethiopian forces invaded Lower Egypt, pressing as far northward as Thebes. The occupation, however, was only temporary. Kashta returned to his capital at Napata, where he resided until his death. See I. E. S. Edwards, "Egypt: From the Twenty-second to the Twenty-fourth Dynasty," *CAH* 3/1. 569–70.

[128]See, for example, K. Baer, "The Libyan and Nubian Kings of Egypt: Notes on the Chronology of Dynasties XXII to XXVI," *JNES* 32 (1973) 7.

[129]Ethiopian meddling in Syro-Palestinian politics continued during the early seventh century. See, for example, Esarhaddon's report on the subjugation of Ba'lu, king of Tyre, who had allied himself with Tirhakah of Ethiopia (*ANET* 290).

cially in light of the long history of Egyptian/Ethiopian support for anti-Assyrian movements.

A new section of the inscription begins in l. 20. Although the text is increasingly uncertain from this point onward, a three-fold division in the material is still apparent. Lines 20–21 report the submission of an unnamed ruler to Assyrian vassalage. Lines 22–23 recount the forcible subjugation of the Meunites,[130] an Arab group located in the vicinity of the "Brook of Egypt" (Wadi Besor).[131] Lines 24–27 concern Samsi, the queen of the Arabs, whose army Tiglathpileser routed at Mt. Saqurri.[132] The organization of this material is unclear. Neither a chronological sequence nor a geographical arrangement is evident.

The precise identity of the ruler mentioned in ll. 20–21 is hard to know. Perhaps he was an Arab leader and for this reason was treated by the Assyrian scribes alongside the Meunites and Samsi.[133] In any case, his decision to submit to Tiglathpileser appears to have been voluntary. If ND4301+4305 rev. 23–25 recount the same incident (see section B6 below), it would appear that emissaries of the ruler journeyed to Calah to do homage before the Assyrian king.

Lines 22–23 are the single extra-biblical reference to the Meunites. The text is very fragmentary at this point and so it is difficult to know whether they submitted peacefully to the Assyrians or offered armed resistance. If the latter, their actions would be understandable. The Meunites probably controlled the overland trade routes along the "Brook of Egypt" at this time and were perhaps reluctant to relinquish that control to the Assyrians.[134] Without new inscriptional evidence, however, the episode remains obscure. In any case, Tiglathpileser's encounter with the Meunites probably occurred in 734/733, when he was campaigning in southern Philistia.

The final lines of ND400 describe Assyrian action against Samsi. Although the text does not refer to her by name, two facts indicate

---

[130]See H. Tadmor, "Philistia under Assyrian Rule," 89; R. Borger and H. Tadmor, "Zwei Beiträge," 250–51.

[131]See N. Na'aman, "The Brook of Egypt," 70.

[132]D. J. Wiseman ("Two Historical Inscriptions," 22, n. 2) locates Mt. Saqurri in northern Syria. The whole of ll. 20–27, he suggests, reports the conquest of towns and peoples which Tiglathpileser encountered as he advanced against Damascus in 733. I. Eph'al (*The Ancient Arabs*, 33–35) contends, however, that a connection between Mt. Saqurri and the defeat of Samsi is apparent in III R 10,2:19 and possibly also in Layard 66:213.

[133]Borger and Tadmor ("Zwei Beiträge," 250) propose an Egyptian ruler. I. Eph'al (*The Ancient Arabs*, 30, n. 80) suggests Ahaz of Judah, but his reasons are not compelling.

[134]This scenario assumes that the Meunites had regained their independence from the Davidic kings, under whom they had been vassals since the reign of Azariah. (See 2 Chr 20:1, where "Meunites" should be read in place of "Ammonites").

that the queen of the Arabs is the focus here. First, the battle reportedly occurred at Mt. Saqurri. In parallel accounts of Samsi's defeat, the toponym is similarly mentioned (see III R 10,2:19 and Layard 66:213). Second, the personal pronouns throughout ll. 24–27 indicate that the leader in question was a woman. Samsi is the likeliest candidate.

The precise whereabouts of Mt. Saqurri and of the battle that ensued there is uncertain. If ll. 20–27 were geographically arranged, one might expect a location somewhere in the vicinity of the Meunites, that is, in the north Sinai. The topography of this region, however, is relatively flat. A more likely location for Mt. Saqurri is to the east of Palestine, perhaps somewhere along the border of the Hauran region. Samsi herself seems to have been dependent on the commerce of international trade and so may have had dominion somewhere in the vicinity of the main north-south highway running along the Transjordanian plateau.[135] Furthermore, we saw above that Layard 72b+73a suggests at least a loose temporal connection between Tiglathpileser's move against Rezin's forces and the battle with Samsi. It is reasonable then to place the latter episode roughly in the area south of Damascus.

Lines 24–27 report the decisive defeat of Samsi's troops. Presumably many of her warriors were slain and her gods and goddess were taken as booty. The queen herself apparently evaded capture. If l. 26 originally read, "to the desert, an arid place, like a wild ass she set her face,"[136] Samsi would seem to have fled the battle scene into the adjacent desert.

6. ND4301+4305

ND4301 and ND4305 are adjoining fragments of a summary inscription found during the 1955 excavations at Nimrud and subsequently published by D. J. Wiseman.[137] Horizontal lines divide the text into paragraphs, each covering a certain area. The original conclusion of the inscription, now lost, might have reported on royal construction at ancient Nimrud.

The reverse side of ND4301+4305 reports on events in Syria and Palestine.

1) ... Ḫata]rikka as far as Mt. S[aue ...
2) ... within] the territory of Assyria I brought back ...

---

[135]See I. Eph'al, *The Ancient Arabs*, 85–86.
[136]See I. Eph'al, *The Ancient Arabs*, 33–36.
[137]D. J. Wiseman, "A Fragmentary Inscription of Tiglath-pileser III from Nimrud," *Iraq* 18 (1956) 117–29.

3) ... the widespread [land of Beth-]Hazael in its entirety from ...
4) [which is on the bor]der[138] of the land of Beth-Omri, into the territory of Assyria [I brought back.

---

5) ... Hi]ram of Tyre who with Rezin of ...
6) ... Mahalab, his stronghold, together with great towns I conquered. Spoil ...
7) ... into] my presence he came and kissed my feet. 20 talents of ...
8) ... decorated [garments], linen garments, officials, singers, songstresses ...

---

9) ... district ... their surrounding areas ...[139]
10) ... Hoshea as ki]ng over them [I set ...[140]
11) ... to Sarrabanu[141] before me ...

---

12) ... 100 talents of silver I seized ...

---

13) ... he fled. Gaza ...
14) ... I made. In the midst of the palace of Gaza ...
15) ... from Egypt ...
16) ... for a trading-center of Assyria ...

---

17) ... with weapons I smote and like ...
18) ... numberless gods ...
19) ... an arid place, like a wild mare ...
20) ... with]in her camp, by fire ...
21) ... female camels with their foals ...
22) ... over her[142] I set and 10,000 warriors ...[143]

---

[138]The first discernible sign of l. 4 is *ti*. Wiseman ("A Fragmentary Inscription," 129) states that the lacuna allows for only one or two signs. Our translation rests on the restoration proposed by H. Tadmor ("The Southern Border," 116, n. 16): [... *ša pat-]ti*. Compare the roughly parallel reading in III R 10,2:6.

[139]So little of the line remains that any translation is unavoidably guesswork. Our translation rests on Wiseman's reading of the Akkadian ("A Fragmentary Inscription," 126): ... -*a] na-gi-[e* ...... *li-]me-ti-šú-nu a-[na* .... (In Wiseman's copy of the cuneiform text, the *me* in *li]metišunu* is not clear.) Recently, R. Borger and H. Tadmor ("Zwei Beiträge," 246) have restored the Akkadian along the lines of III R 10,2:15–18. These scholars read, ... *a-na gi-[mir-ti-šu* ...... *adi mar-š]i-ti-šu-nu a-n[a* ..., and so translate, "in [its] entirety [... together with] their [pos]sessions [I led] to [Assyria ...." It should be noted, however, that the phrase, "together with their possessions" (*adi maršitišunu*) must be restored in III R 10,2:15–18 as well.

[140]The reconstruction of the line is based on the parallel passage in III R 10,2:17–18: *A-u-si' [a-na šarru-ti]-ina eli-šu-nu aš-kun.*

[141]Wiseman ("A Fragmentary Inscription," 123), reads *ka-ra-ba-ni*, apparently deriving the form from the verb *karabu* ("pleading"). The first sign of the cuneiform text, however, is uncertain. Borger and Tadmor ("Zwei Beiträge," 246) read *sar* instead of *ka* and so translate: "... in] Sarrabanu [he came] to me. ..."

[142]Wiseman translates the Akkadian, "over him," but the pronoun (*muḫḫiša*) is feminine. Similarly in l. 20, *karašiša* is best rendered "her camp," not "its camp."

23) ... to the kings my predecessors he had not bowed down ...
24) ... he heard and the awe of my lord Ashur [overwhelmed him ...
25) ... to Kalhu before me ...

---

26) ... 50 talents of gold, 2000 talents of silver ...

---

27) ... before] my presence he did not come. My official ...
28) ... the son of a nobody on the throne ...
29) ... a mule from ...

---

30) ... the kings my ancestors ...
31) ... son of ...

Material relating to the events of 734–731 begins in ll. 3–4.[144] This paragraph summarizes Assyria's final treatment of the "widespread land of Beth-Hazael," that is, the Syrian kingdom of Rezin. Presumably the text once described precisely the extent of the Syrian realm "in its entirety," as far as the Israelite kingdom. Unfortunately, the exact details of the southern boundary are not preserved.[145] We learn only of the kingdom's ultimate fate—its transformation into an Assyrian province.

Lines 5–8 are the only extant account of Assyria's treatment of Tyre in 734–731. Three facts are clear from the text. (1) Hiram, the king of Tyre, was in league with Rezin. (2) The Assyrian campaign against Tyre involved significant military action. Maḥalab,[146] Hiram's "stronghold," and other "great towns" under the king's control were forcibly conquered and booty was taken. (3) At some point in the fighting, Hiram capitulated, submitting personally to Tiglathpileser and paying tribute. In accordance with Assyria's general reluctance to convert the Phoenician and Philistine states into provinces, Hiram was left on the throne.

---

[143]See Eph'al's attempt at reconstructing the *Vorlage* behind this paragraph and the parallel passages in III R 10,2:19–34, II R 67 rev. 2–6, ND400:26–27, and Layard 66: 213–218 (*The Ancient Arabs*, 33–36). Lines 19, 20 and 22 of our text may have read originally: "to the desert, an arid place, like a wild mare she set her face; the rest of her tents, the might of her people, within her camp I set on fire ... a *qepu*-official I appointed over her and 10,000 warriors ... I made bow down to my feet."

[144]Lines 1–2 report the reduction of several cities along the northeastern Mediterranean coast, including Ḥatarikka, to provincial status in 738. The annals of Tiglathpileser give a fuller account of this campaign (see Rost, *Keilschrifttexte*, 20–23, ll. 123ff.)

[145]H. Tadmor ("The Southern Border," 114–122) tries to reconstruct this boundary with the help of parallel passages in III R 10,2 and K2649. See section B7 below.

[146]The town probably should be identified with Khirbet el-Maḥalib, about six kilometers northeast of Tyre. Compare the biblical Ahlab or Meheleb in Judg 1:31 and Josh 19:29.

The precise date of the action against Tyre is uncertain. E. Vogt, followed by J. M. Asurmendi, correlates ll. 5–8 with ND400:2–9 and so dates the campaign to 734.[147] As we argued earlier, however, it seems unlikely that Tiglathpileser would have delayed his march against Philistia to take extensive military action against Hiram's kingdom (see section B5 above). More probably, the Assyrians moved against Tyre in subsequent years, either 733/732 or 732/731. This dating would explain Hiram's absence in the tributary list of 734/733. When the Assyrian king first invaded Palestine, Hiram did not abandon his Syrian ally, but persisted in the revolt.

If Hoshea's name is correctly restored in l. 10, the next paragraph treats Israel. Two considerations support this understanding. The wording of l. 10 is close to that of III R 10,2:18, which mentions Hoshea specifically. Furthermore, the close grouping of Syria, Tyre and Israel in other inscriptions of Tiglathpileser lead us to expect a similar geographical sequence in ND 4301+4305.[148]

The poor preservation of ll. 9–11 handicaps their detailed interpretation. Minimally we gather that Tiglathpileser appointed Hoshea as king in Pekah's place. A similar notice appears in III R 10,2:17–18, where we learn further that Pekah was deposed by his own subjects. Second Kgs 15:30 also reports on Hoshea's rise, stating that he himself "conspired against Pekah the son of Remaliah and attacked him and executed him and ruled in his stead. . . ." The two Assyrian texts and the Kings passage are likely complementary. Tiglathpileser acknowledged Hoshea as the new Israelite king, either after Hoshea's take-over in Samaria in 731/730, or possibly at the beginning of his "conspiracy" in 732/731, when he first "attacked" Pekah. (See the appendix to this chapter.)

Line 11 reports that Hoshea, or his commissioned officers, submitted personally to Tiglathpileser. Where and when this occurred is not altogether clear, for the Akkadian text is critically uncertain at this point. Wiseman reads, *ka-ra-ba-ni a-di maḫ-ri-ia*, and translates, "pleading to my presence." This rendering leaves open the date and place of Hoshea's submission. More recently, R. Borger and H. Tadmor restore the name of the southern Babylonian town, Sarrabanu, at the beginning of the line.[149] On linguistic grounds this reading is preferable to "pleading" (*karabani*). It appears then that Hoshea paid formal homage to Tiglathpileser in Sarrabanu, where the Assyrian king was campaigning during his fourteenth year, Nisan 731 – Nisan

---

[147]E. Vogt, "Die Texte Tiglat-Pilesers," 348–51; J. M. Asurmendi, *La Guerra Siro-Efraimita*, 31.

[148]See Layard 50a+50b+67a (Rost, *Keilschrifttexte*, 26–27, ll. 150–151) and L. D. Levine, *Two Neo-Assyrian Stelae*, 18–19. J. M. Asurmendi (*La Guerra Siro-Efraimita*, 31, 36) especially has drawn attention to the grouping of these three states.

[149]See n. 141 above.

730. The event thus occurred well after the conclusion of the Assyrian campaigns "against Damascus" (Nisan 733 – Nisan 731).

The Assyrian treatment of Israel at large, presumably once described in l. 10, is also uncertain. According to Wiseman's translation, the text refers cryptically to "a district" and "their surrounding areas."[150] Alternatively, Borger and Tadmor restore the Akkadian along the lines of III R 10,2:15–18: "[House of Omri] in [its] en[tirety . . . together with their pos]sessions [I led away] to [Assyria]."[151] This reading is conjectural but possible. If it is correct, the text reports the wholesale deportation of Israel. The truth of this sweeping claim is a separate question, which we will take up only after examining the parallel passage in III R 10,2 (see section B7 below).

What remains of l. 12 reports only that Tiglathpileser confiscated silver. From whom he took the silver is uncertain. Wiseman suggests tentatively that the sum was Judean tribute paid in exchange for Assyrian aid against Syria and Israel.[152] As I. Eph'al has recently noted, however, the language of the text runs counter to this interpretation.[153] The Assyrian scribes normally use the verb, *maḫaru* ("receive"), when recording the reception of tribute. In l. 12 the verb is *nasaḫu* ("seize"), which usually denotes confiscation by force and often refers to the taking of booty in war. Accordingly, even if the account of Ahaz's "gift" in 2 Kgs 16:8 were historical (and this, we will argue, is questionable), we could hardly equate this payment with the confiscation of silver recorded in ND4301+4305.[154] Without new inscriptional evidence, the precise reference of l. 12 remains obscure.

Lines 13–16 summarize the Assyrian campaign against Gaza in 734/733. As in the parallel passages from ND400 and III R 10,2, the text records Hanno's flight to Egypt (l. 13), the placement of images of the Assyrian king and gods in the royal palace (l. 14), and the Philistine king's subsequent return to Gaza (l. 15). Line 16, however,

---

[150] D. J. Wiseman, "A Fragmentary Inscription," 124–26. See n. 139 above.

[151] R. Borger and H. Tadmor, "Zwei Beiträge," 246. See again n. 139 above.

[152] D. J. Wiseman, "A Fragmentary Inscription," 121. Wiseman concedes, however, that l. 12 might record the sum of tribute from all parts of Syria and Palestine.

[153] I. Eph'al, *The Ancient Arabs*, 31, n. 86.

[154] The remarks of Eph'al weigh equally against the proposal by E. Vogt ("Die Texte Tiglat-Pilesers" 351), namely, that l. 12 refers to the voluntary tribute of Philistine cities like Ashkelon. Eph'al's own interpretation correlates l. 12 with ND400:19. Both texts allegedly report on booty which the Assyrians seized at the Brook of Egypt. The common wording of the two lines, however, is not in fact so distinctive as to justify their correlation. Both texts merely record the confiscation of silver. Furthermore, if l. 12 did treat Assyrian action near the Brook of Egypt, it would seem out of place, coming as it does before the report on Gaza in ll. 13–16. The reverse order of events appears in ND400.

adds a new detail to our picture of the campaign: Tiglathpileser established a "trading-center (*karu*) of Assyria."

The precise whereabouts of this center is not absolutely certain. The frequent translation of *karu* as "quay" or "harbor" would suggest a location along the coast, but the Akkadian term can refer more generally to any commercial center, whether coastal or inland. Sargon II reports opening "the sealed *karu* of Egypt" in 720 and there making the Egyptians and Assyrians trade with one another.[155] Quite possibly this *karu* is the same one which Tiglathpileser set up in 734/733, but the question of its location remains debatable. Various proposals by H. Tadmor include El-'Arish, Pelusium or Sile, and a site somewhere on the bay of Sabkhat Bardawil.[156] R. Reich suggests Tell Abu Salima on archaeological grounds, but the evidence that he adduces is too general to support the identification.[157] The most probable location is Gaza itself, as N. Na'aman proposes.[158]

The establishment of a trade-center at or near Gaza reflects the economic motives behind Tiglathpileser's 734/733 campaign. While the invasion of Philistia had several aims, not least of which were military, one objective was to take control of the regional commerce. Gaza was situated at the western end of trade routes which ran across the north Sinai and along which luxury goods from the Arabian peninsula were transported to Syria and Mesopotamia. A *karu* at Gaza would reap tremendous revenue in customs for the Assyrians. From here they could also control overland and sea trade coming up from Egypt. A similar policy is evident in Assyria's treatment of the Phoenician ports.

Lines 17–22 report the Assyrian defeat of Samsi in 733/732 or 732/731. Although the text is poorly preserved, it can be understood with the help of parallel accounts.[159] Tiglathpileser's troops engaged the queen's forces and decisively defeated them (ll. 17–18, 20). The Arabian gods were taken (l. 18) and Arabian equipment or goods were burned in the queen's camp (l. 20). Line 19 alludes to Samsi's flight from the battle scene into the desert. Lines 21–22 report her subsequent submission to Tiglathpileser and the appointment of an

---

[155]See H. Tadmor, "The Campaigns of Sargon II of Assur: A Chronological-Historical Study," *JCS* 12 (1958) 34.

[156]H. Tadmor, "Campaigns of Sargon II," 78, n. 197; idem., "Philistia under Assryian Rule," 92; idem., "The Assyrian Campaigns to Philistia," in *Military History of the Land of Israel in Biblical Times* (ed. J. Liver; Tel-Aviv: Israel Defense Forces Publishing House, 1964) 272.

[157]R. Reich, "The Identification of the 'Sealed *karu* of Egypt,'" *IEJ* 34 (1984) 132–38.

[158]N. Na'aman, "The Brook of Egypt," 83–86.

[159]See n. 143 above.

Assyrian *qepu*-officer over her. The formidable Arabian army also swore allegiance to the Assyrian king.

Of the remaining lines of the inscription, only the report in ll. 27–29 can be related to known historical events. This paragraph probably refers to the insurrection of Uassurme of Tabal and to his replacement by Hulli in 729 or 728.[160] The preceding paragraph, ll. 23–25, reports the submission of a leader, or his officers, to Tiglathpileser in Calah (ancient Nimrud), but the identity of the leader and the date when he or his officers paid homage remain unknown. Line 26 records the reception of gold and silver, but, like l. 12, does not mention when and from whom it was taken. The final paragraph, ll. 30–31, is too fragmentary to interpret.

7. III R 10,2

III R 10,2 is a summary inscription on stone slab discovered by A. H. Layard at Nimrud in 1849. Layard reburied the slab but first made squeeze copies of the inscription. From these G. Smith published the text in 1870.[161] Twenty years later P. Rost published a new edition of the inscription.[162] This version varied from Smith's copy, even though both scholars worked from the very same squeezes. Rost was the last to have seen the squeezes. They have long been lost, along with the original stone slab left by Layard at Nimrud more than a century ago.

Two other factors complicate the textual problem. First, Smith's published copy of the text shows outlines of additional signs in the lacunae. The origin of these is uncertain. Second, there are reportedly differences between Smith's published version and rough drafts of the inscription in his unpublished notebooks.[163]

In the following translation, Rost's version serves as the textual basis for ll. 1–19. At several key points, however, appeal is made to Smith's readings. For ll. 19–34, we rely on the transliterated text provided by I. Eph'al, who had access to the rough drafts in Smith's notebooks.[164] Lines 35–38 are too fragmentary to translate.

1) ... the city of Ḫatarikka as far as Mt. Saue
2) ... the cities of Byblos, Ṣimirra, Arka, Zimarra
3) ... Usnu, [Siannu], Ri'raba, Ri'sisu

---

[160]Wiseman, ("A Fragmentary Inscription," 122) correctly correlates the lines with II R 67 rev. 14–15. For the dating of the reported events, see A. T. E. Olmstead, *Assyrian Historiography*, 34.

[161]For Smith's edition, see H. Rawlinson, *The Inscriptions of Western Asia*, 3. Pl. 10, no. 2. Smith translated ll. 1–23 in his *Assyrian Discoveries* (284–85).

[162]P. Rost, *Keilschrifttexte*, 78–83. He labels the text as "Kleinere Inschriften, I."

[163]I. Eph'al, *The Ancient Arabs*, 27, n. 71.

[164]I. Eph'al, *The Ancient Arabs*, 33–35.

The Assyrian Texts Relating to the Syro-Ephraimitic Crisis 63

4) ... cities on the Upper Sea I subjugated. Six officers
5) ... [as governors over] them I appointed. The town of [Ka]shpuna[165] which is on the shore of the Upper Sea
6) ... the town of Gal'az[a, the town of] Abil-[xxx][166] which are on the border of Beth-Omri
7) ... the widespread [land of Beth-Haza]el[167] in its en[tirety] I brought back within the border of Assyria.
8) [Officers of] mine as governors [over them I ap]pointed. Hanno of Gaza
9) [who before] my [wea]pons fled and to Egypt escaped. Gaza
10) [I conquered. His goods], his possessions, his gods [I carried off ...] of mine[168] and my royal image[169]
11) ... within [his] palace [I set up ...] gods of his land I counted[170] and
12) [tribute and tax] I imposed on them ..... [over]threw him and like a bird
13) ... he fled and ... to his place I restored him and
14) ... [gold], silver, colored garments, linen garments

---

[165]The edition of Rost reads instead, *Ra-aš-pu-na*, commonly identified as Rishpon ('Arsuf), north of Tel Aviv (see E. Forrer, *Provinzeinteilung*, 60; F. M. Abel, *Géographie de la Palestine* [2 vols.; Paris: J. Gabalda, 1933, 1938] 2. 103). Smith's copy, however, shows only a fragment of the first sign. ND400:8 confirms *Ka-aš-pu-na* as the correct reading.

[166]While Rost's edition reads, *A-bi-il-ak-k[a]*, Smith's copy shows only *A-bi-il-[xxx]*. H. Tadmor ("The Southern Border," 114, n. 4) suggests reading *A-bi-il-ma-ka*, identical with the biblical Abel-beth-maacah. For our disagreement, see the discussion of ll. 5–8 below.

[167]The first preserved sign of the line is *li*. F. Hommel (*Geschichte Babyloniens und Assyriens* [Berlin: G. Grote, 1885] 664–65) proposed reading [*Nap-ta*]-*li* (= the biblical Naphtali), but ND4301+4305 rev. 3 confirms *[Ha-za-'-i]-li* (= Hazael) as the correct restoration.

[168]The translation in *TUAT* (1. 373) restores the lacuna: "... [I carried off. Images of the great gods, lords] of mine...."

[169]This translation of the Akkadian, *NA.LUGAL-ti-ia* (*iršu šarru-ti-ia*), makes good sense in context and matches the parallel reading in ND400:16. See *ARAB* 1. 293 and *TUAT* 1. 373. The alternative rendering, "my royal couch," might also make sense, if the reference is to a kind of throne which Tiglathpileser set up for himself in the palace of Hanno. See P. Rost, *Keilschrifttexte*, 79; and G. Smith *Assyrian Discoveries*, 284.

[170]The verb *manu* might mean "count out, distribute" or "count as, reckon for." Smith (*Assyrian Discoveries*, 284–85) decides on the first sense, perhaps suggesting that the Assyrian king gave the gods of Gaza into the charge of a subordinate official responsible for confiscated spoil. Rost decides on the second meaning, thereby construing the line as the king's claim to have set up images of himself and the Assyrian gods as new gods for the people of Gaza. See the similar interpretation in *ARAB* (1. 293) and *TUAT* (1. 373). The translation issue depends partly on one's view of Assyrian religious policies in vassal kingdoms. For discussions of this historical question, see M. Cogan, *Imperialism and Religion*, 42–64; J. W. McKay, *Religion in Judah under the Assyrians, 732–609 B.C.* (SBT II/26; London: SCM, 1973) 60–66; and H. Spieckermann, *Juda unter Assur in der Sargonidenzeit* (FRLANT 129; Göttingen: Vandenhoeck & Ruprecht, 1982) 318–72.

15) ... great .... [I re]ceived. The land of Beth-Omri
16) .... the entirety of his people[171]
17) [together with their possessions to] Assyria I led away. Pekah their king they deposed and Hoshea
18) [for king]ship over them I appointed. Ten talents of g[old] ... talents of silver .... I received and
19) [tribute and tax I imposed on] them.[172] As for Samsi the queen of the Arabs, at Mt. Saqurri
20) ... [I] killed, 1000 + x-hundred people, 30000 camels, 20000 cattle,
21) ... 5000 (bags) of all kinds of spices ... the resting places of her gods
22) ... her property I seized. And she, for the rescue of her life,
23) ... [to the de]sert, an arid place, like a wild ass
24) ... of her, the might of her people, within her camp
25) ... [of] my powerful [wea]pons she became terrified and camels, she-camels
26) ... [be]fore me she brought. A *qepu*-officer over her I appointed and
27) ... The people of Massa', Tema, Saba',
28) ... Hatte, Idib'ilu
29) ... on the border of the western lands
30) ... remote, the praise of my lordship
31) ... my majesty. Gold, silver,
32) ... their tribute as one
33) ... my feet.
34) ... for the wardenship of Egypt I appointed.

Unlike other summary inscriptions, III R 10,2 is not divided by horizontal lines into separate paragraphs. Nevertheless, the geographical arrangement of the text is fairly clear.[173]

ll. 1–5: North Syria
5–8: Kingdom of Damascus
8–15: Gaza
15–19: Israel
19–26: Samsi queen of the Arabs
27–33: Nomadic Arab tribes
34: the Idibi'ilu

Each section recounts the Assyrian treatment of a particular region or people, concluding with a notice on the appointment of an Assyrian governor/*qepu* (ll. 5, 8, and 26) or on the receipt of tribute (ll. 15, 19, and 32–33).

---

[171]The lacuna in l. 16 does contain *il-lut amilu*, but translating the Akkadian is very difficult. See the conjectures of Asurmendi (*La Guerra Siro-Efraimita*, 33) and *TUAT* (1. 374).

[172]For this restoration of the line, see *TUAT* 1. 373. The reading by Rost, "[to Assyria I led] them," is also possible.

[173]See I. Eph'al, *The Ancient Arabs*, 27–28.

Material relating to the events of 734–731 begins in ll. 5–8. Until recently, scholars generally believed that this section had to do with Israel.[174] The conclusion seemed reasonable, for the text mentions Gal'aza (identified as Ramoth-Gilead) and Abil-[xxx] (commonly restored as Abil-akka and identified with the biblical Abel-beth-maacah), both towns traditionally claimed by Israel.[175] Second Kgs 15:29 appeared to point in the same direction, reporting Tiglath-pileser's confiscation of Galilee and Gilead during the reign of Pekah. With F. Hommel's restoration of l. 7, "the widespread [land of the House of Naphta]li," the issue seemed settled.[176]

The discovery of ND4301+4305 in 1955 reopened the question. Lines 3–4 of the reverse side speak of "the widespread [land of Beth-] Hazael." If these lines are parallel to III R 10,2:5–8, as the similar wording of the two passages indicates, "Hazael" rather than "Naphtali" should be restored in l. 7 of III R 10,2. Lines 5–8 appear, then, to recount the final disposition of the kingdom of Damascus in 732/731. The section describes the extent of the kingdom "brought back within the border of Assyria" and then records the appointment of Assyrian governors.

H. Tadmor compares ll. 5–8 closely with the parallel passages in ND4301+4305 and K2649 and reconstructs a fuller text on Damascus.[177]

> The widespread [land of Beth] Hazael in its entirety from M[ount Leba]non as far as the town of Gilead and the town of Abel-Beth-Maacah which are on the borderland of the land of Beth Omri I restored to the territory of Assyria. Officials of mine as governors I appointed.

According to this report, Tadmor explains, the Syrian border ran southward along the length of the Lebanon range and beyond to Abel-beth-maacah. From there it continued along the Jordan River and the east side of the Sea of Galilee, before turning eastward toward Ramoth-Gilead. The Transjordan regions of Bashan and Golan thus lay in Syrian hands on the eve of the kingdom's fall in 734–732. The Galilean hill country, on the other hand, was part of Pekah's kingdom.[178]

---

[174]See for example E. Forrer, *Die Provinzeinteilung*, 59–60; A. Alt, "Erster Feldzug," 155–57.

[175]E. Schrader (*Die Keilinschriften und das Alte Testament* [Giessen: J. Ricker, 1872] 144) was one of the first to make these identifications. The usual, though incorrect, reading of Rashpuna in l. 5 seemed to list a third Israelite town.

[176]F. Hommel, *Geschichte*, 664–65.

[177]H. Tadmor, "The Southern Border," 118. In Rost's edition, K2649 is labeled as "Kleinere Inschriften, III" (*Keilschrifttexte*, 86).

[178]H. Tadmor, "The Southern Border," 118–20.

Under closer examination this reconstruction of the Syrian border appears far from certain. It is based upon three reference points: Mount Lebanon, Ramoth-Gilead, and Abel-beth-maacah. Two of these points are in fact debatable.

While Rost's version of III R 10,2 mentions Abilak[ka] in l. 6, Smith's copy of the text has only Abil-[xxx]. The Hebrew word, *ābēl*, means "meadow" and forms the first part of several compound place-names in the Hebrew Bible: Abel-shittim (Num 33:49), Abel-keramim (Judg 11:33), Abel-meholah (Judg 7:22 and 1 Kgs 4:12), Abel-misraim (Gen 50:11), Abel-maim (2 Chr 16:4), and Abel-beth-maacah (2 Sam 20:14, 18; 2 Kgs 15:29). There were thus many Abels in ancient Israel, many more probably than the Bible records. Without the second part of the compound name in III R 10,2:6, we cannot be sure which town exactly is in mind.

Even if Rost's reading is correct, Abilakka cannot be equated easily with Abel-beth-maacah. We must either assume a scribal error (a *ma* was omitted) or guess that Rost misread an original *ma* as *ak*.[179] Both solutions are textual conjectures in the service of a traditional reading and site identification. We would do just as well to accept Alt's reading and think of an "Abel of Acco" near the coast.[180] In this case, the southern border of the kingdom of Damascus would appear to have enclosed the Galilean hill country as part of Rezin's kingdom.

Tadmor derives the reference to Mount Lebanon from K2649:3.[181] According to Rost's version, however, the Akkadian here reads only [. . .]-*na*. Tadmor's restoration of the name, *KUR La-ba-na-na*, may be correct, but there is no way to confirm it.[182] Yet even if we accept the reading, it hardly provides clear and exact information. Does the text have in mind the entire length of the Lebanon range or only its southern end? The description of the Syrian border begins vaguely, "from Mount Lebanon . . . ." How closely does the western border approach the coast? "Mount Lebanon" is a very general designation for the mountain range north of the Litani River and might apply just as well to its western foothills as to its inland heights.

The uncertainty is further enhanced by the variant reading in III R 10,2:5. In place of the general reference, "Mount Lebanon," the text mentions specifically Kashpuna "on the shore of the Upper Sea." If this Kashpuna is the north Phoenician town in the vicinity of Ṣimirra, the text envisions a long western border along the Lebanon range.

---

[179] H. Tadmor, "The Southern Border," 114, n.4.
[180] See A. Alt, "Erster Feldzug," 156, n.2.
[181] H. Tadmor, "The Southern Border," 117, especially n. 19.
[182] Tadmor (117, n. 19) states that traces of a *na* before the last *na* can still be seen. The copy of the cuneiform text in *CT* XXXV, plate 39, however, shows that these traces are very minimal, so much so that the original sign cannot be restored.

(How closely this border ran along the coast would remain open.) Alternatively, the reference may be to a southern coastal town of the same name. As we noted earlier (see section B5), Nimrud Letter XII might attest to a Kashpuna in the neighborhood of Tyre and Sidon. If III R 10,2 has this southern town in mind, the southern border of Syria-Damascus would seem to have extended far beyond the Jordan River, reaching even to the coast.

Given the fragmentary condition of the Assyrian texts, the precise boundary of the Syrian kingdom during the 730s will remain uncertain. The above considerations, however, have raised the possibility that the kingdom included not only the lands of Bashan and Golan east of the Jordan River, but also the Galilean hill country. The proposal is compatible with both 2 Kgs 15:29 and Layard 29b:230–234. The former text reports Assyria's confiscation of Gilead and Galilee during Pekah's years, but does not state from whom the territory was taken. The latter text records Assyrian military action in Galilee, but again fails to state clearly which kingdom, Syria or Israel, had controlled the region. We suggest that Syrian holdings are at stake in each text.

When precisely the Galilean region would have come under Syrian control is difficult to say, but the last years of Jeroboam II or the early part of Menahem's reign are possibilities. This was a period of Syrian expansion at the expense of Israel.[183] The prophet Amos alludes to the Syrian-Israelite conflict in Transjordan (1:4, 6:13) and seems to anticipate future Syrian aggression (4:3, 6:7, 14). His contemporary, Hosea, also reflects on the same conflict when toward the end of Jeroboam's reign he envisioned Israel's defeat in the Jezreel Valley:

> I (Yahweh) will visit the blood of Jezreel upon the house of Jehu and will put an end to the (extended) realm of the house of Israel. On that day I will break the bow of Israel in the valley of Jezreel (Hosea 1:4–5).

Presumably the prophet here was witnessing Rezin's encroachment on the Galilean region and was anticipating that the Syrian king would successfully push the borders of Damascus as far south as the Jezreel valley.

Lines 8–15 recount the Assyrian treatment of Gaza in 734/733. The description is generally the same as the parallel reports in ND400:14–18 and ND4301+4305 rev. 13–16. Hanno fled to Egypt as the Assyrian army approached (ll. 8–9). The Assyrians captured

---

[183]M. Haran ("The Rise and Decline of the Empire of Jeroboam ben Joash," *VT* 17 [1967] 266–97) argues that Israel expanded into Transjordan during the last years of Jeroboam II (see 2 Kgs 14:23–29). More likely, this expansion occurred during his early or middle years.

Gaza, confiscated booty and the city's gods (l. 10). Tiglathpileser set up an image of himself and possibly one of the Assyrian gods within the royal palace, imposed tribute, and subsequently reinstated Hanno who had returned from Egypt (ll. 10–15).

The next section of the inscription focuses on Israel (ll. 15–19). The report first summarizes Tiglathpileser's action against the nation: "The land of Beth-Omri . . . the entirety of its people [together with their possessions to] Assyria I led away." A note on Pekah's demise then follows. The section concludes with what was probably once a detailed notice on Israelite tribute.

The opening statement exaggerates the Assyrian action against Israel. Not all the people could have been exiled, for some people obviously must have remained for the new king Hoshea to rule. It is noteworthy in this regard that the Israelites themselves, not the Assyrians, are credited with overthrowing Pekah. The notice gives the impression that Tiglathpileser had not yet invaded Israel, or at least the Ephraimite hill country.

In the analyses of Layard 29b and Layard 66, we suggested that Assyria took little, if any, military action against the Israel. Tiglathpileser did seize the regions of Gilead and Galilee, but these may have belonged to Syria. The above study of III R 10,2:5–8 proposed the same understanding of the events. If the reconstruction is correct, Assyrian troops moved to the border of Pekah's kingdom, but never actually invaded. Why they did not push onward is easy to guess: their advance to the Israelite border was enough to catalyze a pro-Assyrian party within Israel, led by Hoshea. This party, popularly supported and perhaps sanctioned by Tiglathpileser, rebelled against Pekah in 732/731, and in effect finished Assyria's campaign in the area.

The grandiose claim about Israel's exile is unlikely more than stock rhetoric glorifying the Assyrian king. The generality of the text is striking here, particularly in comparison to the detail of the following notices on Pekah's fall, Hoshea's "appointment," and Israelite tribute. We suspect that the Assyrian scribes had source material for these latter lines only. The material, however, was problematic to the scribes, for it did not really compliment Tiglathpileser. It recounted, rather, how the Israelites, not the Assyrian king, overthrew Pekah. Accordingly, the Assyrian scribes prefixed to the report the sweeping claim about Israel's exile, thereby covering up their king's secondary role in the subjugation of Israel.

Lines 19–26 provide the fullest extant description of Samsi's defeat at Mount Saqurri (compare Layard 66:213–218, ND400:24–25, and ND4301+4305 rev. 17–22). Lines 20–22 report the dismal outcome in detail: the Assyrians slaughtered many of the queen's troops and confiscated livestock, the Arabian gods, and other spoil. The remainder of the section recounts the queen's escape into the desert, her subsequent submission to the Assyrian king, and the appointment of a *qepu*-officer over her.

The last two sections of the inscription focus respectively on Arab groups of the north Sinai (ll. 27–33) and on the Idibi'ilu (l. 34). The tribute of the former is recounted also in II R 67 rev. 3–5 and Layard 66:218–225. In all three texts, the submission of the Arabs appears to have been voluntary, probably in response to Assyria's new control of the northern end of trade routes. The assignment of the "wardenship of Egypt" to the Idibi'ilu is reported also in II R 67 rev. 6, Layard 29b:240 and Layard 66:226. The Assyrians gave the Idibi'ilu supervisory responsibilities in southwestern Palestine in the vicinity of the "Brook of Egypt."

C. Conclusions

This chapter has closely studied the Assyrian texts relating to the rebellion in Syria and Palestine during the late 730s. While many issues remain uncertain and all conclusions must be viewed as tentative, the following features of the revolt may be suggested on the basis of the preceding analysis.

1. Participants in the Revolt

(1) Several Syro-Palestinian states and peoples were involved in Assyria's effort to suppress rebellion in the west in 734–731. Participants in the anti-Assyrian movement included Rezin of Syria/Damascus, Hiram of Tyre, Pekah of Israel, Mitinti of Ashkelon, Samsi queen of the Arabs, and quite possibly Hanno of Gaza. The Meunites may also have joined the rebellion, but the Assyrian records (ND400:22–23) do not clearly document their involvement. The participation of Edom, Moab, and Ammon is also uncertain. The Assyrian records (II R 67 rev. 10–11) report only their payment of tribute in 734/733. (As we will see, however, the biblical texts indicate that at least the Edomites were initially in league with Syria/Damascus.)

(2) Rezin of Damascus played a leading role in the rebellion. He thus figures conspicuously in the reports on other participants in the revolt, specifically, Hiram of Tyre (ND4301+4305 rev. 5) and Mitinti of Ashkelon (Layard 29b:236). The Eponym List might also hint at the prominent role of Rezin when it cites the Assyrian campaigns "against the land of Damascus" as the most important events of 733/732 and 732/731. (As we will see, the biblical texts describe Pekah of Israel and the Edomites as allies of Rezin and thus also suggest the leadership of the Syrian king in the revolt.)

(3) The Egyptian and/or Ethiopian kingdoms may have encouraged the rebellion against Assyria. Their motive would have been largely economic: Assyrian control of Palestine would have jeopardized Egyptian and Ethiopian trade interests. The Assyrian records hint that some rebel leaders, notably Hanno of Gaza, may have sought military aid from Egypt (ND400:14–19, III R 10,2:15–19). Whatever role the Egyptians actually played in the revolt, however, did not exceed diplomatic support.

(4) Ahaz of Judah was one of the few Palestinian rulers who did not join the rebellion. In 734/733, he submitted voluntarily to Tiglathpileser and paid tribute. The Assyrian records (II R 67 rev. 11) list this payment alongside the tribute of other states in the region.

2. The Assyrian Campaign "against Philistia" in 734/733

(1) The Assyrians responded to the western revolt in 734/733 by marching against Philistia (Eponym List and ND400:1–19). If the campaign followed sometime after Pekah's rise to the Israelite throne, the forces of Tiglathpileser would have invaded the area late in 734 or early in 733. (According to our chronology, Pekah's take-over in Samaria occurred in Tishri 734.)

(2) The strategic goals of the campaign were both military and economic. Tiglathpileser was concerned to cut off any move by Egypt and/or Ethiopia to support the rebel states militarily. The Assyrian king planned also to subjugate the Philistines, particularly Hanno of Gaza, who may have been the strongest participant in the revolt in southwestern Palestine. Finally, control of the Philistine seaports and the overland trade routes in the region was an important objective.

(3) The Assyrian army moved quickly down the eastern Mediterranean coast en route to Gaza (ND400:1–19). Brief military action was taken against Matanbi'il of Arvad and against another unknown opponent further south; otherwise, little resistance was encountered. The sudden appearance of the Assyrians in Palestine apparently caught the Philistine rulers by surprise and so most submitted peacefully.[184]

---

[184]It is possible that the coastal plain north of Philistia was organized at this time into the province of Du'ru (Dor), as known from later Assyrian texts. See A. Alt, "Das System der assyrischen Provinzen," 234–37; idem., "Erster Feldzug," 157. Alt argues that Tiglathpileser confiscated the territory from Israel, but this conclusion is far from certain. As we suggested earlier, the oracles of Amos, Hosea, and Isaiah might indicate that the Phoenicians, Philistines, and Syrians were all encroaching on Israelite territory as early as the reigns of Jeroboam II, Zechariah, and Menahem (see Amos 1:3–5, 6–8, and 9–10; Hos 1:4–5; and Isa 8:23 and 9:10–11). The Sharon plain possibly came under the control of Rezin or one

(4) As the Assyrian troops approached Gaza, Hanno fled to Egypt, possibly to request military aid, and the inhabitants of the city surrendered. Hanno subsequently returned to Gaza and submitted to Tiglathpileser. The Assyrian king reinstated Hanno as an Assyrian vassal, collected tribute and set up a trading-center (*karu*) at Gaza (ND400:14–18; ND4301+4305 rev. 13–16; III R 10,2:8–15).

(5) The Assyrians marched southward to the "Brook of Egypt" (Wadi Besor; ND400:18–19). There they subjugated the Meunites (ND400:22–23) and, perhaps, seized control of the overland trade routes coming up from Egypt and running east-west through the northern Sinai. Tiglathpileser assigned the Idibi'ilu supervisory functions in the region (Layard 29b:240; Layard 66:226; II R 67 rev. 6; III R 10,2:34) and perhaps established an Assyrian defense post.

(6) Other rulers submitted peacefully to Tiglathpileser in 734/733. These included several north Syrian rulers, Ahaz of Judah, Mitinti of Ashkelon, Kaushmalaka of Edom, Salamanu of Moab, Sanipu of Ammon, and Samsi, the queen of the Arabs (II R 67 rev. 7–12; Layard 29b:210). Mitinti, Samsi, and the Transjordanian leaders may have been in league with Rezin previously. If so, their capitulation in 734/733 reflects the partial collapse of the Syrian-led coalition.

3. The Assyrian Campaigns in 733/732 and 732/731

(1) Rezin, Hiram, and Pekah did not submit to the Assyrians in 734/733, but rather continued the resistance for two more years. They were joined, or re-joined, by Mitinti and Samsi. What induced the latter two to reverse their decision of the previous year is difficult to say. Perhaps when Rezin, Hiram, and Pekah showed their determination to hold out against the Assyrians, Mitinti and Samsi reappraised the revolt's chances of success more optimistically. Perhaps also the kings of Syria, Tyre, and Israel exerted strong diplomatic pressure on Mitinti and Samsi. In the case of the Arab queen, that pressure would likely have consisted of economic threats. Samsi's livelihood depended on trade along the routes moving northward through Damascus and westward through the Jezreel Valley to Tyre. If she did not join the revolt and the revolt succeeded, Rezin, Hiram, and Pekah might punish the queen by implementing policies detrimental to her trade interests.

(2) Assyrian action against Syria/Damascus extended over two years (Eponym List). In 733/732, Tiglathpileser campaigned in the southern districts of Syria, defeated Rezin's army in the field, and besieged the capital city (Layard 72b+73a). Probably during the same

---

of his allies several years before the Syro-Ephraimitic crisis. (Note that Hazael of Syria had seized the area during the previous century; see 2 Kgs 12:17.)

year, Assyrian troops also took control of Syria's holdings in Bashan, Golan, and perhaps Galilee (Layard 29b:229–234). Damascus fell in 732/731. Tiglathpileser converted the whole of Rezin's extended kingdom into Assyrian provinces (ND4301+4305 rev. 3–4; III R 10,2:5–8).

(3) The Assyrians defeated the army of Samsi at Mt. Saqurri (probably located east of Palestine, along the border of the Hauran region) in 733/732 (Layard 66:213–218; ND400:24–27; ND4301+4305 rev. 17–22; III R 10,2:1–26). Dating the battle more precisely is difficult, but a time before the initial defeat of the Syrian army and Rezin's retreat to Damascus is plausible (Layard 72b+73a). Samsi fled into the adjacent desert, but subsequently returned to do homage before the Assyrian king. With her submission and payment of tribute, and the oath of allegiance by the Arab troops, Tiglathpileser agreed to leave Samsi in power, but appointed a *qepu*-officer over her.

(4) In 733/732 or 732/731, Assyrian troops also engaged the forces of Hiram (ND4301+4305 rev. 5–8). The campaign involved the conquest of several towns and fortresses under Hiram's control. The Tyrian king eventually capitulated and paid tribute. Like Samsi, he was allowed to retain his throne.

(5) Sometime after Rezin's retreat to Damascus and the Assyrian invasion of Galilee, Assyrian troops marched against Ashkelon (Layard 29b:235–239). Towns under the city's control were conquered and Mitinti himself was possibly assassinated by his own subjects. His son, Rukiptu, ascended the throne and quickly submitted to the Assyrian king. After receiving Rukiptu's tribute and perhaps also entering Ashkelon, Tiglathpileser recognized Rukiptu's kingship.

(6) The Assyrian action against Israel may have been minimal, particularly if, as we suggested, the kingdom of Pekah in 734–731 was limited primarily to the Ephraimite hill country around Samaria. This was an area through which no major trade routes passed and thus an area of little economic value to the Assyrians. Understandably, the subjugation of the other rebel states was a higher priority. Assyria's treatment of Israel may have been determined by another factor as well, namely, Hoshea's revolt against Pekah. The revolt began sometime after Tishri 732 (see the appendix below), and presumably proceeded with at least the tacit approval of Tiglathpileser (Layard 66:228; ND4301+4305 rev. 9–11; III R 10,2:15–19). If the Israelites themselves planned to eliminate Pekah, the Assyrian king would have had little reason to invade Israel. Hoshea eventually captured Samaria, executed Pekah, and paid tribute to Tiglathpileser, while the latter was campaigning in southern Babylonia. According to our chronology, these events occurred after Marheshvan 731.

APPENDIX. THE ROYAL CHRONOLOGY OF ISRAEL AND JUDAH

This dissertation adopts the chronology worked out by J. H. Hayes and P. K. Hooker. They propose the following dates for the reigns of the kings of Israel and Judah during the eighth century.

Judean kings

Azariah: 785/784–760/759
Jotham: 759/758–744/743
Ahaz: 743/742–728/727
Hezekiah: 727/726–699/698

Israelite kings

Jeroboam II: 788/787–748/747
Zechariah: 747
Shallum: 747
Menahem: 746/745–737/736
Pekahiah: 736/735–735/734
Pekah: 750–735/734 (Gilead)
      734/733–731/730 (Samaria)
Hoshea: 730/729-722/721

The chronology involves the following assumptions and hypotheses.

(1) With the exception of a few editorial miscalculations, the figures of the Masoretic text are essentially trustworthy.

(2) A king's reign began officially with his enthronement in the new year festival. In Judah the festival was held in the month of Tishri (September–October), while in Israel it was celebrated a month later in Marheshvan (October–November).

(3) Kings who ruled less than a full year may or may not have been assigned a year's reign, depending on whether they participated in the new year festival. Zechariah and Shallum are examples of Israelite kings who were assassinated before their official enthronement in the new year celebration. They were thus assigned reigns of six months and one month respectively (see 2 Kgs 15:9–10 and 13–15).

(4) In times of political upheaval when no king sat on the throne during the new year festival, a year could pass unassigned. Such was the case in Israel in 747/746. Shallum came to power in Tishri 747, but Menahem prevented his offical enthronement in Marheshvan (see 2 Kgs 15:13–15). The new year festival had passed before Menahem himself gained firm control of Samaria. His reign thus began officially with the next new year celebration in Marheshvan 746.

(5) The years of a king's reign were counted from his official enthronement until his death. This is true even in cases when a king abdicated the throne before he died. Azariah of Judah, for example,

abdicated the throne in 760/759, presumably because of illness (see 2 Kgs 15:5), but he died only after Tishri 734. Events during the interim years were still dated, however, with reference to the beginning of Azariah's reign (compare 2 Kgs 15:1–2, 8, 13, 17, 23, and 27). Hoshea's reign in Israel is a similar case. Although he was captured and imprisoned by the Assyrians in 725/724, the following three years were still counted with reference to his enthronement in 730/29 (see 2 Kgs 17:1–6 and 18:9–10).

(6) The twenty-year reign attributed to Pekah of Israel (2 Kgs 15:27) includes sixteen years when he ruled semi-autonomously in Gilead. He overthrew the regime of Pekahiah at the very beginning of Azariah's fifty-second and last year, Tishri 734 – Tishri 733. Pekah's reign in Samaria began officially with his enthronement in Marheshvan 734.

(7) Several months of civil war preceded the beginning of Hoshea's official reign. He first revolted against Pekah sometime after Tishri 732, that is, during the twelfth year of Ahaz (see 2 Kgs 17:1). Only after Marheshvan 731, however, did he gain control of Samaria, execute Pekah, and send tribute to Tiglathpileser. (Pekah apparently had retained enough support in Samaria to remain in power several months after the fall of Damascus and the departure of the Assyrian army from the region.)

CHAPTER THREE

BIBLICAL ACCOUNTS OF THE
SYRO-EPHRAIMITIC CRISIS

The Assyrian inscriptions document the political conditions and movements in Syria and Palestine during the 730s, but they do not narrate the Syro-Ephraimitic crisis specifically. Only the biblical texts report directly on the episode. This chapter analyzes the two principal accounts, Second Kings 16 and Second Chronicles 28, en route toward a preliminary reconstruction of the war. Material in the book of Isaiah, especially 7:1–17 but other speeches of the prophet also, provides important details about the war and there will be occasion here to refer to these. A full treatment of the Isaianic texts, however, follows in Part II.[1]

A. Second Kings 16

Second Kings 16 recounts the reign of Ahaz. Its focus is thus broader than the Syro-Ephraimitic crisis. The whole of the chapter must be examined, however, in order to identify the editorial tenden-

---

[1] Other biblical texts, for example 2 Kgs 15:29–30 and 37, relate to the prelude and aftermath of the Syro-Ephraimitic crisis and Section C below discusses some of these. A. Alt ("Hosea 5,8–6,6. Ein Krieg und seine Folgen in prophetischer Beleuchtung," *NKZ* 30 [1919] 537–68 = his *KS* II, 163–87) argues that Hos 5:8–6:6 attests to a Judean counterattack against Israel immediately after the abortive siege of Jerusalem. Many commentators accept the interpretation (see J. L. Mays, *Hosea* [Philadelphia: Westminster, 1969] 85–98; H. W. Wolff, *Hosea* [Hermeneia; Philadelphia: Fortress, 1974] 103–30; H. Donner, *Israel unter den Völkern*, 47–51; idem., "The Separate States," 431–32; J. Jeremias, *Der Prophet Hosea* [Göttingen: Vandenhoeck & Ruprecht, 1983] 80–82), but it is not conclusive (see M. Buss, *The Prophetic Word of Hosea: A Morphological Study* [BZAW 111; Berlin: A. Töpelmann, 1969] 36–37). If the Judean counterattack did occur, it was a minor part of the war. None of the speeches of Isaiah refer to it.

cies which shaped not only the overall presentation, but the composite parts as well.

1. The Deuteronomistic Introduction

Deuteronomistic introductory and concluding sections (vv 1–4 and 19–20) bracket the account of selected incidents from the reign of Ahaz (vv 5–18). The introduction merits special attention, for here the polemic of the editors comes to clear expression.[2] The unit exhibits the following structure.

1. Details of Ahaz's reign[3]   1–2a
2. Evaluation of Ahaz's reign   2b–4
   (a) General charge of apostasy   2b–3a
   (b) Listing of Ahaz's sins   3b–4

The general charge of apostasy (vv 2b–3a) divides into two parts. It begins with the typically deuteronomistic formula: "And he did not do what was right in the eyes of Yahweh his God as David his ancestor had done" (v 2b). The expression is comparable to:

"He did what was evil in Yahweh's eyes."[4]

---

[2]Commentators have generally acknowledged the unity of vv 1–4. Recently, however, H. Spieckermann (*Juda unter Assur*, 176) has contended that a second deuteronomistic editor inserted v 3b, thereby reading backwards into the reign of Ahaz an early editor's criticism of Manasseh (2 Kgs 21:6). The arguments of Spieckermann are inconclusive. The adverb, wĕgam, does not follow v 3a as awkwardly as he suggests, especially if it is translated by the emphatic "even" or "indeed." The notice that Ahaz "passed his son through fire" is formulaic. Similar phrasing in 21:6 hardly suggests borrowing. The practice is a typical concern of the deuteronomistic editors who condemn it in Deut 18:10, 2 Kgs 17:17, and Jer 32:35 (see also 2 Kgs 23:10 and Ezek 20:31). There is no compelling reason to think that an original deuteronomistic editor reserved the accusation for Manasseh only. Finally, the reference to the "abominations of the nations whom Yahweh had driven out before the Israelites" is again a typically deuteronomistic formula (compare Deut 18:9 and 1 Kgs 14:9). There is thus little basis for arguing the dependency of 16:3b on 21:2. The whole of vv 1–4 should be assigned to a single redactional level, that of a deuteronomistic editor(s), who, with the help of sources at his disposal, composed the framework of Ahaz's reign.

[3]The editors typically note the king's accession year (synchronized with the regnal year of his Israelite counterpart), parentage, age at accession, and the length and place of his reign. Ahaz is oddly the one Davidic king whose mother is not named.

[4]This formula is applied to all the Israelite kings and to Solomon (1 Kgs 11:6), Jehoram (2 Kgs 8:18), Ahaziah (8:27), Manasseh (21:2), Amon (21:20), Jehoahaz (23:32), Jehoiakim (23:37), Jehoiachin (24:9), and Zedekiah (24:19).

"Judah did what was evil in Yahweh's eyes."[5]
"He did what was right in Yahweh's eyes."[6]

These are usually accompanied by a list of the king's cultic sins and/or his cultic achievements.

The second part of the general charge entails the rare formula, "and he walked in the way of the kings of Israel." In combination with the preceding formula and the list of specific sins that follows, the expression appears to refer to cultic policy. Whether this meaning is original, however, is another matter. Besides Ahaz, only Jehoram (2 Kgs 8:18) and Ahaziah (8:27) are accused of having "walked in the way of the kings of Israel" (or "the house of Ahab"). In both cases, the charge is accompanied by "and he did what was evil in Yahweh's eyes" and so would seem to refer to cultic wrongdoing. On the other hand, the charge in both cases is also explained by a *ki*-clause, which notes the marital ties between the Omride and Davidic houses. Furthermore, it is noteworthy that the accounts of Jehoram and Ahaziah do not actually list specific cultic sins, but focus rather on the political dealings of the two kings. In the case of Ahaziah, such dealings involved his participation in Israel's battles against Syria (8:28–29).

The above evidence is complex and admits no definitive interpretation, but the following conclusions seem plausible. (1) The charge, "he walked in the way of the kings of Israel," is not deuteronomistic. If the editors had coined the expression as "code for the worst imaginable reproach for cultic offence" that could be levelled against a Davidide,[7] one would expect to see its application to Manasseh. In 21:3, however, the editors curiously resort to a circumlocution: Manasseh "erected altars for Baal and made an Asherah, as Ahab the king of Israel had done . . . ." The evidence is thus best explained by the assumption that the editors inherited the formula in 8:18, 8:27, and 16:3 from a source.

(2) The editors combined the formula with their own, "he did what was evil in Yahweh's eyes," and thereby gave it a clear religious meaning. On this redactional level, "walking in the way of the kings of Israel" means imitating the cultic policies of the Israelite kings.[8]

---

[5] The one instance of this expression, 1 Kgs 14:22, may not be textually original. The Septuagint reads "Rehoboam" for "Judah." Second Chronicles 12:14a reads simply, "and he did evil."

[6] The editors apply this formula to the Davidic kings before Manasseh (excepting Solomon, Rehoboam, Jehoram, Ahaziah, and Ahaz) and to Josiah (2 Kgs 22:2).

[7] H.-D. Hoffmann, *Reform und Reformen. Untersuchung zu dem Grundthema der deuteronomistische Geschichtsschreibung* (ATANT 66; Zurich: Theologischer Verlag, 1980) 141.

[8] The apostasy of Jehoram and Ahaziah is also implied by the overall presentation of the two kings and Athaliah. The overthrow of Athaliah, whose previous

(3) In the cases of Jehoram and Ahaziah, the formula originally may have referred to the marital/political connections between the Davidic and Omride houses. The alliance resulted in Judah's support for specifically Israelite military ventures (2 Kgs 8:28).

(4) As originally applied to Ahaz, the formula again might have described his political ties to the Israelite kings. Admittedly, the evidence for this relationship is slim. It may be significant, however, that Hezekiah's mother was a certain Abi, the daughter of Zechariah (18:2). Quite possibly this Zechariah was the last member of the Jehu dynasty whom Shallum brutally assassinated (15:8). If so, it would appear that Ahaz had been married into the Israelite royal house. The political marriage, perhaps arranged by Jotham when Ahaz was still quite young, would have served to buttress an alliance between the two kingdoms that had existed during the first half of the eighth century and possibly had begun as early as the Omride period.[9] The deuteronomistic editors apparently were unaware of any such relationship, understandably so in light of the conflict between Pekah and Ahaz at the time of the Syro-Ephraimitic crisis. The editors construe Ahaz's "walking in the way of the kings of Israel" in a strictly religious sense.

A list of specific sins rounds off the introduction to Ahaz's reign. The charges are typically deuteronomistic. Making one's child "pass through the fire" (v 3b) is proscribed in Deut 18:10 and listed in 2 Kgs 17:17 among the sins which prompted Yahweh to end the Israelite kingdom (compare 2 Kgs 21:6, 23:10, and Jer 32:35).[10] Worship on the

---

usurpation of the Judean throne and seven-year rule are treated by the editors as merely the aftermath of Ahaziah's reign, finds its denouement in the cultic purge of Jerusalem (11:18). The general impression of 8:16–11:20 is thus two-fold. (a) The Baal cult which Ahab, under the influence of Jezebel, had implemented in Israel and which subsequent Omrides had allowed to continue, was introduced into Judah by Jehoram and Ahaziah, who were related to the house of Ahab through Athaliah. (b) The extirpation of Baal worship from the Jerusalem cult at the beginning of Joash's reign (11:18) was parallel to Jehu's purge of the cult in Samaria (10:18–27).

[9]H. Winckler (*Geschichte Israels in Einzeldarstellung* [2 vols.; Leipzig: Pfeiffer, 1895–1900] 1. 88–95, 145–48, 176–80) argues that Judah was an Israelite vassal during the whole of the Omride and Jehu dynasties. Evidence for Judah's subordination during the second half of the ninth century consists mainly in the battle account of First Kings 22, which originally related to the reign of Jehoahaz or Joash. See A. Jepsen, "Israel und Damascus," *AfO* 14 (1941/44) 153–72; J. M. Miller, "The Fall of the House of Ahab," *VT* 17 (1967) 307–24; idem., "The Rest of the Acts of Jehoahaz," *ZAW* 80 (1968) 337–42. Regarding Judah's vassalage during the first half of the eighth century, see M. Haran, "The Empire of Jeroboam," 266–97; and M. Vogelstein, *Jeroboam II: The Rise and Fall of His Empire* (Cincinnati: self-published, 1945).

[10]Scholars usually interpret the expression as a reference to child sacrifice, but the meaning is still debated. See R. R. Wilson, *Prophecy and Society in Ancient*

high places (v 4) is proscribed in Deut 12:2 and again is mentioned in the deuteronomistic peroration on the fall of Israel (2 Kgs 17:9–11).[11] Whether the editors understood these sins as a reversion to Canaanite religion is difficult to say. The comparison with the "abominations of the nations which Yahweh drove out from before the Israelites" seems to suggest so (see Deut 12:2, 18:8, and 2 Kgs 17:8). As we will see below, however, the editors imply that Ahaz's cultic reform (16:10–18) was along Assyrian lines. Their decision nevertheless to set the reform under their evaluation of the king in vv 2b–4 indicates that the charges there have become extremely generalized. They function as schematic rhetoric against non-Yahwistic worship.[12]

2. The Cultic Reform of Ahaz

Verses 5–18 contain accounts of the Syro-Ephraimitic crisis (vv 5–9) and the cultic reform of Ahaz (vv 10–18). The latter divides neatly into the following parts.

1. The new altar	10–16
(a) Erection of the new altar	10–11
(b) Dedication of the new altar and transference of the old sacrificial system	12–16
2. Additional measures relating to the Temple	17–18

The account of the reform does not likely form an original whole with the preceding report on the war. Several reasons support this conclusion. The Judean king in vv 5–9 is consistently designated "Ahaz." This contrasts sharply with "King Ahaz" or simply "the king" in vv 10–18. Significant too are the different spellings of the Assyrian king's name: *Tiglat pĕleser* in v 7 and *Tiglat pil'eser* in v 10. Verses 5–9 are written in a curt reporting style. They focus on the political aspects of the Syro-Ephraimitic war, moving from its crisis (vv 5–6) to a resolution (vv 7–9). The unit needs no continuation. In contrast, the style of vv 10–18 is excursive and the concern is with cultic, not political, matters. The two interests, to be sure, are not incompatible, especially if cultic changes are viewed as the direct result of Ahaz's pact with Assyria. Curiously, however, v 10 presents the construction of the new altar as the king's own decision. Ahaz hap-

---

Israel (Philadelphia: Fortress, 1980) 161 and the bibliography listed there. See also G. Heider, *The Cult of Molek: A Reassessment* (JSOTSup 43; Sheffield: JSOT Press, 1985). Second Kings 3:27 is the parade example of child sacrifice in a military context.

[11] Judean kings accused of patronizing the high places include Rehoboam (1 Kgs 14:22), Asa (15:14), Jehoshaphat (22:43), Jehoash (2 Kgs 12:3), Amaziah (14:4), Azariah (15:4), Jotham (15:35), and Manasseh (21:3).

[12] M. Noth, *Überlieferungsgeschichtliche Studien* (Halle: M. Niemeyer, 1943) 85.

pened to be meeting with Tiglathpileser when he saw the altar in Damascus and decided to copy it. Only the concluding phrase in v 18b, "because of the king of Assyria," suggests a causal relation between the reform and Ahaz's submission to Assyrian vassalage. The notice, however, seems tacked on and is likely redactional.

While vv 5–9 appear self-contained, vv 10–18 need introduction. The circumstantial clause which begins v 10 assumes a knowledge of the Assyrian capture of Damascus and so indicates that the unit could not originally have stood alone. The stylistic and orthographical variations and the different interests highlighted above, however, suggest that vv 5–9 are not its original antecedent material.

Tensions within vv 10–18 indicate that this material is itself composite. (1) Verses 10–16 focus narrowly on the new altar, while vv 17–18 report in desultory fashion miscellaneous changes in the Temple furniture and structures. The latter verses look like an appendix. (2) In vv 10–11 and 15–16, the Judean king is consistently designated "King Ahaz," while in v 12 (and by association, vv 13–14) he is named simply "the king."[13] (3) The series of sacrifices in vv 12–14 is different from the one in v 15.[14] (4) Verse 15 begins, "Then King Ahaz commanded him (*wayṣawwēhû*), Uriah the priest . . . ."[15] Assuming that the verbal form is original, the third person pronominal suffix (*hû*) likely reaches back to "Uriah the priest" in v 11a. Once vv 12–14 were inserted, the antecedent of the pronoun was no longer clear. "Uriah the priest" in v 15 consequently entered the text as a clarifying gloss. (5) The concluding clause of v 11, "before King Ahaz came from Damascus," looks like a gloss,[16] but its clarifying function seems unnecessary in light of v 12a. If v 15 had originally continued v 11ba, however, the temporal sequence of events would have been unclear and so would have begged the clarification which v 11bb provides: Uriah built the new altar while Ahaz was still in Damascus and, by

---

[13]R. Rendtorff (*Studien zur Geschichte des Opfers im Alten Israel* [WMANT 24; Neukirchen-Vluyn: Neukirchener Verlag, 1967] 46–50) and E. Würthwein (*Die Bücher der Könige* [2 vols.; Göttingen: Vandenhoeck & Ruprecht, 1985] 2. 389–91) correctly observe this shift. It is not simply a matter of stylistic variation, as H.-D. Hoffmann (*Reform und Reformen*, 142) suggests.

[14]See R. Rendtorff, *Geschichte des Opfers*, 46–50. H.-D. Hoffmann (*Reform und Reformen*, 143, n. 71) contends that v 15 simply differentiates the sacrifices mentioned in v 13 according to time and to the person offering the sacrifice. This is only partly true. The incongruity between the two series is clear when one compares the *dam-haššĕlāmîm* in v 13b and the *dam ʿōlâ* and *dam-zebaḥ* in v 15a.

[15]This reading repoints the consonantal *wyṣwwhw*. The Masoretic Qere suggests reading *wayṣawweh*, thus omitting what looks to have been originally the pronominal suffix, *hû*.

[16]See E. Würthwein, *Die Bücher der Könige*, 2. 386. The gloss might include the preceding phrase, *kēn ʿāśâ ʾûrîyâ hakkōhēn*. The verse from *kēn* onward is missing in the Septuagint.

implication, received instructions on its use only after the king's return. Both vv 10–11 and 15–16 are neatly rounded off with notices on the priest's compliance.

The above analysis has yielded a complicated picture of 16:10–18. The material includes three originally separate blocks: (a) vv 10–11 and 15–16; (b) vv 12–14; and (c) vv 17–18. The nature of the sources from which these ultimately stem is impossible to determine with certainty. In light of their cultic interest, Temple records or even a Temple history would seem probable, but secular sources, for example, a court history of Ahaz treating, among other topics, royal construction projects, are not out of the question. Equally uncertain is the process through which the three units reached their present assembled form. Possibly the deuteronomistic editors found them as a redacted whole already in a more immediate source, perhaps the "Book of the Chronicles of the Kings of Judah" (*sēper dibrê hayyāmîm lĕmalkê yĕhûdâ*; v 19).[17] They attached the material directly to the account of the Syro-Ephraimitic war in vv 5–9, adding at the same time "because of the king of Assyria" in v 18b as an interpretive end-bracket. Their redaction left the clear impression that Ahaz's alterations in the Temple cult were causally related to the Assyrian alliance.

We have focused on the editorial logic of vv 10–18, especially as this material relates to the preceding account of the Syro-Ephraimitic crisis. Historical remarks about the reform are also in order.

(1) Scholars generally have viewed the reform as an example of how the Assyrians imposed their religion on subject peoples.[18] Recent studies by M. Cogan and J. W. McKay, however, forcefully argue that the Assyrians did not place cultic obligations on satellite and vassal states.[19] Since Ahaz was not even an appointee of Tiglathpileser, he particularly would not have had to meet any religious requirements.

---

[17] Scholars have long debated the nature of this work and its Israelite counterpart. For a recent discussion of the issue, see J. Van Seters, *In Search of History*, 292–302.

[18] See A. T. E. Olmstead, *History of Palestine and Syria to the Macedonian Conquest* (New York/London: Charles Scribner's Sons, 1931) 452; M. Noth, *The History of Israel*, 266; J. Bright, *A History of Israel*, 276; J. A. Montgomery, *A Critical and Exegetical Commentary on the Books of Kings* (2d ed.; Edinburgh: T. & T. Clark, 1976) 459; and J. Gray, *I and II Kings*, 576. H. Spieckermann (*Juda unter Assur*, 367) argues that Ahaz used the old bronze altar, tactfully set to the north side of the Temple, for meeting his cultic obligations to the Assyrian king. The evidence adduced, however, is extremely slim and admits more than one interpretation.

[19] M. Cogan, *Imperialism and Religion*, 42–60; and J. W. McKay, *Religion in Judah*, 60–66. For a different interpretation of the Assyrian texts, however, see H. Spieckermann, *Juda unter Assur*, 318–72.

(2) The Damascus altar which Ahaz copied was likely Syrian, not Assyrian.[20] Two lines of reasoning support this conclusion. Second Chronicles 28:22–23 accuse the king of imitating Syrian religion. The new altar described in the Kings text was probably an instance of this policy. Furthermore, 16:15 reports that the new altar was to be used for burnt offerings. Holocaust altars, however, were unknown in Assyria and the rest of Mesopotamia.[21]

(3) The deuteronomistic editors misleadingly date the reform to the aftermath of the Syro-Ephraimitic crisis. Ahaz would not likely have been imitating Syrian religious practices after the fall of Damascus. More probably, he copied the altar earlier in his reign, when Syrian power was still strong (see 2 Chr 28:23), yet before Syrian-Judean relations had grown acutely hostile.

(4) At least one aspect of the reform may have been related to Ahaz's submission to Tiglathpileser. Verse 17 describes the dismantling of certain items of the Temple furniture. The purpose was possibly to recover the bronze of these items in order to pay Assyrian tribute (compare 2 Kgs 18:16). Whether the removal of the "covered way for the Sabbath" and the "outer entrance for the king" also related to Assyrian demands is hard to say (v 18). The Hebrew text and its meaning are very uncertain.[22]

(5) Ahaz's contemporaries may have seen his changes in the Temple cult as legitimate reform. When viewed apart from the deuteronomistic redaction, the description of the changes seems relatively neutral in tone. Nowhere in vv 10–18 is disapproval clearly expressed or even implied.[23] Furthermore, Uriah the priest apparently implemented the reform without objection. (He is the same priest whom Isaiah chose as a witness to one of his symbolic actions; see Isa

---

[20]H. W. F. Saggs (*Assyriology and the Study of the Old Testament* [Cardiff: University of Wales Press, 1969] 19–22) suggests a third possibility, namely, that the altar was Phoenician. The proposal is not convincing for the reasons elaborated by M. Cogan (*Imperialism and Religion*, 76).

[21]See K. Galling, *Der Altar in den Kulturen des alten Orient. Eine archäologische Studie* (Berlin: K. Curtius, 1925) 43–44, 54–55; A. L. Oppenheim, *Ancient Mesopotamia: Portrait of a Dead Civilization* (Chicago/London: University of Chicago Press, 1964) 186–92.

[22]Instead of the "covered way for the Sabbath" (*mûsak haššabbāt*, according to the Qere), the Septuagint reads "the foundation of the throne" (*themelion tēs kathedras*), which seems to reflect the Hebrew *mûsad haššebet* ("foundation of the throne"). If this reading is correct, it too may reflect Ahaz's need to recover valuable metal for the Assyrian tribute.

[23]See A. Šanda, *Die Bücher der Könige*, 2. 207; J. A. Montgomery, *The Books of Kings*, 459; and J. Gray, *I and II Kings*, 631. E. Würthwein (*Die Bücher der Könige*, 2. 389) and P. R. Ackroyd ("The Reigns of Ahaz and Hezekiah," 252–53) hear derogatory overtones in vv 11, 12bb, 16 and 17, but their explanations are not convincing.

8:1-4. Uriah thus seems to have been fully orthodox, at least in the eyes of the prophet.) The speeches of Isaiah also do not protest the reform.

3. The Syro-Ephraimitic Crisis

Verses 5–9 narrate the Syro-Ephraimitic attack, Rezin's seizure of Elath from the Judeans, Ahaz's appeal to Tiglathpileser, and the Assyrian king's move against Damascus. Although the text on the whole is relatively lucid, two important points of translation merit close attention.

(1) Verse 5bb reports that Rezin and Pekah "were unable to fight" (wĕlōʾ yākĕlû lĕhillāḥēm). The statement seems to suggest that the two kings did not actually attack Ahaz.[24] Verse 5ba indicates, however, that they did in fact besiege the Judean king (wayyāṣūrû ʿal-ʾāḥāz). The verb, lĕhillāḥēm, might mean "conquer," but this sense is infrequent. Besides 2 Kgs 16:5 and the literarily related passage in Isa 7:1, only Zech 10:5 clearly attests to the pregnant meaning of the verb (compare Num 22:11 and 1 Sam 17:9). The Septuagint follows the Masoretic text verbatim (kai ouk edunanto polemein) and so affords little help. The Vulgate also follows the Masoretic text, but "improves" it by adding "him" as the predicate object: non valuerant superare eum. Significantly, the Latin translation attests to the pregnant meaning of lĕhillāḥēm.

Isaiah 7:1 has played an important role in the text-critical debate. It reads:

> In the days of Ahaz the son of Jotham, the son of Uzziah, the king of Judah, Rezin the king of Syria came up with Pekah the son of Remaliah, the king of Israel, to Jerusalem for battle against it (lammilḥāmâ ʿālêhā), but they were [or "he was"] unable to conquer it (wĕlōʾ yākōl lĕhillāḥēm ʿālêhā).

In contrast to the Kings account, the threat here is aimed not against Ahaz personally, but against Jerusalem as a whole. Curiously, the verb yākōl is singular, despite the apparently plural subject, Rezin and Pekah.[25] This datum has led some scholars to think that the verb in 16:5b was originally singular also. K. Budde, for example, suggests that 2 Kgs 16:5b once read: "And they beseiged Ahaz and he [Ahaz!]

---

[24]See E. Würthwein, Die Bücher der Könige, 2. 387. A. Šanda (Die Bücher der Könige, 2. 194) translates v 5b, "They besieged Ahaz, but were unable to wage an (actual) battle."

[25]The plural readings of 1QIsaᵃ, the Septuagint, and the Vulgate are likely attempts to improve the Masoretic text. See H. Orlinsky, "Studies in the St. Mark's Isaiah Scroll, IV," JQR 43 (1952–53) 329–40.

was unable to fight against them" (*wayyāṣūrû ʿal-ʾāḥāz wĕlōʾ yākōl lĕhillāḥēm ʿālēhem*).²⁶ The editor of Isaiah 7 supposedly borrowed the verse, but at the same time altered it by dropping *wayyāṣūrû ʿal-ʾāḥāz* and changing *ʿālēhem* to *ʿālêhā*. The effect of the redaction, Budde explains, was to minimize the threat to Ahaz and to clear Yahweh of any possible guilt in the king's predicament. The singular form, *yākōl*, was allowed to stand, the reader being forced to construe its subject as Rezin and Pekah.²⁷

Budde's reconstruction is ingenious but highly conjectural, without the slightest bit of versional support. Furthermore, it is hard to see why the editors of Isaiah 7 did not change *yākōl*, which supposedly once referred to Ahaz. They certainly did not hesitate to emend other parts of the verse.²⁸ As for 2 Kgs 16:5b, the wording is not so difficult as to demand emendation. The pregnant meaning of *lĕhillāḥēm* is unusual but possible. We retain the Masoretic text and translate: "And they besieged Ahaz but they were unable to prevail."

(2) Most commentators eliminate "Rezin" in v 6a and emend "Syria" (*ʾārām*) to "Edom" (*ʾĕdôm*) throughout the verse.²⁹ The textual changes are supported by the Masoretic *Qere* at the beginning of v 6b and are certainly plausible in view of the similarity between the Hebrew consonants, *r* and *d*. Once the ancient scribes miscopied "Edom" as "Syria," Rezin's name presumably entered the text as a clarifying gloss. Again, however, the ancient versions do not support all of these emendations. The Septuagint, Targum, and Vulgate read "Edomites" in v 6b, but "Rezin " and "Syria" in v 6a (compare the Syriac).

The text-critical decision rests ultimately on a historical consideration: is it likely that Rezin seized Elath from the Judeans? The text speaks specifically of the king's "restoring" (*hēšîb*) Elath to Syria, but everything else known about the city and its surrounding area suggests that the Edomites traditionally claimed it. For years they had

---

²⁶K. Budde, "Isaiah vii. 1 and 2 Kings xvi. 5," *ExpTim* 11 (1899/1900) 327-30; idem., *Jesaja's Erleben*, 32.

²⁷Compare J. Gray's reconstruction of 16:5bb (*I and II Kings*, 573): *wĕlōʾ yākōl lĕhillāḥēm ʿālêhā* ("and he [Ahaz] could not fight for it [Jerusalem]"). R. Bickert ("König Ahas und der Prophet Jesaja," 367–69) also emends *yākēlû* to a singular form, but sees Rezin as its subject.

²⁸The singular verb in 7:1 is not in fact as problematic as Budde suggests. Its subject might be Rezin who, as leader of the attacking coalition, is singled out for special attention.

²⁹For recent examples, see J. Gray, *I and II Kings*, 573; G. H. Jones, *1 and 2 Kings* (2 vols.; Grand Rapids/London: Eerdmans/Marshall, Morgan and Scott, 1984) 2. 535; E. Würthwein, *Die Bücher der Könige*, 2. 386. See also modern translations like the RSV, NEB, JB, and TEV. Compare the KJV and NASB, which read "Syria/Syrians" throughout the verse. The NIV and NJPSV read "Syria" in v 6a and "Edomites" in v 6b.

vied with the Judeans for control of the port (see especially 2 Kgs 14:22, but also 8:20–22, 1 Kgs 9:26–28 and 22:47–50). It is possible that Rezin helped the Edomites to recover Elath, presumably for self-serving reasons. The aid may have been conditional on their support for the revolt against Assyria. Furthermore, by installing his Edomite allies in Elath, Rezin could indirectly control the trade moving up from the port through Transjordan to Damascus. For these reasons, we translate 16:6, "At that time Rezin the king of Syria restored Elath to Edom and drove out the Judeans from Elath. And the Edomites entered Elath and have lived there unto this day."

The account of the war is clearly distinct from the deuteronomistic introduction and the report on Ahaz's cultic reform. In detail, its structure appears:

1. Description of the crisis	5–6
(a) Rezin and Pekah besiege Ahaz in Jerusalem.	5
(b) Rezin restores Elath to Edom.	6
2. Resolution of the crisis	7–9
(a) Ahaz appeals to Tiglathpileser for help against the Syrian and Israelite kings.	7–8
(1) Declaration of vassalage and plea for help	7
(2) Sending of a $\check{s}\bar{o}ḥad$	8
(b) Tiglathpileser moves against Syria.	9
(1) Capture of Damascus and the deportation of its citizens	9a
(2) Execution of Rezin	9b

Internal tensions within the material reflect the use of sources and redaction. Verses 5, 7–9 focus on the Syro-Ephraimitic attack against Ahaz in Jerusalem, while v 6 reports Syria's restoration of Elath to Edomite control. Verse 6 thus appears intrusive. The conclusion is buttressed by the loose temporal connection between the notice and v 5 ("at that time").[30]

Many commentators have viewed vv 7–9 as the original continuation of v 5.[31] Several considerations, however, warrant caution. Verse 5 is a summary statement about the war and its outcome. This fact would cause no great surprise, if it were not for the short length of

---

[30]J. A. Montgomery ("Archival Data in the Book of Kings," *JBL* 53 [1934] 46–52) and H. Tadmor and M. Cogan ("Ahaz and Tiglath-Pileser in the Book of Kings: Historiographical Considerations," *Bib* 60 [1979] 493–98) argue that the formulae, "at that time" ($b\bar{a}^c\bar{e}t\ hah\hat{\imath}^{\supset}$, v 6a) and "then" ($^{\supset}\bar{a}z$, v 5a), mark quotations from archival sources. Their arguments, however, are not conclusive. See J. Van Seters, *In Search of History*, 299–300.

[31]See R. Kittel, *Die Bücher der Könige* (Göttingen: Vandenhoeck & Ruprecht, 1900) 269; J. Gray, *I and II Kings*, 571; E. Würthwein, *Die Bücher der Könige*, 2. 389; and G. H. Jones, *1 and 2 Kings*, 2. 536. Most recently, R. Bickert ("König Ahas und der Prophet Jesaja," 367–71) also seems to treat v 6 as an interpolation.

the account as a whole. It seems strange that a report as brief as this should begin with a summarizing statement.

As the direct continuation of v 5, the imperfect consecutive, *wayyišlaḥ*, at the beginning of v 7 is slightly awkward. The context clearly suggests a pluperfect meaning for the form: "but they *were unable* to prevail (v 5bb) . . . and Ahaz *had sent* messengers to Tiglath-pileser . . . ." (v 7a). Normally, however, this sense of the imperfect consecutive is predicated upon a previous perfect form which also is pluperfect in meaning.[32] In the present case, the antecedent perfect, *yākĕlû*, must be rendered in the simple past. The awkwardness of *wayyišlaḥ* is reflected in the difficulty that translators have in rendering the precise nuance of the conjunction. Following the summary statement of v 5, "so" (RSV), "then" (JB), and the like seem to strain the narrative flow.

Verses 7–9 assume a knowledge of the Syro-Ephraimitic attack and so cannot stand alone. They demand the introduction which v 5 provides. Conversely, however, v 5 does not demand the continuation in vv 7–9. One can easily imagine it standing alone in an earlier source as a short but sufficient notice on the Syro-Ephraimitic war. Perhaps only in the account of the deuteronomistic editors was it filled out in detail with a description of Ahaz's appeal to Assyria and the latter's defeat of Syria. The suggestion becomes more plausible once we attend closely to vv 7–9.

Scholars generally have viewed these verses either as a verbatim quotation from royal archives[33] or as a relatively faithful paraphrase.[34] Consequently, they have considered the historical reliability of the verses reasonably certain. Recently, however, H. Tadmor and M. Cogan have argued forcefully that the terminology of the material reflects the critical attitude of the deuteronomistic editors toward Ahaz.[35] Two phrases are significant in this regard.

(1) Verse 8b characterizes Ahaz's payment as a *šōḥad*. In the overwhelming number of instances, the word has the pejorative meaning, "bribe." If its semantic equivalent is the Akkadian *ṭatu*, as Tadmor and Cogan contend, this too would suggest negative connotations for the term.[36] Official court or temple sources would not

---

[32]See *GKC* 328; also P. Jouon, *Grammaire de l'hébreu biblique* (2d ed.; Rome: Biblical Institute, 1947) 322.

[33]See, for example, J. A. Montgomery, *The Books of Kings*, 36.

[34]See J. Gray, *I and II Kings*, 571–72; and G. H. Jones, *1 and 2 Kings*, 532. A. Šanda (*Die Bücher der Könige*, 2. 207) speaks of the royal annals "shining through the editor's revision in vv 6, 8 and 9." Verse 7, Šanda suggests, derives from a history of Ahaz, but owes its wording to the editor.

[35]H. Tadmor and M. Cogan, "Ahaz and Tiglath-Pileser," 499–508.

[36]It is worth noting the occurrence of the verb *šḥd* in the Sefire inscription, a treaty between KTK and Arpad written in Aramaic and dating to about 750 (see *ANET* 659–61). The end of Stele III reads: "If . . . they bribe whatever king who

likely have applied this kind of derogatory language to a Judean king, but rather would have used a more neutral term like *minḥâ* (see Judg 3:15; 2 Sam 8:2, 6; 1 Kgs 5:1; 2 Kgs 17:3, 4; and Ps 72:10).[37]

(2) Ahaz declares his submission to the Assyrian king in v 7a: "I am your servant and your son" (*ʿabděkā ûbinkā ʾānî*).[38] While the self-designation of a vassal as "servant" accords well with common treaty parlance of the ancient Near East, father-son terminology in a covenant-making context is confined to a single example from Mari in the second millenium B.C.E.[39] Tadmor and Cogan state that in the Assyrian royal correspondence specifically, the writer always refers to himself as "servant" when addressing the king. "A vassal would not have dared to use the term, 'son,' which expressed familial dependency."[40] The combination of the two elements, "your servant" and "your son," within a single covenant-declaration formula is unique in the Hebrew Bible and rare in extra-biblical literature.[41] The authenticity of the formula as used by Ahaz is therefore doubtful. The deuteronomistic editors probably invented the expression and

---

(*wyšḥdn klmh zy*) . . . ." The meaning of the text is debated, but it seems to warn the kings of Arpad against hiring allies against the king of KTK. If so, the verb likely implies disapproval.

[37]C. M. I. Kalluveettil (*Declaration and Covenant: A Comprehensive Review of Covenant Formulae from the Old Testament and the Ancient Near East* [AnBib 88; Rome: Biblical Institute, 1982] 127–26) also views *šōḥad* as a pejorative term. See, however, the different opinion of J. C. Greenfield ("Some Aspects of Treaty Terminology in the Bible," *Papers of the Fourth World Congress of Jewish Studies* [Jerusalem: 1967] 119) and the reservation expressed by P. R. Ackroyd ("The Reigns of Ahaz and Hezekiah," 258, n. 11).

[38]Scholars debate whether this declaration marks Ahaz's first submission to Tiglathpileser, or instead refers to a pre-existing suzerain-vassal relationship between the two. Defenders of the second intepretation argue in one of two ways. (1) Judean vassalage began at least as early as 738, when the Assyrian king subjugated Azariah, the grandfather of Ahaz. (2) The Syro-Ephraimitic crisis followed Tiglathpileser's campaign to Philistia in 734. If Ahaz paid tribute in 734, as the Assyrian inscriptions report (II R 67 rev. 7–12), his appeal to Tiglathpileser during the Syro-Ephraimitic crisis was made as an Assyrian vassal who rightfully expected military help under the terms of a vassal treaty. For a critique of these arguments, see sections C1 and C2 below. Second Kings 16 gives the impression that Ahaz's appeal invited the Assyrians into the life of Judah for the first time.

[39]See C. M. I. Kalluveettil, *Declaration and Covenant*, 98. F. C. Fensham ("Father and Son as Terminology for Treaty and Covenant" in *Near Eastern Studies in Honor of William Foxwell Albright* [ed. H. Goedicke; Baltimore: John Hopkins University Press, 1971] 121–36) discusses instances of father-son language describing suzerain-vassal relations, but these cases occur outside the covenant-making context. The examples derive from second millenium Mari and Amarna.

[40]H. Tadmor and M. Cogan, "Ahaz and Tiglath-Pileser," 504.

[41]Kalluveettil (*Declaration and Covenant*, 129) lists instances of the combined elements outside the covenant-making context. The evidence is slim.

perhaps intended it pejoratively. According to the Judean royal ideology, the Davidic king is the servant and son of Yahweh (see 2 Sam 3:18; 7:14; 1 Kgs 11:13, 34; Pss 2:7, 89:4, 27, 40; 132:10; Hag 2:23). When Ahaz declares that he is the servant and son of Tiglathpileser, his unfaithfulness to Yahweh may be implied.

Far then from being a direct quotation from court or temple records, 2 Kgs 16:7-9 are likely a re-writing of those sources from a deuteronomistic perspective.[42] Consequently, it is open to question what precisely the sources reported about Ahaz's alliance with Assyria. Noteworthy in this regard is the unevenness of the narrative. The account jumps immediately from the Judean king's appeal (vv 7-8) to the fall of Damascus and the execution of Rezin (v 9). The reader is thus forced to fill two logical gaps: the Syro-Ephraimitic siege of Jerusalem left off, once Tiglathpileser responded to Ahaz's call; and Rezin had returned to Damascus before the Assyrians besieged the city. Furthermore, the account is utterly silent about Assyria's treatment of Pekah and Israel.[43] The specific mention of the Israelite king in vv 5 and 7b leads one to expect some mention of his fate in the context of chapter 16, even if only cursory.

In light of these considerations, the compositional history of 16:5-9 seems to have been very complex. Definitive conclusions are impossible, but the following reconstruction is plausible. The deuteronomistic editors inherited vv 5 and 6, either from two separate sources or from two separate sections of a single document. They then filled out the former notice with their own account of Ahaz's appeal and the Assyrian response in vv 7-9. The latter verses, though owing their precise wording to the editors, were based on received information. The unevenness of the narrative, however, suggests that the data at their disposal was disparate. In all likelihood, it included little more than a simple notice that Ahaz at some time paid Assyrian tribute, and a brief report on the fall of Damascus.

Struggling to make sense of this scanty source material, the editors worked it up in a perfectly logical way, namely, on the model of the Asa-Baasha-Benhadad episode in 1 Kgs 15:16-22. In both accounts, a Judean king suffers aggression from an invading power. In

---

[42]H. Tadmor and M. Cogan, "Ahaz and Tiglath-Pileser," 506. See also H. Spieckermann, *Juda und Assur*, 364, especially n. 130.

[43]Tadmor and Cogan ("Ahaz and Tiglath-Pileser," 507-8) suggest that 2 Kgs 15:29 once belonged to the account of Ahaz's reign in 16:5-9, but the editors of Kings removed the notice to their account of Pekah's reign. The orthographic variation in the Assyrian king's name (compare 15:29 and 16:7) weighs against the suggestion. R. Bickert ("König Ahas und der Prophet Jesaja," 367-71) also observes the peculiar silence of 16:7-9 about the fate of Pekah. He draws, however, the wrong conclusion, namely, that the narrative originally referred to Rezin and Syria only.

both, the Judean king finds deliverance by appealing to a third power for military assistance. In both, the appeal for help entails an alliance formula and the payment of a *šōḥad* out of royal and Temple treasuries. With respect both to plot and specific wording, the parallels between the stories are too striking to be accidental.[44] Knowing that the Syro-Ephraimitic siege of Jerusalem had failed (v 5) and that Tiglathpileser had crushed Damascus (v 9), the editors simply assumed that Ahaz escaped his predicament by making a special appeal to the Assyrian king, just as Asa had made to Benhadad of Syria. As argued above, it is likely that the editors did find in their sources a notice on Ahaz's tribute. They, however, interpreted the datum in accordance with First Kings 15: the payment of a "bribe" was a precondition for Assyrian intervention.

If the deuteronomistic editors shaped their account of the Syro-Ephraimitic war along the lines of the Asa-Baasha-Benhadad episode, they also interpreted their source material with an eye to how they would portray Hezekiah and his dealings with the Assyrians. The editorial logic of chapter 16 is a double-logic. (1) Because Ahaz was religiously an apostate king (vv 1–4), enemies afflicted him (vv 5–9). (2) Because Ahaz entered into a political alliance with Assyria, he committed even greater religious sins, reforming the Temple cult along non-Yahwistic lines (vv 10–18). The picture is artificially the reverse of the account of his successor. Hezekiah "did what was right in the eyes of the Lord" (18:3; compare 16:4) . . . trusted in Yahweh the God of Israel (v 5) . . . and held fast to Yahweh" (v 6). Consequently, "Yahweh was with him; wherever he went forth, he prospered. He rebelled against the king of Assyria and would not serve him" (*wĕlōʾ ʿăbādô*, v 7; compare *ʿabdĕkā* in 16:7). In times of distress, Hezekiah appealed to Yahweh for "deliverance from the hand" of his enemy (*hôšîʿēnû nāʾ miyyādô*, 19:19a; compare 16:7b) and Yahweh "heard/answered" his request (*šmʿ*, 19:16, 20; compare 16:9a).

The editors do not spell out their point explicitly, but leave it for the reader to infer from the paratactic juxtaposition of the two accounts.[45] Unlike Hezekiah, Ahaz was powerless before his enemies

---

[44]Compare Kalluveettil's discussion of the structural and verbal parallels (*Declaration and Covenant*, 122). The passages share the following vocabulary: *wayyiqqaḥ, hakkesep wĕhazzāhāb, bêt yhwh, bĕʾōṣĕrôt bêt hammelek, wayyišlaḥ (šalaḥû) šōḥad,* and *wayyišmaʿ*.

[45]J. Van Seters (*In Search of History*, 35–40, 312, and 321) and B. O. Long (*1 Kings with an Introduction to Historical Literature* [FOTL 9; Grand Rapids: Eerdmans, 1984] 19–29) have both investigated parataxis as a compositional device in the books of Kings. Long stresses that the main organizational principle in paratactic literature is analogical. This describes well the connection between the accounts of Ahaz and Hezekiah. The editors present Ahaz as a negative antitype to Hezekiah.

because he was a religiously bad king. In contrast to Hezekiah, who trusted in Yahweh and rebelled against Assyria, Ahaz did not hold fast to Yahweh, but bought the aid of Tiglathpileser against Rezin and Pekah. He was thus to blame for Judah's servitude to Assyria.[46]

B. Second Chronicles 28

Second Chronicles 28 also recounts the reign of Ahaz within the framework of introductory and concluding sections (vv 1–4 and 26–27). The body of the narrative reports the following events.

(1) The Syrians attacked Ahaz and took Judean captives (v 5a). (2) Pekah attacked Ahaz and killed one hundred twenty thousand Judeans (vv 5b–6). (3) Zichri, an Ephraimite warrior, killed Ma'aseiah the king's son (*ben-hammelek*), Azrikam the "commander of the palace" (*nĕgîd habbāyit*), and Elkanah the "next in authority to the king" (*mišnēh hammelek*; v 7). (4) The Israelites took spoil and two hundred thousand Judean captives, but, on the advice of the prophet Oded, they later returned the spoil and captives (vv 8–15).

(5) Ahaz appealed to the king of Assyria (emending the plural *malkê* to *melek* in v 16) for help against the Edomites and Philistines (vv 16–21). The Edomites had attacked Judah and taken captives, while the Philistines had overrun the Shephelah and Negeb. Instead of rescuing the Judean king, Tiglathpileser "came against him and afflicted him" (*wayyābōʾ ʿālāyw tillĕgat pilnĕʾeser melek ʾaššûr wayyāṣar lô wĕlōʾ ḥăzāqô*, v 20). Ahaz sent payment to the Assyrian king, but it was to no avail (v 21).

(6) In "the time of his distress," Ahaz sinned religiously (vv 22–25). He sacrificed to the Syrian gods, cut up the Temple vessels, and closed down the Temple. He also erected altars throughout Jerusalem, set up sanctuaries throughout Judah, and worshipped foreign gods there.

The Chronicler's portrait of Ahaz is far more negative than the Kings account.[47] The extreme criticism of the king is apparent already

---

[46]P. R. Ackroyd's study of the accounts of Ahaz and Hezekiah ("The Reigns of Ahaz and Hezekiah," 248–56) reaches similar conclusions. See also H. Tadmor and M. Cogan, "Ahaz and Tiglath-Pileser," 505–6.

[47]We speak of the "Chronicler" as a matter of convenience and do not mean to imply a single author or editor for First and Second Chronicles, let alone Chronicles-Ezra-Nehemiah. For recent reviews of the literature on the unity and authorship of these books, see J. R. Porter, "Old Testament Historiography," in *Tradition and Interpretation: Essays by Members of the Society for Old Testament Study* (ed. G. W. Anderson; Oxford: Clarendon, 1979) 152–62; H. G. M. Williamson, *1 and 2 Chronicles* (Grand Rapids/London: Eerdmans/Marshall, Morgan & Scott, 1982) 12–17; and P. R. Ackroyd, "The Historical Literature," in *The Hebrew Bible*

in the introduction. The Chronicler here repeats the charges of 2 Kgs 16:2-4, but also lists two additional sins: Ahaz made images for the Baals (v 2b) and he burned incense in the Valley of Hinnom (v 3a). Furthermore, v 3b claims that the Judean king burned several of his sons (*bānāyw*; compare the singular *běnô* in 2 Kgs 16:3). He thus appears to have committed the sin not merely once, as the Kings account suggests, but repeatedly.[48]

Verses 5-21 emphasize the political distress of Ahaz. His circumstances appear far more dire here than in Second Kings 16. The joint Syrian-Israelite invasion, for example, is treated as two separate and fully successful attacks (vv 5-6; compare 2 Kgs 16:5 and 7). The Syrian king first exiled many Judeans to Damascus; then Pekah killed one hundred twenty thousand Judeans (in one day!). The actions of the latter are in turn followed by further Israelite aggression: Zichri killed the king's son and two other high-ranking Judean officials (v 7); the Israelites took great spoil and exiled two hundred thousand Judeans to Samaria (v 8).

Just as the Chronicler divides the Syrian-Israelite attack into two separate invasions, so he also treats the Edomite attack as an independent episode (v 17; compare 2 Kgs 16:6). He adds as well that the Philistines invaded Judah (v 18). Both attacks again appear fully successful.

The treatment of Assyria in vv 16-21 further heightens the distress of Ahaz. Second Kings 16:5-9, we saw above, report how the Judean king survived the Syrian-Israelite attack by sending an appeal and *šōḥad* to Tiglathpileser. In the Chronicler's account, the appeal is connected with the Edomite and Philistine attacks and is said, moreover, to have backfired. The Assyrian king ironically marched against Ahaz, despite the latter's payment (vv 20-21).[49]

Second Chronicles 28 explains the distress of Ahaz and Judah as divine punishment, and in this respect, the account again differs from Second Kings 16. The Deuteronomistic editors imply that the cultic sins of the king led to his political helplessness. They do not, however, make the connection explicitly. In contrast, the Chronicler states unambiguously that Yahweh gave Ahaz into the hands of his enemies (vv 5 and 9). His sins and the apostasy of his people called forth

---

and Its Modern Interpreters (eds. D. A. Knight and G. M. Tucker; Philadelphia/Chico: Fortress/Scholars Press, 1985) 305-8.

[48] See P. R. Ackroyd, "Historians and Prophets," 33-34; and more recently, M. E. W. Thompson, *Situation and Theology*, 93. Compare the view of W. E. Lemke on v 3b ("The Synoptic Problem in the Chronicler's History," *HTR* 58 [1965] 360). He contends that the change from *běnô* to *bānāyw* is nothing more than a plene-defective variation.

[49] The Chronicler speaks disapprovingly of the payment as a matter of the king's "plundering" (*ḥālaq*) the Temple and royal palace.

this punishment. The Judeans had "forsaken Yahweh the God of their fathers" (v 6b; compare v 9); Ahaz had "acted wantonly" (*hiprîaʿ*) in Judah and had "dealt faithlessly" *(ûmāʿôl maʿal)* with Yahweh (v 19b).[50] Consequently, Yahweh "humbled" (*hiknîaʿ*) Judah on account of Ahaz (v 19a).

Verses 22-25 continue the extreme criticism of Ahaz. The focus here is on the religious wrongdoing of the king, and again there are significant differences from the Kings account. The Deuteronomistic editors describe Ahaz's changes in the Temple furniture and structures (2 Kgs 16:10-18) and imply that these reforms were unorthodox and due to Assyrian pressure. The editors, however, do not condemn the changes explicitly. In contrast, 2 Chr 28:22 and 25 strongly denounce the cultic policies of Ahaz as "faithlessness" to Yahweh and the cause of divine anger. Furthermore, the king's religious sins are more flagrant in the Chronicles account. Ahaz is here guilty of worshipping Syrian gods, closing down the Temple cult, and promoting the worship of foreign gods at other sanctuaries (vv 23-25). The Chronicler stresses that these acts of apostasy did not profit the king. Just as his appeal to Tiglathpileser worked to his demise (vv 20-21), so his appeal to foreign gods contributed to his ruin (v 23).[51]

The apostasy of Ahaz is highlighted by the contrasting picture of the Israelites in vv 8-15. (This material is unique to the Chronicler's account.) The prophet Oded here explains that Yahweh punished the Judeans by giving them into the hands of the Israelites. The Israelites, he warns, should not exceed the divine will by using their Judean "brothers" as slaves (vv 9-10a).[52] Harsh treatment of the captives would only compound their own sins against Yahweh (vv 10b-11). The Israelites respond appropriately to this sermon by acknowledging their sins (vv 12-13) and returning the Judean spoil and prisoners (vv 14-16). Their repentance contrasts markedly with the behavior of Ahaz. "In the time of his distress," he did not repent, but instead "acted even more faithlessly with Yahweh" (*wayyôsep limʿôl bayhwh*) by worshipping other gods (vv 22-23).

---

[50]The verb *mʿl* and related forms occur frequently in Chronicles and often refer to religious faithlessness which leads to military defeat and exile (compare 1 Chr 9:1, 10:13, 2 Chr 33:19, and 36:14). See R. Mosis, *Untersuchungen zur Theologie des chronistischen Geschictswerkes* (Freiburger TS 92; Freiburg: Herder, 1973) 29-33.

[51]The repeated use of the verb *ʿzr* and related forms (*laʿzōr*, v 16b; *lěʿezrâ*, v 21b; *maʿzěrîm* and *wěyaʿzěrûnî*, v 23a) reinforces the parallelism.

[52]The Chronicler repeatedly describes the Judeans and Israelites as "brothers" (vv 8, 11, and 15). He thereby emphasizes the essential unity of the northern and southern kingdoms, alludes to their division after Solomon's death, and anticipates their reunion under Hezekiah. See H. W. M. Williamson, *Israel in the Books of Chronicles* (Cambridge: Cambridge University Press, 1977) 118; idem., *1 and 2 Chronicles*, 346; and M. E. W. Thompson, *Situation and Theology*, 97.

Verses 26–27 are a final effort to derogate Ahaz. The deuteronomistic editors report the king's burial "with his fathers in the city of David" (2 Kgs 16:20) The Chronicler, in contrast, emphasizes that the Judeans did not bury Ahaz in the royal tombs (v 27).

The above discussion has highlighted the Chronicler's extreme criticism of Ahaz. Assessing the historical value of the account, however, is a different and more difficult task. It is difficult partly because the extent and nature of the Chronicler's sources are unclear.[53] Certainly he used a version of Samuel and Kings, but this may have differed somewhat from their Masoretic form.[54] Furthermore, he also had access to additional sources, some of which he cites, but others of which he may not have named.[55] Consequently, one cannot simply assume that the Chronicler's departures from Samuel-Kings mark his own editorial work or free composition. Even where source material does underlie his account, the historical issue is still open. The sources used by the Chronicler may themselves have been very tendentious.[56]

The source and historical issues do not admit general and categorical answers. The historian must examine and assess the individual passages separately. With regard to Second Chronicles 28, the following conclusions seem sound.

The theological interests of the Chronicler have shaped his account of Ahaz and the Syro-Ephraimitic crisis. He wants to demonstrate at least three points. (1) The religious sins of Ahaz made him the worst king in Judean history. (2) Yahweh punished the

---

[53] For discussions of the source-critical problem, see M. Noth, *Überlieferungsgeschichtliche Studien*, 131–50; A.-M. Brunet, "Le Chroniste et ses sources," *RB* 60 (1953) 481–508 and *RB* 61 (1954) 349–86; P. Welten, *Geschichte und Geschichtsdarstellung in den Chronikbüchern* (WMANT 42; Neukirchen-Vluyn: Neukirchener Verlag, 1973) 191–94, 201–6; H. G. M. Williamson, *1 and 2 Chronicles*, 17–23; P. R. Ackroyd, "The Historical Literature," 308–9; and T. Willi, *Die Chronik als Auslegung. Untersuchungen zur literarischen Gestaltung der historischen Überlieferung Israels* (FRLANT 106; Göttingen: Vandenhoeck & Ruprecht, 1972) 54–56, 229–41.

[54] See M. Rehm, *Die Bücher der Chronik* (2d ed.; Wuerzburg: Echter Verlag, 1956) 275; W. E. Lemke, "The Synoptic Problem," 360–63; J. R. Porter, "Old Testament Historiography," 155–57.

[55] H. G. M. Williamson, *1 and 2 Chronicles*, 17–21. For a list of the sources cited in Chronicles, see J. M. Myers, *I Chronicles* (AB 12; Garden City, NY: Doubleday, 1965) xlv–xlviii.

[56] Even a critic as skeptical about the Chronicler's reliability as J. Wellhausen conceded that the Chronicler may have used sources in addition to Samuel-Kings (*Prolegomena to the History of Ancient Israel* [Gloucester, MA; Peter Smith, 1973] 222–23; German original, *Prolegomena zur Geschichte Israels* [2d ed.; Berlin: Reimer, 1883] 232–33). He argued, however, that "the historical character of the work is not hereby altered in the smallest degree, it is merely shared by the so-called 'sources'.... The alterations and additions of Chronicles are all traceable to the same fountain-head—the Judaising of the past...."

"faithlessness" of the king by giving him into the hands of his enemies. (3) "In the time of his distress," Ahaz did not repent. He thus received full and just retribution.[57]

This theological agenda accounts for many of the differences between the Chronicler's version of the Syro-Ephraimitic crisis and the Kings account. The Chronicler wants to emphasize the severity of the divine punishment that befalls apostate kings. He thus divides the joint Syro-Ephraimitic crisis into two separate invasions, presents the Edomite attack as yet a third invasion, and transforms all three attacks into fully successful campaigns, each resulting in the exile of Judeans.

For similar reasons the Chronicler recasts the role of Assyria. The deuteronomistic editors, we saw, report how Ahaz survived enemy aggression by appealing to Tiglathpileser for help. This scenario contradicts the Chronicler's dogmatic belief that disaster invariably befalls religiously bad and unrepentant kings.[58] He solves the problem by claiming that the appeal backfired. The Assyrian king is depicted as yet another enemy who, along with the Syrians, Israelites, Edomites, and Philistines, executed Yahweh's punishment of Ahaz. The picture, nevertheless, might approach the historical truth in one respect. Tiglathpileser apparently did not show special consideration or favor to the Judean king (see Section C4.c below).

The account of Oded's sermon and the Israelites' release of Judean captives is historically improbable. Source material might lie behind the narrative, but if so, the Chronicler has thoroughly rewrit-

---

[57]Recent studies of the theological *Tendenz* of Second Chronicles 28 include the works by Ackroyd ("Historians and Prophets," 33–37) and Thompson (*Situation and Theology*, 81–103). See also H. G. M. Williamson, *Israel*, 114–118; and R. Mosis, *Theologie des chronistischen Geschichtswerkes*, 186–92. These studies examine other theological interests of the Chronicler, including the depiction of Ahaz as a second Saul, the exilic motif, and the reunification of the Israelites and Judeans.

[58]Wellhausen (*Prolegomena*, 203) speaks of a "divine pragmatism" in Chronicles, according to which Yahweh's justice responds promptly to the pious or impious behavior of each king. He correctly remarks on the portrayal of Ahaz (206): "Ahaz was a king of little worth, and yet he got fairly well out of the difficulty into which the invasion of the allied Syrians and Israelites had brought him by making his kingdom tributary to the Assyrian Tiglath-Pileser (2 Kings xvi. 1 seq.). But Chronicles could not possibly let him off so cheaply." See the recent discussions of the Chonicler's doctrine of individual retribution by P. Welten, *Geschichte und Geschichtsdarstellung*, 9–186; S. Japhet (*The Ideology of the Book of Chronicles and Its Place in Biblical Thought* [Jerusalem: Bialik Institute, 1977] 154–66); and R. L. Braun ("Chronicles, Ezra, and Nehemiah: Theology and Literary History," in *Studies in the Historical Books of the Old Testament* [ed. J. A. Emerton; VTSup 30; Leiden: E. J. Brill, 1979] 53–56). Compare R. Mosis, *Theologie des chronistischen Geschichtswerkes*, 201.

ten it from his own theological perspective.[59] The account clearly reflects his emphasis on the value of repentance and his concern to highlight by contrast the wickedness of Ahaz.

The notices on Zichri (v 7) and the Philistine invasion (v 18) likely rest on reliable source material. The specific details of both verses lend to them a ring of authenticity and serve no explicit *Tendenz* of the Chronicler. The report on Zichri might refer to an abortive attempt on the life of Ahaz. (The Ephraimite managed to kill the king's son and two high-ranking court officials, but Ahaz himself escaped assassination.) Philistine expansion northward along the coast and westward into the Shephelah might have begun as early as the reign of Jeroboam II and in cooperation with the Syrians (see Isa 9:11; also Amos 1:6–8, where *ʾĕdôm* should perhaps be read as *ʾărām*). When Rezin and Pekah invaded Judah in the late 730s, the Philistines likely encroached further on Judean territory.[60]

C. Reconstructing the Syro-Ephraimitic Crisis

The analyses of Second Kings 16, Second Chronicles 28, and the Assyrian texts (Chapter Two) lay the essential groundwork for reconstucting the Syro-Ephraimitic crisis. The interpretive problems of these sources, we have seen, are difficult, and it is thus not surprising that scholars disagree over the nature and course of the war. The several treatments of the war divide into three basic positions, represented respectively by J. Begrich,[61] H. Donner,[62] and B. Oded.[63]

---

[59]See H. G. M. Williamson, *1 and 2 Chronicles*, 346–47. The Chronicler typically has prophetic and other characters step forward at key points in the history to deliver sermons (for example, 2 Chr 15:1–7, 16:7–9, 20:15–17, 25:7–8, and 32:7–8). See G. von Rad, "Die levitische Predigt in den Büchern der Chronik," in *Festschrift Otto Procksch* (Leipzig: A. Deichert and J. C. Hinrich, 1934) 113–24 = his *GS* (Munich: Chr. Kaiser, 1971) 248–61; A. C. Welch, *The Work of the Chronicler: Its Purpose and Its Date* (London: Oxford University Press, 1939) 42–54; J. M. Myers, "The Kerygma of the Chronicler," *Int* 20 (1966) 259–73; T. Willi, *Die Chronik als Auslegung*, 216–29; and J. D. Newsome, "Towards a New Understanding of the Chronicler and His Purposes," *JBL* 94 (1975) 201–17.

[60]See J. Bright, *A History of Israel*, 274; and C. Shaw, "Micah 1:10–16 Reconsidered," *JBL* 106 (1987) 227–29.

[61]J. Begrich, "Der syrisch-ephraimitische Krieg," 213–37.

[62]H. Donner, *Israel unter den Völkern*, 1–63; idem., "The Separate States," 421–32; idem., *Geschichte des Volkes Israel*, 303–15.

[63]B. Oded, "The Syro-Ephraimite War Reconsidered," 153–65.

1. Joachim Begrich

Begrich examines the Syro-Ephraimitic war as a test case for his chronology of the Israelite and Judean kings.[64] The lasting value of the study, however, is its attempt to highlight the connection of the episode to Assyria's westward expansion.[65] Begrich argues the following points.

(1) Rezin and Pekah would not have invaded Judah while the Assyrian army was near or in the area. The attack therefore must have occurred before Tiglathpileser's Philistine campaign (June/July 734, at the latest). A date during the spring of 734 is likely.[66]

(2) The purpose of the attack was to draw Judah into a broad anti-Assyrian coalition.[67] Besides Rezin and Pekah, members of the alliance included Samsi queen of the Arabs, Hanno of Gaza, Mitinti of Ashkelon, Edom, Ammon, and Moab. Egypt stood in the background as a supporter of the coalition and a potential source of military aid. Assyria's westward expansion could be successfully checked, however, only if all the regional states, including Judah, were united into a single anti-Assyrian block.

(3) Ahaz refused to join the coalition, apparently because he estimated its chances of success as minimal.[68] At the same time, however, he must have realized that he could not escape Assyrian domination by remaining neutral. The Judean king thus submitted to Tiglathpileser and appealed for help in the spring of 734. The decision was politically wise, for Ahaz could expect mild treatment from the Assyrians, if he voluntarily accepted Assyrian vassalage early in the course of events.

---

[64] J. Begrich, "Der syrisch-ephraimitische Krieg," 213; idem., *Die Chronologie der Könige von Israel und Juda und die Quellen des Rahmes der Königsbücher* (Tübingen: J. C. B. Mohr [Paul Siebeck] 1929.

[65] On this point, Begrich is concerned to refute the views of B. Meissner (*Könige Babyloniens und Assyriens* [Leipzig: Quelle & Meyer, 1926] 164) and K. Budde (*Jesaja's Erleben*, 35–36, 41–43). They understand the Syro-Ephraimitic war as a strictly inner-Palestinian conflict.

[66] "Der syrisch-ephraimitische Krieg," 214–15, 235. According to Begrich's chronology, the first regnal year of Pekah began in the fall of 734, but the king had assumed actual power sometime during the previous year. The fall of 735, he claims, is the *terminus a quo* for both Pekah's rise to the throne and the Syro-Ephraimitic war. (Begrich doubts the historical accuracy of 2 Kgs 15:37, which reports the harassment of Judah by Rezin and Pekah as early as the reign of Jotham.)

[67] "Der syrisch-ephraimitische Krieg," 216–20. Begrich reconstructs the coalition on the basis of Layard 72b+73a, 29b, 66, II R 67, and III R 10,2. ND400 and ND4301+4305 were discovered only in the 1950s and so were not available to Begrich.

[68] "Der syrisch-ephraimitische Krieg," 220–22.

(4) Tiglathpileser invaded Palestine in order to crush the anti-Assyrian coalition, not to save Ahaz.[69] The appeal by the Judean king was at most an additional incentive. The Judean embassy may have met the Assyrian army as it was preparing for the campaign or perhaps while it was on the march.

(5) The Assyrian army moved down the eastern Mediterranean coast toward Gaza in the late spring or early summer of 734.[70] The one detour from the coast occurred at Acco, where the Assyrians turned inland to conquer Galilee.[71] The strategic goals of the campaign were to win a quick victory over the southernmost members of the coalition and to cut off possible aid from Egypt. The Assyrians captured Ashkelon and Gezer, received the voluntary tribute of other Philistine rulers, and finally conquered Gaza. Hanno, the king of Gaza, had fled to Egypt for military aid. When the Egyptians refused to help, however, he returned to Gaza, submitted to Assyrian vassalage, and resumed his throne.

(6) In 733–732, the Assyrian army moved from the Philistine coast toward Damascus.[72] In the course of the campaign, Tiglathpileser conquered Gilead and the lands of Bashan and Golan, defeated Rezin's army in the vicinity of Ḥadara, subjugated Samsi, and captured Damascus. After the fall of Damascus, pro-Assyrian forces in Ashkelon assassinated Mitinti, who had rejoined the rebellion in 733. They quickly submitted to Tiglathpileser. Similarly in Israel, Hoshea killed Pekah and paid Assyrian tribute.

2. Herbert Donner

Donner disputes the details of Begrich's reconstruction, particularly as they concern the date of the war.[73] His main objections are two. (1) The Assyrian inscriptions give no indication that Tiglathpileser's Philistine campaign had anything to do with an anti-Assyr-

---

[69]"Der syrisch-ephraimitische Krieg," 222–23.

[70]Begrich ("Der syrisch-ephraimitische Krieg," 223–28) reconstructs the course of the Assyrian campaigns on the basis of III R 10,2, which he mistakenly assumes follows a chronological order (see Chapter Two, section B7). Lines 1–15 supposedly trace the sequential stages of the Philistine campaign in 734.

[71]Begrich ("Der syrisch-ephraimitische Krieg," 227–28) correlates 2 Kgs 15:29 with III R 10,2:6–8 as complementary reports on the seizure of Galilee from Israel. (See Chapter Two, sections B2 and B7, where we suggested that the Assyrians confiscated the region from Syria.) The interpretation forces Begrich to argue that the town of Gal'azu, mentioned in III R 10,2:6 and usually identified with Ramoth-Gilead, was located west of the Jordan.

[72]"Der syrisch-ephraimitische Krieg," 228–34.

[73]*Israel unter den Völkern*, 59–61; "The Separate States," 428–29. Donner also questions whether Egypt played any role in the Syrian-led coalition. On this issue, see Chapter Two, section B5.

ian coalition. (2) The period between the enthronement of Pekah (fall 735, at the earliest) and the Philistine campaign (June–July 734, according to Begrich) is too short to accomodate all the events leading up to and occurring during the Syro-Ephraimitic war. More time would have been required for the initial negotiations between Rezin and Pekah, the first diplomatic contacts between these two kings and Ahaz, the coalition's march against Jerusalem, and Assyria's intervention.[74]

Donner concludes that the coalition did not yet exist at the time of the Philistine campaign. It arose afterward as a response to the new Assyrian presence in Palestine. Accordingly, the Syro-Ephraimitic war also occurred in the aftermath of the Philistine campaign.

Donner proceeds to sketch the Syro-Ephraimitic war in detail.[75] The Assyrians, he argues, marched against Gaza in April/May 734 at the latest. Soon afterwards, negotiations between Rezin, Pekah, and Ahaz probably began. When Ahaz refused to join the coalition, the Syrian and Israelite kings decided to invade Judah. As soon as the Assyrian army had left Palestine (May–July 734), Syrian troops moved into Israel to join the forces of Pekah (Isa 7:1–16). The two armies, however, did not attack Jerusalem for several months. Donner gives three arguments for this delay.

(1) If the Syro-Ephraimitic war took place in the summer of 734, Tiglathpileser would have moved against the coalition at that time. The Assyrian king, however, did not intervene until the spring/summer of 733. It is reasonable to assume that the war and Ahaz's appeal preceded the Assyrian invasion by little more than a week.

(2) Isaiah 7:1–16 reflect conditions in Palestine shortly after the Syrian troops had moved into Israel (v 2). The prophet at this time apparently doubted that the attack would occur (v 4) and anticipated a longer period of tensions (v 16).

(3) If the second child of Isaiah, Immanuel (7:14–16), was born in the summer of 734, the prophet's third child, Maher-shalal-hash-baz (8:1–4), could not have been born before March–July 733. The symbolic names of both children promise deliverance to Ahaz and so reflect the prophet's stance before the Judean king appealed to Assyria.[76]

---

[74]Donner also contends that Rezin and Pekah would not likely have invaded Judah while the Assyrians were in Palestine. Begrich, however, argues the very same point.
[75]*Israel unter den Völkern*, 61–63; "The Separate States," 429–32.
[76]Donner acknowledges the assumptions behind this argument. It is by no means clear that the "young woman" of 7:14 was the "prophetess" of 8:3. Also questionable is whether Immanuel was even a son of Isaiah.

Donner suggests possible reasons for the delay of the Syrian-Israelite attack. If the coalition had arisen suddenly in the summer of 734, ongoing political and strategic disagreements between Rezin and Pekah may have forced them to postpone the invasion. The two kings might also have anticipated a lengthy siege of Jerusalem and feared that their military strength was insufficient. Finally, time for the invasion may have been running out. The Syrian and Israelite troops would have wanted to return home in the fall of 734 to tend their fields.

In the spring of 733, Rezin and Pekah put their plan for invasion into action. Just before their armies reached Jerusalem, Ahaz sent messengers to Tiglathpileser to request his help. The Assyrian king responded immediately and moved against Syria and Israel, thereby forcing the coalition forces to abandon the siege of Jerusalem.[77] In the course of 733 and 732, Tiglathpileser annexed Galilee, Gilead, and the territory of Damascus. Hoshea assassinated Pekah, submitted to Assyrian vassalage, and afterwards ruled over the "rump state of Ephraim."

3. Bustanay Oded

Oded views the Syro-Ephraimitic crisis as an inner-Palestinian conflict. His position is thus directly opposed to Begrich's interpretation of the war. Oded raises three objections in particular.[78]

(1) If Rezin and Pekah had been trying to unite the states of Palestine into an anti-Assyrian coalition, they would not likely have risked an extended siege of Jerusalem. The war would have weakened the coalition militarily and left its northern flank vulnerable to an Assyrian attack.

(2) Most wars between the states of Syria and Palestine were local territorial disputes and power struggles. The Syro-Ephraimitic crisis as sketched by Begrich would be the only instance when armed conflict between the regional states related directly to an effort to check the aggression of an outside superpower.

(3) According to 2 Kgs 15:37, Rezin and Pekah were harassing Judah as early as the reign of Jotham.[79] It thus appears that the Syro-Ephraimitic war extended over several years and only climaxed in

---

[77]Donner follows A. Alt ("Hosea 5,8–6,6," 164–74) in arguing for a subsequent Judean counterattack. See n. 1 above.

[78]"The Syro-Ephraimite War Reconsidered," 153–54.

[79]Begrich, we noted (n. 66), discards the verse as "historically misleading and of no value." Oded, however, gives good reasons for rejecting this argument. R. Kittel (*Die Bücher der Könige*, 268–69), A. Šanda (*Die Bücher der Könige*, 2. 193), J. A. Montgomery (*The Books of Kings*, 453–54), J. Gray (*I and II Kings*, 571), and G. H. Jones (*1 and 2 Kings*, 2. 531) all accept the historical value of 15:37.

the siege of Jerusalem. The cause of the war must have lain elsewhere than in Assyria's westward expansion.

The war, Oded argues, was essentially a struggle between Syria, Israel, and Judah for the control of Transjordan.[80] Judah's ties to the region had begun centuries earlier, but its involvment in the area increased rapidly during the reign of Uzziah/Azariah. The king dominated the Ammonites (2 Chr 26:8) and cooperated with Jeroboam of Israel in controlling northern Transjordan over against Syria (2 Kgs 14:28; compare Amos 6:14, which Oded believes addresses both Judeans and Israelites). With the death of Jeroboam, political chaos erupted in Israel, thus allowing Uzziah to emerge as the dominant power of Syria and Palestine and the sole master of Transjordan. The Syro-Ephraimitic war was an attempt to reverse Judah's superiority in the region.

Oded reconstructs the events of the war in detail.[81] Tiglathpileser allegedly defeated Uzziah in 738, thus clearing the way for a resurgence of Syrian power. Rezin first engineered Pekah's coup in Samaria and thereby reduced Israel to a client state.[82] At the same time, the Syrian border was extended southward as far as Ramoth-Gilead. Rezin and Pekah then tried to expel Jotham, the successor of Uzziah, from the rest of Transjordan. Their plan in part was to encourage Ben Tabeel—an ancestor of the later Tobiads, whom Uzziah had appointed as governor over Judah's holdings bordering on Ammon (see Isa 7:6)—to assert his independence from Judah. Either at this time or later during the reign of Ahaz, Rezin also helped the Edomites to retake Elath. The whole of Transjordan was now directly or indirectly under Syrian control.

The territorial expansion of Rezin climaxed with the Syro-Ephraimitic attack against Jerusalem. Oded dates the invasion to 733. The aim, he contends, was to replace Ahaz with Rezin's own puppet, Ben Tabeel (Isa 7:6). The plan was aborted, however, when Tiglathpileser invaded the region. Ahaz had appealed to the Assyrian king for help, but the latter had his own reasons for taking action. During the Philistine campaign in 734, Tiglathpileser undoubtedly learned of Rezin's aggression and undoubtedly resolved to intervene militarily. The subsequent campaigns of 733 and 732 had no direct connection to the Syro-Ephraimitic war.[83]

---

[80]"The Syro-Ephraimite War Reconsidered," 155–61.
[81]"The Syro-Ephraimite War Reconsidered," 160–65.
[82]Pekah, Oded argues (162–63), had previously governed in northern Transjordan on behalf of Pekahiah. He broke with Samaria and surrendered northern Transjordan to Syria, in exchange for Rezin's support against Pekahiah.
[83]S. Herrmann (*A History of Israel in Old Testament Times* [2d ed.; Philadelphia: Fortress, 1981] 247) apparently reaches the same conclusion when he says that the war "has only indirect relevance to the movements of Assyria."

4. Critique

Two key issues emerge from the preceding review. (1) What were the cause and purpose of the Syro-Ephraimitic war? (2) Did the war precede or follow Tiglathpileser's Philistine campaign? A third issue, though one not raised by Begrich, Donner, and Oded, concerns the payment of Ahaz. Was it really a special appeal for Assyrian help, as 2 Kgs 16:7-8 claims, or simply routine tribute given after the Assyrians had invaded Palestine? The different answers to these questions must be evaluated.

a. The Cause and Purpose of the War

Begrich, Donner, and Oded understand the cause and purpose of the Syro-Ephraimitic war differently. The former two, we saw above, view the war as an attempt to force Judah's participation in an anti-Assyrian coalition. In contrast, Oded argues that the war was strictly a regional struggle for the control of Transjordan, without direct connections to the westward expansion of Assyria. The strength of Oded's case depends partly on his objections to the alternative interpretation. These, however, are not strong. Rezin and Pekah, for example, probably expected to overthrow Ahaz quickly, thereby completing the campaign well before the Assyrian army could respond. Furthermore, the fact that wars between the states of Syria and Palestine were usually regional territorial conflicts should not count much in the assessment of a specific case like the Syro-Ephraimitic war. Finally, 2 Kgs 15:37 requires only slight adjustments in Begrich's view of the war. (1) Pekah was ruling in Gilead as an ally of Rezin during the reign of Jotham. (2) The Syrian king's efforts to form a coalition against Assyria, as well as to dominate Palestine, spanned several years.

Oded's interpretation of the war assumes a powerful Uzziah/Azariah. The extra-biblical evidence consists of two Assyrian fragments traditionally assigned to the annals of Tiglathpileser (*ANET* 282-83; *ARAB* 1. 274-75).[84] These supposedly describe an anti-Assyrian coalition of states led by Azariah in 738. Recently, however, N. Na'aman has shown that one of the fragments actually belongs to the inscriptions of Sennacherib and recounts his defeat of Hezekiah.[85]

---

[84]The fragments are designated as III R 9,2 and III R 9,3. P. Rost (*Keilschrifttexte*, 18-27) presents them as ll. 103-109 and 123-159 of the annals. Tadmor ("Introductory Remarks," 177) contends that III R 9,3 is in fact an eclectic text pieced together from eight or more component parts.

[85]N. Na'aman, "Sennacherib's 'Letter of God' on His Campaign to Judah," *BASOR* 214 (1974) 25-39.

The other fragment mentions an *Azriyau*, but not his country. His identity with Azariah of Judah is by no means certain.[86] Without the Assyrian evidence, Oded's case for the Judean king as the strongest ruler in Syria and Palestine and as the master of Transjordan is greatly weakened.

The biblical evidence is also slim. Second Chronicles 26:8 records how Uzziah dominated the Ammonites (*hāʿammônîm*). The reference, however, is probably a scribal misspelling of "the Meunites" (*hammĕʿûnîm*), who were located to the south of Judah. (Note the mention of the Meunites in v 7 and the Septuagint's reading of Meunites in v 8.) A similar error might lie behind 2 Chr 27:5, which reports Jotham's subjugation of the Ammonites, although textual support for emending this verse is lacking.[87]

Second Kings 14:28 reports that Jeroboam "restored Damascus and Hamath to Judah in Israel." The meaning of the notice is cryptic and its historical value uncertain. In any case, the notice as it stands does not suggest the equal cooperation of Judah and Israel in Transjordan. The phrase, "Judah in Israel," might suggest, rather, the subordinate role of Judah.[88]

First Chronicles 5:17 reports a census in Gilead and Bashan taken "in the days of Jotham king of Judah and in the days of Jeroboam king of Israel." The reference to both kings might reflect their joint rule in the region, as Oded argues, but other explanations are also possible.[89] The equal status of Jotham and Jeroboam in Transjordan is hardly a foregone conclusion.[90]

If 2 Chr 28:15 narrates the return of Judean captives to Jericho "to their kinfolk" (*ʾēṣel ʾăḥêhem*), it would seem to assume the Judean control of Jericho during the reign of Ahaz. However, the Hebrew

---

[86]Compare H. Tadmor, "Azriyau of Yaudi," *ScrHier* 8 (1961) 232–71; M. Haran, "The Empire of Jeroboam," 290–96; M. C. Astour, "Ya'udi," *IDBSup* 975; S. Herrmann, *A History of Israel*, 246; J. Bright, *A History of Israel*, 270; C. M. I. Kalluveettil, *Declaration and Covenant*, 124–27; A. Soggin, *A History of Israel*, 219; and H. Donner, *Geschichte des Volkes Israel*, 305.

[87]Compare I. Benzinger, *Die Bücher der Chronik* (Tübingen/Leipzig: J. C. B. Mohr [Paul Siebeck], 1901) 119; K. Galling, *Die Bücher der Chronik, Esra, Nehemia* (Göttingen: Vandenhoeck & Ruprecht, 1954) 148–49; W. Rudolph, *Chronikbücher* (Tübingen: J. C. B. Mohr [Paul Siebeck], 1955) 288; and H. G. M. Williamson, *1 and 2 Chronicles*, 342.

[88]See M. Vogelstein, *Jeroboam II*, 10; and M. Haran, "The Empire of Jeroboam," 296.

[89]J. M. Myers (*I Chronicles*, 37) argues: "The mention of Jotham with Jeroboam II is simply the writer's way of saying that his list was the official one at that time (i.e., between 750 and 745 B.C.) and he includes the name of the former to accord with his scheme of making the Davidic dynasty the chonologico-religious backbone of his work." Compare W. Rudolph, *Chronikbücher*, 48–49.

[90]M. Vogelstein (*Jeroboam II*, 10) sees 1 Chr 5:17 as evidence of Judah's subordination to Israel.

Biblical Accounts of the Syro-Ephraimitic Crisis   103

can mean "near their kinfolk" and so does not necessarily imply Judah's occupation of the city. In any case, the account as a whole (vv 8–15) is historically suspect and may reflect the political geography of a much later period. Even if we conceded Judah's control of Jericho during the 730s, this fact alone would hardly indicate a Judean foothold in Transjordan.

Other evidence for Judean ties with Transjordan during the eighth century is largely indirect and of little force.[91] If Azariah and Jotham exercised a measure of authority in the region, they likely did so under the protective umbrella of Jeroboam. Consequently, there is little reason to view the Syro-Ephraimitic war as an attempt to reverse Judah's influence in the area.

Oded correctly emphasizes the aggressive designs of Rezin on Palestine. The king sought to create a "Greater Syria," as Hazael had done during the previous century (see 2 Kgs 8:7–15, 28–29; 10:32–33; 12:17–18; 13:3, 22). This plan, however, would inevitably lead to conflict with Tiglathpileser, whose own interests in the region must have soon become clear to the Syrian king. Assyria's westward expansion had begun as early as 743/742 with the seizure of northern Syria from Urartian control. By 739, the lands of Arpad and Unqi had been reduced to Assyrian provinces. By 738, most of the northern coastal cities had been annexed, and the southern Syro-Palestinian states, including Syria-Damascus, Israel, and Tyre, had been forced to pay tribute. It was only a matter of time before Tiglathpileser would tighten his control over Palestine and the trade which moved through it. If Rezin were to gain hegemony in the area, he would have to do it at the expense of and in conflict with Assyria. Unless the Syrian king was very naive, he must have realized the need to check Assyrian expansionism.

Oded's interpretation of the war results partly from his narrow focus on Syria, Israel, and Judah. The full body of biblical and extrabiblical evidence suggests a different and more complicated picture. The Assyrian records, we have seen, document widespread revolt during the late 730s, involving Syria, Israel, Tyre, Ashkelon, Samsi, probably Gaza, and perhaps the Meunites and the Transjordan kingdoms. The inscriptions indicate clearly that Hiram of Tyre was in league with Rezin, and we can reasonably infer the same for Mititi of Ashkelon. Second Kings 16:5–9 reports the alliance between Rezin, Pekah, and the Edomites, and 2 Chr 28:18 might indicate the cooperation of the Philistines. If these states and groups, or at least many of them, were in league with Syria and at the same time at war with Assyria, the idea of an anti-Assyrian coalition, coordinated by Rezin,

---

[91]Particularly unconvincing is Oded's identification of Ben Tabeel as an early Tobiad ruling in Transjordan on behalf of the Davidic kings. Other interpretations are more probable, as we will see in Chapter Five.

is hard to avoid. Similarly, if Ahaz was the one ruler in Palestine who did not join the rebellion, and if the plan of Rezin and Pekah was principally to replace him (Isa 7:6), it is difficult to view the Syro-Ephraimitic war other than as an attempt to depose Ahaz and thereby to obtain complete Judean participation in the war against Assyria.

b. The Date of the War

Begrich and Donner disagree on the date of the Syro-Ephraimitic crisis. The former, we have seen, argues that the war occurred in the spring of 734, sometime before Tiglathpileser's Philistine campaign.[92] In contrast, Donner contends that the Syrian-led coalition arose suddenly during the summer of 734 in response to Assyria's new meddling in the area. Rezin and Pekah attacked Jerusalem the following spring.[93] The arguments of Donner are not convincing.

The Assyrian accounts of the Philistine campaign do not mention the coalition explicitly, but this silence is not as significant as Donner suggests. The inscriptions of Tiglathpileser seldom refer directly to the cooperative relations between Syria and other members of the coalition. (The report on Hiram in ND4301+4305 rev. 5 is the obvious exception. Layard 29b:236 also hints at the alliance between Mitinti and Rezin.) If Donner's reasoning were followed consistently, one might doubt whether a coalition arose at all, either before or after the Philistine campaign. Donner, of course, is not this skeptical.

The accounts of the Philistine campaign report Hanno's flight to Egypt and the initially harsh treatment of Gaza by the Assyrians. These events, we argued earlier, seem to reflect Hanno's deep involvement in some sort of anti-Assyrian activity (see Chapter Two, section B5). While the Assyrian records do not explicitly mention his alliance with Syria and other rebel states, we can reasonably infer it.

The principal members of the coalition apparently did not submit to Tiglathpileser during the Philistine campaign. The conspicuous absence of Rezin, Pekah, and Hiram from the tributary list, II R 67 rev. 7–12, likely reflects their ongoing revolt against Assyria (see Chapter Two, section B4).

Donner contends that the time between Pekah's enthronement (fall 735) and the Philistine campaign is too short for all the events involved in the Syro-Ephraimitic war. His own reconstruction, how-

---

[92]For a similar dating of the war, see M. F. Unger, *Israel and the Arameans*, 100; N. K. Gottwald, *All the Kingdoms of the Earth*, 148–52; Y. Aharoni, *Land of the Bible*, 371; H. Cazelles, "La Guerre Syro-Ephraimite," 73; J. Bright, *A History of Israel*, 274; and M. E. W. Thompson, *Situation and Theology*, 111.

[93]See M. Noth, *The History of Israel*, 259; H. Tadmor, "Azriyau," 263–65 (but compare M. Cogan and H. Tadmor, *II Kings* [AB 11; New York: Doubleday, 1988] 191–92); and S. Herrmann, *A History of Israel*, 247.

ever, does not provide significantly more time.[94] Furthermore, it is not clear that the events would have required much time. Negotiations between Rezin and Pekah may have been quite brief, especially if the two had been allies before Pekah's coup in Samaria. Their subsequent discussions with Ahaz might have collapsed quickly. Syrian troops could have moved into Israel within a week and the joint Syrian-Israelite forces might have reached Jerusalem in a matter of days. The entire sequence of events could have transpired easily within two or three months.

Ironically, Donner has trouble explaining why the events of the war, according to his dating, took so long. The coalition, he claims, arose quickly in the summer of 734, but Rezin and Pekah curiously did not attack Ahaz until the following spring. Donner suggests possible reasons for the delay, but these are sheer conjecture. It is in fact doubtful that the attack was postponed at all.[95]

A great deal of evidence can be interpreted to suggest the following picture of the coalition, particularly its rise. Toward the end of the reign of Jeroboam II, Rezin began to encroach on Israelite territory in northern Transjordan and Galilee (Amos 1:3; Hos 1:5–6; compare Layard 29b:229–234 and III R 10,2:5–8). His actions may have been coordinated with Philistine and Phoenician aggression against Israel. The prophet Amos speaks of Gaza and Tyre "delivering up a whole people" (perhaps Israelite captives) to Syria (Amos 1:6 and 9, emending ʾĕdôm to ʾărām). At about this same time, Pekah led Israelites in Gilead to secede from Jeroboam's kingdom (see Chapter Two, the appendix). It is unlikely mere coincidence that Pekah, Rezin, and the leaders of Philistia and Tyre would form the backbone of the coalition against Assyria during the 730s.

Syrian aggression continued after the death of Jeroboam. During the reign of Menahem, Rezin encroached further on Israelite territory from the east, while his Philistine allies "devoured Israel with open mouth on the west" (Isa 9:11). With Assyrian support, Menahem managed to hold onto the Ephraimite hill country (2 Kgs 15:19). It was only a matter of time, however, before even it would come under Syrian control. The moment came when Pekah overthrew Pekahiah

---

[94]See J. M. Asurmendi, *La Guerra Siro-Efraimita*, 43.
[95]The Isaianic texts adduced by Donner do not clearly attest to the delay. The sequence of the children, Immanuel and Maher-shalal-hash-baz, would be significant only if they were born of the same mother. Isaiah 7:14 and 8:3, however, do not suggest this. Also questionable is Donner's claim that Isaiah initially doubted the imminence of the Syro-Ephraimitic attack. The prophet in 7:4–9 does not doubt that the attack will occur, but only that it will succeed. Furthermore, v 16 does not necessarily anticipate prolonged tensions between the coalition and Judah. The interpretation of the prophet's words here is difficult, but they might imply the coalition's collapse in the near future.

in Samaria (2 Kgs 15:25). Rezin likely engineered the coup, thereby reducing Israel to a client state.

Rezin's actions during the 740s were directed against Judah also. Second Kings 15:37 reports how he and Pekah were moving against Judah during the reign of Jotham. While the exact nature of this harassment is uncertain, the purpose was probably to pressure Judah into the coalition which Rezin was gradually assembling.

Jotham's resistance is understandable in light of Judah's long-standing subordination to Israel. The Davidic kings became more or less vassals of Israel during the Omride era and continued as such throughout the Jehu dynasty.[96] They followed the lead of Samaria particularly in matters of foreign policy, even to the point of fighting wars that were principally in the interests of Israel, not Judah (see 1 Kgs 22:1–38; 2 Kgs 3:4–28; 8:25–29).[97] At the beginning of the eighth century, Amaziah tried to assert his independence from Israel, but the northern king, Jehoash, crushed the revolt (2 Kgs 14:8–14). During the reign of Jeroboam II, Azariah and Jotham may have cooperated with the Israelite king in Transjordan (2 Kgs 14:28 and 1 Chr 5:17), but if so, only as subordinate partners. They perhaps tried to forge even closer relations between the two royal houses by marrying the young Ahaz to the Israelite princess, Abi (compare 2 Kgs 15:8 and 18:2). The purpose of such a marriage would have been to ensure that the future Davidic king would "walk in the way of the kings of Israel" (16:3; compare 8:18 and 27, and see section A1 above). Even after the fall of the Jehu dynasty, Judean subservience probably continued. Consequently, when Menahem rebuffed Rezin and pursued cooperative relations with Assyria, Jotham also refused to join the Syrian cause. Ahaz later took the same stand.

---

[96] Second Kings 8:18 and 27 report that Jehoram and Ahaziah both married into the Omride house, presumably in order to cement relations between the two kingdoms. Since 2 Kgs 8:16–19 do not name the mother of Jehoram, his father Jehoshaphat may also have been married to an Israelite princess.

[97] According to 1 Kgs 22:4 and 2 Kgs 3:7, Jehoshaphat of Judah declared his submissiveness first to Ahab and then to Jehoram: "I will do what you do; my troops shall be your troops, my horses shall be your horses" (NJPSV). The first narrative, however, probably related originally to Jehoahaz of Israel and so also to a Judean king of the late ninth century, perhaps Joash. (See the studies of J. M. Miller listed in n. 9 above.) Similarly in 2 Kgs 3:4–28, Jehoshaphat's name entered the text secondarily. Nevertheless, his cooperation with the Omride rulers is probable. First Kings 22:45 reports that Jehoshaphat "submitted (*wayyašlēm*) to the king of Israel" (NJPSV). His subordination to Ahab may also be reflected in the Assyrian account of the battle at Qarqar (853). The fact that Shalmanesser III does not mention Judah might indicate that the forces of Jehoshaphat were counted as part of Ahab's troops. The assumption would explain the strikingly large contribution of the Israelite king to the coalition's forces (see *ANET* 278–79).

Biblical Accounts of the Syro-Ephraimitic Crisis 107

The situation changed dramatically when Pekah became king in Samaria and brought Israel into league with Syria. He and Rezin probably expected that Ahaz would follow suit and cooperate finally with the coalition. The Judean king, however, refused. Consequently, Rezin and Pekah invaded Judah to replace Ahaz with a more pliant ruler (Isa 7:6), though perhaps not before first arranging Zichri's attempt on the king's life (2 Chr 28:7).

If the above scenario is correct, a long prelude of Syrian aggression led up to the Syro-Ephraimitic crisis. Rezin had been working several years to unite the states of Phoenicia and Palestine into an anti-Assyrian block under his control. The attack on Ahaz was simply the last of many steps taken to solidify the coalition. This view of the war, along with our interpretation of the Assyrian texts, suggest that the Syro-Ephraimitic crisis occurred before Tiglathpileser's Philistine campaign.

A more precise dating of the war is possible, if one accepts the royal chronology advanced in Chapter Two (see the appendix). The *terminus a quo* is Pekah's rise to the throne in Samaria. This event occurred between the Judean new year festival in Tishri 734 and the Israelite celebration a month later. The Philistine campaign is the *terminus ad quem*. Begrich, Donner, and others assume that the Assyrian invasion occurred at the beginning of Tiglathpileser's eleventh year (that is, in the late spring or early summer of 734). The Eponym List, however, does not date it precisely (see Chapter Two, section A). Quite possibly the campaign began as late as January or February of 733. If so, Rezin and Pekah would have attacked Ahaz sometime during the winter months of 734–733.

c. The Payment of Ahaz

Begrich, Donner, and Oded all speak of Ahaz's special appeal and payment to Tiglathpileser. They agree that the Assyrian king invaded Palestine for his own separate reasons, but believe nevertheless that Ahaz sought his intervention. This view rests largely on 2 Kgs 16:5–9. Our analysis of the text, however, suggests that the idea of the appeal and special payment (*šōḥad*) was fabricated by the deuteronomistic editors (see section A3). Ahaz probably paid Assyrian tribute only after Tiglathpileser entered the region. Several considerations support this conclusion.

(1) A special appeal by Ahaz makes poor political sense. The overall pattern of Tiglathpileser's western campaigns indicates that he was bent on controlling the entire Eastern Mediterranean Seaboard (see Chapter Two, section A) and needed no invitation to suppress coalitions directed against Assyrian hegemony in the area. If the Judean king and his advisors had any political sense, they

would have realized that they only needed to wait for Tiglathpileser to move against Rezin and Pekah.

(2) One would expect the Assyrians to have treated Ahaz favorably, if he, one of the few leaders in Palestine who did not join forces with Rezin, had submitted to Assyrian vassalage early in the crisis, calling at the same time for help against the coalition.[98] In fact, they handled the Judean king little differently from other rulers: tribute was imposed[99] and territory lost to the Edomites and Philistines was left unrestored.[100]

(3) II R 67 records the tribute of Ahaz, but makes no special comment about it (see Chapter Two, section B4). The king in fact is listed among other tributaries like Hanno, who had rebelled against Assyria but subsequently surrendered. If the Judean king had made a special appeal for help, the Assyrian scribes might have recorded it to the praise of Tiglathpileser. Not a word, however, is heard in the inscriptions about any appeal.

(4) Isaiah 10:27d–32 (34) might reflect the prophet's support for Ahaz on the very night or morning before the siege of Jerusalem (see Chapter Ten below). If the king still enjoyed Isaiah's favor at this point in the crisis, Ahaz would seem to have waited until the last hour to send messengers to Tiglathpileser. In this case, however, the timing of the decision would have been poor, for members of the coalition now surrounded the Judean king on three sides. Syrian and Israelite troops controlled the highways leading north from Jerusalem. On the west, the Philistines controlled the access to the main coastal highway. On the east, the main route along the Transjordan plateau led through territory controlled by Rezin, Pekah, and Samsi. Only with difficulty could the Judean embassy have made its way past the enemy forces.

D. Summary

A summary sketch of the Syro-Ephraimitic crisis recapitulates the major conclusions of the preceding discussion. The war was the culmination of a long effort by Rezin of Syria to create a coalition of

---

[98]K. Budde ("Jesaja und Ahas," 125–38) also argues this point. He draws, however, the wrong conclusion, namely, that Ahaz's appeal to Assyria was politically unwise.

[99]See II R 67 rev. 7–12. Second Kings 16:8 suggests that the tribute was high, and vv 17–18 might reflect the difficulty that Ahaz had in making the payment (see section A2).

[100]Second Kings 16:6 indicates that the Edomites retained control of Elath long after the Assyrian invasions. The Shephelah and Negeb remained in Philistine hands until the reign of Hezekiah (compare 2 Chr 28:18, 2 Kgs 18:8 and 1 Chr 4:41).

Biblical Accounts of the Syro-Ephraimitic Crisis

states which, under his control, could resist Assyria. Rezin applied pressure first to Jotham and then to Ahaz, but the Judean kings refused to cooperate, following the lead of their Israelite superiors, Menahem and Pekahiah. With Pekah's coup in Samaria (fall 734), Israel joined the Syrian cause, but Ahaz insisted on remaining neutral. He thus asserted the independence of Judah and the Davidic house in foreign affairs for the first time in decades. The Syrian-Israelite attack against Ahaz was intended to enlist total Judean support for the coalition.

Rezin and Pekah besieged Jerusalem late in 734 or early in 733. (At the same time or perhaps earlier, their Philistine and Edomite allies also invaded Judean territory.) The siege, however, was aborted when Tiglathpileser marched against the coalition (early 733), striking first in the Philistine region. Ahaz submitted voluntarily to the Assyrian king and paid tribute after the Assyrians had arrived in the area. Members of the coalition, especially Syria, Israel, and Tyre, continued their resistance two more years.

The study of the speeches of Isaiah in Part II supplements this reconstruction of the Syro-Ephraimitic crisis. We have already referred to one important detail documented in Isa 7:6: Rezin and Pekah intended to replace Ahaz with a certain Ben Tabeel. The plan, we will see, makes good sense in light of his particular identity and Tyre's central role in the coalition. Other details of the war include the peculiar route of the Syrian and Israelite armies as they approached Jerusalem (see Isa 10:27d–32) and the political polarization within Judean society at the time (see Isa 8:6). The latter, we will see, is particularly important for understanding Isaiah. While many Judeans advocated cooperation with Rezin, the prophet strongly supported the neutralist policy of Ahaz.

PART II

ISAIAH AND THE SYRO-EPHRAIMITIC CRISIS

CHAPTER FOUR

THE SOURCE MATERIAL

Part II examines the posture of Isaiah during the Syro-Ephraimitic crisis. At the outset, however, two preliminary issues must be addressed. (1) Which texts in the book of Isaiah relate to the crisis or its immediate prelude? (2) Did the theological interests of editors or collectors significantly shape the presentation of material relating to the war? The latter question calls for a re-examination of the widely accepted *Denkschrift* hypothesis (see Chapter One, sections D and E).

A. The Selection of Texts

Isaiah 7:1–17 narrates the encounter(s) between Isaiah and Ahaz just prior to the Syrian-Israelite siege of Jerusalem. It is thus a third account of the crisis alongside 2 Kgs 16:5–9 and 2 Chr 28:5–21. The narrative is particularly important for our purposes because it purports to present the political-theological stand of the prophet.

Several speeches of Isaiah also relate to the Syro-Ephraimitic war, but scholars debate the exact number of relevant texts. There is a broad concensus that 8:1–4, 5–8, 11–15, and 17:1–6 derive from the eighth-century prophet and fit this context. Different commentators date other passages to the war, for example 3:1–15, 5:25–29 (30), 7:18–25, 8:8b–10, 16–20, 9:7–20 (or 10:4), and 10:27d–34, but the extent of scholarly agreement varies from text to text.

The present work interprets the whole of Isaiah 7–12, with the exception of a few editorial additions and scribal glosses, in connection with the Syro-Ephraimitic crisis. The textual basis of the investigation is thus far broader than that of previous studies.[1] The exegesis of the

---

[1] Compare the more limited selection of texts by H. Donner (*Israel unter den Völkern*, 1–39), N. K. Gottwald (*All the Kingdoms of the Earth*, 150–60), W. Dietrich (*Jesaja und die Politik*, 87–99), J. M. Asurmendi (*La Guerra Siro-Efraimita*, 59–103), and M. E. W. Thompson (*Situation and Theology*, 22–62).

individual texts can alone justify this selection of material. It suffices here to explain our reasons for discounting other passages. Four texts merit special attention.

(1) J. M. Asurmendi suggests dating 3:1–15 to the Syro-Ephraimitic crisis.[2] The references to juvenile rulers in vv 4 and 12, he contends, might allude to the youth and inexperience of Ahaz when he first became king (735, according to Asurmendi's reckoning). The woman rulers mentioned in v 12 may be the queen mother and other women of the royal court, who perhaps guided the young king's political decisions. Asurmendi argues further that the picture of social disorder and injustice throughout the text might reflect the chaotic conditions of Ahaz's reign. Finally, vv 6–9 possibly reflect widespread Judean dissatisfaction with Ahaz and the people's preference for Ben Tabeel as king (compare 7:6, 8:6, 11–15).

This interpretation is not convincing. While the text assumes the disorder and injustice of Judean society, there is little reason to think that such conditions characterized the reign of Ahaz particularly. (Second Kings 16 and Second Chronicles 28 say nothing about social disorder and injustice during the rule of Ahaz.) They might have obtained just as likely during the rule of Jotham. Furthermore, Judean dissatisfaction with Ahaz, correctly observed by Asurmendi in 8:6 and 11–15, is hardly clear in 3:1–15. The text operates on a more general level, imagining first the social chaos which would ensue if untrained persons ruled Judah (vv 4–7), and then declaring that the present leaders of the nation have done no better (vv 8–15). Isaiah condemns and threatens the ruling elite (vv 13–15), but conspicuously excludes the king from the list of officials whom Yahweh will remove (vv 1–3). Finally, Ahaz may not have been the young inexperienced monarch that Asurmendi imagines. According to our chronology, he became king in 743/742 and thus had been ruling almost a decade before the Syro-Ephraimitic crisis (see Chapter Two, the appendix). Dating the 3:1–15 is difficult, but the text may derive from the earliest years of the prophet's career, before the reign of Ahaz.[3]

(2) A few scholars date 5:25–29 (30) to the Syro-Ephraimitic crisis. N. K. Gottwald correlates vv 26–30 with 7:20 and 8:7–8, and assigns

---

[2]*La Guerra Siro-Efraimita*, 96–99; compare J. Steinmann, *Le Pròphete Isaie. Sa vie, son oeuvre et son temps* (2d ed.; Paris: Cerf, 1955) 104–8.

[3]Several passages in Isaiah 1–5 seem to refer to the earthquake that struck Palestine during the days of Azariah (see 1:5–9, 2:9–22, 5:14–17 and 25; compare Amos 1:1, 9:1, and Zech 14:15). Isa 3:1–15 probably belongs to the same general period, that is, if its present literary position is at all an index of its date. See H. L. Ginsburg, "Isaiah in the Light of History," *CJ* 22 (1967) 1–18; idem., "First Isaiah," *EncJud* 9. 49–60; J. Milgrom, "Did Isaiah Prophesy during the Reign of Uzziah," *VT* 14 (1964) 164–82; K. Koch, *The Prophets: The Assyrian Period* (Philadelphia: Fortress, 1983) 105–20; and J. H. Hayes and S. A. Irvine, *Isaiah, the Eighth-Century Prophet: His Times and His Preaching* (Nashville: Abingdon, 1987) 87–92.

the passages to the time immediately after Ahaz supposedly appealed to Assyria.[4] Isaiah predicted that the Assyrians would overrun not only Syria and Israel, but eventually Judah as well. R. E. Clements interprets 5:26–29 similarly.[5] H. Wildberger construes vv 26–29 as a threat against Israel and assigns the passage to the period just before the Syro-Ephraimitic war.[6] If the verses dated any later, he contends, the prophet would not have referred to the Assyrians so vaguely as "a nation afar off."[7]

Like Isa 3:1–15, 5:25–30 might derive from an earlier period, long before the Syro-Ephraimitic war.[8] The arguments for this dating are two. Verse 25 seems to refer to the earthquake that devastated Palestine sometime toward the middle of the eighth century (see Amos 1:1 and Zech 14:5).[9] If we understand the allusion correctly, the larger text would likely date to the same general period as the earthquake. The catastrophe would have been recent enough for the prophet to appeal effectively to it as an example of divine punishment and as an illustration of disaster yet to come. Furthermore, vv 26–30 describe the future invasion of a "nation afar off," but do not name the enemy specifically. Such vagueness is plausibly explained by the assumption that the text dates to a time when Isaiah was still uncertain about the identity of the nation.[10] This would have been the case during the

---

[4]*All the Kingdoms of the Earth*, 155–56.

[5]*Isaiah 1–39*, 69–70.

[6]*Jesaja 1–12*, 211–12. Wildberger views 5:26–29 as the original conclusion of the Outstretched Hand poem in 9:7–20.

[7]Compare H. Donner, *Israel unter den Völkern*, 66–75. Donner views 5:25–29 as the original ending of 9:7–10:4 and assigns the whole to the aftermath of the Syro-Ephraimitic war. This dating depends on the historical allusions in 9:7–20. Verse 13, Donner contends, reflects on the territorial reduction of Israel to the "rumpstate" of Ephraim in 734–732. Verses 17–20 allegedly refer to tribal warfare in the northern kingdom ca. 732/731, "when the disorder caused by the rise of the usurper Hoshea endangered the structure of the rumpstate." This interpretation, however, is not the only possibility. Verses 7–20 might well allude to events before the Syro-Ephraimitic crisis (see Chapter Eight below). In any case, the original connection between 5:25–29 (30) and 9:7–20 (or 10:4) is by no means certain, notwithstanding the wide acceptance of this view (see section B1 below).

[8]See B. Duhm, *Das Buch Jesaja* (5th ed.; Göttingen: Vandenhoeck & Ruprecht, 1968) 61; F. Delitzsch, *Biblical Commentary on the Prophecies of Isaiah* (3d ed.; 2 vols.; New York: Funk & Wagnalls, 1889) 1. 136–42; J. Skinner, *The Book of the Prophet Isaiah. Chapters I–XXXIX* (2d ed.; Cambridge: Cambridge University Press, 1915) 85–86; J. Milgrom, "Did Isaiah Prophesy during the Reign of Uzziah?" 168–69.

[9]J. Skinner (*Isaiah*, 42), G. A. Smith (*The Book of Isaiah* [2 vols.; New York: Armstrong, 1888–90] 1. 50), and G. Fohrer (*Das Buch Jesaja*, 1. 150) similarly understand v 25. Compare H. Wildberger's interpretation of the verse as a metaphorical reference to military disaster (*Jesaja 1–12*, 222).

[10]See J. Milgrom, "Did Isaiah Prophesy during the Reign of Uzziah?" 169.

740s, when Assyria and Urartu were struggling for the control of northern Syria. Only after 740 did Assyria emerge clearly as the dominant power in the Near East.

(3) Most scholars assign 17:1–6 to the period of the Syro-Ephraimitic crisis.[11] This dating rests largely on the following arguments. Verses 1–3 treat Damascus and Israel together, as though they were allies, and thus reflect the political situation in Syria and Palestine during the late 730s. Verse 3a threatens the cessation of kingship in Damascus and thus assumes that the Syrian monarchy has not yet fallen. The announcement must date then before 732, when the Assyrians executed Rezin and made Damascus a province. Verses 4–6 anticipate imminent disaster on Israel: the "glory of Jacob will be brought low" and only a mere remnant of the nation will be left. The prediction assumes an intact Israel and thus must derive from the time before the Assyrians confiscated large parts of the kingdom (733–732).

Several considerations suggest the possibility of dating 17:1–6 to a later period. The text assumes an alliance between Damascus and Israel, but this fact does not necessarily point to the Syro-Ephraimitic crisis. The two were probably in league also in 728–727, when revolt against Assyria again erupted throughout the west.[12] During the re-

---

[11]See, for example, G. Fohrer, *Das Buch Jesaja*, 1. 212–15; H. Donner, *Israel unter den Völkern*, 38–42; E. Vogt, "Jesaja und die drohende Eroberung Palästinas durch Tiglatpileser" in *Wort, Lied und Gottesspruch. Beiträge zu Psalmen und Propheten. Festschrift für Joseph Ziegler* (ed. J. Schreiner; Würzburg: Echter Verlag/Katholisches Bibelwerk, 1972) 249–56; F. Huber, *Die anderen Völker*, 27–34; H. Wildberger, *Jesaja 13–27* (BKAT 10/2; Neukirchen-Vluyn: Neukirchener Verlag, 1978) 633–63; J. M. Asurmendi, *La Guerra Siro-Efraimita*, 99–103; and R. E. Clements, *Isaiah 1–39*, 156–61. Compare, however, the Hellenistic dating of the text by O. Kaiser (*Isaiah 13–39* [London/Philadelphia: SCM/Westminster, 1974] 75–80). A survey of the literature shows wide disagreement over the compositional history of the material. The interpretations range between Fohrer's division of vv 1–6 into six separate speeches and Donner's view of vv 1–3, 4–6, and 10–11 as three strophes of a single poem.

[12]Several sources attest to the uprising. The Assyrian inscription, II R 67 rev. 16, notes that Tiglathpileser sent a *rabšaq* to Tyre and received from Metenna, the ruler of the city, the exorbitant sum of 150 talents of gold. The incident likely reflects political disturbances in the west toward the very end of Tiglathpileser's reign. References in the Eponym List to the events of 728–726 are fragmentary, but probably they once recorded the revolt of Damascus and the subsequent march of the Assyrian army against the city (see Chapter Two, section A). During the fighting, Shalmaneser V apparently succeeded his father and continued the campaign. The Jewish historian, Josephus, reports Shalmaneser's invasion of Syria and Phoenicia, quoting at length the description of the campaign by the Greek author, Menander, who allegedly was dependent on Tyrian archives (*Ant* IX, 283–87). Second Kings 17:3 appears to indicate Hoshea's involvement in the revolt: "Shalmaneser the king of Assyria came up against him and Hoshea became his servant and paid tribute to him." Hosea 10:14 alludes to the brutal mea-

volt, the Syrian monarchy may have revived in Damascus. If so, the prediction of its demise in v 3a would have made sense in 728–727.

The Masoretic text of v 2 announces the desertion of the cities (or citadels) of Aroer (*ʿăzūbôt ʿārê ʿărōʿēr*).[13] Assuming that the verse is senseless in a context that otherwise treats of Damascus and Israel, most scholars either emend the Hebrew[14] or assume that the verse originally belonged elsewhere.[15] Neither proposal, however, is necessary. The Masoretic text should be retained and interpreted as a reference to the military actions of Shalmaneser V in 727, when he suppressed the revolt in Transjordan (compare Hos 10:14 and Isaiah 15–16). Isaiah probably intended the announcement as a warning to Damascus that its own fall would soon follow.

Contrary to the assumption of many scholars, vv 4–6 do not necessarily envision a large Israelite kingdom, as it supposedly existed before the Assyrian campaigns of 733 and 732.[16] The argument loses force particularly if the nation did not in fact lose much territory to Assyria during those years (see Chapter Two above). Be that as it may, the "glory of Jacob" might well refer to Hoshea's kingdom, or possibly to the capital city of Samaria. In either case, the verses make reasonable sense against the background of the revolt in 728–727. Isaiah denounced Israel's involvement in the events and anticipated the brutal response of the Assyrians.

(4) Isaiah 6 reports the prophet's vision of the heavenly divine council, his purification and commission to prevent the repentance of "this people," and the resolve of Yahweh to punish them.[17] Accord-

---

sures of Shalmaneser against Beth-arbel in Transjordan. Finally, Isaiah 15–16 might reflect Moabite participation in the rebellion and the results of the Assyrian response (see G. Smith, "A New Fragment," 328).

[13]The Hebrew Bible knows of different towns by this name: a Moabite Aroer on the northern edge of the Arnon gorge (Num 32:34, Deut 2:36, 2 Sam 24:5, and Jer 48:19); an Aroer in Gad near Rabbah-Ammon, the Ammonite capital (Josh 13:25 and Judg 11:33); and an Aroer south of Beersheba (1 Sam 30:28).

[14]Most scholars accept the reading proposed by P. de Lagarde ("Kritische Anmerkungen zum Buche Isaias," *Semitica* 1 [1878] 30): "Its cities [those of Damascus] are deserted forever" (*ʿăzūbôt ʿārêhā ʿădê ʿad*).

[15]H. Wildberger (*Jesaja 13–27*, 635) and R. E. Clements (*Isaiah 1–39*, 158) suggest that the verse once stood among the sayings against Moab in Isaiah 15–16.

[16]See especially H. Donner, *Israel unter den Völkern*, 41; H. Wildberger, *Jesaja 13–27*, 646–50; and R. E. Clements, *Isaiah 1–39*, 157.

[17]The vast majority of scholars credit the account to the eighth-century prophet, discounting however vv 12–13 as secondary additions. The genuineness of the report is supported not only by its autobiographical style, but also by the ancient cultic, theological, and royal traditions within the text. See W. Schmidt, "Jerusalemer El-Traditionen bei Jesaja: Ein religionsgeschichtlicher Vergleich zum Vorstellungsbereich des göttlichen Königtums," *ZRGG* 16 (1964) 302–13; R. Knierim, "The Vocation of Isaiah," *VT* 18 (1968) 48–57; H. Cazelles, "La Vocation d'Isaie (ch. 6) et les rites royaux," in *Homenaje a Juan Prado* (eds. L. Alvarez

ing to the opening clause of v 1, the vision occurred during the death year of Uzziah (Azariah).[18] If the king died in 734/733, as our chronology proposes (see Chapter Two, the appendix), the vision would date to the period of the Syro-Ephraimitic crisis.[19] The report in Isaiah 6, however, does not reflect directly on the events of the crisis, and for this reason we do not analyze it in detail. Two features of the account, nevertheless, merit comment.

(a) Verses 9–11 speak of the unrepentance and destruction of "this people," but do not specify their precise identity. A. Heschel thinks it unlikely that the mission of the prophet would aim at preventing the repentance and deliverance of his own people. He thus suggests that the prophecy applies to the northern kingdom.[20] Most scholars, however, understand "this people" as a broad reference to the Judeans—both the Davidic king and his subjects alike—who rejected the advice of Isaiah during the Syro-Ephraimitic crisis.

Other sayings of Isaiah against "this people" suggest a different interpretation. Isaiah 8:6 denounces "this people" for supporting the kings of Syria and Israel. The text likely refers to a significant number of Judeans who favored the anti-Assyrian coalition and thus disagreed with the isolationist stand of Ahaz during the Syro-

---

Verdes and E. J. Alonso Hernandez; Madrid: Consejo Superior de Investigaciones Cientificios, 1975) 89–108; and A. Schoors, "Isaiah, the Minister of Royal Anointment?" *OTS* 20 (1977) 85–107. C. F. Whitley ("The Call and Mission of Isaiah," *JNES* 18 [1959] 38–48), O. Kaiser (*Isaiah 1–12*, 118–121), and B. O. Long ("Prophetic Authority as Social Reality," in *Canon and Authority: Essays in Old Testament Religion and Theology* [eds. G. W. Coats and B. O. Long; Philadelphia: Fortress, 1977] 11–13) present lexical, theological, and sociological arguments against Isaiah's authorship, but they are not conclusive.

[18]If the notation were an integral part of the vision report, the report would likely date to a later time, after "the year that King Uzziah died." C. Hardmeier ("Verkündigung und Schrift bei Jesaja, 126–27) thus remarks that "the explicit dating as such is an indication of the distance between the narrated events and the time of the report's composition." The temporal clause in v 1, however, might be a heading secondarily prefixed to the account when it was deposited in the official Judean archives (compare 14:28). If so, there may have been no significant time gap between the vision experience and its report. Compare J. Jenni, "Jesajas Berufung in der neueren Forschung," *TZ* 15 (1959) 329; M. Kaplan, "Isaiah 6:1–11," *JBL* 45 (1926) 255; and R. Knierim, "Vocation," 49.

[19]This interpretation could supplement other arguments against the widespread view of Isaiah 6 as an account of the prophet's inaugural call. In addition to the studies cited above in n. 3, see Y. Kaufmann, *The Religion of Israel: From Its Beginnings to the Babylonian Exile* (Chicago: University of Chicago Press, 1960) 388; F. Horst, "Die Visionsschilderungen des alttestamentlichen Propheten," *EvT* 20 (1960) 198; O. H. Steck, "Bemerkungen zu Jesaja 6," *BZ* 16 (1972) 188–94; and H. Niehr, "Zur Intension von Jes 6.1–9," *BN* 21 (1983) 59–65.

[20]A. Heschel, *The Prophets* (2 vols.; New York/Hagerstown/San Francisco/London: Harper & Row, 1969) 1. 89–90.

Ephraimitic crisis (see Chapter Six below). Isaiah 8:12–15, we will argue, make sense as a reflection of the same political rift within Judean society.[21] If the temple vision of Isaiah dates to the Syro-Ephraimitic crisis, it is reasonable to guess that "this people" in 6:9–11 also refers to the many Judeans who opposed Ahaz. The prophet claimed to have been divinely charged to see that they receive punishment.

(b) The translation and interpretation of 6:13 is difficult.[22] Most commentators view at least the final promise—"the holy seed is its stump"—as an editorial addition or gloss.[23] Similar messages of hope, however, often conclude prophecies of doom in the Near Eastern literature.[24] We accept the verse as the original continuation of v 11[25] and translate it as follows:

> And though a tenth is left in it [the land],
> yet it [the tenth] again will be burned.
> Like the oak and the terebinth when felled,
> a stump [will remain] in it [the land];
> the holy seed is its [the land's] stump.[26]

---

[21]C. Shaw ("Micah 1:10–16 Reconsidered," 223–29) dates Mic 1:10–16 to a time prior to the Syro-Ephraimitic crisis and sees in it the prophet's denunciation of Judean towns in the Shephelah for their anti-Assyrian mood and their disloyalty to the Davidic monarchy.

[22]For text-critical discussions of the verse, see I. Engnell, *The Call of Isaiah: An Exegetical and Comparative Study* (Uppsala/Leipzig: A.-B. Lundequistska/Otto Harrassowitz, 1949) 18–19; W. H. Brownlee, "The Text of Isaiah VI 13 in the Light of DSIa," *VT* 1 (1951) 296–98; F. Hvidberg, F. "The Masseba and the Holy Seed," *NTT* 56 (1955) 97–99; W. F. Albright, "The High Place in Ancient Palestine," *VTSup* 4 (1957) 254; S. Iwry, "*Maṣṣēbāh* and *Bāmāh* in 1 Q Isaiah^A 6:13," *JBL* 76 (1957) 225–32; P. Skehan, "Qumran and the Present State of Old Testament Text Studies: The Masoretic Text," *JBL* 78 (1959) 23; J. W. Sawyer, "The Qumran Reading of Isaiah 6:13," *ASTI* 3 (1964) 11–13; G. R. Driver, "Isaiah I–XXXIX: Textual and Linguistic Problems," *JSS* 13 (1968) 38; G. W. Ahlström, "Isaiah VI. 13," *JSS* 19 (1974) 169–72; and J. A. Emerton, "The Translation and Interpretation of Isaiah VI. 13," in *Interpreting the Hebrew Bible: Essays in Honor of E. I. J. Rosenthal* (eds. J. A. Emerton and S. Reif; Cambridge/New York: Cambridge University Press, 1982) 85–118.

[23]See however K. Budde, "Über die Schranken," 167; E. König, *Das Buch Jesaja* (Gütersloh: Bertelsmann, 1926) 97; F. Feldmann, *Das Buch Isaias* (2 vols.; Muenster: Aschendorff, 1925–26) 1. 76–77; I. Engnell, *The Call of Isaiah*, 46–51; E. J. Kissane, *The Book of Isaiah* (2 vols.; Dublin: Browne and Nolan, 1941–43) 1. 74; G. W. Ahlström, "Isaiah VI. 13," 169–70; and H. Cazelles, "La vocation d'Isaïe," 90–96, 105. These scholars regard v 13 as genuine to the vision report.

[24]See G. W. Ahlström, "Isaiah VI. 13," 169, especially n. 2.

[25]The third-person reference to Yahweh in v 12 marks this verse apart as a secondary interpolation.

[26]This rendering presupposes changing *bām* ("in them") to *bāh* ("in it") at the end of v 13ba. The emendation accords with the reading of several ancient Hebrew manuscripts.

While the first half of the verse concludes the description of disaster soon to befall "this people," the second half speaks hopefully about a "stump" (*maṣṣebet*) and the "holy seed" (*zeraʿ qōdeš*). The language here is metaphorical and thus hard to understand, but it may allude to the royal house.[27] If so, the sense of the saying might be paraphrased: just as the stump of certain kinds of trees is the source of new growth (see Job 14:7–9), so the Davidic house will survive the disaster and flourish (compare Isa 11:1).[28] Isaiah, we will argue, draws the same contrast between the dismal fate of many Judeans and the deliverance of the royal house in 8:5–10 and 11–15 (see Chapter Six below).

B. The Denkschrift Hypothesis

A second issue concerns the possible editorial shaping of Isaiah (6) 7–12. Did distinctive theological interests significantly guide the selection and arrangement of the material? The question has been raised especially in regard to 6:1–9:6, the so-called *Denkschrift* of Isaiah. Scholars debate the original form of the document[29] and its authorship,[30] but most agree that apart from its secondary additions, the

---

[27]The only other reference to the "holy seed" occurs in Ezra 9:2. There, however, the concept has been reinterpreted so as to apply to the post-exilic community. Compare Isa 55:3–5, where the exilic prophet similarly "democratizes" the Davidic tradition.

[28]The term *maṣṣebet* (or *maṣṣēbâ*) might refer also to a dynastic stela in the Jerusalem temple, signifying the perpetuity of the Davidic house. (Compare 1 Kgs 17:5, 2 Kgs 11:14, and 23:3, although the term *ʿammûd* is used in these texts. See H. Cazelles, "La vocation d'Isaie," 90–96.) If so, the Jerusalemite audience of the prophet would certainly have caught this double meaning. Disaster might befall many Judeans, but the royal family and its supporters would survive to become the basis of the nation's revival.

[29]The argument concerns particularly the genuineness of passages like 7:18–25, 8:8b–10, and 8:23b–9:6. Recent commentators generally follow K. Marti's view of 8:16–18 as the original conclusion of the *Denkschrift* ("Der jesajanische Kern," 113–21). See, for example, H. W. Wolff, *Frieden ohne Ende*, 11; O. H. Steck, "Jesaja 6," 198–203; T. Lescow, "Jesajas Denkschrift," 315–31; H.-P. Müller, "Glauben und Bleiben," 25–54; C. Hardmeier, "Verkündigung und Schrift bei Jesaja," 119–34; and W. Werner, "Vom Prophetenwort zur Prophetentheologie. Ein redaktionskritischer Versuch zu Jes 6,1–8,18," *BZ* 29 (1985) 1–30. T. Lescow ("Jesajas Denkschrift," 315–31) is one of the few scholars who regard Isaiah 6 as a secondary addition, albeit authored by Isaiah.

[30]While the majority of scholars attribute the collection of the material to Isaiah the prophet, W. Dietrich (*Jesaja und die Politik*, 62–87) and W. Werner ("Vom Prophetenwort zur Prophetentheologie," 1–30) think of an anonymous redactor who assembled and edited the document. J. Lindblom (*The Immanuel Section*, 3–6) and P. R. Ackroyd ("Isaiah I–XII: Presentation of a Prophet," *VTSup* 29 (1977) 40–44; idem., "Historians and Prophets," 26–33) similarly attribute the collection of

Denkschrift constitutes a cohesive whole which once circulated independently. Expositions of the *Denkschrift* usually assume a high degree of thematic/theological unity for the document, if not also stylistic and structural cohesion. Consequently, the tendentious presentation of the material is sometimes adduced as the reason for why certain details of the Syro-Ephraimitic crisis, for example, the appeal of Ahaz to Assyria, go unmentioned.[31] The issue obviously impinges on our use of the material to sketch the war and the posture of the prophet during it.

In recent years the widespread assumption of a *Denkschrift* has obscured the fact that the existence of such a document is only a theory. R. Kilian aptly remarks in this regard:

> Should not [the assumption] of the *Denkschrift* be questioned more than has been done so far? It is, after all, no more than a hypothesis. Yet one has argued with it during the last decade as though it were beyond all doubt.[32]

Upon review, the arguments which support the hypothesis appear doubtful or inconclusive, and some question persists about the unity of 6:1–9:6. The material is not nearly as streamlined as many scholars suggest.

1. *Isaiah 6:1–9:6 as an Interpolation*

Commentators generally view 6:1–9:6 as a large-scale interpolation into a pre-existing collection of Isaianic speeches: a series of woe-sayings (5:8–24 + 10:1–4a) combined with a long poem on the "outstretched hand" of Yahweh (9:7–20 + 5:25–29).[33] Whether the

---

the material to a redactor and avoid using the label *Denkschrift*, or "memoir," altogether. O. Kaiser (*Isaiah 1–12*, 114–17) contends that exilic and post-exilic editors not only assembled the *Denkschrift*, but composed its component parts as well.

[31] See Chapter One, section E, where we review the argument as set forth by P. R. Ackroyd ("Historians and Prophets," 22–37; idem., "The Reigns of Ahaz and Hezekiah," 250) and O. H. Steck ("Rettung und Verstockung," 77–90).

[32] "Der Verstockungsauftrag Jesajas," in *Bausteine biblischer Theologie. Festgabe für G. Johannes Botterweck zum 60. Geburtstag dargebracht von seinen Schülern* (BBB 50; ed. H.-J. Fabry; Cologne: Hanstein, 1977) 212, n. 15. Compare H. G. Reventlow, "Das Ende der sog. 'Denkschrift' Jesajas," *BN* 38/39 (1987) 62–67. Reventlow disputes the understanding of 6:1–9:6 as Isaiah's memoirs, but still maintains the integrity of the material as a redactional unit.

[33] Compare, however, the variant proposals by H. Donner (*Israel unter den Völkern*, 66–75) and C. E. L'Heureux ("The Redactional History of Isaiah 5.1–10.4," in *In the Shelter of Elyon: Essays in Ancient Palestinian Life and Literature in Honor of G. W. Ahlström* [eds. W. B. Barrick and J. R. Spencer; Sheffield: JSOT Press, 1984] 99–119). Donner claims that 10:1–4 is an original part of the Out-

transposition of 10:1–4a and 5:25–29 from their original places was an accident or the deliberate decision of editors is debated.[34] In either case, 6:1–9:6 appears as an independent unit whose investigation is likely to reveal a distinctive structure, message, and purpose.

This interpretation rests heavily on the view that 5:25–29 and 10:1–4 once belonged to 9:7–20 and 5:8–24 respectively. The arguments for this claim, however, are by no means decisive. The Outstretched Hand poem does not demand the continuation which 5:25–29 would provide. It is true, as Wildberger points out,[35] that the roughly analogous speech in Amos 4:6–12 reviews a number of past divine judgments (vv 6–11), and then concludes with a threat of future punishment (v 12). The text, however, is not exactly parallel to Isa 9:7–20. The refrain which punctuates the Amos passage states only the repeated failure of the people to repent (vv 6a, 8a, 9a, 10a, 11a). A concluding announcement of future punishment is thus to be expected. In contrast, the refrain in Isaiah 9 is itself a proclamation of future judgment. The poem comes to a suitable close in 9:20, or possibly 10:4, by claiming that the hand of Yahweh is still extended against Israel. A detailed description of the disaster such as that which 5:26–29 would provide is not necessary.

The "therefore" of Isa 5:25 does not read smoothly after 9:20 or 10:4. This fact has not been lost on scholars and different explanations have been suggested. One proposal argues that 5:25 originally followed 9:9, while 5:26–29 concluded the Outstretched Hand poem.[36] In this case, however, it is difficult to see how 5:25 was dislodged from the middle of the poem and set with vv 26–29 before the *Denkschrift*.[37]

---

stretched Hand poem. The only passage out of place then is 5:25–29, which originally followed 10:4. Alternatively, L'Heureux attributes 10:1–4 to a redactor, who inserted 6:1–9:6 into the Outstretched Hand poem (5:25 + 9:7–20 + 5:26–29). Both scholars follow the majority of commentators in discounting 5:30 as a secondary addition.

[34]The more recent studies stress the logic of a redactor. See J. Vermeylen, *Du prophète Isaie à l'apocalyptique: Isaie, I–XXXV, miroir d'un demi-millenaire d'expérience religieuse en Israel* (2 vols.; Paris: J. Gabalda, 1977) 1. 169–86; H. Barth, *Die Jesaja-Worte in der Josiazeit. Israel und Assur als Thema einer produktiven Neuinterpretation der Jesajaüberlieferung* (WMANT 48; Neukirchen-Vluyn: Neukirchener Verlag, 1977) 111–17; C. E. L'Heureux, "Isaiah 5.1–10.4," 99–119; and G. T. Sheppard, "The Anti-Assyrian Redaction and the Canonical Context of Isaiah 1–39," *JBL* 104 (1985) 193–98.

[35]*Jesaja 1–12*, 209.

[36]See for example W. Staerk, *Das assyrische Weltreich*, 48; and J. Skinner, *Isaiah*, 42.

[37]One might, of course, argue that a redactor intentionally transposed the verse in order to introduce the motif of Yahweh's outstretched hand into Isaiah 5. He might have accomplished his purpose more easily, however, by leaving 9:7–20 intact and simply copying the refrain into Isaiah 5. So O. Kaiser (*Isaiah 1–12*, 111) suggests that an editor composed 5:25 at the same time that he transposed vv 26–

Another solution sees 5:25–29 as the continuation of 9:20, but assumes the loss (or redactional elimination) of several lines before 5:25. The verse then is only a fragment of a larger strophe.[38] This explanation is certainly possible, but very hypothetical. It is an assumption necessitated by what is itself only a theory, namely, that 5:25–29 originally belonged to 9:7–20. It seems easier to argue that 5:25–29 (or 30) does not fit neatly with the Outstretched Hand poem because the two passages in fact never belonged together.

A few scholars adduce the poetic features of 5:25–29 and 9:7–20 (or 10:4) as evidence of the material's unity. H. Donner contends that 9:7–10:4 + 5:25–29 form a single poem which divides into six strophes, each consisting originally of seven bi-cola in 3+3 meter.[39] The argument, however, is weakened by the fact that it requires numerous emendations of the Masoretic text, the exclusion of several lines and phrases as secondary additions, and a questionable reading of the meter.

C. E. L'Heureux also investigates the strophic structure, meter, and other poetic features of 5:25–29 and 9:7–10:4.[40] He concludes that the Outstretched Hand poem originally included five strophes: 5:25 (a fragment), 9:7–11, 12–16, 17–20, and 5:26–29. Each consists of seven bi-cola predominantly in 3+3 meter and exhibits the abundant use of word-play, inclusio and chiasm.[41]

L'Heureux holds more closely to the Masoretic text than does Donner, but his analysis still requires emendations and deletions. Furthermore, by his own reckoning, several lines deviate from the

---

29 from the end of 9:7–20. This interpretation, however, does away with one of the main reasons for seeing an original connection between 5:25–29 and 9:7–20, namely, that the passages share the "same refrain," and with this reason, one of the principal arguments for viewing 6:1–9:6 as an interpolation.

[38]See, for example, B. Duhm, *Das Buch Jesaja*, 61; G. Fohrer, *Das Buch Jesaja*, 1. 144–52; H. Barth, *Die Jesaja-Worte in der Josiazeit*, 108–12; H. Wildberger, *Jesaja 1–12*, 203–29; R. E. Clements, *Isaiah 1–39*, 66–70. Compare the variant interpretation by C. E. L'Heureux ("Isaiah 5.8–10.4," 105–13). He views 5:26–29 as the direct continuation of 9:20 and construes 5:25 as the remainder of a strophe which originally preceded 9:7.

[39]H. Donner, *Israel unter den Völkern*, 66–68, 178–79.

[40]C. E. L'Heureux, "Isaiah 5:1–10:4," 105–13.

[41]L'Heureux attributes 10:1–4 to the redactor who incorporated 6:1–9:6 (the "Emmanuel Booklet") into the Outstretched Hand poem. In composing the verses, the redactor skillfully imitated the strophic structure, meter, and word-play of the original poem. The woe-form of the material and its focus on social injustice parallels the form and content of 5:8–24. The two blocks together form the outer of two inclusios around 6:1–9:6. The framework of the woe-sayings is intended to suggest that "the events during the Syro-Ephraimitic War which led to Assyrian interference in Judean affairs are due to the corruption of justice in society, even though this is not brought out in the Emmanuel Booklet itself" (114).

3+3 meter (5:25a, 9:7, 9, 11a, 13, 15, 16aa, and 18aba). The metrical evidence cannot count much in the debate over literary unity. L'Heureux must also construe 5:25 as the remainder of a larger strophe and hypothesize that a redactor eliminated its initial lines because their content, whatever it might have been, did not suit his purposes.[42] Finally, the alliteration and word-play which L'Heureux correctly detects in 5:25–29 and 9:7–20 might suggest the common Isaianic authorship of the two passages, but not necessarily their literary unity.

The weightiest argument for viewing 5:25–29 and 9:7–20 (10:4) as parts of a single poem is that the "same refrain" runs throughout (5:25b, 9:11b, 16b, 20b, and 10:4b). However, the reasoning here begs the question, for the statement about Yahweh's anger and outstretched hand in 5:25b appears as the "same refrain" only if one assumes its original connection with 9:7–20 (or 10:4). In Isaiah 5, the statement occurs only once and so is not, properly speaking, a refrain at all. It is easier to argue that the prophet used the same line on two different occasions: once during his early career in the context of Isaiah 5; and again during the Syro-Ephraimitic crisis as a refrain in 9:7–10:4.[43] This interpretation appears all the more preferable if we note again that 5:25–29 (or 30) does not fit neatly with 9:7–10:4.

Equally indecisive is the argument that 10:1–4 once belonged to 5:8–24. The woe-form in both passages is alone no guarantee of their literary unity. Furthermore, the form in 10:1–4, along with the focus on future disaster in vv 3–4, make the unit a fitting climax to the his-

---

[42]The argument here is very tenuous, involving as it does a great deal of guesswork about non-extant material and about the logic of the redactor who eliminated it. According to L'Heureux, the work of the redactor aimed in part at directing the divine punishment of Israel (Isaiah 9) against Judah as well (Isaiah 5) and at extending the motif of Yahweh's outstretched hand over the whole of 6:1–9:6. If this interpretation were correct, however, it would be difficult to see why the redactor did not simply compose the material that he wanted to set at the end of 5:8–24. If he were clever and bold enough to write 10:1–4, as L'Heureux contends, he certainly could have managed, and would not have hesitated, to reproduce the "outstretched-hand" refrain in Isaiah 5 and to compose an announcement of judgment similar to what we find in vv 26–29. This way, too, he could have avoided disturbing the Outstretched Hand poem, robbing it not only of its initial strophe, but of the alleged conclusion that it supposedly demands. In short, L'Heureux imagines a redactor who, in certain instances, exhibits tremendous creativity and skill by composing whole passages, but who, in other instances such as 5:25–29, clumsily resorts to transposing verses from another context, even if it does violence to the traditional material and results in the kind of tensions and inconsistencies that L'Heureux believes reflect redaction. These same criticisms apply to the analysis of H. Barth (*Die Jesaja-Worte in der Josiazeit*, 112).

[43]Section A above gives reasons for dating 5:25–29 (30) to the early years of Isaiah's ministry.

torical review in 9:7–20. Finally, the content of the verses might well be in keeping with the rest of the Outstretched Hand poem. Most scholars construe 10:1–4 as a denouncement of social injustice, similar to those in 5:8–24, but another interpretation is also possible. The "decrees" and "writings" mentioned in v 1 might refer to Israelite edicts which Menahem and Pekah had promulgated and which, in the eyes of Isaiah, had affected the Judeans adversely (see Chapter Eight below). If so, the unit smoothly follows the description of Manasseh and Ephraim "against Judah" in 9:20.

The above considerations have questioned the widespread view of 6:1–9:6 as a large-scale interpolation and thus as an originally independent block. Even if the theory were correct, however, doubts might still remain about the internal cohesion of the material. If 6:1–9:6 is more than a loose concatenation of speeches and narrative relating to the Syro-Ephraimitic crisis, this must be demonstrated from the material itself.

2. Stylistic Cohesion

Some versions of the *Denkschrift* hypothesis argue that Isa 6:1–8:18 (or 9:6) cohere stylistically as the autobiographical testimony of the prophet. However, the "I" style in fact occurs only in 6:1–13 and 8:1–18. Isaiah 7:1–17 refer to the prophet in the third-person (vv 3 and 13; compare v 10) and so appear as a narrative about Isaiah. Scholars have noted the discrepancy and have tried to eliminate it by emending the third-person references in chapter 7 to first-person forms. K. Marti, for example, reads: "Yahweh spoke to me" in v 3; "And I spoke further to Ahaz" in v 10; and "And I said" in v 13.[44] Alternatively, Budde emends the third-person references in vv 3 and 13, but retains the Masoretic text in v 10: "And Yahweh continued to speak to Ahaz."[45] Budde contends, however, that v 10 assumes the agency of the prophet and so refers to Yahweh in the sense, "Yahweh through me [Isaiah]." The verse accords, then, with the autobiographical style elsewhere in the *Denkschrift*.[46]

---

[44]"Der jesajanische Kern," 113–21. See also B. Duhm, *Das Buch Jesaja*, 70–75; T. Lescow, "Jesajas Denkschrift," 21; C. Hardmeier, "Verkündigung und Schrift bei Jesaja," 124. R. Kilian (*Die Verheissung Immanuels*, 14) once argued that the autobiographical style was originally present in 7:3, 10, and 13, but recently he has renounced this view ("Der Verstockungsauftrag Jesajas," 211–212).

[45]"Jesajas Erleben," 35–50. See also H. Donner, *Israel unter den Völkern*, 7–9; and R. E. Clements, *Isaiah 1–39*, 82–89.

[46]Restoring the "I" style in 7:1–17 is particularly important to those scholars who ascribe the *Denkschrift* to Isaiah. If one attributes the document to the followers of the prophet or to a later redactor, the third-person references to Isaiah

These explanations are not convincing. Specifically, it is difficult to see why editors or scribes would have changed only a portion of the *Denkschrift* into a third-person account. If the references to Isaiah arose as explanatory glosses, we might expect to see similar glossing in chapters 6 and 8, where the "I" of the prophet would seem to demand clarification as well. In short, the proposed emendations seem to rest on circular reasoning. On the one hand, the first-person forms in 6:1–8:18 (or 9:6) supposedly attest to the existence of a *Denkschrift* in autobiographical form. On the other hand, the *Denkschrift* hypothesis serves as the basis for changing the third-person references to Isaiah in chapter 7 to first-person forms. If we dispense with hypothetical emendations and hold to the Masoretic text, we are left with stylistically diverse materials. Such diversity would be all the more apparent, if we reckon with passages like 7:18–25 and 8:21–9:6, which are neither autobiographical nor narrative.

3. Thematic and Structural Unity

Proponents of the *Denkschrift* hypothesis frequently discern thematic and structural unity in the document. Several factors, however, figure in the argument, including the distinction between original and secondary passages and the assessment of the document's authorship and purpose. Also the exegesis of difficult passages like the Immanuel saying plays a critical role in the debate over theme and structure. An examination of recent studies demonstrates the interplay of these factors and the assumptions which often underlie the analysis.

According to O. H. Steck, the *Denkschrift* depicts the *Verstockung* or "hardening-of-heart" of Ahaz and the Judeans during the Syro-Ephraimitic war.[47] The commission of Isaiah in the heavenly council first announces this *Verstockung*.[48] Its fulfillment is then documented in the prophet's two encounters with the king and royal house (7:3–9 and vv 10–17), and in 8:1–8a, which relate to the people.[49] The three

---

are more easily retained. See for example H. Wildberger, *Jesaja 1–12*, 269–70; and O. Kaiser, *Isaiah 1–12*, 114–17, 134–36, and 151.

[47] O. H. Steck, "Jesaja 6," 188–206; idem., "Rettung und Verstockung," 73–90; idem., "Jesaja 7,10–17 und 8,1–4," 161–78.

[48] Steck ("Jesaja 6," 190–91, n. 10) discounts 6:12–13 as a secondary addition. The genre of vv 1–11, he argues (189–94), is not an account of call, but rather the "giving of an extraordinary assignment in the heavenly throne-assembly" (*Vergabe eines aussergewöhnlichen Auftrags in der himmlischen Thronversammlung*).

[49] Steck ("Jesaja 6," 193–94, 198–203) contends that this fulfillment is an essential part of the genre of Isaiah 6. Chapters 6–8 thus cohere as a single form-critical unit, allowing however for the secondary additions in 6:12–13, 7:1–2, 15, 18–25, 8:8b–10, and 8:19–9:6.

units contain corresponding elements: Yahweh's offer to save Ahaz/Judah from Syria and Israel (7:3–9a; 11, 14+16; 8:1–4); a warning against or reproach for disbelief in the divine promise (7:4, 9b; 12–13; 8:6); and the threat or announcement of judgment against the Judean king/people (7:9b; 14–17; 8:7–8a).[50] A warning to the followers of Isaiah follows in 8:11–15: they should regard Yahweh as the real opponent of Judah, not the Syrian-Israelite coalition which "this people" fears. The *Denkschrift* concludes with a notice about the written record of Isaiah's words and about the fulfillment of the judgment that he predicted (vv 16–18).

This interpretation depends heavily on Steck's distinction between genuine and secondary passages. He excludes the several clear expressions of salvation in 6:13bb, 8:8b–10, and 9:1–6, which seem extraneous to or in conflict with the *Verstockung*-theme. The sayings of judgment against "the land" (Judah) in 7:18–25 are also discounted, in part because they do not conform to Steck's division of the *Denkschrift* into sections on the king and people respectively. One might retain these several texts and argue that the *Denkschrift* is far more diverse in theme and structure than Steck suggests.[51] This diversity would be all the more apparent, if 7:14–17 and 8:16–18 anticipate genuine salvation for Ahaz and the Davidic dynasty (see Chapter One, section C, and Chapters Five and Six below).[52]

---

[50]"Jesaja 6," 198–203, especially 199, n. 29; "Jesaja 7,10–17 und 8,1–4," 165–78, especially 173, n. 45. The crucial difference between 7:3–9 and vv 10–17, Steck contends, is the king's actual rejection of the divine promise (v 12). The Immanuel saying (vv 14–17) reiterates the demise of Syria and Israel, but deprives the promise of its hopeful implications for Ahaz and the Davidic house. They too will suffer disaster (v 17). Isaiah 8:1–8a shows the same movement of thought in regard to the Judean people.

[51]Steck's remarks ("Jesaja 6," 199, n. 28) on 7:18–25 and 8:8b–10 demonstrate the circularity of his reasoning. "The series of sayings in 7:18–23 (25) interrupts the composition of the three units in 7:1–8:8. . . . The series has no direct connection with the preceding scene, for it is not directed to Ahaz and the royal house and does not develop the disaster especially meant for the dynasty. It also anticipates Judah, which becomes the thematic focus, however, only in 8:1–8a. Isaiah 8:9f similarly does not belong to the original *Denkschrift*. The verses stand isolated in their context, run counter to the direction of the *Denkschrift*'s message, and on account of their undifferentiated expression of salvation, do not stem from Isaiah."

[52]Steck ("Jesaja 7,10–17 und 8,1–4," 162–63) insists on interpreting the Immanuel saying as judgment against Ahaz, partly because of the context (vv 11–13) and the "therefore" (*lākēn*) in v 14 (supposedly an indication of judgment). Chapter Five below will address these arguments. Noteworthy here is the circularity of Steck's reasoning when he adds that the interpretation of 7:14–17 as salvation for Ahaz/Judah "becomes completely untenable, once one recognizes that Isaiah wants to document in these units the fulfillment of the *Verstockung*-command." His remark on 8:17–18 is similar: "In no way do 8:17–18 have a hopeful

Other studies of the *Denkschrift* reckon with at least some of the salvation passages excluded by Steck. They consequently discern a more complex message and structure in the material. H.-P. Müller, for example, underscores the *Verstockung*-theme, but he sees in combination with it an interest in the dialectic of faith.[53] A series of paired expressions, he argues, articulates the two sides of faith. (1) Salvation is in store for Ahaz and Judah insofar as the Syrian-Israelite attack will fail (7:4–9a, 7:16, 8:1–4, 8:9–10). (2) Disaster awaits the king and people, for Assyria will overrun the country (7:9b, 7:17, 8:5–8a, 8:11–15). While the promise of salvation remains unconditional throughout the *Denkschrift*, the threat of disaster in 7:9b changes to an unconditional announcement (7:17, 8:5–8a, 8:11–15), once Ahaz appeals to Assyria for help.

The dialectical pattern which Müller highlights is far from certain. It disappears, for example, in 7:16–17, if one interprets v 17, apart from the secondary "king of Assyria," as an announcement of salvation (see Chapter One, section C, and Chapter Five below). The pattern appears even less consistent, if 7:18–25 is included as part of the *Denkschrift*. Most importantly, Müller is able to accomodate the expressions of salvation in 7:16 and 8:9–10 only by denying them any real implication of hope for Ahaz and/or the Judeans. At least in the case of 8:9–10, however, the jubilant tone of the passage weighs against this interpretation. If one reckons with 6:13bb and 9:1–6, Müller's attempt to reconcile the expressions of salvation and judgment in the *Denkschrift* appears even less successful.

A second way of reconciling the messages of salvation and judgment is to assume that they pertain to different groups. The redaction-critical analysis of 7:1–8:18 by W. Dietrich is a recent example of this approach.[54] Dietrich contends that the material highlights the negative responses of Ahaz and the Judeans to Yahweh's offer of salvation. In the case of the king (7:1–25), the rejection of the divine promise (vv 9b–12) leads to the announcement of judgment (vv 17–20) and the description of its dire consequences (vv 21–25). In contrast, Yahweh's word of salvation to the people (8:1–4) effects a division among them. To those who do not believe, judgment and its severe results are proclaimed (vv 5–8a, 11–15). To those who do believe, salvation is again promised and its positive consequences are described (vv 8b–10, 16–18). At the center of the material stands the

---

outlook, which would contradict the entire flow of the message of the three units [7:3–9, 10–17, and 8:1–8a] and the warning in 8:11–15 . . . ." ("Jesaja 6," 201, n. 33). Steck here begs the very issue, namely, the thematic unity of the *Denkschrift*.

[53] H.-P. Müller, "Glauben und Bleiben," 25–54. See Chapter One, section D above.

[54] W. Dietrich, *Jesaja und die Politik*, 60–87.

double message of the Immanuel sign (7:14–16): judgment for Ahaz and the many Judeans who lack faith; salvation for the few believers.

Dietrich attributes the *Denkschrift* to an anonymous redactor, but says little about the setting, audience, and purpose of the document. His silence on these issues is not surprising, for Dietrich's real concerns are to recover the original speeches of Isaiah and thereby to sketch the stand of the prophet during the Syro-Ephraimitic crisis. In contrast, more recent studies of 6:1–8:18 (or 9:6) are principally interested in the redaction of the material itself and construe its message as one intended specifically for an exilic audience. The analysis of W. Werner is representative.[55]

Werner locates the original *Denkschrift* in 6:1–13, 7:1–17, 18–25, 8:1–4, 5–8a, 11–15, and 16–18.[56] A redactor, influenced by the deuteronomistic prophetic theology, assembled and edited the material, and even assumed the role of the prophet (8:16–18). The document served as instruction and encouragement to the exiles. To them it made the following points.

(a) Unlike Hezekiah, Ahaz and the Judeans lacked faith in the prophetic word. Consequently, Isaiah announced judgment against them (7:1–17, 18–25, 8:5–8a, 11–15).[57]

(b) The faithlessness of the king and people fulfilled the *Verstockung*-command earlier given by Yahweh to Isaiah (6:9–11). Isaiah's status as a genuine prophet was thus vindicated.

(c) The judgment came to pass in the subsequent history of the nation, especially the exile.[58] Again, the validity of the prophetic commission was established.

(d) The exiles should not emulate the example of "this people," that is, the generation of Ahaz, but rather should believe the word of Yahweh's prophets and "fear" God (8:11–13).

(e) Isaiah also spoke reservedly about salvation beyond the judgment (6:12–13), and that hope extends to the exiles. If they truly fear Yahweh, they can expect Yahweh to turn to them in favor.

(f) The redactor and his disciples vouch for the validity of the prophetic commission. They testify to the fulfillment of divine judg-

---

[55] W. Werner, "Vom Prophetenwort zur Prophetentheologie," 1–30. Compare O. Kaiser, *Isaiah 1–12*, 114–17; P. R. Ackroyd, "Isaiah I–XII," 40–46; idem., "Historians and Prophets," 26–33. Ackroyd wisely avoids the term *Denkschrift* or "memoir."

[56] Werner ("Vom Prophetenworte zur Prophetentheologie," 6, n. 30; 16, n. 68) interprets 8:9–10 and 9:1–6 as "eschatological" texts secondarily added to an already expanded *Denkschrift*.

[57] Werner sees secondary expansions in 7:1, 4b, 5b, 8b, 15, 16b, 17b, 21–22, 8:6b, 7ab, 7b, and 8a.

[58] Isaiah 6:12–13 and 8:14–15, Werner argues, look retrospectively on the fall of Jerusalem and the deportation of Judeans in 586.

ment in past history and look forward to Yahweh's merciful dealings with his people in the future (8:16–18).

It is instructive to note how far this version of the *Denkschrift* hypothesis has evolved from the early proposals of K. Budde and K. Marti (see Chapter One, sections A and D). Marti, we have seen, attributes the document to Isaiah, but excludes those passages which anticipate future (eschatological) salvation. Budde, on the other hand, views the whole of 6:1–9:6 as the prophet's memoir, and consequently construes its meaning as a two-fold message: disaster awaits Ahaz and the many Judeans who lack faith, but hope abides for the survival and welfare of a remnant. Werner follows Marti in discounting much of 6:1–9:6 as secondary to the *Denkschrift*, but like Budde, he nevertheless maintains that the original document not only announced judgment, but also expressed a genuine hope in the future. Werner reconciles the two messages, however, by attributing their combination to an exilic redactor. Judgment and salvation are understood to apply respectively to the pre-exilic ancestors and the generation of the exiles.

The above survey has highlighted how the assessment of the message and structure of the *Denkschrift* involves a number of variable factors. It is apparent also, however, that the different interpretations share a common denominator. All assume that, throughout 6:1–9:6, Ahaz and "this people" are closely associated for their lack of faith and Isaiah is pitted against them both. A closer look at 6:1–9:6 raises doubts about this assumption.

Isaiah 8:6 criticizes "this people" because they "rejoice in Rezin and the son of Remaliah [Pekah]." The verse thus suggests that many Judeans supported the Syrian-Israelite coalition that besieged Jerusalem (see Chapter Six below). According to 7:6, the goal of the attack was to replace Ahaz with another king. Interpreted together, 7:6 and 8:6 imply the opposition of many Judeans to Ahaz. If Isaiah denounced the Syrian-Israelite coalition (7:7–9a and 8:1–4) and "this people," who favored the coalition (8:6–8a), he appears to have stood on the side of the Davidic king.

While 6:1–9:6 repeatedly reproaches "this people," little of the material clearly condemns Ahaz specifically. In chapter 8, for example, vv 1–4 threaten Syria and Israel and so function as a promise to the Davidic king. Verses 8b–10, we will argue, may affirm Yahweh's protection of Jerusalem and the royal house against the enemy attack. A similar interpretation is possible also for 8:12–15. These verses likely exhort the Davidic house to revere Yahweh and to trust in the divine protection of Jerusalem and its ruler against Israel and Syria (see Chapter Six below). Isaiah 6:13, 7:1–9, and 9:1–6 might voice the same hopeful message. Even the Immanuel passage can be interpreted as originally an announcement of salvation for Ahaz and the

Davidic dynasty. To be sure, the late addition in 7:17b has transformed the saying into one of judgment. This kind of bias against Ahaz, however, is confined to chapter 7.

In light of these remarks, 6:1–9:6 appears far less streamlined thematically than proponents of the *Denkschrift* hypothesis have suggested. The *Verstockung*-theme, so often proposed as the unifying motif of the material, surfaces clearly only in 6:9–11, and there it may pertain exclusively to the many Judeans who opposed Ahaz during the Syro-Ephraimitic crisis. Isaiah 8:6–8b possibly documents the *Verstockung*, but even this is not certain. The passage criticizes "this people" not because they lacked faith or rejected the prophetic word, but rather because they favored Rezin and Pekah.

Equally questionable is the frequent division of Isaiah 7 and 8 into parallel blocks focusing respectively on the king and people. As we will argue, in chapter 7 the prophet exhorts and encourages Ahaz and the Davidic house (vv 4–9 and 14–17a), but also announces doom for the wider land of Judah (vv 18–25). Isaiah 8 similarly presents a mixture of messages: exhortations and promises to the Davidic house and its supporters (8:1–4, 8b–10, 12–15, and 16–20, and 9:1–6), but also announcements of judgment against "this people" and the Syrian-Israelite coalition (8:4, 6–8a, and 12–15).

Isaiah 6:1–9:6 coheres insofar as it repeatedly voices the divine/prophetic support for Ahaz, the Davidic dynasty, and Jerusalem, against Syria, Israel, and the Judeans. The material, however, does not develop this message schematically. Reproaches, exhortations, warnings, promises, and threats follow one after another, without any clear organization. If a certain thematic consistency is nevertheless apparent, it is not so much due to the careful editing of 6:1–9:6, as it is to the consistency of Isaiah's own thought during the Syro-Ephraimitic crisis.

C. Summary

This chapter addressed two critical issues: the selection of Isaianic texts relevant to the Syro-Ephraimitic crisis, and the possible editorial shaping of that source material. The discussion set forth the following proposals and conclusions.

(1) The detailed exegesis of Isaiah 7–12 will demonstrate that the whole of this material can plausibly be understood against the background of the Syro-Ephraimitic crisis and its immediate prelude.

(2) Different scholars date 3:1–15, 5:25–29 (30), and 17:1–6 to the crisis, but these texts may derive from other periods.

(3) Isaiah 6 is an autobiographical account of a vision which Isaiah experienced in 734/733, the death year of Uzziah. While the vision dates to the time of the Syro-Ephraimitic crisis, the text does not

reflect directly on the events of the war. It is significant for our purposes only insofar as it may attest generally to the different attitudes of Isaiah toward most Judeans ("this people") and the Davidic house at the time.

(4) Scholars look for editorial unity in 6:1–8:18 (or 9:6), partly because they view the material as an originally separate collection secondarily inserted into the middle of 9:7–20 + 5:25–29 (30) and 5:8–24 + 10:1–4a. This redactional theory, however, is not without problems. Isaiah 9:7–10:4 can stand independently as a meaningful speech. Furthermore, 5:25–29 (30) do not fit neatly with 9:7–20, at least as the verses are now preserved. Arguments for the strophic and metrical unity of the material are also doubtful. Finally, the identical wording of 5:25 and the refrain in 9:7–20 (or 10:4) does not alone vouchsafe their original connection. Just as likely, the prophet used the same saying on two different occasions, once in 5:25 during the early part of his career, and again as a refrain in 9:7–10:4 during the Syro-Ephraimitic crisis.

(5) Isaiah 6:1–9:6 does not cohere stylistically. The material includes autobiographical passages (6:1–13 and 8:1–18 [or 20]), a narrative about the prophet (7:1–17), and sayings which fit neither category (7:18–25 and 8:21–9:6). Attempts to recover an original document consistently couched in the "I" style are not convincing.

(6) Arguments for the thematic and structural streamlining of 6:1–9:6 are also not persuasive. An anti-Ahaz bias is apparent in the Immanuel passage, but this is largely due to the late addition in 7:17b. The rest of the material repeatedly attests to the prophet's support of the Davidic king and Jerusalem, and his opposition to many Judeans and the Syrian-Israelite alliance. This two-fold message, however, does not unfold schematically.

The discussion focused on 6:1–9:6, because scholars see there the major deposit of Isaianic material relating to the Syro-Ephraimitic crisis, and because they detect in the material significant editorial shaping. We have challenged both views and the theory of the *Denkschrift* connected with them. It should be added that the prophet's stand in 9:7–12:6 appears much the same as in 6:1–9:6, but here also there is little evidence for a redactional schema.[59] Isaiah 7–12 cohere chronologically, insofar as they relate or date to the Syro-Ephraimitic crisis, but the individual units, we will see, are as much parallel as sequential.

---

[59]Compare R. J. Marshall, "The Structure of Isaiah 1–12," *BR* 7 (1962) 19–33; P. R. Ackroyd, "Isaiah I–XII," 34–46.

CHAPTER FIVE

ISAIAH SEVEN

Isaiah 7 forms a single unit, clearly separate from the vision report in chapter 6 and the prophetic memoir in Isaiah 8. Chapter 7 is not, however, all of one piece. Recent studies yield extremely complicated pictures of the material's redaction, particularly in vv 1–17, but the criteria used for isolating the several editorial layers are often questionable and the results are thus not fully convincing.[1] Nevertheless, at least two stages in the chapter's growth do seem probable.

---

[1]Several scholars observe, for example, the alternation between the singular address to Ahaz (vv 4, 5a, 11, 16b, and 17a) and the plural address to the Davidic house (vv 9b, 13, and 14a). See P. Höffken, "Notizen zum Textcharakter von Jesaja 7,1–17," *TZ* 36 (1980) 323; M. Gorg, "Hiskija als Immanuel. Plädoyer für eine typologische Identifikation," *BN* 22 (1983) 110–15; F. D. Hubmann, "Randbemerkungen zu Jes 7,1–17," *BN* 26 (1985) 40–42; and C. Dohmen, "Verstockungsvollzug und prophetische Legitimation. Literarkritische Beobachtungen zu Jes 7, 1–17," *BN* 31 (1986) 43–55. The shift, however, does not necessarily reflect redaction. It can be explained by the king's status as the representative of the royal house and by the inseparable connection between his fate and the fate of the dynasty.

Other criteria for identifying editorial layers are also questionable. M. Gorg (113) notes the different designations for the deity, "Yahweh" (vv 11–12 and 17a) and "God" or "Lord" (vv 13–14a), but the variation is unlikely significant. F. D. Hubmann (32–33, 40–42) attends to the change in narrative perspective, from the distant reflection on the Syro-Ephraimitic crisis to a more contemporaneous view of the events. This shift is evident in vv 1–2, but not, however, in vv 16–17, as Hubmann argues. There is hardly then much of a basis here for isolating literary layers running throughout the text. O. Kaiser (*Isaiah 1–12*, 116–17), H. Irsigler ("Zeichen und Bezeichnetes in Jes 7,1–17. Notizen zum Immanueltext," *BN* 29 [1985] 82), C. Dohmen (55), and W. Werner, ("Vom Prophetenwort zur Prophetentheologie," 22) see a messianic revision at least in v 15, if not in all of vv 14–16b. The argument rests on their interpretation of what is in fact a very difficult passage, and on the assumption that a messianic message does not fit the preaching of the eighth-century prophet. As will be argued below, the verse or verses need not be viewed as the proclamation of a futuristic messianism at all.

(1) Verses 1–17 circulated as a separate narrative about Isaiah's encounter(s) with the house of David prior to the Syrian-Israelite attack on Jerusalem. The intention of the whole is to document that Isaiah correctly predicted that the Davidic house would survive the enemy threat.

(2) To this account was subsequently appended a series of Isaianic threats originally directed against Judah (vv 18–25).[2] When precisely the prophet uttered these words is difficult to say. It is reasonable to assume, however, that they derive from the same general period of the Syro-Ephraimitic crisis when Isaiah, though remaining a steadfast supporter of Ahaz, vigorously denounced many, if not most, of the Judeans, and proclaimed the devastation of their land.[3]

The editorial combining of vv 1–17 and vv 18–25 resulted in a new understanding of the former. By attaching the threats against Judah to what was originally a word of promise to the Davidic house in vv 14–17a (see section C below), the redactors led the reader to construe that promise as a threat as well. They emphasized the point also by inserting "the king of Assyria" at the end of v 17 as a kind of linchpin between the two blocks of material (see v 20). The coming days of salvation announced in v 17a were thereby reinterpreted as a time of doom and identified with the "that day" of judgment in vv 18–25. Yahweh now appeared to be bringing the Assyrian enemy against both the Davidic house and the Judeans. As we will see, this view of the divine punishment departs widely from the attitude of the historical Isaiah, representing an early attempt to cast Ahaz in a negative light, and as such anticipating the later deuteronomistic criticism of the king in Second Kings 16.

Finally, O. Kaiser (116), H. Irsigler (81), C. Dohmen (48), W. Werner (22), and R. Bickert ("König Ahas und der Prophet Jesaja," 372–74) isolate an historicizing revision of Isa 7:1–17 (25). A number of secondary additions do clarify the historical background of the material, but whether these additions belong together as a single editorial layer is less certain.

[2]K. Budde (*Jesaja's Erleben*, 58–68) and R. G. Rignell ("Das Immanuelszeichen. Einige Gesichtspunkte zu Jes 7," ST 11 [1957] 116–18) argue that the connection between vv 1–17 and vv 18–25 is original, not redactional. Most recent commentators correctly observe, however, that v 17 provides a hard and sharp conclusion to the prophetic narrative. Whatever thematic logic now links the two blocks likely reflects the intention of later editors. See H. Wildberger, *Jesaja 1–12*, 303; and W. Werner, "Vom Prophetenwort zur Prophetentheologie," 24.

[3]Following B. Duhm (*Das Buch Jesaja*, 76), most scholars have viewed the sayings as originally separate fragments, now connected only very loosely by the redactional formulae, "in that day" (*bayyôm hahû*ʾ, v 20) and "it will happen in that day" (*wĕhāyâ bayyôm hahû*ʾ, vv 18, 21, and 23). Whether these formulae invariably reflect the hand of an editor, as many often assume, is debatable. If the sayings in 7:18–25 have been secondarily assembled, their content nevertheless is remarkably cohesive, with the exception of vv 21–22 (see below).

Editorial expansions and glosses are apparent throughout Isaiah 7, but when precisely these entered the text is uncertain. Several of the additions are of an explanatory and/or historicizing nature: vv 4b, 5b, 8b, 10 ("Yahweh") and 20ab.[4] The addition in v 17b ("the king of Assyria") is similar, though as noted above, it effected a radical reinterpretation of vv 14–17a. Verses 21–22 may also be a secondary insertion, perhaps the latest to have entered the text. Their content is difficult to interpret, but the import of the saying seems hopeful.[5] As such, it stands in tension with the prophetic threats that precede and follow. The author of vv 21–22 reinterpreted the diet of Immanuel in v 15, with a view to the blessed life of all those who survive the divine punishment of Judah.

A. Verse 1

Isaiah 7:1 consists of an introductory temporal clause and a terse statement about the Syro-Ephraimitic crisis.

> In the days of Ahaz the son of Jotham the son of Uzziah, the king of Judah, Rezin the king of Syria came up with Pekah the son of Remaliah, the king of Israel, to Jerusalem for battle against it, but he was unable (*wĕlōʾ yākōl*) to conquer it.[6]

---

[4]Many scholars include v 1 as well, but the origin of this verse and its function within the larger narrative remain questions. See section A below.
[5]See R. G. Rignell, "Das Immanuelszeichen," 117; W. McKane, "The Interpretation of Isaiah VII 14–25," *VT* 17 (1967) 216–17; and H. Wildberger, *Jesaja 1–12*, 306. The attempt by G. Fohrer (*Das Buch Jesaja*, 1. 119–20) and R. E. Clements (*Isaiah 1–39*, 91) to discount v 22a as a late eschatological addition to the saying and to construe the remainder as doom is not convincing. Compare also W. Werner, *Eschatologische Texte in Jesaja 1–39* (FB 46; Würzburg: Echter Verlag, 1982) 133–38.
[6]Scholars have long noted the apparent disagreement between the plural subject, Rezin and Pekah, in v 1a and the singular verb, *yākōl*, in v 1b. The discrepancy is often resolved by emending the verb form to *yākĕlû* on the basis of the plural readings in the Septuagint, Syriac, Vulgate, 1QIsa^a, and 2 Kgs 16:5. See for example B. Duhm, *Das Buch Jesaja*, 71; G. B. Gray, *A Critical and Exegetical Commentary on the Book of Isaiah* (2 vols.; Edinburgh: T. & T. Clark, 1912) 1. 114; H. Donner, *Israel unter den Völkern*, 8; and M. E. W. Thompson, *Situation and Theology*, 22, n. 1. The strength of the textual evidence, however, is deceptive, for the versions and the Qumran text are likely ancient attempts to improve the Masoretic text. See H. Orlinsky, "St. Mark's Isaiah Scroll," 329–33, and Chapter Three, section A3 above. We retain *yākōl* in Isa 7:1b and take Rezin as its subject. The tension between *yākōl* and the plural subject in v 1a is considerably lessened by translating the copula connecting Rezin and Pekah (*rĕṣîn melek-ʾărām ûpekaḥ ben-rĕmalyāhû melek-yiśrāʾēl*) in the sense of accompaniment ("with").

As in 2 Kgs 16:5, the text mentions Rezin before Pekah (compare Isa 7:8a-9a, 8:4 and 6). The order may be historically significant, reflecting the superior status of the Syrian king as the leader of the alliance. The conclusion finds support both in the Assyrian texts relating to the war (see Chapter Two, section C1) and in the singular form of the verb that concludes Isa 7:1—"but he [Rezin] was unable" to take the city.[7]

The wording of Isa 7:1 and 2 Kgs 16:5 is very close, though not identical. The main differences between the verses are two. (1) The lengthy temporal clause of 7:1, complete with the genealogy of Ahaz, contrasts with the vague "then" (ʾāz) at the beginning of 2 Kgs 16:5. (2) The Isaiah passage describes the Syrian-Israelite attack as a threat to the city of Jerusalem, while the Second Kings text singles out Ahaz personally as the specific object of the siege.

The precise literary relationship between the two texts is uncertain. Nineteenth-century scholars generally maintained the priority of Isa 7:1,[8] but more recent commentators usually assume the opposite; namely, that the Isaiah passage, apart from its opening clause, derives from 2 Kgs 16:5.[9] A redactor of Isaiah 7 supposedly borrowed the notice in order to locate the prophetic narrative firmly in an historical context.[10] P. R. Ackroyd attaches greater exegetical significance to 7:1. He argues that the Isaianic editor purposefully altered the notice from 2 Kgs 16:5, so as to deemphasize the threat to

---

[7]K. Budde ("Isaiah vii. 1 and 2 Kings xvi. 5," 327–30; *Jesaja's Erleben*, 32) and V. Herntrich (*Der Prophet Jesaja. Kapitel 1–12* [2d ed.; Göttingen: Vandenhoeck & Ruprecht, 1954] 115) argue that the text originally reported Ahaz's inability to fight Rezin and Pekah. See our criticism of the proposal in Chapter Three, section A3 above. R. Bickert ("König Ahas und der Prophet Jesaja," 367–69, 372–74) correctly takes Rezin of Syria as the subject of *yākōl*, but wrongly discounts the reference to Pekah of Israel in v 1a as a late editorial addition. The two kings and/or countries are paired in 7:2, 4, 5, 8a–9a, 16b, 8:4 and 6. Pekah/Israel cannot easily be eliminated as secondary in all these verses.

[8]See, for example, F. Delitzsch, *The Prophecies of Isaiah*, 1. 162; and A. Dillmann, *Der Buch Jesaja* (5th ed.; Leipzig: S. Hirzel, 1890) 64–65.

[9]See, for example, G. B. Gray, *The Book of Isaiah*, 1. 112–13; J. Skinner, *Isaiah*, 53; H. W. Wolff, *Frieden ohne Ende*, 8, 14; G. Fohrer, *Das Buch Jesaja*, 1. 103; H. Donner, *Israel unter den Völkern*, 8; H. Wildberger, *Jesaja 1–12*, 265, 268–69; O. Kaiser, *Isaiah 1–12*, 116, 170–71; and R. E. Clements, *Isaiah 1–39*, 79, 82. Other scholars entertain two possibilities: Isa 7:1 derives either from 2 Kgs 16:5 directly or from the same source from which the deuteronomistic editors extracted 2 Kgs 16:5. See B. Duhm, *Das Buch Jesaja*, 71; V. Herntrich, *Der Prophet Jesaja*, 115; and W. Dietrich, *Jesaja und die Politik*, 66. W. C. Graham ("Isaiah's Part in the Syro-Ephraimitic Crisis," *AJSL* 50 [1933/34] 201–16) is one of the few twentieth-century scholars who argue that 2 Kgs 16:5 derives directly from Isa 7:1.

[10]See the works of O. Kaiser, H. Irsigler, W. Werner, C. Dohmen, and R. Bickert listed in n. 1 above; also R. Kilian *Die Verheissung Immanuels*, 14–15.

Ahaz personally and thereby to highlight the king's lack of faith during the crisis.[11]

A different interpretation is equally plausible. Isaiah 7:1 and 2 Kgs 16:5 may derive from a common source, perhaps the "Book of the Chronicles of the Kings of Judah." Priority would belong to the Isaiah text, insofar as it corresponds closely to the original notice. In the Second Kings text, the notice presumably was modified, so as to denounce Ahaz. In the view of the deuteronomistic editors, the Judean king suffered the attack as a consequence of his religious apostasy (see Chapter Three, section A3).[12]

The events recounted in 7:1 chronologically follow Isaiah's actions and words recorded in vv 2–17 (in fact, all of chapters 7–12). A shift in narrative perspective thus occurs between vv 1 and 2, from reflection on the Syro-Ephraimitic war as an event of the distant past (v 1) to a more contemporaneous view of the crisis prior to its outcome (vv 2–17). Scholars frequently observe the shift as the infelicitous result of redaction, explaining that v 1 is "logically out of place"[13] and that, by anticipating the end of the war, it "robs the narrative of suspense."[14] R. Bartelmus rightly notes, however, that prolepsis occurs elsewhere in Hebrew narrative (for example, Gen 22:1 and 2 Kgs 2:1) and often reflects not so much the work of an editor as a distinctive literary technique (compare Isa 20:1).[15] Regardless of whether Isa 7:1 is redactional, it functions well in context. It is a proleptic summary of the entire crisis, giving the denouement toward which Isaiah's messages to Ahaz and the royal house point. Its concern is not, as Ackroyd contends, to underscore the faithlessness

---

[11]P. R. Ackroyd, "Historians and Prophets," 27–28; compare O. Kaiser, *Isaiah 1–12*, 170–71.

[12]A related but separate question concerns the literary relationship between Isa 7:1 and vv 2–17. Is v 1, or part of it, original to the prophetic narrative? Older scholars, for example B. Duhm (*Das Buch Jesaja*, 70–71) and O. Procksch (*Jesaja I*, 112), contend that the narrative once began with v 2. Most recent scholars, however, include also the opening temporal clause of v 1, either with or without the genealogy of Ahaz, as part of the original introduction. See G. Fohrer, *Das Buch Jesaja*, 1. 103; H. W. Wolff, *Frieden ohne Ende*, 8; H. Donner, *Israel unter den Völkern*, 8; R. Kilian, *Die Verheissung Immanuels*, 8; F. Huber, *Die anderen Völker*, 11; H. Wildberger, *Jesaja 1–12*, 264–65; and O. Kaiser, *Isaiah 1–12*, 134. In contrast, L. G. Rignell ("Das Immanuelszeichen," 100), and R. Bartelmus ("Jes 7,1–17 und das Stilprinzip des Kontrastes," 56) argue that the information of v 1 is essential for understanding the narrative that follows. Compare P. Höffken, "Textcharakter von Jesaja 7,1–17," 324. H. Irsigler ("Zeichen und Bezeichnetes," 81, n. 25) lists reasons against the originality of 7:1, but the argument is not conclusive.

[13]G. B. Gray, *The Book of Isaiah*, 1. 112.

[14]W. Werner, "Vom Prophetenwort zur Prophetentheologie," 16. Compare F. D. Hubmann, "Randbemerkungen," 33–34.

[15]R. Bartelmus, "Jes 7,1–17 und das Stilprinzip des Kontrastes," 56. Compare C. Dohmen, "Literarkritische Beobachtungen," 45–46, especially n. 31.

of the king, nor is it merely to historicize the prophetic narrative. Rather, the verse wants to affirm that the prophet's predictions about the failure of the Syrian-Israelite campaign came true.

B. Verses 2–9

Yahweh commissions Isaiah with a speech of encouragement and warning for Ahaz in vv 3–9. Verse 2 introduces the account by describing the disposition of the Davidic house: "Now when it had been told to the house of David, 'Syria has descended on (nāḥâ ʿal) Ephraim,' its [the house of David's] resolve and the resolve of its people (lĕbābô ûlĕbab ʿammô) wavered as the trees of the forest waver before the wind."[16] The verse functions as a kind of flashback, taking the reader back to the eve of the impending crisis. It notes the irresoluteness of the Davidic house and its supporters in order to explain why a word from the prophet was especially needed at this moment.

The translation and meaning of the report to the Davidic house (v 2a) merit closer attention. The verb nāḥâ appears to derive from the root nûaḥ ("rest").[17] Emended readings, however, are often proposed, including ḥānâ ("encamped") and neʾĕḥâ ("fraternize").[18] Al-

---

[16] The pronominal suffixes of lĕbābô and ʿammô can refer grammatically to Ahaz (v 1a) or to the "house of David" (v 2a). The RSV assumes the former and so reads, "his heart and the heart of his people" (compare the NIV and TEV). H. Wildberger (Jesaja 1–12, 275) argues that at least the suffix of lĕbābô must reach back to Ahaz, "since one cannot speak of the heart of a house." It is possible, however, to treat "house of David" as a collective entity and render the subsequent pronouns as plurals. The NJPSV thus translates v 2b, "their heart and the heart of their people trembled . . . ." Alternatively, one might render lĕbāb as "resolve" and think of the political will of the ruling regime. Our translation follows this interpretation.

[17] If this derivation is correct, the verb and its subject, Syria (ʾărām), are feminine. O. Procksch (Jesaja I, 113) notes the masculine verb accompanying Syria in v 5 (yaʿaṣ) and so suspects the feminine form in v 2. Elsewhere in the Hebrew Bible, Syria appears with feminine verbs (see 2 Sam 8:6, 10:11; Ez 19:12; 1 Chr 19:12). It is joined with a clearly masculine verb only in sentences like Isa 7:5, where the verb precedes the subject (see 2 Sam 10:15, 17, 18, 19; 1 Kgs 20:1; 1 Chr 19:19). In such instances, strict agreement in gender between subject and verb is not expected.

[18] H. Donner (Israel unter den Völkern, 8) advocates the former reading and V. Herntrich (Der Prophet Jesaja, 113) appears to presuppose it. The emendation assumes the metathesis of n and ḥ, which is certainly conceivable. With the preposition ʿal, however, ḥānâ would seem to describe Syria's encampment "against" Israel (not "in" Israel, as Donner proposes; compare Josh 10:5, Judg 6:4, 20:19, 1 Sam 11:1, 2 Sam 12:28, 1 Kgs 16:15, and 2 Kgs 25:1). This meaning does not fit the literary context. Isaiah 7 envisions the hostility between the Syrian-Israelite al-

ternatively, some scholars retain *nāḥâ* but derive the form from *nḥh*. This root usually means "lead or guide" in the Hebrew Bible, but its Semitic cognates might suggest "confederate" as a possible meaning. G. R. Driver thus translates *nāḥâ* as "become allied with," adducing the Arabic *naḥa* ("lean on").[19] O. Eissfeldt notes that in an inscription of the north Syrian king, Idrimi of Alalah, the Akkadian *naḫu* means "to enter a treaty agreement" (see *ANET* 557). *Nāḥâ*, he suggests, has the same sense in Isa 7:2a.[20]

The Masoretic text makes reasonable sense without resorting to hypothetical meanings recovered from cognate languages. *Nāḥâ* derives from *nûaḥ* and has the well-attested sense, "settle, descend on" (compare 7:19, Exod 10:14, and 2 Sam 17:12). The report might refer to the movement of Syrian troops into Israel for the purpose of joining Pekah's forces in an attack on Jerusalem.[21] Another interpretation, however, is also possible. Syria's "descent" on Ephraim may vividly describe Pekah's coup in Samaria in Tishri 734, and with it, the effective takeover of the whole of the northern kingdom by Syria. This conclusion assumes our reconstruction of the events leading to the Syro-Ephraimitic crisis (see Chapters Two and Three above). Long before 734, Rezin had annexed the northern Transjordan and Galilee, and possibly also the coastal Plain of Sharon. As early as the 740s, Pekah had been ruling in Gilead as a Syrian puppet. By the middle 730s, little more than the Ephraimite hill country may have remained of the Israelite kingdom. When Pekah assassinated Pekahiah in 734 and ascended the throne in Samaria, Rezin's control of Israel was effectively complete. Syria had "descended on Ephraim."[22]

---

liance and Ahaz/Jerusalem. For support of his translation, Donner cites Exod 14:2, but the expression there (*taḥănû ʿal-hayyām*) is not comparable to Isa 7:2a.

O. Procksch (*Jesaja I*, 113) suggests the second reading, *neʾĕḥâ*, a nifal form of *ʾḥh*. Compare the older proposal of P. de Lagarde ("Kritische Anmerkungen," 1–30): the Masoretic *nāḥâ* is a contraction of *naʾăḥâ*, a nifal form of *ʾḥh*. Both verbs, however, are hypothetical, attested nowhere else in the Hebrew Bible. (The noun, *ʾāḥ* or "brother," is widespread, of course.)

[19] G. R. Driver, "Linguistic and Textual Problems: Isaiah I–XXXIX," *JTS* 38 (1937) 37.

[20] O. Eissfeldt, "*nûaḥ* 'sich vertragen,'" *SThU* 20 (1950) 71–74 = his *KS* (6 vols.; eds. R. Sellheim and F. Maass; Tübingen: J. C. B. Mohr [Paul Siebeck] 1966) 3. 124–28. Eissfeldt adds that the Akkadian verb occurs with the double preposition *ana eli*, whose second member is equivalent to *ʿal* in Isa 7:2.

[21] See H. Wildberger, *Jesaja 1–12*, 265; compare H. Donner, *Israel unter den Völkern*, 10.

[22] The expression connotes a sense of Syrian aggression (compare 2 Sam 17:12) and so reflects the perspective of the Davidides and Jerusalemites who looked gravely on the coup of Pekah and the political machinations of Rezin presumably behind it.

Verse 2b mentions not only the house of David, but also "its people." Commentators usually understand the text as referring to the wider Judean population. Isaiah 8:6b indicates, however, that many, if not most, Judeans were favorably disposed toward the Israelite and Syrian kings and supported their anti-Assyrian cause. "Its people" in 7:2b should probably be taken, then, in a more restrictive sense, that is, as a reference to the few supporters of the Davidic regime and its policies. These were likely limited to residents of Jerusalem and its environs, and members of the standing army.

Most translations render *lĕbab* (v 2b) as "heart," but the term actually exhibits a wide semantic range in the Hebrew Bible—the inner person, mind, knowledge, memory, conscience, desire, and so forth.[23] Commentators usually construe the word in Isa 7:2 in the sense of courage: the Syro-Ephraimitic threat caused alarm and fear within the Davidic house. *Lĕbab*, however, might also refer to will or resoluteness.[24] We render the term in this sense and suggest that the text has in mind the weakening resolve of the Davidic leadership to persist in its longstanding course of political neutrality.

This interpretation makes sense again in light of the events leading to the Syro-Ephraimitic crisis. Our reconstruction of the history (Chapter Three above) suggested that as early as the reign of Jotham, Rezin of Damascus was pressuring Judah to join the coalition of regional states that would eventually challenge Assyria's expansionism. That pressure perhaps included encouraging Philistine, Meunite, and Edomite encroachment on Judean territory. Prior to 734, Syria did not threaten Judah directly, but with Pekah's coup in Samaria, Syrian hegemony extended to the very border of Judah. Moreover, the Syrian-engineered coup demonstrated clearly that Rezin was prepared to take decisive steps against recalcitrant monarchs.

These circumstances must have forced the Davidides to reevaluate their neutralist stand. Resistance to Syria had already cost Judah significant territory and cut off the country's access to major trade routes. Syrian pressure apparently had begun also to take its toll on the public mood, for many Judeans now favored joining league with

---

[23] See R. C. Dentan, "Heart," *IDB* 2. 549–50; and H.-J. Fabry, "*lēb*," *TWAT* 4. 414–51, especially 437–38.

[24] In 1 Sam 7:3, for example, Samuel exhorts the Israelites: "If with all your heart (*ʾim-bĕkol-lĕbabkem*) you are returning to Yahweh, put aside the foreign gods and the Astaroth from your midst . . . ." The expression, "with all your heart," means in this context "with firm resolve, total commitment, wholeheartedness." The continuation of the speech expresses the same sense: "And make firm your resolve for Yahweh (*wĕhākīnû lĕbabkem ʾel-yhwh*) and serve him only . . . ." Compare Exod 14:5, where "resolve" suitably translates *lĕbab*, but seems to refer more to a specific decision of the will, rather than to resoluteness.

Isaiah Seven 141

Rezin and Pekah (8:6). In the face of internal and external opposition, the national leadership had to reconsider whether it should capitulate to Rezin's demands and join the anti-Assyrian coalition. Heated debate within the administration undoubtedly ensued, some arguing for a reconciliation with Syria, others advocating a continuation of Judean neutrality. Isaiah 7:2b may refer to this controversy, when it reports that the "resolve" of the house of David and its supporters "wavered as trees of the forest waver before the wind."

The divine commissioning of Isaiah follows in vv 3–9. The unit consists of two parts: (a) Yahweh commands the prophet to go forth with his son, She'ar-yashub, to meet Ahaz (v 3); and (b) Yahweh orders Isaiah to deliver to the king a divinely-dictated speech (vv 4–9). That speech, in turn, includes an exhortation to Ahaz (v 4) and a word of assurance and warning to the house of David (vv 5–9a, 9b).[25] The prophet speaks in his own voice in vv 4–6, but then shifts to divine style in vv 7–9.[26] The unit as a whole thus displays the se-

---

[25]This division assumes that vv 5–6 connect syntactically with vv 7–9: "Because (*ya'an kī*) Syria has planned evil (*rā'â*) against you . . . thus Yahweh says . . . ." (For a roughly analogous construction with *ya'an 'ǎšer*, see 1 Kgs 20:28.) Alternatively, M. Saebø ("Formgeschichtliche Erwägungen zu Jes. 7,3–9," *ST* 14 [1960] 54–60) takes vv 5–6 in conjunction with v 4, construing then v 7 as the beginning of an independent sentence. The causal clause, he argues, explains what Ahaz should not fear. (See also K. Budde, *Jesaja's Erleben*, 39; and L. G. Rignell, "Das Immanuelszeichen," 103.) This interpretation is not convincing. *Ya'an*-clauses in prophetic speech normally, though not invariably, precede the main sentence and present the reason for divine action in the future (see D. E. Gowan, "The Use of *ya'an* in Biblical Hebrew," *VT* 21 [1971] 168–79). Outside Isa 7:5–6, the dual conjunction *ya'an kī* occurs five times, four times preceding the main sentence (1 Kgs 13:21; Isa 3:16, 8:6, and 29:13) and once following it (Num 11:20). In all five instances, the causal clause explains the reason for imminent divine punishment. Isa 7:5–6 likely serve a similar function, indicating the situation to which the divine word in vv 7–9 responds (compare Isa 28:15–16). Noteworthy in this regard are the feminine verbs in v 7b, which probably reach back to *rā'â* in v 5a for their subject.

[26]H. Wildberger (*Jesaja 1–12*, 270–72) contends that the divine style begins already in v 4. His reasoning is not explicit, but it seems to involve largely form-critical considerations. The exhortations in v 4, especially *'al-tîrā'* ("don't be afraid"), supposedly distinguish vv 4–9 as an oracle of salvation (*Heilsorakel*). According to J. Begrich ("Das priesterliche Heilsorakel," *ZAW* 52 [1934] 81–92), such exhortations are typically divine speech. It would seem logical to infer that the commands to Ahaz in Isa 7:4 are similarly spoken by Yahweh. The Near Eastern parallels support the conclusion (see, for example, *ANET* 605–6 and 655), although Wildberger does not stress this point.

The oracular formula in v 7a poses real difficulty for this interpretation. If the divine speech begins in v 4, we must envision Yahweh oddly introducing his own response to the Syrian plan, "thus says Lord Yahweh . . . ." M. Saebø ("Formgeschichtliche Erwägungen," 57–58) notes this awkwardness, but wrongly concludes that vv 4–6 and 7–9 are two separate units. (Compare W.

quential embedment of speeches within speeches: Yahweh's words to Ahaz and the royal house (vv 7–9) are quoted in Isaiah's address to the king (vv 4–9), which in turn is quoted in Yahweh's words to the prophet (vv 3–9).

Verse 3 mentions She'ar-yashub, but fails to explain his significance.[27] The name of the child is undoubtedly symbolic (compare 8:3–4 and Hos 1:2–9), but its precise translation and import are uncertain.[28] Two interpretations of She'ar-yashub appear in Isa 10:21 and 22–23, but neither of these necessarily applies in 7:3. The name, we will see, was ambiguous enough to express more than one meaning, depending on the historical and rhetorical situation.[29]

She'ar-yashub is grammatically a verbal sentence, consisting of a subject, $šĕ'ār$, and a predicate, $yāšûb$.[30] The noun derives from the

---

Dietrich, *Jesaja und die Politik*, 82, especially n. 91.) Wildberger himself seems aware of the problem when he states that in 7:4–9, "a very complicated structure arises, in that, within the speech of Yahweh formally considered, a messenger speech is cited and indeed introduced with the formula, *kh ʾmr ʾdny yhwh*." The difficulty disappears, however, if, in the speech that Yahweh dictates to Isaiah (vv 4–9), the prophet first addresses Ahaz in his own voice (vv 4–6) and then quotes the divine message to the king and royal house (vv 7–9). General form-critical considerations should not be allowed to obscure this structure.

[27]The text's silence about the meaning of the name and the role of the child hardly warrants J. Schreiner's discounting the reference as a secondary addition ("Zur Textgestalt von Jes 6 und 7,1–17," *BZ* 22 [1978] 96–97 = his *Segen für die Völker. Gesammelte Schriften zur Entstehung und Theologie des Alten Testaments* [ed. E. Zenger; Würzburg: Echter Verlag, 1987] 69–70).

[28]Scholarly interpretations generally assume that the Masoretic text accurately preserves the original name. J. M. P. Smith ("She'ar yashub," *ZAW* 34 [1914] 220–27), however, changes $yāšûb$ to $yēšēb$ ("remain, abide"), while E. Lipiński ("Le sh'r-yshub d'Isaïe vii 3," *VT* 23 [1973] 245–46) repoints $šĕ'ār$ as $šĕ'ēr$ ("blood"). The former emendation is widely rejected, especially since the discovery of 1QIsaa, which confirms the Masoretic reading. The latter proposal also lacks textual support, and the resultant meaning, "blood [revenge] will return [to the invading Syrians and Israelites]," seems forced.

[29]Most scholars view 10:20–23 as a late editorial passage and so discount the interpretations of She'ar-yashub there as evidence for its meaning in 7:3. See for example B. Duhm, *Das Buch Jesaja*, 101–2; S. Blank, "The Current Misinterpretation of Isaiah's She'ar Yashub," *JBL* 67 (1948) 211–12; G. Fohrer, *Das Buch Jesaja*, 1. 160; H. Wildberger, *Jesaja 1–12*, 278; R. E. Clements, *Isaiah 1–39*, 114–15; and O. Kaiser, *Isaiah 1–12*, 240–42. The argument, however, is by no means conclusive. Both interpretations in Isaiah 10 might derive from the eighth-century prophet (see Chapter Nine below).

[30]L. Köhler ("*She'ar yashub* und der nackte Relativsatz; Syntactica II," *VT* 3 [1953] 85) construes $yāšûb$ as a "bare" relative clause qualifying $šĕ'ār$ ("the remnant that returns"). Alternatively, J. Lindblom (*The Immanuel Section*, 9) understands the name as a "composed nominal sentence" ("a remnant, it will return"). For a negative critique of these proposals in light of the comparative evidence of West Semitic sentence names, see G. Hasel, "Linguistic Considerations

Hebrew root $š^\flat r$ ("remain, be left over") and generally means "remnant."[31] It often refers in Isaiah to the survivors of divine destruction (see 10:18–19, 22–23, 14:22; compare the similar sense of $š\check{e}^\flat ērît$ in 14:30 and 15:9).[32] The verb is an inflected form of $šûb$ ("turn back, return"). While the term exhibits a wide semantic range,[33] two meanings are particularly relevant to the name of Isaiah's son. $Yāšûb$ might have a religious sense: one turns to Yahweh (compare Isa 1:27, 6:10, 9:13, 19:22, and 30:15).[34] The verb can also refer to a return from battle and thus to survival in war (compare 1 Kgs 22:28, Jer 22:22, and Isa 10:22).[35]

The inversion of the normal Hebrew word order in She'ar-yashub is significant. The subject precedes the verb and thereby receives em-

---

Regarding the Translation of Isaiah's *Shear-jashub*: A Reassessment," *AUSS* 9 (1971) 36–46.

[31]Related vocabulary includes $š\check{e}^\flat ērît$ and the nominal and verbal forms of $plṭ$ ("escape"), ytr ("remain over"), and $śrd$ ("escape, survive"). For discussions of the remnant vocabulary and concept in the Hebrew Bible and Near Eastern literature, see W. E. Müller, *Die Vorstellung vom Rest im Alten Testament* [2d ed.; ed. H. D. Preuss; Neukirchen-Vluyn: Neukirchener Verlag, 1973); E. W. Heaton, "The Root $š^\flat r$ and the Doctrine of the Remnant," *JTS* 3 (1952) 27–39; U. Stegemann, "Der Restgedanke bei Isaias," *BZ* 13 [1969] 173–75); and G. Hasel, "Semantic Values of Derivatives of the Hebrew Root $š^\flat r$," *AUSS* 11 (1973) 152–69; idem., *The Remnant: The History and Theology of the Remnant Idea from Genesis to Isaiah* (3d ed.; Berrien Springs: Andrews University Press, 1980) 275–87; idem., "Remnant," *IDBSup* 735–36.

[32]See also the references to the remnant ($š^\flat r$) of Moab, Syria, Israel, and Kedar in Isa 16:14, 17:3, 6, and 21:17. In these passages, divine responsibility is not explicitly stated, but may be implied nevertheless. An oracular word of Yahweh announces the fate of each remnant.

[33]See W. L. Holladay, *The Root shubh in the Old Testament* (Leiden: E. J. Brill, 1958).

[34]Isaiah 10:21 speaks of a remnant returning ($š\check{e}^\flat ār\ yāšûb\ š\check{e}^\flat ār\ ya^c ăqōb$) to $^\flat ēl\ gibbôr$, and so also would seem to have in mind a turning to God. Possibly, however, the text refers to a remnant's renewed attachment to the Davidic king (see Chapter Nine below).

For different assessments of the theme of repentance in Isaiah, see H. W. Wolff, "Das Thema 'Umkehr' in der alttestamentliche Prophetie," *ZTK* 48 (1951) 129–48, especially 138 = his *GS* (2d ed.; Munich: Chr. Kaiser, 1973) 130–50; G. Sauer, "Die Umkehrforderung in der Verkündigung Jesajas," in *Wort, Gebot, Glaube. Beiträge zur Theologie des Alten Testaments. Walter Eichrodt zum 80. Geburtstag* (ATANT 59; ed. H. J. Stoebe; Zurich: Zwingli, 1970) 277–95; H. W. Hoffmann, *Die Intension der Verkündigung Jesajas* (BZAW 136; Berlin: Walter de Gruyter, 1974); and R. Kilian, *Jesaja 1–39*, 107–11.

[35]In the Schweich Lectures of 1909, R. H. Kennett (*The Composition of the Book of Isaiah in the Light of History and Archaeology* [London: H. Frowde, 1910] 11) called attention to this meaning of *yashub* in 1 Kgs 22:28 and suggested interpreting She'ar-yashub in light of it.

phasis.³⁶ Two quite different interpretations, however, are possible. The emphasis might suggest the smallness or insignificance of the remnant: "Only a remnant . . ." or "A mere remnant . . . ." Alternatively, an asseverative meaning may be intended: "A remnant indeed . . ." or less strongly, "At least a remnant . . . ."

The above grammatical and lexical remarks can be summarized by listing the possible translations of She'ar-yashub.

(1) A remnant will indeed turn (to Yahweh).
(2) A remnant will indeed return (i.e. survive).
(3) Only a remnant will turn (to Yahweh).
(4) Only a remnant will return (i.e. survive).

The first and second of these are hopeful declarations, focusing respectively on the repentance of a remnant and on its political-military survival. The third and fourth translations are both pessimistic, but differ from each other in their concern, either with a religious turning to Yahweh or with political survival.

Scholars widely debate which of these meanings Isaiah intended when he and She'ar-yashub met Ahaz.³⁷ S. Blank, R. Kilian, and M. Weiss construe the name as a threat against Judah and/or the Davidic house: a "mere remnant" will survive the Syro-Ephraimitic crisis.³⁸ R. E. Clements, J. Day, and J. J. M. Roberts also interpret She'ar-yashub as a threat, but as one directed against the enemies of Judah: "only a remnant" of the Syrian and Israelite troops will return from battle. For Ahaz and the Judeans, the name thus functions as a promise.³⁹ G. Fohrer similarly sees a hopeful message in She'ar-yashub: as the remnant of all Israel, Judah (as opposed to the north-

---

³⁶G. Hasel ("The Translation of *Shear-jashub*," 39–42) reports that the same word order occasionally occurs not only in other Hebrew names, but also in West Semitic names mentioned in Amorite, Ugaritic, and Phoenician texts.

³⁷The meaning of the name when first given to the child is neither known nor necessarily relevant to its sense in Isa 7:3. G. Hasel (*The Remnant*, 274–75) aptly comments: ". . . One can only speculate about the circumstances in which the name Shear-jashub was given . . . . The crucial question, however, at the time of this historic meeting is, what has the name of the boy to say to Ahaz in this particular situation?" See the similar remarks of M. Weiss ("The Contribution of Literary Criticism to Biblical Research: Illustrated by the Problem of She'ar-Yashub," *ScrHier* 31 [1986] 376–77), who correctly criticizes Wildberger's interpretation of the name on this very point (*Jesaja 1–12*, 278–79).

³⁸S. Blank, "Isaiah's *She'ar Yashub*," 211–15; R. Kilian, *Jesaja 1–39*, 27–39, especially 28–31; idem., "Verstockungsauftrag Jesajas," 217–19; idem., *Die Verheissung Immanuels*, 47–53; and M. Weiss, "The Problem of She'ar-Yashub," 377–86.

³⁹R. E. Clements, *Isaiah 1–39*, 83; J. Day, "Shear-jashub (Isaiah vii 3) and the Remnant of Wrath (Psalm lxxvi 11)," *VT* 31 (1981) 76–78; and J. J. M. Roberts, "Isaiah and His Children," 200–1.

ern kingdom) will survive.[40] T. C. Vriezen, L. Alonso Schökel, and M. E. W. Thompson stress the religious sense of the name: a remnant will "repent."[41] Finally, a number of scholars argue for a combination of meanings in She'ar-yashub: doom and deliverance, repentance and survival. H. W. Wolff's interpretation of the name is typical.

> It presupposes a battle, indeed, a defeat, a decimation of the troops. *Only* a remnant will return! And yet, for this remnant there is hope; it will be saved, it will return. . . . The remnant consists of all who turn back to Yahweh. Those who return to Yahweh survive the judgment.[42]

The several interpretations of She'ar-yashub adduce a variety of evidence. Some appeal to the meaning of Maher-shalal-hash-baz (8:3–4), the symbolic name of Isaiah's second son, who also figured in the message of the prophet during the Syro-Ephraimitic crisis.[43] Others understand She'ar-yashub in light of the Zion theology,[44] or in line with the meaning of similar personal names in Amorite and Ugaritic texts.[45] Many scholars argue on the basis of Isaiah's preaching on

---

[40] G. Fohrer, *Die symbolischen Handlungen der Propheten* (2d ed.; Zurich/Stuttgart: Zwingli, 1968) 30. F. Huber (*Die anderen Völker*, 25) defends this interpretation.

[41] T. C. Vriezen, "Essentials of the Theology of Isaiah," in *Israel's Prophetic Heritage. Essays in Honor of James Muilenberg* (eds. B. W. Anderson and W. Harrelson; New York: Harper, 1962) 138, especially n. 16; L. Alonso Schökel, *Estudios de Poetica Hebrea* (Barcelona: J. Flors, 1963) 376–77; M. E. W. Thompson, *Situation and Theology*, 23–28.

[42] *Frieden ohne Ende*, 17–18. Compare the similar explanation of She'ar-yashub by H. Wildberger (*Jesaja 1–12*, 278): "Isaiah does not deny that there is salvation. However, the salvation depends upon a return to Yahweh. And no one should deceive himself over the fact that only a remnant will find its way back to Yahweh. The name therefore means to say: only a remnant will return from amidst all the catastrophes which will overwhelm Israel, namely, those who turn in faith to Yahweh." See also W. E. Müller, *Die Vorstellung vom Rest*, 64–65; G. Hasel, *The Remnant*, 274–87; and compare J. Lindblom, *The Immanuel Section*, 8–10; A. H. J. Gunneweg, "Heils- und Unheilsverkündigung," 27–34; and S. Herrmann, *Die prophetischen Heilserwartungen im Alten Testament* (BWANT 85; Stuttgart: Kohlhammer, 1965) 127–30.

[43] See for example S. Blank, "Isaiah's *She'ar Yashub*," 214.

[44] See especially J. Day, "Shear-jashub," 77. He suggests that the source behind She'ar-yashub is the tradition of Zion's inviolability in the face of enemy attack (see Pss 46, 48, and 76). He calls attention particularly to Ps 76:11: "Surely thou [Yahweh] dost crush the wrath of man, the remnant of wrath ($šĕ'ērît\ ḥēmōt$)." The idea of a remnant is thus at home in the Zion theology and refers to what survives of the enemy that attacks Zion. Presumably She'ar-yashub has the same meaning in Isaiah 7. (Note that Day relies heavily on J. A. Emerton's rendering of Ps 76:11 ["A Neglected Solution of a Problem in Psalm LXXVI 11," *VT* 24 [1974] 136–46]. The Hebrew of the verse, however, remains uncertain.)

[45] G. Hasel ("Translation of *Shear-jashub*," 44–45) observes that some Ugaritic and Amorite names connect the Common Semitic root *twb* (Hebrew šûb) with the

repentance elsewhere and his other descriptions of a remnant.[46] Most interpretations involve a combination of these arguments and appeal as well to the broad sense of Isa 7:1–9 (or 17).

The immediate narrative context should outweigh other factors in explaining the application of the name in 7:3.[47] Isaiah 7:1–9 (or 17) depict a situation in which the prophet was principally concerned to encourage Ahaz, predicting the failure of the Syrian-Israelite siege.[48] In this instance, accordingly, She'ar-yashub probably expressed a hopeful message, promising the sure survival of a remnant. Isaiah perhaps intended a religious connotation as well: the remnant that turns to Yahweh will return (survive).

On the occasion of Isaiah's meeting with Ahaz outside the walls of Jerusalem, the hopeful announcement of a remnant likely applied

---

name of a divinity or a theophoric element. The "turning" which these names envision is thus a religious one. The evidence, Hasel concludes, supports the argument that the name of Isaiah's first son suggests a return to Yahweh. (As Hasel himself admits, however, the West Semitic names do not parallel She'ar-yashub perfectly. The former speak of a divinity turning to a person, while the name of the prophet's son refers to the turning/returning of a human remnant. The difference is more significant than Hasel acknowledges.)

[46]S. Herrmann (*Heilserwartungen*, 129–30), for example, defends the optimistic and religious meaning of She'ar-yashub by correlating the name with the prophet's words on repentance in Isa 30:15. H. Wildberger (*Jesaja 1–12*, 278) interprets the name more negatively in light of the ominous message in 6:10. S. Blank ("Isaiah's *She'ar Yashub*," 213) and R. Kilian (*Die Verheissung Immanuels*, 49–53; *Jesaja 1–39*, 31–39) review the references to a remnant in 14:30, 17:1–6, and 30:14 and 17, and conclude that She'ar-yashub threatens the political-military decimation of Judah and the Davidic house. Kilian (*Jesaja 1–39*, 107–11; "Verstockungsauftrag Jesajas," 217–19) argues further that the few genuine Isaianic texts which speak of repentance describe it as an impossibility or as a missed opportunity of the past.

[47]M. Weiss ("The Problem of She'ar-Yashub," 373–77) makes a similar methodological point as he evaluates recent interpretations of She'ar-yashub. He goes to an extreme, however, in claiming that the sense of the name in Isaiah 7 can be inferred only from the narrative itself. Furthermore, Weiss does not really heed his own advice. When he construes She'ar-yashub as a threat against Ahaz for planning to appeal to Tiglathpileser of Assyria, he is drawing 2 Kgs 16:7–8 into the exegesis of Isaiah 7. The prophetic narrative itself nowhere hints at this appeal. See Chapter One above, especially section E.

[48]See the studies of R. E. Clements, J. Day, and J. J. M. Roberts listed in n. 39 above, as well as the analysis of F. Huber (*Die anderen Völker*, 24–26). They agree that the narrative recounts the prophet's efforts to reassure the Davidic king. M. Weiss's reading of 7:1–9 ("The Problem of She'ar-Yashub," 377–86) reaches the opposite conclusion, namely, that Isaiah here intends to threaten Ahaz. His interpretation, however, wrongly sets the passage against the background of 2 Kgs 16:7–8. Weiss also overemphasizes the significance of the negative formulation of v 9b. The warning here does not cancel the exhortative, hopeful tone of the preceding verses, and it certainly does not warrant Weiss's claim that Isaiah, from the very start, assumed the king's faithlessness.

to the royal house. The account of the episode in 7:1-9, after all, is primarily concerned with the Davidic regime and its survival (see v 2; also v 9b, where the plural verbs probably address the royal court). Furthermore, 7:6 states clearly that the essential goal of the Syrian-Israelite attack was to replace Ahaz as king in Jerusalem. In these circumstances, the Davidic house had good reason to fear for its continuing existence. Such fear would be all the more understandable, if many of Ahaz's own Judean subjects supported the plan of Rezin and Pekah (see 8:6). With the symbolic name of his son, Isaiah affirmed that Ahaz and the Davidic dynasty would survive the crisis, if they would retain their confidence in Yahweh's promise to safeguard Jerusalem and his anointed. Disaster might befall most Judeans and the land (see 7:18-25 and 8:6-8a), but a remnant would survive—the house of David and its few supporters.

Verse 3b stipulates precisely where Isaiah and She'ar-yashub were to meet Ahaz: "at the end of the conduit to the upper pool, along the Fuller's Field road."[49] The location was undoubtedly outside the walls of Jerusalem (see 2 Kgs 18:17 = Isa 36:2), probably at the southern end of the city, near the Gihon Spring.[50] The text does not explain why Ahaz was there, but it seems likely that he was inspecting the city's fortification and water supply in anticipation of the Syrian-Israelite attack.[51] If this assumption is correct, the king himself

---

[49]J. Schreiner ("Jes 6 und 7,1-17," 69) and R. Bickert ("König Ahas und der Prophet Jesaja," 373) regard the notice as an editorial addition deriving from 2 Kgs 18:17 (= Isa 36:2). Literary borrowing, however, is by no means certain. The mention of the same location in Isaiah 7 and 2 Kings 18 may be due to the simple fact that both texts deal with sieges of Jerusalem.

[50]See M. Burrows, "The Conduit of the Upper Pool," *ZAW* 70 (1958) 221-27. Locations at the northern end of Jerusalem have also been proposed and cannot be ruled out (see O. Procksch, *Jesaja I*, 114; H. Donner, *Israel unter den Völkern*, 10-11).

[51]The majority of scholars share this understanding. See for example H. Donner, *Israel unter den Völkern*, 11; H. W. Wolff, *Frieden ohne Ende*, 16; K. Seybold, *Das davidische Königtum*, 67; W. Dietrich, *Jesaja und die Politik*, 92; H. Wildberger, *Jesaja 1-12*, 277; and M. E. W. Thompson, *Situation and Theology*, 23. Other interpretations of the location, however, are not lacking. F. D. Hubmann ("Randbemerkungen," 37) suggests that the abundant waters at the meeting place prefigure the "going out" of "these two smoldering stubs of fire-wood," that is, the Syrian and Israelite opponents (v 4). The symbolism, however, seems far-fetched. Alternatively, O. Kaiser (*Isaiah 1-12*, 146) and C. Dohmen ("Literarkritische Beobachtungen," 53) see in v 3b a deliberate allusion to 2 Kgs 18:17 (= Isa 36:2). Isaiah 7, Kaiser claims, implies that Ahaz's decision to appeal for Assyrian aid led to dire consequences for the kingdom of Hezekiah in 701. The idea of this appeal, however, is nowhere present in Isaiah 7. Kaiser imports it into the text from 2 Kgs 16:7-8. C. Dohmen argues that the allusion in 7:3 is part of the larger narrative's effort to contrast the faithlessness of Ahaz and Hezekiah's trust in Yahweh. (Compare also W. Werner, "Vom Prophetenwort

was apparently inclined, though not yet decided, to hold out against the demands of the coalition, despite pressure from many Judeans, and perhaps even from some advisers within the royal court. When Isaiah accosted Ahaz, his aim was to encourage the king in this direction.

The speech of the prophet opens in v 4 with a string of commands: "Remain aloof (*hiššāmēr*) and stay calm *(wĕhašqēṭ)*; don't be afraid (*ʾal-tîrāʾ*) and let your resolve not weaken (*ûlĕbābĕkā ʾal-yērak*) on account of these two smoldering stumps of firebrands, that is, the burning anger of Rezin and Syria and the son of Remaliah." According to G. von Rad and others, the prophetic exhortations imitate the address to troops and/or their leader in holy war.[52] Deuteronomy 20:2–4 affords the best example of the genre. There a priest exhorts the army before battle:

> Hear, O Israel, you are drawing near this day for battle against your enemies: let your heart not faint (*ʾal-yērak lĕbabkem*); do not fear (*ʾal-tîrĕʾû*), or tremble, or be in dread of them; for Yahweh your God is he that goes with you, to fight for you against your enemies, to give you the victory.

Other instances of the war address include Exod 14:13–14, Deut 1:29–30, Josh 8:1, 10:8, 25, 11:6, and Judg 7:3. Von Rad interprets Isa 7:4 against the background of these and other similar texts and concludes: "If now in Yahweh's service Isaiah calls for stillness and fearlessness, that can only mean that the prophet declares this war [the Syro-Ephraimitic crisis] to be a holy war for Yahweh."[53]

The verbal evidence for this interpretation is more ambiguous than it might initially appear. The first imperative, *hiššāmēr*, has no role in the war address. *Hašqēṭ* also does not occur in clear examples of the genre, although *ḥrš* may be a synonym in Exod 14:14.[54] The

---

zur Prophententheologie," 17.) Some evidence for this contrast is apparent in 7:10–17 (see below), but not in v 3.

[52] G. von Rad, *Heilige Krieg*, 56–58; see also E. Würthwein, "Jesaja 7,1–9," 131–32; H. W. Wolff, *Frieden ohne Ende*, 18–19; R. Kilian, *Die Verheissung Immanuels*, 17–23; and R. Bartelmus, "Jes 7,1–17 und das Stilprinzip des Kontrastes," 57–59.

[53] *Heilige Krieg*, 57. R. Bartelmus ("Jes 7,1–17 und das Stilprinzip des Kontrastes," 57–59, 63) argues further that Isaiah viewed Ahaz as the divinely commissioned leader in holy war. The Judean king, however, supposedly failed to understand and accept this role.

[54] Even this parallel is not certain. *Hašqēṭ* in Isa 7:4 focuses on the inward attitude of Ahaz. He is to "stay calm" or to "behave calmly." In contrast, *ḥrš* rarely, if ever, refers to the subjective feelings of human beings. It usually means quite simply "be silent." This may be the meaning of the verb in Exod 14:14. After exhorting the Israelites to fearlessness and affirming Yahweh's will to fight for them against the Egyptians, Moses tells the people not to complain further: "As for you, hold your peace (*wĕʾattem taḥărîšûn*)!" (Compare the different translations in the RSV, NEB, and NJPSV.)

command, *ʾal-tîrāʾ*, is a regular element of the war address, as the examples listed above show, but it is not unique to this genre. The last exhortation, *ûlĕbābĕkā ʾal-yērak*, does occur in Deut 20:3, but the same language appears also in Jer 51:46 (there in combination with *yrʾ*), where the specific notion of holy war is not apparent (compare Lev 26:36). The vocabulary of Isa 7:4 does not warrant reading into the text the entire ideology of holy war.

A second and more plausible interpretation of Isa 7:4 views the prophetic exhortations as part and parcel of a typical oracle of deliverance to a king in the face of military danger.[55] The ancient Near East affords numerous examples of the genre, in which similar calls for fearlessness play a prominent role (see *ANET* 451, 655). Oracles of salvation appear frequently in Deutero-Isaiah, but they were likely at home in the cult.[56] Their form usually includes the command, "Do not fear," and a promise of divine help. Priests presumably gave such oracles to individuals in the lament service, but cultic prophets might also have provided them on occasion, especially for the king in preparation for battle (see Ps 21).[57] Isaiah would have been familiar with the practice, and probably imitated it when he addressed Ahaz.[58]

The first imperative, *hiššāmēr*, merits further attention. It is a *nifal* form of the Hebrew root *šmr* and is generally translated "take heed" or "be careful" (see the KJV, RSV, and NIV).[59] Elsewhere in the Hebrew Bible, a stipulation usually follows the command, stating what

---

[55]See H. Wildberger, *Jesaja 1–12*, 270–72; also F. Huber, *Die anderen Völker*, 19.

[56]See J. Begrich, "Das priesterliche Heilsorakel," 91–92. According to E. Conrad (*Fear Not Warrior: A Study of ʾal tîrāʾ Pericopes in the Hebrew Scriptures* [Brown Judaica Studies 75; Chico: Scholars Press, 1985] 77–107 and 120–23), the so-called salvation oracles that Begrich cites in the preaching of Deutero-Isaiah (for example, Isa 41:8–13, 41:14–16, 43:1–4, 43:4–7, and 44:1–5) and other prophets are in fact war oracles. The content and contexts of the passages in question, however, do not clearly support this interpretation.

[57]Compare also Ps 20, a prayer for the king's victory in battle. The king's confession of confidence in vv 7–9 is probably a response to a cultic oracle no longer preserved. See Mowinckel's discussion of Pss 20 and 21 (*The Psalms in Israel's Worship* [2 vols.; Nashville: Abingdon, 1962] 2. 62–63).

[58]It is interesting to compare the language and thought of Pss 20:7–9, 21:6–12, Isa 30:15–16 and 31:1–6. Cultic prayers for victory in battle and the corresponding oracular answers apparently exercised considerable influence on many of Isaiah's speeches.

[59]"Hüte dich" and "sei vorsichtig" are the German equivalents proposed by B. Duhm (*Das Buch Jesaja*, 72), V. Herntrich (*Der Prophet Jesaja*, 113), H. Donner, *Israel unter den Völkern*, 7), H. W. Wolff (*Frieden ohne Ende*, 8), K. Seybold (*Das davidische Königtum*, 67), and H. Wildberger (*Jesaja 1–12*, 264, 279–80). Others translate the verb "pay attention" or "be alert." See the JB and TEV; also O. Procksch, *Jesaja I*, 110; and G. Fohrer, *Das Buch Jesaja*, 1. 104.

one should not do.⁶⁰ Isaiah's meaning in 7:4, however, is not explicit.⁶¹ According to G. von Rad, the prophet was urging Ahaz to forswear all political and defense measures, trusting instead in the miraculous power of Yahweh's protection.⁶² Isaiah, however, was unlikely so naive politically to advocate this radical position. E. Würthwein and H. Donner construe the prophet's purpose more narrowly: he wanted to prevent the king from appealing to Assyria for military help.⁶³ This interpretation involves reading the report of 2 Kgs 16:7-8 into the Isaianic narrative. According to M. E. W. Thompson, Isaiah did not advocate any specific political or military policy, but only urged Ahaz to have faith in Yahweh.⁶⁴ Certainly, however, the prophet must have had some idea of how such faith would manifest itself concretely in political and military decisions.

The simplest interpretation of the prophet's command would view it in relation to the concrete issue that Ahaz and the royal court were facing at the moment; namely, whether to agree finally to join the Syrian-led coalition or to hold out, trusting that Jerusalem could withstand an attack. Isaiah advocated the latter option: Ahaz should "remain aloof," that is, from the coalition. The house of David should abide by its long-standing policy of political neutrality vis-à-vis anti-Assyrian movements (see Chapter Three, section C4b above).

The prophet speaks of the "two smoldering stumps of firebrands" whom Ahaz should not fear, referring to the Syrian and Israelite

---

⁶⁰*Hšmr pen* ("Take heed, lest . . .") occurs in Gen 24:6, Exod 34:12, Deut 4:23, 6:12, 8:11, 11:16, 12:13, 19, 30, and 15:9 (see also Deut 4:9). Other ways of stating the proscribed action include: *min* with the infinitive construct (Gen 31:29 and 2 Kgs 6:9); *kî* ("that") with *lōʾ* and a finite verb (Deut 4:15); and *ʾal* with the jussive (Exod 10:28, Deut 2:4-5, Judg 13:4, Jer 17:21, Job 36:21 and Mal 2:15). The stipulation is formulated positively in Deut 24:8 and Josh 23:11.

⁶¹*Šmr* in the *nifal* form is used absolutely also in 1 Sam 19:2 and 2 Kgs 6:10. F. Huber (*Die anderen Völker*, 22) argues for the meaning, "be alert or on guard," in these two texts and suggests the same for Isa 7:4. The verb in 1 Sam 19:2, however, might be rendered, "Keep to yourself." The continuation of the verse ("stay in secret and hide yourself") suggests this translation. *Nišmar* in 2 Kgs 6:10 might mean, "he was on guard," but "he saved himself" is also possible (see the RSV). Finally, it is unclear why Isaiah would have especially warned Ahaz to be alert or on guard, if, as we suggested above, the king was already taking steps to prepare Jerusalem for the Syrian-Israelite siege.

⁶²*Heilige Krieg*, 57-58; see H. Gressmann, *Der Messias*, 238; F. Weinrich, *Charakter der "prophetischen Politik"*, 38-52; C. A. Keller, "Das quietistische Element in der Botschaft des Jesaja," *ThZ* 11 (1955) 81-97; and G. Fohrer, *Das Buch Jesaja*, 1. 107.

⁶³E. Würthwein, "Jesaja 7,1-9," 54-55; and H. Donner, *Israel unter den Völkern*, 11. K. A. Tångberg (*Die prophetische Mahnrede. Form- und traditionsgeschichtliche Studien zum prophetischen Umkehrruf* [FRLANT 143; Göttingen: Vandenhoeck & Ruprecht, 1987] 67-69) recently argues the same.

⁶⁴*Situation and Theology*, 28-29.

kings.⁶⁵ (Verse 4b is a glossator's sarcastic explanation of the allusion.) Isaiah carefully chose the image to express his estimation of the threat they posed to Ahaz. Just as the ends of firebrands only smoke and, if left alone, soon go out, so also the plans of Rezin and Pekah would come to nothing. In the short run, Yahweh, Israel's "light" and "flame" (see 10:17), would protect Jerusalem and his anointed. In the long run, the Syrian-led coalition would probably collapse. (The alliance, in fact, may have begun to fold in the late winter of 734/733; both Samsi, queen of Arabia, and several Philistine cities temporarily submitted to Tiglathpileser. Resistance to the Assyrians, however, continued another two years, longer than Isaiah perhaps expected.)

A word of assurance follows in vv 5–9a, promising Ahaz that the Syrian-Israelite attack would fail. The intention of the saying is to imbue in the king the political firmness which the preceding imperatives call for. The verses divide into two parts: an extended causal clause quoting the hostile scheme of Rezin (vv 5–6); and Yahweh's response to the Syrian plan (vv 7, 8a, and 9a). (Verse 8b is widely recognized as an addition.) The divine answer in turn consists of a declaration, *lōʾ tāqûm wĕlōʾ tihyeh* (v 7b), and a *kî*-clause (vv 8a, 9a).⁶⁶ The two feminine verbs, *tāqûm* and *tihyeh*, mean synonymously "happen, come to pass" (compare 8:10 and 14:24), and reach back to *rāʿâ* ("evil") in v 5a for their subject.⁶⁷ Verse 7b is thus a declaration against the success of the Syrian plot. The conjunction *kî* which follows (v 8a) is causal in meaning ("for" or "because"). Verses 8a and

---

⁶⁵J. Schreiner ("Jes 6 und 7,1–17," 69) and R. Bickert ("König Ahas und der Prophet Jesaja," 373) argue that only Rezin/Syria originally played a role in 7:1–17, the mention of Pekah/Israel belonging, then, to a later historicizing layer of the narrative. They conclude that, if the metaphor in v 4a refers to both Rezin and Pekah, it logically must be secondary too. The argument collapses, however, if the focus on Syria/Rezin in vv 2 and 5a merely reflects the superior status of Syria/Rezin over Pekah/Israel.

⁶⁶J. Schreiner ("Jes 6 und 7,1–17," 69), P. Höffken ("Textcharakter von Jesaja 7,1–17," 329), H. Irsigler ("Zeichen und Bezeichnetes," 85–86), and R. Bickert ("König Ahas und der Prophet Jesaja," 373–74, 380) view vv 8a and 9a as an editorial expansion of vv 5–7. Their various arguments, however, are not convincing. It is questionable whether Yahweh's brief pronouncement in v 7 would alone have sufficed as encouragement to Ahaz. Some substantiation of the divine claim seems called for. Despite the uncertain meaning of vv 8a and 9a, diachronic solutions to the passage are unwarranted.

⁶⁷*Tāqûm* might have a similar sense in 28:18ab: the pact which the Jerusalemites have made with Sheol will not "succeed" or "prove effective." The larger context, vv 14–22, contrasts the certainty of destruction decreed by Yahweh (v 22) and the inefficacy of human plans for escaping disaster (vv 14–15). Compare, however, O. Kaiser, *Isaiah 1–12*, 134–36, n. 7.

9a thus explain why the "evil" which Rezin plans "will not arise nor come to pass."[68]

The text through v 4 does not describe the Syrian-Israelite threat in any detail, but notes only that Syria "descended" on Ephraim (v 2a) and that their siege of Jerusalem failed (v 1). This changes in vv 5–6, which quote the scheme of the coalition: "Because Syria has plotted (yaʿaṣ) against you, [in league with] Ephraim and the son of Remaliah, saying, 'Let's go up into Judah and terrify it[69] and split it open for ourselves and set up the son of Tabe'al[70] as king in its midst' ...." In their present form, the verses depict Syria and Israel as equal members of the alliance. The reference to Ephraim and the son of Remaliah (v 5b), however, seems tacked on, and it is generally viewed as a late addition. If the text then spoke originally only of Syria's plotting, this might again reflect Rezin's role as the moving force behind the coalition.

The attack against Jerusalem, we argued earlier, was the final step in a long series of Syrian efforts to win the country over as a coalition

---

[68]M. Saebø ("Formgeschichtliche Erwägungen," 60–64) understands the syntax and sense of 7:7–9a differently. He argues that tāqûm and tihyeh (v 7b) mean "endure, last, continue to exist." Verses 8a and 9a are nominal sentences (kî meaning "that"), which function syntactically as the subject of the preceding verbs. The saying as a whole thus announces the demise of Rezin and Pekah and the fall of their two kingdoms. L. G. Rignell ("Das Immanuelszeichen," 101–6), H. W. Wolff (Frieden ohne Ende, 21–22), O. H. Steck ("Rettung und Verstockung," 80–82), F. Huber (Die anderen Völker, 15–19) and O. Kaiser, (Isaiah 1–12, 134–36) similarly understand the passage. The interpretation, however, is not without difficulties. (1) Nominal sentences introduced by kî are usually coupled with masculine verbs (see K. Seybold, Das davidische Königtum, 68, n. 9). The feminine forms in Isa 7:7b are explained well by taking the feminine noun rāʿâ in v 5a as their subject. (2) The verbs qûm and hyh can refer to the continuing existence of a dynasty or nation (see 1 Sam 13:14 and Amos 7:2), but in the speeches of Isaiah specifically, they often describe the failure or fulfillment of divine and human plans (see again 8:10, 14:24, and 28:18). For these and other criticisms of Saebø's interpretation, see especially H. Irsigler, "Zeichen und Bezeichnetes," 82–85.

[69]The verb, ûněqîṣennâ, appears to derive from qûṣ ("feel dread, be afraid"). The root occurs eight other times in the qal, but Isa 7:6 alone attests to the hifil form. P. de Lagarde ("Kritische Anmerkungen," 14) emends the verb to wěnittěṣennâ (from ntṣ, "pull down"), while others, including B. Duhm (Das Buch Jesaja, 72) and recently F. Huber (Die anderen Völker, 12), read ûněṣîqennâ (from ṣûq, "oppress"). S. Speier ("Ûněqîṣenna, Isaiah 7:6a," JBL 72 [1953] xiv) retains ûněqîṣennâ, but construes its sense according to the Arabic ḳāṣa ("rend asunder, destroy"). Elsewhere in the Hebrew Bible, however, qûṣ does not have this meaning. (Speier appeals to yāqîṣû in Job 14:12, but this verb likely derives from qyṣ or yqṣ, and means "awake.") The qal form of the root, kaṣ, occurs in Isa 7:16 and there refers to Ahaz's fear of Rezin and Pekah. The hifil of qûṣ in v 6 likely has the causative meaning, "make afraid, terrify."

[70]This spelling follows the pointing of the Masoretic text. Compare Tabeēl in the Septuagint.

partner (see Chapter Three, section C4b). Earlier diplomatic overtures had failed. Military action against Judean territory, and with it economic pressure, had not worked. Pekah's kingship in Samaria and Israel's subsequent swing to Rezin's side had brought no change in Davidic policy. Even an attempted coup within Jerusalem had come to nothing. The Syrian king must have felt that time had finally run out for the Davidides. If they were still unwilling to join the coalition, Rezin would have to invade and forcibly replace them with a more cooperative regime.

According to v 6a, the Syrian plan to invade Judah involved "splitting it open for ourselves" (wĕnabqīʿennâ ʾēlēnû). The verb is a *hifil* form of *bqʿ* ("divide, cleave, break open or through") with a feminine pronominal suffix. The term frequently refers to the capture of cities (see 2 Kgs 25:4, Jer 39:2, Ezek 26:10, 30:16, and 2 Chr 32:1), and so might seem to describe the siege of Jerusalem in Isa 7:6. The pronominal suffix, however, likely refers to Judah, though Jerusalem certainly was the ultimate objective of the invasion. The RSV translates the whole phrase, "Let us go conquer it for ourselves," but this rendering gives the wrong impression that the coalition was undertaking full-scale military action against the entire country. Rezin was probably not interested in actually annexing Judah, but simply in establishing his effective control over it.[71] This he could do merely by replacing the ruling dynasty with a new regime, just as he had managed in the northern kingdom by means of Pekah's coup.

Two other interpretations are both possible. (1) "Splitting it [Judah] open" might refer specifically to a *Blitzkrieg*, which the Syrian king was planning and which Isa 10:27d–32 describes (see Chapter Ten below). The coalition forces would march southward from Samaria along the watershed route as far as Bethel and from there thrust suddenly into Judean territory. The aim was to besiege the capital city as quickly as possible, avoiding major strongholds of possible resistance, but otherwise terrifying whatever opposition lay in their path. (2) The phrase, wĕnabqīʿennâ ʾēlēnû, might mean, "let us detach it for ourselves."[72] The text accordingly states the purpose of the Syrian-Israelite invasion, namely, to win Judah away from the Davidides and so secure the country as an ally against Assyria.

Verse 6b names the son of Tabe'al (Tabe'el in the Septuatint) as the intended replacement of Ahaz. Neither the Assyrian records nor other biblical texts mention this figure, and so, not surprisingly, scholars widely disagree over his identity. H. Donner contends that

---

[71]Compare K. Budde, *Jesaja's Erleben*, 39–42; idem., "Jesaja und Ahaz," 125–38; and B. Oded, "The Syro-Ephraimite War Reconsidered," 153–65.

[72]G. R. Driver ("Isaiah I–XXXIX: Textual and Linguistic Problems," 39) suggests this translation, though he believes the text refers to peaceful negotiations with Jerusalem.

the son of Tabe'el was a "pliant Aramean" of non-royal descent, probably a servant of the Syrian king.[73] L. G. Rignell construes Tabe'al as a derogatory word-play on the name Rezin, and thus takes the son of Tabe'al as a reference to the Syrian king himself.[74] B. Mazar links Tabe'el with the name Tobiah, suggesting that the son of Tabe'el in Isa 7:6 was a pre-exilic ancestor of the later Tobiads located in Gilead.[75] W. F. Albright takes Tabe'el as the name of a country in northeast Palestine or southeast Syria.[76] The son of Tabe'el, he proposes, was a Judean prince, whose "mother-house" was the land of Tabeel and whose father was either Azariah or Jotham.

The most promising clue to the identity of the son of Tabe'al lies in the Assyrian tributary list published by L. D. Levine.[77] The inscription mentions Tubail, king of Tyre, among other rulers of Anatolia and Syria-Palestine who had paid tribute to Tiglathpileser in 738 or earlier. The Hebrew $tābē^{\jmath}al$ (literally, "good-for-nothing") is likely a deliberate misspelling of the name of the Tyrian king, expressing either Isaiah's or later copyists' pejorative attitude toward the intended replacement of the Davidic king.[78]

If this interpretation is correct, it was a *Tubailide*, a prince of the Tyrian royal house, whom Rezin planned to install as king in

---

[73]*Israel unter den Völkern*, 12; *Geschichte des Volkes Israels*, 307.

[74]"Das Immanuelszeichen," 104. Rignell explains that the original form of the Syrian king's name was *rṣon*, which means "well-being." Tabe'al expresses the opposite sense: "Not-good."

[75]"The Tobiads," *IEJ* 7 (1957) 137–45, 229–38; see also B. Oded, "The Syro-Ephraimitic War Reconsidered," 161–62. Both Mazar and Oded believe that the son of Tabe'el may have been related by blood also to the Davidides. Oded argues further that he functioned as governor over Judean holdings in Transjordan until Rezin encouraged him to sever his ties with Jerusalem and rule independently.

[76]"The son of Tabeel (Isaiah 7:6)," *BASOR* 140 (1955) 34–35. The argument hinges on the mention of the "land of Tabel" in Nimrud Letter XIV (ND 2773). The reading of the toponym in the Akkadian text, however, is disputed. See H. W. F. Saggs, "Nimrud Letters," 131–33; and H. Donner, "Neue Quellen zur Geschichte des Staates Moab in der zweiten Haefte der 8. Jahrhundert v. Chr.," *MIO* 5 (1957) 170–71.

[77]L. D. Levine, *Two Neo-Assyrian Stelae from Iran*, 11–24. See especially A. Vanel, "Ṭâbe'el en Is. VII 6 et le roi Tubail de Tyr," *VTSup* 26 (1974) 17–24; also J. M. Asurmendi, *La Guerra Siro-Efraimita*, 51–54.

[78]Vanel ("Ṭâbe'el en Is. VII 6," 23–24, n. 3) acknowledges and discusses at length the onomastic and phonetic difficulties involved in equating Tubail and Tabe'el. Asurmendi (*La Guerra Siro-Efraimita*, 54) aptly remarks, however, that in light of the different languages and transmission histories of the Akkadian and biblical texts, the exact preservation of the name of the Tyrian king in Isa 7:6 should not be expected. This would be all the more true, if the name in Isaiah were intentionally misspelled.

Jerusalem.[79] Possibly many Judeans supported the scheme, having grown increasingly disgruntled with Davidic rule during the years of Ahaz. Furthermore, there was precedent for a member of the Tyrian royal house occupying the Judean throne: Athaliah, the daughter of Jezebel and granddaughter of Ittoba'al, king of Sidon and Tyre, ruled as queen of Judah for six years during the previous century (see Josephus, *Ant* VIII. 316–18; 1 Kgs 16:29–31; 2 Kgs 8:25–27 and 11:1–4). Rezin certainly could count on the cooperation of his intended appointee, since the present king of Tyre, Hiram, was an ally of the Syrian king (see ND 4301+4305 rev. 5).

The response of Yahweh to the Syrian scheme follows in vv 7, 8a, and 9a: "It shall not arise nor shall it come to pass, for the head of Syria is Damascus and the head of Damascus is Rezin; and the head of Ephraim is Samaria and the head of Samaria is the son of Remaliah." The opening declaration refers to the "evil" which Syria plots against the Davidic house. Yahweh alone decides the fates of nations and rulers. Not as the Syrian "plans" (*ya'aṣ*, v 5a) but as God "plans" do things "arise" (compare 14:24–27; 19:12, 17, 30:1).

The logic of vv 8a and 9a is not altogether clear. They seem on the surface simply to rehearse the political hierarchies within Syria and Israel—the capitals of the two kingdoms and the rulers of those cities. Ahaz, however, certainly did not need divine instruction on these obvious points. Furthermore, such seemingly banal statements do not explain why the Syrian plot would fail. Unless we construe the verses as nominal clauses (*kî* as "that") or dismiss them altogether as an editorial addition, we must assume that their meaning is more implicit than explicit.

Inferring the precise sense of the passage unavoidably involves a degree of uncertainty and scholars, not surprisingly, understand the verses differently. K. Budde construes the verses as an affirmation of the present political order. Syria and Israel and their respective kings have their own fixed boundaries and spheres of influence, and these do not include Judah and Jerusalem.[80] R. Kilian compares the passage to Isa 31:1–3 and suggests that both texts contrast the feebleness of human power and the true power of Yahweh.[81] In Isaiah 7, the prophet contends that the capitals of Syria and Ephraim are *only*

---

[79]Isa 7:6b could refer specifically to Hiram, the immediate successor of Tubail and ally of Rezin, but more likely a lesser member of the royal house is in mind. (On the chronological sequence of Tyrian kings during the 730s, see M. Cogan, "Tyre and Tiglathpileser III," 96–99.)

[80]K. Budde, *Jesaja's Erleben*, 42–43; see also F. Delitzsch, *The Prophecies of Isaiah*, 1. 168; and G. B. Gray, *The Book of Isaiah*, 1. 119.

[81]*Die Verheissung Immanuels*, 26–28. Kilian describes this contrast as a "basic Isaianic theologumenon, which is evident especially in his polemic against every kind of coalition-politics."

Damascus and Samaria, and the rulers of these cities are *only* Rezin and the son of Remaliah. The plan of the coalition is merely human, not divine, and so it stands little chance of success.[82]

Kilian's interpretation moves in the right direction, but does not go far enough. The series of states, capitals, and rulers is likely elliptical, to be completed by the audience of the prophet: "but the head of Judah is Jerusalem, and the head of Jerusalem is the house of David."[83] Isaiah's aim here is to remind Ahaz of his elected status and of Yahweh's commitment to the protection of Jerusalem. While Damascus and Samaria and their two kings lack divine sanction, the head of Judah is Zion, Yahweh's chosen city and the place where he has installed his anointed, the Davidic king. The divine legitimation and protection of the royal city and leadership had long been celebrated during the national festivals and made the centerpiece of theological claims emanating from the royal court (see Pss 2, 46, 48, 89, 110, 122, and 132; 1 Sam 4–6, 2 Sam 6; 1 Sam 16–2 Sam 7). In Isa 7:7–9a, Isaiah urges Ahaz to take these ancient traditions seriously.[84]

Verse 9b is a warning to the entire Davidic court (the verbs are plural): "If you don't stand firm (*ʾim lōʾ taʾămînû*), you won't stand at all" (*kî lōʾ tēʾāmēnû*).[85] The prophet engages here in a clever word-

---

[82]J. Skinner (*Isaiah*, 56) and R. E. Clements (*Isaiah 1–39*, 85) understand vv 8a and 9a similarly. Compare the variations of the interpretation proposed by J. Lindblom (*The Immanuel Section*, 11), H. Donner (*Israel unter den Völkern*, 13), and T. Lescow ("Jesajas Denkschrift," 319–20).

[83]See E. Würthwein, "Jesaja 7,1–9," 140; H. Donner, *Israel unter den Völkern*, 14; H.-P. Müller, "Imperativ und Verheissung im Alten Testament," *EvT* 28 (1968) 565; W. Zimmerli, "Verkündigung und Sprache der Botschaft Jesajas," in *Fides et Communicatio. Festschrift für Martin Doerne zum 70. Geburtstag* (eds. D. Roessler, G. Voigt, and F. Wintzer; Göttingen: Vandenhoeck & Ruprecht, 1970) 446; K. Seybold, *Das davidische Königtum*, 68–69; and H. Wildberger, *Jesaja 1–12*, 282–83. Many older scholars propose concluding the series, "and the head of Jerusalem is Yahweh" (see for example O. Procksch, *Jesaia I*, 116; and V. Herntrich, *Der Prophet Jesaja*, 118). "House of David," however, is a better parallel to "Rezin" and "the son of Remaliah."

[84]R. Kilian (*Die Verheissung Immanuels*, 26), O. Steck ("Rettung und Verstockung," 78–79), and W. Dietrich (*Jesaja und die Politik*, 84) object to this interpretation on two grounds. (1) Isaiah would not have left his essential point unexpressed. (2) The prophet could not assume that his audience would find his meaning obvious and would complete the series in the way that he intended. The first argument holds true only if the second stands. As suggested above, however, there is good reason to think that Ahaz would have easily guessed the implication of Isaiah's words for the safety of Jerusalem and the king's throne. The Zion-Davidic theology, after all, was largely the propaganda of his own court and probably had been rehearsed publicly only a short while earlier during the new year festival in Tishri 734.

[85]According to C. Hardmeier ("Gesichtspunkte pragmatischer Erzähltextanalyse. 'Glaubt ihr nicht, so bleibt ihr nicht'—ein Glaubensappell an schwankende Anhänger Jesajas," *WD* 15 [1979] 33–54), Isa 7:9b is not part of the divine

play: *taʾămînû* and *tēʾāmēnû* not only sound alike, but derive in fact from the same Hebrew root, *ʾmn*. The second verb, a *nifal* form, clearly refers to the political survival of the house of David. The meaning of the first verb, a *hifil* form of *ʾmn* used absolutely, is less certain.[86] Scholars generally translate the term as "believe," but disagree over the prophet's application of the word. G. von Rad sees Isaiah demanding trust in Yahweh's intention and power to defeat the enemy in holy war. Ahaz should leave off all defense measures.[87] E. Würthwein contends that the implied object of "believe" is the Nathan prophecy (2 Samuel 7) and the covenant thereby established between Yahweh and the Davidic house. Isaiah is warning Ahaz not to break that covenant by appealing to Assyria for help.[88] According to H. W. Wolff, the prophet's demand for faith refers directly to the preceding oracle (vv 7–8a, 9a). Ahaz and the royal court should believe Yahweh's proclamation against the success of the Syrian plan, and so should abandon defense measures and the hope in an alliance with Assyria.[89] M. E. W. Thompson argues that Isaiah did not support any particular course of action, but only advocated religious

---

speech that begins in v 7, but rather is the prophet's direct warning to his followers, the audience of the larger *Denkschrift* (6:1–8:18). As such, the half-verse operates on the "meta-communicative" level of the text. The thesis assumes not only the existence of a *Denkschrift*, but also its original autobiographical form in Isaiah 7. Chapter Four above criticized both assumptions. Furthermore, the problems involved in taking v 9b as part of the preceding speech of Yahweh are not as difficult as Hardmeier suggests. The switch from singular to plural address is apparent not only here, but also in vv 10–17, and is adequately explained by the close association of Ahaz with the entire Davidic dynasty. The attachment of a prophetic warning to a salvation oracle may be simply Isaiah's purposeful modification of a traditional form in special circumstances. Finally, there is no significant tension between, on the one hand, the exhortation to fearlessness and the divine promise in vv 4–9a, and on the other hand, the warning in v 9b. They cohere insofar as they contribute to a single rhetorical goal, namely, to convince Ahaz not to capitulate to the demands of the Syrian-Israelite coalition.

[86] For detailed discussions of the meaning and history of *hʾmyn* in the Hebrew Bible, see E. Pfeiffer, "Glaube im Alten Testament. Eine grammatikalisch-lexikalische Nachprüfung gegenwärtiger Theorien," *ZAW* 71 (1959) 151–64; H. Wildberger, "'Glauben.' Erwägungen zu *hʾmyn*," in *Hebräische Wortforschung. Festschrift zum 80. Geburtstag von Walter Baumgartner* (VTSup 16; Leiden: E. J. Brill, 1967) 372–86; R. Smend, "Zur Geschichte von *hʾmyn*," in *Hebräische Wortforschung*, 284–90 = his *Die Mitte des Alten Testaments* (BEvT 99; Munich: Chr. Kaiser, 1986) 118–23; and A. Jepsen, "*ʾmn*," *TWAT* 1. 320–33.

[87] G. von Rad, *Heilige Krieg*, 56–58.

[88] E. Würthwein, "Jesaja 7,1–9," 138–43.

[89] *Freiden ohne Ende*, 23–25. According to this interpretation, the sense of the *hifil* form in Isa 7:9b is declarative or estimative. To "believe" means to acknowledge the reliability of the word of Yahweh. Würthwein's understanding of the verb is in fact similar, although he thinks of the Nathan prophecy as that which Ahaz should regard as certain and dependable.

faith as the context for making all policy decisions.⁹⁰ Finally, H. Wildberger interprets "believe" as a demand for inner firmness. The prophet warns the Davidides to overcome their fear and display confidence on the basis of the ancient divine promises to the regime.⁹¹

These interpretations read too much of a psychological and/or theological meaning into the text. The *hifil* of *ʾmn* can have a non-religious sense and, when used without an object, may mean simply, "to be firm, stand still, or hold steady" (see Job 39:24). This is the import of Isaiah's words in 7:9b. He is warning the Davidides to be firm, refraining from hasty decisions or policy changes (see 28:16).⁹² Specifically, they should maintain their long-standing isolation vis-à-vis the Syrian-led coalition. As we have suggested repeatedly, the royal court in Jerusalem was under tremendous pressure to join the cause with Rezin and Pekah. The prophet advises the Davidic house to resist this pressure, "standing firm" and abiding by its past policy of political neutrality.

Verse 9b thus reinforces the imperatives of v 4: "Remain aloof and stay calm; don't be afraid, and let your resolve not weaken...." Through its conditional and negative formulation, however, v 9b does more than simply repeat the earlier exhortations; it states the consequence of non-compliance: "you won't stand at all" (literally, "you won't be made firm"). By use of the *nifal* form, *tēʾāmēnû*, Isaiah alludes to the Davidic ideology embodied in the Nathan oracle, in which Yahweh vouchsafed the endurance of the Davidic house (2 Sam 7:16).⁹³ There David is assured, "Your house and your kingdom will be established (*neʾĕman*) forever; your throne will be sure for all time" (compare 1 Sam 25:28, 2 Sam 23:5, and Ps 89:3–5, 19–37).⁹⁴ In Isa

---

⁹⁰*Situation and Theology*, 27–29.

⁹¹H. Wildberger, "Glauben," 377; idem., *Jesaja 1–12*, 285. H.-P. Müller ("Glauben und Bleiben," 33–37) argues similarly, when he assigns the *hifil* of *ʾmn* in Isa 7:9b to a group of "inner factitive" *hifil*-formations. Müller, however, contends that, for Ahaz and his advisors, inner firmness (*das Sich-in-Festigkeit-Versetzen*) should have as its basis the proclamation of divine salvation specifically in vv 4–9a.

⁹²In his discussion of Isa 7:4–9, T. Lescow ("Jesajas Denkschrift," 318) comments, "What can 'believe' in the alleged situation mean other than staying calm and avoiding rash steps?" He correctly concludes (319) that "the absolute use of *hʾmyn* in Isa 7:9 is not an especially theological use of the verb ... but rather a general usage which the prophet follows."

⁹³Most scholars recognize the allusion, but a few remain skeptical. See for example G. Fohrer, *Das Buch Jesaja*, 1. 105, n. 48; and T. Lescow, "Jesajas Denkschrift," 320.

⁹⁴In his classic study of 2 Samuel 7, L. Rost (*Die Überlieferung von der Thronnachfolge Davids* [BWANT III/6; Stuttgart: Kohlhammer, 1926] 46–74 = his *Das kleine Credo und andere Studien zum Alten Testament* [Heidelberg: Quell & Meyer, 1965] 159–83) included v 16 as part of the original oracle of Nathan. R. Smend ("Zur Geschichte von *hʾmyn*," 288) contends, however, that the verse belongs to

7:9b, the prophet warns the royal court that this divine promise will be forfeited, if Judah's political neutrality vis-à-vis Syria is not maintained. The text is silent about whatever practical considerations underlay Isaiah's advice. One may surmise, however, that the prophet anticipated tough Assyrian action against the Davidides, should they join the coalition.

C. Verses 10–17

A dispute between the king and prophet follows in vv 10–17. Isaiah instructs Ahaz to ask a sign from Yahweh (v 11), the king refuses (v 12), the prophet reproves Ahaz (v 13), and proclaims the Immanuel "sign" (vv 14–17). J. Schreiner views the material as an originally independent passage, linked secondarily to vv 1–9 by the editorial bridge in v 10.[95] Connections between the two blocks, however, weigh against understanding vv (10) 11–17 as a once independent literary unit.[96] The intelligibility of the passage depends entirely on what is said about Rezin and Pekah in vv 1–6 and on the divine oracle in vv 7–9. Noteworthy, too, is the linguistic link. The coalition intends to "terrify" (ûněqîṣennâ) Judah (v 6); Ahaz is "terrified" (qāṣ) of Rezin and Pekah (v 16). A kind of narrative gap does occur between vv 9 and 10, in that the text does not recount, but simply assumes, the prophet's actual deliverance of the speech dictated in vv 3–9. Such foreshortening, however, is a common technique in Hebrew narrative and provides no basis for Schreiner's redaction-critical conclusion.[97]

Two other features of the text do reflect a degree of tension between vv 1–9 and 10–17. (1) In its present form, v 10 states, "And Yahweh spoke again to Ahaz" (wayyôsep yhwh dabbēr ʾel-ʾāḥāz lēʾmōr).

---

an editorial layer dating to a time long after the eighth-century prophet. This conclusion is by no means certain. Recent literary analyses assign v 16 to a redactional layer dating to the time of Solomon or his successor. See F. M. Cross, *Canaanite Myth and Hebrew Epic: Essays in the History of the Religion of Israel* (Cambridge/London: Harvard University Press, 1973) 241–61; and T. Mettinger, *King and Messiah: The Civil and Sacral Legitimation of the Israelite Kings* (Lund: CWK Gleerup, 1976) 48–63. While the precise compositional history of the text remains uncertain, the divine promise in v 16 was likely an ancient tradition by the time of Isaiah, though not necessrily in its present literary form.

[95] "Jes 6 und 7,1–17," 96.

[96] See R. Kilian, *Die Verheissung Immanuels*, 30–32; P. Höffken, "Textcharakter von Jesaja 7,1–17," 322–25; R. Bartelmus, "Jes 7,1–17 und das Stilprinzip des Kontrastes," 55; and H. Irsigler, "Zeichen und Bezeichnetes," 77–78.

[97] See W. Baumgartner, "Ein Kapitel vom hebräischen Erzählungsstil" in *Eucharisterion. Studien zur Religion und Literatur des Alten und Neuen Testaments. Hermann Gunkel zum 60. Geburtstag* (ed. H. Schmidt; Göttingen: Vandenhoeck & Ruprecht, 1923) 146–48.

In vv 3–9, however, Yahweh speaks directly to the prophet and only through him to the king. Similarly in vv 11–17, Isaiah addresses Ahaz in his own voice, referring to Yahweh in the third-person ("Yahweh your god," v 11; "my God," v 13; "the Lord," v 14; and "Yahweh," v 17).[98] The contradiction is adequately handled by the text-critical assumption that v 10 originally read, "And he [Isaiah] spoke again to Ahaz" (compare the Targum).[99] A glossator mistakenly assumed that Yahweh was the subject of the sentence, perhaps under the influence of 8:5 (compare 8:1 and 11), and also because what precedes in vv 7–9 is divine speech.

(2) The scene and time of action seem to change as the narrative progresses.[100] The first encounter between the king and prophet occurs outside the city walls (v 3). If the "young woman" in v 14b is a Davidic princess, as we will argue below, the second exchange between Isaiah and Ahaz (vv 10–17) would seem to take place within the royal palace and at a different point during the Syro-Ephraimitic crisis. This shift in time and location, however, does not warrant separating vv 1–9 and 10–17 as once independent literary units. Although historically distinct, the two encounters may have been fused in popular memory during the early oral stage of their tradition history.

Verses 10–17 exhibit a legendary character, insofar as they depict Isaiah as a wonder-worker.[101] At the outset, he instructs the king to "ask a sign from Yahweh your God." Signs in ancient Israel functioned in a variety of ways: to call something to remembrance, awaken belief, confirm the truth of a saying, legitimate a speaker, and

---

[98]H. W. Wolff (*Frieden ohne Ende*, 12–13) tries to smooth over the tension by construing Yahweh as the subject of "he said" (*wayyōʾmer*) in v 13. The present form of v 10, he argues, is original and reflects the prophet's concern to focus on the encounter between Ahaz and the word of Yahweh. The several third-person references to Yahweh, however, remain a serious problem for this interpretation.

[99]See G. Fohrer, *Das Buch Jesaja*, 1. 110. The frequently emended reading of the verse, "And I [Isaiah] spoke again to Ahaz," demands similar changes in vv 3 and 13 and rests on the questionable assumption that Isaiah 7 is part of the prophet's personal memoir (see Chapter Four, section B2 above).

[100]A number of scholars observe the shift; see for example O. Procksch, *Jesaja I*, 119; J. Lindblom, *The Immanuel Section*, 15; G. Fohrer, *Das Buch Jesaja*, 1. 112; R. E. Clements, *Isaiah 1–39*, 85–86; and M. E. W. Thompson, *Situation and Theology*, 29. Compare, however, the counter-arguments by H. W. Wolff (*Frieden ohne Ende*, 26) and H. Wildberger (*Jesaja 1–12*, 268).

[101]See G. Quell, *Wahre und Falsche Propheten* (Gütersloh: Bertelsmann, 1952) 171, nn. 1 and 2. P. de Lagarde ("Kritische Anmerkungen," 9–13), H. Gressmann (*Der Messias*, 237), and E. Kraeling ("The Immanuel Prophecy," 277–97) go to an extreme when they characterize the whole of 7:1–17 as legend and thus underestimate the historical worth of the narrative. Equally unconvincing, however, is the position of K. Budde ("Das Immanuelzeichen," 36–54) and H. Wildberger (*Jesaja 1–12*, 273, 286), who deny any elements of legend in Isaiah 7.

so forth.[102] A prophetic sign specifically was usually a vivid illustration of a word about the future, the concrete embodiment of the content of a prophetic prediction.[103] This is the way Isaiah himself seems mainly to have understood the term.[104] The symbolic names of his children, and perhaps his own name as well, were "signs and portents in Israel," illustrating what he had predicted about Jerusalem, the Davidic house, Judah, Syria, and Israel during the Syro-Ephraimitic crisis (8:18). A similar understanding of "sign" appears in Isaiah 20, which relates to the revolt of Ashdod and other regional states against Assyria in 714–711. The prophet's walking about Jerusalem naked or partly clad for three years amounted to a kind of street drama that vividly demonstrated his prediction about the dismal fate of Egypt, Ethiopia, and the Palestinian rebels. He thereby underscored his warning against Judah's involvement in the revolt.

In 7:11, the sign offered to Ahaz is of a different sort. It is not intended to illustrate the content of a prediction, but rather to confirm the veracity of Yahweh's pledge to protect the Davidic dynasty against Syria and Israel (vv 7–9a).[105] Such a sign need not be miraculous, but certainly it must be unusual or unexpected. The choice given to the king—"Let it be as deep as Sheol or as high as heaven" (v 11b)—means to say that Ahaz may ask for any sign whatever, even a miraculous one.

---

[102]For a detailed review of the different types of signs in the Hebrew Bible, see F. Helfmeyer, "'ôt," *TWAT* 1. 182–205.

[103]G. Fohrer ("Die Gattung der Berichte über symbolische Handlungen der Propheten," *ZAW* 64 [1952] 117), G. von Rad (*Old Testament Theology*, 2. 96–97), H. Wildberger (*Jesaja 1–12*, 285), and others stress the Israelite belief in the almost magical efficacy of prophetic signs and symbolic actions. A few biblical texts do in fact assume their power to create history (see for example 2 Kgs 13:14–19), but most passages do not suggest that prophetic signs and symbolic actions were anything more than demonstrations of the content of the prophets' preaching. See for example 1 Kgs 22:10–12, Jer 27:1–7, 28:1–16, and Ezek 4:1–3.

[104]See H. Guthe, "Zeichen und Weissagung in Jes 7,14–17," in *Studien zur semitischen Philologie und Religionsgeschichte. Julius Wellhausen zum siebzigsten Geburtstag* (ed. K. Marti; Giessen: A. Töpelmann, 1914) 177–90; and S. Porúbčan, "The Word 'OT in Isaia 7,14," *CBQ* 22 (1960) 144–59.

[105]According to H. Donner (*Israel unter den Völkern*, 15) and M. Gorg ("Hiskija als Immanuel," 115–21), a sign was probably given to the Davidic king during the enthronement ritual, guaranteeing Yahweh's support for his reign and for the dynasty as a whole. In Isa 7:11, they argue, the prophet offers Ahaz the same kind of royal sign, or at least intends such associations. The interpretation would be more convincing if the biblical allusions to the enthronement ritual actually referred to the giving of a sign. The relevant texts, however, mention only Yahweh's willingness to grant the request of the king: for wisdom to govern well (1 Kgs 3:5–9) and for the domination of the nations (Ps 2:8). In Isa 7:11, the sign likely aims at substantiating the reliability of the divine word specifically in vv 7–9a. To be sure, that word implies the safety of the Davidic house.

The scene bears resemblance to the legendary account of Hezekiah's healing in Isaiah 38. There Isaiah declares to the king: "And this will be for you the sign (*hā᾿ôt*) from Yahweh that Yahweh will do this thing which he has promised. Look, I will make the shadow cast by the declining sun on the dial of Ahaz turn back ten steps" (vv 7 and 8).[106] In this passage and 7:11, the sign bears no conceptual similarity to the content of the prophetic prediction. It is arbitrarily chosen as an unusual, if not miraculous, occurrence that vouchsafes God's power and willingness to carry out what he has announced through the prophet (compare Exod 4:1–9, Judg 6:11–24, Jer 44:29–30).[107]

The Immanuel saying (vv 14–17) also has to do ostensibly with a sign. Isaiah here proclaims to the Davidic house: "Therefore (*lākēn*) the Lord himself will give to you a sign (*᾿ôt*). Look, the young woman is pregnant (*hinnēh hāʿalmâ hārâ*) and is about to bear a son (*wĕyōledet bēn*) and she will call his name (*wĕqārā᾿t šĕmô*) Immanuel.[108] Curds and honey will he eat until he knows (*lĕdaʿtô*) how to reject the bad and choose the good."[109] Scholars debate not only the import of the "sign," whether salvation or disaster or both, but also the question, in what precisely the "sign" consists, whether the child's birth from the "young woman," his name, his diet, or a combination of these. Taken by themselves, however, vv 14b–15 do not appear as the presentation of a sign at all. They are instead simply an announcement of the im-

---

[106]S. Porúbčan ("The Word ᾿OT in Isaia 7,14," 148) contends that the number of steps and the additional years of life granted to Hezekiah (v 5) originally agreed. The argument, however, is not based on any textual evidence, but only on the assumption that the prophetic sign symbolically illustrated the prophetic prediction.

[107]For similar comments on the sign in Isa 7:11, see H. Irsigler, "Zeichen und Bezeichnetes," 102–4.

[108]The Masoretic reading, *wĕqārā᾿t*, is apparently an old third-person feminine singular form (see *GKC*, 206). Exegetical considerations and/or the variant readings of the ancient versions and 1QIsa^a have led some scholars to emend or repoint the Masoretic text: *wĕqārā᾿* ("and one will call"; see H. W. Wolff, *Frieden ohne Ende*, 9), *wĕqārā᾿tā* ("and you [Ahaz] will call"; see L. Dequeker, "Isaie vii 14," VT 12 [1962] 331–35), and *wĕqārā᾿tî* ("I [Isaiah] will call"; see H. Donner, *Israel unter den Völkern*, 9). For a good review of the text-critical issue, see H. Wildberger, *Jesaja 1–12*, 267.

[109]The Hebrew *lĕdaʿtô* can be rendered in different ways: "in order that he learns" (see H. W. Wolff, *Frieden ohne Ende*, 10); "when he knows" (see H. Wildberger, *Jesaja 1–12*, 268; and O. Kaiser, *Isaiah 1–12*, 151); and "until he knows" (see F. Delitzsch, *The Prophecies of Isaiah*, 1. 178; and R. Kilian, *Die Verheissung Immanuels*, 38). The last proposal makes best sense in context (compare v 16), and finds support in the Septuagint's *prin ē gnōnai auton* ("before he knows"). Compare also the Targum.

minent birth of a child and a prediction of his survival.[110] Certainly the name of the child, Immanuel ("God-with-us"), is symbolic; it expresses Yahweh's saving presence.[111] Yet of greater consequence than the name is the child himself—his identity as a royal prince and his survival (see below). That he is born of "the young woman" and expresses the likes and dislikes of normal children[112] is not a sign that illustrates or guarantees the truth of a prediction; rather, it is the concrete fulfillment of the prediction itself. The Syrian and Israelite kings will not succeed in exterminating the Davidic line (vv 5–9a).

How the Immanuel saying came to be characterized as a sign is difficult to say. A conclusive answer is certainly impossible, but the

---

[110]F. Hubmann ("Randbemerkungen," 44–45) also questions whether the Immanuel saying originally had to do with a sign. The birth oracle, he claims, was recast as a sign by later editors.

[111]T. Lescow's interpretation of the name as a cry of distress ("Das Geburtsmotiv," 173–76) is largely dictated by the belief that vv 14–17 are threatening. The context of the saying, however, does not demand this reading, the arguments of Lescow and others notwithstanding. Verse 13 expresses the irritation of the prophet, but not his wholesale rejection of the king (see E. Hammershaimb, "The Immanuel Sign," 134–35; J. Lindblom, *The Immanuel Section*, 16; H. Donner, *Israel unter den Völkern*, 16; W. McKane, "Isaiah VII 14–25," 208–9; and J. J. M. Roberts, "Isaiah and His Children," 197). As a hopeful pronouncement, "God-with-us" was probably at home in the cultic celebration of Zion's status as the inviolable city where Yahweh resides (see Ps 46:8 and 12; W. Vischer, *Die Immanuel-Botschaft*, 333). Isaiah apparently appropriated the liturgical formula for the name of the future child, suggesting thereby that Yahweh would protect Jerusalem against the Syrian-Israelite attack. It is possible that the name also sounded positive overtones of the Davidic covenant, already alluded to in v 9b. (In the dynastic oracle of Nathan, Yahweh says to David, "I have been with you wherever you went" [2 Sam 7:9]. Compare the similar language of Ninlil's promises to Esarhaddon and Ashurbanipal, assuring them that she would protect their kingship; *ANET* 450–51, 605–6.)

[112]The expression in vv 15b and 16a, "knowing how to reject the bad and choose the good," has been understood in different ways: as moral discrimination, the maturity to participate in communal decisions, or the ability and authority to govern. See for example H. S. Stern, "The Knowledge of Good and Evil," *VT* 8 (1958) 415; J. Jensen, "The Age of Immanuel," *CBQ* 41 (1979) 225–27, 231–32; O. Kaiser, *Isaiah 1–12*, 161; and M. Gorg, "Hiskija als Immanuel," 120–21. These interpretations all envision an age of several years for the "child." In this case, however, the Immanuel saying would not have been immediately relevant to Ahaz and the Davidic house during the Syro-Ephraimitic crisis. Isaiah more likely meant to suggest how events and circumstances would unfold in the imminent future and so thought of the child's development within the first year or so after his birth. "Knowing how to reject the bad and choose the good" probably refers to the demonstration of likes and dislikes, especially with regard to different foods. Most infants do this increasingly from ten months of age onward. See R. E. Clements, *Isaiah 1–12*, 88; M. E. W. Thompson, "Isaiah's Sign of Immanuel," *ExpTim* 95 (1983) 68; compare G. B. Gray, *The Book of Isaiah*, 1. 131; and J. Skinner, *Isaiah*, 60–61.

following traditio-historical development seems plausible.[113] At some point during the Syro-Ephraimitic crisis, Isaiah chided the Davidic house—"Is it of so little significance to you to weary men that you weary my God also?"—and then continued with the Immanuel saying. The prophet was criticizing the irresoluteness of Ahaz and his advisers; they delayed in adopting a final stand either against or for the Syrian-led coalition. This meaning, however, was lost on a later generation which no longer understood the precise political issue originally at stake. Popular reflection on v 13 produced a different explanation of the prophet's agitation. Unlike Hezekiah, who accepted a sign from Isaiah confirming a divine promise (Isaiah 38), Ahaz refused a sign verifying the truth of Yahweh's pledge to the Davidic house. The legendary portrayal of the prophet as a great sign- or wonder-worker arose then as an attempt to understand v 13. As a corollary of this popular interpretation, the Immanuel saying also was characterized as a "sign," which Yahweh himself would give in lieu of the sign Ahaz refused.

The above discussion has assumed that the Immanuel saying promises salvation to the house of David. The passage, however, is one of the most debated texts in the Hebrew Bible.[114] Most scholars construe the saying partly or entirely as a threat: disaster will overtake Ahaz and most Judeans. The interpretation rests on two main arguments. (1) The heated altercation between the king and prophet (vv 11–13) suggests that what follows is a word of judgment. After Ahaz refuses the first sign from Yahweh, the second sign must be entirely different, guaranteeing punishment rather than deliverance. A reflection of this change is seen in the different ways of referring to Yahweh: at the outset, he is the God of Ahaz ("your God," v 11), but after the king's refusal of a sign, he is the God of Isaiah alone ("my God," v 13). (2) *Lākēn* ("therefore") at the beginning of v 14 typically introduces announcements of judgment in the Hebrew Bible generally and in genuine Isaianic texts particularly (1:24; 5:13, 14, 24; 8:7;

---

[113]Compare the redaction-critical explanation by F. D. Hubmann ("Randbemerkungen," 44–45). According to our interpretation, the "sign"-motif arose during the oral, not written, stage of the literature.

[114]For reviews of the different interpretations of the Immanuel saying, see J. J. Stamm, "La prophétie d'Emmanuel," *RTP* 32 (1944) 97–123; idem., "Neuere Arbeiten zum Immanuel-Problem," 46–53; idem., "Die Immanuel-Perikope im Lichte neuerer Veröffentlichungen," 281–90; idem., "Die Immanuel-Perikope. Eine Nachlese," *TZ* 30 (1974) 11–22; H. W. Wolff, *Frieden ohne Ende*, 32–40; M. Rehm, *Der königliche Messias im Licht der Immanuel-Weissagungen des Buches Jesaja* (Kevalaer: Butzon & Bercker, 1968) 80–121; W. Dietrich, *Jesaja und die Politik*, 76–78; R. Kilian, *Jesaja 1–39*, 15–26.

10:16; 28:14, 16; 29:14; and 30:7).[115] Its function in the Immanuel saying is likely the same.[116]

Neither argument is particularly strong. *Lākēn* often introduces a prophetic statement about Yahweh's actions in the near future.[117] If such statements usually proclaim judgment, that may be only because the prophets preached doom more often than deliverance, especially during the pre-exilic period. Announcements of salvation do occasionally begin with *lākēn* (see for example 2 Kgs 19:32, 22:20; Isa 51:21, 52:6, 53:12; Ezek 36:22, 37:12; Zech 1:16; compare Hos 2:16–17; Isa 10:24, 27:9, 29:22, and 30:18). If the term suggests doom in Isa 7:14, one must demonstrate this sense from the context.[118]

Ahaz's refusal of the first sign (vv 11–12) and Isaiah's retort (v 13) do not demand a threatening meaning for the Immanuel saying. The saying might well be a second attempt to assure the king of Yahweh's support and to convince him thereby to hold out against the Syrian-led coalition. A rough parallel to the passage appears in a prophetic text from Mari, in which the god Dagan-malik declares to the king: "O Zimri-Lim, even though you for your part have spurned me, I for my part shall embrace you. I shall deliver your enemies into your hand . . . ." (*ANET* 630). Just as a salvation oracle is here granted to the king, despite his reproachable behavior, so also in Isa 7:13–17 a promise of deliverance might well follow the criticism of Ahaz. Closer attention to the details of vv 14–17 bear out the plausibility of this interpretation.

---

[115]See especially J. J. Stamm, "La Prophétie d'Emmanuel," 122; idem., "Die Immanuel-Weissagung. Ein Gespräch mit E. Hammershaimb," *VT* 4 (1954) 31. The argument is partly form-critical, but also literary-critical, insofar as it involves distinguishing between the words of Isaiah and secondary passages. *Lākēn* introduces hopeful messages in Isa 10:24, 27:9, 29:22 and 30:18.

[116]Other arguments for the threatening meaning of the saying concern its internal details, for example, the name and diet of the child (vv 14b and 15), the identity of the "land" that will be deserted (v 16b), and the positive or negative import of v 17. On the significance of the name, Immanuel, see n. 111 above. The other details of the passage are discussed below.

[117]"Therefore" suitably translates the term in most instances, including Isa 7:14. Isaiah and other prophets see a causal connection between, on the one hand, divine actions in the future, and on the other hand, human behavior and situations in the past and present. Compare, however, the alternative renderings of *lākēn* as "if" (G. Fohrer, "Zu Jesaja 7,14 im Zusammenhang von Jesaja 7,10–22," *ZAW* 68 [1956] 54–56) and "in these circumstances" (R. Criado, "El valor de *lākēn* [Vg 'propter'] en Is 7,14. Contribucion al estudio de Emmanuel," *Estudios Eclesiasticos* 34 [1960] 741–51).

[118]J. Lindblom (*The Immanuel Section*, 16) is probably correct in stating that the causal adverb is, in itself, neutral.

The saying is composed of two parts. First, vv 14b and 15 focus exclusively on the Immanuel-child.[119] The prophet draws attention to the pregnancy of "the young woman" and to the fast-approaching birth of her son (v 14b), gives instructions as to the naming of the child (v 14b; compare 2 Sam 12:24–25), and predicts that he will grow up on a diet of curds and honey (probably the normal soft food of infants), "until he knows how to reject the bad and choose the good" (v 15).[120] Second, vv 16 and 17 are an extended causal clause (introduced by *kî*), that presents a two-part prophetic announcement about future political developments. Isaiah first predicts the devastation of Syria and Israel: "The land (*hāʾădāmâ*) before whose two kings you [Ahaz] are in dread will be deserted" (v 16b).[121] The prophet thus implies the

---

[119]Most scholars regard v 15 as a late insertion that disrupts the original connection between the naming of Immanuel (v 14) and the explanation of its meaning (v 16). Verse 16, however, does not in fact explain the name specifically (compare Gen 16:11) and so might attach to vv 14–15 together. The promise in v 15 that Immanuel will grow up is central to the meaning of the entire saying (see below).

[120]Scholars have generally attached great symbolic significance to the diet of Immanuel, but disagree on its hopeful or threatening import. According to one understanding, "curds and honey" (*ḥemʾâ ûdĕbaš*) are nomadic fare or the meager food available during times of invasion and siege. They signify the devastation of the cultivated land and the deprivation that follows. (See for example F. Delitzsch, *The Prophecies of Isaiah*, 1. 178; J. J. Stamm, "La prophétie d'Emmanuel," 113–20; E. J. Kissane, "'Butter and Honey He Shall Eat' (Isaiah 7:15)," *Orientalia et Biblica Lovaniensia* 1 [1957] 169–73; G. Fohrer, *Das Buch Jesaja*, 1. 115; and R. Kilian, *Die Verheissung Immanuels*, 38–39.) Other scholars argue that "curds and honey" are rich foods provided by the fertile land, or the food of the gods, or the nutrition of the messiah and the eschatological age. The diet thus implies salvation in the Immanuel saying. (See for example G. B. Gray, *The Book of Isaiah*, 1. 129–31; J. Skinner, *Isaiah*, 60; H. Gressmann, *Der Messias*, 156, 233; J. Lindblom, *The Immanuel Section*, 23–24; E. Hammershaimb, "The Immanuel Sign," 136–37; and M. Rehm, *Der Königliche Messias*, 66–73.)

These interpretations read far too much into v 15. "Curds and honey" were likely the first solid foods given to a small infant (see R. E. Clements, *Isaiah 1–39*, 88). Isaiah's point is simply that Immanuel will survive the present crisis. The hopeful import of his growing up follows from his identity as a Davidic heir (see below).

[121]K. Budde (*Jesaja's Erleben*, 56–57), G. Fohrer (*Das Buch Jesaja*, 1. 116), R. Kilian (*Die Verheissung Immanuels*, 41–42), O. Kaiser (*Isaiah 1–12*, 171), and P. Höffken ("Textcharakter von Jesaja 7,1–17," 326) discount the relative clause, *ʾăšer ʾattâ qāṣ mippĕnê šĕnê mĕlākêhā*, as a secondary addition. Verse 16b, they contend, originally threatened the land of Judah. The arguments for this interpretation, however, are not convincing. Syntactically, the relative clause is complex, but not impossible nor unparalleled (compare Num 22:30). The term, *ʾădāmâ*, usually refers to agricultural land in the Hebrew Bible generally and in Isaiah specifically (see 1:7, 28:24, and perhaps 6:11), but it can also designate an inhabited area (Amos 3:2; for other references, see J. G. Plöger, "*ʾădāmâ*," *TWAT* 1. 99). The use of the singular *hāʾădāmâ* for the two countries of Syria and Israel is not as prob-

failure of the plot against the Davidic house. He then announces to Ahaz the intention of Yahweh to restore the northern kingdom to Davidic control: "Yahweh will bring upon you (*yābî* *yhwh ʿālêkā*) and upon your people [supporters of the Davidides] and upon your ancestral house [the Davidic dynasty—present and future] days which have not been since the day when Ephraim turned away from Judah" (v 17).[122] The whole of this two-part announcement is introduced by the temporal clause in v 16a: "before (*bĕṭerem*) the child [Immanuel] knows how to reject the bad and choose the good," the prophet's predictions will be fulfilled.[123]

The passage as a whole bears some resemblance to birth announcements elsewhere in the Hebrew Bible.[124] In Gen 16:11, for example, the angel of Yahweh addresses Hagar: "Behold, you are pregnant (*hinnāk hārâ*) and will soon bear a son (*wĕyōledet bēn*): you are to call his name (*wĕqārāʾt šĕmô*) Ishmael ["God-gives-heed"], for (*kî*) Yahweh has given heed to your affliction" (compare Gen 17:19 and Judg 13:3–7). The similarity between the vocabulary and syntax

---

lematic as some scholars have thought (see for example G. B. Gray, *The Book of Isaiah*, 1. 132). The phrasing might simply reflect the fact that after Syria "had descended on Ephraim" (7:2), Isaiah viewed the two countries as a single entity. Finally, the context weighs against the originality of the relative clause only if one assumes at the start that 7:14–17 are entirely threatening to Ahaz and the Davidic house.

[122]Most commentators insist on the threatening sense of v 17: Yahweh will bring against the Davidides days of disaster comparable to the time when Israel seceded from Davidic rule (1 Kings 11–12). The editor who added "the king of Assyria" at the end of the verse clearly understood the saying in this way (compare also the Septuagint's translation). Apart from this addition, however, the verse might well function as a promise: Yahweh will bring upon the Davidides days of political power comparable to the era before Israel broke with the Davidic house. It is true that elsewhere in the Hebrew Bible, the expression *yābîʾ/hēbîʾ ʿal* usually indicates judgment, but this is not invariably the case (see Gen 18:19). The interpretation of Isa 7:17 as a promise corresponds well to the hopeful meaning of Immanuel's name and the threat against Ahaz's enemies in v 16. See Hattendorff, "Zu Jes 7,17," *ZAW* 48 (1930) 324–25; E. Hammershaimb, "The Immanuel Sign," 138; J. Lindblom, *The Immanuel Section*, 26–27; S. Mowinckel, *He That Cometh*, 118–19; W. McKane, "Isaiah VII 14–25," 213; J. J. Scullion, "The Understanding of Isaiah 7,10–17," 299; and J. J. M. Roberts, "Isaiah and His Children," 199.

[123]See H. Irsigler's detailed description of the syntax of vv 16b and 17 ("Zeichen und Bezeichnetes," 92–94). He notes the predicate-subject sequence in both sentences and their subordination to the *bĕṭerem*-clause in v 16a. Irsigler argues, however, that the two sentences, though syntactically parallel, elaborate different senses of the Immanuel "sign," a hopeful meaning (v 16) and a threat (v 17).

[124]For form-critical discussions of birth oracles in the Hebrew Bible, especially Isa 7:14–16, see H.-P. Müller, "Glauben und Bleiben," 38–39; and W. Berg, "Die Identität der 'jungen Frau' in Jes 7,14.16," *BN* 13 (1980) 8–11.

of this text and that of Isa 7:14–17 is obvious. Two pecularities of the Isaiah text, however, are important. (1) The prophet does not stop with the naming of the child, but continues to describe how he will grow up (v 15). Indeed, it is this detail about the child, not his name, that receives emphasis, picked up verbally as it is in v 16a. (2) Although vv 16–17 are formally a causal or explanatory clause, it is unclear how their content "explains" what is said about Immanuel in vv 14–15. They say nothing about the child's mother, nor interpret directly the boy's name ("God-with-us"), nor explain the significance of his growing up. An understanding of these matters is simply assumed. The only direct link between the two halves of the passage occurs in vv 15b and 16a, and even here the relation is not a matter of one thing explaining another. The connection is temporal: the child will grow up "until it knows how to reject the bad and choose the good." Before the child reaches that age, Syria and Israel will suffer destruction (v 16b).

How then should we account for the causal form of vv 16–17? The verses do offer an "explanation," but of a peculiar sort. Assuming that the identity of the Immanuel child and the significance of his growing up for the house of David were obvious to his audience, Isaiah simply lays out as a prediction the political developments that must follow in the near future, "before the child knows how to reject the bad and to choose the good." The prophet's argument is the reverse from what we might expect, but is nonetheless effective. He announces the birth, the naming, and the survival of the child (vv 14–15), and then predicts the realization of the political conditions on which what has been said about the child is premised (vv 16–17).

The identity of Immanuel and of his mother are obviously related questions. The text describes the latter as an ʿalmâ, a term that elsewhere in the Hebrew Bible designates young but post-pubescent women of marriageable age (see Gen 24:43; Exod 2:8; Ps 68:26; Cant 1:3; 6:8; Prov 30:18). With regard to her specific identity, however, scholars disagree widely. The following possibilities have been proposed. (1) The young woman is the wife of the prophet, either identical with the prophetess mentioned in 8:3 or another woman whom Isaiah had married.[125] (2) She is a woman of no particular status, but one who happened to be standing near the prophet as he addressed

---

[125] J. J. Stamm, "La prophétie d'Emmanuel," 97–123; idem., "Ein Gespräch mit E. Hammershaimb," 42; idem., "Die Immanuel-Weissagung und die Eschatologie des Jesaja," *TZ* 16 (1960) 439–55; E. Jenni, "Immanuel," *RGG* 3. 677–78; N. K. Gottwald, "Immanuel as the Prophet's Son," *VT* 8 (1958) 36–47; H. Donner, *Israel unter den Völkern*, 17–18; H. M. Wolf, "A Solution to the Immanuel Prophecy in Isaiah 7:14–8:22," *JBL* 91 (1972) 449–56; J. J. M. Roberts, "Isaiah and His Children," 198.

the royal court.¹²⁶ (3) The young woman stands for a collective entity—either Israel,¹²⁷ the Daughter of Zion,¹²⁸ or any Judean woman who may be pregnant at the time.¹²⁹ (4) She is the mother of the future messiah whom Isaiah perhaps saw in a vision.¹³⁰ (5) She is a mythological figure—the mother-goddess whose pregnancy by the god-king and bearing of a divine child ensure the stability and fertility of the world for the upcoming year.¹³¹ (6) The woman is the Judean queen or a member of the royal harem, that is, a wife of Ahaz, whose son (perhaps Hezekiah) would represent the future of the Davidic dynasty.¹³²

If Isa 7:14–17 is interpretated in close connection with the political crisis of the moment, the last of these interpretations, with slight modification, appears to make the best sense. We recall that the goal of the Syro-Ephraimitic campaign was to replace the Davidic leadership in Jerusalem and thereby to ensure complete Judean cooperation with the anti-Assyrian alliance (vv 5 and 6). This would have entailed

---

¹²⁶T. H. Lescow, "Das Geburtsmotiv," 177–78; R. Bartelmus, "Jes 7,1–17 und das Stilprinzip des Kontrastes," 61.

¹²⁷R. G. Rignell, "Das Immanuelszeichen," 112–13.

¹²⁸H. Kruse, "Alma Redemptoris Mater. Eine Auslegung der Immanuel-Weissagung Is 7,14," *Trier TZ* 74 (1965) 15–36; G. Rice, "A Neglected Interpretation," 220–27.

¹²⁹B. Duhm, *Das Buch Jesaja*, 75; G. B. Gray, *The Book of Isaiah*, 1. 125–26; K. Budde, *Jesaja's Erlebnis*, 51–53; idem., "Das Immanuelszeichen," 22–24; L. Köhler, "Zum Verständnis von Jes 7,14," *ZAW* 67 (1955) 48–50; W. McKane, "Isaiah VII 14–25," 213–14; M. E. W. Thompson, "Isaiah's Sign of Immanuel," 70–71.

¹³⁰For recent variations of the messianic interpretation, see J. Coppens, "La Prophétie de la ʿAlmah," *ETL* 28 (1952) 648–78; H. Junker, "Ursprung und Grundzüge des Messiasbildes bei Jesajas," *VTSup* 4 (1957) 181–96; F. L. Moriarty, "The Emmanuel Prophecies," *CBQ* 19 (1957) 226–33; S. Porúbčan, "The Word ʾOT in Isaia 7,14," 156–59; M. Rehm, *Der Königliche Messias*, 110–21; and J. Jensen, "Age of Immanuel," 220–39. Compare the position of H. W. Wolff (*Frieden ohne Ende*, 38–40). He argues that the ʿalmâ is a woman whom the prophet saw only vaguely in a vision and whose significance he himself probably did not know. Her precise identity is thus a mystery. For a similar conclusion, see H. Gese, "Natus ex virgine," in *Probleme biblischer Theologie. Gerhard von Rad zum 70. Geburtstag* (ed. H. W. Wolff; Munich: Chr. Kaiser, 1971) 85–89.

¹³¹R. Kittel, *Die hellenistische Mysterienreligion und das Alte Testament* (Stuttgart: Kohlhammer, 1924); S. Mowinckel, *He That Cometh*, 110–19; E. Hammershaimb, "The Immanuel Sign," 124–42; J. Lindblom, *The Immanuel Section*, 19–25.

¹³²J. Steinmann, *Le Prophète Isaïe*, 70; S. Mowinckel, *He That Cometh*, 113–17; E. Hammershaimb, "The Immanuel Sign," 134–35; J. Lindblom, *The Immanuel Section*, 19; J. J. Scullion, "The Understanding of Isaiah 7,10–17," 295–90; H.-P. Müller, "Glauben und Bleiben," 40; H. Wildberger, *Jesaja 1–12*, 291–93; W. Berg, "Die Identität der 'jungen Frau,'" 13; F. D. Hubmann, "Randbemerkungen," 43; and H. Irsigler, "Zeichen und Bezeichnetes," 107–8. This identification of the ʿalmâ combines with the mythological interpretation in the works of Mowinckel, Hammershaimb, and Lindblom.

not simply deposing Ahaz, but executing him, along with all possible Davidic heirs to the throne, even those yet unborn. The practice of exterminating the ruling family is attested to in earlier Israelite history.[133] The prophet Ahijah called for the assassination of the entire house of Jeroboam I in the form of a prediction:

> Therefore I [Yahweh] will bring ill upon the house of Jeroboam, I shall cut off from Jeroboam every male [literally, "him who pisses on the wall"], of age or under age [or "born and unborn"], in Israel, and I will make utter riddance of what is left of the house of Jeroboam as one clears away dung (1 Kgs 14:10).

Zimri killed Elah the son of Baasha and then executed "all the house of Baasha; he did not leave him a single male of his kinsmen or his friends" (1 Kgs 16:11). When Jehu toppled the Omride dynasty, he slaughtered the seventy sons of Ahab, as well as all other supporters of that regime (2 Kgs 10:1–11; compare 11:1).[134] The pronouncements of both Amos and Hosea against Jeroboam II call for the extermination of the entire dynastic house (Amos 7:9, 17; Hos 1:3). The wiping out of the dynastic line was probably a real threat to Ahaz and the royal court as they anxiously awaited the approach of Syrian and Israelite troops.

It is this threat—the extermination of the Davidic house—which Isaiah's words in 7:14–17 seek to counter. The young woman (the Hebrew noun is accompanied by the definite article) is neither a metaphorical image nor a collective entity, but a definite person who is in attendance at the court and whose pregnancy and bearing of a child represent in a literal sense the survival of the royal house. If this understanding is correct, only one conclusion can follow: the young woman is a Davidic princess, and her son to be born is a potential heir.[135] That the latter will grow up eating "curds and honey" (again,

---

[133]The story of Abimelech (Judg 9:1–6) provides an example from the Canaanite royal history of Shechem (see A. D. H. Mayes, "The Judges and the Rise of the Monarchy," in *Israelite and Judean History* [eds. J. H. Hayes and J. M. Miller; Philadelphia: Westminster, 1977] 316). A more approximate analogy appears in the Assyrian inscriptions of Esarhaddon. After retaking the throne from his older brothers, the king executed not only the brothers, but their male descendants as well (*ANET* 289–90).

[134]See also 2 Kgs 15:16, which reports Menahem's brutal actions against the citizens of Tappuah (emended from *tipsaḥ*), including ripping open all the pregnant women. If the assassinated king, Shallum, had had his home-base in the Tappuah region, the slaughter of pregnant women by Menahem may have been intended in part to eliminate descendants of Shallum, who might challenge the new king's reign.

[135]The woman and child cannot easily be identified as Abi and Hezekiah. According to our chronology (see Chapter Two, the appendix), Hezekiah rose to the throne in 727/726. If he were twenty-five years old at the time, as 2 Kgs 18:2

the normal soft diet of infants) until it "knows how to reject what is bad and choose what is good" (that is, until it begins to express its likes and dislikes, especially regarding various foods) is tantamount to promising the failure of Rezin's plot and the survival of the Davidic regime. It is the fulfillment of the hope that the child's very name expresses for the house of David: "God is with us."

D. Verses 18–20, 23–25

Isaiah 7:18–20, 23–25 contain words of doom by the prophet. (Verses 21–22 likely derive from a late editor.) Against whom the disaster will come, however, is not explicit. Noteworthy is the absence of any reference to the Davidic house and Jerusalem—for these Isaiah foresaw deliverance. Rather, it is the "land" (*hā'āreṣ*, v 24b) that will be affected. According to E. Hammershaimb, Syria and Israel are here in mind.[136] More likely, Isaiah's words are aimed against the many Judeans who were supportive of Rezin and Pekah and whose punishment at the hands of the Assyrians the prophet thus expected. Yahweh will reduce the countryside to a wild, uncultivated state (vv 23–25). The announcement accords with the prophet's anticipation elsewhere of the devastation of "this people" (6:9–11, 8:6–8a, 11–15).

The material consists of three predictions about the events of "that day" (vv 18, 20, and 23), that is, the day of divine action against the land of Judah. The first two sayings, vv 18–19 and v 20, announce Yahweh's use of surrogate powers to wreak havoc on the land and its inhabitants. The third prediction, vv 23–25, describes the wild condition of the country that will follow in the wake of Yahweh's actions. Here and in vv 18–20, Isaiah resumes the language and motifs of chapter 5, the speech from some years earlier about the "vineyard

---

reports, his birth would date long before the Syro-Ephraimitic crisis. While the twenty-five-year figure for Hezekiah's age may be high, the king was probably older than six or seven years, when he began to rule. C. Dohmen ("Das Immanuelzeichen. Ein jesajanisches Drohwort und seine inneralttestamentliche Rezeption," *Bib* 68 [1987] 314–17) suggests that the *ʿalmâ* was an Assyrian princess whom Tiglathpileser gave to Ahaz as a token of the new diplomatic relations between Assyria and Judah (2 Kgs 16:5–9). The theory is overly speculative and, furthermore, appears predicated on the debatable assumption that the Syro-Ephraimitic crisis occurred after Tiglathpileser's first invasion of Palestine and Ahaz's initial submission to Assyrian vassalage (see Chapter Two, section C4b). It is questionable, too, whether Judah was politically significant enough for the Assyrian king to pursue this kind of diplomacy with Ahaz. The precise identity of Immanuel and his mother is unknown and will likely remain so.

[136]"The Immanuel Sign," 138–39. The verses accordingly would elaborate the threat against the two countries in v 16.

gone bad."[137] The prophet apparently expected to see in the unfolding events of the Syro-Ephraimitic crisis the continuing fulfillment of his previous announcements of doom.

The first prediction (vv 18–19) describes Yahweh's bringing insects against the land: "And on that day Yahweh will whistle (*yišrōq*) for the fly which is at the source of the rivers of Egypt and for the bee which is in the land of Assyria." The greatness of their number is emphasized; "all of them" (*kullām*) will settle on the ravines and rocky clefts, "on all the thorn bushes" (*ûbĕkōl hannaʿăṣûṣîm*) and "on all the pastures" (*ûbĕkōl hannahălōlîm*).[138]

The language here is figurative, referring to the imminent invasion of Judah by foreign powers. Years earlier, Isaiah had voiced the same expectation, using similar vocabulary: "He [Yahweh] will raise a signal for a nation afar off, and whistle (*wĕšāraq*) for it from the ends of the earth" (5:26). The parallelism of the sentence, as well as the larger context (5:27–30), indicate that Yahweh's "whistling" refers to his enlisting a foreign army against Judah and Israel. A similar sense in 7:18–19 is suggested from the description in v 20 of the humiliating treatment of prisoners of war. Elsewhere in the Hebrew Bible, the insect imagery similarly describes military enemies (see Deut 1:44, Ps 118:12).

In the earlier speech of chapter 5, Isaiah did not name the enemy nation for whom Yahweh would "whistle." As we proposed earlier (Chapter Four, section A), this vagueness may have been due to the prophet's own uncertainty as to the identity of the invader. In 734–733, however, the prophet could no longer have been in doubt. Assyria had emerged as the dominant world power, even though still struggling with a troublesome Urartu. Tiglathpileser was an obvious threat to rebellious Syro-Palestinian states and the one whom Isaiah expected to devastate the Judean countryside.

Verse 18 speaks not only of "the bee which is in the land of Assyria," but also of "the fly which is at the source of the rivers of Egypt (*biqṣēh yĕʾōrê miṣrāyim*)." The latter might allude to Egypt gen-

---

[137]For the interpretation of Isa 5:1–30 as a single speech from the time of Menahem's rule in Israel, see J. H. Hayes and S. A. Irvine, *Isaiah*, 98–107.

[138]As a noun meaning "pasture" or "watering-place," *nahălōl* occurs only in Isa 7:19. (In Judg 1:30, it is a proper name for a site in Zebulun.) It derives apparently from the root *nhl*, which frequently in the *piel* means "to lead to a watering-place and cause to rest there." H. Wildberger (*Jesaja 1–12*, 303) argues that one can properly speak only of flies, not bees, settling on watering-places. The objection seems a bit captious, yet even if it holds, it demands only that we rethink the meaning of *nahălōl* in v 19. (Wildberger regards all mention of the fly, Egypt, and watering-places as secondary.) See the translation of O. Kaiser (*Isaiah 1–12*, 172), who, following the suggestion of G. Dalman (*Arbeit und Sitte in Palästina* [2 vol.; Gütersloh: Bertelsmann, 1928–32] 2. 323), renders *nahălōlîm* as "thorn hedges" and thus as a synonmn of *hannaʿăṣûṣîm*.

erally, but more likely it refers specifically to Ethiopia, located at the upper reaches of the Nile River and its tributaries. The reference raises a difficult historical problem: did both Assyria and Ethiopia/ Egypt pose military threats to Judah and other Palestinian states during the late 730s? Most scholars answer negatively and so regard the allusion to Ethiopia as a secondary addition.[139] Whether Isaiah spoke of the fly and bee both, or only of the bee, he supposedly had Assyria alone in mind.

This solution is not altogether satisfactory. None of the historical settings usually proposed for the added reference to Ethiopia/ Egypt—for example, 726, 720, 712, or 701—is really suitable. In these later instances, Ethiopia/Egypt appeared as a potential ally of the Palestinian states, not as an enemy. Isaiah himself never speaks of Ethiopia/Egypt as an agent of divine judgment. Rather, during most of the reign of Hezekiah, the prophet inveighed against Judean participation in any alliance with Ethiopia/Egypt (see 18:1–7; 19:1–15; 20:1–6).

If the whole of v 18 derives from Isaiah, the reference to Ethiopia may have Piye in mind. This pharaoh pressed northward into Lower Egypt, probably in 734, presumably in response to Assyria's increasing control of the east Mediterranean ports and, thus, of the region's entire sea trade (see Chapter Two, section B5). Piye thus might have come within Isaiah's purview during the Syro-Ephraimitic crisis. If the assumption is correct, the prophet apparently thought that Ethiopia might seek to safeguard its economic interests not simply by invading Lower Egypt, but by occupying the southern part, if not the whole, of Palestine as well.[140] (Events, however, did not unfold as the prophet had anticipated. In 734/733, Tiglathpileser marched as far south as the "Brook of Egypt," and in subsequent years, he solidified Assyria's control of Palestine.)

The second saying, v 20, introduces a new image to describe Yahweh's use of surrogate powers against Judah. "With the hired

---

[139] According to G. B. Gray (*The Book of Isaiah*, 1. 137–38), K. Marti (*Das Buch Jesaja*, 79–80), H. Barth (*Die Jesaja-Worte in der Josiazeit*, 199) and R. E. Clements (*Isaiah 1–39*, 90), the two relative clauses in v 18 are editorial. The text originally read, "Yahweh will whistle for the fly and bee." The two insects, they claim, both refer to Assyria. Alternatively, H. Wildberger (*Jesaja 1–12*, 301–3) discounts the mention of the fly, but retains the explicit reference to Assyria in v 18b (without the relative pronoun *ʾăšer*). The saying originally read then: "Yahweh will whistle for the bee in the land of Assyria."

[140] The interpretation here is somewhat similar to the proposal of B. Duhm (*Das Buch Jesaja*, 77), J. Skinner (*Isaiah*, 68), K. Budde (*Jesaja's Erleben*, 61), and G. Fohrer (*Das Buch Jesaja*, 1. 118). In Isa 7:18, they contend, the prophet speaks of Egypt and Assyria both invading Judah. Their collision would mean disaster for Judah, because her territory would become the battlefield for war between the two superpowers.

razor" (bĕta'ar haśśĕkîrâ), Yahweh will shave the head and "hair of the feet" (a euphemism for pubic hair) and the beard.[141] What precisely Isaiah had in mind here is not clear. He may have meant that, by means of the "hired razor," Yahweh will impose harsh conditions of mourning on the many Judeans who favored revolt against Assyria (see Deut 21:10–13; Isa 22:12; Jer 41:4–5; 48:37–39). More likely, however, the background of the imagery is an ancient practice of humiliating slaves and prisoners of war by shaving off their hair (see 2 Sam 10:1–5). Isaiah, then, was portraying the ill treatment that the Judeans would suffer at the hands of enemy troops.

Who is the "hired razor" Yahweh will use against the land? Isaiah himself may not have explained the allusion, but the late addition(s) at the end of the verse, bĕ'ebrê nāhār bĕmelek 'aššûr, likely reflects the prophet's meaning. Yahweh will employ the Assyrian army as mercenaries against the Judeans. The sense is similar to that of 10:5–6 and 15—the Assyrian king functions as the instrument of divine wrath.[142]

---

[141] Syntactically, bĕta'ar haśśĕkîrâ can be translated as a genitive construct ("with the razor of the hired one"). In this case, however, it would be hard to explain the feminine form of haśśĕkîrâ. One could retain the Masoretic text and construe the Hebrew phrase as the apposition of two nouns ("with a razor, [namely] the hired one"). Alternatively, one might repoint bĕta'ar as batta'ar and treat haśśĕkîrâ as an attributive adjective. Elsewhere in the Hebrew Bible, ta'ar is sometimes masculine (see Ps 52:4) and sometimes feminine (see Ezek 5:1). The verb tispeh at the end of Isa 7:20 suggests that the subject ta'ar is feminine here also.

[142] According to K. Budde (Jesaja's Erleben, 61), N. K. Gottwald (All the Kingdoms of the Earth, 156), H. Wildberger (Jesaja 1–12, 306) and others, the "hired razor" alludes to the appeal of Ahaz to Assyria for help against Israel and Syria (2 Kgs 16:7–8). Isaiah 7:20 thus states the ironic consequence of the appeal: Yahweh will use against Ahaz the "razor" that the Judean king himself "hired" against his enemies. H. Tadmor and M. Cogan ("Ahaz and Tiglath-Pileser," 503) argue further that the very term śākîr has a negative sense when refering to the hiring of foreign military aid, much in the same way that śōḥad does. Isaiah thereby voiced his disapproval of the Assyrian alliance.

This interpretation is not convincing for several reasons. (1) Unlike śōḥad, śākîr and related forms are not clearly pejorative elsewhere in the Hebrew Bible (see 2 Sam 10:6, Jer 46:21, and 2 Chr 25:6). In the one example that Tadmor and Cogan cite, 2 Kgs 7:6, the verb śākar seems quite neutral in tone. Also in the Near Eastern literature, the term is not always negative. In the ninth-century inscription of Kilamuwa, the king of Ya'udi boasts of "hiring" (skr) the king of Assyria against his enemies at a bargain price (ANET 654). (2) The rest of Isa 7:18–25 neither mentions nor alludes to Ahaz, the Davidic house, or Jerusalem. The verses threaten "the land," that is, Judah, whose many inhabitants had come to oppose Ahaz because of his refusal to join the anti-Assyrian coalition. (3) As argued at length in Chapter Three above, the Kings account of Ahaz's special appeal to Tiglathpileser is historically suspect. The king likely paid Assyrian tribute only in the wake of the Syro-Ephraimitic crisis.

The third saying (7:23–25) predicts the hard conditions in the land that will ensue in the wake of the enemy invasions. McKane denies the threatening character of the verses, seeing in them rather a positive picture of the ideal Canaan, the pastoral land promised to the people of Yahweh.[143] This interpretation, however, is forced. Once allowance is made for the secondary addition in vv 21–22, the whole of vv 18–25 describes the devastation of the land. Verses 23–25 specifically depict the uncultivated state of the Judean countryside. Briers and thorns will replace the once lush and valuable vines (v 23). Indeed, the wild growth will be so extensive that portions of the previously cultivated land will be used for hunting only (v 24). The once carefully hoed hill country will be neglected; no concern will be given to weeding out the briers and thorns that spring up (v 25a).[144] The formerly cultivated fields will be good only for the grazing of livestock (v 25b).

The parallels between this material and the prophet's earlier speech on the "vineyard gone bad" are numerous. In 5:5, Yahweh states that his vineyard will become a "trampling-ground (*lĕmirmās*)"; in 7:25b, the prophet predicts the Judean farmland will become a place where cattle are let loose and a "trampling-ground (*lĕmirmās*)" for sheep. In 5:6, Yahweh declares that the vineyard shall no longer be pruned or "hoed (*yēʿādēr*)" and, consequently, "briers and thorns (*šāmîr wāšāyit*)" will be allowed to grow up. In 7:23–25, Isaiah proclaims that the Judean hills, which used to be "hoed (*yēʿādērûn*)," will no longer be tended; there will be no worrying over "briers and thorns (*šāmîr wāšāyit*)." Indeed, the "briers and thorns" will overgrow the former vineyards (v 23). The connections between the two texts are too close to be accidental. In 7:18–25, the prophet appears to have intentionally taken predictions from the earlier period and applied

---

[143]W. McKane, "Isaiah VII 14–25," 216–18. His argument involves extending the hopeful meaning of vv 21–22 to vv 23–25.

[144]The syntax and meaning of v 25ab are uncertain. The translation of the RSV construes the verb *tābôʾ* as a second person form and takes the noun *yirʾat* adverbially: ". . . you will not come there for fear of briers and thorns." The JB renders the line similarly, except that it construes *tābôʾ* impersonally: ". . . one will not come there . . . ." G. R. Driver ("Textual and Linguistic Problems: Isaiah I-XXXIX," 39–40) takes *yirʾat* as the feminine subject of *tābôʾ* and translates the noun as a collective term: "Those who fear thorns and briers will not come there" (compare the NEB). The NJPSV construes the syntax of the line similarly, but interprets the sense of the line quite differently: "But the perils of thornbush and thistle shall not spread to any of the hills that could only be tilled with a hoe." Driver and the NJPSV probably understand the syntax of v 25a correctly, but miss the sense of Isaiah's words. The prophet emphasizes the reversion of the once cultivated land to its wild state. *Yirʾat šāmîr wāšāyit* may mean then "concern for [removing] thorns and briers." Isaiah's point is that the land will no longer be tilled, so that briers and thorns may grow up and spread.

them to the unfolding events of 734–732. Assyria, Isaiah expected, would devastate the Judean countryside, reducing Yahweh's vineyard to a desolate land unsuitable for agriculture.

E. Conclusions

The preceding study recognized the compositeness of Isaiah 7, the tendentious character of its redaction, and the legendary features of certain parts. It was possible, nevertheless, to obtain a view of Isaiah's preaching during the Syro-Ephraimitic crisis. The analysis argued the following points.

(1) The issue before Ahaz and the Davidic house in the late fall or winter of 734 was whether they should join the Syro-Palestinian revolt against Assyria. Pressure on them came principally from Rezin and Pekah, who were about to besiege Jerusalem and to replace the Davidic regime with a Tyrian prince, the "son of Tabe'el" (7:1–2, 5–6).

(2) Isaiah met Ahaz outside the walls of Jerusalem and urged him to remain firm in his policy of neutrality (7:3–4). He encouraged the king by predicting that the Syrian plan to overthrow the Davidides would fail (vv 5–7). The promise was based on the old traditions about the divinely elected status of Zion and the Davidic house (vv 8a, 9a). The symbolic name of Isaiah's son, She'ar-yashub, reinforced the hopeful message to the king by implying the survival of a remnant—in this context, the Davidic house and its supporters (vv 2 and 3). The prophet concluded with a warning that, if the Davidides did not hold out against the coalition, they would forfeit Yahweh's protection and eventually fall to the Assyrians (v 9b).

(3) In a second meeting with Ahaz, Isaiah first criticized the Davidides for not adhering confidently to their policy of political neutrality (v 13). He then tried again to bolster the king's confidence in his decision not to participate in the anti-Assyrian coalition (vv 14–17). The Immanuel saying predicted that a Davidic princess would soon bear a royal child who would grow up to express the normal likes and dislikes of infants (vv 14–15). The promise essentially affirmed the survival of the dynasty. At the same time, Isaiah also announced the imminent demise of Ahaz's enemies, Syria and Israel (v 16). The prophet concluded by suggesting that in the wake of the Syro-Ephraimitic crisis, the Davidides might again rule over both the northern and southern kingdoms (v 17).[145]

(4) While Isaiah supported the Davidic house, he predicted doom for many Judeans (7:18–25). Because most of the people favored Rezin and Pekah and opposed the neutralist policies of Ahaz (see 8:6), they would suffer at the hands of foreign invaders, specifically

---

[145]See again n. 122 above.

the Assyrians and possibly the Ethiopians as well (vv 18–20). The consequences of the invasions would be disastrous for the land: the Judean countryside would return to a wild state, unfit for settlement (vv 23–25). The prophet viewed these events as the continuing fulfillment of earlier predictions that Yahweh would destroy his vineyard (see 5:1–7). The Davidic house might survive the judgment as a remnant (see 7:3), but most Judeans would meet disaster.

CHAPTER SIX

ISAIAH 8:1-20

Isaiah 8:1-20 contains genuine Isaianic speeches and reports relating to different phases of the Syro-Ephraimitic crisis. Four originally separate units compose the collection.

(1) A symbolic action report (1-4)
(2) An announcement of disaster against Judah, coupled with a promise of deliverance for Jerusalem and the Davidic house (6-8a, 8b-10)
(3) Admonition and promise to the Davidic house (12-15)
(4) A prophetic confession of confidence and an admonition to the Davidic house and its supporters to abide by Isaiah's word (16-18, 19-20)

The units combine to produce the same picture of the prophet's thought that we saw in chapter 7: the Syrian-Israelite alliance will fail, many Judeans will suffer harsh punishment, Yahweh will protect Ahaz, the Davidic house, and Jerusalem.

The autobiographical style runs throughout vv 1-20. In two instances, however, the prophetic "I" may be secondary. The quotation formula of v 5—"And Yahweh spoke to me again"—leads one to expect divine speech in vv 6-8 (or 10). What follows, however, is not a word from Yahweh, but a prophetic speech that refers to the deity in the third person (v 7). The same discrepancy occurs between v 11 and vv 12-15. The evidence indicates that vv 5 and 11 are redactional additions. Whether these derive from Isaiah himself is less certain, but there are no compelling reasons to assume otherwise.[1] We suggest that at some point prior to the outcome of the Syro-Ephraimitic crisis, Isaiah picked up earlier speeches and wove them together into

---

[1] Elsewhere in the book of Isaiah, the prophet appears to have been involved in the written preservation of his words (see 30:8).

a larger memoir, 8:1–20. His additions in vv 5 and 11 lent coherence to the whole by extending the autobiographical style already present in vv 1–4 and 16–20. The additions also emphasized the divine origin, and thus the reliability, of his announcements and advice during the crisis.[2]

A. Verses 1–4

The symbolic action report in 8:1–4 consists of two parts. Verses 1–2 concern the erection of a public inscription. Here Yahweh orders Isaiah, "Take a large tablet[3] and write upon it in common characters,[4] 'Spoil speeds, prey hastes'" (lĕmahēr šālāl ḥāš baz).[5] The narrative does

---

[2]The picture of the material's composition in recent redaction-critical studies is far more complicated than the one presented here. According to O. Kaiser (*Isaiah 1–12*, 114–17, 178–202), none of vv 1–20 derives from the eighth-century prophet. The foundational layer of chapter 8 comes rather from the hand of a deuteronomistic editor, whose words in turn were expanded with eschatological sayings (vv 8b, 9–10), and still later, with historicizing notices (vv 6b, 7ab, 8aa). W. Dietrich (*Jesaja und die Politik*, 62–75, 90–99) and W. Werner ("Vom Prophetenwort zur Prophetentheologie," 1–16, 29–30) are more generous in ascribing verses to Isaiah. They maintain, nevertheless, that editors thoroughly reworked the prophet's speeches and added several words of their own. The discussion below addresses the arguments of these and other scholars as they pertain to individual passages.

[3]The RSV, NEB, O. Kaiser (*Isaiah 1–12*, 178), and H. Wildberger (*Jesaja 1–12*, 311–12) render the Hebrew gillāyôn gādôl in this way (compare the JB, TEV, NIV, and NJPSV). K. Galling ("Ein Stück judäischen Bodenrechts in Jesaja 8," *ZDPV* 56 [1933] 209–18) construes gillāyôn as a papyrus sheet and emends gādôl to gôrāl ("lot"). He translates the whole, "a notice of common land," and thinks of a formal document attesting to an individual's legal claim to a plot of land. For a critique of this interpretation, see the thorough text-critical analysis by H. Wildberger.

[4]The meaning of ḥereṭ ʾĕnôš is uncertain. The Septuagint and Vulgate translate the Hebrew literally, "a stylus of a man." Modern renderings of the phrase include "a hard stylus" (H. Gressmann, *Der Messias*, 239, n. 1), "a broad stylus" (F. Talmage, "ḥrṭ ʾnwš in Isaiah 8:1," *HTR* 60 [1967] 465–68), "a stylus of disaster" (H. Wildberger, *Jesaja 1–12*, 312), and "in common script" (G. Fohrer, *Das Buch Jesaja*, 1. 122). The last translation assumes metonomy (the instrument of writing substituting for what is written), and construes ʾĕnôš along the lines of ʾîš in ʾammat ʾîš, "an ordinary cubit" (Deut 3:11). The reading of the Targum, "write clearly," correctly paraphrases the sense of the Hebrew. Compare Yahweh's instruction to the prophet Habakkuk: "Write the vision and make it plain on tablets so that he may run who reads it" (kĕtôb ḥāzôn ûbāʾēr ʿal-hallūḥôt lĕmaʿan yārûṣ qôrēʾ bô; Hab 2:2).

[5]Scholars debate the grammar and syntax of the inscribed words. Compare P. Humbert, "Maher Salal Has Baz," *ZAW* 50 (1932) 90–92; S. Morenz, "Eilebeute," *TLZ* 74 (1949) 697–99; H. Donner, *Israel unter den Völkern*, 19; E. Vogt, "Einige hebräische Wortbedeutungen," *Bib* 48 (1967) 63–69; H.-P. Müller, "Glauben und

not actually recount, but simply assumes, that the prophet carried out the command. It adds only that Isaiah secured two reliable witnesses to the event—Uriah the priest (see 2 Kgs 16:10–16) and an otherwise unknown Zechariah, the son of Jeberechiah.[6]

The second part, vv 3–4, reports the conception and birth of the prophet's son by "the prophetess," and then relates Yahweh's instruction for the naming of the child. The latter entails: (a) the divine command, "Call his name Maher-shalal-hash-baz"; and (b) the explanation of the name—"for before the child knows how to call 'Father' and 'Mother,' the wealth of Damascus and the spoil of Samaria will be carried away before the king of Assyria."

The words, *lĕmahēr šālāl ḥāš baz*, connect the inscription and the naming of Isaiah's son. Most scholars take the expression in both instances as the proper name of the child, but the assumption raises problems. Isaiah would not likely have promulgated the name of his son at a time when the child had not yet even been conceived. Furthermore, the recorded order of events suggests that Yahweh revealed the significance of the name only after the child's birth. The prophet would thus not have understood its meaning when he first wrote it down for public reading. This conclusion, however, is most improbable.[7]

Various interpretations struggle to resolve these temporal difficulties. G. B. Gray suggests transposing vv 1–2 and vv 3–4, so that the erection of the inscription would follow the birth and naming of Maher-shalal-hash-baz. The tablet, he argues, would then have a "clear destination; it would be for Isaiah's son. As the text stands, the tablet is inscribed with a name that attaches to no one."[8] Gray, however, does not account for the present order of the passage, nor does he explain why the prophet would have inscribed the name after the child had already been born.

A more frequent interpretation adheres to the present arrangement of the text, but construes the verb tenses in v 3 as pluperfects: "I had approached (*wāʾeqrab*) the prophetess and she had conceived

---

Bleiben," 44; and H. Wildberger, *Jesaja 1–12*, 313. The translation here takes *mahēr* and *ḥāš* as participles and the two nouns, *šālāl* and *baz*, as their subjects. The threatening sense of the words is the same in any case: military defeat and plundering are imminent. The preposition *lĕ* that introduces the saying is an instance of the "lamed inscriptionis" (compare Ezek 37:16; see *GKC* 381–82).

[6]Like Uriah, Zechariah may have been a high religious official. The testimony of both would be particularly appropriate if the prophet's inscription was set up somewhere within the temple area. (Hab 2:2 attests to the custom of prophets writing and posting their oracles in easily readable script.)

[7]Compare H. J. Elhorst, "Jesaja 8,1–4," *ZAW* 33 (1915) 100; and T. C. Vriezen, "Prophecy and Eschatology," *VTSup* 1 (1953) 209, n. 1. Both scholars contend that Isaiah was initially ignorant of the name's meaning.

[8]G. B. Gray, *The Book of Isaiah*, 1. 144.

(*wattahar*) and had borne (*wattēled*) a son and Yahweh had said (*wayyōʾmer*) to me...."[9] The time lapse between the inscription and the naming of the child is thereby eliminated. The series of imperfect consecutive forms, however, reflects a simple narrative style, in which events are recounted sequentially.[10] The Hebrew clearly suggests that the erection of the inscription long preceded the birth and naming of the prophet's son.[11]

A more satisfactory solution is to assume that Isaiah first used the expression, "spoil speeds, prey hastes," as a kind of motto or slogan. It "attaches to no one" in v 1, as Gray notes, because the prophet did not intend it as a proper name.[12] When Isaiah inscribed the saying as a public proclamation, he presumably understood something definite by it, and perhaps used it as a basis for more elaborate preaching. Several months later, when his son was born, Isaiah reused the slogan as a symbolic name for the child. At a still later point during the Syro-Ephraimitic crisis, the prophet recorded both symbolic actions in writing, but he reported the sense of the slogan/name only once (v 4).[13]

When precisely Isaiah first preached "spoil speeds, prey hastes" is difficult to say. Two considerations suggest a date several months before the Syro-Ephraimitic crisis. First, vv 3–4 likely indicate that the prophet applied the saying to his son at a time when Syria and Israel

---

[9] See for example B. Duhm, *Das Buch Jesaja*, 79; K. Marti, *Das Buch Jesaja*, 82; and L. G. Rignell, "Das Orakel 'Maher-salal Has-bas.' Jesaja 8," *ST* 10 (1957) 41.

[10] See S. R. Driver, *A Treatise on the Use of Hebrew Tenses* (3d ed.; Oxford: Clarendon, 1892) sec. 76.

[11] H. Donner (*Israel unter den Völkern*, 20–21) and O. H. Steck ("Jesaja 7,10–17 und 8,1–4," 175–78), among others, make the same observation. Steck, however, draws the wrong conclusion, namely, that the recorded order of events does not reflect their true historical sequence, but rather serves the theological interests of the larger *Denkschrift*, especially the *Verstockung*-theme. Steck's conception of a *Denkschrift* is probably wrong altogether (see Chapter Four above), but even if we were to accept it, his interpretation of 8:1–4 would still be problematic. The readers of the *Denkschrift* would not likely have accepted theological claims based on a presentation of events which they, as contemporaries of the prophet, knew to be wrong. Even Isaiah did not likely enjoy this kind of theological license.

[12] F. Delitzsch (*The Prophecies of Isaiah*, 1. 187) correctly stresses this point: "Most interpreters here [8:1] introduce confusion by taking these words at the same time as the name of a person... this to begin with they are not, though they become so later. In the first instance they are an oracular proclamation of the immediate future...."

[13] According to H. Donner (*Israel unter den Völkern*, 21), Isaiah was guided here by an interest in brevity and good narrative style. As we will see below, another explanation is also possible. Between the erection of the inscription and the naming of the prophet's son, political circumstances may have changed, and with them Isaiah's precise understanding of *mahēr šālāl ḥāš baz*. Naturally, however, he recorded only the updated interpretation, now given in v 4.

were allies against Assyria and, presumably, also a threat to the Davidic house.[14] The birth and symbolic naming of the child occurred, then, between Pekah's coup in Samaria (Tishri 734) and the first Assyrian campaign to Palestine (the winter of 733).[15] Second, the narrative sequence of events in 8:1–4 indicates that the inscription preceded the birth of Maher-shalal-hash-baz by at least nine months. Taken together, these two facts point to the early part of 734 (either the winter or early spring) as the occasion when Isaiah first preached "spoil speeds, prey hastes." This was a time when Tiglathpileser was campaigning in the eastern part of the empire and Rezin of Syria was strongly pressuring both Pekahiah of Israel and Ahaz of Judah to join the coalition against Assyria. By means of the inscribed slogan, Isaiah expressed his estimation of the revolt's chances of success: the Assyrians would defeat and pillage Syria. If this interpretation is correct, the implications of the prophet's message for Ahaz and Jerusalem would have been clear: they should remain aloof from the coalition.

Nine or more months after the inscription, Isaiah named his newborn son, Maher-shalal-hash-baz. The reuse of the slogan in this way may have been motivated by two political developments. (1) Assyria had not dealt with Rezin as quickly as the prophet had anticipated. Throughout the winter and early spring of 734, or possibly longer, Tiglathpileser was still bogged down in the east with Urartu and had not yet taken action against the budding revolt in the west. (2) With Pekah's coup in Samaria, Israel swung to the side of Syria. The coalition's prospects for success perhaps looked better than ever in the fall of 734, and the pressure on the Davidides to join the cause was certainly rising. In these circumstances, the Jerusalemite public and the royal court must have wondered whether Isaiah's previous prediction and advice had been correct.

The response of the prophet to such doubt was firm. Boldly he repeated the threat, "spoil speeds, prey hastes," appropriating the slogan for the symbolic name of his son. At the same time, he extended its reference so as to include Syria and Israel together. Perhaps with an eye to quelling increased skepticism over his powers

---

[14]Compare W. Dietrich, *Jesaja und die Politik*, 91. He argues that the "wealth of Damascus" and the "spoil of Samaria" (v 4) refer to spoil which Rezin and Pekah had seized from Judah. He dates the saying to a time after the Syrian-Israelite invasion of Judah.

[15]This is also the approximate period for the birth and naming of the royal child, Immanuel. The two symbolic names express the two sides of the same message—salvation for the Davidic house and disaster for its enemies, Syria and Israel. Compare the interpretation of H. Donner (*Israel unter den Völkern*, 21–22), who separates the births of the two children by ten or eleven months. His argument assumes that Immanuel and Maher-shalal-hash-baz are both sons of the prophet by the same woman.

of prognostication, he added too a temporal limit, within which the saying would be fulfilled: "before the child knows how to cry 'Father' and 'Mother'"—that is, within a year—Assyria would crush the coalition.

B. Verses 6–8a, 8b–10

Isaiah 8:6–10 contain a threat against "this people," the Judeans (vv 6–8a), and a promise of deliverance for Jerusalem and/or the Davidic house (vv 8b–10).[16] Scholars usually treat these as two separate sayings,[17] but they belong together as parts of a single speech, linked by the perfect consecutive form, *wĕhāyâ*, at the beginning of v 8b. The force of the conjunction is adversative: Yahweh is bringing disaster against "this people," *but* "us" God will protect.

Historical allusions within 8:6–10 help date the passage. If vv 7–8a speak of an Assyrian invasion of Judah as a future event, the speech likely anticipates Tiglathpileser's first campaign to Palestine in the early months of 733.[18] (As events actually transpired, the

---

[16]L. G. Rignell ("Maher-salal Has-baz," 41–42) identifies "this people" as the Israelites. The passage would then continue the thought of vv 1–4. The argument rests largely on the assumption that, if "this people" supported Rezin and Pekah, as 8:6b states, they were propably the Israelites, not the Judeans. Verse 6a, however, accuses "this people" of having "rejected (*māʾas*) the waters of Shiloah." The allusion here is most likely to the Judeans. Note further that v 8a explicitly anticipates the Assyrian invasion of Judah. The reference is not made merely in passing, as Rignell is forced to argue. See K. Fullerton, "The Interpretation of Isaiah 8:5–10," *JBL* 43 (1924) 254–64; also H. Donner, *Israel unter den Völkern*, 24, n. 3; and H. Wildberger, *Jesaja 1–12*, 323.

[17]See for example B. Duhm, *Das Buch Jesaja*, 79–82; G. B. Gray, *The Book of Isaiah*, 1. 144–50; J. Lindblom, *The Immanuel Section*, 32; G. Fohrer, *Das Buch Jesaja*, 1. 126–29; H. Donner, *Israel unter den Völkern*, 22–27; W. Dietrich, *Jesaja und die Politik*, 134–35, 159–61; H.-P. Müller, "Glauben und Bleiben," 45–49; H. Wildberger, *Jesaja 1–12*, 321–33; R. E. Clements, *Isaiah 1–39*, 96–98; and W. Werner, "Vom Prophetenwort zur Prophetentheologie," 11–12. While they agree that 8:5–10 is not all of one piece, they debate two related questions. (1) Does v 8b belong with what precedes or what follows? (2) Do vv 8b and 9–10 derive from Isaiah or later editors? See the discussion of these issues below, especially in nn. 49 and 54.

[18]Compare W. Dietrich, *Jesaja und die Politik*, 159–60. He treats vv 6–8a and vv 9–10 as separate speeches and dates both to the period of Sennacherib's invasion (705–701). The later dating, especially in regard to vv 6–8a, rests on questionable arguments. (1) Dietrich dismisses the explicit reference to Rezin and Pekah in v 6b as a redactor's addition, and then observes that the remainder of the passage does not clearly allude to the Syro-Ephraimitic crisis. The case against the authenticity of v 6b, however, is not strong. If the line is original to Isaiah, as we will argue below, the speech would date to 734/733. (2) Dietrich assumes that Tiglathpileser's invasion of Palestine was motivated in part by Ahaz's appeal for help against Syria and Israel (2 Kgs 16:7–9). In these circumstances, Dietrich rea-

Assyrian army moved along the Mediterranean coast toward Gaza, without penetrating the heartland of Judah.) Furthermore, if the reference to "nations" and "far-off lands" and the assertion that their plans will not "arise" (vv 9–10a) have as their background the designs of Rezin and Pekah upon Jerusalem (7:5–6), the passage would date shortly before the Syrian-Israelite siege of the capital city. Finally, the address to Immanuel in v 8b and the play on his name at the end of v 10 might reflect the recent birth of the royal child. The birth would have inspired the prophet with confidence in the survival of the Davidic house and so may have prompted these verses.[19]

Verses 6–8a combine a reproach of "this people" (v 6) with a threat of divine punishment (vv 7–8a). The two parts are connected syntactically (*ya'an kî . . . wĕlākēn*; "because . . . therefore"), and also by means of a single metaphor: the people have spurned the "gently flowing waters of the Shiloah;" Yahweh is about to bring against them the "mighty and many waters of the River" (Euphrates).

The interpretation of the verses depends largely on the text-critical assessment of v 6b: *ûmĕśôś ʾet-rĕṣîn ûben-rĕmalyāhû*. The Hebrew means literally, "and rejoicing with Rezin and the son of Remaliah."[20] Most scholars consider the line corrupt, not only for linguistic reasons, but also because of its supposedly impossible sense. H.

---

sons, Isaiah's threat that Assyria would invade Judah (vv 7–8a) would make little sense. The argument collapses, however, if the idea of the appeal is a deuteronomistic invention (see Chapter Three above). Isaiah might well have expected the Assyrians to move against Judah, if as v 6b indicates, many Judeans favored Rezin and Pekah. (3) Dietrich sees in v 6a a condemnation of Hezekiah's tunnel connecting the Gihon Spring and the Pool of Siloam (see 2 Kgs 20:20; 2 Chr 32:30). The allusion, however, is doubtful, especially if v 6b is original. The vast majority of scholars correctly interpret 8:6–8a against the background of the Syro-Ephraimitic crisis.

[19] According to most scholars, Isa 8:5–8 are the prophet's response to Ahaz's recent appeal to Assyria. See for example H. Donner, *Israel unter den Völkern*, 24; H. Wildberger, *Jesaja 1–12*, 322–23; and R. E. Clements, *Isaiah 1–39*, 96. Wildberger suggests further that, at the time of 8:5–8, Tiglathpileser had already responded to the appeal and had intervened in Syria-Palestine. The interpretation wrongly includes Ahaz and the Davidides among "this people," and then imports 2 Kgs 16:7–8 all too quickly into the exegesis of Isaiah.

[20] The noun *mĕśôś* is apparently a construct form of *māśôś*, "exultation," from the root *śûś/śîś*, "rejoice." The *ʾet* which follows is either the preposition "with" or the accusative particle. According to *GKC* (421), the construct state occasionally connects with prepositions, especially in prophetic or poetic style. Besides Isa 8:6b, however, no other examples for the combination of the construct state and the preposition *ʾet* specifically are listed. Jer 33:22 possibly attests to the combination of the construct state with the accusative particle (*mĕšārĕtê ʾōtî*). Some scholars, however, question the correctness of this phrase also; see W. Rudolph, *Jeremia* (3d ed; Tübingen: J. C. B. Mohr [Paul Siebeck], 1968) 218; J. Bright, *Jeremiah* (AB 21; Garden City: Doubleday, 1965) 194. The syntax of both Isa 8:6b and Jer 33:22, though perhaps not impossible, is certainly unusual.

Wildberger's comment on the passage is typical in this regard: "Who in Jerusalem would have rejoiced in Rezin and the son of Remaliah, where apparently everyone lived in fear before the two kings?"[21]

Textual reconstructions of the verse usually involve changing *měśôś* to a *qal* form of *mss*, "dissolve, melt (in fear)."[22] Variations of the proposal lie behind the following translations.

> Because this people reject the waters of Shiloah which run gently and dispersing away . . .[23]
>
> Because this people scorn the waters of Shiloah which flow gently and languish because of Rezin and the son of Remaliah . . .[24]
>
> Because this people spurns the gently running waters of Shiloah and melt in fear because of the arrogance of Rezin and the son of Remaliah . . .[25]
>
> Because this people scorns the gently flowing waters of Shiloah because of the uproar of Rezin and the son of Remaliah . . .[26]

---

[21]*Jesaja 1–12*, 323. Compare, however, L. G. Rignell, "Maher-salal Has-baz," 41–42. He argues that v 6b makes good sense, if "this people" in v 6a refers to the Syrians and Israelites (see n. 16 above). K. Fullerton ("Isaiah 8:5–10," 269–70) sets forth a similar interpretation, though he is careful to state that it pertains only to the present form of the text. A glossator, he claims, inserted v 6b, as well as the phrase *'ălêhem* ("upon them") in v 7aa. The additions reinterpreted v 6a as a condemnation of the Israelites. Isaiah originally had the Judeans in mind.

[22]The *qal* infinitive construct of *mss* appears to occur in Isa 10:18: *wěhāyâ kimsōs nōsēs* ("and it will be as when a sick person wastes away"). The Hebrew here is difficult, however, and may be corrupt (see Chapter Nine, n. 36 below). Most other instances of the verb are *nifal* forms. When *mss* means "fear," its grammatical subject is usually *lēb* (a person's "heart melts"; see Deut 1:28, 20:8, Josh 2:11, 5:1, 7:5, Isa 13:17, 19:1, Ezek 21:12, Pss 22:15; compare 2 Sam 17:10).

[23]See F. Giesebrecht, "Die Immanuel-Weissagung," *TSK* (1888) 227. The reading discards *'et-rěṣîn ûben-rěmalyāhû* as an explanatory gloss to the "waters of Shiloah," changes *měśôś* to *měsôs*, and takes the emended form as a parallel to *lě'aṭ* ("gently"). The proposals of V. Herntrich (*Der Prophet Jesaia*, 143), O. Procksch (*Jesaja I*, 131) and R. E. Clements (*Isaiah 1–39*, 96) are similar. It is difficult, however, to see how "Rezin and the son of Remaliah" explains the "waters of Shiloah." See the understandably skeptical comments of K. Fullerton ("Isaiah 8:5–10," 268).

[24]So B. Duhm (*Das Buch Jesaja*, 80) reads the verse, emending *měśôś* to *māsas* and *'et-rěṣîn* to *měrěṣîn*. Compare the reconstruction of the line by K. Marti (*Das Buch Jesaja*, 84): *ûmāsōs mippěnê/millipnê rěṣîn ûben-rěmalyāhû*.

[25]H. Wildberger (*Jesaja 1–12*, 321) suggests this reading, emending *měśôś* to *māsôs* and *'et-rěṣîn to miśśě'ēt rěṣîn*. Compare K. Budde's reconstruction of the text: *māsôś miśśě'ēt rěṣîn ûben-rěmalyāhû* ("Jes 8,6b," *ZAW* 44 [1926] 65–67). He construes *māsôs* as the infinitive absolute of the root *mśś*, supposedly a bi-form of *mss* meaning "despair." (H.-P. Müller ["Glauben und Bleiben," 45, n. 4] recently argues the same.) *Mśś* is unattested elsewhere in the Hebrew Bible.

[26]H. Donner, *Israel unter den Völkern*, 22–23. The reading calls for emending *ûměśôś 'et-* to *miśśō'at*.

Because this people rejects the gently running waters of Shiloah and dissolves together with Rezin and the son of Remaliah . . .[27]

Several reasons weigh against these and similar readings. (1) Textual evidence for emending v 6b is altogether lacking. The ancient versions all seem to assume a Hebrew text similar, if not identical, to the Masoretic text.[28] (2) Emending *měśôś* to a form of *mss* does not alone resolve the line's difficult syntax. Further alterations of the text are usually required, thus weakening the force of the argument.[29]

(3) With one minor adjustment in the Masoretic pointing, *ûměśôś* to *ûmāśôś*, it is possible to explain the unusual Hebrew of v 6b as an example of legitimate poetic license.[30] If the syntax of the line were normal, one would see a verbal form of *śûś/śîś* followed by the preposition *b* or *ʿal* ("rejoice in or over [someone]"). As v 6b stands, the noun *māśôś* is followed by the accusative particle or the preposition *ʾēt*. Isaiah may have intentionally phrased the line in assimilation to the Hebrew of v 6a, *māʾas* . . . *ʾēt*. The deviation from normal syntax skillfully produces verbal assonance, while still conveying the general sense of "this people's rejoicing in Rezin and the son of Remaliah."

(4) The sense of Isa 8:6b is not impossible. Only if one insists that the Davidic king and Judean people alike feared Rezin and Pekah (and so appealed to Assyria for help; 2 Kgs 16:5–9) does the meaning of the verse seem wrong. Without textual evidence to the contrary, however, the Masoretic text should be retained and the historical background understood accordingly.

Alongside the text-critical issue is the literary-critical question, Does v 6b belong originally to the prophet's speech? W. Dietrich, among others, is doubtful.[31] He contends that the line disrupts the close connection between the "gently flowing waters of Shiloah" (v 6a) and the "mighty and many waters of the River" (v 7aa). Dietrich

---

[27]So J. Lindblom (*The Immanuel Section*, 44) translates the verse, changing *měśôś* to *māsos*, but retaining *ʾet* as the preposition "with."

[28]The Septuagint reads: "but desired to have Rasin and the son of Romelias as king over them." The Targum is similar: "and are pleased with Rezin and the son of Remeliah." Compare also the Vulgate: "and has rather taken Rasin, and the son of Romelia."

[29]An exception is the proposal of A. M. Honeyman ("Traces of an Early Diacritic Sign in Isaiah 8:6b," *JBL* 63 [1944] 45–50). His reconstruction of the verse is limited to emending *ûměśôś* to *ûmāśô* (the infinitive absolute of *mšh*). The resulting translation, however, seems forced: "and [this people] drew up (out of the water) Rezin and the son of Remaliah." Nevertheless, Honeyman senses correctly that 8:6b alludes to the favorable attitude of most Judeans toward the Syrian and Israelite kings.

[30]See H. Klein, "Freude an Rezin. Ein Versuch, mit dem Text Jes. viii 6 ohne Konjektur auszukommen," *VT* 30 (1980) 229–234.

[31]*Jesaja und die Politik*, 64–65.

consequently sets v 6b aside, along with "the king of Assyria and all his glory" in v 7ab, as late explanatory additions.[32]

Again, several considerations weigh against this conclusion. First, compared with some other glosses in Isaiah, the expressions "rejoicing in Rezin and the son of Remaliah" and "the king of Assyria and all his glory" are more elaborate in their phrasing (compare "the king of Assyria" at the end of 7:17 and 20a). They are not the briefly worded notes that characteristically derive from glossators or historicizing editors. Second, if we are correct about the verbal assonance between vv 6b and 6a, v 6b again does not look like a simple explanatory note. Glossators and historicizing editors do not usually engage in this kind of wordplay. Third, the expressions do explain "rejecting the waters of the Shiloah" and "the waters of the River," but this alone hardly indicates that the lines are secondary. They are, rather, the prophet's deliberate elucidation of the metaphorical imagery he is using.[33] To claim, as Dietrich does, that such explanation "makes Isaiah a bad stylist" is at best an overstatement.[34]

The above remarks argue for retaining 8:6b (without emendation) and v 7ab as original parts of Isaiah's speech. The decision is important particularly with respect to v 6b, for here we receive a rare but clear glimpse into the complex political dynamics within Judah on the eve of the Syro-Ephraimitic crisis.

The prophet begins with an accusation against "this people" (v 6a). The same reference occurs in 6:9 and 8:11–12, and in all three passages, Judeans are probably in mind.[35] The threat "against them"

---

[32]The same conclusion is reached by J. Skinner (*Isaiah*, 73), G. B. Gray (*The Book of Isaiah*, 1. 146–47), G. Fohrer (*Das Buch Jesaja*, 1. 125–28), O. Kaiser (*Isaiah 1–12*, 186), R. E. Clements (*Isaiah 1–39*, 96–97), and W. Werner ("Vom Prophetenwort zur Prophetentheologie," 11–12). Other commentators, for example, B. Duhm (*Das Buch Jesaja*, 80) and W. Wildberger (*Jesaja 1–12*, 321–22), ascribe v 6b (in emended form) to Isaiah, but still regard v 7ab as secondary. H. Donner (*Israel unter den Völkern*, 22–25) is one of the few recent scholars who retain both lines (v 6b emended) as part of the prophet's speech.

[33]See A. M. Honeyman, "An Early Diacritic Sign in Isaiah 8:6b," 46; and H. Klein, "Freude an Rezin," 230–31.

[34]H. Klein ("Freude an Rezin," 229–30) in fact argues precisely the opposite, namely, that as the verses now stand, 8:6–7a form a six-line strophe with a balanced structure and meter. To excise vv 6b and 7ab would only obscure the care with which Isaiah composed the passage.

[35]For a detailed discussion of the expression, "this people," in Isaiah and elsewhere, see J. Boehmer, "Dieses Volk," *JBL* 45 (1926) 134–48. In Isa 9:15 and 28:11, the expression refers to the Israelites. The same identification, however, is not possible in 8:6, as Rignell ("Maher-salal Has-baz," 41–42) believes (see n. 16 above and n. 36 below).

(ʿălêhem) in 8:7-8a supports this identification: into Judah will Yahweh bring the rising waters of the "River" (v 8a).³⁶

Isaiah charges that Judeans have rejected the "waters of the Shiloah" (mê haššilōaḥ). The reference is unique in the Hebrew Bible and, for this reason, not altogether clear. Presumably some sort of water canal for Jerusalem is meant.³⁷ Excavations in Jerusalem at the end of the nineteenth century uncovered two canals that, before the construction of Hezekiah's tunnel, led off the overflowing waters of the Gihon Spring southward along the east side of the city.³⁸ Isaiah 8:6 probably refers to one of these.

Still unclear is what "rejecting" the waters of the Shiloah means. According to J. Lindblom, the reproach refers concretely to measures taken by Ahaz for improving and securing water service in Jerusalem, especially in times of siege.³⁹ More probably, the language of Isaiah is figurative, and its interpretation depends on rightly seeing the symbolic import of "the waters of the Shiloah." Most scholars construe the expression as an allusion to Yahweh—either his protecting presence in Jerusalem, or his ability to steer world history, or the word of Yahweh.⁴⁰ Ahaz and the Judeans, so it is argued, spurned Yahweh by appealing to Assyria for help against Rezin and Pekah. The interpretation usually demands either the elimination or

---

³⁶According to F. Delitzsch (*The Prophecies of Isaiah*, 1. 193) and L. G. Rignell ("Maher-salal Has-baz," 42–43), the passage envisions first the advance of the River's waters against the Israelites (v 7), and then the inundation of Judah (v 8). K. Fullerton ("Isaiah 8:5-10," 256, 264, and 269) sees the same sequence, but credits it to a glossator who added v 6b and "against them" in v 7. Verses 7–8, however, do not clearly depict the movement that these scholars see. Verse 7a focuses on Yahweh's role in the disaster: he is the one who causes the waters of the River to rise "against them," that is, the Judeans. Verses 7b and 8b describe the result: the River rises over its banks and flows into Judah.

³⁷Nehemiah 3:15 mentions a "pool of the Shelah [leading] to the garden of the king" (bĕrēkat haššelaḥ lĕgan-hammelek), which may be a later development of a water system dating back to the time of Ahaz or earlier. See D. J. Clines, *Ezra, Nehemiah, Esther* (Grand Rapids/London: Eerdmans/Marshall, Morgan & Scott, 1984) 155.

³⁸See M. Burrows, "The Conduit of the Upper Pool," 226; J. Simons, *Jerusalem in the Old Testament* (Leiden: E. J. Brill, 1952) 176.

³⁹*The Immanuel Section*, 43. See also B. Stade, *Geschichte des Volkes Israel* (2 vols.; Berlin: G. Grote, 1887) 1. 593; and H. Gressmann, *Der Messias*, 237. Stade claims that, despite the testimony of 2 Kgs 20:20 and 2 Chr 32:30, "Hezekiah's tunnel" may actually date to the reign of Ahaz. Isaiah 8:6 supposedly alludes to its construction as a substitute for the older Shiloah canal. Compare W. Dietrich, *Jesaja und die Politik*, 159–60.

⁴⁰See for example B. Duhm, *Das Buch Jesaja*, 80; K. Fullerton, "Isaiah 8:5–10," 262; O. Procksch, *Jesaja I*, 133; G. Fohrer, *Das Buch Jesaja*, 1. 125–27; O. Kaiser, *Isaiah 1–12*, 185; H. Wildberger, *Jesaja 1–12*, 324–25; and M. E. W. Thompson, *Situation and Theology*, 34.

emendation of v 6b, and for this there is little support. Furthermore, in light of its doubtful historicity, the appeal cannot be cited to explain the prophet's criticism of "this people."

The key to understanding "the waters of the Shiloah" might lie in the significance of the Gihon Spring, whose overflow the Shiloah drained. The spring is mentioned elsewhere in the Hebrew Bible and in connection with highly important events. First Kings 1:33-40 records that Zadok the priest and Nathan the prophet escorted the young Solomon to the Gihon and there privately anointed him as the successor to the throne. Although the anointing ritual is described only in this one instance, the ceremony was likely repeated for each new Davidic king, or perhaps even annually.[41]

In view of the Shiloah's connection to the Gihon Spring, it would hardly be surprising if the canal also became in some way associated with the anointment ritual. Traces of this association may appear in Psalm 110, a royal psalm composed for the coronation. Psalm 110:7 seems to describe part of the ritual itself—the king drinks "from the brook by the road" (*minnaḥal badderek*). The allusion here is unlikely to the Gihon, but rather to the Shiloah, which led off from it.[42] Also noteworthy in this regard is the Syriac and Aramaic translations of 1 Kgs 1:33. These locate the anointment of Solomon at the Shiloah. The translations admittedly derive from the early centuries C.E., but they may testify to a genuinely ancient association between the canal and the royal ceremony. In Isa 8:6a, the prophet possibly assumes this association, and thus refers to the Davidic kingship metaphorically as the "waters of Shiloah." The interpretation finds support in the Targum's rendering of the verse: "Because this people despised the kingdom of the house of David which leads them gently as the waters of Shiloah that flow gently, and are pleased with Rezin and the son of Remaliah...."[43]

The prophet's reproach reveals how strong Judean opposition to the Davidic house had grown during the 730s.[44] Ahaz, and perhaps

---

[41]Second Kings 11 describes the enthronement of Joash in the royal palace. For a discussion of both the anointment and enthronement ceremonies, see G. von Rad, "Das judäische Königsritual," *TLZ* 72 (1947) 211-16 = his *GS* (Munich: Chr. Kaiser, 1971) 205-13; also S. Mowinckel, *He That Cometh*, 63-65.

[42]Compare S. Mowinckel, *The Psalms in Israel's Worship*, 1. 63-64; H.-J. Kraus, *Psalmen* (BKAT 15; 2 vols.; 5th ed.; Neukirchen-Vluyn: Neukirchener Verlag, 1978) 2. 936.

[43]Compare again the reading of the Septuagint: "Because this people reject the water of Siloam which flows gently and desire to have Rasin and the son of Romelias as king over them...." While the translators do not refer explicitly to the Davidic house, they clearly imply that kingship over "this people," the Judeans, was at stake during the Syro-Ephraimitic crisis.

[44]A number of nineteenth and early twentieth century scholars reckoned with an anti-Davidic, pro-Syrian party in Judah. See for example B. Stade, *Geschichte*,

Jotham earlier, had refused to align themselves with the anti-Assyrian coalition at high territorial and economic cost (2 Kgs 16:6; 2 Chr 28:16–19), and many of their subjects must have questioned in retrospect the wisdom of their leadership. With Pekah's coup and Israel's subsequent alliance with Rezin, most Judeans probably looked forward to Ahaz's following suit, and thus to cooperative relations with the Syrians (see Chapter Three, secs. C4b and D above). However, when the king persisted in an isolationist course, Judean discontent with the Davidic house reached a high. On the eve of the Syrian-Israelite invasion, a large part of the country was ready to accept a new non-Davidic leadership that would cooperate with the Syrian and Israelite kings.[45] Rezin's plan to replace Ahaz with a Tyrian prince (Isa 7:6), and thereby to secure Judah as an ally, held hope of success because many Judeans would be willing to fight in Syria's cause against Assyria.

Isaiah staunchly supported Ahaz and encouraged him to hold out against the coalition (7:1–17). He also tried to muster popular support for the Davidic policy, at least within Jerusalem. The Syrians and Israelites, the prophet argued, were no match for the Assyrians and would soon suffer defeat and plunder (8:1–4). If the wider Judean public outside the capital city and its environs opposed the Davidic regime and "rejoiced in Rezin and the son of Remaliah," disaster would overtake them as well.[46]

---

1. 596; and F. Wilke, *Jesaja und Assur*, 28–30. In more recent times, J. M. Asurmendi (*La Guerra Siro-Efraimita*, 66–68) and H. Klein ("Freude an Rezin," 231–33) set forth similar interpretations of Isa 8:6. H. Wildberger concedes the possibility of a small minority in Jerusalem who supported "the son of Tabeel" as a replacement for Ahaz. He asserts, however, that the vast majority of Judeans, to whom "this people" in 8:6 refers, "undoubtedly approved the politics of the court." The claim, however, is only an assumption, and Wildberger does not defend it.

[45]Micah 1:10–16 likely dates to the period prior to the Syro-Ephraimitic crisis and reflects the strained relations between, on the one hand, Jerusalem and the Davidic house, and on the other hand, the other cities of Judah. See C. Shaw, "Micah 1:10–16 Reconsidered," 227–29.

[46]Compare this interpretation with the following remarks of K. Fullerton ("Isaiah 8:5–10," 261, n. 19). "Wilke's view [*Jesaja und Assur*] that Isaiah was resisting a popular demand to join the anti-Assyrian Syro-Ephraimitic coalition and was attempting to win adherence to the peace-policy of the Davidic dynasty (pp. 28–30) throws away the most important clue we have for the interpretation of cc. 7 and 8 for the sake of 8:6b. This clue is the pro-Assyrian policy of Ahaz (2 K. 16). To this policy Isaiah was firmly opposed. Instead of the prophet attempting to dissuade the people from an anti-Assyrian policy, every datum in cc. 7 and 8 except 8:6b indicates that he was doing his utmost to allay the popular *fear* of the Syro-Ephraimitic coalition in order to prevent both court and people from appealing to Assyria for help. Unfortunately, Isaiah's efforts were in vain." Fullerton, like so many others, simply assumes the reliability of the Kings text,

The prophet's threat against the Judeans follows in vv 7–8a: Yahweh will soon bring against them the "mighty and many waters of the River, (that is) the king of Assyria and all his glory."[47] The development of the flood metaphor in vv 7b–8aα vividly expresses Isaiah's sense of impending doom. Should the Judeans, who favor Rezin and Pekah, actively join the rebel cause, the Assyrians would overrun the country, crush the resistance, and impose harsh penalities on the people. The final line (v 8aβ), however, appears to qualify the threat. The flood will reach "up to the neck" and, by implication, no further, thus leaving the head above water. The prophet may be suggesting here that Jerusalem, the "head" of Judah, and Ahaz, the "head" of Jerusalem (see 7:8–9), will not "go under," but survive. If this interpretation is correct, the line serves as a transition to the second part of Isaiah's speech, his words concerning the house of David and Jerusalem (vv 8b–10).[48]

Verse 8b is directed to Immanuel, the royal infant whose birth and survival Isaiah had predicted earlier (7:14–16): "But the outspreading of his [the Lord's] wings will fill the breadth of your realm, O Immanuel."[49] The address to the infant is only a rhetorical device. In Isaiah's eyes, Immanuel is the embodiment of the Davidic house

---

and so infers Isaiah's opposition to both Ahaz and "this people." In fact, the material in Isaiah 7 and 8 does not refer to the appeal, let alone denounce the king for making it.

[47]The phrase, "all his glory" (wĕ'et-kol-kĕbôdô), might imitate the language of the Assyrian royal inscriptions that speak frequently of the "splendor" (melemmu or melammu) of Assur, the Assyrian god, overwhelming the enemy in battle (see for example ANET 287). Certainly familiar with this kind of boast, Isaiah turns it against the Judeans, qualifying it by naming Yahweh as the hidden will behind events.

[48]K. Fullerton ("Isaiah 8:5–10," 27–72) objects that the rhetorical character of 8:5–8 does not allow one to infer a sense of hope in v 8aβ. His arguments, however, are not conclusive, especially if the promise in vv 8b–10 continues the speech. (Compare also H. Wildberger, Jesaja 1–12, 327.) F. Delitzsch (The Prophecies of Isaiah, 1. 193), J. Meinhold (Der Heilige Rest [Bonn: A. Marcus and E. Weber, 1903] 114), and J. Skinner (Isaiah, 74) recognize that v 8aβ places a limit on the divine punishment. They do not, however, understand the line in light of the basic split between most Judeans, on the one side, and Jerusalem and the Davidic regime, on the other. Isaiah does envision the salvation of a remnant, as Meinhold argues, but he has in mind specifically the capital city and the royal house there.

[49]The majority of commentators since Duhm ascribe the line to a late editor, but disagree on whether it implies disaster or salvation. Compare K. Fullerton, "Isaiah 8:5–10," 276–89; G. Fohrer, Das Buch Jesaja, 1. 127; H. Wildberger, Jesaja 1–12, 327; R. E. Clements, Isaiah 1–39, 97; and W. Werner, "Vom Prophetenwort zur Prophetentheologie," 12. Verse 8b does introduce a new metaphor, but this fact alone does not weigh against its Isaianic authorship, nor against its original connection with vv 6–8a. Its message is hopeful, reflecting the shift in Isaiah's focus from "this people" to Jerusalem and the Davidic house.

Isaiah 8:1–20   193

and the guarantee of its ongoing reign. In addressing the child, the prophet in effect addresses the regime as a whole.

The words to Immanuel depict Yahweh as a great bird.[50] J. Skinner, among others, interprets the image in a threatening sense, that is, as a bird of prey,[51] but elsewhere in the Hebrew Bible it usually connotes divine protection (see Deut 32:11, Ruth 2:12, and Mal 3:20). Particularly the psalms often speak of refuge in "the shadow of Yahweh's wings" (Pss 17:8; 36:8; 57:2; and 63:8; see also 61:5 and 91:4). The language in some of these texts may be more than metaphorical. Persons accused of certain crimes may have sought legal asylum in the Jerusalem temple, where, in the "holy of holies," the outstretched wings of two cherubic figures reached from wall to wall (1 Kgs 6:23–28).[52] In any case, the temple iconography is probably the source of Isaiah's metaphor. He employs the bird image to describe Yahweh's protection of the Davidic realm, that is, Jerusalem and its immediate vicinity (see Isa 31:5).[53]

This interpretation finds support in vv 9–10,[54] which continue the prophet's speech.[55] Isaiah rhetorically addresses the enemy nations of

---

[50] Nineteenth-century scholars frequently took v 8b as a continuation of the preceding threat and so misconstrured "his/its wings" (*kĕnāpāyw*) as the wings/flanks of the Assyrian army or as the small streams branching off from the flooding River (a figure for the Assyrian army). See for example F. Delitzsch, *The Prophecies of Isaiah*, 1. 194. (The interpretation is in fact ancient, reflected already in the reading of the Targum: ". . . and the people of his [the Assyrian king's] armies will fill the open places of your land, O Israel.") Nowhere else in the Hebrew Bible, however, does the noun *kānāp* refer either to military troops or to the offshoots of a river. In v 8b, Isaiah introduces a new metaphor for Yahweh's action vis-à-vis Jerusalem and the Davidic house. (The possessive pronoun, "his," reaches back to ʾădōnāy in v 7a.)

[51] J. Skinner, *Isaiah*, 74; compare B. Duhm, *Das Buch Jesaja*, 81; G. Fohrer, *Das Buch Jesaja*, 1. 127; and W. Eichrodt, *Der Heilige in Israel. Jesaja 1–12* (BAT 17/1; Stuttgart: Calwer, 1960) 98–100.

[52] See W. Beyerlin, *Die Rettung der Bedrängten in den Feindpsalmen der Einzelnen auf institutionelle Zusammenhänge untersucht* (FRLANT 99; Göttingen: Vandenhoeck & Ruprecht, 1970), especially 108–9.

[53] The Hebrew of 8:8b speaks literally of the "width" of Immanuel's "land" (*rōhab ʾarṣĕkā*) and so might seem, on first reading, to refer to the whole of Judah. Certain considerations, however, point toward a different conclusion. During the years preceding the Syro-Ephraimitic crisis, the territory over which the Davidides exercised firm control had shrunk considerably. Both the Edomites and Philistines had encroached upon Judah from the south and west, and large parts of the country openly challenged the authority of the Davidic leadership. On the eve of the Syrian-Israelite invasion, Ahaz's effective rule was likely limited to the dynasty's essential power base, Jerusalem and its environs.

[54] The Isaianic authorship of these verses is widely debated. For a survey of the scholarly discussion, see K. Fullerton, "Isaiah 8:5–10," 282–89; and H. Wildberger, *Jesaja 1–12*, 330–31. Note also the recent analyses of the passage by F. Huber (*Die anderen Völker*, 69–82), H. Barth (*Die Jesaja-Worte in der Josiazeit*, 178), and

the world; mockingly he summons them to battle: "Band together,[56] you peoples, and be dismayed; give ear, all you far-off countries!

W. Werner (*Eschatologische Texte*, 168–78). If the vocabulary of the verses does not point decisively to Isaiah, certainly it is in keeping with his language elsewhere. (See the lexical evidence as reviewed and assessed by Wildberger, Huber, and Werner.) The "we"-style of the passage appears also in Isa 2:5 and 9:5, which, contrary to the assumption of Huber and others, may derive from the eighth-century prophet. (Even if 2:5 and 9:5 were secondary, 8:[8b] 9–10 might still be taken as the one instance in which the prophet plays upon the name of Immanuel and so adopts the "we"-style.)

Many scholars argue that the thought of 8:9–10 does not fit the overall message of Isaiah. According to Werner, for example, the verses reflect the eschatology of the post-exilic period (see also G. Fohrer, *Das Buch Jesaja*, 1. 128). Their content in fact does not demand this interpretation. The motif of the enemy attack is part of the Zion tradition inherited by Isaiah (see H.-M. Lutz, *Jahwe, Jerusalem und die Völker. Zur Vorgeschichte von Sach. 12,1–8 und 14,1–5* [WMANT 27; Neukirchen-Vluyn: Nerkirchener Verlag, 1968] 215–16). Huber, among others, objects that the unconditional nature of the promise in 8:9–10 is uncharacteristic of the eighth-century prophet (see also K. Budde, *Jesaja's Erleben*, 80). However, if statements like 9:6 derive from Isaiah, as we and many other scholars believe (see Chapter Seven below), it appears that the prophet, on occasion, did pronounce future divine blessing and salvation, without stipulating conditions. (Our interpretation of 7:14–17a construed this passage similarly.) Finally, Huber claims that the hopeful message of the passage is an editor's attempt to "neutralize" or "correct" the preceding threat (compare H. Barth, *Die Jesaja-Worte in der Josiazeit*, 180; and R. E. Clements, *Isaiah 1–39*, 97–98). As we argued above, however, the shift from a threat to a promise is adequately explained as a reflection of the prophet's changing focus, from the Judeans, who "rejoice" in Rezin and Pekah (vv 6–8a), to Jerusalem and the Davidic regime (vv 8b–10). The speech as a whole contrasts the dismal fate of the former with the divine protection of the latter. In short, the thought of vv (8b) 9–10 is perfectly conceivable in the mouth of the eighth-century Jerusalemite prophet and quite in keeping with his overall message of salvation for the capital city and the royal house during the Syro-Ephraimitic crisis.

[55]Wildberger (*Jesaja 1–12*, 322) contends that the imperatives in v 9 clearly mark the beginning of a new unit. Verses 8b–10, however, share the same hopeful, if not triumphant, tone, and the theme throughout is Yahweh's protecting presence with Jerusalem and the Davidic house. The play on the name of Immanuel (vv 8b and 10b) also ties the verses together.

[56]Scholars debate the correctness and meaning of *rōʿû*. For detailed reviews of the text-critical issue, see M. Saebø, "Zur Traditionsgeschichte von Jesaja 8,9–10," *ZAW* 76 (1964) 132–34; and H. Wildberger, *Jesaja 1–12*, 329. The translation here construes the verb as an imperative form of *rʿh* II ("associate"). The reading is supported by the Greek translations of Aquila, Symmachus, and Theodotion (*sunathroisthēte*), the Targum (*ʾthbru*), and the Vulgate (*congregamini*). Compare, however, the suggestion of H. Schmidt ("Jesaja 8,9 und 10," in *Stromata. Festgabe des Akademisch-theologischen Vereins zu Giessen im schmalkaldener Kartell anlässlich seines 50. Stiftungstages* [ed. G. Bertram; Leipzig: Hinrich, 1930] 3–10): he derives *roʿu* from *ruaʿ* and translates, "Raise a shout." Saebø ("Traditionsgeschichte," 132–43) musters tradition-historical arguments in support of the proposal and many others accept it. (See for example H.-M. Lutz, *Yahwe, Jerusalem und die*

Gird yourselves and be dismayed, gird yourselves and be dismayed! Hatch a plot and it will come to nothing; contrive a plan and it shall not arise, for God is with us" (*kî ʿimmānû ʾēl*). Underlying the taunt is the ancient tradition of Zion's inviolability (see Pss 2; 46; 48; and 76).[57] As the place where Yahweh resides, Zion enjoys divine protection. Enemy nations may conspire to storm the city, but their plans "come to nothing." Yahweh "terrifies them in his fury" (Ps 2:5). He "breaks the weapons of war" (Ps 76:3); the besieging forces panic and take flight (Ps 48:5). Zion's residents live securely, confident in the claim, "Yahweh of hosts is with us" (Ps 46:7). The belief is clearly echoed in the concluding line of the prophet's speech, "for God is with us" (v 10b). The phrase, however, is also a play on the name of the royal child addressed in v 8b: Yahweh's protection of "your land, O Immanuel" is his protection of Jerusalem, the seat of the Davidic house and the city where Yahweh resides.

Isaiah framed the taunt as a general address to the "peoples" (*ʿammîm*) and "far-off countries" (*merḥaqqê-ʾāreṣ*; literally, "those from the ends of the earth"), but he likely had Syria and Israel particularly in mind.[58] Their plan to set aside the Davidic house involved besieging the capital city. Isaiah had already denounced the plan and declared against its success, "It shall not arise" (*lōʾ tāqûm*; 7:7). An echo of the same promise resounds in 8:10: "Contrive a plan, but it will not

---

Völker, 40–47; G. Fohrer, *Das Buch Jesaja*, 1. 128; and W. Werner, *Eschatologische Texte*, 168.)

[57]See H.-P. Müller, "Glauben und Bleiben," 47–49; and H. Wildberger, *Jesaja 1–12*, 332. M. Saebø ("Traditionsgeschichte," 135–42) argues strongly that the verses imitate the genre of the war-summons. The combination of this form with the content of the Zion tradition is understandable, for the latter typically envisions the siege of Zion by enemy nations. Saebø recognizes correctly the ironic tone of the imperatives.

[58]K. Marti (*Das Buch Jesaja*, 85), among others, objects to this interpretation: "If the 'peoples' of v 9 could be Ephraim and Syria, the verses might refer to the protection of Judah in the Syro-Ephraimitic war. But the peoples are addressed universally and the Syrians and Ephraimites do not live at the end of the earth." The passage, Marti concludes, derives from a post-exilic writer who, typically, promises the eschatological salvation of Judah before the onslaught of the heathen nations of the world. H. Donner (*Israel unter den Völkern*, 26–27) ascribes the verses to Isaiah and dates them to the Syro-Ephraimitic crisis, but he concedes at the same time that "peoples" does not likely refer to Syria and Israel alone. He suggests instead that the address has in mind the entire anti-Assyrian coalition, "which presumably was much broader than the Old Testament sources indicate." Isaiah declares that their plans for revolt against Assyria will not succeed. Our interpretation follows M. Saebø ("Traditionsgeschichte," 140–42) in seeing the general address to the "peoples" and "far-off countries" as part and parcel of the traditio-historical background of vv 9–10, that is, the war-summons and/or the Zion tradition. See also H.-P. Müller, "Glauben und Bleiben," 48; compare J. Lindblom, *The Immanuel Section*, 32–33; L. G. Rignell, "Maher-salal Has-baz," 43–44.

arise" (*dabbĕrû dābār wĕlōʾ yāqûm*).⁵⁹ Repeatedly, then, during the Syro-Ephraimitic crisis, Isaiah showed himself as one who took the Zion-Davidic theology seriously and who urged the royal house to do likewise. Ahaz, he argued, should hold out against Rezin and Pekah, confident in the promise that Yahweh would sustain his reign and protect Jerusalem against enemy attack.

C. Verses 12–15

Isaiah 8:12–15 present several interpretive problems. These include the uncertain identity of the prophet's audience, the unclear meaning of the conspiracy charge in v 12, the possible corruption of the Hebrew text in vv 12–14, and the questionable integrity of the passage as a single speech of Isaiah. The following analysis argues that, except for one slight emendation at the beginning of v 14, the Masoretic text should be retained.⁶⁰ Verses 12–15 form a single speech by the eighth-century prophet,⁶¹ which he delivered to a plural

---

⁵⁹Note also the connection between *ʿuṣû ʿēṣâ* in 8:10 and *yāʿaṣ* in 7:5. The similar vocabulary and thought of the two passages reflect their common Isaianic authorship and their relation to the same historical episode. Compare W. Werner, *Eschatologische Texte*, 169.

⁶⁰For discussions of the text-critical issue, see N. Lohfink, "Isaias 8,12–14," *BZ* 7 (1963) 98–104; and C. A. Evans, "An Interpretation of Isa 8,11–15 Unemended," *ZAW* 97 (1985) 112–13. The scholarly debate focuses largely on *qešer* in v 12a, *taqdîšû* in v 13a, and *lĕmiqdāš* in v 14a. Both Lohfink and Evans correctly retain the Masoretic text. The following analysis, however, disagrees with their translations and interpretations of the verses.

⁶¹Compare the redaction-critical analyses of O. Kaiser (*Isaiah 1–12*, 189–94), W. Dietrich (*Jesaja und die Politik*, 69–74, 96–97), and W. Werner ("Vom Prophetenwort zur Prophetentheologie," 7–11). According to Kaiser, vv 11–15 derive largely from a post-exilic author concerned to explain the fall of Israel (722) and Judah (586). A second hand, Kaiser argues, later substituted *taqdîšû* and *miqdāš* for the original *taqšîrû* and *maqšîr* in vv 13a and 14a, thereby extending a hope of salvation to the post-exilic community. Dietrich and Werner ascribe part of 8:11–15 (18) to the eighth-century prophet, but envision the extensive reworking of his words by a redactor. Dietrich detects two speeches of Isaiah in the material: 8:12–13 and 8:16, 14 (*wĕhāyâ lĕmiqdāš* emended to *lihyôt* or *wĕhāyâ*), 15b. Werner isolates a single speech of the prophet: 8:11 (*kōh ʾāmar yhwh* only), 12a, 13a, 14a, 14ba, 15a (without *rabbîm*), and 15b (*wĕnāpĕlû wĕnišbārû* only).

In lieu of a detailed evaluation of these analyses, the following criticisms suffice. (1) Verses 14–15 do not clearly reflect backwards on the fall of Israel and Judah, as Kaiser claims. The threat against the "two houses of Israel" is intelligible against the background of the Syro-Ephraimitic crisis, when Israel and most Judeans opposed Ahaz, Yahweh's anointed king in Jerusalem. (2) The tensions which Dietrich sees between vv 12–13 and vv 14–15 are not nearly as significant as he imagines. They provide little basis for distinguishing between two originally separate speeches. (3) Werner argues that vv 12b and 13b focus on a general theological issue, namely, the contrast between false fear and the fear of God. As

audience.⁶² The text does not specify the identity of Isaiah's audience, but the verses make sense as an address to the Davidic house and its supporters prior to the Syrian-Israelite advance against Jerusalem in 734/733.⁶³ (Compare the plural address to the royal court in 7:9b.) The message reiterates what the prophet had said on other occasions during the same crisis: Ahaz should not capitulate to Rezin and Pekah, for Yahweh would deliver him and the capital city.

The speech exhibits a two-part structure. (a) Isaiah admonishes the Davidides and their supporters to dissent from the political leanings of "this people" (vv 12–13). (b) The prophet promises that Yahweh will protect Zion against the "two houses of Israel" (Judah and Israel) and safeguard the throne of its king (vv 14–15). How the admonition and promise relate is not explicit. Isaiah may have understood the former as a precondition of the latter. If so, the prophet's logic could be paraphrased: if the Davidides revere Yahweh and, accordingly, hold out against the demands of Syria, Israel, and the Judean people, Yahweh will defend Zion and its leadership against all opponents.

The prophetic admonition is first couched in negative terms: "Do not consider conspiracy (*qeŝer*) all that this people considers conspiracy" (*qāŝer*; v 12a).⁶⁴ Isaiah's words are less than clear and have in-

---

such, they are supposedly the addition of an editor, who "sought to extend the actual warning of Isaiah to later readers and listeners, for whom the political constellations of Isaiah's time were no longer relevant." If the verses carry political overtones, as we will argue below, they would fit well with the prophet's warning about "conspiracy."

⁶²Verses 12 and 13 contain several second-person plural forms: *lōʾ-tōʾmĕrûn, lōʾ-tîrĕʾû wĕlōʾ taʿărîṣû, taqdîŝû, môraʾăkem,* and *maʿărîṣkem*.

⁶³According to most scholars, the speech addresses the few followers of the prophet. They and Isaiah supposedly stood in opposition to Ahaz and the rest of "this people" who feared Rezin and Pekah, rejected the advice of the prophet, and favored appealing to Assyria for help. (See G. B. Gray, *The Book of Isaiah,* 1. 150; O. Procksch, *Jesaja I,* 136; L. G. Rignell, "Maher-salal Has-baz," 45; H. Donner, *Israel unter den Völkern,* 28; N. Lohfink, "Isaias 8,12–14," 101, especially n. 15; H. Wildberger, *Jesaja 1–12,* 336; and C. A. Evans, "Isaiah 8,11–15 Unemended," 113.) The evidence for this kind of prophetic circle, however, is slim in the case of Isaiah. Reference is frequently made to the "disciples" in 8:16, but the Hebrew there is uncertain and capable of other renderings (see below). Furthermore, the interpretation rests on the same assumption that we have questioned repeatedly, namely, that the king and people stood together in their opposition to the prophet. The analysis of the prophetic speeches so far has argued that Isaiah supported Ahaz against his own subjects, who "favored Rezin and the son of Remaliah" (8:6).

⁶⁴BH suggests reading *qādōŝ* ("holy") for *qeŝer/qāŝer*. The proposal apparently was first made by Archbishop Secker and published by R. Lowth (*Isaiah: A New Translation* [London: J. Dodsley and T. Cadell, 1778]). More recently, G. R. Driver ("Two Misunderstood Passages of the Old Testament," *JTS* 6 [1955] 82–84)

vited several interpretations. According to K. Marti and L. G. Rignell, the conspiracy charge refers to the Syrian-Israelite alliance.[65] B. Duhm, G. Fohrer, and J. Lindblom think instead of pro-Syrian dissidents within Jerusalem, who schemed to overthrow Ahaz.[66] According to O. Procksch, H. Donner, and R. E. Clements, "this people" accused Isaiah of conspiracy, either because he denounced Ahaz, or because in counseling against the king's appeal to Assyria, he seemed to favor Syrian and Israelite interests, or because in advising against Judah's cooperation with Rezin and Pekah, he appeared to represent the concerns of Assyria.[67]

Each of these proposals has problems. The noun *qešer* and the related verb *qšr* usually refer to an internal coup, that is, an attempt to overthrow the ruling regime by a party within the state.[68] Less frequently the terms describe a king's revolt against his suzerain (2 Kgs 17:4). The Syrian-Israelite invasion of Judah does not fit either meaning.[69] Possibly the charge in Isa 8:12 describes plots against the Da-

---

retains *qešer*, but translates the term as "difficulty." For the negative assessment of both views, see N. Lohfink, "Isaias 8,12–14," 99–100.

[65] K. Marti, *Das Buch Jesaja*, 86; L. G. Rignell, "Maher-salal Has-baz," 45. See also N. K. Gottwald, *All the Kingdoms of the Earth*, 156, n. 77; T. Lescow, "Jesajas Denkschrift," 325; W. Dietrich, *Jesaja und die Politik*, 94–95; and W. Werner, "Vom Prophetenwort zur Prophetentheologie," 9.

[66] B. Duhm, *Das Buch Jesaja*, 83; J. Lindblom, *The Immanuel Section*, 30; and G. Fohrer, *Das Buch Jesaja*, 1. 130–31.

[67] O. Procksch, *Jesaja I*, 136; H. Donner, *Israel unter den Völkern*, 28–29; and R. E. Clements, *Isaiah 1–39*, 99. See also C. A. Evans, "Isa 8,11–15 Unemended," 113. According to Evans, the theologians of the royal court accused Isaiah of *qešer* because the prophet opposed the treaty with Assyria. Understood in this way, *qešer* involves speaking out against the official policy of the king.

[68] Examples include 2 Sam 15:12, 31; 1 Kgs 15:27; 16:9, 16, 20; 2 Kgs 9:14; 10:9; 11:14; 12:21; 14:19; 15:10, 15, 25, 30; 21:23–24; compare Amos 7:10. N. Lohfink ("Isaias 8,12–14," 100) correctly stresses this meaning. He goes to an extreme, however, when he claims that "an external political alliance is never designated by the word *qešer* in biblical Hebrew; the word is rather a technical term of internal politics and means a revolution, the plan for assassinating a king . . . ." Nehemiah 4:2 is one clear instance in which *qšr* designates the confederation of external enemy forces for aggressive action against a state, city, or community.

[69] Compare N. Lohfink, "Isaias 8,12–14," 100; H. Wildberger, *Jesaja 1–12*, 337; and W. Dietrich, *Jesaja und die Politik*, 94–95, especially n. 31. Dietrich underestimates the force of the lexical evidence when he remarks, "The fact that the Old Testament seldom speaks of an external political *qešer* is easily explained by the predominant interest of the text in the internal affairs of Israel." He argues further: "Above all, v 12 emphasizes that the entire people were afraid of the *qešer*. The statement does not suggest the quarrel or power struggle of inner-Judean parties, but rather the unanimous fear before the external enemy." Verse 12, however, does not in fact say that the people feared a *qešer*. Moreover, Isa 8:6 contradicts Dietrich's interpretation: "this people rejoice in Rezin and the son of Remaliah."

vidic house arising within Jerusalem itself. In this case, however, it is hard to imagine how someone as politically astute as Isaiah could discount the seriousness of such plots so lightly. If 2 Chr 28:7 alludes to an attempt on Ahaz's life (see Chapter Three, section B above), it would seem that at least one abortive coup nearly succeeded.

The conspiracy charge is not likely an accusation against Isaiah. Several reasons count against this interpretation. (a) There is no clear evidence that the prophet ever broke with Ahaz.[70] The Immanuel saying and 8:6–10 can, in fact, be interpreted to suggest the opposite conclusion, namely, that Isaiah supported the king throughout the Syro-Ephraimitic crisis. (b) Despite the claim of 2 Kgs 16:7–9, Ahaz did not likely enlist Assyria's help against the coalition (see Chapter Three, sections A3 and C4c above). The alleged appeal cannot be made the bone of contention between the prophet and "this people." The Judeans had little reason to suspect Isaiah of having Syrian and Israelite loyalties. To the contrary, the prophet made his stand against the coalition repeatedly clear (7:7–9, 16; 8:1–4). (c) It is not impossible that some Judeans misconstrued Isaiah's opposition to the coalition as a pro-Assyrian stand. At least as it has been framed, however, the proposal does not adequately explain the conspiracy charge, especially if, as most scholars think, the Davidic house itself favored an alliance with Assyria.[71] Furthermore, while the prophet described Assyria as the agent of Yahweh's wrath (7:18b, 20; 8:4, 7–8a), he also criticized the arrogance of the Assyrians and announced the divine punishment that would eventually overtake them (10:5–27c; see Chapter Nine below). No one would likely have understood such a position as pro-Assyrian.

The conspiracy charge in 8:12 makes sense as an accusation against Ahaz. "This people" favored the Syrian-led coalition and advocated Judah's participation (8:6). Popular discontent with the isolationist stand of Ahaz was growing during the 730s, and many must have hoped that, with Pekah's coup in the fall of 734 and Samaria's swing to Rezin's side, Ahaz too would change his position. When the king still refused to cooperate with the coalition, the Judeans accused him of conspiracy.

The charge is understandable in the light of Judah's subordination to Israel since the Omride era (see Chapter Three, section C4b above). With few exceptions, the Davidic kings had long supported their northern counterparts, especially in matters of foreign policy. Their cooperation continued as late as the 740s and early 730s. Ahaz

---

[70]In Isa 7:13, the prophet criticizes Ahaz and the Davidic house for hesitating to take a firm stand against the coalition. The reproach, however, does not signal Isaiah's decisive rejection of the king. See the discussion of the passage in Chapter Five, section C above.

[71]See H. Donner, *Israel unter den Völkern*, 29.

followed the example of Menahem and Pekahiah, refusing to join the anti-Assyrian movement led by Rezin of Damascus. All this changed, however, with Pekah's coup and the subsequent pro-Syrian policy of Israel. Ahaz's refusal to cooperate with the coalition constituted blatant defiance of his Israelite superior. The significance of this decision cannot be underestimated. Ahaz was the first Judean king since Amaziah to attempt to assert his independence from the northern kingdom (see 2 Kgs 14:8–14). Pekah must have viewed Ahaz as a renegade, and in this opinion many Judeans apparently concurred. They denounced Ahaz's revolt against his Israelite superior as "conspiracy."

This interpretation finds support in Isa 8:12b. There, Isaiah urges the Davidic house: "and do not revere nor regard with awe the one whom they revere" (wĕʾet-môrāʾô lōʾ-tîrĕʾû wĕlōʾ taʿărîṣû). The verb, tîrĕʾû, and its object, môrāʾô, derive from the root yrʾ and usually are translated with the meaning of "fear" or "be afraid" (see the RSV, NEB, JB, TEV, and NIV; compare the NJPSV). Frequently in the Hebrew Bible, and particularly in Deuteronomy, yrʾ has the sense of "revere" or "respect" and, furthermore, carries political overtones, expressing the properly obedient attitude of a vassal toward a suzerain.[72] The expression occurs often in the diplomatic language of the ancient Near East, in which a suzerain demands the undivided loyalty of a subjugated people or ruler.[73] We propose this political use as the background of Isa 8:12b. While most Judeans urged Ahaz to honor his obligations to Pekah, his Israelite superior, Isaiah encouraged the king to renounce such claims on his loyalty.

The prophet's advice in 8:13 is formulated positively: "Yahweh of hosts—him you should declare holy (ʾōtô taqdîšû) and he is the one whom you shall revere (môraʾăkem) and regard with awe (maʿăriṣkem)." In accordance with the above interpretation of v 12, the second half of v 13 would appear to state that Yahweh, not Pekah of Israel, is the one whom the Davidides should respect as sovereign. Such respect, of course, would entail their following Yahweh's instruction—holding out against Rezin and Pekah.

The meaning of v 13a is more difficult to determine. B. Duhm, followed by others, questions whether the command makes sense in

---

[72] See M. Weinfeld, *Deuteronomy and the Deuteronomic School* (Oxford: Clarendon, 1972) 83 and 332–33. In Deuteronomy and related literature, yrʾ expresses Israel's posture before its divine king, Yahweh. Typical phrases include yrʾ ʾt yhwh ("to fear Yahweh"), lmd lyrʾh ʾt yhwh ("to learn to fear Yahweh"), and yrʾ ʾt yhwh kl hymym/kl ymy hyyk ("to fear Yahweh all the days/as long as you live"). Weinfeld lists specific references.

[73] See M. Weinfeld, *Deuteronomy and the Deuteronomic School*, 83, especially n. 6, and 332–33. The verb palāḫu in the Neo-Assyrian vassal treaties is the Akkadian equivalent to yrʾ.

context, and so changes the text to read as a threat: "Yahweh of hosts, him shall you regard as a conspirator (ʾōtô taqšîrû)."[74] The emendation presumes a corruption of the Hebrew text, which scribally is plausible enough: the Hebrew letters r and d are graphically similar and thus frequently confused, and the metathesis of r/d and š is easy to imagine.[75] The proposal falters, however, on two facts. (1) The ancient versions and 1QIsaᵃ all agree with the taqdîšû of the Masoretic text. (2) Taqšîrû in Isa 8:13 would be the only instance of qšr in the hifil form. (Elsewhere in the Hebrew Bible, the root appears in the qal, nifal, piel, pual, and hithpael.) The proposal thus amounts to emending the Hebrew text only to create a new hapax legomenon.[76] It is best to retain the Masoretic text and explore anew its possible meanings.

"To declare Yahweh holy" is an infrequent expression in the Hebrew Bible, occurring only in Num 20:12; 27:14; Isa 29:23; and 8:13. In the first two instances, the phrase seems to mean the acknowledgment of Yahweh's awesome power. Moses and Aaron are reproached for not having credited Yahweh with the miracle at Meribah. A similar sense is present in Isa 29:23. When the Israelites see their children, "the work of my (Yahweh's) hands," they will confess the power of their God. If the same meaning were present in 8:13, the prophet would seem to be urging the Davidides to acknowledge the power of Yahweh on their behalf. The exhortation would make sense alongside Isaiah's promises elsewhere that Yahweh will protect the Davidic house and Zion against the attacks of Rezin and Pekah.

The context of v 13a, however, is one in which the question of Ahaz's loyalties is particularly at issue. The overall sense of vv 12–13

---

[74] B. Duhm, *Das Buch Jesaja*, 83; see K. Marti, *Das Buch Jesaja*, 86; G. Fohrer, *Das Buch Jesaja*, 1. 129–31; W. Dietrich, *Jesaja und die Politik*, 70; O. Kaiser, *Isaiah 1–12*, 190; and H. Wildberger, *Jesaja 1–12*, 334–35. G. R. Driver ("Two Misunderstood Passages," 82–84) adopts this emendation, but renders the threat, "him you will find difficult." J. Lindblom (*The Immanuel Section*, 30) also reads ʾōtô taqšîrû, but understands the line in a hopeful sense: "Yahweh of hosts you shall have as an ally." O. Procksch (*Jesaia I*, 136–37) emends ʾōtô taqdîšû to ʾittô tiqšōrû and translates, "with him you will conspire." All of these proposals assume that the verb in v 13a closely corresponds to the use of qešer in v 12.

[75] Alternatively, one might see the corruption as an intentional scribal or editorial change. See O. Kaiser, *Isaiah 1–12*, 194; and H. Wildberger, *Jesaja 1–12*, 324.

[76] The readings proposed by J. Lindblom, G. R. Driver, and O. Procksch (see n. 74 above) are equally problematic. Lindblom argues that the hifil of qšr gives only another nuance to the qal meaning of the root, conceiving the act of "binding" (or "allying") as an ongoing state. The fact remains, however, that the hifil form, whatever its precise nuance may be, is simply unattested, despite the relative frequency of the verb (forty-four times). The same criticism applies to Driver's translation. O. Procksch avoids the problem by restoring a qal form of qšr and emending ʾōtô to the prepositional phrase ʾittô. This construction, however, is also anomalous. Qšr combines usually with ʿal ("against"), occasionally with b or ʾim ("with"), but never with ʾēt ("with").

is that the Davidic king should honor Yahweh as suzerain, not Pekah of Israel. Is it possible that "declaring Yahweh holy" also carries political overtones? The interpretation is supported by Psalm 99. This composition is an enthronement psalm in which the declaration of Yahweh's holiness functions like a refrain (vv 3, 5, and 9).[77] Confessing Yahweh's holiness, then, is precisely what one did in the ritual celebration of the divine kingship over the world at large and over Israel specifically. The particular expression, "Yahweh is holy," likely carried connotations of Yahweh's sovereignty.[78] Certainly Isaiah and his audiences would have been familiar with this tradition, and might have understood 8:13a in this light.[79] If so, the line would fit well with the meaning of its overall context: the Davidides should acknowledge Yahweh as overlord, not Pekah of Israel.[80]

In vv 14 and 15, Isaiah describes the future action of Yahweh. Again, however, the interpretation of the material involves text-critical issues. The RSV translates the Hebrew of v 14: "And he will become a sanctuary (*lĕmiqdāš*), and a stone of offense, and a rock of stumbling to both houses of Israel, a trap and a snare (*lĕpaḥ ûlĕmôqēš*) to the inhabitants (*lĕyôšēb*) of Jerusalem." Many commentators argue that "sanctuary" is hardly a suitable parallel to "stone of offense" and "rock of stumbling." B. Duhm thus emends *lĕmiqdāš* to *lĕmôqēš* ("snare"), which matches the use of *môqēš* and *nôqĕšû* in vv 14b and

---

[77] See M. Mowinckel, *The Psalms in Israel's Worship*, 1. 106–9, 117, 156, 165, and 185; J. Schreiner *Sion-Jerusalem Jahwes Königsitz. Theologie der Heiligen Stadt im Alten Testament* (SANT 7; Munich: Kösel, 1963) 199–202; compare H.-J. Kraus, *Psalmen*, 2. 849–55.

[78] Psalm 22:4 also testifies to the close connection between the holiness and royal status of the deity: "And yet thou [God] art enthroned in holiness (*wĕʾattâ qādōš yōšēb*), thou art he whose praises Israel sings" (NEB; compare the RSV and NJPSV). Note too the response of the men of Beth-shemesh to the return of the Ark, the throne of Yahweh, from the Philistines: "Who can stand before Yahweh, this holy God?" (1 Sam 6:20; compare 4:4 and 2 Sam 6:2). Here again, divine kingship and holiness are associated.

[79] Note that the Temple vision of Isaiah closely connects the kingship and holiness of Yahweh (Isa 6:1–3 and 5). There, however, it is not the human community, but the heavenly seraphim, who proclaim the holiness of God.

[80] Compare M. E. W. Thompson's remark on 8:13 (*Situation and Theology*, 37): "Isaiah is to regard Yahweh as holy, and this idea, far from having little if any meaning in this context, means that Yahweh is to be acknowledged as truly sovereign in creation and history and absolutely in control of world events. He is the one who is to cause the prophet fear and dread (v. 13)." Thompson seems to recognize the political connotations of Yahweh's "holiness," but construes the statement in too broad a way. Isa 8:12–13 are not concerned so much with Yahweh's sovereignty over the world in general, but with his sovereignty over the Davidic house and Judah specifically. He is the king whom they should obey.

15b.[81] Alternatively, O. Kaiser and H. Wildberger propose reading *maqšîr* ("conspiracy" or "conspirator"), thus bringing the line into conformity with *qešer* in v 12 and *taqšîrû* (emended from *taqdîšû*) in v 13a.[82] K. Marti and W. Dietrich excise the term altogether.[83] The force of these proposals is the same: Yahweh's future action is altogether threatening, against the two houses of Israel and the residents of Jerusalem.

Several considerations weigh against these emendations. (a) There is no textual evidence for excising *lĕmiqdāš*. The ancient versions all assume some noun in v 14a. (b) The Septuagint and Vulgate both read "sanctuary" and so support the Masoretic text. Similarly, 1QIsa[a] reads *lmqdš*. Only the Targum construes the line as a threat: "And his [Yahweh's] Memra will become among you an avenger (*purʿan*). (c) *Miqdāš* and the proposed reading, *môqēš*, are not very close scribally. One could justify the change only by hypothesizing that later editors or tradents intentionally substituted *miqdāš*. (d) *Maqšîr* is a more plausible emendation, but the term is unattested. The reading thus results only in a new hapax legomenon. (e) Elsewhere in Isaiah 7 and 8, we have argued, the prophet distinguishes between the fate of Zion and that of Israel and Judah in general. Yahweh will protect the former (7:7–9a and 8:8b–10) and punish the latter (7:16, 18–25; 8:1–4, 5–8a). It would be surprising if, in 8:14, Isaiah were to predict disaster for both.

Isaiah 8:14 makes good sense as a promise of divine protection for Zion and the Davidic house.[84] Except for one alteration, the Masoretic text should be retained and translated: "Then he [Yahweh] will become for the sake of his holy domain[85] a stone of offense and a rock

---

[81]*Das Buch Jesaja*, 83–84; see also J. Skinner, *Isaiah*, 75–76; and J. Lindblom, *The Immanuel Section*, 31. G. Fohrer's translation, "He will become a snare (*Fallstrick*)," seems to assume the same emendation (*Das Buch Jesaja*, 1. 129).

[82]O. Kaiser, *Isaiah 1–12*, 190, 194; H. Wildberger, *Jesaja 1–12*, 334–35; see also R. E. Clements, *Isaiah 1–39*, 99; and compare H.-P. Müller, "Glauben und Bleiben," 50, n. 2. G. R. Driver ("Two Misunderstood Passages," 82–84) reads *maqšîr*, but translates the term, "cause of difficulty."

[83]K. Marti, *Das Buch Jesaja*, 86–87; W. Dietrich, *Jesaja und die Politik*, 70, 96. O. Procksch (*Jesaia I*, 136–37) deletes "sanctuary" and the following phrase, "and a stone of stumbling."

[84]Compare C. A. Evans, "Isa 8,11–15 Unemended," 113; and M. E. W. Thompson, *Situation and Theology*, 37. They correctly see a promise of deliverance in the passage, but misunderstand it as one intended for the prophet and his few followers only, not Ahaz and Jerusalem.

[85]The conjunction *û* that now precedes *lĕʾeben negep* ("stone of offense") was perhaps originally the pronominal suffix *ô* ("his"), qualifying *lĕmiqdāš*. The noun, in this context, does not mean "sanctuary," but more broadly "holy domain" (compare Ps 114:2), and refers to Zion, the city of Yahweh's residence and protection (compare Isa 4:5–6). The preposition, *lĕ*, expresses interest or advantage and so means "for the sake of" or "in behalf of."

of stumbling to the two houses of Israel [Israel and Judah], a trap and a snare for the sake of the ruler of Jerusalem."[86] The passage thus articulates the same message that Isaiah delivered on other occasions during the same period. If the Davidides honor Yahweh's sovereignty and follow his instructions, holding out against the demands of the coalition as well as those of many Judeans, Yahweh will defend Zion, "his holy domain," and its ruler, Ahaz. Verse 15 pronounces the disaster that will befall the Israelites and most Judeans: "Many of them will stumble and fall and be shattered and be snared and trapped."

D. Verses 16–20

Isaiah 8:16–20 conclude the collection of reports and speeches that began in 8:1. The Hebrew text is difficult, particularly in vv 19–20, and the various translations suggest very different meanings.[87] A related issue concerns whether vv 16–18 signal the prophet's withdrawl from public affairs to a private life within a small circle of loyal followers.[88] Finally, many scholars question the authenticity of the material, especially vv 19–20, to Isaiah.[89]

---

[86]$Yôšēb$ here does not mean "resident(s)," but rather "the one who sits or is enthroned" (compare Ps 55:20, Amos 1:8, and Isa 9:8). It refers to the Davidic king. The preposition $lĕ$ that precedes the noun ($lĕyôšēb$) again expresses interest or advantage. The text contrasts the salvation of the Davidic king and the punishment of Israel and Judah.

[87]For discussions of the text and its translation, see H. L. Ginsberg, "An Unrecognized Allusion to Kings Pekah and Hoshea of Israel," ErIsr 5 (1958) 61–65; P. W. Skehan, "Some Textual Problems in Isaia," CBQ 22 (1960) 47–55; G. R. Driver, "Isaianic Problems," in Festschrift für Wilhelm Eilers (ed. G. Wiessner; Wiesbaden: Otto Harrasowitz, 1967) 43–57; H.-P. Müller, "Das Wort von dem Totengeistern Jes. 8,19f.," WO 8 (1975) 65–76; C. F. Whitley, "The Language and Exegesis of Isaiah 8:16–23," ZAW 90 (1978) 28–43; and R. P. Carroll, "Translation and Attribution in Isaiah 8.19f.," BT 31 (1980) 126–34.

[88]According to most scholars, opposition to Isaiah's message from both the Davidic house and the Judeans at large forced the prophet to retire among his "disciples," at least for a time. See for example J. Lindblom, The Immanuel Section, 47–48; and H. Wildberger, Jesaja 1–12, 344–47; compare H.-P. Müller, "Glauben und Bleiben," 52–53; R. E. Clements, Isaiah 1–39, 100–1; C. Hardmeier, "Verkündigung und Schrift bei Jesaja," 119–31, especially 130–31; and M. E. W. Thompson, Situation and Theology, 37–40. R. P. Carroll ("Ancient Israelite Prophecy and Dissonant Theory," Numen 24 [1977] 135–51) and R. R. Wilson (Prophecy and Society in Ancient Israel [Philadelphia: Fortress, 1980] 273) see essentially the same picture, but recast it in social-scientific jargon.

The interpretation assumes that $bĕlimmūdāy$ in v 16 means "with my disciples." The text and translation here are in fact uncertain, and other renderings are not only possible, but more likely (see below). The evidence for a small "peripheral" group of Isaiah's followers is extremely slim, if extant at all. H. L. Ginsberg ("An

The following interpretation takes 8:16–20 as a single speech of the eighth-century prophet. As in the preceding unit, the audience of Isaiah is not specified, but the verses can be plausibly understood as an address to the Davidic court prior to the end of the Syro-Ephraimitic crisis.[90] The prophet calls for the official securing of his earlier words, presumably in a written document to be deposited in royal or temple archives, and claims for them an authoritative sta-

---

Unrecognized Allusion," 62) is correctly skeptical when he states that the disciples of Isaiah are "phantoms attested only by our problematic *blmdy* in v. 16." See also Y. Kaufmann, *The Religion of Israel*, 354, n. 7; and P. R. Ackroyd, "Isaiah I–XII," 26–29. If one talks at all of the prophet's "support group," one should think of the Davidic house, who, unlike "this people," did not oppose Isaiah, but decided to follow his advice during the Syro-Ephraimitic crisis.
There is also little evidence in the book of Isaiah for the prophet's withdrawl from public ministry. P. R. Ackroyd ("Isaiah I–XII," 28) comments: "The fact that we have no historical references in the Isaianic material for the period between the Syro-Ephraimite war in the reign of Ahaz (so vii and viii) and the threat to Ashdod in 713–711 (so xx) is no basis for the supposition that Isaiah did not speak publicly during that period." Actually, the prophetic speeches in Isaiah 13–19 and 28–33 can be understood in connection with international events from 731 to 720. They would thus testify to the prophet's continued activity in the wake of the Syro-Ephraimitic crisis. See J. H. Hayes and S. A. Irvine, *Isaiah*, 220–66 and 320–70; and compare G. Smith, "A New Fragment of the Assyrian Canon," 328–29.

[89]W. Werner ("Vom Prophetenwort zur Prophetentheologie," 1–7) contends that the vocabulary and thought of 8:16–18 reflect the hand of a deuteronomistic redactor (compare W. Dietrich, *Jesaja und die Politik*, 72–73). The lexical arguments, however, are not conclusive, and the thought of the passage can be interpreted in line with the prophet's message elsewhere. Most scholars doubt the authenticity of vv 19–20 only. (See for example B. Duhm, *Das Buch Jesaja*, 86; H.-P. Müller, "Das Wort von den Totengeistern," 74–75; R. P. Carroll, "Inner Tradition Shifts in Meaning in Isaiah 1–11," *ExpTim* 89 [1978] 302–3; R. E. Clements, *Isaiah 1–39*, 101–2; and H. Wildberger, *Jesaja 1–12*, 343–44; but compare L. G. Rignell, "Maher-salal Has-baz," 48–49; G. Fohrer, *Das Buch Jesaja*, 1. 134; and W. Eichrodt, *Jesaja 1–12*, 93–98, 103–4.) The reasons against their Isaianic authorship are not strong. The sequence of the terms *tĕʿûdâ* and *tôrâ* in v 16 is reversed in v 20a, but this variation alone hardly proves the hand of a redactor. Neither do the two terms have a new sense in v 20a. The dependence of the passage on Isa 47:10b–12 is far from clear. The verbal similarities are limited to *šaḥrāh* in 47:11 and *šaḥar* in 8:20, and even this parallel is not certain (see below). The content of the two passages is not particularly close. BHS distinguishes the prose style of 8:19–20 from the poetry of vv 16–18. The division, however, is doubtful, for meter is not clearly apparent in any of the material. Finally, the statement in v 19 about resorting to necromancy and wizardry does not necessarily assume the hard circumstances of the exile (see below).

[90]Compare the comments of B. Duhm (*Das Buch Jesaja*, 86) on v 19. He recognizes that, if Isaiah composed the verse, it must address Ahaz and his advisors. Duhm rejects the interpretation, however, simply because the verse's "instructional, pedagogical tone is not suitable for a political speech."

tus.[91] They should serve as the standard by which Ahaz and the royal court might assess the truth of the oracles of other intermediaries.

The speech opens in v 16 with the command, "Bind up the testimony (*tĕʿûdâ*), seal up the instruction (*tôrâ*)...."[92] Both nouns refer to Isaiah's earlier speeches during the Syro-Ephraimitic crisis,[93] but the precise nuance of each term is somewhat uncertain. The first, *tĕʿûdâ*, occurs outside of Isa 8:16 and 20 only in Ruth 4:7.[94] There it means "attestation" and describes a specific symbolic act accompanying property transactions. In the Isaiah text, the term appears closer in meaning to the related nouns *ʿēdâ* and *ʿēdût*, both usually translated "testimony." While these generally refer to the divine will as encapsulated in specific laws or law codes, *tĕʿûdâ* in 8:16 designates the divine will as articulated by the prophet. The term may also have the additional sense of "protest" or "admonition."[95] The prophet's "testi-

---

[91]Compare the metaphorical interpretations of v 16 by J. Lindblom (*The Immanuel Section*, 47–48), H. Wildberger (*Jesaja 1–12*, 344–45), and M. E. W. Thompson (*Situation and Theology*, 38–39). Their arguments rest, at least partly, on the assumption that *bĕlimmūdāy* means "in my disciples."

[92]The two verbs, *ṣôr* and *ḥătôm*, are apparently singular imperative forms of *ṣrr* and *ḥtm*. If one assumes that the concluding phrase, *bĕlimmūdāy*, means "with/in my disciples," the commands appear to be Yahweh's address to Isaiah. (See J. Boehmer, "'Yahwes Lehrlinge' im Buch Jesaja," *ARW* 33 [1936] 171–75.) Divine speech in v 16, however, would be strangely isolated, since the "I" in vv 17 and 18 is clearly Isaiah. H. Wildberger (*Jesaja 1–12*, 342–43) therefore construes the verbs as infinitive absolutes and translates the line as an indicative statement of the prophet: "I bind [*ṣôr*, from *ṣûr*] the testimony, I seal [*ḥătôm*] the teaching in my disciples." B. Duhm (*Das Buch Jesaja*, 84), G. B. Gray (*The Book of Isaiah*, 1. 155–57), and K. Marti (*Das Buch Jesaja*, 87) suggest similar readings, though they derive *ṣôr* from *ṣrr* (compare J. Skinner, *Isaiah*, 76; G. Fohrer, *Das Buch Jesaja*, 1. 132; and M. E. W. Thompson, *Situation and Theology*, 37, n. 93). Alternatively, E. J. Kissane (*The Book of Isaiah* [2 vols.; Dublin: Browne and Nolan, 1941–43] 1. 99–101) emends the verbs to passive participles and translates, "The testimony is bound up [*ṣārûr*], the teaching sealed [*ḥātûm*] in my disciples."

These proposals are unnecessary, for the speaker and addressee in v 16 become questions only if one insists on translating *limmūdāy* as "my disciples." The term in fact can be rendered in other ways that obviate the problem (see below). The plene spellings of the two imperatives are nevertheless unusual, and the proposed infinitive absolutes involve only slight changes in the Masoretic pointings. Whether the verbs are imperatives or infinitive forms, they have in either case the force of a command. Before the royal court and its supporters, Isaiah calls for the securing of his "testimony" and "instruction."

[93]Compare R. E. Clements, *Isaiah 1–39*, 100–101. He suggests that the terms refer specifically to *mahēr šālāl ḥāš baz* inscribed on the tablet in 8:1.

[94]The noun probably derives from *ʿād*, "bear witness." Other roots have been suggested, including *ydʿ* and *ʿdd*, but these are less likely. See G. Rice, *The Syro-Ephraimite Crisis*, 272; and H. L. Ginsberg, "An Unrecognized Allusion," 62.

[95]See J. Lindblom, *The Immanuel Section*, 47. Note that the verb *ʿād* can mean "warn, charge, exhort."

mony" reproached and threatened the opponents of the Davidic house, while warning Ahaz to hold to a neutralist course.

The second noun, *tôrâ*, frequently means "law," but also more generally "instruction."[96] The term can perhaps refer specifically to the political advice a counselor gives the king or the people, although clear instances of this meaning are lacking.[97] Isaiah uses the verb *yrh* in 28:9, where he questions the political wisdom of Israelite plans for rebellion against Assyria.[98] A similar political connotation may be present in Isa 8:16, since the prophetic speeches that composed the "instruction" were essentially political advice to the royal court and its supporters.[99] Isaiah, of course, regarded such instruction not simply as prudent counsel, but as the authoritative will of Yahweh (see 8:3b, 5, 11, and 18).

The concluding phrase of v 16, *bĕlimmūdāy*, is usually translated "in/among my disciples" and taken as a reference to a small circle of Isaiah's followers. The reading, however, is by no means certain. Among the ancient versions, only the Vulgate gives this translation (*in discipulis meis*). The Septuagint, Targum, and the Syriac vary in their readings, but none of them refers to a distinct prophetic group. Whether the Masoretic text is retained or emended, the following renderings and/or interpretations make as good, if not better, sense.

(1) The Hebrew may mean "with the things taught by me" (compare the Syriac). We would then translate v 16, "Bind up the testimony, seal up the instruction with my teaching."

(2) *Bĕlimmūdāy* might be rendered "with my learned ones." The reference in this case would be to court or temple personnel, perhaps

---

[96] In Proverbs, *tôrâ* describes parental teaching (1:8; 4:1; and 6:20), a wife's advice to her husband (31:26), and the wisdom of the sages (13:14). For studies of the word in the Hebrew Bible and in Isaiah specifically, see W. J. Beecher, "Torah: A Word-Study in the Old Testament," *JBL* 24 (1905) 1–16; L. Smith, "The Use of the Word torah in Isaiah, Chapters 1–39," *AJSL* 46 (1929) 1–21; J. Begrich, "Die priesterliche Tora," *BZAW* 66 (1936) 63–88 = his *GS*, 232–60; G. Ostborn, *Tora in the Old Testament* (Lund: Hgakan Ohlssons, 1945); J. Jensen, *The Use of tora by Isaiah: His Debate with the Wisdom Tradition* (CBQMS 3; Washington: CBA, 1973); also S. Wagner, "*yrh* II," *TWAT* 3. 920–30.

[97] Note however Prov 29:18: "For lack of prophetic vision (*ḥāzôn*) a people lose restraint, but happy is he who heeds instruction (*tôrâ*)." The saying is grouped with proverbs apparently intended for the training of royal heirs (see vv 4, 12, and 14). If the use of v 18 were similar, *tôrâ* might describe the political advice that a prophet gives to a king.

[98] See J. H. Hayes and S. A. Irvine, *Isaiah*, 320–30.

[99] Compare J. Jensen, *The Use of tora by Isaiah*, 110, especially n. 197; and M. E. W. Thompson, *Situation and Theology*, 38. They contend that *tôrâ* and *limmūdāy* in Isa 8:16 are "scholastic" terms.

Uriah and Zechariah mentioned in 8:2, who were in charge of securing official documents.[100]

(3) One might emend *bĕlimmūdāy* to *kĕlimmūd* and translate the verse, "Bind up the testimony, seal up the instruction in accordance with what is customary."[101] In this case, the prophet asks simply that his written speeches be handled in the manner standard for all documents entered into the royal or temple archives.[102]

(4) *Bĕlimmūdāy* may be a corruption of *bĕlimmūdêhā*, "upon its ties."[103] Mishnaic texts attest to this meaning for *limmūd*, and biblical examples offer support.[104] If Isaiah understands the term in this sense, v 16 graphically describes the handling of his written speeches. The document (presumably papyrus) would first be folded up and tied with string; then "upon its ties" a wax seal would be affixed.[105]

---

[100] See L. G. Rignell, "Maher-salal Has-baz," 48; and R. E. Clements, *Isaiah 1–39*, 100.

[101] Ancient scribes frequently misread *b* for *k*. The possessive suffix perhaps arose in part through dittography: the *w* that begins v 17 was written twice and then construed by later scribes as *y*. Note that neither the Septuagint nor the Targum reads the first-person pronoun here.

[102] The precise procedure is uncertain. Isaiah may intend simply for the document of his speeches to be deposited in a container of some sort, or more generally in the royal or temple archives. (The Qumran sectarians preserved scrolls in clay vessels, and Jer 32:14 testifies to the same practice.) Alternatively, the prophet may have in mind the more elaborate steps for folding up, tying, sealing, and depositing a papyrus document. Examples of sealed writings at Elephantine illustrate the procedure, and Jer 32:9–15 seems to describe a similar practice (compare Isa 29:11; Job 14:17; Dan 12:4; Neh 9:38; 10:1; 1 Kgs 21:8; and Esth 8:8). See N. H. Tur-Sinai, *The Book of Job: A New Commentary* (Jerusalem: Kiryath Sepher, 1957) 240–41; also N. Avigad, *Hebrew Bullae from the Time of Jeremiah: Remnants of a Burnt Archive* (Jerusalem: Israel Exploration Society, 1986) 120–30.

[103] See H. Torczyner (N. H. Tur-Sinai), *Lachish I (Tell ed Duweir): The Lachish Letters* (London: Oxford University Press, 1938), 16; idem., *Job*, 240–41. The scribal error is easy enough to imagine, if one writes the end of v 16 and the beginning of v 17 as a continuous line of letters without spacing: *blmdyhwḥkyty*. The graphic similarity of *yh* and *wḥ* could have resulted in haplography, the *h* of *blmdyh* being dropped accidently.

[104] Compare the following expressions: "a roped heifer" (*ʿeglâ mĕlummādâ*, Hos 10:11); "like an unhitched heifer" (*kĕʿēgel lōʾ lummād*, Jer 31:18); and "a wild ass bound to the wilderness" (*pereh limmūd midbār*, Jer 2:24). Concerning the possible connection between the Hebrew *lmd* and the Ugaritic *mdl* ("hitch, harness, yoke"), see M. H. Goshen-Gottstein, "'Ephraim is a well-trained heifer' and Ugaritic *mdl*," *Bib* 41 (1960) 64–66.

[105] Three other proposed readings should be noted, though they seem less plausible than those listed above: *baylādîm* ("in the children"; H. L. Ginsberg, "An Unrecognized Allusion," 61–62); *bal-lĕmōd* ("not to learn"; G. R. Driver, "Isaianic Problems," 44); and *blmd* ("from the learned"; C. F. Whitney, "Isaiah 8:16–23," 29).

The prophet proclaims his confidence in v 17: "And I will wait (wĕḥikkîtî) for Yahweh, who is about to hide his face from the house of Jacob, and will hope in him" (wĕqiwwêtî-lô). The words are reminiscent of lament psalms, in which the distressed worshiper declares his or her faith in divine deliverance, "waiting for" and "hoping in" Yahweh (see Pss 25:3, 5, 21; 27:14; 39:8; 69:7–21; 130:5; compare Jer 14:22).[106] Isaiah here identifies with Jerusalem and the Davidic house, both seriously threatened by Syria and Israel and opposed by many Judeans as well. He is sure that Yahweh will save Ahaz and the capital city from the present crisis.

The statement reflects Isaiah's firm belief in the truth of his "testimony" and "instruction." The earlier speeches announced the demise of Ahaz's enemies, and 8:17 affirms the prediction. Yahweh is about to "hide his face from the house of Jacob."[107] The Israelites and most Judeans, the prophet believes, will suffer at the hands of the Assyrians (compare 8:4, 7–8a, 14–15). Their defeat coincides, in part, with Yahweh's salvation of the Davidic house and Jerusalem; for this Isaiah "waits" and "hopes" (compare 8:8b–10 and 14).[108]

In verse 18, Isaiah draws special attention to himself and his children: "Look! I and the children whom Yahweh has given me are

---

[106]See C. Westermann, "Das Hoffen im Alten Testament," in his *GS* (Munich: Chr. Kaiser, 1964) 219–65. W. Werner ("Vom Prophetenwort zur Prophetentheologie," 1–4) and W. Dietrich (*Jesaja und die Politik*, 72) doubt the authenticity of the language to Isaiah, but their skepticism is not justified. The prophet frequently draws on the terminology of the cult. The two verbs, qwh and ḥkh, occur elsewhere in Isaiah, though the authorship of several of the passages is disputed (see 5:2, 4, 7; 25:9; 26:8; 30:18; and 33:2).

[107]The idiom occurs frequently in the psalms and generally describes Yahweh's giving someone over to terror and distress (see Pss 13:2; 22:25; 27:9; 69:18; 88:15; 102:3; 104:29; 143:7; 144:25; also Deut 32:20; and Mic 3:4). In Isa 8:16, "house of Jacob" may designate the northern kingdom alone, but more probably the majority of Judeans as well. (Note that the Septuagint [Codex Vaticanus] speaks of "the houses of Jacob" in 8:14 and presumably has in mind both Israel and Judah.) The prophet anticipates their deliverance into the hands of adversaries (compare Ezek 39:20 and Jer 33:5).

[108]Compare the interpretations of G. Fohrer (*Das Buch Jesaja*, 1. 132–34), J. Lindblom (*The Immanuel Section*, 49) and M. E. W. Thompson (*Situation and Theology*, 39–40). According to Fohrer, Isaiah anticipates the future intervention of Yahweh as one entirely of judgment. However, the expressions, "waiting for Yahweh" and "hoping in Yahweh," normally suggest an expectation of divine deliverance. J. Lindblom recognizes the positive tone of the passage, but construes the prophet's message as an eschatological statement. Isaiah, he argues, "looked forward to the age to come, when a new Israel was created, living in quite new conditions, under the sceptre of a new Davidide, an ideal king." Thompson speaks of the "double message of the presence of Yahweh." He argues that Isaiah saw Yahweh as a source of hope for the "faithful" (the prophet and his followers), but as the cause of disaster for Ahaz and others who do not "believe."

signs and portents against Israel from Yahweh Sebaoth who resides on Mt. Zion." The logical connection with what precedes is not altogether clear, but two interpretations are possible.

(1) If the "testimony" were sealed up so that its message were no longer accessible, public signs might be necessary to call it to mind. The symbolic names of the prophet's children, both of which had hopeful import for the Davidic house, and possibly Isaiah's own name as well ("Yahweh delivers"), would serve this function.[109]

(2) Isaiah might mean to emphasize that, as signs and portents, he and his children are "from Yahweh." Their message is therefore authoritative and certain to come true. In this case, the prophet's reference to himself and the children may be a shorthand way of characterizing the content of the "testimony" and "instruction." It is directed, we have argued, against Israel, Syria, and the majority of Judeans, but is intended also as assurance to Ahaz and Jerusalem. Isaiah's confidence in the truth of his preaching rests on his conviction that he and the children stand in the commission of Yahweh.

The description of Yahweh as "the one who resides on Mt. Zion" reinforces the hopeful import of the passage. The expression is probably formulaic and at home in the liturgy of the Jerusalem temple (see Pss 74:2; 135:21; Joel 4:17). It encapsulates the Zion tradition, which could have only promising overtones in the ears of the Davidides. The God who commissions the prophet and his children as signs and portents protects Zion against all enemies. Those who live within the city, particularly the royal leadership, must stand firm in the ancient promise: if they hold out against the Syrian-Israelite forces and against the pressure of most Judeans, Yahweh will defend them in his holy city.

An admonition to the Davidic court and its supporters follows in vv 19–20: they are to abide by Isaiah's word, now contained in the "testimony" and "instruction," even in the face of differing predictions from other intermediaries. The actual rendering of the saying is difficult, and accordingly, scholars interpret the verses in very different ways. The following serves as a tentative translation.

> 19. And if they say to you, "Consult (*diršû*) the necromancers and wizards who chirp and mutter; should not (*hălô'*) a people consult (*yidrōš*) its spirits (*'ĕlōhāyw*), the dead on behalf of the living?" 20. [Look] to the instruction and testimony (*lĕtôrâ wĕlitʿûdâ*) if (*'im-lō'*) they [the necromancers and wizards] do not speak according to this word [the instruction and testimony] for which there is no desire (*šāḥar*).

---

[109]Their continuing prominence in the public eye would effectively substitute for the open copy of a document normally drawn up for ongoing consultation (see Jer 32:9–15).

The saying appears to consist of a complex conditional sentence.[110] The protasis (v 19) hypothetically quotes popular advice to the royal court: they are to confer with other specialists in divination, presumably for help in understanding the present crisis and in charting policy.[111] The named specialists—necromancers (ʾōbôt) and wizards (yiddĕʿōnîm)—are later proscribed in the Deuteronomic literature (Deut 18:11), and here, already by Isaiah, may be derogated as ones who "chirp and mutter." The prophet implies that their oracles and advice hardly deserve equal consideration alongside his own "testimony."

Isaiah does not specify who might urge the Davidides to consult other intermediaries. Probably he had in mind the many Judeans who opposed Ahaz's neutralist stance and the counsel of Isaiah upon which that policy was based. These understandably might have pressured the king and court to consult other specialists, hoping that the latter would support their own political views. The rhetorical style of v 19b fits well with this assumption. Isaiah anticipates the arguments of the Judeans and thereby weakens their force.

The reply of the prophet in v 20 is elliptical. If the implied verb of the line is "consult" (drš, as in v 19), the response might mean, "Refer to the instruction and testimony, rather than consulting necromancers

---

[110] For a detailed discussion of the syntax of the saying, see H.-P. Müller, "Totengeistern," 65–68, 72–74. He compares the verses to the Lachish Ostraca no. 3, ll. 8–12, and no. 4, ll. 4–6. See also P. W. Skehan, "Some Textual Problems," 47–55.

[111] For a detailed discussion of the attribution of words in 8:19–20, see R. P. Carroll, "Translation and Attribution," 126–34. The RSV concludes the quotation with v 19a, presenting what follows as the prophet's reply: "Should not a people consult their God? Should they consult the dead on behalf of the living?" If one grants for the moment that v 19a consists of two rhetorical questions, the interrogative hălōʾ ("should not") would likely govern both, and so would call for an affirmative answer to each. It is hard, though, to imagine Isaiah suggesting that a people "consult the dead on behalf of the living." The most straightforward reading of v 19b would take the line as a single question in which "its spirits" (see 1 Sam 28:13 for this rendering of ʾĕlōhîm) and "the dead" stand in apposition as dual objects of the verb yidrōš. In this way, the advice quoted by the prophet extends to the end of v 19 and suggests that a people, particularly its leadership, might legitimately confer with dead spirits for advice in critical situations.

Less certain is whether the quotation continues into v 20a. The NEB translates the text in this way: ". . . a nation may surely seek guidance of its gods, of the dead on behalf of the living, for an oracle or a message?" (compare the NJPSV). This reading forces one to construe the ʾim-lōʾ that immediately follows in an asseverative sense, "Surely they will say . . . ." Isaiah's reply would then take the form of an oath formula in which the principal sentence (e.g., "May Yahweh do harm to me if . . .") has been suppressed. While this interpretation is certainly possible, it is by no means the most straightforward syntactically. The text makes equally good sense if one begins the prophet's answer in v 20a.

and wizards." However, the preposition *lĕ*, translated above as "to," can also have the sense of "according to," thus setting forth Isaiah's "instruction and testimony" as the norm by which the royal court should steer foreign affairs. The verse might thus be rendered: "Hold to the instruction and testimony . . . ." This reading fits well with the continuation, "if they do not say according to this word . . . ." The prophet proposes his earlier speeches as the authoritative word of Yahweh (also the firm basis for foreign policy!), by which the advice and prognoses of other specialists should be judged.

The final relative clause of v 20, *ʾăšer ʾên-lô šāḥar*, has tried the ingenuity of scholars.[112] Our translation of the Hebrew rests on the following decisions. (1) The clause is original to v 20.[113] (2) It qualifies "this word" (*kaddābār hazzeh*), that is, the "instruction and testimony" of Isaiah.[114] (3) *Šāḥar* means "desire" and describes the negative response which Isaiah's preaching had evoked from many.[115] Rendered along these lines, v 20 exhorts the Davidic court to abide by the prophet's political advice, even though "this people" (the majority of Judeans) had no "desire" for it, and encouraged their leadership to seek a different message from other sources.

Another interpretation is also possible. *Šāḥar* may be a corruption of *šōḥad* ("bribe").[116] If the emendation is made, the saying

---

[112] See the text-critical studies listed in n. 87 above.

[113] Compare P. W. Skehan, "Textual Problems," 47–55. He views the clause as a gloss on v 21a: the one who "passes through it [the land?]" has no "dawn," that is, hope. The metaphor does fit with the darkness motif of vv 22–23, yet one would expect a gloss on v 21a to identify the cryptic identity of its subject.

[114] This is the most straightforward understanding of the verse's syntax. However, modern translations and commentaries usually interpret the final clause as a negative comment on the advice previously quoted and/or on the futility of necromancy and wizardry. See H. Wildberger, *Jesaja 1–12*, 352; O. Kaiser, *Isaiah 1–12*, 199–202; R. E. Clements, *Isaiah 1–39*, 102; and H.-P. Müller, "Totengeistern," 72–74; compare the RSV, NEB, NJPSV, and JB.

[115] Although other instances of this meaning are lacking, the verb *šḥr* frequently has the sense of "seek eagerly, diligently, or with longing" (see Ps 78:34 and Prov 7:15, where the term is parallel to *drš* and *bqš*; also Hos 5:15; Ps 63:2; and Isa 26:9). The traditional rendering of *šāḥar* as "dawn" is impossible if the final clause comments on the "instruction and testimony" of the prophet. (Note that among the ancient versions, only the Vulgate reads "dawn" [*matutina lux*].) The same conclusion applies to G. R. Driver's translation of the term as "force" ("Isaianic Problems," 45; compare H.-P. Müller, "Totengeistern," 73–74; O. Kaiser, *Isaiah 1–12*, 199, n. 3; and H. Wildberger, *Jesaja 1–12*, 343). C. F. Whitley ("Isaiah 8:16–23," 30–31) sees correctly that *šāḥar* in 8:20 has to do with "seeking" Yahweh's will through the testimony of Isaiah. However, he interprets the line, along with v 16, as a statement about the inaccessibility of the testimony to "the learned," and thus about the inability of "this people" to communicate with Yahweh.

[116] The graphic similarity of the Hebrew letters *d* and *r* would explain the scribal error. Note that the readings of the Septuagint and Syriac assume the Hebrew *šōḥad*.

implies that the testimony of Isaiah is reliable because it has not been bought. (Compare Micah's charge during the same period that Jerusalem's "prophets divine for money"; 3:11.) The same presumably could not be said of prognoses that differ from "this word."

E. Summary

The analysis of 8:1–20 focused on the attitude of Isaiah toward Ahaz, Jerusalem, the Judeans, and the Syrian-Israelite alliance. As stated at the outset, the same portrait of the prophet can be seen in the material as the one we discerned in chapter 7: Isaiah was an ardent defender of the Davidic king and a proponent of the Zion theology. The details of this picture can be summarized quickly.

(1) Several months prior to the Syro-Ephraimitic crisis, the prophet erected a public inscription with the words, "spoil speeds, prey hastes" (8:1–2). The saying predicted the demise of Syria and so encouraged the Davidides in their isolationist policy.

(2) After Pekah's coup in Samaria and Israel's swing to the side of Rezin, Isaiah reappropriated the saying as the symbolic name of his newborn son (8:3–4). At the same time, he extended its threatening message to address both Syria and Israel, and set a time limit for Assyria's action against the coalition. The advice to the Davidides was implicit but clear: stay out of the rebellion.

(3) Isaiah denounced the many Judeans who opposed Ahaz and supported instead the Syrian and Israelite kings (8:6). While they accused the Davidic king of "conspiracy" against his Israelite superior, the prophet urged Ahaz to revere his true sovereign, Yahweh, by holding to a neutralist course (8:12–13). Yahweh would deliver the Davidic king and Zion from the present crisis, and use the Assyrians to punish the Judeans and Israelites (8:7–10, 14–15).

(4) The prophet claimed that his preaching was the reliable word of Yahweh and so the only legitimate basis for policy-making (8:16–20). Popular opposition to the neutralist stand which Isaiah advocated, and which Ahaz was following, put tremendous pressure on the king to consult other specialists in divination. Isaiah dismissed the value of any advice that might differ from his own "testmony" and "instruction."

CHAPTER SEVEN

ISAIAH 8:21–9:6

Interpretations of Isa 8:21–9:6 disagree widely on several issues. The translation is in doubt at many points, particularly in 8:21–23.[1] The verb tenses throughout the passage are open to question and, consequently, it is debatable which verses, if any, anticipate future developments and which verses reflect on past events and/or present circumstances.[2] The compositional unity of the material is also contested,[3] as well as its authorship and date.[4] Finally, scholars disagree on the identity of the royal child mentioned in 9:5.[5]

---

[1] For detailed discussions of the text and translation, see H. L. Ginsberg, "An Unrecognized Allusion," 61–65; G. R. Driver, "Isaianic Problems," 43–49; J. A. Emerton, "Some Linguistic and Historical Problems in Isaiah VIII 23," *JSS* 14 (1969) 151–75; and C. F. Whitley, "Isaiah 8:16–23," 28–43.
[2] The issue has been raised particularly in regard to 8:23–9:6. Compare H. Barth, *Die Jesaja-Worte in der Josiazeit*, 145–48; and W. Werner, *Eschatologische Texte*, 23–35.
[3] Most commentators agree on a break between 8:21–22 (23aa) and v 23ab. (Compare however H. L. Ginsberg, "An Unrecognized Allusion," 61, 65. He contends that "the former" and "the latter" in v 23abb refer back to "his king(s)" in v 21b.) The connection between 8:23abb and 9:1–6 is more debated. H. Wildberger (*Jesaja 1–12*, 365–67) follows A. Alt ("Jesaja 8,23–9,6. Befreiungsnacht und Krönungstag," in *Festschrift Alfred Bertholet* [Tübingen: J. C. B. Mohr [Paul Siebeck] 1950] 29–49 = his *KS* II. 206–25) in taking the verses as a single original unit. H. W. Wolff (*Frieden ohne Ende*, 60–63), O. Kaiser (*Isaiah 1–12*, 203–6), and R. E. Clements (*Isaiah 1–39*, 103–5), among others, remain doubtful. W. Werner (*Eschatologische Texte*, 20–22) recently presents a full list of reasons for seeing a new beginning in 9:1, but the argument is not conclusive.
[4] Opinions range between two extremes: attributing all the material to Isaiah, though perhaps allowing for a gloss in v 23aa; and assigning the verses to various exilic or post-exilic writers. Advocates of the first view include H. L. Ginsberg ("An Unrecognized Allusion," 61–65), H. Wildberger (*Jesaja 1–12*, 355–57), and M. E. W. Thompson ("Isaiah's Ideal King," 79–88; *Situation and Theology*, 14, 40–42, 45–48). The second interpretation is defended by O. Kaiser (*Isaiah 1–12*, 199–206). (Compare H. Barth, *Die Jesaja-Worte in der Josiazeit*, 141–77, especially

The following interpretation of 8:21–9:6 differs sharply from most previous treatments in taking the verses as a single speech of the eighth-century prophet. The passage is understandable as an address to a Jerusalemite audience shortly after Pekah's coup in Samaria and Ahaz's move toward independence from the northern kingdom. The speech celebrates this assertion of independence, predicts the continued well-being of the Davidic dynasty, and promises divine support.

A. Verses 21–22

Verses 21–22 are usually thought to describe the oppressive conditions either in Israel, following the Assyrian campaigns in 734–732, or in Jerusalem/Judah, after the Babylonian invasion in 588–587.[6] The latter proposal obviously assumes that the passage does not derive from the eighth-century prophet. However, neither the language nor the content of the verses counts against Isaiah as their author.[7] The former proposal rests on the widespread but debatable belief that the northern kingdom suffered tremendously at the hands of Tiglathpileser. He supposedly converted much of its territory into Assyrian provinces. According to our reconstruction of the history, the provinces in question may have been established mostly on land confiscated from Syria. If so, it would seem that Israel received rela-

---

152–54 and 170–74. He dates vv 21–22 to the exilic period, but 8:23–9:6 to the last third of the seventh century.) R. E. Clements (*Isaiah 1–39*) 101–9) represents a mediating position, attributing 8:21–22, 23aa, and 23abb to different late editors and glossators, but retaining 9:1–6 for the eighth-century prophet.

[5]For a review of the various proposals, see M. Rehm, *Der königliche Messias*, 168–84; and R. Kilian, *Jesaja 1–39*, 5–10.

[6]Compare for example H. Wildberger, *Jesaja 1–12*, 357–58; and H. Barth, *Die Jesaja-Worte in der Josiazeit*, 153–54. Despite their different datings of the verses, both scholars view the material as a reflection on the present difficult circumstances of the speaker/writer. O. Kaiser (*Isaiah 1–12*, 200) characterizes the saying as a *vaticinium ex eventu*. In contrast, L. G. Rignell ("Maher-salal Has-baz," 49–50) dates 8:21–22 to the Syro-Ephraimitic crisis and interprets them as a genuine anticipation of future conditions, when the oracle against Syria and Ephraim (8:1–4) would come to pass.

[7]See especially the comments of H. Wildberger (*Jesaja 1–12*, 357) on the vocabulary and imagery of the text. According to B. Duhm (*Das Buch Jesaja*, 86–87), J. Skinner (*Isaiah*, 77), K. Marti (*Das Buch Jesaja*, 90), G. B. Gray (*The Book of Isaiah*, 1. 157), V. Herntrich (*Der Prophet Jesaja*, 57), and G. Fohrer (*Das Buch Jesaja*, 1. 134), the prophet's authorship of the verses, if not certain, is at least possible. H. Barth (*Die Jesaja-Worte in der Josiazeit*, 153–54), O. Kaiser (*Isaiah 1–12*, 200, 202), and R. E. Clements (*Isaiah 1–39*, 102–3) attribute the passage to an exilic or post-exilic writer on the assumption that the third-person feminine suffix *bāh* ("through her") refers to Jerusalem (compare 3:25 and 5:14), destroyed by the Babylonians in 587. The suffix, however, can refer to the "land" mentioned subsequently in v 22.

tively lenient treatment from the Assyrians in the aftermath of the Syro-Ephraimitic crisis (see above Chapter Two, secs. B2, B3, B7, and C3).

The passage makes sense against the background of political developments in Israel just prior to the Syro-Ephraimitic crisis. This interpretation, however, depends on the following translation.

> 21. So he passes over into it [the land], fierce and hungry. And when he becomes ravenous and works himself into a rage, then he revolts against his king and his God and turns [to go] upward. 22. And he sets his sights on the land [Israel]. And look, there is distress and darkness, the gloom of oppression and widespread calamity.

The opening line is curiously cryptic: "So he passes over into it, fierce and hungry (*wĕʿābar bāh niqšeh wĕrāʿēb*)."[8] Neither here nor in what follows does Isaiah clearly identify the subject of the action. Assuming that the passage depicts a general situation of hardship, modern translations often render the third-person verbs with the impersonal "they" (RSV, NEB, NIV) or "people" (TEV).[9] It is possible, however, that the "he" throughout the verses refers to a specific figure, namely, Pekah. Pekah, we have argued, had been ruling in Gilead for several years, but in the fall of 734, he and fifty Gileadite troops managed to assassinate Pekahiah, and Pekah ascended the throne in Samaria (2 Kgs 15:25). Isaiah 8:21 may allude to the usurper and his co-conspirators, describing their passage from Transjordan into the northern kingdom. If so, the description of Pekah as "fierce" (literally, "hardened"), "hungry," and "in a rage" (*wĕhitqaṣṣap*, v 21ba) would dramatize his firm intent on overthrowing the regime of Pekahiah.[10]

---

[8]H. L. Ginsberg ("An Unrecognized Allusion," 62) construes *niqšeh* as the subject of *ʿābar*, *bāh* as the pre-exilic equivalent to *bô*, and *wĕrāʿēb* as a second verb. He thus translates the verse, "Upon him shall come hardship, so that he will hunger." There is no evidence, however, for *niqšeh* as a noun meaning "hardship." The term is a *nifal* participle of *qšh* ("be hard, severe, fierce"), functioning as an adjective in 8:21a. As such, it is parallel to *rāʿēb*, also an adjective qualifying the unnamed subject of *ʿābar*.

[9]Most commentators understand the verse similarly. See for example G. Fohrer, *Das Buch Jesaja*, 1. 134–35; O. Kaiser, *Isaiah 1–12*, 199; and H. Wildberger, *Jesaja 1–12*, 355, 358.

[10]The anonymous "he" throughout 8:21-22 and the vague reference to "it" in v 21a suggest to many scholars that the passage is only a fragment. Antecedent material presumably has been lost. (See B. Duhm, *Das Buch Jesaja*, 87; J. Skinner, *Isaiah*, 77; G. B. Gray, *The Book of Isaiah*, 1. 160; P. Skehan, "Some Textual Problems," 48; and H. Wildberger, *Jesaja 1–12*, 356; compare L. G. Rignell, "Mahersalal Has-baz," 49; and H. Barth, *Die Jesaja-Worte in der Josiazeit*, 153.) Elsewhere, however, Isaiah begins a commentary on current political events in a similar way (see the discussion of Isa 10:27d-34 in Chapter Ten below). If the coup of Pekah

The description of events continues in v 21bb, "he revolts against his king and his God" (wĕqillēl bĕmalkô ûbēʾlōhāyw). The verb is a *piel* form of *qll* and normally means "curse." Most commentators thus render the line, "he will curse his king and his God," presumably because of the hard times that have befallen the land.[11] This sense, however, would normally demand the introduction of "his king" and "his God" with the accusative particle ʾ*et*. In 8:21, they are governed by the preposition *b*, and so would seem to be those *by* which "he" curses. F. Delitzsch thus translates the line, "they curse by their king and by their god."[12] G. B. Gray, however, correctly objects that this rendering leaves unnamed the object cursed, and envisions, moreover, the unusual case of cursing by the name of the king.[13] A better interpretation takes the verb *qll* as an equivalent to the Akkadian *qullulu* ("offend or revolt") and construes the preposition *b* in an adversative sense, "against."[14] Translated in this way, the line would have a clear political meaning and could refer to the conspiracy of Pekah against Pekahiah.[15]

The final clause of v 21 and the opening of v 22 are frequently interpreted together and translated, "[and they will] turn their faces upward (ûpānâ lĕmāʿĕlâ); and they will look to the earth (wĕʾel-ʾereṣ yabbîṭ)." Given this rendering, two senses would be possible. (1) The

---

was quite recent, the prophet could assume his audience's familiarity (indeed their preoccupation!) with it. He could thus begin simply, "So he passes over into it." The residents of Jerusalem and the Davidic house would have easily sensed whom and what the prophet was describing.

[11]See for example B. Duhm, *Das Buch Jesaja*, 87; O. Procksch, *Jesaja I*, 141–42; O. Kaiser, *Isaiah 1–12*, 199; H. Wildberger, *Jesaja 1–12*, 355–59; and M. E. W. Thompson, *Situation and Theology*, 40; also the KJV, RSV, JB, NIV, and TEV.

[12]*The Prophecies of Isaiah*, 1. 203–4.

[13]*The Book of Isaiah*, 1. 161. The translation of C. F. Whitley ("Isaiah 8:16–23," 32) avoids the second difficulty: "And he will curse by his idol and by his god." The rendering of *malkô* as "his idol" is based partly on the assumption that the larger context, 8:16–23, concerns the idolatry of the nation in hard times. The consultation of "spirits" is mentioned in vv 19–20, but these verses conclude the preceding speech, as well as the larger memoir in 8:1–20. Verses 21–22 themselves do not clearly suggest anything about idolatry.

[14]See G. R. Driver, "Isaianic Problems," 46, 49; and H. L. Ginsberg, "An Unrecognized Allusion," 62, 64; also the NEB and NJPSV.

[15]Despite the autonomy of Pekah in Gilead since the 740s or earlier, Isaiah still referred to Pekahiah as "his king." Pekah's authority in Gilead was perhaps initially under the auspices of the Israelite king in Samaria. Jeroboam II probably had appointed him as a high-ranking official over the region. After Pekah broke with Samaria and began to rule independently in Gilead, neither the Israelite royal annals nor Isaiah acknowledged Pekah's new status, but continued to view him as a renegade subject. Second Kings 15:25 thus refers to Pekah as the *šāliš* ("captain," RSV) of Pekahiah. Similarly, Isa 8:21 describes Pekahiah as "his [Pekah's] king." See M. Vogelstein, *Jeroboam II*, 6, n. 13.

distressed inhabitants of the land search the heavens above and the earth below for a sign or omen of an imminent turn of fate. (2) "Upward" and "to the earth" are opposites that together express the idea, "everywhere." The people look around on all sides. Both interpretations assume that the continuation of the saying in v 22b states what the distressed inhabitants in fact see: "distress and darkness, the gloom of oppression and widespread calamity." The text supposedly describes the hopeless circumstances in the land after a foreign invasion.

If the passage is interpreted against the background of Pekah's coup in 734, a different translation with a more political sense suggests itself. The final clause of v 21 might mean, "and he turns to go upward," alluding to the ascent of Pekah and his troops into the central Ephraimite hill country toward Samaria. There, in the capital city, they would overthrow Pekahiah (2 Kgs 15:25). Verse 22a would refer similarly to Pekah's takeover in Israel: "And he sets his sights on the land [Israel]," that is, to acquire it.[16]

Verse 22b describes the adverse consequences of the coup: "And look, there is distress and darkness, the gloom of oppression (*mĕʿûp ṣûqâ*) and widespread calamity (*waʾăpēlâ mĕnuddāḥ*)."[17] The prophet here may be exaggerating matters, especially if many, or most, Israelites favored the change in leadership. Nevertheless, a certain amount of confusion and some oppressive measures would have been inevitable. The new king probably took steps to establish his control over the whole country, perhaps tracking down and executing whatever supporters Pekahiah had once had. If Isaiah exaggerates the distress, he does so for rhetorical purposes. His

---

[16] The verb *yabbîṭ* derives from *nbṭ* and generally means "look" or "gaze." In certain contexts, however, it is best translated as "regard, give thought to" (see Isa 22:8 and 11 in the NJPSV). *Nbṭ* can also have the more specific nuance, to regard something with desire or envy (see Ps 92:12 and 1 Sam 2:32). A similar sense may apply in Isa 8:22a.

[17] Compare the different translations of G. R. Driver ("Isaianic Problems," 46, 49) and H. L. Ginsberg ("An Unrecognized Allusion," 62–64). Driver repoints *mĕʿûp* (a hapax legomenon) as *mēʿûp* (the preposition *min* with *ʿûp*, "escape") and *mĕnuddāḥ* as *minnĕdōaḥ* (*min* with *ndḥ*, "put away"). He thus renders the line: "Everywhere is distress and darkness that cannot be escaped, constraint and gloom that cannot be avoided." Ginsberg repoints *mĕʿûp* as *mēʿîp* (*min* with *ʿyp*, "shine"), emends *mĕnuddāḥ* to *minnĕgōah* (*min* with *ngh*, "shine or brightness"), and translates: "Distress and darkness beyond glimmering, straitness and gloom beyond brightening." Both readings might still reflect Pekah's takeover in Israel. Nevertheless, it is better to hold more closely to the Masoretic text. *Mĕʿûp* is intelligible as a noun meaning "darkness" or "gloom" (from *ʿûp* II, "be dark"). Its pointing and the Masoretic accentuation of the line suggest that the term is a construct form bound closely to *ṣûqâ*. *Mĕnuddāḥ* is possibly a pual participle of *ndḥ* meaning "widespread" (see A. Guillaume, "Paronomasia in the Old Testament," *JSS* 9 [1964] 289–90).

ultimate aim is to highlight how favorably the fate of Ahaz and his kingdom compares with that of the former Israelite regime.

B. Verse 23aa

Commentators generally doubt the Isaianic authorship of 8:23aa.[18] They take the verse instead as the comment of a glossator or editor on v 22b,[19] or as an editor's bridge between the dark picture in vv 21–22 and the hopeful pronouncement in 8:23ab–9:6.[20] While the line does function as a transition, there is no reason to assign it to a late hand.[21] Viewed within the larger context of 8:21–9:6, v 23aa makes sense as a decisive turning point in Isaiah's presentation. In vv 21–22, we suggested above, the prophet relates the coup of Pekah and the resulting fallout in the northern kingdom. In 8:23–9:6, Isaiah shifts his focus to the kingdom of Ahaz. The comparison between their different fates is expressed by the adversative $kî$, which opens the line: "but" (RSV) or "nevertheless" (NIV) or "on the other hand."[22]

If this interpretation is correct, v 23aa summarizes the bright future of Ahaz's realm: "But there will not be gloom ($kî$ $lō'$ $mû'āp$) for her who has been oppressed ($la'ăšer$ $mûṣāq$ $lāh$)."[23] Neither here nor in

---

[18]The exception is H. L. Ginsberg ("An Unrecognized Allusion," 61–65), who apparently understands 8:16, 19–23 + 5:30 + 9:1–6 as a single speech of the eighth-century prophet. He translates v 23aa as a subordinate clause to what follows: "For if (emending $lō'$ to $lû$) there were glimmering for him for whom there is straitening...."

[19]See for example B. Duhm, *Das Buch Jesaja*, 88; G. Fohrer, *Das Buch Jesaja*, 1. 134–35; H. Wildberger, *Jesaja 1–12*, 356, 360; and O. Kaiser, *Isaiah 1–12*, 200–1. The interpretation assumes two things: (1) that the content of v 23aa is pessimistic; and (2) that v 22b needs the clarification that v 23aa supposedly tries to provide. Both assumptions are debatable.

[20]See R. E. Clements, *Isaiah 1–39*, 104; compare H. Barth, *Die Jesaja-Worte in der Josiazeit*, 155.

[21]The break between v 22b and v 23 is not as sharp as H. Wildberger (*Jesaja 1–12*, 356) and others believe, especially if the $kî$ at the beginning of v 23aa introduces a contrast. The line does take up the vocabulary of v 22b in slightly different forms (compare $mû'āp$ and $mě'ûp$, $mûṣāq$ and $ṣûqâ$), but the changes do not necessarily reflect the hand of a glossator.

[22]H. Barth (*Die Jesaja-Worte in der Josiazeit*, 154) argues for a similar meaning (*aber*), though he ascribes 8:23aa to a glossator.

[23]More literally, the line reads: "But there will not be gloom for the one that there was (has been) oppression to her." The difficult Hebrew syntax and the uncertain meanings of $mû'āp$ (a hapax legomenon) and $mûṣāq$ have given rise to a variety of other translations. (For a review of the different proposals, see C. F. Whitley, "Isaiah 8:16–23," 33–34.) The rendering suggested here holds to the Masoretic text and rests on the following decisions. (1) $Mû'āp$ is a noun from the root $'ûp$ II ("be dark"). (2) The construction, $lō'$ $mû'āp$, is unusual ($'ên$ would normally negate the noun), but not impossible. The tense of the clause is ambiguous, but a

the verses that follow does Isaiah clearly identify the referent of "her," but the allusion may be to Jerusalem, the capital of the Davidides. For years they had been subordinate to the northern kings, fighting Israelite wars and perhaps paying Israelite tribute. The Syrians, Israelites, and most Judeans probably expected that the same relationship would continue between Pekah and Ahaz. It did not. Ahaz asserted his independence by refusing to follow Pekah into the Syrian-led coalition. To be sure, the Davidic king vacillated on the issue up to the Syrian-Israelite invasion (see 7:13). Isaiah 8:21–9:6 might indicate, however, that Ahaz initially declared his break with Israel only weeks or even days after Pekah's coup. The prophet applauded the move and proclaimed a new era of prosperity.

C. 8:23ab–9:6

Isaiah 8:23ab–9:6 celebrate the new independence of Ahaz and promise the continued support of Yahweh for the Davidic house.[24]

---

future meaning is possible, if not probable (see the RSV). (3) *Mûṣāq* is a noun, "oppression" (from *ṣûq*, "constrain, press upon, bring into straits"), related to "her" by the preposition *l*, "to" or "for." (4) The tense of *mûṣāq lāh* is also ambiguous, but a past meaning makes sense (see again the RSV). J. Skinner (*Isaiah*, 79) and G. B. Gray (*The Book of Isaiah*, 1. 163) object that the shift in tense is arbitrary. Other translations, however, are at least as arbitrary and often involve more conjecture. This is true even of Duhm's reading, which Gray and Skinner both favor, though with some reservation.

[24] Scholars have suggested a variety of other historical settings for (8:23ab) 9:1–6. For reviews of the different proposals, see G. B. Gray, *The Book of Isaiah*, 1. 166–68; and M. E. W. Thompson, "Isaiah's Ideal King," 79–84. Scholars who assign the verses to Isaiah think of the following periods or occasions: the early stage of the prophet's ministry, before the Syro-Ephraimitic crisis (M. E. W. Thompson, "Isaiah's Ideal King," 85–85); the decade between 732 and 722 (A. Alt, "Isaiah 8,23–9,6," especially 46–48); the accession of Hezekiah in 725 (R. E. Clements, *Isaiah 1–39*, 103–5); the birth of Hezekiah in 734–732 (J. Lindblom, *The Immanuel Section*, 41); Hezekiah's preparations for revolt in 705–701 (H. W. Wolff, *Frieden ohne Ende*, 63); and the end of the abortive siege of Jerusalem by Sennacherib in 701 (J. Mauchline, *Isaiah 1–39*, 117).

Among the scholars listed above, Lindblom alone assigns 9:1–6 to the period of the Syro-Ephraimitic crisis. While the details of his interpretation are doubtful, the dating has the advantage of taking seriously the present location of the passage alongside other materials relating to the war (Isaiah 7 and 8). Thompson admits this advantage, but still rejects the proposal. He reasons that Isaiah would not have used the "extravagant language of victory" in 9:1–4 to describe Jerusalem's survival of the Syrian-Israelite attack. The prophet, after all, had never considered the coalition a serious threat (7:4). The objection, however, loses much of its force, if 9:1–6 refer to Ahaz's break with Israel. If the Davidic house had long been subservient to the kings of Samaria, Isaiah might well have used the "extravagant language of victory" to celebrate its move toward independence in 734.

They are thus an elaboration of the preceding declaration. The verses divide into three parts. In 8:23ab–9:2, the prophet describes the good fortune of the people and their rejoicing. The reasons for celebration follow in vv 3–5, climaxing in a review of the king's exalted status. Verse 6 predicts the eternal rule of the Davidic house, concluding with a pledge of divine support.

Isaiah prefaces the description of the people's good fortune with a reflection on earlier events (v 23abb). Understanding the historical allusions is difficult, partly because the Hebrew syntax and the meaning of the verbs are uncertain.[25] Our interpretation assumes the following translation.

> Like the time (kāʿēt) the former one (hāriʾšôn) made contemptible (hēqal) the land of Zebulon and the land of Naphtali, and the latter one (wĕhāʾaḥărôn) made harsh (hikbîd) the Way of the Sea, Beyond the Jordan, Galilee of the Nations . . . .

This reading rests on three decisions. First, the perfect verb forms, hēqal and hikbîd, both refer to past events and describe the sad fate of the land.[26] Second, hāriʾšôn and hāʾaḥărôn are the subjects of hēqal and hikbîd, and refer to specific persons.[27] Third, 8:23abb is an extended

---

[25] Emerton's study ("Problems in Isaiah VIII 23," 151–75) illustrates well how closely the linguistic and historical problems of the passage are related.

[26] Compare the translation of the RSV: ". . . he brought into contempt . . . he will make glorious . . . ." The NIV, TEV, and JB assume the same shift in tense and meaning. (See also L. G. Rignell, "Maher-salal Has-baz," 51; H. Wildberger, *Jesaja 1–12*, 363; and K. Seybold, *Das davidische Königtum*, 81.) G. R. Driver ("Isaianic Problems," 46–47, 49) renders both verbs in the past, but assigns them opposite meanings: ". . . the first (invader) has dealt lightly . . . the second (invader) has dealt heavily . . . ." Compare H. Barth's translation (*Die Jesaja-Worte in der Josiazeit*, 141–45): ". . . he made contemptible . . . he made honorable . . . ." (See similarly M. E. W. Thompson, *Situation and Theology*, 45; and J. M. Asurmendi, *La Guerra Siro-Efraimita*, 75.) C. F. Whitley ("Isaiah 8:16–23," 36–37) emends hēqal to qal (restoring the initial h to the end of hāriʾšôn) and construes hikbîd in a negative sense ("conquered, made heavy, burdened"). He thus translates the verbs: ". . . he hastened to . . . he subdued . . . ."

[27] So H. L. Ginsberg ("An Unrecognized Allusion," 61–65) and G. R. Driver ("Isaianic Problems," 47) understand the Hebrew. (J. A. Emerton ["Problems in Isaiah VIII 23," 58–60] also takes the two terms as personal subjects, but interprets their combination as an expression of totality: "Everyone, from first to last, treated with contempt and harshness . . . .") Most other scholars construe hāriʾšôn and hāʾaḥărôn as adjectives qualifying ʿēt, and thus see the verse as a description of "the former time" and "the latter time" when "he" (presumably Yahweh) took and/or takes actions for and against the land. (See for example B. Duhm, *Das Buch Jesaja*, 141–45; K. Marti, *Das Buch Jesaja*, 91; and more recently, H. Barth, *Die Jesaja-Worte in der Josiazeit*, 141–45.) Driver and Emerton rightly object, however, that ʿēt is a feminine noun, while hāriʾšôn and hāʾaḥărôn are masculine in form. C. F. Whitley resolves the discrepancy by adding the feminine ending â to the two

prepositional phrase, "like the time (*kāʿēt*) . . . ." It sets forth a previous history, against which the new situation of the "people" (9:1–2) is understood.

Scholars generally agree that part or all of 8:23 reflects on Israel's territorial losses during and after the Syro-Ephraimitic crisis. Variations of this interpretation include the following.

(1) Isaiah 8:23 describes two invasions of Israel, either by Tiglathpileser and Shalmaneser V,[28] or by Tiglathpileser alone on two separate occasions.[29]

(2) The two lines of the saying use different names to designate the same three regions: the coastal plain, the Galilean hill country, and Gilead. The first line describes how, in 734–732, Tiglathpileser invaded these areas and organized them into the provinces of *Du'ru*, *Magido*, and *Gal'azu*. The second line anticipates their liberation in the near future.[30]

(3) The two lines of the saying are parallel reflections on Tiglathpileser's annexation of Israelite territory in 734–32.[31]

---

adjectives. The proposal, however, still leaves the verbs without a clear subject. (The implicit "he" of the verse, Whitley argues, refers to Tiglathpileser.) A. Alt ("Jesaja 8,23–9,6," 32–35) supplies a subject by inserting *yhwh* after *hēqal*, but the addition has no textual support. Like Whitley, H. Wildberger (*Jesaja 1–12*, 363–64) changes *harīʾšôn* and *haʾaḥărôn* to feminine forms and connects them with *ʿēt*. The resulting noun clauses, he suggests, are the explicit subjects of *hēqal* and *hikbîd*. The verse thus reads: "As the earlier time brought humiliation . . . so the future brings honor . . . ." It is questionable, however, whether this translation in fact corresponds to ancient Hebrew idiom. In any case, the proposal demands minor, but still unnecessary, emendations of the text. Good sense can be made of the verse as it now stands.

[28]See G. R. Driver, "Isaianic Problems," 48.

[29]So C. F. Whitley, ("Isaiah 8:16–23," 41–42) understands the verse. The first line, he argues, vividly describes how Tiglathpileser "hastened" (emending *hēqal* to *qal*) to the lands of Zebulon and Naphtali in 734. The second line supposedly recounts his second expedition in 733/732, when he marched through the Jordan Valley. Even if Whitley's translation were correct, the interpretation rests on a doubtful reconstruction of the king's campaigns (see Chapter Two above).

[30]A. Alt ("Jesaja 8,23–9,6," 32–38, 45–49) advocates this interpretation. In the first line of 8:23, he inserts "the Plain of Sharon" and "the hill country of Gilead" alongside the lands of Zebulon and Naphtali. The list of regions is thereby made to agree more closely with the series of areas in the second line. Alt also assumes that the two verbs, *hēqal* and *hikbîd*, are different in tense and opposite in meaning. They mean respectively "brought into contempt" and "will glorify."

[31]See J. A. Emerton, "Problems in Isaiah VIII 23," 156. Emerton recognizes that the lands of Zebulon and Naphtali are not coterminous with "the Way of the Sea, Beyond the Jordan, Galilee of Nations." He nevertheless rejects the two-campaign interpretation, as well as emendations of the verse that aim at bringing the two lines into exact agreement. He reasons instead that "Isa. viii. 23 names two of the principal tribes in the region, but not every tribe concerned, and then lists more fully the three provinces into which the northern part of Israel was or-

(4) The verse laments the fact that Hoshea, the "latter one," did not recover the Israelite regions which Pekah, the "former one," had lost to Tiglathpileser in 734–32.[32]

(5) Isaiah 8:23 describes the beginning and end of Assyria's domination of Israel. The first line refers to the first of Tiglathpileser's two campaigns against the northern kingdom during the Syro-Ephraimitic crisis. The second alludes to the decline of Assyria during the late seventh century and the concomitant liberation of all the Israelite territories that Tiglathpileser had siezed a century earlier.[33]

Despite their obvious differences, these proposals all rest on the same belief, namely, that the Assyrians reduced Israel to the "rump state" of Ephraim in 734–32. This assumption, we have argued, is far from certain (see Chapters Two and Three above). Second Kings 15:29 reports Tiglathpileser's seizure of Gilead and Galilee during the reign of Pekah, but fails to state from whom he captured them. The Assyrian reports on the campaigns of Tiglathpileser in Galilee and Transjordan are also ambiguous, but they may view the regions as part of Rezin's kingdom. Israel would have lost the territory to Syria and/or its allies long before the Syro-Ephraimitic crisis. If this reconstruction is correct, Isa 8:23 possibly reflects this earlier period, during which "Greater Israel" was gradually reduced to Samaria and the surround-

---

ganized by the Assyrians . . . . The historical background of Isa. viii. 23 is thus Tiglathpileser's annexation of the northern part of Israel c. 732 and his organization of it into three provinces. This interpretation is possible without altering the Hebrew text."

[32]See H. L. Ginsberg, "An Unrecognized Allusion," 61–65. He takes the whole of 8:23 as a single sentence and translates: "For if there were glimmering for him for whom there is straitening, (only) the former (king) would have brought shame upon the land of the Zebulunite and the land of the Naphtalite, but the latter would have brought honour to the Way of the Sea, the Other Side of the Jordan, Galilee of the Nations." The verse, Ginsberg explains, tells how Hoshea would be different from Pekah if the opening premise were true. However, Hoshea's failure to "bring honour" to Israel's lost regions shows that the premise is in fact false: there is not "glimmering for him for whom there is straitening." Isaiah supposedly concluded that the circumstances of the northern kingdom could become still worse, that his earlier prophecy against the nation (8:4) would eventually come to pass in full.

[33]See H. Barth, *Die Jesaja-Worte in der Josiazeit*, 141–66. The interpretation rests heavily on the assumption that the second line of the saying tells how Yahweh "brought honor" to the coastal plain, Gilead, and Galilee. The allusion, Barth contends, must be to the liberation of these areas during the reign of Josiah. If the first line describes the humiliation of Zebulon and Naphtali only, it must refer to Tiglathpileser's first expedition in 733. This was the occasion, Barth explains, when these specific regions came under Assyrian control.

ing Ephraimite hill country. The responsibility for the decline, Isaiah claims, belongs to two Israelite kings.[34]

The "former one" might refer to Jeroboam II. During the later years of his reign, the Syrians and others began to encroach on the peripheral territories of his kingdom. Amos 1:3–5, 13–15, and 6:13 attest to the king's troubles in Gilead: the Syrians, Ammonites, and Israelites all struggled to control the region. Amos 1:6–8 and 9–10 may allude to Philistine and Phoenician actions against Israelite and Judean holdings along the coast. Land and prisoners were taken, possibly in close cooperation with Syria (reading *ărām* for *ědôm* in vv 6 and 9). Hosea 1:5 may reflect Jeroboam's difficulties in Galilee. The saying appears to anticipate Israel's loss of the Jezreel Valley and with it, by implication, all of the hill country to the north. Behind the prophet's words is perhaps a situation in which Syria was challenging Jeroboam's control of the region. While Hos 1:5 still looks forward to Israel's complete loss of the area, Isa 8:23ab reflects on it as a past event. Jeroboam had "made contemptible the land of Zebulun and the land of Naphtali."

The "latter one" would be Menahem. After months of civil war in the northern kingdom, he ascended the throne in Samaria (746/745). He was able to secure his rule, however, only after great struggle and with Assyrian assistance (see 2 Kgs 15:19–20). The period, then, was one of extreme internal weakness for Israel. Consequently, it was also an opportune time for Syria and its allies to capitalize on earlier made inroads into Israelite territory. Isaiah 9:11 may relate in part to this period: "Syrians on the east and Philistines on the west devoured Israel with open mouth." The last part of 8:23 can be seen as an allusion to the same situation. By the end of Menahem's reign, Israel had completely lost the "Way of the Sea, Beyond the Jordan, Galilee of the Nations."

Against the background of Israel's earlier territorial losses, Isa 9:1 describes the recent break between the southern and northern kingdoms.[35]

---

[34]Compare H. L. Ginsberg, "An Unrecognized Allusion," 61–65. He also sees a reference to two Israelite kings and identifies them as Pekah and Hoshea. "Make contemptible" (*hēqal*) and "make harsh" (*hikbîd*) admittedly seem a somewhat strange way of describing how two Israelite kings lost territory. It is important to note, however, that the selection of verbs is largely determined by Isaiah's interest in word-play. *Hēqal* and *hikbîd* mean literally "make light" and "make heavy." The saying thus has an ironic twist: "Light" and "heavy" treatment amount to the same thing—the loss of Israelite territory. The word-play may explain the peculiar phrasing of the text.

[35]Commentators frequently translate 9:1, along with the verses that follow, in the present tense and interpret the text as, in part, a promise about future deliverance. (See for example H. Wildberger, *Jesaja 1–12*, 366, 370; K. Seybold, *Das davidische Königtum*, 90; W. H. Schmidt, "Die Ohnmacht des Messias. Zur Über-

... [so now] the people who were walking in darkness have seen a great light, upon those who were living in a land of deep darkness a light has shined.

How broadly "people" should be understood is not altogether certain, but the reference probably includes only the Davidic house and its supporters.[36] For seventy or more years, they had been subservient to the kings of Samaria. Ahaz's move toward independence in the fall of 734 brought this relationship to an end. At the same time, it marked the last phase of a twenty-year history in which Israel gradually lost all holdings and/or influence beyond the hill country of Ephraim.

Isaiah celebrates this turn of events for the Davidic realm in a style reminiscent of thanksgiving psalms.[37] This is particularly clear

---

lieferungsgeschichte der messianischen Weissagungen im Alten Testament," *KD* 15 [1969] 19–21; and H. W. Wolff, *Frieden ohne Ende*, 64, 69–72.) However, most of the verbs throughout the passage are either perfects or imperfect consecutives, which normally refer to past events. In v 2bb, Isaiah uses the imperfect, but there it is part of a simile: The people "have rejoiced . . . just as they rejoice (*ka'ăšer yāgîlû*) when dividing up spoil." Also in vv 4 and 6, Isaiah uses the imperfect and perfect consecutive. Here and only here does his focus genuinely shift to the future. For opposing analyses of the issue, compare H. Barth, *Die Jesaja-Worte in der Josiazeit*, 145–47; and W. Werner, *Eschatologische Texte*, 23–25. Note also the recent study of 8:23b by J. Høgenhaven ("On the Structure and Meaning of Isaiah VIII 23B," *VT* 37 [1987] 218–21). He explains that "the 'real' time-aspect of viii 23b–ix 6 is that of the future. . . . The hymn, however, celebrates the events envisaged as if they had already taken place, thus creating a kind of literary fiction within which the future is anticipated." He adds further in a note, "The 'real' time-aspect, however, is revealed through the imperfect *tēšh* ix 6." Høgenhaven's argument illustrates well the kind of contorted reasoning one must resort to, if one insists on the future orientation of the entire passage.

[36]Compare the interpretation of A. Alt ("Jesaja 8,23–9,6"). He argues that the whole of 8:23–9:6 was intended as an address to the northern kingdom. The oracle anticipates Yahweh's deliverance of Israelite territories from Assyrian control, the accession of a new Davidic king in Jerusalem, and the re-unification of Israel and Judah under Davidic rule. The "people" in v 1 thus refers to the Israelites. M. E. W. Thompson ("Isaiah's Ideal King," 80–81) rightly objects, however, that a northern audience would not likely have received this message favorably, as long as an Israelite king still ruled in Samaria. Isaiah, moreover, must have known this. If Judah and Jerusalem were the primary locus and concern of the prophet's preaching, 8:23–9:6 likely address and speak about a southern audience. Isaiah 8:6 indicates that, on the eve of the Syro-Ephraimitic crisis, the prophet denounced the majority of Judeans ("this people") and proclaimed their imminent destruction. If 9:1, then, celebrates the deliverance of the "people" in 734, the statement probably focuses narrowly on the royal court and the capital city.

[37]See F. Crüsemann, *Studien zur Formgeschichte von Hymnus und Danklied in Israel* (WMANT 32; Neukirchen-Vluyn: Neukirchener Verlag, 1969). Drawing on the results of Cruesemann's study, H. Barth (*Die Jesaja-Worte in der Josiazeit*, 148–

in v 2. Here the prophet addresses the deity directly, crediting Yahweh for the people's new found hope.

> You have made rejoicing great [reading *haggîlâ* for *haggôy lō’*), you have increased gladness. They have rejoiced before you as with the joy of harvest time, just as they rejoice when dividing up spoil.

The words reflect the strong backing Ahaz enjoyed among his supporters, particularly in Jerusalem. Cultic celebrations were possibly held within the capital city, thanking Yahweh for the liberation of the Davidic kingdom from Israelite domination.[38]

Verses 3–5 list specific reasons for rejoicing, each beginning with the conjunction *kî*. The first of these alludes most clearly to the people's new independence.

> For (*kî*) his burdensome yoke (*ʿōl subbŏlô*) and the staff against his shoulder (*maṭṭēh šikmô*), the rod of the one who was oppressing him (*šēbeṭ hannōgēś bô*), you [Yahweh] have broken just as [on] the day of Midian.

The language here has obvious political overtones, describing the oppression of foreign rule.[39] The expressions make sense as references to the long domination of the Davidic kingdom by Israel. Isaiah describes the end of this domination as Yahweh's doing, and compares it to a traditional example of the people's liberation—the defeat of the Midianites in pre-monarchical times.[40]

---

51) lists the formal similarities between the individual thanksgiving psalm and Isa (8:23b) 9:1–6. These include the alternation between direct address to Yahweh and statements about Yahweh, the use of the "we"-style when speaking directly to the audience, the description of divine deliverance from past distress, and the use of the deictic *kî* to introduce the reasons for thanksgiving. Whether the Isaiah text is in fact a thanksgiving psalm, as Barth claims, is debatable. See the critical comments of W. Werner (*Eschatologische Texte*, 22–23) on this point, as well as his review of other genre labels suggested for the passage.

[38] Whether the terms of the verse, especially *gîlâ* ("rejoicing") and *śāmēḥû lēpānēkā* ("rejoiced before you"), are actually technical expressions from the cult is uncertain. For reviews and different assessments of the lexical evidence, compare H. Wildberger, *Jesaja 1–12*, 374; and W. Werner, *Eschatologische Texte*, 31–32. In any case, the text likely has in mind the ritual rejoicing of Isaiah's own audience, not the eschatological rejoicing imagined by a post-exilic writer, as Werner argues.

[39] Compare Deut 28:48 (*ʿōl barzel*); Isa 10:27 (*subbŏlô mēʿal šikmekā wĕʿullô mēʿal ṣawwāʾrekā*); 14:4–5 (*nōgēś, maṭṭēh rĕšāʿîm, šēbeṭ mōšĕlîm*); 14:25 (*ʿullô wĕsubbŏlô mēʿal šikmô*); Jer 28:2 (*ʿōl melek bābel*); 30:8 (*ʿullô mēʿal ṣawwāʾrekā*); and Zech 9:8 (*wĕlōʾ-yaʿăbōr ʿălêhem ʿôd nōgēś*). All of these texts refer to the domination of Yahweh's people by foreign powers.

[40] Some scholars interpret the prophet's meaning in light of the specific details of the full-blown tradition now found in Judges 6–8. According to A. Alt ("Jesaja

A second reason for celebration follows in v 4.

> For (*kî*) every boot of the trampling soldier in battle tumult and [every] mantle rolled in blood will be burned [*wĕhāyĕtâ liśrēpâ*] as fuel for a fire.

The perfect consecutive, *wĕhāyĕtâ*, likely signals Isaiah's shift to the future tense.[41] Having described in v 3 the breaking of Israel's political strength, Isaiah now predicts an end to the nation's military power.[42] As in 8:1–4, the prophet is probably anticipating Assyria's

---

8,23–9,6," 38–39), for example, Isaiah expected an act of divine deliverance, which, like the rout of the Midianites in Judges 7:9–25, would occur suddenly in a single night. H. Wildberger (*Jesaja 1–12*, 376) suggests, though with some reservation, that the ideas of holy war and miraculous divine intervention might carry over from the Judges text into Isa 9:3. W. Harrelson ("Nonroyal Motifs in the Royal Eschatology," in *Israel's Prophetic Heritage*, 152–53) believes that Isaiah's reference to the "day of Midian" (along with the names of the child listed in 9:5) calls to mind the charismatic leaders of pre-monarchical Israel, particularly Gideon, and intends to cast the future ruler of the people (v 5) in the same mold. The allusion in 9:3 is far too brief to justify these interpretations. Possibly the prophet knew the tradition of the Midianite defeat only in a shorter and less dramatic form, as it was rehearsed in the cult (see Ps 83:10–12). In any case, it is hazardous to read the specific details and notions of the Judges text into the prophetic speech.

[41] Compare O. Kaiser, *Isaiah 1–12*, 204, n. 11. He apparently treats v 4a as a *casus pendens*, and so thinks it possible to translate *wĕhāyĕtâ* in the past tense. See *GKC*, 337 and 458.

[42] Scholars have long argued that 9:4 looks forward to the destruction of Assyrian forces. See for example F. Delitzsch, *The Prophecies of Isaiah*, 1. 209–10, B. Duhm, *Das Buch Jesaja*, 89; A. Alt, "Jesaja 8,23–9,6," 37–40, 46–49; H. W. Wolff, *Frieden ohne Ende*, 57–63; K. Seybold, *Das davidische Königtum*, 79–80, 88–89; and R. A. Carlson, "The Anti-Assyrian Character of the Oracle in Is. IX 1–6," *VT* 24 (1974) 130–35; compare M. E. W. Thompson, *Situation and Theology*, 46. In defense of this interpretation, Wolff and Carlson both note the hapax legomenon, *sĕʾôn* ("boot"). The noun, they claim, is a loan-word from the technical military terminology of the Assyrians (*šenu* in Akkadian), and thus a clear pointer to the Assyrian army as the object of the prophet's threat.

The argument is not as strong as it might first appear. The Akkadian *šenu* is not confined to the Neo-Assyrian period, but is found also in Old Assyrian, Middle Babylonian, and Neo-Babylonian. Furthermore, the noun is not clearly a technical military term. It frequently means more generally "shoe" or "sandal." Finally, the word appears in other cognate languages, including Old Aramaic (*šʾn*), New Aramaic (*sena*), and possibly Ugaritic (*sʾn*). (See W. von Soden, *Akkadisches Handwörterbuch* [3 vols.; Wiesbaden: Otto Harrassowitz, 1965–81].) The widespread testimony to the word in several Semitic languages from many periods makes it hard to know precisely how it came to Isaiah. (Compare J. Vollmer, "Zur Sprache von Jesaja 9,1–6," *ZAW* 80 [1968] 345–46.) Despite the lack of evidence, *sĕʾôn* may in fact have belonged to the Hebrew language already in the eighth century. The assumption is probable, for otherwise the prophet's Jerusalemite audience would not likely have understood the term. (Commenting on *sĕʾôn*, Wolff states, "We thereby see clearly once again that the prophet did not

move against the Syrian-Israelite alliance. The rhetorical aim of the prediction is to assure the Davidides and their supporters that their new independence from the northern kingdom is not a short-term affair, but will continue into the distant future.

Verse 5 presents a final reason for rejoicing—the "birth" of a royal "child." Here the prophet addresses his Jerusalemite audience directly.

> For (kî) a child (yeled) has been born for us (yullad-lānû), a son (bēn) has been appointed for us (nittan-lānû). And authority has fallen (wattĕhî) upon his shoulder and he has been named (wayyiqrāʾ šĕmô) Wonderful Counselor, Mighty God, Everlasting Father, Prince of Peace.

This translation highlights Isaiah's conspicuous return to the past tense. The Hebrew verbs are either perfect forms or imperfect consecutives. The verse, then, does not predict a future "child," but reflects on a past event and its significance for the present.[43]

The identity of the royal "child" is widely debated. Many scholars defend a future messianic interpretation,[44] but this understanding must be ruled out, if the verbs genuinely refer to a past event. Two major alternatives remain. (1) The child is a recently born heir to the Davidic throne, perhaps Immanuel. According to this view, the language of v 5aa is literal. The prophet heralds the birth of the prince as the dawning of a new age of salvation for Yahweh's people and of

---

shy away from using in his preaching words that hitherto were quite unknown in Israel and that were imported into the land only by the Assyrian occupational forces." The Assyrian army, however, did not invade and occupy Judah/Jerusalem in 734–732, nor during the 720s. Unless one is willing to date (8:23) 9:1–6 to the last phase of Isaiah's career, it is hard to imagine that his southern audience would have been familiar with Assyrian military jargon.) One is inclined to take sĕʾôn as an Assyrian loan-word only if one is already convinced that 9:1–6 concerns the liberation of the "people" from Assyrian rule.

[43] J. Lindblom (*The Immanuel Section*, 33–34) especially emphasizes this point; see also H. Barth, *Die Jesaja-Worte in der Josiazeit*, 145–48. According to H. Wildberger (*Jesaja 1–12*, 366, 370), v 5a is the only part of 9:1–6 which genuinely refers to a past event. The recent birth of the child, he claims, assures the future fulfillment of the promises in vv 1–4. See the criticism of this view in n. 35 above.

[44] See for example B. Duhm, *Das Buch Jesaja*, 89; J. Skinner, *Isaiah*, 80–84; O. Procksch, *Jesaia I*, 144–50; J. Coppens, "Le roi idéal d'Is., IX, 5–6 et XI, 1–5, est-il une figure messianique?" in *A la rencontre de Dieu. Mémorial A. Gelin* (Lyon: 1961) 85–108; H. W. Wolff, *Frieden ohne Ende*, 66–70; and M. Rehm, *Der königliche Messias*, 181–84. These scholars attribute the messianic message of the passage to the eighth-century prophet. Others understand the text as an expression of exilic or post-exilic messianism. See for example K. Marti, *Das Buch Jesaja*, 94–96; G. Fohrer, *Das Buch Jesaja*, 1. 137–43; J. Vollmer, "Zur Sprache von Jesaja 9,1–6," 343–50; W. Werner, *Eschatologische Texte*, 25–40, 45, 81–88; and R. Kilian, *Jesaja 1–39*, 9–10.

glory for the Davidic house.[45] (2) "Child" and "son" are metaphorical designations for a contemporary Davidic king who, having gone through the enthronement ritual, now has the status of Yahweh's adopted "son" (compare Pss 2:7, 89:27, and 2 Sam 7:14).[46] This second interpretation is the more likely.[47] Verse 5 is not a royal birth announcement, but a prophetic statement about the exalted standing of the actual Davidic ruler by virtue of his formal enthronement.[48]

---

[45]See for example J. Lindblom, *The Immanuel Section*, 37; H.-J. Kraus, "Jesaja 9,5–6 (6–7)," in *Herr, tue meine Lippen auf* (5 vols.; 2d ed.; ed. G. Eichholz; Wuppertal: E. Mueller, 1961) 5. 43–53; H. Wildberger, *Jesaja 1–12*, 376–77; compare S. Mowinckel, *He That Cometh*, 108–10; and H. Barth, *Die Jesaja-Worte in der Josiazeit*, 167–68.

[46]Compare A. Alt, "Jesaja 8,23–9,6," 39–46; and G. von Rad, "Das judäische Königsritual," 211–16; idem., *Old Testament Theology*, 2. 169–72. According to these scholars, 9:5–6 alludes to the enthronement of a future Davidic ruler. Von Rad particularly stresses the messianic character of the passage. In contrast, N. K. Gottwald (*All the Kingdoms of the Earth*, 166–67), R. E. Clements (*Isaiah 1–39*, 105–9), and J. M. Asurmendi (*La Guerra Siro-Efraimita*, 75–79) argue that 9:5–6 refer to the enthronement of Hezekiah, or at least to his initial association with the throne as co-regent with Ahaz.

[47]Certain considerations weigh against the first interpretation, at least as it is defended by J. Lindblom (*The Immanuel Section*, 34–38) and H. Wildberger (*Jesaja 1–12*, 376–77). Both scholars understand the advent of the child in 9:5 as the fulfillment of the promise of Immanuel's birth in 7:14. The text, however, provides little basis for this equation. More importantly, 9:5abb describes the child as someone already invested with the authority of government and given throne names. These were normally conferred upon kings during the enthronement ceremony. The language of 9:5 thus points most naturally to a ruler already installed on the throne. Lindblom is aware of the problem and tries to solve it by arguing that Isaiah thought of the royal infant as "having already at his birth been entrusted by Yahweh with the rule in his kingdom . . . in this case birth and enthronization coincide." The explanation, however, is only an expedient for rescuing what is in fact a problematic interpretation. Wildberger tries to support it with the help of Near Eastern analogies, but the one Egyptian parallel which he cites ("The Myth of the Birth of the Pharaoh") cannot bear the weight of his case. More plausible is the proposal of H. Barth (*Die Jesaja-Worte in der Josiazeit*, 167–68). He suggests that the text reflects first on the birth of the king (v 5aa) and then on his later enthronement (v 5abb). While this interpretation is certainly possible, it remains questionable whether the text really envisions two distinct events, separated, as it were, by a gap of several years.

[48]H. Barth (*Die Jesaja-Worte in der Josiazeit*, 167–68) musters four arguments against this interpretation, at least as it concerns v 5aa. (1) According to Ps 2:7, the newly enthroned king is designated specifically as Yahweh's son. In contrast, the Isaiah text refers to the king simply as "child" and "son." (2) Isaiah 9:5 speaks of the child/son as one given "to us," that is, to the speaker and his audience. Again, in the enthronement ceremony, the king does not become the son of the people generally, but rather the son of Yahweh specifically. (3) In Ps 2:7, an adoption formula clearly announces the new status of the enthroned king: "You [the king] are my [Yahweh's] son (*bēn*), today I have begotten you" (*yĕlidtîkā*). If Isa 9:5aa alludes to the same liturgical event, it is difficult to explain the ambigu-

The names ascribed to the king are the traditional throne names which he received during the ritual.[49]

Scholars who share this understanding of v 5 usually identify the "child" and "son" as Hezekiah.[50] Interpreted against the background of the Syro-Ephraimitic crisis, however, the text appears to refer to Ahaz. Contrary to the assumption of most scholars, Isaiah did not reject this king, but supported him, applauding particularly his break with the northern kingdom in the fall of 734. In 9:5, the prophet cites Ahaz's exalted royal status as reason for celebration. Whether the verse reflects back on the recent renewal of his kingship or simply reviews the king's standing as proclaimed at the beginning of his reign is difficult to say. In either case, the implication of the prophet's statement would have been clear to his Jerusalemite audience, given current political developments. Ahaz's break with Pekah realized the ideal claims of the royal theology. He no longer ruled in the shadow of an Israelite king, but rather as a fully independent king with divine legitimation. "Authority has fallen upon his shoulder" and will remain. (Note the play on the word, "shoulder" [šĕkem], in vv 3 and 5.)

The speech ends in v 6 with a promise of continued well-being for the Davidic house.[51] While the general meaning of the prophet seems

---

ous passive construction of the line. (4) The Isaiah text refers to the "giving" (ntn) of a "child" (yeled). These terms do not belong to the language and thought of the enthronement ceremony.

The detailed discrepancies between the phrasing of 9:5 and the language of the enthronement ritual cannot be denied. They are not as significant, however, as Barth and others believe (see H. W. Wolff, *Frieden ohne Ende*, 66–68; and H. Wildberger, *Jesaja 1–12*, 377). The Isaiah text is a prophetic speech composed for an audience outside the cult. There is no reason to expect it to conform exactly to the phrasing of Ps 2:7. The prophet reflects on the previous enthronement of the king "from a distance," freely recasting in his own words the technical formulaic language of the ritual. (Although T. Lescow ["Geburtsmotif," 184] doubts the Isaianic authorship of 9:1–6, his remarks on vv 5–6 parallel our own here: "We can reckon [in vv 5–6] with the appropriation of the content of the royal protocol, but we may not suppose that we encounter that content in a pure form. Isaiah 9:5–6 may be in this respect far less a quotation than Ps 2:7–9." He adds further [186]: "And vv 5b–6 do not *quote* a royal protocol, but *reflect* it . . . .")

[49]For discussions of the names, especially their traditio-historical background, see H. Wildberger, "Die Thronnamen des Messias, Jes. 9,5b," *TZ* 16 (1960) 314–32; idem., *Jesaja 1–12*, 381–84; W. Harrelson, "Nonroyal Motifs in the Royal Eschatology," 152–53; K. Seybold, *Das davidische Königtum*, 82–87; and R. A. Carlson, "Is. IX 1–6," 131–35.

[50]See the works of Gottwald, Clements, and Asurmendi cited in n. 46 above.

[51]The verb, taʿăśeh ("will do," v 6bb), signals a change in focus to the future. H. Barth (*Die Jesaja-Worte in der Josiazeit*, 146) tries to avoid this shift by construing the final line as a nominal sentence: "It is the zeal of Yahweh Sebaoth that does (taʿăśeh) such a thing." The imperfect form, Barth contends, expresses the "progressive duration" of present circumstances. See the criticisms of this translation by W. Werner, *Eschatologische Texte*, 24–25.

clear enough, translating the verse is nonetheless difficult. The Hebrew might be rendered as follows:

> Of the greatness of authority (*lĕmarbēh hammiśrā*) and of security (*ûlĕšālôm*) there will be no end for the throne (*kissē'*) of David and for its sovereignty (*mamlaktô*), establishing (*lĕhākîn*) it and sustaining (*ûlĕsaʿădāh*) it with justice and righteousness, from this time forth and forevermore. The zeal of Yahweh will do this![52]

The subject of the action is not clearly indicated, but in view of the final sentence, Yahweh is likely intended.[53] He establishes and upholds the Davidic throne.

The conclusion aims at assuring Isaiah's audience that their recent independence from Israel will last into the future, "from this time forth and forevermore." Significantly, the promise picks up the traditional language and thought of the royal theology. Yahweh "establishes" (*kûn*) the "throne" (*kissē'*) of each Davidic king, "sustains" (*sʿd*) his "reign" or "sovereignty" (*mamlākâ*), and endows the king with divine "justice" (*mišpāṭ*) and "righteousness" (*ṣĕdāqâ*; compare 2 Sam 7:12–16, Pss 18:36, 20:3, 72:1–2, and 89:28–37). Isaiah holds up these traditional beliefs to the Davidic court and the residents of Jerusalem, and urges them to take the claims seriously. "From this time forth and forevermore," the Davidic regime will stand firmly with divine support. "The zeal of Yahweh will do this!"

D. Summary

This chapter interpreted 8:21–9:6 as a single speech of Isaiah to a Jerusalemite audience in the fall of 734. The verses respond to the

---

[52]This translation rests on three decisions. (1) Contrary to the efforts of many scholars, an additional throne name is not to be sought at the beginning of the verse. One cannot assume an exact correspondence between the Judean royal protocol and the Egyptian practice, where five throne names were the norm. Compare H. Wildberger, *Jesaja 1–12*, 365, 384; W. Zimmerli, "Vier oder fünf Thronnamen des messianischen Herrschers in Jes. IX 5b.6," *VT* 22 (1972) 249–52; K. D. Schunck, "Der fünfte Thronname des Messias (Jes. IX 5–6)," *VT* 23 (1973) 108–10; and R. A. Carlson, "Is. IX 1–6," 131–35. (2) The final *m* in *lemarbēh* is orthographically incorrect. One should change the letter to its medial form, following the marginal *Qere*, and translate, "of greatness." The term stands parallel to *ûlĕšālôm* ("and of security"), both being governed by *'ēn-qēṣ* ("there will be no end"). Compare W. Zimmerli, "Vier oder fünf Thronnamen," 249–52; and H. Barth, *Die Jesaja-Worte in der Josiazeit*, 169. (3) The *hifil* infinitives, *lĕhākîn* and *ûlĕsaʿădāh*, express neither purpose nor result, but simply accompanying circumstances. See *GKC*, 351; and H. Wildberger, *Jesaja 1–12*, 384.

[53]Compare H. Wildberger, *Jesaja 1–12*, 384. He argues that the task of "establishing and sustaining it," that is, the throne of David, belongs to the royal "child" of v 5.

usurpation of Pekah in Samaria and to the subsequent break of Ahaz from the northern kingdom. The speech applauds the new independence of the Davidic house, and promises Yahweh's continued support for the regime. The details of Isaiah's message include the following.

(1) The fallout of Pekah's coup in Israel is severe. Confusion and oppression are widespread in the land (8:21–22). In comparison, the fate of Jerusalem and the Davidic kingdom appears favorable (v 23aa).

(2) Ahaz's refusal to follow Pekah into the anti-Assyrian coalition marks the beginning of an age of salvation and glory for the capital city and the Davidic house. Furthermore, their liberation from the northern kingdom is ultimately the work of Yahweh (9:1–4).

(3) The new independence of the Davidic house is only the most recent stage in the long steady decline of Israel. Just as the northern kingdom lost its peripheral territories during the reigns of Jeroboam II and Menahem (8:23abb), so now at the very beginning of Pekah's rule in Samaria, the nation has lost control of the southern kingdom (9:1–4).

(4) The status of Ahaz as the adopted son of Yahweh legitimates his rule as an independent king in Jerusalem. The "authority of government" belongs to him by virtue of his formal enthronement. His break with Israel represents in fact the full realization of this traditional Davidic claim (v 5).

(5) The recent turn of fate for the Davidic house is by no means a short-term affair. Yahweh will sustain the throne of Ahaz and the stability of the dynasty "from this time forth and forevermore" (v 6).

CHAPTER EIGHT

ISAIAH 9:7–10:4

Scholars generally ascribe 9:7–10:4 to Isaiah, but doubt the cohesion of the verses as a single speech. The woe-saying in 10:1–4 is usually associated with 5:8–24, while 5:25–29 (30) is thought to have once concluded the Outstretched Hand poem in 9:7–20. Chapter Four above (see section B1) argued against this interpretation. The following analysis construes 9:7–10:4 as a single speech given by Isaiah to a Jerusalemite audience on the eve of the Syro-Ephraimitic crisis. The refrain in vv 11b, 16b, 20b, and 10:4b binds the material together and sounds its principal theme—the continuation of divine punishment against Israel. The purpose of the speech was likely to support the recent move of the Davidic house toward independence from the northern kingdom.

The speech reviews past events in Israelite history (9:7–20) before turning to the current situation and future developments (10:1–4).[1] Isaiah describes these events as instances of divine punishment when Yahweh stretched forth his hand to strike the nation. Despite the

[1] The verbs of the speech are a puzzling mixture of perfect, imperfect consecutive, imperfect, participial, and perhaps perfect consecutive forms. The tenses are thus open to question. (For a good review of the issue, see G. B. Gray, *The Book of Isaiah*, 1. 180–82.) A number of older scholars take the perfects (and imperfect consecutives) as expressions of prophetic certainty, and so understand the material entirely as a prediction of future events. See for example B. Duhm, *Das Buch Jesaja*, 92–95; K. Marti, *Das Buch Jesaja*, 96–100; and V. Herntrich, *Der Prophet Jesaia*, 172–83. J. Skinner (*Isaiah*, 86), however, rightly objects that "such a lavish and continuous use of the prophetic perfect would be as unique in the O. T. as the point of view presupposed by it is unnatural." He and most recent scholars interpret 9:7–20 as an historical review. See G. Fohrer, *Das Buch Jesaja*, 1. 144–52; H. Donner, *Israel unter den Völkern*, 66–75; N. K. Gottwald, *All the Kingdoms of the Earth*, 152–53; H. Wildberger, *Jesaja 1–12*, 203–29; and R. E. Clements, *Isaiah 1–39*, 66–70. Note that the somewhat analogous speech in Amos 4:6–12 rehearses a number of divine punishments in the past before announcing a still future judgment.

severity of each blow, the divine wrath did not abate. According to the conclusion in 10:1–4, Yahweh's anger extends into the present moment and beyond, bringing new disaster upon the northern kingdom. The primary interest of the prophet lies here, in the future "day of punishment." The prediction of disaster gains credibility when set against the background of Israel's sinful past and the relentlessness of God's anger.

The historical allusions of the speech are difficult to interpret. According to H. Donner, the verses largely reflect on developments in Israel between 733 and 722; for example, the campaigns of Tiglathpileser and the territorial reduction of Israel (vv 12–16), tribal warfare in Ephraim after Hoshea seized power (vv 17–20), social chaos and injustice during the last years of the northern kingdom (10:1–2).[2] In contrast, H. Wildberger dates 9:7–20 (+ 5:25–29) to the eve of the Syro-Ephraimitic crisis, and so sees references to events before 734. The speech, he argues, alludes to Syrian and Israelite attacks during the eleventh, tenth, and ninth centuries (v 11), the revolution of Jehu in the 840s (vv 12–16), and the war between Amaziah of Judah and Joash of Israel at the beginning of the eighth century (v 20ab).[3] O. Procksch also dates 9:7–10:4 (+ 5:25–30) to the period just before the Syro-Ephraimitic crisis. According to him, however, the material reviews events from the time of Menahem to the reign of Pekah.[4]

While the details of Procksch's interpretation may need adjustment, it correctly tries to understand 9:7–10:4 against the background of the recent past leading up to the Syro-Ephraimitic crisis. As in 8:23–9:6, the range of Isaiah's vision extends from the last years of Jeroboam II to the current situation in 734. This was a stretch of history which the prophet and his audience themselves had experienced

---

[2]*Israel unter den Völkern*, 66–75. Verses 7–11, Donner argues, alone concern an earlier period of Israelite history. They refer to Syrian and Philistine attacks during the ninth and first half of the eighth centuries. Compare R. E. Clements, *Isaiah 1–39*, 67–69. He takes 9:8 as an allusion to Assyria's actions against Israel in 733. Verse 11, he argues, possibly reflects Israelite disagreements with Syria after the Assyrian disposition of the region in 732. The rest of the material (vv 12–20) supposedly documents the deteriorating social and political conditions in the northern kingdom during its final decade.

[3]H. Wildberger, *Jesaja 1–12*, 210–22. The interpretation of G. Fohrer (*Das Buch Jesaja*, 1. 146–50) is similar. In 9:17–20, however, he sees a reflection of the civil war in Israel that followed the overthrow of the Jehu dynasty.

[4]O. Procksch, *Jesaia I*, 100–7. He sees allusions to the following episodes: Tiglathpileser's invasion of Palestine and Menahem's tribute in 738 (v 9); Syrian and Philistine attacks in response to Menahem's pro-Assyrian policy (v 10–11); the assassination of Pekahiah in 735 (v 13); fighting between the parties of Pekah and Pekahiah (v 20a); and the start of the Syro-Ephraimitic war, when Pekah (in league with Rezin) attacked Judah (v 20b). For a similar interpretation of 9:7–20, see N. K. Gottwald, *All the Kingdoms of the Earth*, 152–53; compare also J. Skinner, *Isaiah*, 86–90.

and could vividly recall. The episodes which Isaiah describes all damaged Israelite society. These, we suggest, include the earthquake that struck Palestine during the 750s or 740s (vv 7–9); the encroachment of Syrians and Philistines on Israelite territory toward the end of Jeroboam's reign and during the years of Menahem (vv 10–11a); Shallum's coup and the fall of the house of Jehu (vv 12–16a); the civil war and internal strife in the Shallum-Menahem-Pekah conflicts (vv 17–20); and perhaps the current activity of Pekah and Israel in the anti-Assryian rebellion (10:1–2). The end of the speech turns to the future and anticipates the forthcoming attack of the Assyrians against Israel and the rest of the anti-Assyrian coalition (10:3–4a).

The refrain of the speech divides the material into four parts.

(1) Earthquake and enemies (vv 7–11)
(2) Internal turmoil and strife (vv 12–16)
(3) Civil hostilities and warfare (vv 17–20)
(4) "Iniquitous decrees" and future judgment (10:1–4)

The sequence of the units is roughly chronological.

A. Verses 7–11

The opening verses recount the first of several disasters which befell Israel, and the response of the nation to it.

7. A word the Lord sent against Jacob,
    and it fell upon Israel.
8. But the people reasoned,[5] all of them,
    Ephraim and the ruler of Samaria,
    in pride and arrogance, saying:[6]

---

[5]D. W. Thomas ("A Note on the Meaning of yd^c in Hosea ix.7 and Isaiah ix.8." *JTS* 41 [1940] 43–44) translates the verb, $w\check{e}y\bar{a}d\check{e}^c\hat{u}$, after the meaning of the Arabic $wadu^ca$, "be humiliated" (see also the NEB). This sense, however, is not clearly attested for yd^c elsewhere in the Hebrew Bible. H. Wildberger (*Jesaja 1–12*, 203) renders the verb as "experienced" (*erfuhr*), but he must then supply the object "it." (Compare G. Fohrer, *Das Buch Jesaja*, 1. 144; and O. Kaiser, *Isaiah 1–12*, 219.) Yd^c can mean "consider, think, or reason." This sense fits well with the $l\bar{e}^\jmath m\bar{o}r$ ("saying") at the end of v 8 and the quotation of the response of the people in v 9. The NJPSV understands the Hebrew similarly.

[6]Many scholars add a verb at the beginning of v 8b in order to improve the supposedly awkward syntax of the verse as a whole. B. Duhm (*Das Buch Jesaja*, 92–93) and H. Donner (*Israel unter den Völkern*, 68) suggest restoring $k\hat{\imath}\ y\bar{o}^\jmath m\check{e}r\hat{u}$ ("since they will say") or $h\bar{a}^\jmath\bar{o}m\check{e}r\hat{\imath}m$ ("who say"). O. Procksch (*Jesaia I*, 100–1) and O. Kaiser (*Isaiah 1–12*, 219) both read $hammitga^\jmath\bar{a}weh\ b\check{e}ga^\jmath\bar{a}w\hat{a}\ \hat{u}b\check{e}g\bar{o}del\ l\bar{e}b\bar{a}b$ ("who boast in arrogance and haughtiness"), assuming that the initial participle was lost through haplography. These and other emendations of v 8b are unnecessary, if yd^c in v 8a means "reason" (see n. 5).

9. "Bricks have fallen,
   but with dressed stones we will rebuild;
   the sycamore has collapsed,
   but with cedar we will replace it!"

The prophet here employs several different terms to designate the northern kingdom. The sequence may be historically significant, for it seems to equate Jacob/Israel (v 7) with Ephraim and Samaria (v 8a). Isaiah may thus be thinking of a time when the northern kingdom had already been reduced in size, now consisting primarily of the central hill country west of the Jordan. As Chapters Two and Three above suggested, the territorial reduction of Israel may have begun during the last years of Jeroboam II.

Isaiah does not name the concrete disaster, but refers to it theologically as a divine "word" (*dābār*) against the nation. H. Donner argues that the term encapsulates all of Yahweh's past judgments against Israel.[7] According to H. Wildberger, "word" means particularly the prophetic word and refers to the activity of earlier prophets whom Isaiah saw as his predecessors.[8] Both scholars agree that v 7 functions as a short-hand description of a long sequence of past catastrophes. Correspondingly, vv 8–9 are thought to quote a popular Israelite saying or song as a typical example of the people's pride and of their obstinate refusal throughout the past to take correction from God.[9]

This interpretation is certainly possible, but a different understanding is just as likely, if not more so. The specificity of the allusions in vv 10–20 might suggest that vv 7–9 also concern a particular episode. The saying ascribed to the people in v 9 hints at the event: "Bricks have fallen . . . the sycamore has collapsed . . . ." The words here make sense as an allusion to the earthquake that struck Palestine sometime during the 750s or 740s.[10] While Amos 1:1 only notes the

---

[7]*Israel unter den Völkern*, 70. According to Donner, "word" is in "hypostatic form." The continuation of the speech reviews some of the specific instances of divine punishment which this "word" includes.

[8]*Jesaja 1–12*, 213.

[9]Donner (*Israel unter den Völkern*, 71) explains: "The pride which Isaiah condemns can hardly be characterized more clearly than by the song of progress cited in v 9." The song has to do with the extension of royal building privileges to the increasingly affluent aristocracy. "Isaiah can see in this nothing other than satiety, corruption, and the loss of connection to Yahweh." Wildberger (*Jesaja 1–12*, 215) argues similarly when he describes v 9 as "a proverbial saying of defiance, which helps a person to get over severe blows." Isaiah quoted the saying in order to illustrate the kind of pride which continually had prevented the people from discerning Yahweh's hand in past disasters.

[10]For a similar interpretation, see E. J. Kissane, *The Book of Isaiah*, 1. 111–12. Other scholars see instead a reference to military events. According to O. Procksch (*Jesaia I*, 103), v 9 reflects Tiglathpileser's invasion of Palestine in 738 (2 Kgs 15:19). The Assyrians presumably destroyed domestic houses and cut down

event, the post-exilic author of Zech 14:4–5 compares it to the eschatological judgment, and so gives an indication of its devastating consequences.

> ... and the Mount of Olives shall be split in two from east to west by a very wide valley; so that one half of the Mount shall withdraw northward, and the other half southward ... and you shall flee as you fled from the earthquake in the days of Uzziah king of Judah.

Earlier addresses of Isaiah, for example 1:2–20, 2:6–20, and 5:25, reflected on the earthquake as an instance of divine punishment,[11] and 9:7–9 may focus on it too. The saying notes particularly the destruction of houses and other buildings, cheaply built with mudbrick and sycamore timber.

If this interpretation is correct, the "word" of Yahweh in v 7 might refer to the earlier preaching of Amos. In Amos 9:1, the prophet reports a vision, in which Yahweh stands beside the altar and apparently calls for an earthquake. Isaiah was possibly familiar with the prophecy and believed that it had come to pass.

Despite the widespread devastation of the land, the northerners apparently continued to assume an optimistic, even arrogant, attitude. The quotation in v 9 is meant to illustrate their defiance: they will rebuild the collapsed houses with stronger and costlier materials. Their words express the feeling of "better next time."

Verses 10–11 recount a second instance of divine punishment. Because the earthquake did not bring about the repentance of the people, Yahweh struck Israel again, this time by means of foreign enemies.

10. So Yahweh exalted the oppressors [in the charge] of Rezin[12] over it, and stirred up its enemies;

---

forests outside the cities before Menahem finally paid tribute. R. E. Clements (*Isaiah 1–39*, 67) contends that the saying refers to the destruction of the northern kingdom during the later Assyrian campaign in 733.

[11]See J. H. Hayes and S. A. Irvine, *Isaiah*, 69–78, 83–87.

[12]The vast majority of scholars consider ṣārê rěṣîn of the Masoretic text (literally, "the oppressors of Rezin") impossible in context. Ṣārê is usually changed to ṣārāyw or ṣōrěrāyw ("its oppressors"), and the reference to Rezin is deleted as a gloss. See for example B. Duhm, *Das Buch Jesaja*, 93; O. Procksch, *Jesaia I*, 100–1; H. Wildberger, *Jesaja 1–12*, 203–5; O. Kaiser, *Isaiah 1–12*, 219; and R. E. Clements, *Isaiah 1–39*, 68; also the RSV, NEB, JB, TEV; compare the NIV and NJPSV. The emendation has the further advantage of bringing the two halves of the verse into closer correspondence: ṣārāyw would be an exact parallel to ʾōyěbāyw ("its enemies").

The textual evidence for emending v 10a is nevertheless ambiguous. The Isaiah scroll from Qumran and the Vulgate agree with the Masoretic reading. Verse 10 in the Septuagint runs: "Though God will dash down those who rise up against

11. Syria from the east and the Philistines from the west devoured Israel by the mouthful.

The verses are understandable against the background of Israel's territorial reduction during the last part of Jeroboam's reign and the early years of Menahem. Under the leadership of Rezin, Syria and/or surrogate powers encroached on Israelite holdings in Transjordan and the Galilee. At the same time, Syria and Philistia together may have overrun the Sharon Plain. The aggression of both countries fits into a larger pattern of Syrian expansionism and anti-Assyrian movements during the second half of the eighth century. Rezin was intent on two related goals: (1) re-establishing a "Greater Syria" that would dominate Palestine; and (2) leading other western powers into a coalition that could eventually check Assyrian efforts to control the Eastern Mediterranean Seaboard. It was inevitable that pro-Assyrian countries like Israel would suffer at the hands of Rezin and his allies.

B. Verses 12–16

Neither the earthquake nor enemy attacks brought Israel to its senses; the people refused to repent (v 12). Consequently, the "outstretched hand" of Yahweh struck the nation again.

13. Yahweh cut off from Israel head and tail,
    palm branch and reed, in one day!
14. Elder and the honored one, that is the head;
    and prophet teaching falsehood, that is the tail.[13]
15. And the leaders of this people[14] became wanderers,
    and the followers became misguided.

---

him on Mount Zion, and disperse his enemies . . . ." This reading does not mention Rezin, but the poor sense of the Greek impairs its value as a textual witness. The Targum refers to "the adversary of Israel, Rezin," apparently reflecting the Hebrew ṣārô (or ṣōrěrô) rěṣîn. Finally, a number of late Hebrew manuscripts improve the Masoretic text by reading ṣārê rěṣîn ("the princes of Rezin").

If one retains the Masoretic text, one must construe ṣārê rěṣîn in the sense of "oppressors in the charge of Resin." Alternatively, one might follow the Targum, emending ṣārê to ṣārô and taking Rezin as a noun in apposition. Finally, one might view the reference to the Syrian king as a gloss, which nevertheless explains correctly the sense of the verse. Rezin was likely the ringleader of the various attacks against Israel.

[13]The vast majority of scholars correctly view v 14 as an explanatory gloss.

[14]H. Wildberger (Jesaja, 218) contends that "the leaders of this people" (měʾaššěrê hāʿām-hazzeh) refers to the "spiritual leaders" of the Israelites. The piel of the verb ʾšr in 9:15 probably is equivalent to the Akkadian ešeru, and means more generally "lead or govern." Isaiah thus might have in mind a variety of officials, but especially the kings. See H. Niehr, "Zur Etymologie und Bedeutung von ʾšr I," UF 17 (1986) 231–35.

16. Thus the Lord would not rejoice over its youngsters,
and would show no mercy to its orphans and widows;[15]
because everyone was defiled and an evildoer,
and every mouth was speaking foolishness.

The generality of the language here makes it hard to determine Isaiah's exact referents. The overall picture of social upheaval, political anarchy, and revolution might reflect events in Israel during the early 740s (see 2 Kgs 15:8–22). According to our chronology (see Chapter Two, the appendix), Zechariah succeeded Jeroboam II in the spring of 747, but ruled only six months before falling victim to the conspiracy of Shallum (15:8–10). Shallum in turn reigned only one month before his assassination in a countercoup led by Menahem (vv 13–14). Menahem carried out brutal actions to suppress opposition, including sacking the town of Tuppuah and ripping open the wombs of its pregnant women (v 16). His rule was fully secured only later, perhaps in 743, through the assistance of Tiglathpileser (vv 19–20).

In describing the upheaval within Israel, Isaiah uses two word-pairs: "head and tail, palm branch and reed" (v 13). Their meaning is unclear. According to the gloss in v 14, "head and tail" refer to the nation's leaders: the elder, honored one, and prophet. Isaiah himself possibly alludes to specific figures, for example, Zechariah (the head and palm branch) and his assassin, Shallum (the tail and reed). These identifications, however, are highly speculative and perhaps wrong-headed altogether. The two word-pairs may simply express the opposite ends of the social spectrum, that is, the leadership and aristocracy as well as the common people (compare Deut 28:13, 44; and Isa 19:15). The Septuagint suggests this sense when it construes "palm branch and reed" to mean "great and small" (*megan kai mikron*).[16]

---

[15]The two verbs, *yiśmaḥ* ("rejoice") and *yĕraḥēm* ("show mercy"), are not as parallel in meaning as one might expect. The Isaiah scroll from Qumran has *yhmwl* ("spare") in place of the first verb. Whether this reading is the more original, however, is uncertain. The Masoretic text is supported by the Septuagint's *euphranthēsetai* ("be glad"). The Qumran sectarians probably borrowed *yhmwl* from v 18 as a better parallel to *yĕraḥēm*. BHS suggests retaining *yiśmaḥ*, but construing it in the sense of the Arabic *samuḥu* ("be merciful"). This meaning certainly fits well in context, but remains hypothetical. Elsewhere in the Hebrew Bible, *śmḥ* invariably means "rejoice, be glad."

[16]Compare H. Donner, *Israel unter den Völkern*, 72–73. He notes that in Egyptian literature, "head and tail" refer to the forward frontier and hinterland of a country. When Isaiah states that Yahweh cut these off, he is reflecting on the territorial reduction of Israel in 733–32. It is questionable, however, whether the prophet and his audience were as familiar with Egyptian symbolism as Donner assumes. His interpretation of the palm branch and reed as royal insignia which Israelite and Judean kings took over from the Egyptian pharaohs is similarly unconvincing.

If this interpretation is correct, the text describes the extent of the national anarchy. The sequential political coups in Israel victimized not only the leaders, but the people also (v 15). Conditions worsened to the point that Yahweh forsook even the care of the defenseless and underprivileged (v 16aa). The whole society was contaminated and wicked, civil strife cutting across all echelons of the society (v 16ab). Isaiah views the chaos as divine punishment, which, despite its severity, still failed to make Israel repent: "For all this, his [Yahweh's] anger did not abate and his hand was still outstretched" (v 16b).

C. Verses 17–20

This section continues the theme of civil strife, but focuses on the period leading up to Pekah's takeover in Samaria. According to v 20aa, the conflict involved "Manasseh against Ephraim, and Ephraim against Manasseh." Such a situation was possibly produced by the following concrete developments. Menahem, apparently from Tirzah in the tribal territory of Manasseh (2 Kgs 15:14), assassinated Shallum in 747, ascended the throne, and crushed the opposition centered in Tappuah and its vicinity in northern Ephraim. (On the mixture of tribal elements in this area, see Josh 16:8–9 and 17:7–8.) For several years, however, he had to contend with Syrian aggression, and perhaps as well with dissent within Ephraim itself. At the same time, Pekah was ruling as a rival monarch in the Manassite territory of northern Gilead. He had risen to power during the last years of Jeroboam, probably with the support of Rezin, the Syrian king. Isaiah 9:20 could refer to the strife between Pekah and the kings of Samaria. It had begun as early as the reign of Jeroboam, but greatly intensified during the years of Menahem and Pekahiah. It is quite possible that the forces of Pekah played a part in Syria's "devouring Israel from the east" (9:11), and so confronted Ephraimite troops directly on the battle field.

Verse 20ab notes also that Manasseh and Ephraim "together were against Judah."[17] The prophet may have in mind the following actions.

---

[17] J. Skinner (*Isaiah*, 90), G. B. Gray (*The Book of Isaiah*, 1. 188), and R. E. Clements (*Isaiah 1–39*, 69) view the reference as a secondary addition that disrupts the otherwise exclusive focus of the speech on the northern kingdom. According to Skinner and Gray, the line derives from a scribe or editor who had in mind the Syro-Ephraimitic war. Clements argues that the addition means to explain the final defeat of Israel as the consequence of the people's refusal to reunite with Judah and to accept Davidic rule.

These arguments are not convincing. While the larger speech concerns primarily the northern kingdom, the events involved in the nation's turmoil had serious repercussions in Judah. If the historical review in 9:7–20 aims at denouncing Is-

(1) Ephraimite opposition to Judah could refer to decisions of the government in Samaria, which adversely affected the southern kingdom. One such decision might have been connected with Menahem's payment to Tiglathpileser for the temporary use of Assyrian mercenaries. According to 2 Kgs 15:19–20, Menahem needed the soldiers to strenthen his hold on the kingdom, especially against the threat of his rival, Pekah, in Transjordan.[18] As a subordinate state within "Greater Israel," Judah might have been forced to bear some of the financial burden. If so, Judean obligations to Israel, which may normally have included providing contingency troops, reached a new level of demand during the reign of Menahem.

(2) Manasseh's or Pekah's hostility toward Judah probably began as early as the 740s. Second Kings 15:37 states explicitly that during the reign of Jotham, "Yahweh began to send Rezin the king of Syria and Pekah the son of Remaliah against Judah." The notice does not record specific aggressive actions, but two incidents may be relevant. First, Pekah might have cooperated with Rezin in seizing territory in northern Transjordan, where Jotham perhaps had previously had some influence (see 1 Chr 5:17). Second, Pekah's troops may have helped Rezin wrest the port of Elath from Judean control (see 2 Kgs 16:6).

Verses 17–19 describe the civil discord within Israel in two ways. On the one hand, v 18aba credits Yahweh with the disaster: his wrath burned the land and made the people "like fuel for the fire" (kĕmaʾăkōlet ʾēš). On the other hand, v 17 states that wickedness raged like a wildfire through the land, "consuming" (tōʾkēl) the briers and thorns (compare 5:6 and 7:23–25). Here, Isaiah ascribes the destruction of the society to human behavior. The same notion is expressed in vv 18bb–19.

> No one would spare his fellow citizen.
> 19. Each snatched on the right, but was still hungry,
> each snatched on the left, but was not satisfied.
> Each consumed (yōʾkēlû) the flesh of his offspring.[19]

---

rael as the object of God's continual wrath, it is hardly surprising that Isaiah, a southern prophet speaking to a southern audience, mentions the oppression of the southern kingdom as one of Israel's sins. Furthermore, the reference in v 20 does not necessarily point to the Syro-Ephraimitic crisis. Ephraimite and Manassite action against Judah likely began during the previous decade and took several different forms (see below). As for the interpretation of Clements, it reads far too much into v 20.

[18] For this understanding of the incident, see especially T. R. Hobbs, *2 Kings* (WBC 13; Waco, Texas: Word Books, 1985) 198–200.

[19] The Masoretic reading, "the flesh of his arm" (bĕśar-zĕrōʿô), is unlikely original. H. Wildberger (*Jesaja 1–12*, 204–6), O. Kaiser (*Isaiah 1–12*, 220, n. 10), R. E.

The language of "consumption" here describes the northern strife in terms of cannibalism and fratricide.

D. Isaiah 10:1–4

While 9:7–20 review past calamities in the northern kingdom, the last section of the speech, 10:1–4, focuses on current conditions in Israel and future developments. Several features of the text signal this shift: the "woe" introduction; the predominance of participial and imperfect verb forms; the second-person address, particularly in v 3; and the clear reference to coming disaster in vv 3–4a. The future orientation of the final lines brings the entire speech to a suitable close.

Verses 1–2 condemn a number of practices.

1. Woe to those who promulgate iniquitous decrees,
    and who publish oppressive edicts,
2. turning aside the powerless from justice,
    and robbing of their rights the afflicted of my people,
    with widows becoming their spoil,
    and the fatherless their plunder.

Scholars interpret this reproach in two different ways.

(1) Many argue that the verses concern judicial administration within Judah.[20] Either new, unjust social laws were promulgated to the benefit of the wealthy and/or ruling classes, or existing laws were interpreted so as to deprive the weak of their goods and property. This approach views the condemned actions as a reflection of general conditions, rather than of specific actions and circumstances. The saying belongs alongside similar reproaches against Judah in 5:8–24.[21]

Clements (*Isaiah 1–39*, 69), and others suggest changing *zĕrōʿô* to *rēʿô*, "neighbor" (see also the RSV and JB). The Targum and Septuagint both support this emendation. It is possible, however, to make sense of the text simply by repointing *zĕrōʿô* as *zarʿô*, "his seed or offspring." Rabbinic discussions of 9:19 advocate this reading. See A. M. Honeyman, "An Unnoticed Euphemism in Isaiah IX 19–20?" *VT* 1 (1951) 221–23; M. Wallenstein, "An Unnoticed Euphemism in Isaiah IX 19–20?" *VT* 2 (1952) 179–80; also the NEB, NIV and TEV. Compare the verse with Deut 28:53–57.

[20] See for example J. Skinner, *Isaiah*, 90–91; J. Vermeylen, *Du prophète Isaïe à l'apocalyptique*, 1. 169–77, 185–86; H. Wildberger, *Jesaja 1–12*, 175–83, 198–201; and R. E. Clements, *Isaiah 1–39*, 60–62. Compare C. E. L'Heureux, "Isaiah 5.1–10.4," 111–16. Isaiah 10:1–4, he argues, blame the leaders of Judean society for social injustice, but the verses derive from a seventh-century redactor.

[21] E. J. Kissane (*The Book of Isaiah*, 1. 107–12) also views 10:1–4 as a warning to Judah's leaders about their abuse of the poor. He nevertheless retains the verses in their present place as the conclusion of 9:7–10:4. Isaiah, he believes, is concerned throughout the speech with the whole of Yahweh's people, Israel and Judah together. (Compare J. Vermeylen, *Du prophète Isaïe à l'apocalyptique*, 1. 178–

Isaiah 9:7–10:4 245

(2) According to H. Donner, 10:1–4 condemns social and judicial discrimination in the northern kingdom between 732 and 722.[22] This second approach still views the saying as a reflection of general conditions, but takes seriously the present place of the verses in a speech about Israel.

Chapter Four above argued for taking 10:1–4 as the continuation of 9:7–20, and thus it supports, in this one respect, Donner's interpretation. His understanding of the text, however, is otherwise questionable. The allusions in 9:7–20 probably do not refer to the Syro-Ephraimitic war and its aftermath, as Donner believes, but rather to the events leading up to 734. The roughly chronological progression of the historical review likely indicates that the final section of the speech, 10:1–4, treats of the situation on the eve of the Syro-Ephraimitic crisis.[23]

If our interpretation is correct, the reproach in 10:1–2 might be understood in two ways. It could refer to social conditions in the northern kingdom during the reign of Pekahiah and at the beginning of Pekah's rule. In light of the pressing political issues of this period, however, Isaiah would not likely have been much concerned with the domestic problems of Israel. All the evidence suggests instead that the prophet focused at this time on political events. His criticism in 10:1–2 makes better sense against the background of international developments just before and during the Syro-Ephraimitic crisis. The decrees promulgated would thus have emanated from the Israelite court in Samaria, and would have regarded Israelite-Judean relations.

79.) This interpretation is sustained with the help of certain assumptions. (1) "Jacob" and "Ephraim" in 9:7 include both the northern and southern kingdoms. (2) The reference to "Ephraim and the inhabitants of Samaria" in v 8ab is secondary. (3) The mention of Rezin in v 10a is also a later interpolation. At least the first two of these assumptions are doubtful. It is difficult to deny the primary focus of the material on the northern kingdom. Compare the position of O. Procksch (*Jesaia I*, 101–2, 107). He takes 9:7–10:4 as a single speech, but nevertheless sees a clear shift in the prophet's focus from Israel (vv 7–20) to Judah (10:1–4).

[22]*Israel unter den Völkern*, 74.

[23]Compare B. Duhm, *Das Buch Jesaja*, 92–97. The passage, he argues, denounces and threatens Israelite leaders for injustice to the poor, and so continues the concern of 9:7–20 with the northern kingdom. Duhm assigns the entire speech, 9:7–10:4 + 5:25–29, to the earliest period of Isaiah's preaching, long before the Syro-Ephraimitic crisis. He reasons that if 5:26–29 describe the Assyrian enemy in such vague, ideal terms, the speech as a whole likely belongs to a time when the Assyrians were not yet an urgent threat. The argument, of course, collapses if one questions the association of 5:25–29 with 9:7–10:4. Furthermore, Duhm's interpretation assumes that 9:7–20 prophesies future events. If the verses instead reflect on past disasters during the last years of Jeroboam and throughout the reigns of Menahem and Pekahiah, Duhm's early dating of the material is out of the question.

This approach has two advantages. On the one hand, it interprets the verses within their larger literary context (that is, as the conclusion of the speech on Israel beginning in 9:7) and within a specific historical setting. On the other hand, it discerns a thematic link between 10:1–4 and the statement about Judah's oppression in 9:20.[24]

The language of v 1 merits closer attention. The prophet speaks first of "those who promulgate iniquitious decrees" (*haḥōqĕqîm ḥiqqê-ʾāwen*). The verb and noun frequently refer to customs, cultic stipulations, and civil laws of varying kinds. On occasion, however, they also carry the idea of an official governmental edict. Joseph, for example, is said to have issued a "decree" (*ḥōq*) requiring the Egyptians to render annually a fifth of their harvest to Pharaoh (Gen 47:26). David similarly is reported to have made a "statute" (*ḥōq*) for the distribution of spoil taken in battle (1 Sam 30:25). Isaiah 10:1a may have in mind edicts of the royal court in Samaria which the prophet considered, if not illegal, then certainly unjust.

Verse 1b mentions those who "publish oppressive edicts" (*ûmiktĕbê ʿāmāl kittēbû*).[25] Like *ḥōq*, *miktāb* can refer to governmental enactments. Second Chronicles 36:22 (= Ezra 1:1) thus speaks of the "edict" (*miktāb*) of Cyrus allowing Jewish exiles to return to Jerusalem and to rebuild the temple (compare 2 Chr 35:4; and *kĕtāb* in Esth 3:14, 4:8, 8:8 and 13). Isaiah probably intends a similar sense in 10:1b. The *piel* form of the verb *ktb* occurs only here, and so its precise nuance remains unclear. It may suggest repetitive action, and so mean something like "constant writing." If so, Isaiah would seem to emphasize the zeal with which the royal court constantly issued new decrees. Alternatively, the *piel* of *ktb* might be comparable to the modern notion of "publish," that is, putting something into public circulation.

Which specific edicts does Isaiah have in mind? The turbulent history of Israel from 750 onward saw several changes in dynasty, as well as the conflicts between Pekah (Manasseh) and Menahem (Ephraim). These undoubtedly provided numerous occasions for royal decrees affirming or changing policies. Verse 2 helps to narrow the focus somewhat, by indicating the negative impact of the decrees. Furthermore, if 10:1–2 relate at all to the thought of 9:20, it would seem that the edicts adversely affected the southern kingdom in particular. In light of these considerations, three possibilities suggest themselves.

---

[24]Compare O. Procksch, *Jesaia I*, 101–2, 107; also A. Dillmann, *Der Prophet Jesaja*, 95–96, 100. Both view the mention of Judah in 9:20 as a transition to 10:1–4. The latter verses, they assume, concern legal and social injustice in the southern kingdom.

[25]This reading emends the *ûmĕkattĕbîm* of the Masoretic text to the plural construct form (see *BHS*).

(1) Isaiah may be thinking of various decrees requiring Judah to share in Israelite payments to Assyria. The first such decree probably was issued during the late 740s, when Menahem had to raise revenue to pay for the use of Assyrian mercenaries (2 Kgs 15:19–20). In later years, the northern kingdom was obliged to send annual tribute to the Assyrian king. Menahem, and later Pekahiah, perhaps promulgated new sets of demands on Judah, requiring or increasing the monetary contributions of the southern kingdom.

(2) Pekah's takeover in Samaria and the subsequent swing of the northern kingdom to the side of Rezin were probably the occasion of a special edict. This would have declared not only Israel's participation in the Syrian-led coalition, but also the support of the Davidic house and Judah. Perhaps also included was a statement of the specific obligations of both kingdoms to the coalition. Isaiah, of course, would have vehemently denounced the decree.

(3) Isaiah may be alluding to a special proclamation of Pekah in the fall of 734, denouncing Ahaz as a renegade. The Davidic king opposed the new foreign policy of Israel and refused to join forces with Syria. He and Judah were thus open to charges of insubordination and "conspiracy" (see 8:12). The edict of Pekah presumably was intended to intimidate the government in Jerusalem, as well as to turn Ahaz's own Judean subjects against him.

Verse 2 focuses on the adverse impact of the decrees on the "powerless" (*dallîm*), the "afflicted of my [Yahweh's] people" (*ănîyê ʿammî*), the "widows" (*ʾalmānôt*), and the "fatherless" (*yĕtômîm*). If the terms here are meant literally, Isaiah may be suggesting the far-reaching effects of the Israelite edicts: they touched even the lowest rungs of the social ladder. The leadership and aristocracy of Israel and Judah probably passed much of the burdern of the Assyrian payments onto the common people in the form of higher prices and taxes. The lowest classes had little choice but to endure the hardship. Whatever protests they might have made doubtlessly fell on deaf ears. The prophet might thus speak of the powerless being denied the opportunity to plead their case, of the afflicted being robbed of their rights, and of widows and orphans becoming "spoil" (*šālāl*) and "plunder" (*yābōzzû*). Like Amos, Isaiah condemns such practices as injustice.

An alternative interpretation understands the language of v 2 metaphorically. The various terms would thus refer to Judeans in general, or to the citizens of Jerusalem specifically, whom the Israelite kings had dominated for decades. The latest instance of such oppression may have been the decrees of Pekah, either volunteering Judah's support for the Syrian-led coalition, or denouncing the Davidides for their refusal to join the cause. In this case, the language of v 2 might sound political overtones. Pekah's decrees all but cancelled Judean self-government, and denied the Davidic house any right to formulate its own foreign policy. The ruling establishment of Jerusalem had become like powerless widows and orphans before the government in Samaria.

In v 3, Isaiah rhetorically addresses the writers of the decrees:

> What then will you do on the day of punishment,
>   and in the storm that comes from afar?
> To whom will you flee for help,
>   and where will you leave your glory?

The day of "punishment" or "visitation" (*yôm pĕquddâ*) is equivalent to the "day of Yahweh" described elsewhere by Isaiah and other prophets (see, for example, Isa 2:10–21 and Amos 5:18–20). It refers to a time of reckoning, when divine judgment overtakes the nation. The expression in Isa 10:3 is general enough to encompass both the coming day of Yahweh's punishment and the movement of Assyrian troops against Israel and the coalition. Similarly, the "storm from afar" (*šô'â mimmerḥāq*) could denote either Yahweh's advent or the arrival of Tiglathpileser from Assyria. The words of the prophet imply the helplessness of Israel before Yahweh/Assyria, the inescapability of Israel's ruin on the "day of punishment."

In v 3ba, Isaiah asks specifically: "To whom will you flee (*tānûsû*) for help (*lĕ'ezrâ*)?" In view of the many psalms describing God as the "help" (*'ezrâ*) and "refuge" (*mānôs*) of distressed persons, one would normally answer the prophet's question by naming Yahweh. Isaiah, however, likely has in mind the position advocated in Exod 22:22–24. This text stipulates:

> You shall not afflict any widow or orphan. If you do afflict them, and they cry out to me, I will surely hear their cry; and my wrath will burn, and I will kill (*wĕhāragtî*) you with the sword, and your wives shall become widows and your children fatherless.

According to this law, anyone guilty of the charges in Isa 10:1–2 could not appeal to Yahweh for assistance, but rather would have to flee from him. Perhaps this attitude toward the abusers of widows and the fatherless partly explains Isaiah's choice of social classes in v 2. His aim would be to emphasize the inevitability of disaster soon to befall the northern kingdom.

The final question of Isaiah (v 3bb) refers to the "glory" (*kābôd*) that the Israelites will "leave behind" (*ta'azbû*) when disaster strikes. Since "glory" does not seem to fit the context, various translations propose other meanings: "wealth" (RSV), "riches" (JB, NIV), "children" (NEB), and "carcasses" (NJPSV). Another interpretation, however, merits consideration. *Kābôd* might be translated as "Glory" or "Glorious One" and taken as an allusion to Yahweh. In light of the cult's strong emphasis on *kābôd* as an attribute of God (see Pss 19:2,

29:1, 3; 24:7-10, 104:31; 138:5; and 145:5, 11), it would hardly be surprising if Isaiah were to use the term metonymically to refer to Yahweh. It may be, however, that *kābôd* had long been coined as a divine epithet. In Ps 149:5, the psalmist urges the congregation to "exult in the Glorious One" (*yaʿlĕzû ḥăsîdîm bĕkābôd*).[26] In what appears to be a condemnation of Judean idolatry, the prophet Jeremiah speaks of Yahweh's people having "exchanged their Glorious One for that which does not profit" (*hēmîr kĕbôdô bĕlôʾ yôʿîl*, 2:11b).[27]

If *kābôd* refers to Yahweh in Isa 10:3bb, the verb *taʿazbû* (normally, "forsake, leave behind") would mean something like "escape" (or more colloquially, "ditch"), and so would provide a close parallel to *tānûsû* ("flee") in the preceding question (v 3ba). Understood in this way, the line emphasizes that there is no safe refuge from Yahweh when he comes to punish the Israelites: they cannot escape "their Glorious One." The prophet's use of the epithet would be sarcastic.

In v 4a, Isaiah himself answers the preceding questions with an announcement of judgment that clearly anticipates the Assyrian invasion of Israel. However, textual problems in the first half of the line, *biltî kāraʿ taḥat ʾassîr*, cloud the precise meaning of the prophet.[28] A plausible solution involves emending the Hebrew to *bēlet yikraʾ taḥat ʾassîr/ʾōsēr*.[29] This reading in turn might be translated in two ways.

---

[26]For this translation, see M. Dahood, *Psalms* (3 vols.; AB 16, 17, 17A; Garden City: Doubleday, 1965-70) 3. 356-57.

[27]Compare the accusation against the priests in Hos 4:7b: "Their Glorious One (*kĕbôdām*) they exchanged (emending *ʾāmîr* to *hēmîrû*) for shame." Note also the words of the daughter-in-law of Eli in 1 Sam 4:22: "The Glorious One (*kābôd*) has departed from Israel, for the ark of God has been captured."

[28]For detailed discussions of the Hebrew and its translation, see G. B. Gray, *The Book of Isaiah*, 1. 193-94; and H. Wildberger, *Jesaja 1-12*, 179-80. Some scholars propose a different pointing and word division of the text, so as to recover an allusion to Egyptian deities: "Belthis is sinking, Osirus has been broken" (*beltî kōraʿat hat ʾōsîr*). Supposedly the Israelites or Judeans worshipped these gods and looked to them for help in times of distress. See for example B. Duhm, *Das Buch Jesaja*, 97; J. Steinmann, *Le Prophète Isaie*, 114; G. Fohrer, *Das Buch Jesaja*, 1. 90; and H. Donner, *Israel unter den Völkern*, 66-69, 74. J. Skinner (*Isaiah*, 91), Gray, and Wildberger rightly object, however, that there is little, if any, evidence that Belthis and Osirus were venerated in Israel and Judah during the eighth century. Gray himself changes *biltî kāraʿ* to *lĕbiltî kĕrôaʿ* and translates the line, "To avoid crouching under (?) the prisoners." Wildberger retains the consonants of the Masoretic text, but repoints *kāraʿ* as the infinitive absolute *kārôaʿ*. He takes the line to mean something like "Nothing remains but to crouch like a prisoner."

[29]See C. J. Labuschagne, "Ugaritic *blt* and *biltî* in Is. X 4," *VT* 14 (1964) 97-99. He translates the emended text, "No, he will crouch among the prisoners and among the slain will they fall." By the emphatic "no" (*bēlet*), the prophet supposedly cuts off possible responses to the preceding questions, because God alone has the answer: captivity and death are inevitable for the disobedient. More likely, *bēlet* in this context means "nowhere." The word itself bluntly answers Isaiah's questions.

(1) "Nowhere! One will crouch among the prisoners" (ʾassîr). (2) "Nowhere! One will squat down underneath the captor" (ʾōsēr). The first rendering emphasizes that captivity is certain. The second graphically depicts the sexual abuse of prisoners of war.[30] In either case, the ignominious treatment of the Israelites by the Assyrians is clear. The second part of v 4a concludes the threat: "and they will fall beneath the slain (hărûgîm)." It is perhaps signficant that the verb *hrg* occurs also in the law of Exod 22:22–24. Isaiah might be suggesting that Yahweh will employ Assyria to enforce the penalty for abusing "widows and orphans."

E. Summary

The analysis understood 9:7–10:4 against the background of events and conditions in Israel leading up to the Syro-Ephraimitic crisis. Most of the speech consists of an historical review of past calamities from the 750s onward: the earthquake (9:7–9); Syrian and Philistine aggression (vv 10–11); the fall of the house of Jehu and the subsequent anarchy (vv 13–16); and the internecine strife involved in the Shallum-Menahem-Pekah conflicts (vv 17–20). The descriptions combine to produce an impressive picture of ongoing Israelite sin, relentless divine anger and punishment, and the slow but sure ruin of the northern kingdom.

The climax of the speech, it was argued, comes in 10:1–4. Here Isaiah focuses on Israelite sin as it affected the southern kingdom (vv 1–2). In particular, he denounces various edicts of the royal court in Samaria, which perhaps required Judah to share the burden of Assyrian tribute, or volunteered Judah's support for the Syrian-led rebellion, or denounced the Davidic house for refusing to cooperate with the coalition. The prophet concludes by predicting the imminent Assyrian invasion of Israel (vv 3–4).

If the speech dates to the eve of the Syro-Ephraimitic crisis, its aim is likely to discourage any second thoughts of Ahaz and the Davidic court about their isolationist foreign policy. The dismal record of their northern counterparts, the suffering of Judah at the hands of "Ephraim and Manasseh," the continuity of divine anger toward Israel in the past and present, and the future judgment of the nation by means of the Assyrian: all justify the south's break with the northern kingdom.

---

[30]Compare the sexual meaning of *krʿ* in Job 31:9–10: "If my heart has been enticed to a woman . . . then let my wife grind for another and let others crouch down (yikrĕʿûn) on top of her."

CHAPTER NINE

ISAIAH 10:5–27C

Isaiah 10:5–27c focus largely on the role of Assyria in international politics. The material opens with a woe-cry (*hôy*) over Assyria and a reference to its commission as the instrument of divine wrath (v 5).[1] The conclusion (vv 24–27c) predicts an end to Yahweh's anger and his punishment of Assyria. The vocabulary here matches the language of v 5 and so reinforces the thematic cohesion of the material (see below). The description of the march of an unnamed army in vv 27d–32 marks the beginning of a new unit.

Scholars usually envision a complicated history of redaction behind 10:5–27c. Most agree on an original Isaianic core in vv 5–9 and 13–15,[2] dating sometime between 717 and 711.[3] This speech subse-

---

[1]The RSV translates the *hôy* as a simple exclamation ("Ah"), but it is likely a true woe-particle as in 5:8, 11, 18, 21, and 10:1. As for the genuineness of the *hôy* in Isa 10:5, only a few scholars have raised doubts. K. Marti (*Das Buch Jesaja*, 105), for example, suspects the "woe" because "it seems incomplete," without any elaboration in the speech that follows (vv 5–9, 11, 13–14). Marti is right to look for this elaboration, but he draws the wrong conclusion. If the material does not elaborate the disaster implied by the woe-cry, it is not because the "woe" is secondary, but because Marti wrongly discerns the limits of the speech. It continues in vv 15–19 and there presents the announcement of judgment that one would expect. Compare K. Fullerton, "The Problem of Isaiah, Chapter 10," *AJSL* 34 (1917/1918) 170–84. Fullerton suggests that the original speech of Isaiah neither threatened nor even reproached Assyria for overextending its divinely appointed task. The prophet's aim, rather, was simply to contrast two theories of Assyria's conquests. "Were these [the conquests] due to Assyria's own power or to Yahweh's?" (184). This interpretation, of course, excludes vv 16–19 from the speech, but also requires excising vv 7b–8 and the whole of vv 10–12.

[2]See for example W. Dietrich, *Jesaja und die Politik*, 115–20; R. E. Clements, *Isaiah 1–39*, 109–13; and H. Wildberger, *Jesaja 1–12*, 390–94, 398. Others include v 11 as a genuine part of the speech; see O. Procksch, *Jesaia I*, 162–68; and G. Fohrer, *Das Buch Jesaja*, 1. 153–58. B. Duhm (*Das Buch Jesaja*, 98–101), K. Marti (*Das Buch Jesaja*, 102–5), and H. Donner (*Israel unter den Völkern*, 142–43) view the whole of v 15 as

quently underwent a series of expansions in vv 10–12, 16–19, 20–23, and 24–27c. Scholars disagree about the origin(s) of the additions, and suggestions range from Isaiah himself[4] to a seventh-century editor[5] to various redactors of the late post-exilic period.[6]

Whether complex editing of this sort in fact underlies 10:5–27c is debatable. Certain considerations might suggest otherwise.

(1) One might expect the woe-cry (v 5) and the extended reproach of Assyria (vv 7–15) to lead into an announcement of punishment.[7]

---

a secondary addition. A few scholars take 14:24–27 as the original continuation of Isaiah's words in 10:5–15; see T. K. Cheyne, *Introduction to the Book of Isaiah* (London: A. and C. Black, 1895) 79–80; N. K. Gottwald, *All the Kingdoms of the Earth*, 183; F. Huber, *Die anderen Völker*, 41–50; and compare O. Procksch, *Jesaia I*, 163, 172.

[3]See the works of O. Procksch, W. Dietrich, R. E. Clements, and H. Wildberger listed in n. 2 above; also J. Schreiner, *Sion-Jerusalem*, 265; and H. Barth, *Die Jesaja-Worte in der Josiazeit*, 26. Verse 9, they argue, reflects backward on Assyria's capture of several Syrian cities and Samaria. These cities were conquered between 722 and 717. Verse 9 does not mention the fall of Ashdod (711), as one would expect if Isa 10:5–15 dated later. The speech is thus assigned to the period between 717 and 711.

Other scholars assign 10:5–15 to the time of Sennacherib's invasion in 701. See for example the works of B. Duhm, K. Marti, N. K. Gottwald, and G. Fohrer listed above in n. 2; also B. Childs, *Isaiah and the Assyrian Crisis*, 39–44.

[4]O. Procksch (*Jesaia I*, 168–74), for example, views 10:16–19 as a genuine threat of the prophet, yet one originally aimed against Israel, not Assyria. Also vv 20–21, he believes, derive from Isaiah. Procksch views vv 24–27 as the original continuation of the prophet's speech in 10:5–15. Compare J. J. M. Roberts, "Isaiah and His Children," 200–1. He suggests that parts of vv 16–19 and 20–24a not only derive from Isaiah, but may date to the time of the Syro-Ephraimitic crisis.

[5]H. Barth (*Die Jesaja-Worte in der Josiazeit*, 30–34) and R. E. Clements (*Isaiah 1–39*, 113–14) include 10:16–19 as part of a full-scale redaction of the book of Isaiah during the reign of Josiah. Clements (114–17) also assigns vv 20–27 to the Josianic editor(s).

[6]See for example B. Duhm, *Das Buch Jesaja*, 101–3; K. Marti, *Das Buch Jesaja*, 105–8; G. Fohrer, *Das Buch Jesaja*, 1. 158–62; and H. Wildberger, *Jesaja 1–12*, 406–8, 413–14, and 418–19. Compare O. Kaiser, *Isaiah 1–12*, 238–41.

[7]Compare H. Wildberger, *Jesaja 1–12*, 392; and H. Barth, *Die Jesaja-Worte in der Josiazeit*, 18. They argue that the opening *hoy* already hints at doom and so does not require subsequent elaboration. The point is well-taken: prophetic woe-speeches do not invariably contain explicit statements of judgment. Nevertheless, such statements usually are present and often are introduced by *hinnēh* or *lākēn*, just as in 10:16. (For detailed studies of the prophetic woe-speech, see E. Gerstenberger, "The Woe-Oracles of the Prophets," *JBL* 81 [1962] 249–63; R. J. Clifford, "The Use of HOY in the Prophets," *CBQ* 28 [1966] 458–64; G. Wanke, "ʾôy und hôy," *ZAW* 78 [1966] 215–18; J. G. Williams, "The Alas-Oracles of the Eighth Century Prophets," *HUCA* 38 [1967] 75–91; and C. Westermann, *Basic Forms of Prophetic Speech* [Philadelphia: Westminster, 1967] 190–94.) In First Isaiah specifically, woe-sayings of the eighth-century prophet connect with explicit statements of disaster in 5:8–10, 11–13, 22–24a; 10:1–4; 28:1–4; 29:1–3 (5); 30:1–5; and 31:1–3.

The rhetorical question in v 15 does not bring the speech to a suitable close.[8] The verse likely functions, rather, as a transition to a prediction of disaster such as one finds in vv 16–19.[9]

(2) While vv 5–19 cohere form-critically as a speech of judgment against Assyria, it would hardly be surprising if Isaiah continued with an elaboration on the Assyrian problem as it related to Israel, Jerusalem, and the Davidic house. His audience understandably would have wanted clarity on these aspects of the issue and the prose commentary in vv 20–27c provided it.[10]

(3) Key terms recur throughout 10:5–27c and so contribute to the unity of the material: "rod" and "staff" (*šēbeṭ* and *maṭṭeh*, vv 5, 15, 24, and 26); "anger" and "wrath" (*ʾap* and *zaʿam*, vv 5 and 25); "send" (*šlḥ*, vv 6 and 16); "do/work" (*ʿśh*, vv 11, 13, and 23); "destroy/end" (*klh*; vv 18, 22, 23, and 25); and "all the earth" (*kol-hāʾāreṣ*, vv 14 and 23).

By means of the repeated vocabulary, the verses present a set of related themes and motifs and their reversal. Yahweh will appoint Assyria as the "rod/staff" of his "anger/wrath," but this "rod/staff" will presume to have a power of its own (compare vv 5 and 15). The Assyrian will claim that he himself "works" disaster against the nations, taking "all the earth" into his control. Yahweh, however, is the

---

The list would be longer, if the threat in 5:24a were a summarizing pronouncement to the three woes in vv 18, 20, 21, and 22. The woe-saying in 33:1 also includes a statement of punishment, but most scholars doubt its genuineness to Isaiah. Compare, however, J. H. Hayes and S. A. Irvine, *Isaiah*, 360–65.

[8]H. Barth (*Die Jesaja-Worte in der Josiazeit*, 17 and 18, n. 6) and W. Dietrich (*Jesaja und die Politik*, 120, n. 27) contend that the picture of an instrument in v 15 refers back to the thought of v 5 and so rounds off the speech nicely. (Barth speaks of a "ring composition.") The same, however, could be said of the language and thought of vv 24–27c, which also match the opening in v 5 (see below). The comment of O. Procksch (*Jesaia I*, 168) on v 15 is absolutely correct: "We are eager to see how, after these words, God will act. He must intervene now."

[9]O. Procksch (*Jesaia I*, 163, 168, and 172) rightly sees that vv 5–15 are incomplete without an accompanying threat. He discounts vv 16–19, however, as the original continuation of the speech and looks instead to vv 24–27c + 14:24–27. See the similar interpretations of F. Huber (*Die anderen Völker*, 47–48) and N. K. Gottwald (*All the Kingdoms of the Earth*, 183); and compare H. Donner, *Israel unter den Völkern*, 145. G. von Rad (*Old Testament Theology*, 2. 163) is one of the few modern scholars who take vv 5–19 as an original whole.

[10]Compare the different opinion of G. B. Gray on 10:20–27: "Isaiah wrote prose as well as poetry, but there is no reason to believe that he allowed fine poems to dribble out in prose conclusions" (*The Book of Isaiah*, 1. 203). The statement might be more correct, if the prophet were as concerned with literary aesthetics as Gray seems to suppose. Isaiah, however, was a skilled orator chiefly interested in persuading his audience. From a rhetorical perspective, prose conclusions might indeed be the best way to instruct the prophet's listeners on key points of his speech.

one truly at "work" in "all the earth" (compare vv 11, 13, 14, and 23). He will use Assyria to wrack "destruction," but afterwards the divine "anger and wrath" will come to an "end," and Yahweh will then make an "end" of Assyria (compare vv 5, 18, 22, 23, and 25). God will "send" disaster against the nation whom he earlier "sent" against Israel (compare v 6 and 16). After Assyria, the "rod" and "staff" of divine wrath, has fulfilled its purpose, Yahweh will raise a "staff" against it (compare vv 5 and 25–26).

(4) Scholars have long recognized genuine Isaianic terms and images in vv 16–27c, but have seen the material as the work of late editors who took up, and elaborated on, the vocabulary and imagery of the eighth-century prophet in other passages.[11] However, it seems equally possible that Isaiah himself used the same language and imagery on more than one occasion. It is true that the terms and phrases are often applied in different ways, but this alone does not necessarily reflect the hand of a redactor. The generality of the language facilitates a variety of applications, not just by late editors, but by the prophet as well.

(5) While 10:5–27c cohere thematically and in the repeated use of key vocabulary, the diversity of the material cannot be overlooked. The verses include poetry and prose, divine and prophetic speech, a variety of forms, and a number of individual, though not unrelated, points. Such diversity, however, need not be seen as the result of editing. Rather, it may reflect simply the complexity of Isaiah's topic (the role and fate of Assyria), his concern to treat it fully, and his need of different styles and forms to instruct and persuade his audience.

The following analysis understands 10:5–27c as a single speech of Isaiah, though allowing for secondary additions in vv 10, 12, and perhaps 18b (see below secs. B and C). In it he gives a full treatment of Assyria: its function as the agent of Yahweh's wrath, its arrogance and pride, the divine judgment that will overtake Assyria, and the future deliverance of Israel and Zion from Assyrian domination. The material divides into several parts.

---

[11]See B. Duhm, *Das Buch Jesaja*, 101–5; K. Marti, *Das Buch Jesaja*, 105–8; G. B. Gray, *The Book of Isaiah*, 1. 199–206; H. Wildberger, *Jesaja 1–12*, 405–22; and R. E. Clements, *Isaiah 1–39*, 113–17. Clements, for example, sees the following lines of dependence: 10:16 ("a wasting sickness") on 17:4; 10:17 ("light" and "thorns and briers") on 5:6 and 9:1; 10:18 (the forest image and "both body and soul") on 9:13, 17:4 and 6; 10:19 ("the remnant of his trees") on 17:6; 10:20 ("him that smote them") on 9:12; 10:21 ("A remnant will return" and "to the mighty God") on 7:3 and 9:5; 10:22 ("overflowing") on 8:8; 10:23 ("make a full end") on 6:11; 10:24 ("smite with the rod") on 9:3; 10:25 ("my indignation will come to an end") on 5:25, 9:11, 16, and 20; 10:26 ("Midian") on 9:3; and 10:27 ("his burden will depart") on 9:4. Clements describes these parallels as instances of a "midrashic" exegesis that he believes is typical of a Josianic redactor. See also H. Barth, *Die Jesaja-Worte in der Josiazeit*, 30–34 and 234–36.

(1) Yahweh's statement about Assyria's role (5–7)
(2) A hypothetical speech attributed to the Assyrian king (8–9, 11, 13–14)
(3) A prophetic promise of Assyria's eventual destruction (15–19)
(4) A prophetic prediction of the survival of an Israelite remnant (20–23)
(5) A divine promise to Zion and a prophetic assurance of Zion's redemption from Assyria (24–25, 26–27c)

Dating this speech is difficult, but a setting during the Syro-Ephraimitic crisis is plausible.[12] This interpretation rests on the following arguments.

(a) Most commentators, we noted, take 717 as a terminus a quo, at least for vv 5–15. The dating assumes that v 9 reflects on the actual fall of Syrian cities and Samaria between 722 and 717. The verse, however, is part of a hypothetical speech placed in the mouth of the Assyrian king (vv 8–14). The words are a quotation of what the Assyrian *will* say (*kî yōʾmar*, v 8a), after Yahweh sends him against Israel.[13] The material then does not refer to past or present events, but anticipates future Assyrian attitudes and actions. If so, Isa 10:5–27c derive from a time before 722–717, possibly as early as the Syro-Ephraimitic crisis.

(b) It should occasion no surprise that in 734 Isaiah could accurately list Assyrian conquests that in fact would follow some years later. All involved major western cities that, with the possible exception of Carchemish, had fought in anti-Assyrian coalitions during the early years of Tiglathpileser (Arpad, Hamath, and Calno/Calneh) or were about to revolt against Assyria in 734 (Damascus and Samaria). The prophet fully appreciated the strong spirit of resistance that continually resurged in these cities and anticipated their fall to Assyria.

(c) It is reasonable to assume that, sometime during the Syro-Ephraimitic crisis, Isaiah would have had to address the issue of Assyria directly and fully. Certainly Ahaz and the Davidic house would have wanted a prophetic statement on the matter, if they were going to follow the prophet's advice and hold out against Syria and Israel. Earlier speeches of Isaiah had named the Assyrians as the divinely summoned threat against the coalition and Judah (7:18–20, 8:4, and 8:7–8a), but none had given a detailed assessment of Assyria. In 10:5–27c, the prophet offered a full exposition of his understanding of the relationship between Yahweh and Assyria and of the future course of events he envisioned.

---

[12]Note that G. Smith ("A New Fragment," 328) suggested this setting for the whole of Isaiah 7–10.

[13]The finite verbs thoughout vv 5–8a are all imperfects: *ʾăšallĕḥennû* and *ʾăṣawwennû* in v 6a; *yĕdammeh* and *yaḥšōb* in v 7a; and *yōʾmar* in v 8a. Many modern translations render the verbs as present tenses (see the RSV, NIV, NEB, and NJPSV), but the Septuagint and the Vulgate correctly recognize the future orientation of the passage.

(d) Isaiah plays on the names of Maher-shalal-hash-baz and She'ar-yashub in vv 6b and 21–22. Apart from these references, no other texts from the prophet's later ministry allude to the children. During the Syro-Ephraimitic crisis, however, both sons figured prominently in Isaiah's preaching (7:3 and 8:1–4). The play on the names in chapter 10 likely reflects the same setting.[14]

(e) The narratives and speeches preceding 10:5–27c, we have argued, relate to the Syro-Ephraimitic crisis. This setting is certain in 7:1–8:20; it is less clear, but still plausible, in 8:21–9:6 and 9:7–10:4. Isaiah 10:27d–12:6, we will argue below (see Chapter Ten), also make sense against the background of the events of 734. The larger literary context of 10:5–27c might thus suggest a similar date for this speech.

A. Verses 5–7

The speech begins with a divine statement about the proper role of Assyria. Yahweh describes the nation as the "rod ($šēbeṭ$) of my anger and the staff ($maṭṭeh$) of my wrath" (v 5).[15] The image here is not altogether clear. $Šēbeṭ$ and $maṭṭeh$ can designate the scepter of a king (see Gen 49:10; Amos 1:5 and 8; Jer 48:17; Ezek 19:11–14; Pss 2:9 and 45:7). If this meaning applies in 10:5, Isaiah would seem to be suggesting that Yahweh will exercise his royal authority over international affairs by means of Assyria. Alternatively, $šēbeṭ$ and $maṭṭeh$ may suggest the picture of a parent disciplining a wayward child. (The first term is particularly frequent in references to corporal punishment; see for example Prov 13:24, 22:15, 23:13–14, and 29:15.) Yahweh is the parent and Assyria is the stick that he will use. The same metaphor of corporal punishment also occurs in 1:2b–3 and 5–6. The refrain in 9:7–10:4 ("For all this his [Yahweh's] hand is still stretched out") may suggest it as well. Whatever the exact image might be in

---

[14] Note that the play on Maher-shalal-hash-baz might suggest Israel as the identity of the "profane nation" and "the people of my [Yahweh's] wrath" in v 6b (compare 8:4). If so, the larger speech would surely date to a time before the fall of the northern kingdom in 722.

[15] As it now stands, the Hebrew of v 5b makes poor sense: $ûmaṭṭeh$-$hû$' $bĕyādām$ $za'mî$ ("and a rod it is in their hand my wrath"). B. Duhm (*Das Buch Jesaja*, 98), G. B. Gray (*The Book of Isaiah*, 1. 195, 201), H. Barth (*Die Jesaja-Worte in der Josiazeit*, 22–23 and 26), and others are probably correct in viewing $hû$' $bĕyādām$ as an explanatory gloss (so also the RSV). The reading proposed by G. R. Driver ("Linguistic and Textual Problems: Isaiah I–XXXIX," 36–50), however, is also possible: $wmṭṭh$ $z'my$ hw' $bydm$ ("the rod of my wrath—it is in their hand"). Compare the NIV, NEB, and NJPSV.

10:5, *šēbeṭ* and *maṭṭeh* are associated with Yahweh's fury. They are clearly negative symbols for divine punishment.[16]

Verse 6 describes further the appointed role of Assyria: "Against an ungodly nation (*běgôy ḥānēp*) I [Yahweh] will send him and against the people of my wrath (*wěʿal-ʿam ʿebrātî*) I will command him." The text does not explicitly name the nation that God will punish, but in view of the allusion to Maher-shalal-hash-baz in v 6b, Israel is probably intended.[17] The northern kingdom is reproached as *ḥānēp* (compare 9:16). Modern translations usually render the term as "godless" or "ungodly" (see the RSV, JB, NEB, NIV, and NJPSV), but elsewhere the word often means "polluted" or "contaminated."[18] Whichever sense applies in 10:6, it is easy to guess the concrete wrongdoing of the nation: Israel's violation of its treaty with Assyria, and perhaps also its threats against Jerusalem and the Davidic house. Isaiah views these acts as the immediate cause of Yahweh's wrath.

The two verbs, "send" (*šlḥ*) and "command" (*ṣwwh*), have a quasi-official sense, connoting the formal commissioning of the Assyrians. The prophet thereby indicates that the forthcoming move of Assyria against Israel will not be an accident of history, or even primarily the action of a foreign power. The invasion is credited to the will of God.

The specific task planned for Assyria is two-fold: "to take spoil and seize plunder (*lišlōl šālāl wělābōz baz*) and to trample it [Israel] down like mud in the street" (v 6b).[19] The first half of the line plays

---

[16]H. Wildberger (*Jesaja 1–12*, 394–95) argues that *maṭṭeh* in 10:5 refers specifically to a magic rod. The lexical evidence, however, does not clearly support this interpretation. The rods of the Egyptian magicians, Aaron, and Moses have magical power (see Exod 4:2–4; 7:12, 19–20; and 17:5), but this sense is not apparent in Jer 48:17, Ezek 19:11, and Ps 110:2.

[17]This is also the conclusion of O. Procksch (*Jesaja I*, 164) and J. Schreiner (*Sion-Jerusalem*, 264). Compare B. Duhm, *Das Buch Jesaja*, 98; J. Skinner, *Isaiah*, 94; K. Fullerton, "Isaiah, Chapter 10," 178; and G. Fohrer, *Das Buch Jesaja*, 1. 155. They understand vv 5–7 as a very general statement about Assyria's divinely appointed role, and so argue against identifying the "ungodly nation" with any particular country. The meaning, Skinner explains, is that "Jehovah sends the Assyrian against any nation that incurs His anger." (According to this view, the imperfect verbs express frequentative or habitual action.) Still other scholars propose all Israel (the northern and southern kingdoms together) as the object of Yahweh's threat. See for example R. E. Clements, *Isaiah 1–39*, 110–11.

[18]For a full discussion of *ḥānēp*, see K. Seybold, "*Ḥānēp*," *TWAT* 3. 41–48.

[19]F. Huber (*Die anderen Völker*, 45–47) excises v 6b as a late addition. The line (along with other insertions in vv 7b and 8–12) supposedly disturbs the clearer structure of the original speech. The argument, however, is not convincing, for the organizational symmetry that Huber seeks is excessively precise. Moreover, even he concedes the possible correspondence between the commission of Assyria in v 6b and its transgression in v 14. Huber must then adduce metrical

on the symbolic name or slogan, Maher-shalal-hash-baz. Isaiah had used it earlier in a threat against Syria and Israel (8:1-4). As severe as the disaster might be, it is not unlimited. The divine intent is punishment, not the annihilation of the people and state.

The focus of the speech shifts in v 7, from Yahweh's plans for Assyria to Assyria's own intentions. Here begins the reproach that the opening woe-cry (v 5) leads one to expect. Yahweh will employ Assyria as an instrument of punishment, but the nation, or its king, "will not so intend (*yĕdammeh*) and his mind will not plan (*yaḥšōb*) so" (v 7a). His resolve, rather, will be "to destroy (*lĕhašmîd*) and to cut off (*ûlĕhakrît*) many nations" (v 7b).[20] The disobedience of the Assyrian regards both the purpose and extent of his commission. Yahweh intends punishment (v 6b), but the Assyrian plans annihilation (v 7b). God commands him against an "ungodly nation" (Israel, v 6a), but he intends to conquer "many nations" (v 7b), indeed, "all the earth" (v 14), including Jerusalem (v 11). Underlying such disobedience is, of course, Assyria's failure to recognize its role as an agent of Yahweh (v 5).[21]

The saying here shows how realistically Isaiah viewed Assyria. However firmly the prophet believed in Yahweh's guidance of foreign powers and international events, this theological conviction never blinded him to Assyria's own self-image and goals. Years of observing Tiglathpileser had taught Isaiah and his contemporaries how ambitious the king's designs on the entire Eastern Mediteranean Seaboard were. They had learned as well how brutally Assyria could deal with revolts. When the Assyrian king campaigned in the west, he often did more than "take spoil, seize plunder, trample," and then leave; he frequently conquered and liquidated the states of the region. Isaiah was in no way naive on this point. He clearly saw that

---

and lexical arguments against the line, but these cannot bear much weight. (The lexical argument is particularly weak.)

[20] The last half of the line reads literally, "to cut off nations not a few" (*lōʾ mĕʿāt*). The Targum translates the final phrase with *lʾ bḥys* ("without pity"); see S. Speier, "Zu drei Jesajastellen. Jes. 1,7; 5,24; 10,7," *TZ* 21 (1965) 312–13.

[21] K. Fullerton ("Isaiah, Chapter 10," 178–84) and F. Huber (*Die anderen Völker*, 46–47) discount v 7b as a redactor's addition. Huber excises the line because it duplicates vv 13b–14 as the structural counterpart to v 6a. Again, however, he looks for an overly precise symmetry in Isaiah's speech (see n. 19 above). Fullerton reasons that the original speech contrasted two theories about Assyria's conquests. (a) The conquests were due to the nation's own initiative and power. (b) They were due to Yahweh's will and power. Verse 7b (along with vv 8–12) introduces into the speech another contrast, one between the plan of Yahweh (chastisement) and the plan of Assyria (annihilation). The two thoughts, however, are certainly compatible, as Fullerton himself admits. Indeed, they are closely related. The thematic diversity that Fullerton emphasizes is too slight to warrant excising v 7b.

the divine and Assyrian plans for Israel would sharply differ in their intent and ultimate outcome.

B. Verses 8–9, 11, 13–14

Verses 8–9, 11, and 13–14 are a hypothetical speech placed by Isaiah in the mouth of the Assyrian king.[22] The prophet envisions the king bragging over the conquest of several cities, including Samaria, and threatening Jerusalem as well. The future orientation of the quotation is indicated by the imperfect verbs in vv 6–7 and especially at the beginning of v 8—"For he will say." Isaiah thus anticipates that, at some time in the future, the Assyrian king will make such a speech.

The words ascribed to the king articulate his self-understanding and intentions, and thus illustrate the accusation in v 7: "But he will not intend so and his mind will not plan so; rather, his resolve will be to destroy and cut off many nations." The speech brilliantly imitates the braggadocio of Assyrian monarchs in their own inscriptions, and thus reflects Isaiah's familiarity with Assyrian propaganda.[23] Four boasts are placed in the king's mouth.

(1) The king asks rhetorically, "Is not each of my commanders (*śāray*) a king?" (v 8b). The question suggests that even the subordinates of the Assyrian monarch are on an equal footing with foreign

---

[22]B. S. Childs (*Isaiah and the Assyrian Crisis*, 43) and H. Barth (*Die Jesaja-Worte in der Josiazeit*, 23–25) include v 12b as part of Isaiah's speech, but the majority of scholars are probably correct in viewing the whole verse as a late addition. The passage disrupts the words ascribed to the Assyrian king and prematurely anticipates the divine punishment of Assyria described in vv 16–19. In regard to the meaning of v 12, see P. W. Skehan, "A Note on Is 10,11b–12a," *CBQ* 14 (1952) 236; H. Donner, *Israel unter den Völkern*, 143; and H. Wildberger, *Jesaja 1–12*, 402.

A more difficult question concerns the genuineness of v 10. Many commentators object that the verse introduces a foreign thought into Isaiah's speech by criticizing the idolatry of Samaria and Jerusalem (see for example R. E. Clements, *Isaiah 1–39*, 111–12; and H. Wildberger, *Jesaja 1–12*, 401). This, however, does not seem to be the intention of the verse. If an editor (or the prophet) wanted to make this criticism, he would not have placed it in the mouth of the Assyrian king, for he himself is guilty of pride and ignorance, and so is hardly a credible witness to the religious wrongs of Samaria and Jerusalem.

There are other reasons, however, for doubting the genuineness of v 10. If taken with v 11, it appears grammatically as an anacoluthon. While v 9 assumes the capture of Samaria, v 10 seems to suppose that the city and Jerusalem have not yet fallen. Finally, the interrogative form of v 11 (*hălō*ʾ) matches that of v 9 (*hălō*ʾ in v 9a; ʾ*im-lō*ʾ in v 9b), and the content of the verses flows smoothly. Note that references to the conquest of Samaria conclude and begin vv 9 and 11 respectively.

[23]See P. Machinist, "Assyria and Its Image in the First Isaiah," *JAOS* 103 (1983) 719–37.

rulers. (Isaiah plays here on the similarity between the Hebrew *śar*, "subordinate officer," and the Akkadian *šarru*, "king.") By implication, the Assyrian king is without rival in status and power. The boast is typical of the grandiose claims in the Assyrian royal inscriptions.[24]

(2) The king recounts his capture of six major Syrian and Palestinian cities: "Is/Was not (*hălō'*) Calno like Carchemish, Hamath like Arpad, Samaria like Damascus?" (v 9). The cities are all placed on the same level: each fell when the Assyrian "stretched forth his hand" (compare v 14). Historically, they were subjugated or conquered at different times: Carchemish in 738 and 717; Calno or Calneh (Kullani in the Assyrian texts) in 738 and possibly again in 717; Hamath in 738 and 720; Arpad in 740, 738, and 720; Damascus in 732 and 720; Samaria in 722 and 720. Since the time frame for the speech is an imaginary future, after these cities have been taken, the dates of their actual capture are irrelevant to dating the verses. Speaking in 734, Isaiah envisioned all of the cities falling to the Assyrian monarch as he campaigned westward. Verse 9 lists them geographically from north to south, and so roughly in the order that an Assyrian army would encounter them in the march from Mesopotamia to southern Palestine. The approaching threat to Jerusalem is thereby implied.

(3) The Assyrian monarch imagines extending his list of conquests to include Jerusalem: "Just as I dealt with Samaria and its idols (*wěle'ĕlîlêhā*), will I not do the same to Jerusalem and its images (*wělaʿăṣabbêhā*)?" (v 11). The reference here to idols and images in Samaria and Jerusalem should not be understood as a denunciation of cultic wrong-doing.[25] Isaiah is simply wording matters as might the Assyrian king, whom he is imitating.[26] The spoliation of the gods of conquered peoples was a standard Assyrian practice and the

---

[24]Compare for example the self-praise of Ashur-nasir-pal II (883–859): "I, great king, strong king, king of the universe, king of Assyria, king of all the four quarters, sun (god) of all people, prince, vice-regent of Ashur, valiant man, who acts with the support of Ashur and the god Shamash and has no rival among the princes of the four quarters . . . ." (*ARI* 2. 712).

[25]Compare H. Wildberger's commentary on vv 10–11. The addition "apparently intends—post festum—to explain why Jerusalem, the city of God, despite all the promises that had been made about the city, fell to the enemy just as the other cities. Like them, Jerusalem trusted in idols" (*Jesaja 1–12*, 401). This kind of polemic, which Wildberger believes is deuteronomistic, simply does not make sense in the mouth of the Assyrian king (see n. 22 above). Compare too the remarks of R. E. Clements on v 11: "Strikingly the redactional addition recognizes that Jerusalem too is guilty of idolatry, like Samaria . . ." (*Isaiah 1–39*, 112). The saying is not nearly as judgmental as Clements imagines. The Assyrian king does not denounce the "idols" and "images" of Samaria and Jerusalem as sin or a matter of guilt. He suggests only that the idols and images cannot save the cities from him. The king's attitude here reflects, of course, his ignorance (see below).

[26]See the similar interpretation of K. Marti, *Das Buch Jesaja*, 103.

frequent boast of Assyrian monarchs in their inscriptions.[27] The prophet has the Assyrian king planning to do the same to Jerusalem and "its images."

The boast reflects not only the arrogant pride of the Assyrian, but also his three-fold ignorance. (a) The king believes that he has conquered Samaria on his own initiative and by his own power. In fact, Yahweh sent him against Israel (v 6). (b) The king sets Jerusalem on the same level as Samaria and the other cities that have fallen to Assyria. In fact, Jerusalem is not like the other cities, for Yahweh resides in it and will protect it.[28] (c) The Assyrian monarch believes that the god of Jerusalem belongs to the same category as the powerless idols of Samaria. In fact, Yahweh the God of Jerusalem is also the Lord of history and the very one who commissioned the Assyrian king.[29]

(4) The king ascribes the success of his campaigns to his own power and wisdom (v 13a).[30] The boast then continues with a review of his mighty deeds in a style reminiscent, again, of the Assyrian royal inscriptions.[31] The accomplishments include: (a) annihilating sovereign states, incorporating them into the Assyrian provincial system (v 13a); (b) dethroning foreign rulers (v 13bb); and (c) plundering the wealth of other peoples (vv 13ba and 14).[32] The last is described at

---

[27]For a detailed discussion of Assyria's confiscation of the gods of foreign peoples, see M. Cogan, *Imperialism and Religion*, 22–41.

[28]See the interpretation of Isa 7:7–9a, 8:8b–10, 8:14–15, and 8:18 in Chapters Five and Six above, and compare 14:32, 17:12–14, 18:1–7, and 31:4–5. In recent years, the antiquity of the Zion tradition and the place of the tradition in Isaiah's preaching have been questioned, but the arguments are not convincing. For a detailed review of the issues and of the different scholarly opinions, see R. Kilian, *Jesaja 1–39*, 40–97. Particularly doubtful is the extreme position of Kilian himself, who thinks it possible to view all the Zion texts in First Isaiah as editorial additions.

[29]B. S. Childs (*Isaiah and the Assyrian Crisis*, 42–43) and H. Barth (*Die Jesaja-Worte in der Josiazeit*, 23, 26) correctly observe that the words of the king in v 11 make him guilty of blasphemy against Yahweh. This theme, however, is not nearly as intrusive in the speech as Childs and Barth believe. There is no need to remove it, as they do, by eliminating "its idols" and "its images" from v 11.

[30]The phrase, *kî ʾāmar* ("for he said"), at the beginning of v 13 is unlikely original. It was necessitated by the editorial addition in v 12, which disrupted the Assyrian's speech. Note that the perfect form, *ʾāmar*, contrasts with the imperfect *yōʾmar* in v 8a.

[31]See P. Machinist, "Assyria and Its Image," 722 and 724.

[32]Some scholars suspect that v 13bb is scribally corrupt, and so use the ancient versions to reconstruct the Hebrew. See for example the emendations proposed B. Duhm (*Das Buch Jesaja*, 100), K. Marti (*Das Buch Jesaja*, 104), and H. Wildberger (*Jesaja 1–12*, 390–91). With slight repointing, however, the Masoretic text makes reasonably good sense: "Like a hero [literally, a mighty one] I brought down rulers (*waʾôrîd kěʾābîr yôšěbîm*). The simile here may call to mind an ancient title of God in the Jerusalem cult—"the Mighty One of Jacob" (*ʾăbîr yaʿăqōb*; see Ps

length with the use of a bird/nest simile. The king claims that, just as one might take eggs from a nest when the bird is gone, so he took the wealth of the peoples and "gathered up the whole earth" (v 14). The continuation of the image expresses the ease with which the monarch plundered the world: "Not a wing flapped nor did a mouth open and squawk." In an earlier speech, Isaiah described Yahweh as a great bird protecting the realm of Immanuel, that is, Zion (8:8b; compare 31:5). The prophet may understand the boast of the Assyrian king in 10:14 as a challenge to this idea.

In Isaiah's version of the king's self-praise, everything is stated in terms of the royal "I," without reference to any deity. The piling up of first-person forms gives the impression of a vastly inflated ego: "I did ... I will do ... my power and my wisdom ... I have understanding ... I brought down ... my hand came upon ... I gathered up ...." While the royal "I" figures largely also in the Assyrian inscriptions, it does not do so to the same extent as here. The Assyrian monarchs speak of their divine commission and credit their victories and dominance to the gods, especially Ashur. Isaiah's omission of divine references is deliberate. It creates a stronger sense of hubris on the part of the Assyrian king. It also avoids postulating the existence of the Assyrian deities, and thus leaves unchallenged the assertion that Yahweh alone fashions the Assyrian power. Finally, the king's failure to mention any god makes him guilty of the very charge that Assyrian monarchs often made against their enemies, namely, that they "trusted in their own strength" and "did not fear the oath of the gods."[33]

C. Verses 15–19

In vv 15–19, Isaiah speaks in his own voice and promises his audience that Yahweh would eventually destroy Assyria. The prophet begins with two rhetorical questions (v 15).

> Does the axe vaunt itself over the one who cuts with it,
>   or the saw magnify itself over the one who wields it?
> As though a rod would wield the one who lifts it,[34]

---

[13] 2:2 and 5; compare Gen 49:24). In Isa 1:24, the prophet himself calls Yahweh "the Mighty One of Israel" (ʾăbîr yiśrāʾēl). If the simile in 10:13bb sounds overtones of this title, the prophet again portrays the Assyrian king arrogantly aspiring to the status of Yahweh.

[33] See P. Machinist, "Assyria and Its Image," 734.

[34] This translation assumes that the mĕrîmāyw of the Masoretic text ("the ones who lift it") is a scribal error for mĕrîmô. Compare H. Barth, *Die Jesajaworte in der Josiazeit*, 23. He retains mĕrîmāyw as an instance of the "royal plural."

or a staff should lift him who is not of wood!³⁵

The obvious response, of course, is "no." Isaiah invites his listeners to make a simple deduction on the common-sense assumption that the user of an instrument is superior to the instrument itself. The aim of the prophet is to suggest the absurdity of the Assyrian king's boast. Yahweh is the user of Assyria, and therefore Assyria, the instrument, should not claim a higher status. Verse 15bb picks up the language with which the speech opened (v 5), and thereby makes the prophet's point clear: Assyria, the "rod" and "staff" of Yahweh's anger, will overstep its appointed task and thus will incur Yahweh's wrath.

Verses 16–19 proclaim the punishment of Assyria, and so elaborate the details of the doom implied in the opening woe-cry (v 5). The prediction gives an ironic twist to the initial commission of Assyria. Yahweh will "send" (*šlḥ*) the nation against Israel (v 6), but he eventually will "send" (*šlḥ*) disaster against Assyria (v 16). The "therefore" (*lākēn*) at the beginning of v 16 links the threat directly to the boast of the Assyrian king (vv 8–9, 11, 13–14). Because of his pride and his intention to "destroy and cut off many nations" (v 7), the agent of God's wrath will become himself the object of divine anger.

The details of the punishment are difficult to understand, but the verses seem to focus on the land of Assyria.³⁶ The picture of devastation consists of the following threats. A "barrenness" (*rāzôn*) will

---

³⁵B. Duhm, K. Marti, and H. Donner view v 15 as an editorial addition (see n. 2 above), but K. Fullerton ("Isaiah, Chapter 10," 177) and H. Wildberger (*Jesaja 1–12*, 393) correctly observe that the interrogative style and the thought of the verse are characteristic of Isaiah. The rhetorical questions, moreover, appropriately follow the Assyrian's words in vv 13–14. Wildberger does regard the last part of v 15 ("As though a rod . . .") as an explanatory gloss, but this conclusion is unnecessary. See also H. Barth, *Die Jesaja-Worte in der Josiazeit*, 23; and compare R. E. Clements, *Isaiah 1–39*, 113.

³⁶Most commentators see several images in vv 16–19, including the affliction of the Assyrian's body (vv 16 and 18b) and the destruction of his land (vv 17, 18a, and 19). They credit the mixture of different pictures to the incompetence of a late editor. (See for example B. Duhm, *Das Buch Jesaja*, 101; G. B. Gray, *The Book of Isaiah*, 1. 199; and K. Marti, *Das Buch Jesaja*, 106; but compare H. Barth, *Die Jesaja-Worte in der Josiazeit*, 32–33.) It is possible, however, to interpret at least v 16 as referring to the Assyrian landscape (see below). As for v 18b, the image of a sick man "wasting away" (so the RSV) is by no means certain. The Hebrew here is quite difficult and probably corrupt. See the different readings proposed by E. Robertson ("Some Obscure Passages in Isaiah," *AJSL* 49 [1932/33] 320–22); O. Procksch (*Jesaia I*, 169–70); K. Marti (*Das Buch Jesaja*, 105); and G. R. Driver ("Isaiah I–XXXIX: Textual and Linguistic Problems," 41–42). G. B. Gray (*The Book of Isaiah*, 1. 196, 201–2) and H. Barth (28–30) wisely leave the line untranslated. It may be, in any case, a late addition to vv 16–19, as Wildberger (*Jesaja 1–12*, 406) and others suggest.

come upon its "fertile regions" (*mišmannāyw*, v 16a).³⁷ Its "glorious area" (*kĕbōdô*) will be burned (v 16b).³⁸ The fire will consume even its briers and thistles (v 17b). The forests and garden-lands of Assyria will be utterly destroyed, so that only an insignificant remnant of its trees will remain (vv 18a, 19). The devastation, the prophet asserts, will be the work of Yahweh. The "light of Israel" (*ʾôr-yiśrāʾēl*) and "its Holy One" (*ûkĕdōšô*) will be the "fire" and "flame" that destroy Assyria's land (v 17a).³⁹

The description of disaster may echo the braggadocio of the Assyrian kings in their own inscriptions. The monarchs frequently tell how they marched to the west and there cut down trees for use in their homeland (see *ANET* 275–76, 278, 280). In Isa 10:16–19, the prophet appears to turn this boast against the Assyrian: his own trees will be destroyed (v 19). Again in the Assyrian texts, the kings brag constantly how they burned the cities of their enemies and on occa-

---

³⁷H. Barth (*Die Jesaja-Worte in der Josiazeit*, 28–29) translates *rāzôn* and *mišmannāyw* respectively as "emaciation" and "his fat." The line would then envision the Assyrian as a stout man afflicted with disease. The threat against Israel in Isa 17:4 presents a similar image: "and the fat of his [Jacob's] flesh will grow lean" (*ûmišman bĕśārô yērāzeh*). In 10:16, however, the noun *mišman* appears in the plural form and so more likely means something like "fat ones." (O. Kaiser [*Isaiah 1–12*, 238, n. 2] suggests that the plural form refers to the fat parts of the Assyrian's body, but the proposal seems forced.) Two specific interpretations are possible. (a) The line might threaten the troops of the Assyrian king (literally, "his stout or strong ones") with disease. (For this sense of *mišman*, see Ps 78:31, where *mišmannêhem* ["their strong ones"] is parallel to *baḥûrê yiśrāʾēl* ["the picked men of Israel"].) (b) Verse 16a might threaten the "fertile areas" of Assyria with "barrenness." (*Mišman* has this meaning in Dan 11:24. Note also that in Num 13:20, the adjectives, *šāmēn* and *rāzeh*, occur together and refer to the quality of land, whether fertile or barren.) This second interpretation fits reasonably well with the meaning of vv 17, 18a, and 19, and possibly also with the sense of v 16b (see below).

³⁸H. Wildberger (*Jesaja 1–12*, 405, 409) similarly takes *kābôd* as a reference to the *Pracht* ("splendor") or *Üppigkeit* ("luxuriant growth") of the land of Assyria. Compare Isa 4:2 and 5, where *kābôd* is used to describe the "fruit of the land" and "the whole site of Mount Zion." H. Barth (*Die Jesaja-Worte in der Josiazeit*, 28–29, 32–34) construes v 16b as a description of the fever within the Assyrian's body. (See also G. B. Gray, *The Book of Isaiah*, 1. 200; G. R. Driver, "Isaiah I–XXXIX: Textual and Linguistic Problems," 41–42; and O. Kaiser, *Isaiah 1–12*, 239.) This interpretation is certainly possible. Its disadvantage, however, is that the line so understood does not fit well with the imagery of the verses that follow. Barth is then forced to guess at the complicated logic of a hypothetical Josianic redactor who supposedly composed vv 16–19.

³⁹This interpretation assumes that the two parts of v 17a are synomously parallel. Compare the different understanding of the line by D. Grossberg ("Pivotal Polysemy in Jeremiah XXV 10–11A," *VT* 36 [1986] 481–85). He translates *ʾôr yiśrāʾēl* as "the field of Israel," and construes "his Holy One" (Yahweh) as the agent who will burn it.

sion destroyed the outlying gardens and forests. Tiglathpileser III, for example, describes his campaign against Kin-zer in Babylonia in the following way:

> Kin-zer, son of Amukkani, I shut up in Sapie, his royal city. Many (of his people) I slew in front of his (city) gate. The mulberry (?) groves which were (planted) along his (city) walls, I cut down; not one was left (*lit.*, escaped). The date-palms within the confines of his land I destroyed. His ----- I cut off (?) and filled the fields (with them, *or*, it). All of his cities I destroyed, I devastated, I burned with fire ... (*ARAB* 2. 285).[40]

According to Isaiah, Yahweh will do the same to the forests and gardens of Assyria. The divine punishment is ironically fitting. If the king is guilty of the same pride and false confidence that he ascribes to his enemies, then he should suffer the same disaster (see sec. B above).

Although it goes unsaid in vv 15–19, the context makes clear that the destruction of Assyria is expected to take place after the nation has fulfilled its purpose as the instrument of Yahweh's judgment. The text envisions the following scenario. (1) As the agent of divine wrath, Assyria will attack the Syro-Ephraimitic forces (and the western anti-Assyrian coalition). (2) The Assyrians will not only punish Israel and others by plundering and trampling (thus carrying out the will of Yahweh), but also will overextend their divinely ordained function by annexing territory and eradicating native monarchies. (3) The Assyrian monarch will brag about his achievements and engage in self-glorification, as if his accomplishments were his own self-inspired achievements. (4) The Assyrian monarch will even set his eyes on Jerusalem, as if it too were his for the taking. (5) Because the instrument (Assyria) moves to challenge the user (Yahweh) and vaunts itself against the user (that is, he has thoughts about taking Jerusalem), Yahweh will take action against the Assyrians and destroy their land.

D. Verses 20–23

In vv 20–23, Isaiah turns his attention to the fate of Israel (the northern kingdom) "in that day."[41] The temporal clause is a general

---

[40]Compare also the king's description of his campaign against Rezin in 733/732: "I assembled in the vicinity of his [Rezin's] city and like a bird in a cage I shut him in. His gardens ... trees without number I cut down and left not one standing" (Layard 72b+73a; see Chapter Two, section B1 above).

[41]Many scholars assume that the passage concerns Judah and that v 20 refers to the nation's relationship with Assyria. However, they then find it impossible to locate the saying in the historical circumstances of Isaiah's career, and so attribute it to a late editor. B. Duhm (*Das Buch Jesaja*, 101) thus formulated the

designation for the future course of events described in vv 5–19.⁴² The prophet assumes that some of the northerners will survive the Assyrian invasion of their land. He thus speaks of them in v 20 as the "remnant of Israel" (šěʾār yiśrāʾēl) and "the fugitives of the house of Jacob" (ûpělêṭat bêt-yaʿăqōb).⁴³ Two actions of these survivors, one negative and the other positive, are described.

(a) The remnant will not again depend or lean on the one who previously "smote it" (makkēhû; v 20a). The prophet may refer here to Israel's role as a puppet of Syria, which, prior to Pekah's takeover, had harrassed Israel, confiscated its territory, and encouraged nations in the region to encroach upon its land (see 9:10–11a).⁴⁴ With Pekah's coup in Samaria, Israel's foreign policy changed and the nation became a subordinate ally of Syria.

(b) The positive action is that the remnant will lean on Yahweh "in truth" (beʾĕmet; v 20b). Here Isaiah simply assumes that reliance on Syria reflected a lack of faith in Yahweh. The concluding phrase "in truth" is difficult to interpret, but it might suggest that Israel viewed its participation in the anti-Assyrian coalition as the will of God. The prophet disagreed totally and spoke of the future, when Israel would "truly" lean on Yahweh.

In v 21, the prophet plays on the symbolic name of his son, She'ar-yashub. According to 7:3, Isaiah earlier had taken the child to a meeting with Ahaz. In that context, we argued, the name implied

---

problem: "Ahaz leaned upon Assyria (Second Kings 16), but was not struck, while Hezekiah did not lean upon Assyria, but was struck." See also K. Marti (*Das Buch Jesaja*, 106), H. Wildberger (*Jesaja 1–12*, 413), and O. Kaiser (*Isaiah 1–12*, 240–41), all of whom quote Duhm. The difficulty, however, is avoided by taking "Israel" and "the house of Jacob" in v 20 as references to the northern kingdom. The verse then makes good sense as a description of the nation's past and present relations with Syria (see below).

⁴²In the analysis of 7:18–25, we questioned whether the expressions, "in that day" and "it will happen in that day," are invariably the formulae of redactors, as is assumed so often (see Chapter Five, n. 3). The same issue arises in 10:20. We propose that the temporal clause here (wěhāyâ bayyôm hahûʾ) derives from Isaiah and marks a transition in his thought.

⁴³These two expressions may not designate the same group. The "remnant" could refer to those who will survive the war, while the "fugitives" might denote those who flee south before the hostilities with Assyria erupt.

⁴⁴S. Blank ("The Current Misinterpretation," 212), R. P. Carroll ("Inner Tradition Shifts," 302), R. E. Clements (*Isaiah 1–39*, 115) and others observe that Isaiah understands makkēhû in 9:12 as a reference to Yahweh. They conclude that the expression in 10:20 does not likely derive from the prophet, if here it refers to a human enemy. The discrepancy, however, is more apparent than real. In 9:12, Isaiah does describe Yahweh as "the one who smote him [Israel]," but the actual agent of the divine punishment is clearly Syria, whose actions against Israel are recounted in the preceding verse. It is hardly then a radical shift in meaning if makkēhû in 10:20 describes Syria.

the survival of the Davidic house, and so functioned as encouragement to the king. In 10:21, She'ar-yashub is given a different application in reference to the northern kingdom. Here the prophet declares: "A remnant shall return (šĕ'ār yāšûb), a remnant of Jacob (šĕ'ār ya'ăqōb) to 'ēl gibbôr."

Modern translations usually render 'ēl gibbôr as "Mighty God" (see the RSV, NJPSV, JB, NIV, and NEB), and so understand v 21 as a synonymously parallel statement to v 20b. However, one might interpret 'ēl gibbôr as a title of the Davidic king, in this case, Ahaz (see 9:5).[45] Understood in this way, 10:21 anticipates that the northerners who survive the Assyrian onslaught will return to the Davidic monarch. The Israel that survives will become again part of the Davidic realm. Isaiah implied the same message in an earlier speech to the royal court (see Isa 7:17a).

The tenor of the speech changes in v 22 from optimism to gloom. The shift, however, does not necessarily reflect the hand of a redactor, as many scholars believe.[46] In the preceding verses, Isaiah promised his Jerusalemite audience that Israelites in the future would again give their allegiance to the Davidic house. In v 22, the prophet emphasizes that the northern kingdom must first suffer Yahweh's judgment by the hand of the Assyrians. The statement is rhetorically addressed to Israel, and thereby the threat is carefully directed away from Isaiah's actual audience, the Davidic court and the citizens of Jerusalem. On the eve of the Syro-Ephraimitic crisis, the latter must have welcomed the prediction of Israel's imminent demise. Perhaps, too, they took the pronouncement as a warning of the peril involved in joining the western coalition.

The threat against Israel emphasizes the certainty of disaster: "Even if your people, O Israel, were as the sand of the sea, only a remnant of it shall return (šĕ'ār yāšûb bô). Destruction is decreed (killāyôn ḥārûṣ), overflowing with righteousness" (šôṭēp ṣĕdāqâ). Here the prophet declares that even if the hypothetical ideal—an Israel innumerable (Gen 22:12; 32:12; Josh 11:4; Hos 2:1)—should exist, still

---

[45]Compare the different interpretation of R. P. Carroll ("Inner Tradition Shifts in Meaning," 302). He begins with the assumption that the verse derives from a time after the monarchy had fallen. 'Ēl gibbôr can only then refer to Yahweh. This meaning, he concludes, departs from Isaiah's understanding of the expression in 9:5 as a title of the Davidic king. Carroll's argument is clearly circular. Compare the equally problematic reasoning behind S. Blank's remarks on 'ēl gibbôr ("The Current Misinterpretation," 211).

[46]O. Procksch (Jesaia I, 171), for example, remarks that, in vv 20–21, "the emphasis is on the expected salvation of the remnant that turns to God. . . . In contrast, v. 22f. stress that only a pitiful remnant of the people will be saved. Optimism predominates there, pessimism here. Though composed in the same meter as v. 20f., v. 22f. nevertheless proves to be an addition that does not derive from Isaiah." Compare H. Wildberger, Jesaja 1–12, 412–13, 415.

only a fraction will survive when the Assyrians attack. The reason is that God has already decreed disaster for the nation.

The meaning of the final phrase, *šôṭēp ṣĕdāqâ*, is not altogether clear. The term *šṭp* ("overflow, flood") refers in 8:8 to the Euphrates River rising over its banks and sweeping into Judah. The metaphor, of course, describes an Assyrian invasion. In 10:22, however, Isaiah speaks of *ṣĕdāqâ* overflowing. Two interpretations are possible. The term may mean "righteousness," as it is translated above, and so may refer to the actions of Yahweh (through the Assyrians) to restore the order disrupted by Israel, when it transgressed its treaty with Assyria. Alternatively, *ṣĕdāqâ* may mean simply "retribution." In this case, the concluding clause of v 22 would be a short statement on the certainty and severity of Israel's punishment: "Retribution shall come like a flood!" (NJPSV). The threat would allude to the imminent Assyrian invasion.

Verse 23 reinforces v 22: "Surely it is a destructive and decreed thing (*kālâ wĕneḥĕrāṣâ*) that the Lord Yahweh Sebaoth is doing in the midst of the whole earth" (*ʿōśeh bĕqereb kol-hāʾāreṣ*). As noted earlier, the final clause picks up the vocabulary of the speech attributed to the Assyrian king (see especially v 11, 13a, and 14a). The point is thereby made that Yahweh, not the Assyrian, is truly the one at work in international politics.[47]

E. Verses 24–27c

After describing the future punishment of Israel, the prophet focuses on the situation and fate of his audience, the Jerusalemites (vv 24–27c).[48] Here he assures them that they have nothing to fear from Assyria and that eventually they will attain their political freedom even from this imperial power.

> 24. Therefore, thus says the Lord Yahweh Sebaoth, "Do not be afraid of Assyria, O my people dwelling in Zion, when it smites with a rod, and wields its staff against you on the road to Egypt. 25. For after a little while my wrath will be finished, and my anger will be directed toward their [Assyria's] destruction." 26. And Yahweh Sebaoth will brandish a whip against him, as when he smote Midian at the Rock of Oreb; and his staff will extend to the sea, and he will wield it on the road to Egypt.

---

[47]K. Marti (*Das Buch Jesaja*, 106–7), S. Blank ("The Current Misinterpretation," 212), H. Wildberger (*Jesaja 1–12*, 415), and others contend that vv 22b–23 envision a universal judgment such as that depicted in late apocalyptic writings. If the passage does not fit squarely within the thought of apocalyptic, they argue, it at least moves in that direction. Neither the language nor the thought of vv 22b–23 demands this conclusion.

27. And in that day, its [Assyria's] burden will be removed from your shoulder; and its yoke from upon your neck will be broken.⁴⁹

Verses 24-25 are formally a divine oracle, consisting of both an exhortation (v 24) and a promise (v 25). The saying seeks to encourage the residents of Zion, in view of the forthcoming Assyrian invasion of Palestine. In v 24, Isaiah seems to assume that the campaign might threaten Jerusalem (compare v 11). This is not surprising, for much of Ahaz's kingdom was inclined to support the anti-Assyrian efforts of Rezin and Pekah (see 8:6). The prophet envisions the Assyrians marching down the coastal highway, the road to Egypt (probably the same as the "Way of the Sea" in 8:23). (When Tiglath-pileser took action against the western coalition in late 734 or early 733, he in fact moved down the Mediterranean coast into Philistine territory and to the border of Egypt—that is, along the road to Egypt. There is no evidence, however, that either Judah or Jerusalem was threatened at the time.) The campaign, Isaiah argues, should not alarm the Jerusalemites, for (*kî*, v 25) after Yahweh has vented his anger against Israel, his wrath will turn against the Assyrians.

The word of salvation continues in vv 26-27c, but no longer as an oracle of Yahweh. Isaiah now speaks in his own voice as he elaborates on the preceding promise. After Yahweh has used Assyria as an instrument of judgment, he will take action against Assyria. To illustrate the nature of the Assyrian defeat (v 26a), Isaiah alludes to Israel's victory over Midian (see Judg 7), a victory gained in spite of great numerical inferiority (compare 9:4). The threat continues in v 26b, but the meaning of the line is uncertain. The statement about Yahweh's staff extending to the sea (that is, the Mediterranean) may simply assert that Yahweh will not only end Assyrian dominance over Jerusalem, but also will break the nation's hold on the coastal region. If this interpretation is correct, the prophet appears to have appreciated what would be a principal goal of Tiglathpileser's invasion of southern Palestine in 734/733, namely, the control of the Mediterranean seaports and their lucrative trade. The destruction of

---

⁴⁸The Masoretes understood all of v 27 as a sense unit. The last part of the verse, however, probably belongs with v 28 and forms the beginning of a new speech. See Chapter Ten, sec. A below.

⁴⁹The translation rests on the following assumptions. (a) *Běderek miṣrāyim* in vv 24 and 26 is a geographical reference, not an allusion to the Exodus tradition (compare H. Wildberger, *Jesaja 1-12*, 417, 419). (b) *Zaʿam* in v 25b was originally *zaʿmî* and so was parallel to the *ʾappî* that follows. (c) The frequent emendation of *ʿal-tablîtām* in v 25b is unnecessary. (For a review of the different proposals, see H. Barth, *Die Jesaja-Worte in der Josiazeit*, 44.) The Hebrew, as it stands, makes reasonably good sense: Yahweh declares that his anger will shift from Israel to Assyria. The promise is the basis for the prophet's exposition in v 26. (d) *Wěḥubbal* in v 27c should be changed to *yěḥubbal*.

Assyrian hegemony in Palestine, Isaiah thus suggests, will include even that part of the region that the Assyrians prized most.

The consequence of Yahweh's eventual action against Assyria will be the people's redemption from Assyrian dominance (v 27a–c). "In that day," the "burden" and "yoke" of service will be removed and broken.[50] Prior to 734/733, the Judeans had not been directly related to Assyria in a state of vassalage. Judah's relationship to Assyria had been through Israel. Nevertheless, the Judeans and Jerusalemites, as subordinate entities within "Greater Israel," probably had felt the burdern of Assyrian policies for years, and had shared in the tribute payments of the northern kingdom. Isaiah, no doubt, guessed that, with Tiglathpileser's action against Israel and his invasion of southern Palestine, the Davidides would formally become Assyrian vassals. Hardship under foreign dominance would thus continue for a time, though "in that day" Yahweh would end it. Verses 24–27c may thus be less optimistic than a first reading would indicate. In an earlier speech, the prophet had celebrated Jerusalem's independence from Israel (8:21–9:6), but here in Isaiah 10, he makes clear that complete freedom from foreign powers lies still in the future. In the time immediately ahead, the "burden" of Assyria must still be borne and its "yoke" carried.

F. Summary

The above interpretation of 10:5–27c viewed the material (excluding vv 10, 12, and 18b) as a single speech of the eighth-century prophet, dating to the period of the Syro-Ephraimitic crisis. In it, Isaiah sets forth to a Jerusalemite audience his understanding of Assyria's role in international politics, and of the ultimate fates that await Assyria, Israel, the Davidic house and Zion. The following specific points are made.

(1) Yahweh will employ Assyria as an agent of punishment against Israel (vv 5–6). Because the northern kingdom has broken its treaty with Assyria and also is planning an assault against Ahaz in Jerusalem, God will command Assyria to move against Israel (and presumably the other members of the western coalition as well).

---

[50]The term, *sōbel* ("burden"), could refer to a vassal's specific obligations to an overlord (see 1 Kgs 11:28, where the variant, *sēbel*, refers to forced labor). These might have involved not only the payment of tribute, but also the requirement to supply contingents of troops or other special forces.

The image of a "yoke" (*ʿōl*) is frequent in the Assyrian inscriptions, where it refers to the subjugation of other states and peoples, or to a vassal's rebellion against Assyria ("throwing off the yoke"). See P. Machinist, "Assyria and Its Image," 734.

(2) The Assyrian king himself will not acknowledge his divine commission (v 7a). He instead will ascribe his conquests to his own power and initiative (vv 8–9, 11, 13–14). Furthermore, the king will overextend his appointed task by seeking to annihilate, not chastise, Israel, and by planning to conquer many nations (v 7b), indeed "all the earth" (v 14). Even Jerusalem, the very seat of Yahweh, may be threatened (v 11).

(3) The Assyrian's intentions are absurd and a reflection of his arrogant pride (v 15). Yahweh will therefore punish Assyria by destroying its own land (vv 16–19), though not until the nation has served its purpose in Yahweh's plan for Israel (vv 22–23).

(4) In the wake of the Assyrian invasion, a fraction of the Israelites will survive and genuinely obey Yahweh's will (v 20). Perhaps also they will again give their allegiance to the Davidic king, Yahweh's anointed in Zion (v 21).

(5) The Davidic house and the residents of Jerusalem should expect to bear the burden of Assyrian vassalage for a time (v 24). They are not, however, to fear or lose hope, for their full political freedom lies ahead. Yahweh's anger will turn against the Assyrians and he will put an end to their rule (vv 25–27). The present moment is not the time of liberation, but it will come.

If this interpretation of 10:5–27c is correct, the speech appears to have served a number of goals. It encouraged the Davidic court to hold out against Israel and Syria by affirming Yahweh's plan to send Assyria against the coalition. At the same time, the speech also demonstrated that Isaiah's political advice rested on a realistic appraisal of Assyria. The prophet acknowledged that the nation would dominate Jerusalem and its leadership, but argued that such domination would not last forever. In the immediate future, Ahaz and the Jerusalemites should not try to resist Assyria's might.

CHAPTER TEN

ISAIAH 10:27d–12:6

Isaiah 10:27d–12:6 concludes the material in First Isaiah relating to the Syro-Ephraimitic crisis (chapters 7–12). This section constitutes a single speech delivered on the very eve of Jerusalem's siege by Rezin and Pekah. In it, Isaiah predicts the failure of the forthcoming attack and looks forward to the future prosperity of the Davidic house. Yahweh will defend Zion against the enemy forces; afterward, Davidic sovereignty will eventually extend over a united Israel and Judah and over the surrounding nations. The promise aims at encouraging Ahaz and the residents of Jerusalem to hold out against the coalition, trusting in the ancient claims of the Zion and Davidic traditions.

This interpretation contrasts sharply with other treatments of the material. Scholars generally see 10:27d–12:6 as the product of a long and complex process of literary growth, in which a few short sayings of Isaiah were expanded by several late redactors.[1] The following analysis understands the different sayings (including the presumed

---

[1]The analysis of R. E. Clements (*Isaiah 1–39*, 117–29) is typical in this regard. He assigns the verses to six or more different hands. Isaiah 10:27d–32 alone is credited to the eighth-century prophet. A seventh-century redactor expanded the saying in vv 33–34. A post-exilic editor is responsible for 11:1–9, which may actually be a combination of two originally separate promises (vv 1–5 and vv 6–9). Another post-exilic editor appended vv 11b, 12–16. Verse 10 subsequently entered the text as a transitional passage between the promises in 11:1–9 and vv 11–16. Chapter 12 is yet another expansion, though when precisely it occurred is uncertain. The gloss in v 11b is one of the latest additions to the book.

This interpretation demonstrates the extreme to which a redaction-critical approach can lead. For a similar analysis of the material, see O. Kaiser, *Isaiah 1–12*, 245–72. Wildberger's treatment (*Jesaja 1–12*, 417–86) is somewhat more moderate, in that he takes 10:27d–34 and 11:1–9 as whole speeches and assigns both to Isaiah. The remainder of the material, however, is again divided into a number of editorial passages.

editorial additions) as parts of one speech by Isaiah. The verses divide into three sections.

(1) A description of the Syro-Ephraimitic march against Jerusalem (10:27d–32)
(2) A prediction that the attack will fail (vv 33–34)
(3) A promise of future prosperity for the Davidic regime and kingdom (11:1–12:6)

The last section, in turn, consists of several sub-parts. (a) Verse 1 states generally that the Davidic house will survive and thrive. (b) Verses 2–9 describe the Davidic king—his charismatic endowment, his function as righteous judge, and the paradisiacal peace of his reign. (c) Verse 10 predicts the future prestige of the Davidic regime and the greatness of Zion among the nations. (d) Verses 11–16 look forward to the reconstitution of a great Davidic kingdom. This will include both Israel and Judah, now reconciled, as well as the subjugated peoples of Philistia, "the children of the east," Edom, Moab, and Ammon. (e) Isaiah 12:1–6 anticipate the future thanksgiving of Isaiah's Jerusalemite audience.

A. Isaiah 10:27d–32

This section describes a military invasion of Judah and the panic of towns lying in its path.[2]

27d. He came up from Samaria;[3]
28.   he arrived at Aiath.
    He passed through Migron;
    at Michmash he stowed his gear.[4]

---

[2]B. Duhm (*Das Buch Jesaja*, 104) and K. Marti (*Das Buch Jesaja*, 108–9) deny the verses to Isaiah for the following reasons. (1) The extensive word-play in the passage is uncharacteristic of the prophet. (2) The verses place special emphasis on Jerusalem, whereas Isaiah is usually more concerned with the land of Judah. (3) The description of the invasion is too objective to have been made by a prophet contemporary with the crisis. For counter-arguments to these points, see G. B. Gray, *The Book of Isaiah*, 1. 207–8. Most scholars correctly attribute 10:27d–32 to Isaiah.

[3]The line in the Masoretic text is senseless: *wĕḥubbal ʿōl mippĕnê-šāmen*. The verb probably belongs with v 27a–c and so concludes the preceding speech. The rest of the line should be emended to *ʿālâ mippĕnê šōmĕrôn* (see below).

[4]H. Donner (*Israel unter den Völkern*, 30–31) argues that *kēlî* usually refers to military equipment and weapons. If this sense applies in 10:28, he reasons, the verb *yapqîd* (a *hifil* form of *pqd*) must mean "muster, inspect," not "store," as it is usually translated. Donner thus renders the verse, "He crossed over Migron to Michmash, he inspected his military equipment." As Wildberger (*Jesaja 1–12*, 424) rightly objects, however, *pqd* means "muster, inspect" only in the *qal*. In the *hifil*,

29. He crossed the Geba pass;
      [there] he bivouacked.[5]
     Ramah trembled!
      Gibeah of Saul fled!
30. Raise your voice, O daughter of Gallim!
      Watch out, O Laishah!
      Sound a warning, O Anathoth![6]
31.   Madmenah is in flight!
      The inhabitants of Gebim flee for safety.
32. Standing at Nob this very day,
      he will shake his fist
      at the mountain of the daughter of Zion,
      the hill of Jerusalem.

Most of the place-names here are identifiable: Aiath (et-Tell), Michmash (Muchmas), the Geba "pass" (crossing over the Wadi es-Suwenit en route to Jeba'), Ramah (er-Ram), Geba/Gibeah of Saul (Jeba'), Anathoth (Ras el-Ḥarrube), and Nob (probably located on Mt. Scopus, just opposite Jerusalem).[7] Most scholars identify Migron with Tell-Maryam, southwest of Muchmas on the northern side of the

---

the verb means "commit, entrust, deposit, appoint." The noun *kēlî* can refer generally to baggage (see, for example, 1 Sam 17:22).

[5]The plural forms, *ʿāběrû* and *lānû*, contrast with the singular verbs in the preceding lines. G. Fohrer (*Das Buch Jesaja*, 1. 162), H. Wildberger (*Jesaja 1–12*, 423–24), and O. Kaiser (*Isaiah 1–12*, 246) retain the Masoretic text, construe *lānû* as "for us, our," and take v 29ab as a quotation of the advancing army. The whole of v 29a would then read, "They cross through the pass, 'Let Geba be our quarters for the night!'" (see also the NIV and NJPSV). The quotation, however, intrudes abruptly in the itinerary of the army, Wildberger's appeal to the lively style of the text notwithstanding. A more likely solution is to take both *ʿāběrû* and *lānû* as verbs, emend them to singular forms (*ʿābar* and *lān*; see 1QIsaa and the Septuagint), and change *maʿbārâ gebaʿ* to *maʿbārat gebaʿ*. See H. Donner, *Israel unter den Völkern*, 31.

[6]The *ʿăniyâ ʿănātôt* of the Masoretic text ("poor/suffering is Anathoth") makes poor sense. The first term should probably be repointed to *ʿănîhā* (literally, "Respond to it," that is, to the invasion).

[7]Following W. F. Albright (*Excavations and Results at Tell el-Ful (Gibeah of Saul)* [New Haven: Yale University Press, 1924]), most scholars treat Geba and Gibeah of Saul as separate sites, identifying the first as modern Jeba' and the second as Tell el-Ful. See for example Y. Aharoni, *The Land of the Bible*, 393; H. Donner, *Israel unter den Völkern*, 34–35; H. Wildberger, *Jesaja 1–12*, 430; and O. Kaiser, *Isaiah 1–12*, 248–51. J. M. Miller ("Gibeah/Geba of Benjamin," *VT* 25 [1975] 145–66) and P. M. Arnold (*Gibeah in Israelite History and Tradition* [dissertation, Emory University, 1986] 66–121) have made a strong case for taking Geba and Gibeah as variant names of the same city and for identifying it as Jeba'.

Suwenit, but the toponym might refer to the Suwenit itself.[8] The locations of Gallim, Laishah, Madmenah, and Gibim are unknown.[9]

The route of the invasion is unusual. North-south travel in the area normally followed the main watershed highway linking Shechem, Bethel, Mizpah, Ramah, and Jerusalem. The army in 10:27d–32, however, seems to have branched off southeastward at Bethel, taking the more difficult road through Michmash and Geba, and then picking up the main highway again just north of Jerusalem. While the reasons for this detour can only be guessed, it seems reasonable to assume that the invading force sought to by-pass the Judean fortress at Mizpah (Tell en-Nasbah).[10]

Textual corruption in v 27d has obscured the starting point of the campaign. As it stands, the Hebrew makes little sense: *wĕḥubbal ʿōl mippĕnê-šāmen* ("and a yoke will be broken because of fatness").[11] The majority of scholars correctly assign the verb, *wĕḥubbal*, to v 27a–c and change *ʿōl* to *ʿālâ*. Verse 27d then reports the outset of the enemy invasion: "he came up from . . . ." The toponym at the end of the line is uncertain. Several readings have been proposed in place of *šāmen*: *yĕšîmôn* or "wilderness";[12] *ṣāpôn* or "the North";[13] *bêt-ʾēl* or Bethel;[14]

---

[8] See P. M. Arnold, "Migron," in the *Anchor Bible Dictionary* (forthcoming).

[9] See, however, the identifications suggested by H. Donner (*Israel unter den Völkern*, 35; and "Der Feind aus dem Norden: Topographische und archäologische Erwägungen zu Jes. 10,27b–34," *ZDPV* 84 [1968] 46–54).

[10] See H. Donner, *Israel unter den Völkern*, 36; idem, "Der Feind aus dem Norden," 47. Compare the different explanation by J. Skinner (*Isaiah*, 100): ". . . Isaiah is thinking of a *surprise attack*, in which the enemy's movements would be screened from observation till he was within striking-distance of the capital."

[11] O. Kaiser (*Isaiah 1–12*, 243) translates the line, "and the yoke will be shattered for fat." He sees the sentence as a gloss on vv 24–27, which "is concerned with the sudden strengthening of the people of God as indicated in 9:3f." Attempts to hold to the Masoretic text result in forced interpretations of this sort. Compare H. Gilead, "*wĕḥubbal ʿōl mippĕnê-šemen*," *Beth Mikra* 31 (1985/86) 134–36 (Hebrew).

[12] See D. L. Christensen, "The March of Conquest in Isaiah X 27c–34," *VT* 26 (1976) 385–99. The reading *yĕšîmôn*, he claims (389), "is reasonable from a textual point of view, requiring no real emendation since the phenomenon of shared consonants is well attested." He concedes (392), however, that the initial *y* might have been lost through haplography. The route in vv 27–32 is supposedly the traditional path of a cultic procession of the Ark from the Yeshimon or "wilderness" (near Gilgal) to Jerusalem. Isaiah, Christensen argues, envisions Yahweh the Divine Warrior marching against Jerusalem along the same route.

This interpretation is not convincing for several reasons. (1) The evidence for a ritual procession from the area of Gilgal to Jerusalem is extremely slight. Christensen adduces only Ps 68:8–9, 28–30, and even this text does not clearly support his thesis. (2) The route described in Isa 10:27–32 would be as strange for a ritual procession as it is for an actual military campaign. (3) Verses 28b and 29a state that the enemy stored his baggage at Michmash, crossed the Geba pass, and then set up camp for the night. These details do not likely refer to Yahweh the Divine Warrior.

rimmôn or Rimmon;[15] and *šōměrôn* or Samaria.[16] The last proposal is the most likely, but the decision depends in part on the identification of the enemy.

Nowhere in 10:27d–32 is the invader explicitly named. This fact might indicate the loss of antecedent material once identifying the enemy.[17] It is possible, however, that v 27d marks an absolute beginning. If the speech were given just prior to the army's arrival at Jerusalem, as v 32 indicates, Isaiah certainly did not need to name the invader for his audience. If the siege were to begin "this very day," they could hardly have been in doubt as to the referent of the anonymous "he" of these verses.

The location of the verses after a speech about the Assyrians (10:5–27c) would seem to suggest that the Assyrians are the subject here also. Three interpretations of the passage follow this line of thought. First, 10:27d–32 describes Sennacherib's campaign against Jerusalem in 701.[18] Second, the verses chart the advance of Assyrian troops possibly dispatched by Sargon II from Samaria in 715–711. The march presumably aimed at discouraging Hezekiah and other Judean

---

[13]See J. Simons, *The Geographical and Topographical Texts of the Old Testament* (Leiden: E. J. Brill, 1959) par. 1588; and compare W. R. Smith, "Old Testament Notes, II. Isaiah X. 27, 28," *Journal of Philology* 13 (1885) 62–65. This reading is not impossible, but the spelling is not particularly close to the Masoretic text. Furthermore, the list of cities in vv 28–32 leads one to expect the name of a city in v 27d as well.

[14]See G. Dalman, "Palästinische Wege und die Bedrohung Jerusalems nach Jesaja 10," *PJB* 12 (1916) 45. The suggestion is geographically plausible, in that Bethel (Beitin) lies on the main north-south highway, only a few kilometers north of et-Tell. It is hard, however, to see how *bêt-ʾēl* could have evolved through corruption into the *šāmen* of the Masoretic text.

[15]See B. Duhm, *Das Buch Jesaja*, 103; K. Marti, *Das Buch Jesaja*, 108; G. B. Gray, *The Book of Isaiah*, 1. 206–10; H. Donner, *Israel unter den Völkern*, 30; also the RSV. Against this proposal, W. F. Albright ("The Assyrian March on Jerusalem, Isa. X, 28–32," *AASOR* 4 [1924] 135) correctly argues that "there is not a rarer corruption in the whole gamut of possibilities than of *resh* to *shin*." Furthermore, the road from Rimmon (Rammun) does not lead directly to Ai, as 10:27d–28 would require, but to Michmash. It is also an extremely difficult road. Rimmon, in any case, is an unlikely starting point for a military invasion.

[16]See for example O. Procksch, *Jesaia I*, 174–76; E. J. Kissane, *The Book of Isaiah*, 1. 127–32; V. Herntrich, *Der Prophet Jesaja*, 201–2; G. Fohrer, *Das Buch Jesaja*, 1. 162; H. Barth, *Die Jesaja-Worte in der Josiazeit*, 18, n. 7; H. Wildberger, *Jesaja 1–12*, 423–24; and R. E. Clements, *Isaiah 1–39*, 119.

[17]G. Fohrer (*Das Buch Jesaja*, 1. 162–63) and H. Wildberger (*Jesaja 1–12*, 425) suggest this conclusion. H. Barth (*Die Jesaja-Worte in der Josiazeit*, 64–69) and O. Kaiser (*Isaiah 1–12*, 247) argue instead that the verses are a redactional construction.

[18]J. Mauchline, *Isaiah 1–39. Introduction and Commentary* (London/New York: SCM/Macmillan, 1962) 125–26; and apparently G. Fohrer, *Das Buch Jesaja*, 1. 162–64.

leaders from further involvement in the current Ashdod revolt.[19] Third, the passage is purely visionary; that is, it does not describe an actual campaign, but only the imagined route of an Assyrian invasion yet to take place.[20]

Each of these proposals is problematic. Second Kings 18–19 indicate that the troops of Sennacherib approached Jerusalem from the southwest, that is, from the direction of Lachish in the Shephelah (18:14, 17; 19:9).[21] The route described in Isa 10:27d–32 can hardly be correlated with the campaign of this king. It is possible that the verses describe troops dispatched by Sargon II during the Ashdod revolt, but the interpretation is highly conjectural. There is no evidence, besides this text, for an Assyrian invasion of Judah from the north and the siege of Jerusalem in 715–711.[22] Finally, interpreting the verses as a visionary account does not square with the detail of the description (for example, "at Michmash he stowed his gear . . . [there—at the Geba pass] he bivouacked"), nor with the unusual route of the campaign.[23] Furthermore, the perfect verb forms that predominate in this passage probably refer to past action, and so reflect an actual march.

These difficulties cast doubt on the original assumption, namely, that 10:27d–32 describe an Assyrian campaign. If one examines the verses apart from the preceding speech and asks again which known military campaigns did approach Jerusalem from the north during Isaiah's times, an answer comes easily to mind: the Syrian-Israelite invasion of Judah in 734/733.[24] Second Kings 16:5 and Isa 7:6 firmly

---

[19]See O. Procksch, *Jesaia I*, 175; H. Wildberger, *Jesaja 1–12*, 427–28; compare R. E. Clements, *Isaiah 1–39*, 117–20.

[20]See L. Féderlin, "A propos d'Isaie 10:29–31," *RB* 3 (1906) 266; G. Dalman, "Palästinische Wege," 37–57; W. F. Albright, "Isa. X, 28–32," 134–40. G. B. Gray, *The Book of Isaiah*, 1. 206–7; J. Skinner, *Isaiah*, 92, 100–1; J. Steinmann, *Le Prophète Isaie*, 235–38; and E. Jenni, *Die politischen Voraussagen der Propheten* (ATANT 29; Zurich: Zwingli, 1956) 18, n. 13; compare D. L. Christensen, "The March of Conquest," 389–90, 395–99.

[21]For a discussion of the route and strategy of Sennacherib's campaign, see N. Na'aman, "Sennacherib's 'Letter to God,'" 25–39.

[22]A. K. Jenkins ("Isaiah's Fourteenth Year: A New Interpretation of 2 Kings xviii 13—xix 37," *VT* 26 (1976) 289–98) claims that the account(s) of Sennacherib's invasion in Second Kings 18–19 really relate to the time of Sargon II and the Ashdod revolt. His arguments for dissociating the material from Sennacherib's campaign, however, are not strong. In any case, the Kings text does not describe the advance of an enemy army from the north, as does Isa 10:27d–32.

[23]See especially H. Donner, *Israel unter den Völkern*, 32–33. The counter-arguments of H. Barth (*Die Jesaja-Worte in der Josiazeit*, 65–66) are not convincing.

[24]Recent proponents of this interpretation include especially H. Donner (*Israel unter den Völkern*, 30–38; "Der Feind aus dem Norden," 46–54), but also R. B. Y. Scott ("The Book of Isaiah," *IB* 5. 245–46), G. E. Wright (*Isaiah* [London: SCM, 1964] 48–49), N. K. Gottwald (*All the Kingdoms of the Earth*, 157), and B. S. Childs (*Isaiah and the Assyrian Crisis*, 61–62). According to J. Skinner (*Isaiah*, 100–1),

document the campaign, and 10:27d–32 contain nothing that seriously challenges this identification. Although the passage does not describe the invading army as a combination of separate forces, Syrian and Israelite, this may reflect the status of Rezin as the superior member of the alliance.[25] Isaiah 7:1 and 5 might similarly testify to the dominant role of the Syrian king.[26]

If 10:27d–32 refer to the Syro-Ephraimitic invasion of Judah, it is reasonable to restore Samaria at the beginning of the speech. From the capital city of the northern kingdom, the forces of Rezin and Pekah set out southward along the main watershed highway. At Bethel, the coalition army picked up the less traveled road leading through Michmash in order to avoid possible fighting at Mizpah, a Judean fortress (v 28). The invading troops crossed the Geba pass and then made camp, leaving for the next day an easy eight-mile march to Jerusalem (v 29a). Isaiah's speech seems to have been delivered at this point of the campaign. The prophet comments on the panic of towns still lying more or less in the invader's path (vv 29b–31), and anticipates his imminent arrival at Nob opposite Jerusalem (v 32).

Verse 32 is clearly the climax of the entire description: "Standing at Nob this very day, he will shake his fist at the mountain of the daughter of Zion, the hill of Jerusalem." The vivid image serves to underscore the arrogance of the enemy. It is Zion itself, Yahweh's own residence, that the Syrian-Israelite forces attack.

B. Verses 33–34

Verses 33–34 predict Yahweh's action against the arrogant enemy.[27] The announcement of judgment proceeds in metaphorical terms.

10:28–32 contain Isaiah's vision of a future Assyrian attack, but the prophet's memory of the Syrian-Israelite invasion during the reign of Ahaz might underlie the vision as its "psychological basis."

[25]Compare H. Wildberger, *Jesaja 1–12*, 427.

[26]R. E. Clements (*Isaiah 1–39*, 118) raises one other objection to the above interpretation, namely, that 10:27d–32, if understood in connection with the Syrian-Israelite alliance, conflict with Isaiah's low estimation of the alliance as a threat to Ahaz in 7:1–9 (17). The messages in the two texts are not in fact contradictory. In chapter 7, Isaiah says only that Rezin's plan to conquer Jerusalem and to replace Ahaz will not succeed, and that, if left alone, the western coalition would eventually collapse. The prophet does not claim that the invasion of Judah will not materialize. In chapter 10, he describes the invasion and the fright of Judean towns lying in its path, but he continues in vv 33–34 (taken by Clements as an editorial addition) to declare how Yahweh will defeat the attack.

[27]According to H. Wildberger (*Jesaja 1–12*, 425–28) and D. L. Christensen ("The March of Conquest," 390–99), the verses declare Yahweh's punishment of Jerusalem. This interpretation assumes that the preceding lines describe either

33. Behold the Lord Yahweh Sebaoth[28]
    is about to lop off the boughs with a crash!
    And the great in height is about to be cut down
    and the exalted will be brought low.
34. And the thickets of the forest will be cut down with iron
    and the Lebanon with its majesty will fall.

Many scholars deny these verses to Isaiah,[29] but there are good reasons for accepting their genuineness.[30] The divine title, *hāʾādôn yhwh ṣĕbāʾôt* ("the Lord Yahweh of Hosts"), is employed elsewhere by the prophet (see 1:24; 3:1; 10:16 and 23; and 19:4), and the vocabulary of the verses is generally in keeping with Isaiah's language.[31] The forest/tree metaphor appears in other speeches by the prophet (compare 1:29–30; 10:18–19; 14:8; and 18:5), and the basic theme of the passage—Yahweh's humbling of the proud—figures prominently in Isaiah's preaching (see for example 2:9–22). Most importantly, vv 33–34 provide the necessary continuation of vv 27d–32, which alone

---

the march of the Divine Warrior (Christensen) or the advance of an Assyrian army during the period of the Ashdod revolt (Wildberger). If vv 27d–32 relate to the Syrian-Israelite invasion of Judah in 734–733, vv 33–34 likely announce Yahweh's defense of Zion against the enemy. (See especially H. Donner, *Israel unter den Völkern*, 30–38.) The same promise, we argued earlier, is made in 7:5–9a, 8:8b–10, and 8:14–15.

[28]D. L. Christensen ("The March of Conquest," 390–92) changes *hāʾādôn* ("the Lord") to *ʾărôn* ("ark") on the assumptions that vv 27–34 describe Yahweh's march against Zion and that the route of his advance reflects the periodic ceremonial transport of the ark from Gilgal to Jerusalem. There is no textual evidence, however, for the emendation, and Christensen's interpretation of the passage is problematic on other grounds (see n. 12 above). H. Donner (*Israel unter den Völkern*, 30, 38) strikes *hāʾādôn* for metrical reasons, but the argument is not strong, given the different approaches to Hebrew prosody. (Compare Donner's reading of the meter, which involves counting accents, to the analysis of Christensen, who counts syllables.) The Septuagint, Targum, and Vulgate all agree with the *hāʾādôn yhwh ṣĕbāʾôt* of the Masoretic text.

[29]See for example B. Duhm, *Das Buch Jesaja*, 104; K. Marti, *Das Buch Jesaja*, 110; N. K. Gottwald, *All the Kingdoms of the Earth*, 158; G. Fohrer, *Das Buch Jesaja*, 1. 164; and R. E. Clements, *Isaiah 1–39*, 120–21.

[30]See P. Auvray, *Isaie 1–39* (Paris: J. Gabalda, 1972) 138–41; H. Wildberger, *Jesaja 1–12*, 425–28; and D. L. Christensen, "The March of Conquest," 390–91. All three view vv 33–34 as the continuation of Isaiah's words in the preceding lines. H. Donner (*Israel unter den Völkern*, 30–31, 38) takes v 33 as the conclusion of the speech, assigning then v 34 to a glossator. H. Barth (*Die Jesaja-Worte in der Josiazeit*, 57–64) regards only v 33a genuine to Isaiah, and connects the line with 11:1–5.

[31]Compare for example the use of *špl*, *gbh*, and *rûm* in 10:33 and 2:9–17. Even B. Duhm (*Das Buch Jesaja*, 104), who regarded the passage as an editorial addition, conceded that the verses employ many Isaianic expressions.

would have little significance.³² To the arrogant onslaught of the Syro-Ephraimitic enemy, Yahweh will respond with awesome power, bringing "the exalted low."³³

The prediction is rooted in the ancient Zion tradition. Celebrated in the cult, it rehearsed Yahweh's defeat of the nations who assemble against the holy city (see Pss 46, 48, and 76). In 10:33–34, Isaiah applies the tradition to actual circumstances: Yahweh will protect Zion against the attack of Rezin and Pekah (compare 8:8b–10).

The metaphor, however, derives from a different source. Cutting down the forest of Lebanon is a frequent boast of the Assyrian kings in their own inscriptions (see *ANET* 275 and 276) and one which Isaiah certainly knew (see Isa 14:8; compare 37:24). The prophet picks up the language and applies it to Yahweh in 10:33–34. The appropriation is apt, for the actual destruction of the Syro-Ephraimitic forces would come at the hands of the Assyrians, Yahweh's instrument of wrath (see 8:4–7 and 10:5).³⁴

C. Isaiah 11:1–12:6

The third and longest section of Isaiah's speech predicts a bright future for the Davidic regime and kingdom (11:1–12:6). The promise logically follows the preceding material, for here the prophet contrasts the glorious future of the attacked with the dismal fate of the attackers. (The conjunction at the beginning of 11:1, wĕyāṣāʾ, likely has an adversative meaning, "but" or "on the other hand.") Isaiah facilitates the transition by continuing the tree metaphor. Yahweh

---

³²R. E. Clements (*Isaiah 1–39*, 117–21) concludes just the opposite, namely, that 10:27d–32 can stand independently as a meaningful speech. His argument, however, assumes that the passage dates to the Ashdod revolt, envisions the attack of an Assyrian army, and intends to dissuade Hezekiah from further involvement in the anti-Assyrian movement. This interpretation was criticized above. If the passage relates to the Syro-Ephraimitic war, it demands continuation. G. B. Gray (*The Book of Isaiah*, 1. 207) makes the same point, but draws the wrong conclusion. The passage, he reasons, does not describe the Syrian-Israelite invasion because it ends with v 32, and so "threatens Jerusalem without an alleviating promise, and is therefore inconsistent with Isaiah's attitude at the time of the Syro-Ephraimitisch war (c. 7) . . . ." Verses 33–34 supply the "alleviating promise" which Gray correctly believes is required.

³³G. B. Gray (*The Book of Isaiah*, 1. 207) and, more recently, H. Barth (*Die Jesaja-Worte in der Josiazeit*, 68) emphasize the disparity between the straightforward description in vv 27d–32 and the figurative language in vv 33–34. The shift in style clearly occurs, but the change does not necessarily reflect the hand of a redactor. Gray also contends that the meter of the two sections is not the same. The prosody of the material is too uncertain to count much in the debate.

³⁴Compare B. S. Childs, *Isaiah and the Assyrian Crisis*, 62; and H. Barth, *Die Jesaja-Worte in der Josiazeit*, 68.

will cut down the "boughs," the "great in height," the "thickets of the forest," and the "Lebanon with its majesty" (10:33–34), but "the stock/stump of Jesse" will flourish (11:1).[35]

Verse 1 states the prophet's principal claim, namely, that the Davidic house will not only survive, but also will flourish. Interpreting the verse precisely is difficult, however, for the translation is not altogether certain. The RSV renders the Hebrew:

> There shall come forth a shoot
> from the stump of Jesse (*miggēzaʿ yīšāy*)
> and a branch will grow out of his roots.

If the translation, "stump of Jesse," is correct, the text seems to reflect the territorial reduction of the Davidic kingdom during Isaiah's time. This reduction, we have argued, occurred in the years preceding, but especially during, the Syro-Ephraimitic crisis, when much of Judah sided with Rezin and Pekah. In the fall of 734, Ahaz had absolute control of Jerusalem and its environs only. The prophet claims that this "stump" of a kingdom will not only survive, but also revive and prosper.

The translation "stump," however, is not the only possibility. The Hebrew *gēzaʿ* occurs two other times in the Hebrew Bible: Job 14:7 and Isa 40:24. In the first passage, the term clearly refers to the stump of a cut tree.[36] In Isa 40:24, however, *gēzaʿ* refers to the stalk of a recently planted tree, before branches have sprouted. It is thus possible to translate the phrase in 11:1, "the stock of Jesse," and to understand it as a simple reference to the Davidic house. (The Targum translates *gēzaʿ yīšāy* as "the sons of Jesse.") The text, then, would not emphasize the reduced state of the Davidic kingdom, only that the regime will prosper.

A third interpretation of 11:1 depends again on a particular translation. Reading against the late Masoretic accentuation of the verse, one might render the Hebrew: "But the shoot from the stock of Jesse will grow forth and the sapling from its roots will sprout" (emending

---

[35]Most scholars take 11:1 as the beginning of a new unit, but a few correctly observe the close link between the verse and 10:33 (34). See J. G. Herder, *Vom Geist der Ebräischen Poesie* (3d ed.; Leipzig: J. A. Barth, 1824) 206–8; O. Procksch, *Jesaia I*, 152; B. Childs, *Isaiah and the Assyrian Crisis*, 62; J. Schreiner, *Sion-Jerusalem*, 263; and H. Barth, *Die Jesaja-Worte in der Josiazeit*, 63–64. Most recently, W. Werner (*Eschatologische Texte*, 48–49) objects that 10:33 (34) and 11:1 do not in fact belong to the same "imagination field." The discrepancy which he emphasizes, however, is not as significant as he believes.

[36]T. Lescow ("Das Geburtsmotiv," 190) cites this use of *gēzaʿ* and assumes a similar meaning in Isa 11:1. The verse, he concludes, presupposes the fall of the Davidic dynasty.

yipreh to *yiprah*).³⁷ The subjects of the sentence, "the shoot from the stock of Jesse" and "the sapling from its roots" may reflect a traditional honorific title of the Davidic king. The prophet Zechariah applies a similar title (*ṣemaḥ*, "the Shoot") to Zerubbabel, the future Davidic king (Zech 3:8 and 6:12; compare Jer 23:5 and 33:15).³⁸ A close parallel appears also in an Assyrian inscription, in which Esarhaddon is called "precious branch of Baltil ... an enduring shoot" (*pir'u Baltil šūquru ... kisitti ṣâti; IA* 20. 17). Isaiah's point in 11:1 would again be that the Davidic kingship will flourish.

The differences among these interpretations are slight. Whichever one chooses, two points should be stressed. First, the text does not necessarily assume the fall of the Davidic kingdom and thus the events of 586, as many scholars have thought.³⁹ Verse 1 makes good sense as a reflection of the reduced state of the kingdom in 734. Second, the verse need not be seen as an expression of hope for a future messiah, but rather can be understood in reference to the contemporary Davidic monarch, Ahaz.⁴⁰ Other speeches of Isaiah, we have

---

³⁷The *yipreh* ("be fruitful") of the Masoretic text is not as parallel to the preceding *wĕyāṣā'* ("go forth") as one might expect. The readings of the Septuagint (*anabēsetai*), Targum (*ytrby*), Syriac (*nafraʿ*), and Vulgate (*ascendet*) seem to translate *yiprah*.

³⁸S. Mowinckel (*He That Cometh*, 161) and M. Fishbane (*Biblical Interpretation in Ancient Israel* [Oxford: Clarendon, 1985] 474, n. 36) note that "the righteous shoot" (*ṣemaḥ ṣedeq*) frequently appears as a royal title in Northwest Semitic inscriptions (see *KAI* 43. 10).

³⁹See for example K. Marti, *Das Buch Jesaja*, 110–13; G. B. Gray, *The Book of Isaiah*, 1. 213–14; T. Lescow, "Das Geburtsmotiv," 190; G. Fohrer, *Das Buch Jesaja*, 1. 166–67; R. E. Clements, *Isaiah 1–39*, 121–22; and W. Werner, *Eschatologische Texte*, 49–51. Compare H. Gressmann, *Der Messias*, 247; H. Wildberger, *Jesaja 1–12*, 443; and J. Jensen, *Isaiah 1–39* (Wilmington, Deleware: Michael Glazier, 1984) 131.

⁴⁰The vast majority of scholars assume the messianic character of 11:1–9. See for example B. Duhm, *Das Buch Jesaja*, 104–8; K. Marti, *Das Buch Jesaja*, 110–14; H. Gressmann, *Der Messias*, 246–48; S. Mowinckel, *He That Cometh*, 160, 175, 178–79, 182; G. von Rad, *Old Testament Theology*, 2. 169–70; T. Lescow, "Das Geburtsmotiv," 188–92; H. Wildberger, *Jesaja 1–12*, 436–62; J. Bright, *A History of Israel*, 291; W. Werner, *Eschatologische Texte*, 46–88; and R. Kilian, *Jesaja 1–39*, 10–12. For a detailed review of the messianic interpretations, see especially M. Rehm, *Der königliche Messias*, 185–234. Only a few commentators understand the passage in reference to a contemporary king, usually Hezekiah. See R. B. Y. Scott, "Isaiah," 247; A. S. Herbert, *The Book of the Prophet Isaiah. Chapters 1–39* (Cambridge: Cambridge University Press, 1973) 88–90; and compare M. B. Crook, "A Suggested Occasion for Isa. 9:2–7 and 11:1–9," *JBL* 68 (1949) 213–24.

Scholars who understand 11:1–9 as a messianic saying but still ascribe the verses to Isaiah usually assume that the eighth-century prophet rejected Ahaz (and later Hezekiah), and so looked forward to a future Davidic king. J. Bright (*A History of Israel*, 291) thus remarks: "In spite of his conviction that Ahaz had betrayed his office, perhaps because of it, Isaiah treasured the dynastic ideal as this

argued, reflect the same support and great expectations for Ahaz (see 7:4–9, 14–17a; 8:14; and especially 9:5–6). The context of 11:1, furthermore, might point in the same direction. If 10:27d–34 predict Yahweh's destruction of the Syrian-Israelite forces attacking Ahaz in Jerusalem, it is natural to see in the speech's continuation a promise of prosperity for this king's reign.

Verses 2–9 describe the Davidic king in detail. The portrait begins by reviewing his charismatic endowment: "And upon him will rest the spirit of Yahweh (*rûaḥ yhwh*), a spirit of wisdom and understanding (*rûaḥ ḥokmâ ûbînâ*), a spirit of counsel and might (*rûaḥ ʿēṣâ ûgĕbûrâ*), a spirit of knowledge and reverence for Yahweh" (*rûaḥ daʿat wĕyirʾat yhwh*; v 2).

The attributes derive largely from the traditional royal ideology.[41] First Samuel 16:13, for example, narrates how the spirit of Yahweh attached to David after his anointment, and remained upon him "from that day forward" (compare 1 Sam 11:6, 2 Sam 23:2, Zech 4:6, and Isa 61:1).[42] Extraordinary wisdom and understanding are attributed to David in 2 Sam 14:7, but especially to Solomon in First Kings 3 and 10:1–10 (compare Prov 8:14–16). The royal titles in Isa 9:5 include "Wonderful Counselor" and "Mighty God," indicating that counsel and might were also traditional qualities of the Davidic king. Finally, "fear" or reverence before Yahweh is mentioned as an essential characteristic of the Davidic ruler in 2 Sam 23:3b (compare Deut 17:19) and also in Isa 8:13, Isaiah's exhortation to the royal court.[43]

---

had been perpetrated in the cult (e.g. Ps. 72) and himself gave classic expression to the expectation of a scion of David's line who would fulfill that ideal (Isa. 9:2–7; 11:1–9), exhibiting the charismatic gifts supposedly reposing in the dynasty (ch. 11:2), establishing justice as Ahaz so notably had not, and bringing the national humiliation forever to an end." Compare the similar comments of G. von Rad (*Old Testament Theology*, 2. 170–71), O. H. Steck (*Friedensvorstellungen im alten Jerusalem* [Zurich: Theologischer Verlag, 1972] 57, n. 154), J. Jensen (*Isaiah 1–39*, 131), and H. Wildberger, *Jesaja 1–12*, 443.

The interpretation rests heavily on the negative portrayals of Ahaz in Second Kings 16 and Second Chronicles 28. Examined on their own, the speeches of Isaiah do not clearly denounce the king. We have in fact argued the opposite conclusion. The prophet not only put stock in the the Davidic tradition, but supported as well the present representative of the dynasty, Ahaz.

[41] See K. Seybold, *Das davidische Königtum*, 92–93; also S. Mowinckel, *He That Cometh*, 65–66 and 175.

[42] For a detailed review of the biblical texts in which the *rûaḥ yhwh/ʾĕlōhîm* attaches to different royal and prophetic figures, see W. Werner, *Eschatologische Texte*, 63–66. The evidence does not justify his late dating of Isa 11:1–9.

[43] According to W. Werner (*Eschatologische Texte*, 66, 74), the differentiation of Yahweh's spirit into various spiritual gifts (for example, wisdom, understanding, counsel, and so on) indicates a post-exilic date for the passage. The terminology, he claims further, has connections with late wisdom writing. Again, however, the

Verses 3b–4 describe the king's function as righteous judge, protector of the poor and weak against the "violent" (emending *ereṣ* to *ʾāriṣ* in v 4b) and wicked. The picture is again thoroughly traditional.[44] Psalm 72, for example, petitions God to grant the king "justice" and "righteousness" so that he may "judge thy people with righteousness and thy poor with justice . . . defend the cause of the poor of the people, give deliverance to the needy, and crush the oppressor" (vv 1–4; compare vv 12–14 and Jer 22:15–17). Similarly, Psalm 101, a composition possibly used in the coronation ceremony, presents the king's pledge to govern justly (compare 2 Sam 23:3b). The theme is not uniquely Israelite, but characteristic of the royal ideology in Mesopotamia and Syria as well (see *ANET* 149, 151, 164–65, and 178).

If Ahaz is the concrete referent of the description in 11:3b–4, as we propose, Isaiah appears to be applying to Ahaz the kind of high-flung court rhetoric that the Davidides themselves typically used to describe their rule. It is part of the royal ideal rehearsed in the enthronement ceremony, but no doubt on other occasions as well. Behind this stock language in Isaiah 11, however, there may also lie special edicts issued by Ahaz in 734/733, favoring the lower classes in order to gain their support at a time when the king's popularity outside the capital city and its immediate environs was low. The strategy of such edicts would correspond to the *mīšarum* of Mesopotamian kings, who, upon ascending to the throne or on other special occasions, granted concessions and favors to various constituencies (see the edict of Ammisaduqa; *ANET* 526–28).

The portrait of the Davidic king concludes by describing the paradisiacal peace that will accompany his reign (vv 6–9).[45] Animosity and conflict between weak and strong members of the animal kingdom and between the animal world and the human realm will end. "They shall not hurt or destroy on my holy mountain [Zion], for the

---

textual evidence that Werner cites (for example, Prov 1:1–4, 7a; 8:12–21; Exod 28:3, and Deut 34:9) does not justify his conclusion.

[44]See K. Seybold, *Das davidische Königtum*, 85–88, and 94.

[45]A number of scholars regard these verses as a secondary addition to 11:1–5; see for example W. H. Schmidt, "Die Ohnmacht des Messias," 23, especially n. 8; T. Lescow, "Das Geburtsmotiv," 188; H.-J. Hermisson, "Zukunftserwartung und Gegenwartskritik in der Verkündigung Jesajas," *EvT* 33 (1973) 58–61; H. Barth, *Die Jesaja-Worte in der Josiazeit*, 60–62; J. Vermeylen, *Du prophète Isaïe à l'apocalyptique*, 1. 275–76; and O. Kaiser, *Isaiah 1–12*, 253. Their primary argument is that the picture of peace within the animal kingdom is unrelated to the preceding description of the ideal king or messiah. For a rebuttal of this and other arguments, see especially H. Wildberger, *Jesaja 1–12*, 444; also M. Rehm, *Der königliche Messias*, 209–228; and K. Seybold, *Das davidische Königtum*, 94–96. W. Werner (*Eschatologische Texte*, 48) also makes a strong case for the integrity of 11:1–9, although he dates the whole to the post-exilic period.

land will be full of the knowledge of Yahweh, as the waters cover the sea" (v 9).[46]

Two ancient traditions underlie vv 6-9, namely, the Zion tradition and the royal ideology. The first typically depicts Jerusalem in ideal, even mythological, terms. Out of Yahweh's holy city the river of paradise flows (Ps 46:5). Divine blessing rests on Zion—provisions for her are abundant, even for the city's poor (Ps 132:15). Fraternal peace prevails in Zion (Ps 133:1), and there Yahweh has "commanded the blessing, life for evermore" (v 3).[47]

The royal ideology claims that peace, good fortune, and fertility accompany the reign of the righteous king. Thus Ps 72 prays for divine blessing on the king: "In his days may righteousness flourish and peace abound . . . . May there be abundance of grain in the land . . . may its fruit be like Lebanon and may people blossom forth from the cities like the grass of the field" (vv 7 and 16). This claim is also typical of royal ideology in the wider ancient Near East (see *ANET* 159, 164–65, 606, and 626–27).[48]

These examples demonstrate again how seriously Isaiah takes the Zion and Davidic traditions. The prophet picks up their language and applies it to the era he believes will surely dawn—the reign of Ahaz, after his deliverance from the Syro-Ephraimitic attack and his eventual liberation from the Assyrian "yoke."

Verse 10 describes the future prestige of the Davidic regime among the nations: "And in that day the root of Jesse that endures will become a signal for peoples; nations will seek him and his dwelling place will be glorious" (compare the NJPSV). The exalted standing of Zion is also stressed here. While "dwelling place" (*měnūḥâ*) refers to the whole of Palestine in Ps 95:11 and Deut 12:9, it refers specifically to Zion in Ps 132:8, part of the liturgy commemorating God's election of Zion and the Davidic house. If the same sense applies in Isa 11:10, the text looks forward to the pilgrimage of nations to Zion, there to "seek" the Davidic king.

Most scholars doubt Isaiah's authorship of 11:10.[49] Their arguments include the following. (a) "In that day" (*wěhāyâ bayyôm hahû'*)

---

[46]W. Werner (*Eschatologische Texte*, 69) argues that the description of peace in vv 6-9 takes up and changes the similar picture in Isa 65:25; see also O. Kaiser, *Isaiah 1–12*, 253. The direction of dependence, however, may be the reverse.

[47]For a detailed study of the conception of peace in the Jerusalemite cult tradition, see O. H. Steck, *Friedensvorstellungen*, 25–50.

[48]See H. Gressmann, *Der Messias*, 151; S. Mowinckel, *He That Cometh*, 27–56; and M. Rehm, *Der königliche Messias*, 218–28.

[49]See for example G. Fohrer, *Das Buch Jesaja*, 1. 170; J. Becker, *Isaias—der Prophet und sein Buch* (SBS 30; Stuttgart: Katholisches Bibelwerk, 1968) 62; J. Vollmer, *Geschichtliche Rückblicke und Motive in der Prophetie des Amos, Hosea und Jesaja* (BZAW 119; Berlin: Walter de Gruyter, 1971) 184; H. Barth, *Die Jesaja-Worte in der Josiazeit*, 59; J. Vermeylen, *Du prophète Isaïe à l'apocalyptique*, 1. 277; H. Wildberger,

is a redactional formula, marking v 10 apart as an addition. (b) Verse 10 functions as a bridge between the promises in vv 1–9 and vv 11–16. The wording of the verse shows the dependence of the writer on 11:1 and v 12. If 11:11–16 are post-exilic, as their reference to the ingathering of dispersed Judeans and Israelites would suggest, so must v 10 be similarly late. (c) Verse 1 refers to "the branch of his [Jesse's] roots" (*neṣer miššārāšāyw*), while v 10 mentions simply "the root of Jesse" (*šōreš yīšay*). The discrepancy reflects the hand of an editor, who was either careless in imitating the metaphor in v 1[50] or intent on reinterpreting the metaphor as a reference to the post-exilic community.[51] (d) In 11:1–9 the Davidic king is important for the salvation of Judah/Israel only, while in v 10 he has universal significance as a "signal" (*nēs*) or rallying point for the peoples and nations of the world. This second view of the king's role derives from a late editor, intent on expanding the prophet's meaning.

These arguments are not decisive. The expression, "in that day" (*wĕhāyâ bayyôm hahû'* or simply *bayyôm hahû'*) often introduces secondary additions to a prophetic speech, but it can also belong to the original words of the prophet (see Isa 2:11b, 17b, 20a; 3:18; 4:2; 7:18–25; and 10:20).[52] "Root of Jesse" varies only slightly from the phrasing in 11:1. The small difference hardly justifies seeing the careless hand of a late writer.[53] Verse 10 connects closely with vv 11–16, but the latter may also derive from Isaiah (see below). Most importantly, the exalted status of the king and of Jerusalem among the nations is part and parcel of the royal Zion tradition, upon which Isaiah relies so heavily. It is not in the least surprising that the prophet, after describing the reign of the king in vv 2–9 and alluding to Zion specifically in v 9, should in v 10 elaborate on the Zion tradition, predicting the pilgrimage of the nations to the holy city (see Isa 2:2–4; Pss 2:8–11;

Jesaja 1–12, 439, 458; O. Kaiser, *Isaiah 1–12*, 262–63; W. Werner, *Eschatologische Texte*, 164–65; and R. E. Clements, *Isaiah 1–39*, 125–26.

[50]So H. Wildberger, *Isaiah 1–12*, 437, 458.

[51]So J. Becker, *Isaias*, 62; H. Barth, *Die Jesaja-Worte in der Josiazeit*, 59; J. Vermeylen, *Du prophète Isaïe à l'apocalyptique*, 1. 277; and R. E. Clements, *Isaiah 1–39*, 125.

[52]The genuinness of the formula(s) in these and other passages has, of course, been questioned, but often the argument is little more than the assumption that "in that day" is a redactor's device. If the content and language of the passages allow one to understand the verses as extensions of Isaiah's own thought, there is no reason to discount them as editorial additions.

[53]As in 11:1, v 10 refers to the Davidic monarchy, not a future messiah or the post-exilic community (see E. J. Kissane, *The Book of Isaiah*, 1. 126). Compare the analyses of J. Becker, H. Barth, J. Vermeylen, and R. E. Clements listed in n. 51 above).

18:45–46; 68:29–33; 72:8–11; compare Zech 8:22–23). There they will "seek (*yidrōšû*) the root of Jesse."⁵⁴

Verses 11–16 anticipate the reunion of Judah and Israel and their domination over the surrounding nations. The material divides roughly into four parts: the ingathering of dispersed Judeans and Israelites by Yahweh (vv 11–12); the reconciliation between Judah and Israel (v 13); the defeat and/or subjugation of the Philistines, "children of the east," Edomites, Moabites, and Ammonites (v 14); and Yahweh's guiding of the "remnant of his people" out of Assyria (vv 15–16). The first and last parts correspond in theme, forming then a kind of inclusio.

Despite the nearly unanimous agreement among scholars that this material does not derive from Isaiah,⁵⁵ only two lines should be ascribed to a later writer: v 11b (from "Egypt" onward) and v 15aa ("And Yahweh will destroy the tongue of the sea of Egypt"). The first addition presumably arose under the influence of v 12b, which speaks of "the four corners of the earth" from which the dispersed will return.⁵⁶ The second expansion was probably prompted by the allusion in v 16b (there in the form of a comparison) to the exodus from Egypt, and also by the exodus imagery applied to Assyria in v 15ab-b.⁵⁷ The remainder of the verses speaks only of a return from Assyria and from the "four corners of the earth," over which Assyr-

---

⁵⁴The verb *drš* generally means "resort to, consult, inquire of." It can also have a technical meaning, "to ask for an oracle." In 11:10, Isaiah probably thinks of the Davidic monarch as the adjudicator of international disputes. The picture is similar to the pilgrimage of nations described in 2:2–4. In that text, however, Yahweh judges between the nations; in 11:10, the nations "consult" his anointed king for legal decisions.

⁵⁵See for example H. Barth, *Die Jesaja-Worte in der Josiazeit*, 58; H. Wildberger, *Jesaja 1–12*, 466–67; W. Werner, *Eschatologische Texte*, 102–9; and R. E. Clements, *Isaiah 1–39*, 125–27. (E. J. Kissane [*The Book of Isaiah*, 1. 126–27] is one of the few commentators who takes at least vv 13–14 as genuine to the eighth-century prophet.) The major arguments for dating the material to the post-exilic period include the following. (a) The redactional formula, *wĕhāyâ bayyôm hahûʾ*, marks a new beginning in v 11. (b) References to the "remnant" of Yahweh's people in v 11 and to the "dispersed" of Israel and Judah in v 12 assume the events of the exile in 586. (c) The enmity between "Israel" and "Judah" (v 13) was typical of conditions in Palestine during the post-exilic period. (d) The hope for the reunion of the northern and southern kingdoms (v 13) is characteristic of prophetic eschatology from the time of Ezekiel onward. (e) Verse 16 alludes to the exodus tradition, but Isaiah never uses this tradition in his preaching. The references to a second exodus and to the "highway" on which the dispersed will return are similar to, if not dependent on, the preaching of Deutero-Isaiah. For a rebuttal to these arguments, see Kissane's discussion and the analysis below.

⁵⁶See O. Procksch, *Jesaia I*, 156–59; and H. Wildberger, *Jesaja 1–12*, 465.

⁵⁷See H. Wildberger, *Jesaja 1–12*, 465–66. The "River" in v 15ab refers to the Euphrates (compare 8:7).

ian kings typically claimed to rule (see *ANET* 274, 276, 281, and 289). This and other themes in the material can be understood as part of Isaiah's message during the Syro-Ephraimitic crisis.

The gathering of the dispersed is a thoroughly traditional theme.[58] In ancient Mesopotamia, it became an essential element of the royal ideology. As the righteous ruler commissioned by the gods for the protection of the people, the king is to restore the scattered and exiled to their native lands.[59] The motif came to figure prominently also in the prophecies of salvation in Israel and Judah. This was true not only of the exilic and post-exilic periods (see for example Ezek 3:27 and Isa 56:8), but possibly of the pre-exilic era also—that is, if one is willing to entertain the authenticity of texts like Mic 2:12, 4:6, and Jer 30:11.[60]

In Isa 11:11–16, however, the theme is perhaps more than stock prophetic rhetoric. At an earlier point in the Syro-Ephraimitic crisis, Isaiah had denounced both the Israelites and the Judeans, and had predicted their harsh punishment by the Assyrians (see 7:18–20; 8:4 and 7). He may have expected at least limited deportations in accordance with the general Assyrian policy toward rebellious peoples. In Isaiah 11, the prophet possibly assumes this exile proleptically, and proceeds to look beyond it to a brighter future. Yahweh will restore the "remnant of his people" (*šĕ'ār ʿammô*) to their place,[61] and there they will prosper under the rule of the Davidic king. Isaiah describes the return from exile by the analogy of the exodus: through the midst of the River (Euphrates), they will cross dryshod and will return on a broad secure highway (vv 15ab–16). (For the later development of this theme by Deutero-Isaiah, see 40:3–5.)

Associated with Yahweh's gathering of the dispersed are the reconciliation between Judah and Israel (v 13) and their joint domination of the surrounding nations (v 14). These predictions are in keeping with what we would expect from Isaiah. The prophet had witnessed rising tensions between the two countries since the days of Menahem

---

[58]For a good discussion of the theme in biblical and Near Eastern literature, see G. Widengren, "Yahweh's Gathering of the Dispersed," in *In the Shelter of Elyon: Essays on Ancient Palestinian Life and Literature in Honor of G. W. Ahlström* (eds. W. B. Barrick and J. R. Spencer; Sheffield: JSOT Press, 1984), 227–45.

[59]Widengren ("Yahweh's Gathering," 234–37) reviews numerous examples of the idea from Assyria and Babylonia, and highlights the formulaic language which accompanies it. The stereotypical vocabulary includes *sapaḫu* ("scatter"), *puḫḫuru* ("gather"), and *turru ašrišu* ("restore to its place").

[60]See again G. Widengren, "Yahweh's Gathering," 227–34, 237–41. Like the Mesopotamian texts, the biblical passages express the idea with certain fixed expressions, for example, *qbṣ* ("gather"), *'sp* ("assemble"), *hēpîṣ* ("scatter"), *nidḫê yiśrā'ēl* ("the dispersed of Israel"), and *hēšîb šĕbût* ("restore").

[61]For the role of the remnant motif in Isaiah's preaching, see also 7:3 and 10:20–23.

(see 9:20) and open conflict between their leaders during the Syro-Ephraimitic crisis. Isaiah was thoroughly familiar with the "jealousy of Israel" and the "hostility of Judah." Furthermore, during the crisis, Isaiah had expressed the hope for the reunion of the northern and southern kingdoms under Davidic rule (7:17a). The same expectation appears in chapter 11. Relying on traditional ideas about the extent of the Davidic state, Isaiah suggests that the revived kingdom will also dominate Edom, Moab, Ammon, Philistia, and "the children of the east" (probably desert tribes). He thus holds out to Ahaz the hope for a return of the monarchy's greatest glory.

The speech concludes with a description of the future celebration by the king and the people (12:1–6).[62] In these verses, the prophet appears to be quoting traditional material from hymnic and/or thanksgiving psalms (vv 1–2 and vv 4–6).[63] His special contribution lies in the way he presents the psalm excerpts as prophecy (wĕʾāmartā

---

[62]Practically all commentators attribute 12:1–6 to a late redactor (or redactors), who supposedly appended the verses as an epilogue to Isaiah 1–11. See for example B. Duhm, *Das Buch Jesaja*, 11; G. Fohrer, *Das Buch Jesaja*, 1. 172–75; H. Wildberger, *Jesaja 1–12*, 479–80; R. E. Clements, *Isaiah 1–39*, 127–29; and J. Jensen, *Isaiah 1–39*, 36–37. This understanding is so widespread that recent analyses simply assume it as the starting point for studying further the editorial function of the passage within the book of Isaiah. See for example P. R. Ackroyd, "Isaiah I–XII," 36–40; and G. T. Sheppard, "The Canonical Context of Isaiah 1–39," 196–98.

The arguments against the Isaianic authorship of 12:1–6 are by no means conclusive. The fact, for example, that the verses quote or allude to other hymns in the Hebrew Bible hardly points to the hand of an editor. The eighth-century prophet could use traditional material just as easily as an editor might. (This suggestion is plausible especially in light of the material's probable origin in the Jerusalem cult.) Themes and words in 12:1–6 certainly have parallels elsewhere in chapters 1–11, but these parallels may suggest only that the several texts in question all derive from Isaiah. Isaiah 12:1–6 does presuppose the message of hope in 11:11–16, as Clements correctly observes. Such dependence, however, is precisely what one would expect to see in sequential parts of a single speech. Wildberger objects that the vagueness of 12:1–6 contrasts with the concrete pictures of salvation in genuinely Isaianic passages (for example, 2:2–4, 9:1–6, and 11:1–9). The picture in 12:1–6 may be more concrete than Wildberger supposes, describing the new year festival that the prophet's audience will celebrate in the future. In any case, the preceding parts of the speech (10:27d–11:16) already depict the future salvation in detailed terms. Other reasons against ascribing 12:1–6 to Isaiah are equally inconclusive.

[63]If 2:2–5 derive from Isaiah, this passage presents an interesting analogue to the prophet's use of traditional material in 12:1–6. (For a detailed discussion of the authorship of 2:2–5, see H. Wildberger, *Jesaja 1–12*, 76–81.) In 2:2–4, Isaiah recites an old confession (probably part of a Zion hymn) regarding the status and role of the ideal Zion. (Compare the modification of the same confession in Mic 4:1–4.) In v 5, the prophet urges his Jerusalemite audience to live up to the ideal image of the city.

*bayyôm hahû*ʾ, v 1aa; *waʾămartem bayyôm hahûʾ*, v 4aa).⁶⁴ He sets them forth as songs to be sung "in that day," after Yahweh, "the Holy One of Israel" dwelling in Zion (v 6), has defeated the Syro-Ephraimitic enemy and all other hostile forces.⁶⁵ This future orientation is reinforced by the prophet's promise in v 3. The line likely refers to part of the traditional new year festival, which Isaiah's audience would celebrate in the future (see below).

Verses 1–6 abound with stylistic variations and present a mixture of formal elements.⁶⁶ Particularly conspicuous is the change from singular address in v 1 (*wĕʾāmartā*) to plural address in vv 3–4 (*ûśĕʾabtem . . . waʾămartem*). This shift and other apparent inconsistencies may be adequately explained by assuming a change in the addressee. In vv 1–2, the prophet addresses the king specifically, quoting to him part of a psalm that he will sing "in that day." In vv 3–6, Isaiah turns to his larger Jerusalemite audience.⁶⁷ The address here begins with a promise (v 3) and then quotes a traditional hymn that the audience will recite "in that day" (vv 4–6).⁶⁸

---

⁶⁴F. Crüsemann (*Hymnus und Danklied in Israel*, 50–56) and H. Wildberger (*Jesaja 1–12*, 478, 480) see the expressions as imitations of the formulaic introduction to instructions for heralds. W. Werner (*Eschatologische Texte*, 166) correctly remarks, however, that the genre distinction is of little help in understanding 12:1–6, for the formulas here do not introduce the calls of heralds.

⁶⁵Compare 26:1–6, which similarly presents a song to be recited "in that day." A majority of scholars has long denied the passage, along with the whole of chapters 24–27, to Isaiah, but dissident voices have not gone unheard (see for example J. Mauchline, *Isaiah 1–39*, 23–24). For a review of the issue and an overview of scholarship, see G. W. Anderson, "Isaiah XXIV–XXVII Reconsidered," *VTSup* 9 (1963) 118–26. Much of Isaiah 24–27, including 26:1–6, may derive from the eighth-century prophet. See J. H. Hayes and S. A. Irvine, *Isaiah*, 294–320.

⁶⁶Many commentators make the same observation, and so speak of the "mosaic" character of 12:1–6. (See for example B. Duhm, *Das Buch Jesaja*, 111; J. Steinmann, *Le Prophète Isaïe*, 237; O. Kaiser, *Isaiah 1–12*, 268–72; and H. Wildberger, *Jesaja 1–12*, 478–80; but compare L. Alonso Schökel, "Is. 12: De duabus methodis pericopam explicandi," *VD* 34 [1956] 154–60.) However, they attribute the combination of the different elements to a late editor (or editors). It is just as possible that the eighth-century prophet assembled the material out of traditional pieces and addressed them to different members of his audience (see below).

⁶⁷For this division of the passage, see B. Duhm, *Das Buch Jesaja*, 111; A. S. Herbert, *Isaiah 1–39*, 93; also the RSV and NJPSV; and compare P. R. Ackroyd, "Isaiah I–XII," 36. Others take vv 1–3 as a sub-unit; see for example J. Mauchline, *Isaiah 1–39*, 132–33; G. Fohrer, *Das Buch Jesaja*, 1. 172–73; H. Wildberger, *Jesaja 1–12*, 478–79; and W. Werner, *Eschatologische Texte*, 165–66; also the NEB. This interpretation rests largely on the parallel phrasing of vv 1aa and 4aa: "And you will say on that day . . . ." Verse 3, however, does not fit formally with the individual thanksgiving psalm in vv 1–2. The plural verb forms of v 3 link it with what follows.

⁶⁸The feminine singular imperatives and pronoun in v 6 (*ṣahălî wārōnnî, bĕqirbēk*) address the "inhabitant of Zion" (*yôšebet ṣîyôn*). The latter is probably a

The psalm fragment quoted to the king (vv 1–2) probably derives from a traditional song of individual thanksgiving.[69] In the introduction, the psalmist speaks directly to Yahweh: "I will give thanks to you, O Yahweh." The reason for thanksgiving then follows: "for you had been angry with me, but your anger turned away and you comforted me."[70] In v 2, the psalmist turns to the larger congregation and declares his trust in Yahweh as the God of his salvation.[71]

A closer look at the psalm fragment reveals a possible connection with royal and/or enthronement psalms.[72] The psalmist declares in v 2b: "For Yahweh is my strength and my song and he has become my salvation." The line has a close parallel in Ps 118:14 (compare v 21). This text appears, at first glance, to be part of a royal thanksgiving for deliverance in battle (see vv 10–12). The Mishnah, however, relates Psalm 118 to the autumnal Feast of Tabernacles (*Sukkah* 4:5) and thus to the festival of Yahweh's enthronement.[73] That Isaiah would quote, in 12:1–2, part of a similar liturgy accords well with v 3, where the prophet refers explicitly to part of the new year ritual (see below).[74] Whatever the precise genre of Psalm 118 may be, the "I" in v 14, as well as in Isa 12:1–2, is likely the king.[75]

---

collective expression for all the residents of Jerusalem. H. Wildberger (*Jesaja 1–12*, 477–78) correctly translates the vocative, "you citizens of Zion" (*du Zionsbürgershaft*). The verse thus continues Isaiah's words to his Jerusalemite audience in vv 3–5. Compare P. R. Ackroyd, "Isaiah I–XII," 36.

[69]See J. Mauchline, *Isaiah 1–39*, 132; A. S. Herbert, *Isaiah 1–39*; 93; W. Werner, *Eschatologische Texte*, 166; R. E. Clements, *Isaiah 1–39*, 128; H. Wildberger, *Jesaja 1–12*, 478. G. Fohrer (*Das Buch Jesaja*, 1. 173) describes the verses as an "eschatological thanksgiving song." The label is misleading, however, insofar as it is meant to refer to the thanksgiving which the "end"-community (*die endzeitliche Gemeinde*) will sing in the distant future.

[70]Verse 1b in the Masoretic text resembles the style of a lament: *yāšōb ʾappěkā ûtěnaḥămēnî* ("May your anger turn away and may you comfort me"). After the opening in 12:1a, one would expect instead a declarative statement about the end of Yahweh's wrath. The tension is removed by emending *yāšōb* and *ûtěnaḥămēnî* to *wayyāšob* and *wattěnaḥămēnî* respectively. The Septuagint, Syriac, and Vulgate support these changes, and most modern translations seem to assume them (see the RSV, JB, NEB, NIV, and NJPSV). Compare however H. Wildberger, *Jesaja 1–12*, 477–78.

[71]Such confessions typically appear in psalms of lament, but they are not out of place in songs of thanksgiving. The experience of deliverance naturally gives rise to expressions of confidence. See S. Mowinckel, *Psalms in Israel's Worship*, 2. 41.

[72]See S. Mowinckel, *Psalms in Israel's Worship*, 1. 123, n. 58.

[73]See S. Mowinckel, *Psalms in Israel's Worship*, 1. 120; 123, n. 58; and 131; also O. Kaiser, *Isaiah 1–12*, 271–72. Note the allusion to a temple procession in vv 19–20 and the reference to a special ritual at the altar in v 27.

[74]Note that v 2b also appears in Exod 15:2, part of the so-called Song of the Sea, which also shows some similarities to enthronement psalms, especially in v 18.

[75]According to O. Kaiser (*Isaiah 1–12*, 270), the transition to the plural address in 12:3–5 shows that the preceding "I" stands for the community. He is hard-

In v 3, the prophet turns from the king and addresses the larger Jerusalemite audience: "And you will draw water with rejoicing from the wells of salvation." According to the Mishnah, the rite alluded to here was performed on the night between the sixth and seventh days of the Feast of Tabernacles. Water from Siloam was carried in stately procession to the Temple courtyard, where the high priest poured it on the altar, thereby ensuring abundant rain in the upcoming year (*Sukkah* 4:9–10). In 12:3, the prophet promises the residents of Jerusalem that they will perform this ritual in the future, just as they have in past years.[76] The implication of the prediction is clear: the prophet's audience will survive the present crisis and be able to celebrate the new year festival again and to enjoy the blessings it brings upon themselves and their king.

Isaiah proceeds in vv 4–6 to quote to his audience a song that they will all sing "in that day." The style of the verses is that of the "imperative" hymn,[77] and the content is thoroughly traditional. The original setting of the psalm is hard to determine, but its connection with the new year festival is a plausible assumption, that is, if vv 1–3 relate to this same occasion. The concluding reference to God's dwelling in Zion (v 6) serves as a fitting end to the prophet's entire speech. The inhabitants of Jerusalem will survive the Syro-Ephraimitic attack, and so will be able to declare "in that day" that the protecting presence of Yahweh is in their midst.

D. Summary

The preceding analysis understood Isa 10:27d–12:6 as one long address by the eighth-century prophet, dating shortly before the Syrian-Israelite siege of Jerusalem. The several parts of the speech combine to produce an impressive picture of the city's deliverance and of the glorious future that awaits Zion and the Davidic house. The message of the prophet includes the following points.

---

pressed then to explain the variation: "We cannot rule out the possibility that the choice of the first person singular in vv. 1 and 2 has been affected by the fact that in Israel only the individual thanksgiving was a special genre, while the role of the popular thanksgiving was played by the hymn in praise of God." The argument is not convincing, for one would think that that the redactor whom Kaiser envisions could easily have found a way to avoid the confusion. The change from the "I"-forms to the plural "you"-forms, however, makes sense as a reflection of Isaiah's changing focus, from what the king specifically will say (vv 1–2) to what the larger audience will do and say "in that day" (vv 3–6).

[76] According to W. Werner (*Eschatologische Texte*, 166), v 3 predicts the eschatological reversal of the situation described in Isa 8:6. The connection between the two texts, however, seems far-fetched.

[77] See F. Crüsemann, *Hymnus und Danklied in Israel*, 55–56.

(1) The forces of Rezin and Pekah have invaded Judah and will besiege Jerusalem "this very day" (10:27d–32). The attack against Zion, Yahweh's own residence, illustrates the arrogance of the enemy.

(2) The siege will fail, for Yahweh will defend the city and destroy the attackers (vv 33–34). The ancient tradition about the divine protection of Zion is no empty claim, but holds true in the actual circumstances of the Syro-Ephraimitic war.

(3) In contrast to the defeat of Syria and Israel, the Davidic house and kingdom will flourish (11:1–10). After Ahaz's deliverance from the Syrian-Israelite forces and his eventual liberation from Assyrian domination, the ideal claims of the Zion and Davidic traditions will be realized. Such claims include the wise and just rule of the Davidic king (vv 2–5), the peace of his reign (vv 6–9), and the exalted status of the king and Zion among the nations of the world (v 10).

(4) The Assyrians may soon deport some Israelites and Judeans for their involvement in the rebellion, but Yahweh will eventually return the exiles (vv 11–12 and 15–16). Furthermore, the northern and southern kingdoms will reunite under Davidic rule, and together they will dominate the surrounding peoples and states (vv 13–14). The future will thus bring a restoration of the Davidic monarchy's greatest glory.

(5) "In that day," the Jerusalemites and their king will celebrate the new year festival, giving thanks to Yahweh for their deliverance from the present crisis and for their subsequent good fortune (12:1–6).

PART III

CONCLUSION

CHAPTER ELEVEN

CONCLUSION

This study began with a statement about the importance of historical reconstruction for understanding the roles of the prophets in the politics of their day. The work has sought to demonstrate the truth of this claim in the case of Isaiah, Ahaz, and the Syro-Ephraimitic crisis. The analysis of the relevant Assyrian and biblical texts allows for a new understanding of the episode, particularly as it concerns the isolationist policies and actions of Ahaz, and the polarized relations between the king and most Judeans at the time. Our proposed reconstruction permits a radical reappraisal of Isaiah's political posture during the war, and of his relations to Ahaz especially.

From the seminal studies of K. Budde to recent works on Isaiah and the Syro-Ephraimitic crisis, scholarship has generally seen the prophet and Ahaz as antagonists. Isaiah supposedly rejected the king for soliciting Assyrian aid against the Syrian-Israelite invasion, and so for showing a lack of faith in the protection of Yahweh. The opposition between the king and prophet has been a central assumption in studies of the Immanuel saying, the prophet's use of traditions, the eschatology of his preaching, the interpretation of the so-called *Denkschrift*, and so on.

A major concern of this dissertation was to emphasize that the above picture of the king and prophet does not derive directly from the narratives and speeches in Isaiah. It depends, rather, on the correlation of the prophetic material with the negative deuteronomistic presentation of Ahaz's reign in Second Kings 16, particularly the notice there on his request for Assyrian aid. This correlation, we argued, has been made far too quickly, with too little thought as to the reliability of the Kings report.

Once one scrutinizes the Kings text closely, its tendentious character becomes apparent, and the idea of the king's appeal looks increasingly like a deuteronomistic fiction. Scholars have taken the appeal as the factual background of Isaiah's speeches, arguing indeed that, without a knowledge of the Assyrian alliance, the prophetic material would remain "a sealed book." This study has argued the opposite. The report of the appeal in Second Kings 16 has done more to obscure the political posture of Isaiah than any other factor in the exegesis of his speeches.

Reassessing the prophet's message, especially as it relates to Ahaz, involved rethinking the issues and events of the Syro-Ephraimitic crisis, and the political dynamics that obtained during the war. Our examination of the Assyrian and biblical texts makes the following picture plausible.

(1) The Syro-Ephraimitic crisis was not simply an inner-Palestinian conflict. The episode related directly to a broader anti-Assyrian movement in the southwestern part of the Assyrian empire. Rezin of Damascus led the movement and other members of the coalition included Hiram of Tyre, Mitinti of Ashkelon, Hanno of Gaza, Pekah of Israel, Samsi queen of the Arabs, probably the Edomites, and perhaps the Ammonites, Moabites, and Me'unites. Egypt and/or Ethiopia probably supported the revolt, at least diplomatically.

(2) The anti-Assyrian coalition did not arise suddenly in 734/733, but had been several years in the making. Rezin and his allies had been pressuring Israel and Judah to join the alliance as early as the reigns of Menahem and Jotham, but the Israelite and Judean kings persistently refused to participate. They apparently chose instead to bear the burden, and rely on the protection, of Assyrian vassalage. As late as 734/733, the coalition was still incomplete, for it still did not include Judah.

(3) Prior to 734, Pekah had been ruling in Transjordan as a Syrian stooge. With his coup in Samaria in Tishri 734, Israel joined the western coalition led by Rezin. Ahaz of Judah, however, held to a neutralist course. The decision marked the first time in several decades that a Judean king did not follow the lead of his Israelite superior. Ahaz's policy amounted to an assertion of Davidic/Judean independence, and Pekah and Rezin must have denounced the king as a renegade vassal.

(4) On the eve of the Syro-Ephraimitic crisis, Judean society was politically polarized. On the one hand, the Davidic house elected to hold out against the overtures and pressures of the western coalition. In this decision, the royal court was probably supported by the residents of Jerusalem and perhaps the military. On the other hand, most Judeans ("this people," in Isaiah's language) favored Rezin and Pekah, and opposed the foreign policy of their own Davidic leadership. Many southerners apparently shared the view of the Syrian and Israelite kings, accusing Ahaz of "conspiracy" or treason against his

Israelite superior. They probably supported Rezin's plan to install a new regime in Jerusalem.

(5) The Syrian-Israelite attack on Jerusalem took place sometime during the last months of 734 or at the beginning of 733. The siege of the capital city aimed at replacing Ahaz with a certain "ben Tabe'al." The identity of this figure as a Tyrian prince ensured that he would cooperate with the coalition and so bring Judah into the alliance against Assyria.

(6) Rezin and Pekah abandoned the siege, once the Assyrian army marched westward to Philistia in the winter of 733. Second Kings 16 attributes the campaign to the special appeal and payment of Ahaz, but the claim is unlikely historical. The Assyrians were motivated by other concerns—crushing insurrection in the west; securing Syria and Palestine against Egyptian and/or Ethiopian meddling; extending and tightening Assyria's control of the region's overland and sea trade. The Judean king paid tribute to Tiglathpileser after the Assyrians had invaded Palestine.

(7) With the Assyrian campaign to Philistia, the western coalition began to collapse. The major partners of the alliance (Syria, Tyre, Israel, Ashkelon, and Samsi, queen of the Arabs) managed to regroup, however, and offered Assyria staunch resistance for two more years. Samsi and Hiram of Tyre eventually submitted to Tiglathpileser and so managed to retain their thrones. Mitinti of Ashkelon was apparently assassinated by his own subjects and replaced by his son, Rukiptu, who accepted Assyrian vassalage. After two years of fighting Rezin, the Assyrians captured Damascus, executed Rezin, and incorporated the Syrian kingdom into the Assyrian provincial system. Hoshea of Israel led a revolt against Pekah in 732/731, probably with Assyrian approval. In 731/730, he took Samaria, executed Pekah, and sent tribute to Tiglathpileser in southern Babylonia.

Against the background of the Syro-Ephraimitic crisis as understood above, the dissertation reinterpreted the Isaianic literature relating to the war. This material, we argued, is far more extensive than most scholars suppose. It includes the narrative in 7:1–17; the string of sayings in 7:18–20, 23–25; a prophetic memoir in 8:1–20, compiled by Isaiah using earlier speeches; and several long addresses of the prophet in 8:21–9:6, 9:7–10:4, 10:5–27c, and 10:27d–12:6. The narrative in chapter 7 exhibits, in places, a certain legendary character and even a degree of bias against Ahaz. This bias, however, is far less extreme than the negative polemic of the deuteronomistic editors and the Chronicler in Second Kings 16 and Second Chronicles 28. The narrative still provides details of the circumstances that actually obtained during the Syro-Ephraimitic crisis, and the historian can recover from the text a fairly reliable picture of the prophet's preaching at the time. The speeches that follow to the end of chapter 12 all derive from the same general period, and together they present a trustworthy and seemingly complete picture of Isaiah's posture during the war.

The analysis of Isaiah 7–12 argued that, on the eve of the Syro-Ephraimitic crisis, the main policy decision confronting Ahaz was whether to capitulate to the demands of Rezin, Pekah, and most Judeans, and to join the coalition against Assyria. Despite some vacillation and insecurity on the issue at the height of the crisis, the Judean king held to a neutralist course. In this decision, he was strongly supported by Isaiah. The prophet applauded Ahaz's break with Israel and urged the king to stand firm. Throughout the course of the war, Isaiah remained a faithful legitimist of the Davidic regime and the most fervent proponent of its isolationist policy. His support for Ahaz was largely responsible for the king's successful assertion of Davidic independence from the leadership in Samaria.

The specific preaching of Isaiah during the crisis elaborated several distinct but related themes. (1) Yahweh will abide by his ancient promises to protect Zion against enemy attacks and to maintain the throne of the Davidic king. (2) Syria, Israel, and the rest of the western coalition will meet with disaster, for Yahweh will punish them by means of the Assyrians. (3) The Judean population has incurred Yahweh's anger by siding with Rezin and Pekah. They too will suffer harsh treatment by the Assyrians. (4) Ahaz and the royal court should revere Yahweh as their true sovereign, not Pekah of Israel. Such reverence involves following the advice of Isaiah, Yahweh's prophet, and holding out against the coalition. If the Davidides do not stand firm, they will not survive, for the Assyrians will remove them from power. (5) While the Assyrian king will execute Yahweh's punishment, he will arrogantly transgress his divinely given task and ascribe his military achievements to his own power and initiative. For a time, Ahaz and Jerusalem will have to bear the "yoke" of Assyrian vassalage, but Yahweh will eventually break the power of Assyria, destroy its land, and liberate Zion. (6) When the day of liberation comes, Israel and Judah will reunite under the rule of the Davidic house; together they will regain their dominance over the surrounding nations; and they will enjoy the peace and justice that ideally accompany the reign of the Davidic king.

These messages combine in the service of a single goal, namely, to persuade Ahaz to stand confidently on the belief of Yahweh's protection, and so to maintain a neutralist position during the Syro-Ephraimitic crisis. The rhetorical force of Isaiah's preaching is evidenced by the fact that the Davidic king followed his advice, despite the tremendous pressure on Ahaz to do otherwise.

Prophets of ancient Israel and Judah are often pictured as figures who opposed the kings of their day, challenged the easy confidence of their society in national traditions of salvation, and reinterpreted those traditions to proclaim judgment. The characterization may fit some prophets, but it does not cover all the prophets. This, of course, has always been acknowledged, but the fact is often forgotten in the actual treatment of those figures considered "great" prophets. Some "great" prophets had the task of holding up to their audiences age-old traditions of divine favor and protection, urging them to believe in those traditions and to conduct the affairs of their lives in light of them, despite the apparent risks. Isaiah was a prophet of this kind, at least during the Syro-Ephraimitic crisis. In a time of great danger to Ahaz and Jerusalem, Isaiah emphasized Yahweh's commitment to the Davidic king and Zion and exhorted them to take the divine promises seriously.

BIBLIOGRAPHY

Abel, F.-M. *Geògraphie de la Palestine*. 2 vols. Paris: J. Gabalda, 1933, 1938.
Ackroyd, P. R. "History and Theology in the Writings of the Chronicler," *CTM* 38 (1967) 501–15.
_____. "Historians and Prophets," *SEÅ* 33 (1968) 18–54.
_____. "The Theology of the Chronicler," *LTQ* 8 (1973) 101–16.
_____. "Isaiah." In *The Interpreter's One-Volume Commentary on the Bible*, 329–71. Edited by C. M. Layman. Nashville/London: Abingdon, 1971.
_____. "Chronicles, Books of," *IDBSup* 156–58.
_____. "The Chronicler as Exegete," *JSOT* 2 (1977) 2–32.
_____. "Isaiah I–XII: Presentation of a Prophet," *VTSup* 29 (1977) 16–48.
_____. "Isaiah 36–39: Structure and Function." In *Von Kanaan bis Kerala. Festschrift J. P. M. van der Ploeg*, 3–21. Edited by W. C. Delsman et al. Kevalaer/Neukirchen-Vluyn: Butzon & Bercker/Neukirchener Verlag, 1981.
_____. "The Biblical Interpretation of the Reigns of Ahaz and Hezekiah." In *In the Shelter of Elyon: Essays on Ancient Palestinian Life and Literature in Honor of G. W. Ahlström*, 247–59. Edited by W. B. Barrick and J. R. Spencer. Sheffield: JSOT Press, 1984.
_____. "The Historical Literature." In *The Hebrew Bible and Its Modern Interpreters*, 297–323. Edited by D. A. Knight and G. M. Tucker. Philadelphia/Chico: Fortress/Scholars Press, 1985.
Aharoni, Y. *The Land of the Bible: A Historical Geography*. 2d ed. Philadelphia: Westminster, 1979.
Ahlström, G. W. "Isaiah VI. 13," *JSS* 19 (1974) 169–72.

Albright, W. F. "The Assyrian March on Jerusalem, Isa. X, 28–32," *AASOR* 4 (1924) 134–40.

———. *Excavations and Results at Tell el-Ful (Gibeah of Saul).* New Haven: Yale University Press, 1924.

———. "The Gezer Calendar," *BASOR* 92 (1943) 16–26.

———. "The Chronology of the Divided Monarchy of Israel," *BASOR* 100 (1945) 16–22.

———. "The Son of Tabeel (Isaiah 7:6)," *BASOR* 140 (1955) 34–35.

———. "The High Place in Ancient Palestine," *VTSup* 4 (1957) 242–58.

———. "Prolegomenon." In the reissue of C. F. Burney's, *The Book of Judges with Introduction and Notes* and *Notes on the Hebrew Text of the Books of Kings*, 1–38. New York: Ktav, 1970.

Alonso Schökel, L. "Is. 12: De duabus methodis pericopam explicandi," *VD* 34 (1956) 154–60.

———. "Is. 10:28–32: Análisis estilístico," *Bib* 40 (1959) 230–36 = (slightly revised) "Isaiah 10:27b–32: Stylistic Analysis." In his *Hermeneutica de la Palabra. II. Interpretacion Literaria de Textos Biblicos*, 351–57. Madrid: Cristiandad, 1987.

———. "Two Poems of Peace: A Stylistic Study of Isaiah 8:23–9:6 and 11:1–16." In his *Hermeneutica de la Palabra. II. Interpretacion Literaria de Textos Biblicos*, 329–49. Madrid: Cristiandad, 1987.

———. *Estudios de Poética Hebrea.* Barcelona: J. Flors, 1963.

Alt, A. "Hosea 5,8–6,6. Ein Krieg und seine Folgen in prophetischer Beleuchtung," *NKZ* 30 (1919) 537–68.

———. "Das System der assyrischen Provinzen auf dem Boden des Reiches Israel," *ZDPV* 52 (1929) 22–42.

———. "Neue assyrische Nachrichten über Palästina," *ZDPV* 67 (1945) 128–46.

———. "Jesaja 8,23–9,6. Befreiungsnacht und Krönungstag." In *Festschrift Alfred Bertholet*, 29–49. Tübingen: J. C. B. Mohr (Paul Siebeck), 1950.

———. "Menschen ohne Namen," *ArOr* 18 (1950) 9–24.

———. "Tiglathpilesers III. erster Feldzug nach Palästina." In his *KS* II. 150–63. Munich: C. H. Beck, 1953.

———. "Historische Geographie und Topographie des Negeb." In his *KS* III. 382–459. Munich: C. H. Beck, 1959.

Andersen, K. T. "Die Chronologie der Könige von Israel und Juda," *ST* 23 (1969) 67–119.

Anderson, B. W. "'God with Us'—In Judgment and in Mercy: The Editorial Structure of Isaiah 5–10 (11)." In *Canon, Theology, and the Old Testament Interpretation. Essays in Honor of Brevard S. Childs*, 230–45. Edited by G. M. Tucker, D. L. Petersen, and R. R. Wilson. Philadelphia: Fortress, 1988.

Anderson, G. W. "Isaiah XXIV–XXVII Reconsidered," *VTSup* 9 (1963) 118–26.

Arnold, P. M. *Gibeah in Israelite History and Tradition*. Dissertation, Emory University, 1986.

———. "Hosea and the Sin of Gibeah," *CBQ* 51 (1989) 447–60.

———. "Migron." In the *Anchor Bible Dictionary* (forthcoming).

Astour, M. C. "Ya'udi," *IDBSup* (1962) 975.

Asurmendi, J. M. *La Guerra Siro-Efraimita: Historia y Profetas*. Valencia/Jerusalem: Institutión San Jerónimo, 1982.

———. "Isaie dans son temps: Isaie et la politique," *MDB* 49 (1987) 36–37.

Auvray, P. *Isaie 1–39*. Paris: J. Gabalda, 1972.

Avigad, N. *Hebrew Bullae from the Time of Jeremiah: Remnants of a Burnt Archive*. Jerusalem: Israel Exploration Society, 1986.

Baer, K. "The Libyan and Nubian Kings of Egypt: Notes on the Chronology of Dynasties XXII to XXVI," *JNES* 32 (1973) 4–25.

Barnes, W. H. *Studies in the Chronology of the Divided Monarchy of Israel*. Dissertation, Harvard University, 1986.

Barnett, R. D. and Faulkner, M. *The Sculptures of Tiglatpileser III (745–727 B.C.) from the Central and Southwest Palaces at Nimrud*. London: Trustees of the British Museum, 1962.

Bartelmus, R. "Jes 7,1–17 und das Stilprinzip des Kontrastes. Syntaktisch-stilistische und traditionsgeschichtliche Anmerkungen zur 'Immanuel-Perikope,'" *ZAW* 96 (1984) 50–66.

Barth, H. *Die Jesaja-Worte in der Josiazeit. Israel und Assur als Thema einer productiven Neuinterpretation der Jesajaüberlieferung*. WMANT 48. Neukirchen-Vluyn: Neukirchener Verlag, 1977.

Baumgartner, W. "Ein Kapitel vom hebräischen Erzählungsstil." In *Eucharisterion. Studien zur Religion und Literatur des Alten und Neuen Testaments. Hermann Gunkel zum 60. Geburtstag*, 145–57. Edited by H. Schmidt. Göttingen: Vandenhoeck & Ruprecht, 1923.

———. "Zur Form der assyrischen Königsinschriften," *OLZ* 27 (1924) 313–17.

Becker, J. *Isaias—der Prophet und sein Buch*. SBS 30. Stuttgart: Katholisches Bibelwerk, 1968.

Beecher, W. J. "Torah: A Word-Study in the Old Testament," *JBL* 24 (1905) 1–16.

Beer, G. "Zur Zukunftserwartung Jesajas." In *Studien zur semitischen Philologie und Religionsgeschichte. Julius Wellhausen zum siebzigsten Geburtstag*, 13–35. Edited by K. Marti. Giessen: A. Töpelmann, 1914.

Begrich, G. "Der wirtschaftliche Einfluss Assyriens auf Südsyrien und Palästina," *TLZ* 102 (1977) 309–12.

Begrich, J. "Der syrisch-ephraimitische Krieg und seine weltpolitischen Zusammenhänge," *ZDMG* 83 (1927) 213–37.

_____. *Die Chronologie der Könige von Israel und Juda und die Quellen des Rahmes der Königsbücher*. Tübingen: J. C. B. Mohr (Paul Siebeck), 1929.

_____. "Jesaja 14, 28–32. Ein Beitrag zur Chronologie der israelitischen-judäischen Königszeit," *ZDMG* 86 (1933) 66–79.

_____. "Das priesterliche Heilsorakel," *ZAW* 52 (1934) 81–92.

_____. "Die priesterliche Tora," *BZAW* 66 (1936) 63–88.

_____. *Gesammelte Studien*. Edited by W. Zimmerli. Munich: Chr. Kaiser, 1964.

Bennet, Crystal-M. "Some Reflections on Neo-Assyrian Influence in Transjordan." In *Archaeology in the Levant. Essays for Kathleen Kenyon*, 165–71. Edited by R. Moorey and P. Parr. Warminster: Aris and Phillips, 1978.

Benzinger, I. *Die Bücher der Chronik*. Tübingen/Leipzig: J. C. B. Mohr (Paul Siebeck), 1901.

Berg, W. "Die Identität der 'jungen Frau' in Jes 7,14.16," *BN* 13 (1980) 7–13.

Beyerlin, W. *Die Rettung der Bedrängten in den Feindpsalmen der Einzelnen auf institutionelle Zusammenhänge untersucht*. FRLANT 99. Göttingen: Vandenhoeck & Ruprecht, 1970.

Bickert, R. "König Ahas und der Prophet Jesaja. Ein Beitrag zum Problem des syrisch-ephraimitischen Krieges," *ZAW* 99 (1987) 361–84.

Bin-Nun, S. R. "Formulas from Records of Israel and Judah," *VT* 18 (1968) 414–32.

Biran, A. "Tell Dan—Five Years Later," *BA* 43 (1980) 168–82.

_____. "Dan." In *Archaeology and Biblical Interpretation. Essays in Memory of D. Glenn Rose*, 101–11. Edited by L. G. Perdue, L. E. Toombs, and G. L. Johnson. Atlanta: John Knox, 1987.

Björndalen, A. J. "Zur Einordnung und Funktion von Jes 7,5f.," *ZAW* 95 (1983) 260–63.

Blank, S. "The Current Misinterpretation of Isaiah's *She'ar Yashub*," *JBL* 67 (1948) 211–15.

_____. "Immanuel and which Isaiah?" *JNES* 13 (1954) 83–86.

_____. "Traces of Prophetic Agony in Isaiah," *HUCA* 27 (1956) 81–92.

Boehmer, J. "Der Glaube und Jesaja. Zu Jes. 7,9 und 28,16," *ZAW* (1923) 84–93.

_____. "Dieses Volk," *JBL* 45 (1926) 134–48.

_____. "'Yahwehs Lehrlinge' im Buch Jesaja," *ARW* 33 (1936) 171–75.

Borger, R. and Tadmor, H. "Zwei Beiträge zur alttestamentliche Wissenschaft aufgrund der Inschriften Tiglathpilesers III," *ZAW* 94 (1982) 244–51.

Boutflower, C. *The Book of Isaiah Chapters [I–XXXIX] in the Light of Assyrian Monuments*. London/New York: Society for Promoting Christian Knowledge, 1930.

Braun, R. L. "A Reconsideration of the Chronicler's Attitude to the North," *JBL* 96 (1977) 59–62.

_____. "Chronicles, Ezra and Nehemiah: Theology and Literary History." In *Studies in the Historical Books of the Old Testament*, 52–65. VTSup 30. Edited by J. A. Emerton. Leiden: E. J. Brill, 1979.

Bright, J. "Isaiah." In *Peake's Commentary on the Bible*, 489–515. Edited by M. Black and H. H. Rowley. London/New York: T. Nelson, 1962.

_____. *Jeremiah*. AB 21. Garden City: Doubleday, 1965.

_____. *A History of Israel*. 3d ed. Philadelphia: Westminster, 1981.

Brinkman, J. A. *A Political History of Post-Kassite Babylonia, 1158–722 B.C.* AnOr 43. Rome: Pontificium Institutum Biblicum, 1968.

Brossier, F. "Isaie et le messianisme: 2. Un roi ideal le futur," *MDB* 49 (1987) 42.

Brownlee, W. H. "The Text of Isaiah VI 13 in the Light of DSIa," *VT* 1 (1951) 296–98.

Brunet, A.-M. "Le Chroniste et ses sources," *RB* 60 (1953) 481–508; 61 (1954) 349–86.

Brunet, G. *Essai sur l'Isaie de l'histoire: Étude de quelques textes notamment dans Isa. VII, VIII & XXII.* Paris: A. & J. Picard, 1975.

Buber, M. *Der Glaube der Propheten.* Zurich: Manesse, 1950.

Buchanan, G. W. "The Old Testament Meaning of the Knowledge of Good and Evil," *JBL* 75 (1956) 114–20.

Budde, K. "Isaiah vii. 1 and 2 Kings xvi. 5," *ExpTim* 11 (1899/1900) 327–30.

_____. *Geschichte der althebräischen Litteratur.* Leipzig: C. F. Amelangs Verlag, 1906.

_____. "Über die Schranken, die Jesajas prophetischen Botschaft zu setzen sind," *ZAW* 41 (1923) 154–203.

_____. "Jes 8,6b," *ZAW* 44 (1926) 65–67.

_____. *Jesaja's Erleben. Eine gemeinverständliche Auslegung der Denkschrift des Propheten (Kap. 6,1–9,6).* Gotha: L. Klotz, 1928.

_____. "Zu Jesaja 8, Vers 9 und 10," *JBL* 49 (1930) 423–28.

_____. "Jesaja und Ahas," *ZDMG* 84 (1931) 125–38.

_____. "Das Immanuelzeichen und die Ahaz-Begegnung Jesaja 7," *JBL* 52 (1933) 22–54.

Burrows, M. "The Conduit of the Upper Pool," *ZAW* 70 (1958) 221–27.

Buss, M. *The Prophetic Word of Hosea: A Morphological Study.* BZAW 111; Berlin: A. Töpelmann, 1969.

Buxenbaum, Y. "Shear-Yashub (On Isaiah 7–8)," *Beth Mikra* 33 (1987/1988) 33–50 (Hebrew).

Carlson, R. A. "The Anti-Assyrian Character of the Oracle in Is. IX 1–6," *VT* 24 (1974) 130–35.

Carroll, R. P. "Inner Tradition Shifts in Meaning in Isaiah 1–11," *ExpTim* 89 (1977/78) 301–4.

_____. "Ancient Israelite Prophecy and Dissonant Theory," *Numen* 24 (1977) 135–51.

_____. "Translation and Attribution in Isaiah 8.19f.," *BT* 31 (1980) 126–34.

Cazelles, H. "La Vocation d'Isaie (ch. 6) et les rites royaux." In *Hommenaje a Juan Prado,* 89–108. Edited by L. Alvarez Verdes and E. J. Alonso Hernandez. Madrid: Consejo Superior de Investigaciones Cientificios, 1975.

_____. "Problèmes de la Guerre Syro-Ephraimite," *ErIsr* 14 (1978) 70–78.

_____. *Historie politique d'Israël des origines à Alexandre le Grand*. Paris: Desclee, 1982.

_____. "Isaie et le messianisme: 1. La foi dans l'oint de YHWH," *MDB* 49 (1987) 41.

Cheyne, T. K. *The Prophecies of Isaiah*. 2d ed. London: K. Paul, Trench, 1882.

_____. *Introduction to the Book of Isaiah*. London: A. and C. Black, 1895.

Childs, B. S. *Isaiah and the Assyrian Crisis*. SBT II/3. London: SCM, 1967.

Christensen, D. L. "The March of Conquest in Isaiah X 27c–34," *VT* 26 (1976) 385–99.

Clements, R. E. *Isaiah 1–39*. Grand Rapids/London: Eerdmans/Marshall, Morgan & Scott, 1980.

Clifford, R. J. "The Use of HOY in the Prophets," *CBQ* 28 (1966) 458–64.

Clines, D. J. "The Evidence for an Autumnal New Year in Pre-exilic Israel Reconsidered," *JBL* 93 (1974) 22–40.

_____. *Ezra, Nehemiah, Esther*. Grand Rapids/London: Eerdmans/Marshall, Morgan & Scott, 1984.

Cogan, M. "Tyre and Tiglathpileser III: Chronological Notes," *JCS* 25 (1973) 96–99.

_____. *Imperialism and Religion: Assyria, Judah, and Israel in the 8th and 7th Centuries B.C.E.* SBLMS 19. Missoula: Scholars Press, 1974.

Cogan, M. and Tadmor, H. "Gyges and Ashurbanipal: A Study in Literary Transmission," *Or* 46 (1977) 65–85.

_____. *II Kings*. AB 11. New York: Doubleday, 1988.

Conrad, E. *Fear Not Warrior: A Study of ʾal tiraʾ Pericopes in the Hebrew Scriptures*. Brown Judaica Studies 75. Chico: Scholars Press, 1985.

_____. "The Royal Narratives and the Structure of the Book of Isaiah," *JSOT* 41 (1988) 67–81.

Cook, H. J. "Pekah," *VT* 14 (1964) 121–35.

Coppens, J. "La Prophétie de la ʿAlmah," *ETL* 28 (1952) 648–78 = *La Prophétie de la ʿAlmah*. ALBO II/35. Louvain: Publications universitaires de Louvain, 1952.

_____. "Le roi idéal d'Is., IX, 5–6 et XI, 1–5, est-il une figure messianique?" In *A la rencontre de Dieu. Mémorial A. Gelin,* 85–108. Lyon: 1961.

Cornill, C. H. "Die Komposition des Buches Jesajas," *ZAW* 4 (1884) 83–105.

Crenshaw, J. L. "A Liturgy of Wasted Opportunity (Am 4:6–12; Isa 9:7–10:4; 5:25–29)," *Semitics* 1 (1970) 27–37.

Criado, R. "El valor de *laken* (Vg 'propter') en Is 7,14. Contribucion al estudio de Emmanuel," *Estudios Eclesiasticos* 34 (1960) 741–51.

Crook, M. "A Suggested Occasion for Isa. 9:2–7 and 11:1–9," *JBL* 68 (1949) 213–24.

Cross, F. M. *Canaanite Myth and Hebrew Epic: Essays in the History of the Religion of Israel.* Cambridge/London: Harvard University Press, 1973.

Crüsemann, F. *Studien zur Formgeschichte von Hymnus und Danklied in Israel.* WMANT 32. Neukirchen-Vluyn: Neukirchener Verlag, 1969.

Dahood, M. *Psalms.* AB 16, 17, 17A. 3 vols. Garden City: Doubleday, 1965–70.

Dalman, G. *Arbeit und Sitte in Palästina.* 2 vols. Gütersloh: Bertelsmann, 1928–32.

_____. "Palästinische Wege und die Bedrohung Jerusalems nach Jesaja 10," *PJB* 12 (1916) 37–57.

Day, J. "Shear-jashub (Isaiah vii 3) and the Remnant of Wrath (Psalm lxxvi 11)," *VT* 31 (1981) 76–78.

Delitzsch, F. *Biblical Commentary on the Prophecies of Isaiah.* 2 vols. 3d ed. New York: Funk & Wagnalls, 1889.

Dentan, R. C. "Heart," *IDB* 2. 549–50.

Dequeker, L. "Isaie vii 14," *VT* 12 (1962) 331–35.

Dietrich, W. *Jesaja und die Politik.* BEvT 74. Munich: Chr. Kaiser, 1976.

Dillmann, A. *Der Prophet Jesaja.* 5th ed. Leipzig: S. Hirzel, 1890.

Dohmen, C. "Verstockungsvollzug und prophetische Legitimation. Literarkritische Beobachtungen zu Jes 7,1–17," *BN* 31 (1986) 37–51.

_____. "Das Immanuelzeichen. Ein jesajanisches Drohwort und seine inneralttestamentliche Rezeption," *Bib* 68 (1987) 305–29.

Donner, H. "Neue Quellen zur Geschichte des Staates Moab in der zweiten Häfte der 8. Jahrhundert v. Chr.," *MIO* 5 (1957) 155–84.

_____. *Israel unter den Völkern. Die Stellung der klassischen Propheten des 8. Jahrhunderts v. Chr. zur Aussenpolitik der Könige von Israel und Juda*. VTSup 11. Leiden: E. J. Brill, 1964.

_____. "Der Feind aus dem Norden: Topographische und archäologische Erwägungen zu Jes. 10,27b–34," *ZDPV* 84 (1968) 46–54.

_____. "The Separate States of Israel and Judah." In *Israelite and Judean History*, 381–434. Edited by J. H. Hayes and J. M. Miller. Philadelphia: Westminster, 1977.

_____. *Geschichte des Volkes Israel und seiner Nachbarn in Grundzügen*. Göttingen: Vandenhoeck & Ruprecht, 1987.

Driver, G. R. "Linguistic and Textual Problems: Isaiah I–XXXIX," *JTS* 38 (1937) 36–50.

_____. "Three Notes," *VT* 2 (1952) 356–57.

_____. "Two Misunderstood Passages of the Old Testament," *JTS* 6 (1955) 82–84.

_____. "Isaianic Problems." In *Festschrift für Wilhelm Eilers*, 43–57. Edited by G. Wiessner. Wiesbaden: Otto Harrasowitz, 1967.

_____. "Isaiah I–XXXIX: Textual and Linguistic Problems," *JSS* 13 (1968) 36–57.

Driver, S. R. *A Treatise on the Use of Hebrew Tenses*. 3d ed. Oxford: Clarendon, 1892.

Duhm, B. *Das Buch Jesaja*. 5th ed. Göttingen: Vandenhoeck & Ruprecht, 1968.

Eaton, J. H. "The Origin of the Book of Isaiah," *VT* 9 (1959) 138–57.

Edwards, I. E. S. "Egypt: From the Twenty-second to the Twenty-fourth Dynasty." In *The Cambridge Ancient History*, 3/1. 534–81. 2d ed. Edited by J. Boardman, I. E. S. Edwards, N. G. L. Hammond, and E. Sollberger. Cambridge/London/New York: Cambridge University Press, 1982.

Eichrodt, W. *Der Heilige in Israel. Jesaja 1–12*. BAT 17/1. Stuttgart: Calwer, 1960.

Eissfeldt, O. "nûaḥ 'sich vertragen,'" *SThU* 29 (1950) 71–74 = his *KS* 3. 124–28. 6 vols. Edited by R. Sellheim and F. Maass. Tübingen: J. C. B. Mohr (Paul Siebeck), 1966.

Elat, E. "The Economic Relations of the Neo-Assyrian Empire with Egypt," *JAOS* 98 (1978) 20–34.

Elhorst, H. J. "Jes 8,1–4," *ZAW* 35 (1915) 98–101.

Elliger, K. "Prophetie und Politik," *ZAW* 53 (1935) 3–22.

Emerton, J. A. "Some Linguistic and Historical Problems in Isaiah VIII 23," *JSS* 14 (1969) 151–75.

_____. "A Neglected Solution of a Problem in Psalm LXXVI 11," *VT* 24 (1974) 136–46.

_____. "The Translation and Interpretation of Isaiah VI. 13." In *Interpreting the Hebrew Bible: Essays in Honor of E. I. J. Rosenthal*, 85–118. Edited by J. A. Emerton and S. Reif. Cambridge/New York: Cambridge University Press, 1982.

Engnell, I. *The Call of Isaiah: An Exegetical and Comparative Study*. Uppsala/Leipzig: A.-B. Lundequistska/Otto Harrassowitz, 1949.

Eph'al, I. "Assyrian Dominion in Palestine." In *WHJP* 4/1. 276–89.

_____. "Israel: Fall and Exile." In *WHJP* 4/1. 180–91.

_____. *The Ancient Arabs: Nomads on the Borders of the Fertile Crescent: 9th-5th Centuries B.C.* Jerusalem/Leiden: Magnes/E. J. Brill, 1982.

Evans, C. A. "An Interpretation of Isa 8,11–15 Unemended," *ZAW* 97 (1985) 112–13.

_____. "On Isaiah's Use of Israel's Tradition," *BZ* 30 (1986) 92–98.

Ewald, H. *Die Propheten des Alten Bundes*. 3 vols. 2d ed. Göttingen: Vandenhoeck & Ruprecht, 1867–68.

Fabry, H.-J. "*leb*," *TWAT* 4. 414–51.

Farrar, F. W. *The Second Book of Kings*. London: Hodder and Stroughton, 1894.

Féderlin, L. "A propos d'Isaie X, 29–31," *RB* 3 (1906) 266–73.

Feldmann, F. *Das Buch Isaias*. 2 vols. Münster: Aschendorff, 1925–26.

Fensham, F. C. "Father and Son as Terminology for Treaty and Covenant." In *Near Eastern Studies in Honor of William Foxwell Albright*, 121–36. Edited by H. Goedicke. Baltimore: John Hopkins University Press, 1971.

Feuillet, A. "Le signe propose a Achaz et l'Emmanuel (Isaie 7.10–25)," *RSR* 30 (1940) 129–51.

Fey, R. *Amos und Jesaja. Abhängigkeit und Eigenständigkeit des Jesaja*. WMANT 12. Neukirchen-Vluyn: Neukirchener Verlag, 1963.

Fichtner, J. "Jahwes Plan in der Botschaft des Jesaja," *ZAW* 63 (1951) 16–33.

Finkelstein, J. J. "Mesopotamian Historiography," *PAPS* 107 (1963) 461–72.

Fishbane, M. *Biblical Interpretation in Ancient Israel.* Oxford: Clarendon, 1985.

Fohrer, G. "Die Gattung der Berichte über symbolische Handlungen der Propheten," *ZAW* 64 (1952) 101–20.

_____. *Das Buch Jesaja.* 2 vols. 2d ed. Zurich/Stuttgart: Zwingli, 1966.

_____. "Zu Jesaja 7,14 im Zusammenhang von Jesaja 7,10–22," *ZAW* 68 (1956) 54–56.

_____. "The Origin, Composition and Tradition of Isaiah I–XXXIX," *ALUOS* 3 (1962) 3–38.

_____. "Wandlungen Jesajas." In *Festschrift für Wilhelm Eilers,* 58–71. Edited by G. Wiessner. Wiesbaden: Otto Harrassowitz, 1967.

_____. *Die symbolischen Handlungen der Propheten.* 2d ed. Zurich/Stuttgart: Zwingli, 1968.

Forrer, E. *Die Provinzeinteilung des assyrischen Reiches.* Leipzig: J. C. Hinrichs, 1920.

Fullerton, K. "Isaiah's Earliest Prophecy against Ephraim," *AJSL* 33 (1916/17) 9–39.

_____. "The Problem of Isaiah, Chapter 10," *AJSL* 34 (1917/18) 170–84.

_____. "Viewpoints in the Discussion of Isaiah's Hopes for the Future," *JBL* 41 (1922) 1–101.

_____. "The Interpretation of Isaiah 8:5–10," *JBL* 43 (1924) 253–89.

Galling, K. *Der Altar in den Kulturen des alten Orient. Eine archäologische Studie.* Berlin: K. Curtius, 1925.

_____. "Ein Stück judäischen Bodenrechts in Jesaia 8," *ZDPV* 56 (1933) 209–18.

_____. *Die Bücher der Chronik, Esra, Nehemia.* Göttingen: Vandenhoeck & Ruprecht, 1954.

Gehman, H. S. "The Ruler of the Universe: The Theology of First Isaiah," *Int* 11 (1957) 269–81.

Gerstenberger, E. "The Woe-Oracles of the Prophets," *JBL* 81 (1962) 249–63.

Gese, H. "Natus ex virgine." In *Probleme biblischer Theologie. Gerhard von Rad zum 70. Geburtstag*, 73–89. Edited by H. W. Wolff. Munich: Chr. Kaiser, 1971.

Gilead, H. "*wĕḥubbal ʿōl mippĕnê-šāmen*," *Beth Mikra* 31 (1985/86) 134–36 (Hebrew).

Ginsberg, H. L. "An Unrecognized Allusion to Kings Pekah and Hoshea of Israel," *ErIsr* 5 (1958) 61–65.

_____. "Isaiah in the Light of History," *CJ* 22 (1967) 1–18.

_____. "Reflexes of Sargon in Isaiah after 715 B.C.E.," *JAOS* 88 (1968) 47–53.

_____. "First Isaiah," *EncJud* 9. 49–60.

Gitay, Y. "Isaiah—The Impractical Prophet," *BRev* 4 (1988) 10–15.

Godbey, A. H. "The Kepu," *AJSL* 22 (1905) 81–88.

Goldbaum, F. J. "Two Hebrew Quasi-Adverbs: *laken* and *ʾaken*," *JNES* 23 (1964) 132–35.

Goldingay, J. "The Chronicler as a Theologian," *BTB* 5 (1975) 99–126.

Goldstein, J. *I Maccabees*. AB 41. Garden City: Doubleday, 1976.

_____. *II Maccabees*. AB 41A. Garden City: Doubleday, 1983.

Gorg, M. "Hiskija als Immanuel. Plädoyer für eine typologische Identifikation," *BN* 22 (1983) 107–25.

Goshen-Gottstein, M. H. "'Ephraim is a well-trained heifer' and Ugaritic *mdl*," *Bib* 41 (1960) 64–66.

Gottlieb, H. "Jesaja, Kapitel 12," *DTT* 37 (1974) 29–32.

Gottwald, N. K. "Immanuel as the Prophet's Son," *VT* 8 (1958) 36–47.

_____. *All the Kingdoms of the Earth: Israelite Prophecy and International Relations in the Ancient Near East*. New York/Evanston/London: Harper & Row, 1964.

Gouders, K. "Die Berufung des Propheten Jesaja (Jes 6,1–13), 2. Teil," *BibLeb* 13 (1972) 172–84.

Gowan, D. E. "The Use of *yaʿan* in Biblical Hebrew," *VT* 21 (1971) 168–85.

Graham, W. C. "Isaiah's Part in the Syro-Ephraimitic Crisis," *AJSL* 50 (1933/34) 201–16.

Gray, G. B. *A Critical and Exegetical Commentary on the Book of Isaiah*. 2 vols. Edinburgh: T. & T. Clark, 1912.

Gray, J. *I and II Kings*. Philadelphia: Westminster, 1963.

Grayson, A. K. *Assyrian and Babylonian Chronicles.* Locust Valley, NY: J. J. Augustin, 1975.

_____. "Histories and Historians of the Ancient Near East: Assyria and Babylonia," *Or* 49 (1980) 140–94.

Greenfield, J. C. "Some Aspects of Treaty Terminology in the Bible." In *Papers of the Fourth World Congress of Jewish Studies.* Jerusalem: 1967.

Gressmann, H. *Der Messias.* Göttingen: Vandenhoeck & Ruprecht, 1929.

Grollenberg, L. H. *Zwischen Gott und Politik. Der Prophet Jesaja.* Stuttgart: KBW, 1971.

Grossberg, D. "Pivotal Polysemy in Jeremiah XXV 10–11A," *VT* 36 (1986) 481–85.

Guillaume, A. "Paronomasia in the Old Testament," *JSS* 9 (1964) 282–90.

Gunneweg, A. H. J. "Heils- und Unheilsverkündigung in Jes. VII," *VT* 15 (1965) 27–34.

_____. *Prophetie und Politik.* Bonn: Evangelisches Kirchenamt für die Bundeswehr, 1978.

Guthe, H. "Zeichen und Weissagung in Jes 7,14–17." In *Studien zur semitischen Philologie und Religionsgeschichte. Julius Wellhausen zum siebzigsten Geburtstag*, 177–90. Edited by K. Marti. Giessen: A. Töpelmann, 1914.

Habel, N. "The Form and Significance of the Call Narratives," *ZAW* 77 (1965) 297–323.

Hallo, W. W. "From Qarqar to Carchemish: Assyria and Israel in Light of New Discoveries," *BA* 23 (1960) 33–61.

Hallo, W. W. and Simpson, W. K. *The Ancient Near East: A History.* New York: Harcourt, Brace, Jovanovich, 1971.

Hammershaimb, E. "The Immanuel Sign," *ST* 3 (1949) 124–42 = his *Some Aspects of Old Testament Prophecy from Isaiah to Malachi*, 9–28. Copenhagen: Rosenkilde og Bagger, 1966.

Haran, M. "The Rise and Decline of the Empire of Jeroboam ben Joash," *VT* 17 (1967) 266–97.

Hardmeier, C. "Gesichtspunkte pragmatischer Erzältextanalyse. 'Glaubt ihr nicht, so bleibt ihr nicht'—ein Glaubensappell an schwachende Anhänger Jesajas," *WD* 15 (1979) 33–54.

_____. "Jesajas Verkündigungsabsicht und Jahwes Verstockungsauftrag." In *Die Botschaft und die Boten. Festschrift H. W.*

Wolff, 235–51. Edited by J. Jeremias and L. Perlitt. Neukirchen-Vluyn: Neukirchener Verlag, 1981.

_____. "Verkündigung und Schrift bei Jesaja. Zur Entstehung der Schriftprophetie als Oppositionsliteratur im alten Israel," *TGl* 73 (1983) 119–34.

Harrelson, W. "Nonroyal Motifs in the Royal Eschatology." In *Israel's Prophetic Heritage*, 147–65. Edited by B. W. Anderson and W. Harrelson. New York: Harper, 1962.

_____. "Prophetic Eschatological Visions and the Kingdom of God." In *The Quest for the Kingdom of God: Studies in Honor of George E. Mendenhall*, 117–26. Edited by H. B. Huffmon, F. A. Spina, and A. R. W. Green. Winona Lake: Eisenbrauns, 1983.

Hasel, G. "Linguistic Considerations Regarding the Translation of Isaiah's *Shear-jashub*: A Reassessment," *AUSS* 9 (1971) 36–46.

_____. "Semantic Values of Derivatives of the Hebrew Root *shʾr*," *AUSS* 11 (1973) 152–69.

_____. *The Remnant: The History and Theology of the Remnant Idea from Genesis to Isaiah*. 3d ed. Berrien Springs: Andrews University Press, 1980.

_____. "Remnant," *IDBSup* 735–36.

Hattendorff. "Zu Jes 7,17," *ZAW* 48 (1930) 324–25.

Hayes, J. H. "The Tradition of Zion's Inviolability," *JBL* 82 (1963) 419–26.

_____. *Amos, the Eighth-Century Prophet: His Times and His Preaching*. Nashville: Abingdon, 1988.

Hayes, J. H. and Hooker, P. K. *A New Chronology for the Kings of Israel and Judah and Its Implications for Biblical History and Literature*. Atlanta: John Knox, 1988.

Hayes, J. H. and Irvine, S. A. *Isaiah, the Eighth-Century Prophet: His Times and His Preaching*. Nashville: Abingdon, 1987.

Hayes, J. H. and Miller, J. M., eds. *Israelite and Judean History*. Philadelphia: Westminster, 1977.

Heaton, E. W. "The Root *šʾr* and the Doctrine of the Remnant," *JTS* 3 (1952) 27–39.

Heider, G. *The Cult of Molek: A Reassessment*. JSOTSup 43. Sheffield: JSOT Press, 1985.

Helfmeyer, F. J. "*ʾôt*," *TWAT* 1. 182–205.

Herbert, A. S. *The Book of the Prophet Isaiah. Chapters 1–39*. Cambridge: Cambridge University Press, 1973.

Herder, J. G. *Vom Geist der ebräischen Poesie*. 3d ed. Leipzig: J. A. Barth, 1825.

Hermisson, H.-J. "Zukunftserwartung und Gegenwartskritik in der Verkündigung Jesajas," *EvT* 33 (1973) 54–77.

Herntrich, V. *Der Prophet Jesaja. Kapitel 1–12*. 2d ed. Göttingen: Vandenhoeck & Ruprecht, 1954.

Herrmann, S. *Die prophetischen Heilserwartungen im Alten Testament*. BWANT 85. Stuttgart: Kohlhammer, 1965.

_____. *A History of Israel in Old Testament Times*. 2d ed. Philadelphia: Fortress, 1981.

Heschel, A. *The Prophets*. 2 vols. New York/Hagerstown/San Francisco/London: Harper & Row, 1969.

Hesse, F. *Das Verstockungsproblem im Alten Testament*. BZAW 74. Berlin: A. Töpelmann, 1955.

Hobbs, T. R. *2 Kings*. WBC 13. Waco: Word Books, 1985.

Höffken, P. "Notizen zum Textcharakter von Jesaja 7,1–17," *TZ* 36 (1980) 321–37.

Hoffmann, H.-D. *Reform und Reformen. Untersuchung zu dem Grundthema der deuteronomistische Geschichtsschreibung*. ATANT 66. Zurich: Theologischer Verlag, 1980.

Hoffmann, H. W. *Die Intension der Verkündigung Jesajas*. BZAW 136. Berlin: Walter de Gruyter, 1974.

Høgenhaven, J. "On the Structure and Meaning of Isaiah VIII 23B," *VT* 37 (1987) 218–21.

_____. *Gott und Volk bei Jesaja. Eine Untersuchung zur biblische Theologie*. Leiden/New York/Copenhagen/Cologne: E. J. Brill, 1988.

Holladay, W. L. *The Root shubh in the Old Testament*. Leiden: E. J. Brill, 1958.

_____. *Isaiah: Scroll of a Prophetic Heritage*. Grand Rapids: Eerdmans, 1978.

Hommel, F. *Geschichte Babyloniens und Assyriens*. Berlin: G. Grote, 1885.

_____. "Assyria," *HBD* 1. 176–90.

Honeyman, A. M. "Traces of an Early Diacritic Sign in Isaiah 8:6b," *JBL* 63 (1944) 45–50.

_____. "An Unnoticed Euphemism in Isaiah IX 19–20?" *VT* 1 (1951) 221–23.

Hooke, S. H. "The Sign of Immanuel." In his *The Siege Perilous: Essays in Biblical Anthropology and Kindred Subjects*, 222–34. London: SCM, 1956.

Horst, F. "Die Visionsschilderungen des alttestamentlichen Propheten," *EvT* 20 (1960) 193–205.

Huber, F. *Yahwe, Juda, und die anderen Völker beim Propheten Jesaja*. BZAW 137. Berlin/New York: Walter de Gruyter, 1976.

Hubmann, F. D. "Randbemerkungen zu Jes 7,1–17," *BN* 26 (1985) 27–46.

Hughes, J. R. A. *The Secrets of the Times: Recovering Biblical Chronologies*. Sheffield: JSOT Press, 1989.

Humbert, P. "Mahēr Šalāl Ḥāš Baz," *ZAW* 50 (1932) 90–92.

Hvidberg, F. "The Masseba and the Holy Seed," *NTT* 56 (1955) 97–99.

Irsigler, H. "Zeichen und Bezeichnetes in Jes 7,1–17. Notizen zum Immanueltext," *BN* 29 (1985) 75–114.

Iwry, S. "*Maṣṣēbāh* and *Bāmāh* in 1 Q Isaiah[A] 6:13," *JBL* 76 (1957) 225–32.

Janzen, W. *Mourning Cry and Woe Oracle*. BZAW 125. Berlin/New York: Walter de Gruyter, 1972.

Japhet, S. "The Supposed Common Authorship of Chronicles and Ezra-Nehemiah Investigated Anew," *VT* 18 (1968) 330–71.

_____. "Chronicles, Book of," *EncJud* 5. 517–34.

_____. *The Ideology of the Book of Chronicles and Its Place in Biblical Thought*. Jerusalem: Bialik Institute, 1977 (Hebrew).

Jenkins, A. K. "Isaiah's Fourteenth Year: A New Interpretation of 2 Kings xviii 13–xix 37," *VT* 26 (1976) 289–98.

Jenni, J. *Die politischen Voraussagen der Propheten*. ATANT 29. Zurich: Zwingli, 1956.

_____. "Jesajas Berufung in der neueren Forschung," *TZ* 15 (1959) 321–39.

_____. "Immanuel," *RGG* 3. 677–78.

Jensen, J. *The Use of tora by Isaiah. His Debate with the Wisdom Tradition*. CBQMS 3. Washington: CBA, 1973.

_____. "The Age of Immanuel," *CBQ* 41 (1979) 220–39.

_____. *Isaiah 1–39*. Wilmington, Delaware: Michael Glazier, 1984.

_____. "Yahweh's Plan in Isaiah and in the Rest of the Old Testament," *CBQ* 48 (1986) 443–55.

Jeppesen, K. "Call and Frustration: A New Understanding of Isaiah VIII 21-22," *VT* 32 (1982) 145-57.

Jepsen, A. "Israel und Damascus," *AfO* 14 (1941/44) 153-72.

_____. *Die Quellen des Königsbuches*. 2d ed. Halle: Niemeyer, 1956.

_____. "Die Nebiah in Jes 8,3," *ZAW* 72 (1960) 267-68.

_____. "ʾmn," *TWAT* 1. 313-48

Jepsen, A. and Hanhart, R. *Untersuchungen zur israelitischen-jüdischen Chronologie*. BZAW 88. Berlin: A. Töpelmann, 1964.

Jeremias, J. *Der Prophet Hosea*. Göttingen: Vandenhoeck & Ruprecht, 1983.

Jirku, A. "Zu 'Eilebeute' in Jes 8,1.3," *TZ* 15 (1950) 118.

Jones, D. R. "The Traditio of the Oracles of Isaiah of Jerusalem," *ZAW* 67 (1955) 226-46.

Jones, G. H. *1 and 2 Kings*. 2 vols. Grand Rapids/London: Eerdmans/Marshall, Morgan & Scott, 1984.

Jouon, P. *Grammaire de l'hébreu biblique*. 2d ed. Rome: Biblical Institute, 1947.

Junker, H. "Ursprung und Grundzüge des Messiasbildes bei Jesajas," *VTSup* 4 (1957) 181-96.

Kaiser, O. *Isaiah 1-12*. 2d ed. London/Philadelphia: SCM/Westminster, 1983.

_____. *Isaiah 13-39*. London/Philadelphia: SCM/Westminster, 1974.

Kalluveettil, C. M. I. *Declaration and Covenant: A Comprehensive Review of Covenant Formulae from the Old Testament and the Ancient Near East*. AnBib 88. Rome: Biblical Institute, 1982.

Kaplan, M. "Isaiah 6:1-11," *JBL* 45 (1926) 251-59.

Kaufmann, Y. *The Religion of Israel: From Its Beginnings to the Babylonian Exile*. Chicago: University of Chicago Press, 1960.

Keller, C. A. "Das quietistische Element in der Botschaft des Jesaja," *TZ* 11 (1955) 81-97.

Kennett, R. H. *The Composition of the Book of Isaiah in the Light of History and Archaeology*. Schweich Lectures, 1909. London: H. Frowde, 1910.

Key, A. F. "The Magical Background of Is. 6:9-13," *JBL* 86 (1967) 198-204.

Kilian, R. *Die Verheissung Immanuels*. *Jes 7,14*. SBS 35. Stuttgart: Katholisches Bibelwerk, 1968.

_____. "Prolegomena zur Auslegung der Immanuelsverheissung," *FB* 2 (1972) 207–15.

_____. "Der Verstockungsauftrag Jesajas." In *Bausteine biblischer Theologie. Festgabe für G. Johannes Botterweck zum 60. Geburtstag dargebracht von seinen Schülern*. BBB 50. Edited by H.-J. Fabry. Cologne: Hanstein, 1977.

_____. *Jesaja 1–39*. EF 200. Darmstadt: Wissenschaftliche Buchgesellschaft, 1983.

Kissane, E. J. *The Book of Isaiah*. 2 vols. Dublin: Browne and Nolan, 1941–43.

_____. "'Butter and Honey Shall He Eat' (Isaiah 7:15)," *Orientalia et Biblica Louvaniensia* 1 (1957) 169–73.

Kitchen, K. A. *The Third Intermediate Period in Egypt (1100–650 B.C.)*. Warminster: Aris and Philips, 1973.

Kittel, R. *Die Bücher der Könige*. Göttingen: Vandenhoeck & Ruprecht, 1900.

_____. *Die hellenistische Mysterienreligion und das Alte Testament*. Stuttgart: Kohlhammer, 1924.

Klauber, E. *Assyrisches Beamtentum nach Briefen aus der Sargonidenzeit*. Leipzig: J. C. Hinrichs, 1910.

Klein, H. "Freude an Rezin: Ein Versuch, mit dem Text Jes. viii 6 ohne Konjektur auszukommen," *VT* 30 (1980) 229–34.

Knierim, R. "The Vocation of Isaiah," *VT* 18 (1968) 48–57.

Knutson, F. B. "Political and Foreign Affairs." In *Ras Shamra Parallels*, 2. 111–29. Edited by L. R. Fisher. 3 vols. Rome: Pontificum Institutum Biblicum, 1975.

_____. "Literary Genres in PRU IV." In *Ras Shamra Parallels*, 2. 153–214. Edited by L. R. Fisher. 3 vols. Rome: Pontificum Institutm Biblicum, 1975.

Koch, K. *The Prophets: The Assyrian Period*. Philadelphia: Fortress, 1983.

Köhler, L. "She'ar yashub und der nackte Relativsatz; Syntactica II," *VT* 3 (1953) 85.

_____. "Zum Verständnis von Jes 7,14," *ZAW* 67 (1955) 48–50.

König, E. *Das Buch Jesaja*. Gütersloh: Bertelsmann, 1926.

Kraeling, E. G. "The Immanuel Prophecy," *JBL* 50 (1931) 277–97.

Kraus, H.-J. *Die Königsherrschaft Gottes im Alten Testament*. Tübingen: J. C. B. Mohr (Paul Siebeck), 1951.

_____. *Prophetie und Politik*. Munich: Chr. Kaiser, 1952.

_____. "Jesaja 9,5-6 (6-7)." In *Herr tue meine Lippen auf*, 5. 43–53. 5 vols. 2d ed. Edited by G. Eichholz. Wuppertal: E. Müller, 1961.

_____. *Psalmen*. BKAT 15. 2 vols. 5th ed. Neukirchen-Vluyn: Neukirchener Verlag, 1978.

Kruse, H. "Alma Redemptoris Mater. Eine Auslegung der Immanuel-Weissagung Is 7,14," *Trier TZ* 74 (1965) 15–36.

Küchler, F. *Die Stellung des Propheten Jesajas zur Politik seiner Zeit*. Tübingen: J. C. B. Mohr (Paul Siebeck), 1906.

L'Heureux, C. E. "The Redactional History of Isaiah 5.1–10.4." In *In the Shelter of Elyon: Essays in Ancient Palestinian Life and Literature in Honor of G. W. Ahlström*, 99–119. Edited by W. B. Barrick and J. R. Spencer. Sheffield: JSOT Press, 1984.

Laato, A. *Who Is Immanuel? The Rise and the Foundering of Isaiah's Messianic Expectations*. Abo: Abo Academy Press, 1988.

Labuschagne, C. J. "Ugaritic *blt* and *bilti* in Is. X 4," *VT* 14 (1964) 97–99.

Lack, R. *La symbolique du libre d'Isaie. Essai sur l'image littéraire comme élément de structuralisme*. Rome: Biblical Institute Press, 1973.

Lagarde, P. de. "Kritische Anmerkungen zum Buche Isaias," *Semitica* 1 (1878) 1–30.

Lance, H. D. "Gezer in the Land and in History," *BA* 30 (1967) 34–47.

Lange, F. "Exegetische Problems zu Jes. 11," *LR* 23 (1975) 115–27.

Layard, A. H. *Ninevah and Its Remains*. New York: G. P. Putnam, 1851.

_____. *Discoveries in the Ruins of Ninevah and Babylon*. London/New York: J. Murray/G. P. Putnam, 1853.

Lemke, W. E. "The Synoptic Problem in the Chronicler's History," *HTR* 58 (1965) 349–63.

Lescow, T. "Das Geburtsmotiv in den messianischen Weissagungen bei Jesaja und Micha," *ZAW* 79 (1967) 172–207.

_____. "Jesajas Denkschrift aus der Zeit des syrisch-ephraimitischen Krieges," *ZAW* 85 (1973) 315–31.

Levine, L. D. "Menahem and Tiglat-Pileser; A New Synchronism," *BASOR* 206 (1972) 40–42.

_____. *Two Neo-Assyrian Stelae from Iran*. Toronto. Royal Ontario Museum, 1972.

_____. "The Second Campaign of Sennacherib," *JNES* 32 (1973) 312–17.

Liebrich, L. J. "The Position of Ch. 6 in the Book of Isaiah," *HUCA* 25 (1954) 37–40.

_____. "The Compilation of the Book of Isaiah," *JQR* 46 (1955–56) 259–77; 47 (1956–57) 114–38.

Lindblom, J. *A Study on the Immanuel Section in Isaiah. Isa. vii,1–ix,6.* Lund: CWK Gleerup, 1958.

Lipiński, E. "Le *sh°r-yshub* d'Isaie vii 3," *VT* 23 (1973) 245–46.

Lohfink, N. "Isaias 8,12–14," *BZ* 7 (1963) 98–104.

Long, B. O. "Reports of Visions among the Prophets," *JBL* 95 (1976) 353–65.

_____. "Prophetic Authority as Social Reality." In *Canon and Authority: Essays in Old Testament Religion and Theology*, 3–20. Edited by G. W. Coats and B. O. Long. Philadelphia: Fortress, 1977.

_____. *1 Kings with an Introduction to Historical Literature.* FOTL 9. Grand Rapids: Eerdmans, 1984.

Lowth, R. *Isaiah: A New Translation.* London: J. Dodsley and T. Cadell, 1778.

Lutz, H.-M. *Jahwe, Jerusalem und die Völker. Zur Vorgeschichte von Sach. 12,1–8 und 14,1–5.* WMANT 27. Neukirchen-Vluyn: Neukirchener Verlag, 1968.

McCarthy, D. J. "Notes on the Love of God in Deuteronomy and the Father-Son Relationship between Yahweh and Israel," *CBQ* 27 (1965) 144–47.

M'Clymont, J. A. "Hezekiah," *HBD* 1. 376–79.

Machinist, P. "Assyria and Its Image in the First Isaiah," *JAOS* 103 (1983) 719–37.

McKane, W. "The Interpretation of Isaiah VII 14–25," *VT* 17 (1967) 208–19.

McKay, J. W. *Religion in Judah under the Assyrians, 732–609 B.C.* SBT II/26. London: SCM, 1973.

Maisler, B. (see Mazar).

Marshall, R. J. "The Structure of Isaiah 1–12," *BR* 7 (1962) 19–33.

_____. "The Unity of Isaiah 1–12." *LQ* 14 (1962) 21–38.

Marti, K. *Das Buch Jesaja.* Tübingen: J. C. B. Mohr (Paul Siebeck), 1900.

_____. "Der jesajanische Kern in Jes 6,1–9,6," *BZAW* 34 (1920) 113–21.

Mattingly, G. L. "The Role of Philistine Autonomy in Neo-Assyrian Foreign Policy," *NEASB* 14 (1979) 49–57.

Mauchline, J. *Isaiah 1–39. Introduction and Commentary.* London/New York: SCM/Macmillan, 1962.

Mays, J. L. *Hosea.* Philadelphia: Westminster, 1969.

Mazar, B. [B. Maisler]. "Ancient Israelite Historiography," *IEJ* 2 (1952) 82–88.

_____. "The Tobiads," *IEJ* 7 (1957) 137–45, 229–38.

_____. "The Aramean Empire and its Relations with Israel," *BA* 25 (1962) 97–120.

Meinhold, J. *Der Heilige Rest.* Bonn: A. Marcus and E. Weber, 1903.

Meissner, B. "Palästinensische Städtebilder aus der Zeit Tiglatpilesers IV.," *ZDPV* 39 (1916) 261–63.

_____. *Könige Babyloniens und Assyriens.* Leipzig: Quelle & Meyer, 1926.

Mettinger, T. *King and Messiah: The Civil and Sacral Legitimation of the Israelite Kings.* Lund: CWK Gleerup, 1976.

Meyer, E. *Geschichte des Altertums.* 5 vols. 2d ed. Stuttgart/Berlin: J. G. Cotta'sche, 1931.

Milgrom, J. "Did Isaiah Prophesy during the Reign of Uzziah?" *VT* 14 (1964) 164–82.

Miller, J. M. "The Fall of the House of Ahab," *VT* 17 (1967) 307–24.

_____. "The Rest of the Acts of Jehoahaz," *ZAW* 80 (1968) 337–42.

_____. "Gibeah/Geba of Benjamin," *VT* 25 (1975) 145–66.

Miller, J. M. and Hayes, J. H. *A History of Ancient Israel and Judah.* Philadelphia: Westminster, 1986.

Montgomery, J. A. "Archival Data in the Book of Kings," *JBL* 53 (1934) 46–52.

_____. *A Critical and Exegetical Commentary on the Books of Kings.* 2d ed. Edinburgh: T. & T. Clark, 1976.

Morenz, S. "Eilebeute," *TLZ* 74 (1949) 697–99.

Moriarty, F. L. "The Immanuel Prophecies," *CBQ* 19 (1957) 226–33.

_____. "Isaiah 1–39," *JBC*, 265–82.

Mosis, R. *Untersuchungen zur Theologie des chronistischen Geschichtswerkes.* Freiburger TS 92. Freiburg: Herder, 1973.

Motyer, J. A. "Context and Content in the Interpretation of Isaiah 7.14," *Tyndale Bulletin* 21 (1970) 118–26.

Mowinckel, S. "Die vorderasiatischen Königs- und Fürsteninschriften. Eine stilistische Studie." In *Eucharisterion. Studien zur Religion und Literature des Alten und Neuen Testaments. Hermann Gunkel zum 60. Geburtstag*, 278–322. Edited by H. Schmidt. Göttingen: Vandenhoeck & Ruprecht, 1923.

_____. *Propheten Jesaja*. Oslo: Aschehoug, 1925.

_____. "Die Chronologie der israelitischen und judäischen Königen," *AcOr* 10 (1932) 161–277.

_____. "Die Komposition des Jesajabuches Kap. I–XXXIX," *AcOr* 11 (1933) 267–92.

_____. *He That Cometh*. Oxford/Nashville: B. H. Blackwell/Abingdon, 1956.

_____. *The Psalms in Israel's Worship*. 2 vols. Nashville: Abingdon, 1962.

Müller, H.-P. "Uns is ein Kind geboren . . . Jes. 9,1–6 in traditionsgeschichtlicher Sicht," *EvT* 21 (1961) 408–19.

_____. "Imperativ und Verheissung im Alten Testament," *EvT* 28 (1968) 557–71.

_____. "Glauben und Bleiben. Zur Denkschrift Jesajas Kapitel vi 1–viii 18," *VTSup* 26 (1974) 25–54.

_____. "Das Wort von dem Totengeistern Jes. 8,19f.," *WO* 8 (1975) 65–76.

Müller, W. E. *Die Vorstellung vom Rest im Alten Testament*. 2d ed. Edited by H. D. Preuss. Neukirchen-Vluyn: Neukirchener Verlag, 1973.

Murray, D. F. "The Rhetoric of Disputation: Re-examination of a Prophetic Genre," *JSOT* 38 (1987) 95–121.

Myers, J. M. *I Chronicles*. AB 12. Garden City: Doubleday, 1965.

_____. "The Kerygma of the Chronicler," *Int* 20 (1966) 259–73.

Na'aman, N. "Sennacherib's 'Letter to God' on His Campaign to Judah," *BASOR* 214 (1974) 25–39.

_____. "The Brook of Egypt and Assyrian Policy on the Border of Egypt," *TA* 6 (1979) 68–90.

_____. "Historical and Chronolgoical Notes on the Kingdoms of Israel and Judah in the Eighth Century B.C.," *VT* 36 (1986) 71–92.

Newsome, J. D. "Towards a New Understanding of the Chronicler and His Purposes," *JBL* 94 (1975) 201–17.

Niehr, H. "Zur Intension von Jes 6.1–9," *BN* 21 (1983) 59–65.

_____. "Zur Etymologie und Bedeutung von ʾšr I," *UF* 17 (1986) 231–35.

Nielsen, K. "Is 6:1–8:18 as Dramatic Writing," *ST* 40 (1986) 1–16.

North, R. "Does Archaeology Prove Chronicles' Sources?" In *Light unto My Path: Studies in Honor of J. M. Myers*, 375–401. Edited by E. H. Bream. Philadelphia: Temple University Press, 1974.

Noth, M. *The History of Israel*. 2d ed. New York/Evanston: Harper & Row, 1960.

_____. *Überlieferungsgeschichtliche Studien*. Halle: M. Niemeyer, 1943.

Oded, B. "Observations on Methods of Assyrian Rule in Transjordan after the Palestinian Campaign of Tiglathpileser III," *JNES* 29 (1970) 177–86.

_____. "The Historical Background of the Syro-Ephraimite War Reconsidered," *CBQ* 34 (1972) 153–65.

_____. "The Phoenician Cities and the Assyrian Empire in the Time of Tiglathpileser III," *ZDPV* 90 (1974) 38–49.

Olivier, J. P. J. "The Day of Midian and Isaiah 9:3b," *JNSL* 9 (1981) 143–49.

Ollenburger, B. C. *Zion the City of the Great King: A Theological Symbol of the Jerusalem Cult*. JSOTSup 41. Sheffield: JSOT Press, 1987.

Olmstead, A. T. E. "The Assyrian Chronicle," *JAOS* 34 (1915) 344–68.

_____. *Assyrian Historiography: A Source Study*. The University of Missouri Studies. Social Science Series III/1. Columbia, MO: University of Missouri Press, 1916.

_____. *History of Palestine and Syria to the Macedonian Conquest*. New York/London: Charles Scribner's Sons, 1931.

Oppenheim, A. L. *Ancient Mesopotamia: Portrait of a Dead Civilization*. Chicago/London: University of Chicago Press, 1964.

Orlinsky, H. "Studies in the St. Mark's Scroll, IV," *JQR* 43 (1952–53) 329–40.

Ostborn, G. *Tora in the Old Testament*. Lund: Hgakan Ohlssons, 1945.

Parpola, S. *Neo-Assyrian Toponyms*. AOAT 6. Kevelaer: Butzon & Bercker, 1970.

Paul, S. "A Literary Reinvestigation of the Authenticity of the Oracles against the Nations of Amos." In *De la Torah au Messie*, 189–204. Edited by M. Carrez et al. Paris: Desclee, 1981.

Pavlovsky, V. and Vogt, E. "Die Jahre der Könige von Juda und Israel," *Bib* 45 (1964) 321–47.

Pitard, W. T. *Ancient Damascus: A Historical Study of the Syrian City-State from Earliest Times until Its Fall to the Assyrians in 732 B.C.E.* Winona Lake: Eisenbrauns, 1987.

Pfeiffer, E. "Glaube im Alten Testament. Eine grammatikalisch-lexikalische Nachprüfung gegenwärtiger Theorien," *ZAW* 71 (1959) 151–64.

Plöger, J. G. "*ʾădāmâ*," *TWAT* 1. 99–105.

Porter, J. R. "Old Testament Historiography." In *Tradition and Interpretation: Essays by Members of the Society for Old Testament Study*, 125–62. Edited by G. W. Anderson. Oxford: Clarendon, 1979.

Porúbčan, S. "The Word *ʾOT* in Isaia 7,14," *CBQ* 22 (1960) 144–59.

Priest, J. "The Covenant of Brothers," *JBL* 84 (1965) 400–6.

Procksch, O. *Jesaia I.* KAT 9. Leipzig: A. Deichert, 1930.

———. *Der Staatsgedanke in der Prophetie.* Gütersloh: Bertelsmann, 1933.

Quell, G. *Wahre und Falsche Propheten.* Gütersloh: Bertelsmann, 1952.

Rad, G. von. "Die levitische Predigt in den Büchern der Chronik." In *Festschrift Otto Procksch*, 113–24. Leipzig: A. Deichert and J. C. Hinrich, 1934.

———. "Das judäische Königsritual," *TLZ* 72 (1947) 211–16.

———. *Der Heilige Krieg im alten Israel.* ATANT 20. Zurich: Zwingli, 1951.

———. *Old Testament Theology.* 2 vols. New York: Harper and Row, 1965.

———. *Gesammelte Studien.* Munich: Chr. Kaiser, 1971.

Rawlinson, H. C. *Cuneiform Inscriptions of Western Asia.* 5 vols. London: British Museum, 1861–1909.

Reade, J. "Mesopotamian Guidelines for Biblical Chronology," *Syro-Mesopotamian Studies* 4/1 (1981) 1–9.

Redford, D. B. "Studies in Relations between Palestine and Egypt during the First Millenium B.C.: II. The Twenty-second Dynasty," *JAOS* 93 (1973) 3–17.

Rehm, M. *Die Bücher der Chronik.* 2d ed. Würzburg: Echter Verlag, 1956.

_____. *Der königliche Messias im Licht der Immanuel-Weissagungen des Buches Jesaja.* Kevelaer: Butzon & Bercker, 1968.

Reich, R. "The Identification of the 'Sealed *karu* of Egypt,'" *IEJ* 34 (1984) 132–38.

Rendtorff, R. *Studien zur Geschichte des Opfers im Alten Israel.* WMANT 24. Neukirchen-Vluyn: Neukirchener Verlag, 1967.

Reventlow, H. G. "A Syncretistic Enthronement Hymn in Isa. 9:1–6," *UF* 3 (1971) 321–25.

_____. "Das Ende der sog. 'Denkschrift' Jesajas," *BN* 38/39 (1987) 62–67.

Rice, G. *The Syro-Ephraimite Crisis and the Witness of Isaiah, Chapters Seven and Eight, to the Prophet's Involvement.* Dissertation, Columbia University, 1969.

_____. "The Interpretation of Isa 7:15–17," *JBL* 96 (1977) 363–69.

_____. "A Neglected Interpretation of the Immanuel Prophecy," *ZAW* 90 (1978) 220–27.

Rignell, L. G. "A Study of Isaiah 9:2–7," *LQ* 7 (1955) 31–35.

_____. "Das Immanuelszeichen. Einige Gesichtspunkte zu Jes 7," *ST* 11 (1957) 99–119.

_____. "Das Orakel 'Maher-salal Has-bas.' Jesaja 8," *ST* 10 (1957) 40–52.

Roberts, J. J. M. "The Davidic Origin of the Zion Tradition," *JBL* 92 (1973) 329–44.

_____. "Isaiah and His Children." In *Biblical and Related Studies Presented to Samuel Iwry*, 193–203. Edited by A. Kort and S. Morschauser. Winona Lake: Eisenbrauns, 1985.

_____. "Isaiah 2 and the Prophet's Message to the North," *JQR* 75 (1985) 290–303.

Robertson, E. "Some Obscure Passages in Isaiah," *AJSL* 49 (1932/33) 320–22.

Rost, L. *Die Überlieferung von der Thronnachfolge Davids.* BWANT III/6. Stuttgart: Kohlhammer, 1926 = his *Das kleine Credo und andere Studien zum Alten Testament*, 119–253. Heidelberg: Quell & Meyer, 1965.

Rost, P. *Die Keilschrifttexte Tiglat-Pilesers III.* Leipzig: E. Pfeiffer, 1893.

Rudolph, W. "Problems in the Books of Chronicles," *VT* 4 (1954) 401–9.

_____. *Chronikbücher.* Tübingen: J. C. B. Mohr (Paul Siebeck), 1955.

———. *Jeremiah*. 3d ed. Tübingen: J. C. B. Mohr (Paul Siebeck), 1968.

Saebø, M. "Formgeschichtliche Erwägungen zu Jes. 7,3–9," *ST* 14 (1960) 54–69.

———. "Zur Traditionsgeschichte von Jesaia 8,9–10," *ZAW* 76 (1964) 132–44.

Saggs, H. W. F. "Nimrud Letters, 1952—Part II," *Iraq* 17 (1955) 126–60.

———. *Assyriology and the Study of the Old Testament*. Cardiff: University of Wales Press, 1969.

———. *The Might That Was Assyria*. London: Sidgewick and Jackson, 1984.

Šanda, A. *Die Bücher der Könige*. 2 vols. Münster: Aschendorff, 1911–12.

Sauer, G. "Die Umkehrforderung in der Verkündigung Jesajas." In *Wort, Gebot, Glaube. Beiträge zur Theologie des Alten Testaments. Walter Eichrodt zum 80. Geburtstag*. ATANT 59. Edited by H. J. Stoebe. Zurich: Zwingli, 1970.

Sawyer, J. "The Qumran Reading of Isaiah 6:13," *ASTI* 3 (1964) 11–13.

Scharbert, J. *Die Propheten Israels bis 700 v. Chr*. Cologne: J. P. Bachem, 1965.

———. "Was versteht das Alte Testament unter Wunder?" *BK* 22 (1967) 37–42.

Schmid, H. H. *Shalom: Frieden im Alten Orient und im Alten Testament*. SBS 51. Stuttgart: Katholisches Bibelwerk, 1971.

Schmidt, H. "Jesaja 8,9 und 10." In *Stromata. Festgabe des Akademisch-theologischen Vereins zu Giessen im schmalkaldener Kartell anlässlich seines 50. Stiftungstages*, 3–10. Edited by G. Bertram. Leipzig: Hinrich, 1930.

Schmidt, J. M. "Gedanken zum Verstockungsauftrag Jesajas (Is. VI)," *VT* 21 (1971) 68–90.

Schmidt, W. "Wo had die Aussage: 'Yahweh der Heilige,' ihren Ursprung?" *ZAW* 74 (1962) 62–66.

———. "Jerusalemer El-Traditionen bei Jesaja: Ein religionsgeschichtlicher Vergleich zum Vorstellungsbereich des göttlichen Königtums," *ZRGG* 16 (1964) 302–13.

Schmidt, W. H. "Die Ohnmacht des Messias. Zur Überlieferungsgeschichte der messianischen Weissagungen im Alten Testament," *KD* 15 (1969) 18–34.

Schoors, A. *Jesaja*. Roermond: J. J. Romen, 1972.

_____. "Isaiah, the Minister of Royal Anointment?" *OTS* 20 (1977) 85–107.

Schrader, E. *Die Keilinschriften und das Alte Testament*. Giessen: J. Ricker, 1872.

Schramm, W. *Einleitung in die assyrischen Königsinschriften*. Handbuch der Orientalistik I/5, part 2. Leiden/Cologne: E. J. Brill, 1973.

Schreiner, J. *Sion-Jerusalem Jahwes Königssitz. Theologie der heiligen Stadt im Alten Testament*. SANT 7. Munich: Kösel, 1963.

_____. "Zur Testgestalt von Jes 6 und 7,1–17," *BZ* 22 (1978) 92–97 = his *Segen für die Völker. Gesammelte Schriften zur Entstehung und Theologie des Alten Testaments*, 65–71. Edited by E. Zenger. Würzburg: Echter Verlag, 1987.

Schroeder, O. "*wmśwś* eine Glosse zu *rāṣon*," *ZAW* 32 (1912) 301–2.

Schunk, K. D. "Der fünfte Thronname des Messias (Jes. IX 5–6)," *VT* 23 (1973) 108–10.

Scott, R. B. Y. "The Literary Structure of Isaiah's Oracles." In *Studies in Old Testament Prophecy*, 175–86. Edited by H. H. Rowley. New York: Scribner, 1950.

_____. "The Book of Isaiah." *IB* 5. 151–381.

Scullion, J. J. "An Approach to the Understanding of Isaiah 7:10–17," *JBL* 87 (1968) 288–300.

Seybold, K. *Das davidische Königtum im Zeugnis der Propheten*. FRLANT 107. Göttingen: Vandenhoeck & Ruprecht, 1972.

_____. "*Ḥānēp*," *TWAT* 3. 41–48.

Shaw, C. "Micah 1:10–16 Reconsidered," *JBL* 106 (1987) 223–29.

Shea, W. "Menahem and Tiglath-Pileser III," *JNES* 37 (1978) 43–49.

Sheppard, G. T. "The Anti-Assyrian Redaction and the Canonical Context of Isaiah 1–39," *JBL* 104 (1985) 193–216.

Simons, J. *Jerusalem in the Old Testament*. Leiden: E. J. Brill, 1952.

_____. *The Geographical and Topographical Texts of the Old Testament*. Leiden: E. J. Brill, 1959.

Skehan, P. W. "A Note on Is 10,11b–12a," *CBQ* 14 (1952) 236.

_____. "Qumran and the Present State of Old Testament Text Studies: The Masoretic Text," *JBL* 78 (1959) 21–25.

_____. "Some Textual Problems in Isaia," *CBQ* 22 (1960) 47–55.

Skinner, J. *The Book of the Prophet Isaiah. Chapters I–XXXIX*. 2d ed. Cambridge: Cambridge University Press, 1915.

Smend, R. "Zur Geschichte von *hʾmyn*." In *Hebräische Wortforschung. Festschrift zum 80. Geburtstag von Walter Baumgartner*, 284–90. VTSup 16. Leiden: E. J. Brill, 1967 = his *Die Mitte des Alten Testaments*, 320–33. BEvT 99. Munich: Chr. Kaiser, 1986.

Smith, G. "On a New Fragment of the Assyrian Canon Belonging to the Reigns of Tiglath-pileser and Shalmaneser," *TSBA* 2 (1873) 321–32.

_____. *Assyrian Discoveries*. London: S. Low, Marston, Searle, and Rivington, 1876.

Smith, G. A. *The Book of Isaiah*. 2 vols. New York: Armstrong, 1888–90.

Smith, J. M. P. "*Sheʾar yashub*," *ZAW* 34 (1914) 220–27.

Smith, L. "The Use of the Word torah in Isaiah, Chapters 1–39," *AJSL* 46 (1929) 1–21.

Smith, W. R. "Old Testament Notes, II. Isaiah X. 27, 28," *Journal of Philology* 13 (1885) 62–65.

Soden, W. von. *Akkadisches Handwörterbuch*. Wiesbaden: Otto Harrassowitz, 1965–81.

Soggin, A. *A History of Israel*. London/Philadelphia: SCM/Westminster, 1984.

Spalinger, A. "Esarhaddon and Egypt: An Analysis of the First Invasion of Egypt," *Or* 43 (1974) 295–326.

Speier, S. "*Ûněqîṣennah*, Isaiah 7:6a," *JBL* 72 (1953) xiv.

_____. "Zu drei Jesajastellen (Jes. 1,7; 5,24; 10,7)," *TZ* 21 (1965) 310–13.

Spieckermann, H. *Juda unter Assur in der Sargonidenzeit*. FRLANT 129. Göttingen: Vandenhoeck & Ruprecht, 1982.

Stade, B. *Geschichte des Volkes Israel*. 2 vols. Berlin: G. Grote, 1887.

Staerk, W. *Das assyrische Weltreich im Urteil der Propheten*. Göttingen: Vandenhoeck & Ruprecht, 1908.

Stamm, J. J. "La prophétie d'Emmanuel," *RTP* 32 (1944) 97–123.

_____. "Die Immanuel-Weissagung: Ein Gespräch mit E. Hammershaimb," *VT* 4 (1954) 20–33.

_____. "Neuere Arbeiten zum Immanuel-Problem," *ZAW* 68 (1956) 46–53.

_____. "Die Immanuel-Weissagung und die Eschatologie des Jesaja," *TZ* 16 (1960) 439–55.

_____. "Die Immanuel-Perikope im Lichte neuerer Veröffentlichungen," *ZDMGSup* 1 (1969) 281–90.

_____. "Die Immanuel-Perikope. Eine Nachlese," *TZ* 30 (1974) 11–22.

Staub, J. J. "A Review of the History of the Interpretations of Isaiah 8:11–9:6." In *Jewish Civilization: Essays and Studies*, 1. 89–107. Edited by R. A. Brauner. Philadelphia: Reconstructionist Rabbinical College, 1979.

Steck, O. H. "Bemerkungen zu Jesaja 6," *BZ* 16 (1972) 188–206.

_____. *Friedensvorstellungen im alten Jerusalem*. Zurich: Theologischer Verlag, 1972.

_____. "Beiträge zum Verständnis von Jesaja 7,10–17 und 8,1–4," *TZ* 29 (1973) 161–78.

_____. "Rettung und Verstockung. Exegetische Bemerkungen zu Jesaja 7,3–9," *EvT* 33 (1973) 73–90.

Stegemann, U. "Der Restgedanke bei Isaias," *BZ* 13 (1969) 161–86.

Steinmann, J. *Le Prophète Isaie. Sa vie, son oeuvre et son temps*. 2d ed. Paris: Cerf, 1955.

Stern, H. S. "The Knowledge of Good and Evil," *VT* 8 (1958) 405–18.

Tadmor, H. "The Campaigns of Sargon II of Assur: A Chronological-Historical Study," *JCS* 12 (1958) 22–40, 77–100.

_____. "Azriyau of Yaudi," *ScrHier* 8 (1961) 232–71.

_____. "The Southern Border of Aram," *IEJ* 12 (1962) 114–22.

_____. "The Assyrian Campaigns to Philistia." In *Military History of the Land of Israel in Biblical Times*, 261–85. Edited by J. Liver. Tel-Aviv: Israel Defense Forces Publishing House, 1964 (Hebrew).

_____. "Philistia under Assyrian Rule," *BA* 29 (1966) 86–102.

_____. "Introductory Remarks to a New Edition of the Annals of Tiglath-pileser III," *Proceedings of the Israel Academy of Sciences and Humanities* II/9 (1967) 168–87.

_____. "The Historical Inscriptions of Adad-nirari III," *Iraq* 35 (1973) 141–50.

_____. "Assyria and the West: The Ninth Century and Its Aftermath." In *Unity and Diversity: Essays in the History, Literature, and Religion of the Ancient Near East*, 36–48. Edited by H. Goedicke and J. J. M. Roberts. Baltimore: John Hopkins University Press, 1975.

_____. "Observations on Assyrian Historiography." In *Essays on the Ancient Near East in Memory of J. J. Finkelstein*, 209–13.

Memoirs of the Connecticut Academy of Arts and Sciences 19. Edited by M. D. Ellis. Hamden, CT: Archon, 1977.

———. "The Chronology of the First Temple Period: A Presentation and Evaluation of the Sources," *WHJP* 4/1. 44–60, 318–20 = J. A. Soggin, *A History of Ancient Israel*, 368–83, 408–11. London/Philadelphia: SCM/Westminster, 1984.

Tadmor, H. and Cogan, M. "Ahaz and Tiglath-Pileser in the Book of Kings: Historiographical Considerations," *Bib* 60 (1979) 491–508.

Talmage, F. "*ḥrṭ ʾnwš* in Isaiah 8:1," *HTR* 60 (1967) 465–68.

Talmon, S. "Divergences in Calendar-Reckoning in Ephraim and Judah," *VT* 8 (1958) 48–74 = (slightly revised) "The Cult and Calendar Reform of Jeroboam I." In his *King, Cult and Calendar in Ancient Israel: Collected Essays*, 113–39. Jerusalem: Magnes, 1986.

Tånberg, K. A. *Die prophetische Mahnrede. Form- und traditionsgeschichtliche Studien zum prophetischen Umkehrruf.* FRLANT 143. Göttingen: Vandenhoeck & Ruprecht, 1987.

Thiele, E. R. "The Chronology of the Kings of Judah and Israel," *JNES* 3 (1944) 137–86.

———. "Pekah to Hezekiah," *VT* 16 (1966) 83–103.

———. "Coregencies and Overlapping Reigns among the Hebrew Kings," *JBL* 93 (1974) 174–200.

———. *The Mysterious Numbers of the Hebrew Kings: A Reconstruction of the Chronology of the Kingdoms of Israel and Judah*. 3d ed. Grand Rapids: Zondervan, 1984.

Thomas, D. W. "A Note on the Meaning of yd^c in Hosea ix.7 and Isaiah ix.8," *JTS* 41 (1940) 43–44.

Thompson, M. E. W. *Situation and Theology: Old Testament Interpretations of the Syro-Ephraimite War*. Sheffield: Almond, 1982.

———. "Isaiah's Ideal King," *JSOT* 24 (1982) 79–88.

———. "Isaiah's Sign of Immanuel," *ExpTim* 95 (1983) 67–71.

Torczyner, H. (see Tur-Sinai).

Troeltsch, E. "Das Ethos der hebräischen Propheten," *Logos* 6 (1916) 1–28.

Tur-Sinai, N. H. [H. Torczyner]. *Lachish I (Tell ed Duweir): The Lachish Letters*. London: Oxford University Press, 1938.

———. *The Book of Job: A New Commentary*. Jerusalem: Kiryath Sepher, 1957.

Unger, M. F. *Israel and the Arameans of Damascus*. Grand Rapids: Zondervan, 1957.

Ungnad, A. "Eponym." In *Reallexikon der Assyriologie*, 2. 412–57. 6 vols. Edited by E. Ebling and B. Meissner. Berlin: Walter de Gruyter, 1932.

Vanel, A. "Ṭâbe'el en Is. VII 6 et le roi Tubail de Tyr," *VTSup* 26 (1974) 17–25.

Van Seters, J. *In Search of History: Historiography in the Ancient World and the Origins of Biblical History*. New Haven/London: Yale University Press, 1983.

Vaux, R. de. *Ancient Israel: Its Life and Institutions*. New York: McGraw-Hill, 1961.

Vermeylen, J. *Du prophète Isaie à l'apocalyptique: Isaie, I–XXXV, miroir d'un demi-millénaire d'expéreince religieuse en Israel*. 2 vols. Paris: J. Gabalda, 1977.

Vischer, W. *Die Immanuel-Botschaft im Rahmen des königlichen Zionsfestes*. Zurich: Evangelischer Verlag, 1955.

Vogelstein, M. *Jeroboam II: The Rise and Fall of His Empire*. Cincinnati: self-published, 1945.

Vogt, E. "'Filius Tab'el' (Isa 7:6)," *Bib* 37 (1956) 263–64.

_____. "Die Texte Tiglat-Pilesers III. über die Eroberung Palästinas," *Bib* 45 (1964) 348–54.

_____. "Einige hebräische Wortbedeutungen," *Bib* 48 (1967) 57–74.

_____. "Jesaja und die drohende Eroberung Palästinas durch Tiglatpileser." In *Wort, Lied und Gottesspruch. Beiträge zu Psalmen und Propheten. Festschrift für Joseph Ziegler*, 249–56. Edited by J. Schreiner. Würzburg: Echter Verlag/Katholisches Bibelwerk, 1972.

Vollmer, J. "Zur Sprache von Jesaja 9,1–6," *ZAW* 80 (1968) 343–50.

_____. "Jesajanische Begrifflichkeit [9.1–6]," *ZAW* 83 (1971) 389–91.

_____. *Geschichtliche Rückblicke und Motive in der Prophetie des Amos, Hosea und Jesaja*. BZAW 119. Berlin: Walter de Gruyter, 1971.

Vriezen, T. C. "Prophecy and Eschatology," *VTSup* 1 (1953) 199–229.

_____. "Essentials of the Theology of Isaiah." In *Israel's Prophetic Heritage. Essays in Honor of James Muilenberg*. Edited by B. W. Anderson and W. Harrelson. New York: Harper, 1962.

Wagner, N. E. "A Note on Isaiah vii 4," *VT* 8 (1958) 438.

Wagner, S. "*yrh* II," *TWAT* 3. 920–30.

Wallenstein, M. "An Unnoticed Euphemism in Isaiah IX 19–20?" *VT* 2 (1952) 179–80.

Wanke, G. "ʾoy and hoy," *ZAW* 78 (1966) 215–18.

Watts, J. D. W. *Isaiah 1–33.* WBC 24. Waco: Word Books, 1985.

Weinfeld, M. *Deuteronomy and the Deuteronomic School.* Oxford: Clarendon, 1972.

Weinrich, F. *Der religiös-utopische Charakter der "prophetischen Politik."* Giessen: A. Töpelmann, 1932.

Weippert, M. "Heiliger Krieg in Israel und Assyrien," *ZAW* 84 (1972) 460–93.

_____. "Menahem von Israel und seine Zeitgenossen in einer Steleninschrift des assyrischen Königs Tiglathpileser III. aus dem Iran," *ZDPV* 89 (1973) 26–53.

Weiss, M. "The Contribution of Literary Criticism to Biblical Research: Illustrated by the Problem of She'ar-Yashub," *ScrHier* 31 (1986) 373–86.

Welch, A. C. *The Work of the Chronicler: Its Purpose and Its Date.* London: Oxford University Press, 1939.

_____. *Kings and Prophets of Israel.* Edited by N. W. Porteous. London: Lutterworth, 1952.

Wellhausen, J. *Prolegomena to the History of Ancient Israel.* Gloucester, MA: Peter Smith, 1973. (German original, *Prolegomena zur Geschichte Israels.* 2d ed. Berlin: Reimer, 1883).

Welten, P. *Geschichte und Geschichtsdarstellung in den Chronikbüchern.* WMANT 42. Neukirchen-Vluyn: Neukirchener Verlag, 1973.

Werner, W. *Eschatologische Texte in Jesaja 1–39.* FB 46. Würzburg: Echter Verlag, 1982.

_____. "Vom Prophetenwort zur Prophetentheologie. Ein redactionskritischer Versuch zu Jes 6,1–8,18," *BZ* 29 (1985) 1–30.

Westermann, C. "Das Hoffen im Alten Testament." In his *GS*, 219–65. Munich: Chr. Kaiser, 1964.

_____. *Basic Forms of Prophetic Speech.* Philadelphia: Westminster, 1967.

Whedbee, J. W. *Isaiah and Wisdom.* Nashville/New York: Abingdon, 1971.

Whitley, C. F. "The Call and Mission of Isaiah," *JNES* 18 (1959) 38–48.

_____. "The Language and Exegesis of Isaiah 8:16–23," *ZAW* 90 (1978) 28–43.

Widengren, G. "Yahweh's Gathering of the Dispersed." In *In the Shelter of Elyon: Essays on Ancient Palestinian Life and Literature in Honor of G. W. Ahlström*, 227–45. Edited by W. B. Barrick and J. R. Spencer. Sheffield: JSOT Press, 1984.

Wifall, W. R. "The Chronology of the Divided Monarchy of Israel," *ZAW* 80 (1968) 319–37.

Wildberger, H. "Die Thronnamen des Messias, Jes. 9,5b," *TZ* 16 (1960) 314–32.

———. "'Glauben'. Erwägungen zu hʾmyn." In *Hebräische Wortforschung. Festschrift zum 80. Geburtstag von Walter Baumgartner*, 372–86. VTSup 16. Leiden: E. J. Brill, 1967.

———. *Jesaja 1–12*. BKAT 10/1. 2d ed. Neukirchen-Vluyn: Neukirchener Verlag, 1980.

———. *Jesaja 13–27*. BKAT 10/2. Neukirchen-Vluyn: Neukirchener Verlag, 1978.

Wilke, F. *Jesaja und Assur. Eine exegetisch-historische Untersuchung zur Politik des Propheten Jesaja*. Leipzig: Dieterich'sche Verlagsbuchhandlung, 1905.

———. *Die politische Wirksamkeit der Propheten Israels*. Leipzig: Dieterisch'sche Verlagsbuchhandlung, 1913.

Willi, T. *Die Chronik als Auslegung. Untersuchungen zur literarischen Gestaltung der historischen Überlieferung Israels*. FRLANT 106. Göttingen: Vandenhoeck & Ruprecht, 1972.

Williams, J. G. "The Alas-Oracles of the Eighth Century Prophets," *HUCA* 38 (1967) 75–91.

Williamson, H. G. M. *Israel in the Books of Chronicles*. Cambridge: Cambridge University Press, 1977.

———. *1 and 2 Chronicles*. Grand Rapids/London: Eerdmans/Marshall, Morgan & Scott, 1982.

Wilson, R. R. *Prophecy and Society in Ancient Israel*. Philadelphia: Fortress, 1980.

Winckler, H. *Geschichte Israels in Einzeldarstellung*. 2 vols. Leipzig: Pfeiffer, 1895–1900.

Winckler, H. and Zimmern, H., eds. *Die Keilschriften und das Alte Testament*. 3d ed. Berlin: Reuther and Reichard, 1902–3.

Wiseman, D. J. "Two Historical Inscriptions from Nimrud," *Iraq* 13 (1951) 21–28.

———. "A Fragmentary Inscription of Tiglath-pileser III from Nimrud," *Iraq* 18 (1956) 117–29.

Wolf, H. M. "A Solution to the Immanuel Prophecy in Isaiah 7:14–8:22," *JBL* 91 (1972) 449–56.

Wolff, H. W. "Das Thema 'Umkehr' in der alttestamentliche Prophetie," *ZTK* 48 (1951) 129–48 = his *GS*, 130–50. 2d ed. Munich: Chr. Kaiser, 1973.

_____. *Frieden ohne Ende. Jesaja 7,1–17 und 9,1–6 ausgelegt.* BibS(N) 35. Neukirchen-Vluyn: Neukirchener Verlag, 1962.

_____. *Hosea.* Hermeneia. Philadelphia: Fortress, 1974.

Wolverton, W. I. "Judgment in Advent: Notes on Isaiah 8:5–15 and 7:14," *ATR* 37 (1955) 284–91.

Worschech, U. F. C. "The Problem of Isaiah 6:13," *AUSS* 12 (1974) 126–38.

Wright, G. E. *Isaiah.* London: SCM, 1964.

Würthwein, E. "Jesaja 7,1–9. Ein Beitrag zu dem Thema: Prophetie und Politik." In *Theologie als Glaubenswagnis. Festschrift für Karl Heim zum 80. Geburtstag,* 47–63. Hamburg: Furche-Verlag, 1954 = his *Wort und Existenz. Studien zum Alten Testament,* 127–43. Göttingen: Vandenhoeck & Ruprecht, 1970.

_____. *Die Bücher der Könige.* 2 vols. Göttingen: Vandenhoeck & Ruprecht, 1985.

Yadin, Y. *Hazor: The Rediscovery of a Great Citadel of the Bible.* New York: Random House, 1975.

Zimmerli, W. "Verkündigung und Sprache der Botschaft Jesajas." In *Fides et Communicatio. Festschrift für Martin Dörne zum 70. Geburtstag,* 441–54. Edited by D. Rössler, G. Voigt, and F. Wintzer. Göttingen: Vandenhoeck & Ruprecht, 1970.

_____. "Vier oder fünf Thronnamen des messianischen Herrschers in Jes. IX 5b.6," *VT* 22 (1972) 249–52.

_____. "A Neglected Solution of a Problem in Psalm LXXVI 11," *VT* 24 (1974) 136–46.

AUTHOR INDEX

Abel, F.-M., 63
Ackroyd, P. R., 16–17, 82, 87, 90–91, 93–94, 120, 121, 129, 132, 136–37, 205, 290–92
Aharoni, Y., 32–33, 39, 104, 275
Ahlström, G. W., 119
Albright, W. F., 119. 154, 275, 277, 278
Alonso Schökel, L., 145, 291
Alt, A., 33, 37, 46–52, 66, 70, 75, 99, 215, 221, 223, 226–28, 230
Anderson, G. W., 291
Arnold, P. M., 275–76
Astour, M. C., 102
Asurmendi, J. M., 2, 8–10, 32–33, 41, 44, 46, 59, 64, 105, 114, 116, 154, 191, 230–31
Auvray, P., 280
Avigad, N., 208

Baer, K., 54
Barnes, W. H., 23
Barnett, R. D., 36
Bartelmus, R., 11, 137, 148, 159, 169
Barth, H., 122–24, 173, 193–94, 215–17, 220, 222, 224, 226–27, 229–32, 252–54, 256, 259, 261–64, 269, 277, 278, 280–82, 285–88
Baumgartner, W., 159
Becker, J., 286, 287
Beecher, W. J., 207

Begrich, J., 4, 23, 39, 95–99, 101, 104, 107, 141, 149, 207
Benzinger, I., 102
Berg, W., 167, 169
Beyerlin, W., 193
Bickert, R., 23, 84–85, 88, 134–36, 147, 151
Biran, A., 34
Blank, S., 142, 144–46, 266–68
Boehmer, J., 188, 206
Borger, R., 45–46, 55, 57, 59–60
Braun, R. L., 94
Bright, J., 33, 81, 95, 102, 104, 185, 283–84
Brinkman, J. A., 25
Brownlee, W. H., 119
Brunet, A.-M., 93
Buber, M., 2, 10
Budde, K., 2, 3–6, 10, 13, 15–16, 83–84, 96, 108, 119, 125, 130, 134, 135, 141, 153, 155, 160, 166, 169, 173–74, 186, 194, 297
Burrows, M., 147, 189
Buss, M., 75

Carlson, R. A., 228, 231, 232
Carroll, R. P., 204, 205, 211, 266–67
Cazelles, H., 39, 104, 117, 119, 120
Cheyne, T. K., 252
Childs, B. S., 2, 252, 259, 261, 278, 281, 282

Christensen, D. L., 276, 278–80
Clements, R. E., 11, 115–17, 123, 135, 136, 142, 144, 146, 156, 160, 163, 166, 173, 184–86, 188, 192, 194, 198, 203, 204–6, 212, 215–16, 220–21, 230–31, 235–36, 239, 242, 244, 251–52, 254, 257, 259–60, 263, 266, 273, 277–81, 283, 287–88, 290, 292
Clifford, R. J., 252
Clines, D. J., 189
Cogan, M., 28, 41, 51, 63, 81–82, 85–90, 104, 155, 174, 261
Conrad, E., 149
Coppens, J., 12, 169, 229
Criado, R., 165
Crook, M., 283
Cross, F. M., 159
Crüsemann, F., 226, 291, 293

Dahood, M., 249
Dalman, G., 172, 277, 278
Day, J., 144–46
Delitzsch, F., 115, 136, 155, 162, 166, 182, 189, 192–93, 218, 228
Dentan, R. C., 140
Dequeker, L., 162
Dietrich, W., 2, 11, 113, 120, 128–29, 136, 142, 147, 156, 164, 180, 183–85, 187–89, 196, 198, 201, 203, 205, 209, 251–53
Dillmann, A., 136, 246
Dohmen, C., 133–34, 136, 137, 147, 171
Donner, H., 1–2, 12, 33, 39, 46, 52–53, 75, 95, 97–99, 101–2, 104–5, 107, 115–17, 121–23, 125, 135–39, 147, 149, 150, 153–54, 156, 161–63, 168, 180, 182–86, 188, 195, 197–99, 203, 235–38, 241, 245, 249, 251–52, 253, 259, 263, 274–78, 280
Driver, G. R., 119, 139, 153, 175, 197–98, 201, 204, 208, 212, 215, 218–19, 222–23, 256, 263–64

Driver, S. R., 182
Duhm, B., 115, 123, 125, 134–37, 142, 149, 152, 169, 173, 182, 184, 186, 188–89, 192, 193, 198, 200–3, 205, 206, 216–18, 220, 222, 228, 229, 233, 235, 237, 239, 245, 249, 251–52, 254, 256, 257, 261, 265–66, 274, 280, 283, 290, 291

Edwards, I. E. S., 54
Eichrodt, W., 193, 205
Eissfeldt, O., 139
Elhorst, H. J., 181
Elliger, K., 2
Emerton, J. A., 119, 145, 215, 222–24
Engnell, I., 119
Eph'al, I., 29, 31, 37–41, 45–46, 55–56, 58, 60, 62, 64
Evans, C. A., 196–98, 203

Fabry, H.-J., 140
Faulkner, M., 36
Féderlin, L., 278
Feldmann, F., 119
Fensham, F. C., 87
Fishbane, M., 283
Fohrer, G., 11, 115, 116, 135–37, 142, 144–45, 149, 150, 158, 160–61, 165–66, 173, 180, 184, 188–89, 193–95, 198, 201, 203, 205–6, 209, 216–17, 220, 229, 235–37, 249, 251–52, 257, 277, 280, 283, 286, 290–92
Forrer, E., 29, 33, 39, 63, 65
Fullerton, K., 184, 186, 189, 191–93, 251, 257, 258, 263

Galling, K., 82, 102, 180
Gerstenberger, E., 252
Gese, H., 169
Giesebrecht, F., 186
Gilead, H., 276
Ginsberg, H. L., 114, 204–6, 208,

215, 217–20, 222, 224–25
Godbey, A. H., 39
Goldstein, J., 48
Gorg, M., 133, 161, 163
Goshen-Gottstein, M. H., 208
Gottwald, N. K., 2, 12, 104, 113–15, 168, 174, 198, 230–31, 235–36, 252–53, 278, 280
Gowan, D. E., 141
Graham, W. C., 136
Gray, G. B., 135–37, 155, 163, 166–67, 169, 173, 181–82, 184, 188, 197, 206, 216–18, 221, 235, 242, 249, 253, 254, 256, 263–64, 274, 277–78, 281, 283
Gray, J., 34, 81–82, 84–86, 99
Grayson, A. K., 24–26, 28
Greenfield, J. C., 87
Gressmann, H., 7, 8, 10, 16, 150, 160, 180, 189, 283, 286
Grossberg, D., 264
Guillaume, A., 219
Gunneweg, A. H. J., 145
Guthe, H., 161

Hammershaimb, E., 9, 12, 163, 166–69, 171
Haran, M., 67, 78, 102
Hardmeier, C., 14, 118, 120, 156–57, 204
Harrelson, W., 228, 231
Hasel, G., 142–46
Hattendorf, 167
Hayes, J. H., 23, 24, 30, 73–74, 114, 172, 205, 207, 239, 253, 291
Heaton, E. W., 143
Heider. G., 79
Helfmeyer, F. J., 161
Herbert, A. S., 283, 291
Herder, J. G., 282
Hermisson, H.-J., 285
Herntrich, V., 136, 138, 149, 156, 186, 216, 235, 277
Herrmann, S., 100, 102, 104, 145, 146

Heschel, A., 116
Hobbs, T. R., 243
Höffken, P., 133, 137, 151, 159, 166
Hoffmann, H.-D., 77, 80
Hoffmann, H. W., 143
Høgenhaven, J., 226
Holladay, W. L., 143
Hommel, F. 63, 65
Honeyman, 187–88, 244
Horst, F., 118
Huber, F., 2, 116, 145–46, 149–50, 152, 193–94, 252–53, 257–58
Hubmann, F. D., 133, 137, 147, 163, 164, 169
Hughes, J. R. A., 23
Humbert, P., 180
Hvidberg, F., 119

Irsigler, H., 133–34, 136, 137, 151, 152, 159, 162, 167, 169
Irvine, S. A., 114, 172, 205, 207, 239, 253, 291
Iwry, S., 119

Japhet, S., 94
Jenkins, A. K., 278
Jenni, J., 118, 168, 278
Jensen, J., 11, 163, 169, 207, 283, 284, 290
Jepsen, A., 78, 157
Jeremias, J., 75
Jones, G. H., 84–86, 99
Jouon, P., 86
Junker, H., 169

Kaiser, O., 11, 116, 118, 121, 122, 126, 129, 133–34, 136–37, 142, 147, 151–52, 162–63, 166, 172, 180, 188–89, 196, 201, 203, 212, 215–18, 220, 228, 237, 239, 243, 252, 264, 266, 273, 275–77, 285–86, 291–93
Kalluveettil, C. M. I., 87, 89, 102

Kaplan, M., 118
Kaufmann, Y., 118, 205
Keller, C. A., 150
Kennett, R. H., 143
Kilian, R., 8, 11, 121, 125, 136, 137, 143–44, 146, 148, 155, 156, 159, 162, 164, 166, 216, 229, 261, 283
Kissane, E. J., 119, 166, 206, 238, 244, 277, 287–88
Kittel, R., 85, 99, 169
Klein, H., 187–88, 191
Knierim, R., 117–18
Koch, K., 114
Köhler, L., 142, 169
König, E., 119
Kraeling, E. G., 6, 12, 16, 160
Kraus, H.-J., 2, 8, 190, 202, 230
Kruse, H., 169
Küchler, F., 1–2

L'Heureux, C. E., 121–24, 244
Labuschagne, C. J., 249
Lagarde, P. de, 117, 139, 152
Lance, H. D., 36
Lemke, W. E., 91, 93
Lescow, T., 12, 13–14, 120, 125, 156, 158, 163, 169, 198, 231, 282–83, 285
Levine, L. D., 28, 38, 41, 59, 154
Lindblom, J., 10, 12, 120, 142, 145, 156, 160, 163, 165–67, 169, 184, 187, 189, 195, 198, 201, 203, 204, 206, 209, 221, 229, 230
Lipiński, E., 142
Long, B. O., 89, 118
Lowth, R., 197
Luckenbill, D. D., 29, 32, 38, 40
Lutz, H.-M., 194

Machinist, P., 259, 261–62, 270
McKane, W., 135, 163, 167, 169, 175
McKay, J. W., 63, 81
Marshall, R. J., 132

Marti, K., 13, 120, 125, 130, 173, 182, 186, 195, 198, 201, 203, 206, 216, 235, 251–52, 254, 260, 261, 263, 265, 268, 274, 277, 280, 283
Mattingly, G. L., 52–53
Mauchline, J., 221, 277, 291–92
Mayes, A. D. H., 170
Mays, J. L., 75
Mazar, B., 154
Meinhold, J., 192
Meissner, B., 36, 96
Mettinger, T., 159
Meyer, E., 35
Milgrom, J., 114–15
Miller, J. M., 23, 30, 78, 106, 275
Montgomery, J. A., 81–82, 85, 86, 99
Morenz, S., 180
Moriarty, F. L., 169
Mosis, R., 92, 94
Mowinckel, S., 10, 148, 167, 169, 190, 202, 230, 283, 284, 286, 292
Müller, H.-P., 14, 120, 128, 156, 158, 167, 169, 180, 184, 186, 195
Müller, W. E., 143, 145
Myers, J. M., 93, 95, 102

Na'aman, N., 24, 39, 45–46, 50–52, 54–55, 61, 101, 278
Newsome, J. D., 95
Niehr, H., 118, 240
Noth, M., 33, 39, 79, 81, 93, 104

Oded, B., 23, 49, 52, 95, 99–100
Olmstead, A. T. E., 40, 62, 81
Oppenheim, A. L., 82
Orlinsky, H., 83, 135
Ostborn, G., 207

Pitard, W. T., 35
Pfeiffer, E., 157
Plöger, J. G., 166

Porter, J. R., 90, 93
Porúbčan, S., 161–62, 169
Procksch, O., 2, 137, 138–39, 147, 149, 156, 160, 186, 189, 197, 198, 201, 203, 218, 229, 236, 237, 238, 239, 245–46, 251–52, 257, 263, 267, 277–78, 282, 288

Quell, G., 160

Rad, G. von, 3, 7, 10, 95, 148, 150, 157, 161, 190, 230, 253, 283–84
Rawlinson, H. C., 40, 62
Reade, J., 24
Rehm, M., 93, 164, 166, 169, 216, 229, 283, 285–86
Reich, R., 61
Rendtorff, R., 80
Reventlow, H. G., 121
Rice, G., 2, 169, 206
Rignell, L. G., 134–35, 137, 141, 152, 154, 169, 182, 184, 186, 188–89, 195, 197–98, 205, 207, 216–17, 222
Roberts, J. J. M., 12, 144, 146, 163, 167–68, 252
Robertson, E., 263
Rost, L., 158
Rost, P., 27–28, 29, 37–38, 40–41, 46, 48, 50, 58, 62–66, 101
Rudolph, W., 32, 102, 185

Saebø, M., 141, 152, 194–95
Saggs, H. W. F., 45, 47, 49, 53, 82, 154
Šanda, A., 34, 82–83, 86, 99
Sauer, G., 143
Sawyer, J., 119
Schmidt, W., 117
Schmidt, W. H., 225, 285
Schoors, A., 118
Schrader, E., 65
Schramm, W., 40
Schreiner, J., 142, 147, 151, 202, 252, 257
Schunk, K. D., 232
Scott, R. B. Y., 283
Scullion, J. J., 12, 167, 169
Seybold, K., 8, 10, 11, 147, 149, 152, 156, 222, 225, 228, 231, 257, 284–85
Shaw, C., 95, 119, 191
Sheppard, G. T., 122, 277
Skehan, P. W., 119, 204, 211–12, 217, 259
Skinner, J., 115, 122, 136, 156, 163, 166, 173, 188, 192–93, 203, 206, 216–17, 221, 229, 235–36, 242, 244, 257, 276, 278–79
Smend, R., 157–59
Smith, G., 25, 32, 37, 40, 62–63, 117
Smith, G. A., 115
Smith, J. M. P., 142
Smith, L., 207
Spalinger, A., 39
Speier, S., 152, 258
Spieckermann, H., 63, 76, 81
Stade, B., 189, 190
Staerk, W., 2, 122
Stamm, J., 10, 164–66, 168
Steck, O. H., 17, 118, 120–21, 126–28, 152, 156, 182, 284, 286
Stegemann, U., 143
Steinmann, J., 114, 169, 249, 278, 291
Stern, S., 163

Tadmor, H., 24, 26–29, 32–33, 36, 41, 45–46, 48, 52, 55, 57–61, 63, 65–66, 85–90, 102, 104, 174
Talmage, F., 180
Tånberg, K. A., 150
Thomas, D. W., 237
Thompson, M. E. W., 2, 10, 11, 15, 91–92, 104, 113, 135, 145, 147, 157, 160, 163, 169, 189,

202, 204, 206–7, 209, 215, 218, 221–22, 226, 228
Troeltsch, E., 2
Tur-Sinai, N. H., 208

Unger, M. F. 34–35
Ungnad, A., 24

Vanel, A., 154
Van Seters, J., 28, 81, 85, 89
Vermeylen, J., 122, 244, 285–87
Vischer, W., 8–10, 11, 163
Vogelstein, M., 78, 102, 218
Vogt, E., 45–47, 59–60, 116, 180
Vollmer, J., 228, 229, 286
Vriezen, T. C., 145, 181

Wagner, S., 207
Wallenstein, M., 244
Wanke, G., 252
Weinfeld, M., 200
Weinrich, F., 2, 7, 150
Weippert, M., 42–43
Weiss, M., 144, 146
Welch, M., 95
Wellhausen, J., 93–94
Welten, P., 93–94
Werner, W., 120, 129–30, 133–37, 147, 180, 184, 188, 192, 194–96, 198, 205, 209, 215, 226, 227, 229, 231, 282–88, 291–93
Westermann, C., 209, 252
Whitley, C. F., 118, 204, 208, 212, 215, 218, 220, 222–23
Widengren, G., 289
Wildberger, H., 11, 115–17, 123, 126, 134–37, 139, 141–42, 144–47, 149, 156–58, 160–62, 169, 172–74, 180–81, 184, 185–86, 188–89, 191–95, 197–98, 201, 203–6, 212, 215–18, 220, 222–23, 225, 227–32, 235–40, 243, 244, 249, 251–52, 254, 257, 259–61, 263–69, 273–75, 277–80, 283–88, 290–92
Wilke, F., 2, 191
Willi, T., 93, 95
Williams, J. G., 252
Williamson, H. G. M., 90, 92–95, 102
Wilson, R. R., 78, 204
Winckler, H., 1, 78
Wiseman, D. J., 44–47, 55–57, 59–60, 62
Wolf, H. M., 168
Wolff, H. W., 9–12, 75, 120, 136, 137, 143, 145, 147–49, 152, 157, 160, 162, 164, 169, 215, 221, 226, 228–29, 231
Würthwein, E., 7–8, 17, 80, 82–85, 148, 150, 156–57

Yadin, Y., 34

Zimmerli, W., 156, 232

Subject Index

Abel-beth-maacah, 63, 65, 66
Abi, 78, 106, 170
Ahab, 34, 77, 106, 170
Ahaz (Jehoahaz), 1, 4–19, 41, 70, 71, 74, 75–109, 118–19, 121, 126–32, 134–39, 141–42, 144, 146–53, 157–67, 169–71, 174, 176, 179, 183–85, 189–93, 196–201, 203–7, 209–11, 213, 216, 220–21, 226, 230–31, 233, 247, 250, 255, 266–67, 269, 270, 273, 279, 282–86, 290, 297–301
Ahaziah, 76, 77–78, 106
Amaziah, 79, 106, 200, 236
Ammon (Ammonites), 41, 69, 71, 96, 100, 102, 225, 274, 288, 290, 298
Amos, 35, 67, 70, 105, 170, 239, 247
Anatolia, 41, 43, 154
Apocalyptic, 268
Arabia (Arabs), 37–39, 42, 64, 69
Arpad, 24, 25, 86–87, 103, 255, 260
Arvad, 41, 43, 46–49, 70
Asa, 79, 88–89
Ashdod, 41, 43, 49, 54, 161, 205, 252, 278, 280–81
Ashkelon, 32–33, 35–37, 41, 43, 51, 52, 60, 72, 97, 103, 299
Athaliah, 77–78, 155
Azriyau, 102

Baasha, 34, 88–89, 170
Bashan, 65, 67, 72, 97, 102
Benhadad I, 34, 88–89
Brook of Egypt, 39, 45, 46, 51, 52, 54–55, 60, 69, 71, 173

Calno (Kullani), 25, 255, 260
Carchemish, 42, 255, 260
Chronology, 23–24, 70, 72, 73–74, 96, 107, 114, 118
Conspiracy, 10, 59, 197–200, 247, 298
Covenant, 8, 87, 157, 163
Cult, 9, 12, 76–83, 89–92, 149, 163, 202, 209–10, 227–28, 231, 248–49, 260–61, 276, 281–82, 285–86, 290, 292–93

Damascus, 25, 29–31, 33, 35–36, 39, 40, 50, 56, 64–67, 69, 71–72, 74, 80, 82–83, 85, 89, 97, 116–17, 155–56, 181, 252, 255, 260, 299
Davidic Dynasty/House, 3, 8, 14–15, 18, 77–78, 102, 106, 109, 120, 127, 130–34, 138–41, 144, 146–47, 150, 153–58, 161–64, 167, 169–71, 174, 176–77, 179, 183–85, 190–95, 197–205, 207, 209–10, 216, 218, 221–22, 226–27, 231–33, 235, 247, 250, 253, 255, 257, 267, 270–71,

273–74, 281–82, 286–87, 290, 293–94, 298, 300
Davidic Tradition, 8–10, 88, 157–59, 161, 176, 196, 231, 232–33, 273, 284–86, 294, 301
Denkschrift, 2–7, 13–14, 17, 120–32, 157, 297
Disciples (of Isaiah), 9, 12, 14–15, 197, 204–6
Divination, 210–12, 213
Dor (*Du'ru*), 70, 223

Earthquake, 114, 237–39, 250
Edom (Edomites), 41, 69, 71, 84–85, 90, 91, 94, 96, 100, 103, 108–9, 140, 193, 274, 288, 290, 298
Egypt (Egyptians), 39, 47, 51, 52–55, 61, 69, 70, 96, 97, 161, 172–73, 268–69, 298–99
El Gibbor (Mighty/Heroic God), 10, 143, 229, 231, 267
Elath, 83–85, 100, 108, 243
Elephantine, 208
Enthronement, 73, 230–33, 285
Ephraim, 39, 68, 72, 99, 105, 115, 125, 138, 139, 152, 155, 167, 195, 216, 219, 224–26, 236–38, 242–43, 245, 246, 250
Eponymn List, 24–26, 69, 107
Esarhaddon, 27, 53, 54, 163, 170, 283
Eschatology, 13, 130, 166, 194–95, 209, 227, 239, 288, 292, 297
Ethiopia (Ethiopians), 54, 69, 70, 161, 173, 176, 298–99
Exile(s), 60, 68, 94, 205, 216, 288–89
Exodus, 196, 269, 288–89

Faith, 4–5, 7, 9, 14, 16–17, 88, 92, 94, 128–31, 137, 145, 147, 150, 157–58, 209, 266, 297

Galilee, 32–36, 65–68, 72, 97, 99, 105, 139, 222–25, 240

Gaza, 37, 39, 41, 43, 45–46, 50–54, 60–61, 63–64, 67–68, 71, 98, 103–5, 185
Gezer, 36, 97
Gideon, 9, 228
Gihon Spring, 147, 185, 189–90
Gilead, 48, 65, 68, 74, 97, 99, 101–2, 105, 139, 154, 217–18, 223–25, 242
Glory, 248–49
Golan, 65, 67, 72, 97

Hamath, 46, 255, 260
Hanno, 37, 45, 51–55, 60, 63, 67–71, 96, 104, 108, 298
Hazael, 34–35, 70, 103
Hezekiah, 3, 6, 30, 32, 36–37, 78, 89–90, 92, 101, 129, 147, 162, 169–71, 173, 185, 189, 230–31, 266, 277, 281, 283
Hiram, 25, 41, 43–44, 47, 53, 57–59, 69, 71, 72, 103, 104, 108, 155, 298, 299
Holiness, 200–2
Holy War, 7, 9, 148–49, 157, 228
Hosea, 67, 70, 170
Hoshea, 34, 59, 68, 72, 74, 97, 115–17, 224–25, 236, 299

Idibi'ilu, 32, 36–40, 69, 71
Idolatry, 159–61
Immanuel, 3–6, 9–13, 98, 105, 126, 127, 129, 130, 132, 135, 162–71, 176, 183, 185, 192–95, 199, 229–30, 262, 297
Injustice, 114, 123, 125, 236, 244–47

Jehoahaz (of Israel), 34, 78, 106
Jehoash/Joash (of Israel), 35, 78–79, 106, 236
Jehoram (of Judah), 76, 77–78, 106
Jehoshaphat, 79, 106
Jehu (Dynasty), 78, 106, 170,

Subject Index

236, 250
Jeroboam II, 35, 67, 70, 95, 100, 102–3, 105–6, 170, 218, 225, 233, 236–38, 240–42, 245
Jerusalem, 4, 9–10, 75, 83, 98–100, 104–5, 109, 113, 120, 129–32, 135, 139–40, 147, 150–53, 155–56, 161, 169, 171, 174, 176, 179, 183–85, 189, 191–97, 203, 209, 210, 213, 216, 221, 226–27, 232–33, 247–48, 253, 257–61, 265, 267, 269–71, 273–74, 276–79, 282, 286, 294, 298–99, 301
Jezreel (Valley), 67, 71, 225
Josiah (Josianic), 224, 252, 254
Jotham, 73, 78, 79, 96, 99–103, 106, 109, 114, 140, 154, 191, 243, 252

Kashpuna, 45–50, 63, 66–67
Kullani (Calneh/Calno), 25, 260

Maher-shalal-hash-baz, 4, 98, 105, 145, 180–84, 206, 210, 256–58
Manasseh
  king, 76, 77, 79
  tribe, 125, 242–43, 246, 250
Matanbi'il, 41, 49, 70
Mati'ilu, 25
Menahem, 25, 35, 43, 67, 70, 73, 105–6, 109, 125, 170–72, 200, 225, 233, 236–38, 240–43, 245–47, 250, 289, 298
Messiah (Messianism), 133, 166, 169, 229–30, 283, 285, 287
Meunites, 55–56, 71, 102–3, 140, 298
Micah, 3, 213
Midian (Midianites), 227–28, 269
Mitinti, 32–33, 35–36, 41–43, 51, 69, 71–72, 96–97, 103–4, 298–99
Moab (Moabites), 41, 69, 71, 96, 117, 274, 288, 290, 298

Naphtali, 63, 65, 222–25
Nathan (Prophecy of), 8, 157, 158–59, 163
New Year Festival, 73–74, 107, 156, 290–94

Oded, 90, 92, 94
Omri (Omrides), 33–35, 40, 77–78, 106, 170, 199

Pekah, 4, 8, 11, 12, 14, 23, 33–35, 39–41, 43–44, 50, 52, 59, 64, 65, 68–72, 74, 78, 83–84, 88, 90, 91, 95–101, 103–9, 125, 130–31, 135, 139–41, 147, 151–53, 158–59, 171, 176, 183–92, 194, 197–202, 213, 216–19, 221, 224–25, 231, 233, 236–37, 242–43, 245–47, 250, 266, 269, 273, 279, 281–82, 294, 298–300
Pekahiah, 74, 100, 105, 109, 139, 183, 200, 217–19, 236, 242, 245, 247
Philistia (Philistines), 25, 39, 41, 43, 44, 47, 48, 50–51, 52–55, 59–61, 70, 87, 90–91, 94–95, 97, 103, 105, 108–9, 140, 151, 193, 225, 236–37, 240, 250, 269, 274, 288, 290, 299
Phoenicia (Phoenicians), 46, 48–50, 52–53, 61, 70, 71, 82, 105, 116, 225
Piye, 54, 173

Ramoth-Gilead, 65, 66, 97, 100
Remnant, 4–6, 12, 13, 130, 142–47, 176–77, 192, 266–67, 288–89
Repentance, 14, 92–93, 143–46, 239, 240, 242
Rezin, 4, 8–9, 11–12, 14, 18, 23, 25, 29–31, 33, 35–36, 40–44, 52, 56, 59, 66–67, 69–72, 83–85, 88, 90–91, 96–101, 103–9, 130–31, 135–36, 139–41, 147,

151–59, 171, 176, 183–87, 189, 190–92, 194, 197–201, 213, 224, 236, 239–40, 242, 245, 247, 265, 269, 273, 279, 281–82, 294, 298–300
Righteousness, 232, 268, 285
Rukiptu, 33, 36, 72, 299

Samaria, 34, 38–40, 50, 59, 72–74, 91, 100, 104–5, 117, 153, 155–56, 181, 183, 217, 219, 221, 224, 226, 232–33, 237–38, 242–43, 245–48, 250, 252, 255, 259–61, 266, 277, 279, 298–300
Samsi, 29, 31, 37–39, 41, 43, 53, 55–56, 61–62, 64, 68–69, 71, 72, 96, 97, 103, 108, 151, 298, 299
Sargon II, 49, 61, 277–78
Sennacherib, 101, 184, 221, 252, 277
Shallum, 73, 78, 170, 237, 241–42, 250
Shalmaeser III, 54, 106
Shalmaneser V, 25, 116–17, 223
Sharon (Plain of), 50, 70–71, 139, 223, 240
She'ar-yashub, 3, 4, 13, 141–47, 176, 210, 256, 266–67
Sheol, 151, 161
Shephelah, 90, 95, 108, 278
Shiloah, 9, 184–85, 188–90
Sidon, 34, 47, 48, 53, 155
Sign, 5, 6, 8, 9, 12, 129, 160–65, 210, 219
Ṣimirra, 45–46, 48, 49, 66
Sinai, 36, 39, 54, 56, 69, 71
Solomon, 10, 76, 190, 284
Syria (Aram), 11, 14, 18, 23, 25, 29–31, 33–36, 39–40, 41–44, 47, 50, 52–54, 58–59, 60, 61, 65–70, 77, 84, 86, 90–92, 94, 95, 99–105, 107–9, 115–16, 118, 127, 130–31, 138–40, 151–53, 155, 159, 161, 166–68, 171, 174, 176, 182–84, 186, 191, 195, 197–99, 209, 210, 213, 216, 224–25, 236–37, 240, 247, 250, 255, 258, 266, 271, 294, 299, 300

Tabeel (Ben Tabe'al), 4, 100, 109, 114, 152–55, 176, 191, 299
Tabernacles (Feast of), 292–93
Temple, 81, 82, 90, 205, 207–8, 210, 293
Tiglathpileser, 5, 6, 14, 18, 19, 23–31, 33, 36, 38–44, 47–56, 58–62, 68, 70–72, 74, 80–83, 87–91, 94, 96–101, 103–4, 107–9, 116, 146, 151, 154, 171–72, 174, 183–85, 216, 223–24, 236, 238, 241, 243, 248, 255, 258, 265, 269–70, 299
Torah, 207
Trade, 34, 39, 47, 49, 50, 52, 53, 55–56, 61, 69–72, 85, 103
Transjordan, 34, 35, 41, 43, 56, 65, 67, 71, 85, 100–3, 105–6, 108, 117, 139, 154, 224, 240, 243, 298
Tyre, 34, 41–44, 47–48, 53, 58–59, 71, 103, 105, 109, 116, 154–55, 299

Urartu, 24–25, 103, 116, 172
Uriah, 80, 82–83, 181, 183, 208
Uzziah/Azariah, 55, 73–74, 79, 87, 100, 101–3, 106, 114, 118, 154, 239

Vassalage, 31, 38–39, 42–43, 51–53, 63, 72, 81, 82, 87, 96–97, 108, 200, 270, 298–300

Zabibe, 25, 31, 43
Zebulon, 172, 222–25
Zechariah (of Israel), 70, 73, 78, 241
Zechariah (son of Jeberechiah), 181, 208
Zichri, 90, 91, 95, 107, 199

Zion (Theology), 4, 8, 145, 147, 156, 163, 169, 176, 194–97, 201, 203–4, 210, 213, 254, 261, 262, 264, 268–71, 173, 274, 279–81, 285–87, 290–92, 293–94, 300, 301

SCRIPTURE INDEX

Genesis
16:11 .... 166, 167
17:19 167
22:11 137
22:12 267
24:6 150
24:43 168
31:29 150
32:12 267
47:26 246
49:10 256
49:24 262
50:11 66

Exodus
2:8 168
4:1–9 162
4:2–4 257
7:12 257
7:19–20 257
10:14 139
10:28 150
14 7
14:5 140
14:13–14 148
14:14 148
15:2 292
15:18 292
17:5 257
22:22–24 .... 248, 249
28:3 285
34:12 150

Leviticus
26:36 149

Numbers
11:20 141
13:20 264
20:12 201
22:11 83
22:30 166
27:14 201
32:34 117
33:49 66

Deuteronomy
1:28 186
1:29–30 148
1:44 172
2:4–5 150
2:36 117
3:11 180
4:9 150
4:15 150
4:23 150
6:12 150
8:11 150
11:16 150
12:2 79
12:9 286
12:13 150
12:19 150
15:9 150
17:19 284
18:8 79

18:9	76
18:10	76, 78
18:11	211
12:30	150
20:2–4	7, 148
20:3	149
20:4	9
20:8	186
21:10–13	174
24:8	150
28:13	241
28:44	241
28:48	227
32:11	193
32:20	209
34:9	285

Joshua

2:11	186
5:1	186
6	7
7:5	186
8:1	148
10:5	138
10:8	148
10:25	148
11:4	267
11:6	148
13:25	117
16:8–9	242
17:7–8	242
19:29	58
23:11	150

Judges

1:30	172
1:31	58
3:15	87
6–8	227
6:4	138
6:11–24	162
6:12	9
6:14–24	9
6:16	9
6:24	10

6:36–40	9
7	269
7:3	148
7:9–25	228
7:22	66
9:1–6	170
11:33	66, 117
13:3–7	167
13:3–5	9
13:4	150
13:18–19	10
20:19	138

Ruth

2:12	193
4:7	206

1 Samuel

2:32	219
4–6	156
4:4	202
4:22	249
6:20	202
7:3	140
11:1	138
11:6	284
13:14	152
14	7
16:13	284
17:9	83
17:22	275
19:2	150
25:28	158
28:13	211
30:25	246
30:28	117

2 Samuel

3:18	88
6	156
6:2	202
7	157
7:9	10, 163
7:12–16	232
7:14	10, 88, 230

7:16	8, 158
8:2	87
8:6	87, 138
10:1–5	174
10:6	174
10:11	138
10:15	138
10:17	138
10:18	138
10:19	138
12:24–25	166
12:28	138
14:7	284
15:12	198
15:31	198
17:10	186
17:12	139
20:14	66
20:18	66
23:2	284
23:3	284, 285
23:5	158
24	7
24:5	117

1 Kings

1:33–40	90
1:33	190
3	284
3:5–9	161
4:12	66
5:1	87
6:23–28	193
9:26–28	85
10:1–10	284
11–12	167
11:6	76
11:13	88
11:28	270
11:34	88
13:21	141
14:9	76
14:10	170
14:22	77, 79
14:25–28	53
15:14	79
15:16–22	88–89
15:27	198
15:30	34
16:9	198
16:11	170
16:15	138
16:16	198
16:20	198
16:29–31	155
17:5	120
20:1	138
20:28	141
21:8	208
22:1–38	106
22:4	106
22:10–12	161
22:28	143
22:43	79
22:45	106
22:47–50	85

2 Kings

2:1	137
3:4–8	106
3:7	106
6:9	150
6:10	150
7:6	53, 174
8:7–15	103
8:16–11:20	78
8:18	76, 77, 106
8:20–22	85
8:25–29	106
8:25–27	155
8:27	76, 77, 106
8:28–29	77, 103
8:28	78
9:14	198
10:1–11	170
10:9	198
10:32–33	34, 103
11	190
11:1–4	155
11:1	170

11:14	120, 198
12:3	79
12:17–18	103
12:17	34, 71
12:21	198
13:3	103
13:7	34
13:14–19	161
13:22	103
14:4	79
14:8–14	106, 200
14:19	198
14:20	35
14:22	77, 85
14:23–29	67
14:25	35
14:28	100, 102, 106
15:4	79
15:5	74
15:8–22	241
15:8–10	241
15:8	78, 106
15:9–10	73
15:10	198
15:13–15	73
15:13–14	241
15:14	242
15:15	198
15:16	170, 241
15:19–20	43, 225, 241, 243, 247
15:19	105
15:25	106, 198, 217–19
15:27	74
15:29–30	75
15:29	33–34, 39, 66–67, 97, 224
15:30	34, 39, 59, 198
15:35	79
15:37	75, 96, 99, 101, 106, 243
16	13, 16, 18, 19, 75–91, 114, 134, 191, 266, 284, 297–99
16:1–4	76–79
16:3	76–78, 106
16:5–9	4–5, 6, 15, 79–80, 83–91, 103, 107, 171, 187
16:5	83–84, 91, 135–37, 278
16:6	84–85, 91, 108, 191, 243
16:7–9	85–88, 184, 199
16:7–8	146, 147, 150, 174
16:7	87–88, 91
16:8	60, 86–87, 108
16:10–18	79–83, 92
16:10–16	181
16:17–18	108
16:20	93
17:1–6	74
17:1	74
17:3	87, 116
17:4	54, 87, 198
17:8	79
17:9–11	79
17:17	76, 78
18–19	278
18	147
18:2	78, 106, 170
18:3	89
18:5	89
18:7	89
18:8	108
18:9–10	74
18:14	278
18:16	82
18:17	147, 278
18:19–25	54
19:8–9	54
19:9	278
19:16	89
19:19	89
19:20	89
19:32	165
20:20	189
21:2	76, 77
21:3	79
21:6	76, 78

21:20	76
21:23–24	198
22:20	165
23:3	120
23:10	76, 78
23:32	76
23:37	76
24:9	76
24:19	76
25:1	138
25:4	154

1 Chronicles

4:41	108
5:17	102, 106, 243
9:1	92
10:13	92
19:12	138
19:19	138

2 Chronicles

12:14	77
16:4	66
20:1	55
25:6	174
26:8	100, 102
27:5	102
28	16, 18, 90–95, 114, 284, 299
28:1–4	90, 91
28:5–21	91
28:7	90, 91, 95, 107, 199
28:8–15	92, 94–95, 103
28:15	102
28:16–21	90, 91
28:16–19	191
28:18	91, 95, 103, 108
28:22–25	90, 92
28:22–23	82
28:26–27	90, 93
32:1	153
32:20	189
33:19	92
35:4	246
36:14	92
36:22	246

Ezra

1:1	246
9:2	120
19:12	138

Nehemiah

3:15	189
4:2	198
9:38	208
10:1	208

Esther

3:14	246
4:8	246
8:8	246
8:13	246

Job

14:7–9	120
14:7	282
14:12	152
14:17	208
36:21	150
39:24	158

Psalms

2	156, 195
2:5	10, 195
2:7	10, 88, 230–31
2:8–11	287
2:8	10, 161
2:9	256
13:2	209
17:8	193
18:36	232
18:45–46	288
19:2	248
20	149
20:3	232
20:5	10
20:7–9	149
20:7–8	10
21	149

Reference	Page
21:6–12	149
21:9–12	10
22:4	202
22:15	186
22:25	209
24:7–10	249
24:8	10
25:3	209
25:5	209
25:21	209
27:9	209
27:14	209
29:1	249
29:3	249
36:8	193
39:8	209
45:7	10, 256
46	145, 156, 195, 281
46:5	286
46:7	195
46:8	163
46:12	163
48	145, 156, 195, 281
48:5	195
52:4	174
55:20	204
57:2	193
61:5	193
63:2	212
63:8	193
68:8–9	276
68:26	168
68:28–30	276
68:29–33	288
69:7–21	209
69:18	209
72	284–86
72:1–2	232
72:7	10
72:8–11	288
72:10	87
74:2	210
76	195, 281
76:3	195
76:11	145
78:34	212
78:31	264
83:10–12	228
88:15	209
89	156
89:3–5	158
89:3	88
89:15	10
89:19–37	158
89:20	10
89:26	88
89:27–28	10
89:27	230
89:28–37	232
89:39	88
91:4	193
92:12	219
95:11	286
97:2	10
99	202
101	285
102:3	209
104:29	209
104:31	249
110	156
110:2	257
110:7	190
114:2	203
118:10–12	292
118:12	172
118:14	292
118–21	292
122	156
130:5	209
132	156
132:2	262
132:5	262
132:8	286
132:10	88
132:15	286
133:1	286
133:3	286
135:21	210
138:5	249
143:7	209

144:25	209
145:5	249
145:11	249
149:5	249

Proverbs

1:1–4	285
1:7	285
1:8	207
4:1	207
6:20	207
7:15	212
8:12–21	285
8:14–16	284
13:14	207
13:24	256
22:15	256
23:13–14	256
29:15	256
29:18	207
30:18	168
31:26	207

Canticles

1:3	168
6:8	168

Isaiah

1–5	3, 114
1:2–20	239
1:2–3	256
1:5–6	256
1:7	166
1:24	164, 262, 280
1:27	143
1:29–30	280
2:2–5	290
2:2–4	287, 288, 290
2:5	194
2:6–20	239
2:9–22	280
2:9–17	280
2:10–21	248
2:11	287
2:17	287
2:20	287
3:1–15	113, 114, 131
3:1	280
3:16	141
3:18	287
3:24	216
4:2	264, 287
4:5–6	203
4:5	264
5	122, 124, 171–72
5:1–7	177
5:2	209
5:4	209
5:5	175
5:6	175, 243, 254
5:7	209
5:8–24	121–25, 132, 235, 244
5:8–10	252
5:8	251
5:11–13	252
5:11	251
5:13	164
5:14	164, 216
5:18	251, 253
5:20	253
5:21	251, 253
5:22–24	252
5:22	253
5:24	164, 252
5:25–30	113–15, 131
5:25–29	113–15, 121–24, 132, 235–36, 245
5:25	115, 122–24, 132, 239
5:26	172
5:30	122
6:1–9:6	2–7, 120–32
6–8	4
6:1–8:18	132, 157
6	3, 13–14, 117–20, 125–26, 129, 131–33
6:1–11	13, 126
6:1–3	200
6:1	118

6:5 202	153–55, 191, 203
6:9–13 4	7:7–9 .... 11, 130, 152, 155–59,
6:9–11 .... 118–19, 129, 131,	161, 199, 203, 261
171	7:7 195
6:9 188	7:8–9 136
6:10–12 4	7:8 .... 135, 151
6:10 .... 143, 146	7:9 .... 8, 127, 128, 133,
6:11 .... 166, 254	146, 156–59, 176
6:12–13 .... 126, 129	7:10–17 .... 3, 8, 9, 126–27,
6:12 119	159–71
6:13 .... 4, 119–20, 127–28,	7:10–13 .... 5, 6, 15
130	7:10 .... 125, 135, 159–60,
7–12 .... 113, 120, 131–32,	245
137, 273, 300	7:11 .... 133, 160–62, 164
7–10 255	7:13 .... 125, 133, 160,
7:1–8:18 128	164–65, 199, 221
7 .... 4, 15–17, 126, 128,	7:14–17 .... 10–12, 127–28,
131, 133–77, 179,	131, 134–35, 162–71,
192, 279	176, 194, 285
7:1–17 .... 16, 75, 113,	7:14–16 .... 5, 6, 14, 98, 129,
125–26, 129,	133, 167, 192
132–34, 191, 299	7:14 .... 4, 9, 98, 105, 133,
7:1–16 98	160, 164–67, 230
7:1–9 .... 8, 13, 130, 146–47,	7:15 .... 135, 166–68
159–160, 259	7:16 .... 105, 128, 133,
7:1 .... 3, 83–84, 135–38,	136, 152, 166–68,
279	176, 199, 203
7:2–9 138–59	7:17 .... 6, 14, 15, 128, 131,
7:2 .... 137, 138–41, 167	132, 133, 134, 135,
7:3–9 .... 3, 17, 126–28, 138,	160, 166–67,
141–42, 160	177, 188, 267, 290
7:3 .... 3, 4, 125, 142–48,	7:18–25 .... 6, 15, 126–29,
160, 176–77, 254,	131–32, 134, 147,
256, 266, 289	171–77, 203, 266,
7:4–9 .... 6, 7, 14, 105, 128,	287
131, 142, 284	7:18–20 .... 255, 289, 299
7:4 .... 127, 133, 135, 136,	7:18–19 172
148–51, 158, 221	7:18 .... 172–73, 199
7:5–9 .... 151, 163, 280	7:19 139
7:5–7 10	7:20 .... 114, 134, 173–74,
7:5–6 .... 152–55, 185	188, 199
7:5 .... 133, 135–36, 138,	7:21–22 .... 134, 135, 171, 175
151–52, 196, 279	7:22 135
7:6 .... 100, 104, 107, 109,	7:23–25 .... 175–76, 243, 299
114, 130, 147,	8 .... 6, 16, 17, 126,

8:1–20 .... 179–213, 218, 299
 130–31, 133, 180, 192
8:1–18 .... 125, 132
8:1–8 .... 13, 126–27, 128
8:1–4 .... 14, 83, 98, 113,
 127–31, 180–84,
 191, 199, 203, 216,
 228, 256, 258
8:1–2 .... 180–81, 213
8:1 .... 160, 180, 182, 206
8:2 208
8:3–4 .... 142, 145, 181–83,
 213
8:3 .... 4, 98, 105, 168,
 181–82, 207
8:4 .... 136, 182–83, 199,
 209, 224, 255, 256,
 289
8:5–10 .... 120, 184
8:5–8 .... 13, 15, 113, 128,
 129, 185, 203
8:5 .... 160, 179–80, 206
8:6–10 .... 184–96, 213
8:6–8 .... 14, 130, 147, 171,
 184–92, 194
8:6 .... 9, 109, 114, 118,
 127, 130, 136, 141,
 147, 176, 180, 184,
 185–91, 198, 199,
 213, 226, 269, 293
8:7–8 .... 114, 184, 189, 192,
 199, 209, 255
8:7 .... 164, 180, 186–88,
 289
8:8–10 .... 13, 113, 120,
 127–28, 130–31,
 184, 192–96, 203,
 209, 261, 280, 281
8:8 .... 180, 184, 192–93,
 195, 254, 262, 268
8:9–10 .... 10, 14, 128, 193–96,
 180, 184–85
8:10 .... 151, 152, 193–96
8:11–15 .... 9–10, 13–15, 113,
 114, 120, 127–29,
 171, 196
8:11–12 188
8:11 .... 160, 179–80, 207
8:12–15 .... 119, 130, 131,
 196–204
8:12–13 .... 196–97, 201–2,
 213
8:12 .... 196, 197–200, 247
8:13 .... 196, 200–2, 284
8:14–15 .... 129, 196, 202–4,
 209, 213, 261, 280
8:14 .... 196, 209, 285
8:16–20 .... 131, 180, 204–13
8:16–18 .... 13, 14, 120,
 127–30, 205
8:16 .... 197, 204–8, 212
8:17 .... 208, 209
8:18 .... 161, 207, 209–10,
 261
8:19–20 .... 210–13, 205, 218
8:21–9:6 .... 126, 132, 215–33,
 256, 270, 299
8:21–22 .... 215, 216–20, 233
8:21 .... 212, 217–18
8:22–23 212
8:22 218–19
8:23–9:6 .... 6, 10, 120, 215–16,
 220, 221–32, 236
8:23 .... 70, 215, 220–25,
 233, 269
9:1–6 .... 2, 13, 127–31,
 215–16, 221, 229,
 231, 290
9:1 .... 225–26, 254
9:2 .... 226, 227
9:3–5 227–31
9:3 .... 227–28, 254, 276
9:4 .... 228, 254, 269
9:5–6 284
9:5 .... 194, 215, 229–33,
 254, 267, 284
9:6 .... 222, 231–32
9:7–12:6 132
9:7–10:4 .... 115, 123, 132,
 235–50, 256, 299

Scripture Index

9:7–20 .... 113, 115, 121–25, 132, 142, 235–36, 244–45
9:7–11 237–40
9:7 245
9:8 .... 204, 236, 237, 245
9:9 238–39
9:10–11 .... 43, 70, 239–40, 266
9:11 .... 95, 105, 225, 236, 242
9:12–16 .... 236, 237, 240–42
9:12 .... 240, 254, 266
9:13 .... 143, 241, 254
9:14 240–41
9:15 .... 188, 242
9:16 .... 242, 257
9:17–20 .... 236, 237, 242–44, 250
9:20 .... 125, 236, 242–43, 246, 290
10:1–4 .... 121–22, 124–25, 132, 235–36, 244–50
10:1–2 244–47
10:1 .... 246, 251
10:3 .... 244, 248–49
10:4 149–50
10:5–27c 199, 251–71, 277, 299
10:5–19 253
10:5–15 .... 252, 253, 255
10:5–7 256–59
10:5–6 174
10:5 .... 252–54, 256, 258, 263, 281
10:6 .... 256–58, 261, 163
10:7 .... 258, 259, 263, 271
10:8–9 259–60
10:8 .... 255, 259
10:9 .... 25, 252, 255, 259–60
10:10–12 .... 251, 252
10:10 .... 254, 259, 270
10:11 .... 251, 259–61, 268–69, 271
10:12 .... 254, 259, 261, 270
10:13–14 .... 259, 261–62, 263, 271
10:15–19 .... 251, 262–65
10:15 .... 174, 251, 253, 263, 271
10:16–27 254
10:16–19 .... 251–53, 259, 263–65, 271
10:16 .... 165, 252, 254, 263, 280
10:17 .... 151, 254, 264
10:18–19 .... 143, 280
10:18 .... 186, 254
10:19 .... 254, 264
10:20–27c 252, 253
10:20–23 .... 142, 252, 265–68, 289
10:20 .... 254, 265–66, 271, 287
10:21 .... 10, 142–43, 254, 266–67, 271
10:22–23 .... 142, 143, 268, 271
10:22 .... 143, 254, 267–68
10:23 .... 268, 280
10:24–27c 251–53, 268–70, 276
10:24 .... 165, 254
10:25 254
10:26 254
10:27d–12:6 ...... 256, 273–94, 299
10:27d–34 .... 113, 217, 273, 280, 284
10:27d–32 .... 108–9, 153, 251, 273–80, 293
10:27 .... 227, 254 274, 276–77
10:32 279
10:33–34 .... 273, 279–81, 282, 294
11:1–12:6 281–94
11:1–9 .... 273, 283–85, 287, 290
11:1–5 .... 273, 280, 285
11:1 .... 120, 281–84, 287
11:2–9 .... 274, 284–86, 287
11:2 .... 10, 284

Reference	Page(s)
11:3–5	10
11:3–4	285
11:6–9	10, 273, 285–86, 294
11:10	273, 274, 286–88, 294
11:11–16	273–74, 287–90, 294
12:1–6	273–74, 290–93
13–19	205
13:17	186
14:4–5	227
14:8	280, 281
14:22	143
14:24–27	155, 252, 253
14:24	151, 152
14:25	227
14:28	118
14:30	143, 146
14:32	261
15–16	117
15:9	143
16:14	143
17:1–6	113, 116–17, 131, 146
17:3	143
17:4	254, 264
17:6	143, 254
17:12–14	261
18:1–7	173, 261
18:5	280
19:1–15	173
19:1	186
19:4	280
19:12	155
19:15	241
19:17	155
19:22	143
20	161
20:1–6	173
20:1	137
21:17	143
22:8	219
22:11	219
22:12	174
24–27	291
25:9	209
26:1–6	291
26:8	209
26:9	209
27:9	165
28–33	205
28:1–4	252
28:9	207
28:11	188
28:14	165
28:15–16	141
28:16	158
28:18	151, 152
28:24	166
28:29	10
29:1–3	252
29:11	208
29:13	141
29:14	10, 165
29:22	165
29:23	201
30:1–17	15
30:1–7	54
30:1–5	252
30:1	155
30:7	165
30:8	179, 227
30:14	146
30:15–16	149
30:15	143, 146
30:17	146
30:18	165, 209
31:1–6	149
31:1–5	15
31:1–3	54, 155, 252
31:4–5	261
31:5	193, 262
32:1	10
33:1	253
33:2	209
36:2	147
37:24	281
38	162, 164
40:3–5	289

40:24	282
41:8–13	149
41:14–16	149
43:1–4	149
43:4–7	149
44:1–4	149
47:10–12	205
51:21	165
52:6	165
53:12	165
56:8	289
61:1	284
62:25	286

Jeremiah

2:4	208
2:11	249
14:22	209
17:21	150
22:15–17	285
22:22	143
23:5	283
27:1–7	161
28:1–16	161
28:2	227
30:11	289
31:18	208
32:14	208
32:9–15	208, 209
32:35	76, 78
33:5	209
33:15	283
33:32	185
39:2	153
41:4–5	174
44:29–30	162
46:21	174
48:17	256, 257
48:19	117
51:46	149

Ezekiel

3:27	289
4:1–3	161
5:1	174
19:11–14	256
19:11	257
20:31	76
21:12	186
26:10	153
30:16	153
36:22	165
37:12	165
37:16	181
39:20	209

Daniel

11:24	264
12:4	208

Hosea

1:2–9	142
1:3	170
1:4–5	67, 70
1:5	225
1:5–6	105
2:16–17	165
4:7	249
5:8–6:6	75
5:15	212
7:11	54
10:11	208
10:14	116–17

Joel

4:17	210

Amos

1:1	114, 115, 238
1:3–5	70, 225
1:3	105
1:4	67
1:5	256
1:6–8	70, 95, 225
1:6	105
1:8	204, 256
1:9–10	70, 225
1:9	105
1:13–15	225
3:2	166

4:3 67
4:6–12 .... 122, 235
5:18–20 248
6:2 25
6:7 67
6:13–14 35
6:13 .... 67, 225
6:14 .... 67, 100
7:2 152
7:9 170
7:10 198
7:17 170
8:14 35
9:1 .... 116, 239

Micah
1:10–16 .... 119, 191
2:12 289
3:4 209
3:11 213
4:6 289
5:4 10

Habakkuk
2:2 181

Haggai
2:23 88

Zechariah
1:16 165
3:8 283
4:6 284
6:12 283
8:22–23 288
9:8 227
10:5 83
14:5 .... 114, 116, 239

Malachi
2:15 150
3:20 193

1 Maccabees
5:26 48

2 Maccabees
12:13 48

www.ingramcontent.com/pod-product-compliance
Lightning Source LLC
Chambersburg PA
CBHW021959160426
43197CB00007B/182